Al-Māturīdī and the Development of Sunnī Theology in Samarqand

Islamic History and Civilization

STUDIES AND TEXTS

VOLUME 100

The titles published in this series are listed at *brill.com/ihc*

Al-Māturīdī and the Development of Sunnī Theology in Samarqand

By

Ulrich Rudolph

Translated by

Rodrigo Adem

BRILL

LEIDEN | BOSTON

Cover illustration: Ulugh Beg Madrassah in Registan Ensemble. Samarkand, Uzbekistan. ciStock.com/Humancode.

Library of Congress Cataloging-in-Publication Data

Rudolph, Ulrich.
[Al-Maturidi und die sunnitische Theologie in Samarkand. English]
Al-Maturidi and the development of Sunni theology in Samarqand / by Ulrich Rudolph ; translated by Rodrigo Adem.
pages cm. — (Islamic history and civilization / Studies and texts ; v. 100)
Includes bibliographical references and index.
ISBN 978-90-04-23415-4 (hardback : alk. paper) — ISBN 978-90-04-26184-6 (e-book) 1. Islam—Doctrines—History. 2. Islam—Uzbekistan—Samarqand—History. 3. Maturidiyah. 4. Maturidi, Muhammad ibn Muhammad, -944 or 945. I. Adem, Rodrigo. II. Title.

BP166.1.R8313 2015
297'.204109587—dc23

2014034960

This publication has been typeset in the multilingual "Brill" typeface. With over 5,100 characters coverin
Latin, IPA, Greek, and Cyrillic, this typeface is especially suitable for use in the humanities.
For more information, please see www.brill.com/brill-typeface.

ISSN 0929-2403
ISBN 978-90-04-23415-4 (hardback)
ISBN 978-90-04-26184-6 (e-book)

This book is printed on acid-free paper.

Contents

Preface ix
List of Abbreviations x

Introduction 1
1 The Famous Unknown 1
2 The First Image: al-Māturīdī as Faithful Successor to Abū Ḥanīfa 4
3 The Second Image: al-Māturīdī as Eastern Counterpart to al-Ashʿarī 7
4 The State of Research and Current Conceptualizations 11

PART 1
Preliminary History and Conditions: The Ḥanafite Tradition in Northeastern Iran

1 **The Foundation and Establishment of Ḥanafite Theology in the Second/Eighth and Early Third/Ninth Centuries** 23
1.1 The Preparatory Role of the Murjiʾa 23
1.2 Abū Ḥanīfa (d. 150/767) and the Letters to ʿUthmān al-Battī 28
1.2.1 *The First* Risāla 28
1.2.2 *The Second* Risāla 36
1.3 Abū Muqātil al-Samarqandī (d. 208/823) and the *Kitāb al-ʿĀlim wa-l-mutaʿallim* 42
1.4 Abū Muṭīʿ al-Balkhī (d. 199/814) and the *Kitāb al-Fiqh al-absaṭ* 53

2 **Development in the Third/Ninth Century** 72
2.1 Stagnation in Theology and a Lack of Sources: Abū Bakr al-Samarqandī (d. 268/881–2) 72
2.2 Ḥanafite Elements in Ibn Karrām's Theology (d. 255/869) 75

3 **The State of Theology during al-Māturīdī's Lifetime** 81
3.1 Abū Muṭīʿ Makḥūl al-Nasafī (d. 318/930) and the *Kitāb al-Radd ʿalā ahl al-bidaʿ wa-l-ahwāʾ* 81
3.2 Al-Ḥakīm al-Samarqandī (d. 342/953) and the *Kitāb al-Sawād al-aʿẓam* 97

PART 2
The Emergence of al-Māturīdī

4 Life and Activity 125
- 4.1 Biographical Reports 125
- 4.2 Teachers 132
  - 4.2.1 *Abū Bakr al-Jūzjānī* 132
  - 4.2.2 *Abū Naṣr al-ʿIyāḍī* 134
- 4.3 Students 137
  - 4.3.1 *Abū Aḥmad al-ʿIyāḍī* 137
  - 4.3.2 *Abū l-Ḥasan al-Rustughfanī* 140
  - 4.3.3 *ʿAbd al-Karīm al-Pazdawī* 144

5 Theological Opponents 148
- 5.1 The Wide Spectrum of Polemic 148
- 5.2 The Muʿtazilite Challenge 156
  - 5.2.1 *Abū l-Qāsim al-Balkhī al-Kaʿbī and the Baghdad School* 158
  - 5.2.2 *The Basran School* 159
  - 5.2.3 *Ibn al-Rāwandī* 160
  - 5.2.4 *Muḥammad b. Shabīb* 162
- 5.3 The Ḥanafite Rivals: al-Najjār and the School of Rayy 163
- 5.4 The Focal Point of the Discussion: Refutation of the Dualists and the "Dahrīya" 166

6 Works 180
- 6.1 Lost Works 180
- 6.2 Extant Texts 183
  - 6.2.1 *The* Taʾwīlāt al-Qurʾān *or* Taʾwīlāt ahl al-sunna 183
  - 6.2.2 *The* Kitāb al-Tawḥīd 189

PART 3
Al-Māturīdī's Theology

7 Structures and Their Forerunning Models 201
- 7.1 The Structure of the *Kitāb al-Tawḥīd* 201
- 7.2 The Bipartite Nature of the Work 214
- 7.3 Possible Sources 223

8 An Outline of al-Māturīdī's Teachings 231
Prolegomena: Epistemology 231
8.1 The World 233
8.1.1 *The Contingency of the World* 233
8.1.1.1 Al-Māturīdī's Proofs 233
8.1.1.2 The Background of the Argument 236
8.1.2 *The Ontological Structure of the World* 242
8.1.2.1 Bodies and Accidents 242
8.1.2.2 Natures 253
8.1.2.3 Informing Factors and Exemplary Models 260
8.2 God 262
8.2.1 *God's Existence* 262
8.2.2 *God's Knowability* 264
8.2.2.1 The Rationalistic Position of the Ḥanafites 264
8.2.2.2 Inferring the Unseen from that which is Seen 266
8.2.3 *God's Oneness* 268
8.2.4 *The Otherness of the One* 274
8.2.5 *God's Attributes* 278
8.2.5.1 Earlier Ḥanafite Views 278
8.2.5.2 Al-Māturīdī's Contribution 282
8.2.6 *The Ambiguous Descriptions of God in the Qur'ān* 287
8.2.6.1 Earlier Ḥanafite Views 287
8.2.6.2 Al-Māturīdī's Contribution 291
8.2.7 *God's Wisdom* 296
8.3 Human Beings 300
8.3.1 *Human Rationality* 300
8.3.2 *Human Actions* 302
8.3.2.1 The Conceptualization of the Ḥanafites and the Karrāmites 302
8.3.2.2 Al-Māturīdī's Contribution 304
8.3.3 *Belief and Sin* 308

Concluding Observations 313
1 Al-Māturīdī's Position in Islamic Theology 313
2 The Relationship to Abū Ḥanīfa 317
3 The Relationship to al-Ashʿarī 317
4 The Formation of the Māturīdīya 319

Appendix: Inauthentic and Doubtful Texts 325
1 Inauthentic Texts 325
1.1 Sharḥ al-Fiqh al-akbar 325
1.2 Risāla fī l-ʿaqāʾid 329
1.3 Kitāb al-Tawḥīd 329
1.4 Risāla fī-mā lā yajūz al-waqf ʿalayhi 329
2 Doubtful Texts 330
Fawāʾid 330

Bibliography 332
Index of People 349
Index of Religious and Political Movements 353
Index of Arabic Terms 355

Preface

This volume is the edited English version of my book, *Al-Māturīdī und die sunnitische Theologie in Samarkand*, originally published in 1997 by E.J. Brill. In addition to the original publication it includes a number of corrections and addenda as well as references to more recent publications on al-Māturīdī, including the Istanbul edition of his Qur'ān commentary which was completed in 2011 (see the introductory chapter of "The State of Research and Current Conceptualizations").

The publication of this English translation was made possible by the personal dedication of several people whom I would like to thank by name: Wadād al-Qāḍī (Chicago), Sebastian Günther (Göttingen), and Hinrich Biesterfeldt (Bochum) who were ready from the outset to include the book in the series *Islamic History and Culture*, Kathy van Vliet from E.J. Brill, who diligently saw the work through to completion, and Nicolas Hintermann (Zurich), who prepared the index. The greater part of this project, however, was the result of the inexhaustible efforts of Rodrigo Adem, a former student of Wadād al-Qāḍī who is currently completing his PhD thesis at the University of Chicago. He not only expended considerable personal effort to translate the book, but also carried on innumerable discussions with me on its theological topics. In this respect he was the ideal translator, combining linguistic fluency with knowledge of the field, interest in the subject matter, and a keen sense of judgment.

List of Abbreviations

BCH	*Bulletin de correspondance hellénique*
BEO	*Bulletin d'études orientales*
EI^{1}	*Encyclopaedia of Islam*, First Edition
EI^{2}	*Encyclopaedia of Islam*, Second Edition
EIr	*Encyclopaedia Iranica*
GAL	Brockelmann: *Geschichte der arabischen Litteratur*
GAS	Sezgin: *Geschichte des arabischen Schrifttums*
ILO	Institut de Lettres Orientales
IS	*Islamic Studies*
JA	*Journal Asiatique*
JAOS	*Journal of the American Oriental Society*
JRAS	*Journal of the Royal Asiatic Society*
MIDEO	*Mélanges de l'Institut Dominicain d'Études Orientales*
MUSJ	*Mélanges de l'Université Saint-Joseph*
MW	*Muslim World*
OLZ	*Orientalistische Literaturzeitung*
REI	*Revue des études islamiques*
REJ	*Revue des études juives*
RSO	*Rivista degli Studi Orientali*
SI	*Studia Islamica*
ZA	*Zeitschrift für Assyriologie und verwandte Gebiete*
ZDMG	*Zeitschrift der Deutschen Morgenländischen Gesellschaft*

Introduction

1 The Famous Unknown

Abū Manṣūr Muḥammad b. Muḥammad al-Māturīdī (d. 333/944) is among the few Islamic theologians whose significance needs no emphasis nor special reminder. His reputation as a groundbreaking *mutakallim* is long undisputed; his influence on later generations, which manifested in its own school of theology, is acknowledged by all. This legacy has raised him to the rank of a leading teacher of the Islamic faith, and al-Māturīdī is still referred to as such to this day in nearly every handbook and survey on Islam.

Yet, despite this high estimation and ubiquitous accolade, a certain uncertainty is to be found. With all due respect to the oft-cited *mutakallim*, one still feels at a loss to describe his theology with precision, and to explain the means by which he distinguished himself from the other representatives of his discipline. Up to this point, what has been said about al-Māturīdī describes his aforementioned historical status considerably more than it does his actual work or personage. We hear, for instance, that he was, next to al-Jubbāʾī (d. 303/915–6), Abū Hāshim (d. 321/933), al-Kaʿbī (d. 319/931), and al-Ashʿarī (d. 324/935–6), one of the greatest thinkers of the early classical era of *kalām*.[1] Most prominently emphasized after this point is that the second Sunnī school of *kalām*, the influence of which has lasted over hundreds of years, can be traced back to him.[2] Yet, the very basis of this latter achievement, i.e., al-Māturīdī's specific doctrine itself, is still not known in all of its specifics. One does find publications on his doctrine that are somewhat informative, but the overall picture remains irritatingly vague. Indeed, its contours are so lacking

1 Richard M. Frank, "Notes and Remarks on the *ṭabāʾiʿ* in the Teaching of al-Māturīdī," in *Mélanges d'Islamologie: Volume dédié à la mémoire de Armand Abel par ses collègues, ses élèves et ses amis*, ed. P. Salmon (Leiden, 1974), 137. Likewise see idem, *Beings and Their Attributes: The Teaching of the Basrian School of the Muʿtazila in the Classical Period* (Albany, NY, 1978), 111; cf. Alnoor Dhanani, *The Physical Theory of Kalām: Atoms, Space, and Void in Basrian Muʿtazilī Cosmology* (Leiden, 1994), 6 and others.

2 According to the most frequent descriptions; cf. the typical example of Macdonald, *EI*[1], s.v. "Māturīdī"; Ignaz Goldziher, *Vorlesungen über den Islam*, ed. Franz Babinger (Heidelberg, 1925) 117f.; A.S. Tritton, *Muslim Theology* (London, 1947), 174; Louis Gardet and M.M. Anawati, *Introduction à la théologie musulmane: Essai de théologie comparée* (Paris, 1981), 60f.

 | DOI 10.1163/9789004261846_002

in focus that even in the more recent literature one can still come across such articles as "The Obscurity of al-Māturīdī" or "The Problem of al-Māturīdī."[3]

Modern research is not to be blamed for this strange divide between the fame of our theologian and our knowledge of his work. The problem begins much earlier, in the medieval Arabic sources themselves. There we encounter the surprising phenomenon that in a large number of classical representations of the divisions in Islamic theology where one would most expect to see al-Māturīdī prominently mentioned, his name is strikingly absent. The reason for this was not a conscious disregard, but a certain historical or geographical configuration, so to speak. Al-Māturīdī did not live in Iraq or another central region of the Islamic world, but carried out his scholarly activity in Samarqand, i.e., at the far eastern border of the Oecumene. Ideas from other regions reached that area, but local intellectual developments did not interest anyone further to the west, even in Baghdad. As a consequence, al-Māturīdī was initially unknown, and his influence was restricted for a long time to Samarqand and his Transoxanian homeland.

This changed only in the middle of the fifth/eleventh century, as the Seljuks, coming from the northeast, expanded their rule successfully into the core dominions of Islam.[4] As they advanced, they brought with themselves the theology that they had become familiar with in Transoxania, and made sure as well, though not always through the most judicious means, to make this theology known in these central Islamic territories as well. At first this led to turbulence, especially in Iran, and opened old wounds between the Ḥanafites and Shāfiʿites who consequently faced off anew—this time as followers of al-Māturīdī and al-Ashʿarī, respectively.[5] Later however, they came to a reconciliation that, significantly, was initiated in Syria. The Zangid ruler Nūr al-Dīn (r. 541–68/1146–74) paved a way by which he would advocate the strengthening of Sunnism as a whole, which meant toleration of the differences between the

---

3 Both titles are from Montgomery Watt. "The Obscurity ..." is the title of the pertinent chapter in his *The Formative Period of Islamic Thought* (Edinburgh, 1973), 312; "The Problem ..." is an essay of his that appeared in the *Mélanges d'Islamologie: Volume dédié à la mémoire de Armand Abel par ses collègues, ses élèves et ses amis*, ed. P. Salmon (Leiden, 1974), 264–269.

4 On the following, compare Madelung's foundational work, which is extraordinarily rich in material, Wilferd Madelung, "The Spread of Māturīdism and the Turks," in *Actas do IV Congresso de Estudos Árabes e Islâmicos, Coimbra-Lisboa 1968* (Leiden, 1971), 109–168, esp. 124ff.

5 On this see idem, *Religious Trends in Early Islamic Iran* (Albany, NY, 1988), 26ff. (with the chapter title: "The Two Factions of Sunnism: Ḥanafism and Shāfiʿism"); Tilman Nagel, *Die Festung des Glaubens. Triumph und Scheitern des islamischen Rationalismus im 11. Jahrhundert* (Munich, 1988), 363f.

individual Sunnī schools.[6] What he instituted found appeal and a following among the Ayyūbids (from 564/1169), and was upheld most notably in the subsequent century, when the Mamlūks came to power (from 648/1250). Within their territory they established the definitive principle of the equal authority of all the Sunnī legal schools; and if this was initially intended for the four great schools of law, then in principle it could be extended to theology. It is certainly not a coincidence that in Syria of the eighth/fourteenth century, voices could be heard articulating what to us today seems to go without saying: in Sunnī Islam there are two recognized *kalām* methodologies, one the doctrine of al-Ashʿarī, and the other the Māturīdite doctrine from distant Transoxania.[7]

Thus did al-Māturīdī finally gain general recognition, and to a degree that only a few Islamic theologians have been similarly granted. But this relatively late acknowledgment had its own share of consequences; such a delay was ultimately responsible for the fact that his teachings are not described or even alluded to in any of the well-known Islamic heresiographies—which almost all originate from before the eighth/fourteenth century. The fact that al-Ashʿarī fails to mention the man from Samarqand in his *Maqālāt al-Islāmīyīn* is not surprising if one reflects on its early date of composition (ca. 300/912–3). It is noteworthy, however, that the same observation can be made of considerably later heresiographers such as ʿAbd al-Qāhir al-Baghdādī (d. 429/1037), Ibn Ḥazm (d. 456/1064), al-Shahrastānī (d. 548/1153) and others. Even Ibn Khaldūn (d. 808/1406), who shows himself to be an expert on *kalām* in his *Muqaddima*, mentions numerous thinkers by name without including al-Māturīdī in his presentation.[8]

This was of direct consequence for the course taken by modern research, since for a long period of time its conception of early Islamic theology was determined by such heresiographical works: Its first important source was the *K. al-Milal wa-l-niḥal* of al-Shahrastānī, which was widely accessible by the middle of the nineteenth century.[9] Soon thereafter followed other heresiographies that initially attracted great interest because it was believed that early *kalām* in particular would be objectively and systematically laid out in them.

6 Madelung, "The Spread," 155ff.

7 Compare the third section of this introduction: "The Second Image: al-Māturīdī as Eastern Counterpart to al-Ashʿarī."

8 Cf. Ibn Khaldūn, *Al-Muqaddima*, as vol. 1 of *Taʾrīkh al-ʿAllāma Ibn Khaldūn*, ed. Y.A. Daghir (Beirut, 1965–67), 830 ult.ff. and 852.10ff. In English translation see *The Muqaddimah: An Introduction to History*, trans. Franz Rosenthal (New York, 1958), vol. 3, 46ff., 61ff.

9 The edition of the text, procured by Cureton, appeared in 1842 and 1846; the German translation of Haarbrücker appeared in 1850 and 1851.

But, as it would happen, when these sources were silent on a certain theologian, a void arose beyond which it was hardly possible to proceed further. This is precisely what happened in the case of Abū Manṣūr al-Māturīdī. He was discovered—only around the turn of the century—through other texts, where one could read how significant he had been as a theologian. But the typical heresiographical "reference books" that an Islamicist could refer to at the time did not offer any further information. And so initially the opportunity to attain more precise information on the teachings and ideas of the highly-praised *mutakallim* was simply unavailable.

2 The First Image: al-Māturīdī as Faithful Successor to Abū Ḥanīfa

That the heresiographies remain silent does not necessarily mean that al-Māturīdī was entirely neglected or passed over in the pertinent medieval literature. On the contrary, there are two other genres of sources in which observations on his doctrines are to be culled; these even provide a specific interpretive image to his name. Yet in order to properly categorize these representations of al-Māturīdī, one must first consider the geographical and temporal circumstances in which they emerged and were conveyed.

The first remarks on our theologian naturally originate from the region in which he was active, namely, Transoxania. When reflecting on the nature of their theological tradition, scholars of that region from the fifth/eleventh century held that it had been decidedly imprinted by al-Māturīdī's contributions. This is the sense of the testimony given by Abū l-Yusr al-Pazdawī (d. 493/1100),[10] for instance, and by his younger contemporary Abū l-Muʿīn al-Nasafī (d. 508/1114), who expressed the same thoughts even more pronouncedly.[11] Neither of them, intended to identify al-Māturīdī as the founder of Sunnī theology in Transoxania, however. To them he was rather an outstanding representative of the same; not as a founder, but as a thinker who masterfully laid out and interpreted a long-standing theological doctrine. Instead, they were in agreement on placing Abū Ḥanīfa (d. 150/767) at the original genesis of the school. He was remembered as having provided the correct answers to all definitive questions in matters of faith, and what he taught is supposed to have been transmitted

10 Abū l-Yusr Muḥammad al-Pazdawī, *K. Uṣūl al-dīn*, ed. Hans Peter Linss (Cairo, 1383/1963), 2.-2ff. Hereafter cited as *Uṣūl*.

11 Abū l-Muʿīn Maymūn b. Muḥammad al-Nasafī, *Tabṣirat al-adilla*, ed. Claude Salamé (Damascus, 1990–93), vol. 1, 358.15ff. Hereafter cited as *Tabṣira*.

and elaborated upon by all his successors in Bukhārā and Samarqand without detectable alteration.

In the writings of al-Pazdawī, this position is expressed in two ways. First, he calls his own school, not the "Māturīdīya," but deliberately *aṣḥāb Abī Ḥanīfa.*[12] Having said this, he repeatedly endeavors to reiterate to the reader that one or another particular doctrine had, of course, already been professed by Abū Ḥanīfa.[13] Al-Nasafī's remarks are even more explicit and systematic. He does not merely rely on the fact that the great Kufan is cited by name in northeastern Iran every now and then. His goal was to prove that Abū Ḥanīfa's doctrine had in fact been passed on from generation to generation intact and without interruption. To that end, he used the topic of God's attributes as an instructive example, writing what was to be understood as an affirmation of tradition and a program for the future: Al-Nasafī begins this with the statement that in the entirety of Transoxania and Khurāsān, all the leading figures of Abū Ḥanīfa's companions (*inna aʾimmata aṣḥābi Abī Ḥanīfa... kullahum*) that followed his way in the principles (*uṣūl*) as well as the branches (*furūʿ*), and that stayed away from *iʿtizāl* (i.e., the doctrine of the Muʿtazilites), had already "in the old days" held the same view (on God's attributes) as he did.[14] In order to prove this, a historical digression follows, in which names of earlier prominent Ḥanafites of Transoxania are listed. In this presentation, al-Nasafī describes the history of the Samarqand school, running through a contiguous chain of scholars with apparently equivalent theological perspectives. This chain begins with Abū Ḥanīfa, continues with Muḥammad b. al-Ḥasan (al-Shaybānī), and continues through the ranks on to al-Māturīdī and his successors.[15] Al-Māturīdī is viewed in this presentation as a member—albeit a prominent one—of a homogenous series of theologians. His merit is supposed to have come from advocating theological doctrine in a particularly brilliant and astute manner; this was a doctrine, however, that all the other scholars followed in principle as well. Because of this, al-Nasafī repeats in several places that al-Māturīdī always deferred to the statements of the school founder from Kufa,[16] and when he praises al-Māturīdī it is with the honorific of "the most knowledgeable person on the views of Abū Ḥanīfa" (*aʿraf al-nās bi-madhāhib Abī Ḥanīfa*).[17]

---

12 *Uṣūl*, 190.9.

13 On the doctrine of attributes (ibid., 70.11f.); on human capability for action (ibid., 115.14ff.); on the concept of belief (ibid., 152.6ff.).

14 *Tabṣira*, vol. 1, 356.6–8.

15 Ibid., vol. 1, 356.8–357.9.

16 For example, ibid., vol. 2, 705.9ff. and 829.1f.

17 Ibid., vol. 1, 162.2f.

It is noteworthy that we can detect an apologetic undertone with al-Pazdawī as well as with al-Nasafī. This was directed at the Ashʿarites of Nishapur, who had apparently censured the Transoxanians for allowing unacceptable innovations in their theology. At the focal point of this critique was the doctrine of divine attributes professed in Samarqand and the surrounding areas. This was denounced by the Ashʿarites as a heretical innovation of the fifth/eleventh-century that none of the predecessors (*salaf*) had adhered to.[18] Such a critique, however, was obviously easy to disprove on a historical basis: It was undeniable that al-Māturīdī had been active at the turn of the fourth Islamic century, contemporaneous with al-Ashʿarī, one might add.[19] An even more convincing counter-argument aimed to antedate al-Māturīdī: If Abū Ḥanīfa stood behind the entire Transoxanian theological tradition, then the circumstances could be explained and vindicated from every doubt: in this light, the *aṣḥāb Abī Ḥanīfa* of Samarqand not only adhered to proper doctrine, but could maintain its legitimacy through the important Islamic principle of historical seniority.

Admittedly this apologetic argument did not promulgate any entirely novel view of things, but for this same reason it must have been viewed as cogent and rather plausible, given the established custom which stood behind it. Indeed, Abū Ḥanīfa's name had been cited in Transoxania in this manner for a long period of time. Already by the third/ninth century, texts named him as the highest authority, and al-Māturīdī, too, did not fail to demonstrate his reverence for him in many instances.[20] Thus if al-Pazdawī and al-Nasafī pointed to the great Kufan as the actual authority of Transoxanian theology, this was not decisive for Abū Ḥanīfa's lauded status, but rather against al-Māturīdī's, or to be more precise, against the conceivable possibility of selecting him as the new leader and eponym of the school. His emergence did not signify a break in the teachings of faith; his doctrine was in no way a new paradigm. What really mattered was the tradition itself, and by paying homage to this tradition arose the image of Abū Ḥanīfa as school founder, with Abū Manṣūr al-Māturīdī as his brilliant interpreter.

---

18 Ibid., vol. 1, 310.8ff.: compare also al-Pazdawī's reaction, *Uṣūl*, 69.10ff. and 70.5ff. On this general theme, see Rudolph, "Das Entstehen der Māturīdīya," *ZDMG* 147 (1997): 393–404.

19 The chronological comparison with al-Ashʿarī must have played a role in the polemic, as *Tabṣira*, vol. 1, 240.8ff. shows, where it is explicitly stated that al-Māturīdī adhered to a particular doctrine that was only later adopted by the Ashʿarīya.

20 Cf. Abū Manṣūr Muḥammad b. Muḥammad al-Māturīdī, *K. al-Tawḥīd*, ed. Fathalla Kholeif (Beirut, 1970), 303.15, 304.1, 369.21, 382.19 [hereafter cited as *Tawḥīd*]; idem, *Taʾwīlāt al-Qurʾān*, ed. Ahmet Vanlıolu (Istanbul, 2005), vol. 1, 81.8, 105.7, 121.8, 158.10, 193.8, 231.1, 343.11, 354.4, 369.14, 393.2, 408.5 and many others (cf. the indices of the other volumes) [hereafter cited as *Taʾwīlāt*].

Once this decision was taken, it gained credency in times to follow. It is thus unsurprising that we commonly read in later literature about the Abū Ḥanīfa-school of northeastern Iran. Ibn al-Dāʿī, for example, a Shīʿite author of the sixth/twelfth century, relates that the theologians of Transoxania of his time are Ḥanafites with determinist leanings.[21] Tāj al-Dīn al-Subkī (d. 771/1370) described the doctrine of the Māturīdīya two hundred years later, saying that it was the doctrine of *aṣḥāb Abī Ḥanīfa*.[22] Even the Ottoman scholar Kamāl al-Dīn al-Bayāḍī (d. 1078/1687), committed without a doubt to al-Māturīdī's ideas, also rotely cited the same tradition: His main theological work bears the title *Ishārāt al-marām ʿan ʿibārāt al-imām*, and states after just a few lines that the foundation of all religious knowledge is to be found in the articulations of the "leader of leaders" (*imām al-aʾimma*), i.e., Abū Ḥanīfa.[23]

3 The Second Image: al-Māturīdī as Eastern Counterpart to al-Ashʿarī

The two latter authors named, al-Subkī and al-Bayāḍī, lead us to the second image that was developed in the Islamic sources. Tāj al-Dīn al-Subkī in particular played a prominent role in this development since he seems, as far as we know, to be its first exponent. In order to understand his conceptualization of things, we must recall that the famous Shāfiʿite *qāḍī* was neither from Transoxania nor in a situation comparable to that of al-Pazdawī or al-Nasafī. Born in Cairo in the eighth/fourteenth century many generations after their lifetimes, he spent the greater part of his life in Syria, where he carried out his scholarly activity. The distinct environment and new era was characterized by conditions that differed fundamentally from those mentioned previously. For al-Subkī, the rivalry between the Māturīdite-Ḥanafites and other Sunnī currents of thought no longer stood in the foreground. His experience was imprinted much more by the *Religionspolitik* of the Mamlūks, whose highest goal consisted of bringing about the accommodation and mutual recognition of all the Sunnī schools.

---

21 In Ibn al-Dāʿī, *K. Tabṣirat al-ʿawāmm fī maʿrifat maqālat al-anām*, ed. ʿAbbās Iqbāl (Tehran, 1313/1934), 91.9: "*Ḥanafiyān-i bilād-i Khurāsān u-kull-i mā-warāʾa-nahr u-Farghāna u-bilād-i Turk jabrī bāshand.*"

22 See the following section.

23 Kamāl al-Dīn al-Bayāḍī, *Ishārāt al-marām min ʿibārāt al-imām*, ed. Yūsuf ʿAbd al-Razzāq (Cairo, 1368/1949), 18.5f. with an enumeration of works attributed to Abū Ḥanīfa (in this edition, page 18 is the first page of text of the *Ishārāt*).

Al-Subkī's contribution to this development was no small one. He was, as stated from the outset, a Shāfiʿite judge whose work, *Ṭabaqāt al-Shāfiʿīya al-kubrā*, has remained significant for identifying and chronicling his legal school. The aim of this work, however, was not to advance a polemic against the other *madhhabs*; it was characterized by a reconciliatory attitude which is nowhere as evident as in those passages related to our inquiry.

The theme al-Subkī's addresses there is the prolonged success of Ashʿarite theology. He clearly viewed this as definitive, because according to his thesis, all true Sunnīs by his time had either come to follow this method or at least one that was comparable. This he supports first by mentioning the Shāfiʿites that of course generally adhered to Ashʿarite teachings.[24] Still, al-Subkī's intention goes beyond this obvious assertion. He thus goes on to maintain that one could (with only three insignificant exceptions) legitimately equate al-Ṭāhāwī's[25] teachings (to which many in Egypt still adhered) with those of al-Ashʿarī. And in the following sentence the Mālikites are also named as good Ashʿarites.[26]

The greatest challenge to this notion, and the one that also requires the most explanation, is addressed in the last relevant excerpt of this text. It is represented in those whom al-Subkī calls "the Ḥanafites,"[27] which means those Ḥanafite and Māturīdite scholars who had come from the East and become so numerous in Damascus and Aleppo since the sixth/twelfth century.[28] The *qāḍī* had apparently read their books and thereby come to a reassuring conclusion: What they taught did not deviate foundationally from the doctrine of al-Ashʿarī. The differences (*khilāfāt*) were restricted, in fact, to thirteen points in total, of

---

24 See al-Subkī, *Ṭabaqāt al-Shāfiʿīya al-kubrā*, ed. ʿAbd al-Fattāḥ Muḥammad al-Ḥulw and Maḥmūd Muḥammad al-Ṭanāḥī (Cairo, 1964–76), vol. 2, 261.10ff.

25 We still lack a clear image of Ṭāhāwī (d. 321/933), a traditionist oriented Ḥanafite from Egypt. His juristic works have been variously examined. On his life, see the introduction to Jeanette Wakin's *The Function of Documents in Islamic Law: The Chapters on Sales from Ṭāhāwī's Kitāb al-Shurūṭ al-Kabīr* (Albany, NY, 1972), 23f. where she has presented the most important reports. His creed is of theological interest, and has been translated repeatedly (first in Joseph Hell, *Von Mohammed bis Ghazâlî* (Jena, 1915), 37ff.) but has not been examined yet. Cf. for the moment Arent Jan Wensick, *The Muslim Creed: Its Genesis and Historical Development* (Cambridge, 1932), 140f., and W. Montgomery Watt, *Formative Period,* index.

26 Al-Subkī, 261.-10ff.

27 Ibid., 261.-2.

28 The reports on these Ḥanafites have been collected by Madelung, "The Spread," 149ff. The significance of Syria is moreover attested to by the fact that al-Subkī, in the entire excerpt mentioned, disputes with the Ḥanafite scholar Abū l-ʿAbbās known as Qāḍī al-ʿAskar (d. 767/1365 in Damascus), cf. al-Subkī, 261.4.

which six were real issues of content (*ma'nawī*), while the other seven were mere differences in articulation (*lafẓī*).[29] This, according to al-Subkī, ought not be a motive for accusing the other side of disbelief or innovation (*takfīr* and *tabdī'* respectively).[30] Even the Ash'arīya had issues which they disputed among themselves.[31] At the end of the day it could be maintained that all of the methodologies that claimed to be Sunnī were in agreement on all theological questions of consequence.

Al-Subkī stood by the conclusion of this evaluation in a *Nūnīya*, which as he himself affirms, had already become notably popular during his lifetime.[32] One of his students, a certain Nūr al-Dīn Muḥammad b. Abī al-Ṭayyib al-Shirāzī who came to Damascus in 757/1356 from Jīlān, even authored a commentary on it.[33] Its influence should not be underestimated. Abū 'Udhba revived it (ca. 1125/1713)[34] when he wrote on the same theme almost four hundred years later. His text, *al-Rawḍa al-bahīya fī mā bayna al-Ashā'ira wa-l-Māturīdīya*, does not go conceptually beyond al-Subkī's,[35] but this makes clear to us precisely how farsighted the views of the Mamlūk *qāḍī* from the eighth/fourteenth century had truly been. His views were in accordance with a general exigency toward harmonization that not only distinguished its own time period but would continue ultimately to become a part of Sunnī self-conception.

The relationship between the *Nūnīya* and the *Rawḍa al-bahīya* has long been known in the available research, and has also given occasion to many examinations and analyses.[36] Less obvious is the observation that the texts of al-Subkī, al-Shirāzī, and Abū 'Udhba were by no means the only Islamic articulations of the congruity between al-Ash'arī and al-Māturīdī. Rather, it seems that a whole genre of literature was developed on this particular theme. This is especially true in Ottoman times, to which an entire series of relevant texts attests.

---

29 Ibid., 261.-3ff.

30 Ibid., 261 ult. f.

31 Ibid., 262.5f.

32 The wording of the *qaṣīda* is reproduced ibid. 262.-12ff.; on its popularity see ibid. 262.9ff.

33 Ibid., 262.11ff.

34 We know almost nothing about him; see the brief reports of Jean Spiro in "La Théologie d'Aboû Manṣoûr al-Mâtourîdy," in *Verhandlungen des XIII. Internationalen Orientalisten-Kongresses (Hamburg 1902)* (Leiden, 1904), 293f.; *GAL*, vol. 1, 195 and suppl. vol. 1, 346.

35 Abū 'Udhba, *al-Rawḍa al-bahīya fī-mā bayna'l-Ashā'ira wa-l-Māturīdīya* (Hyderabad, 1322). Right from the beginning Abū 'Udhba (3.12–14) emphasizes that the two *kalām* schools are coequal. The adherents of both are situated on the path of guidance.

36 On this see the following chapter.

One of these is by ʿAbd al-Ghanī al-Nābulūsī (d. 1143/1730)[37] and carries the title *Taḥqīq al-intiṣār fī ittifāq al-Ashʿarī wa-l-Māturīdī ʿalā khalq al-ikhtiyār*. It had long been considered lost, but has recently been identified from a Damascus manuscript and is now also available in a printed edition.[38] Two further texts on the theme have been known for longer and were already available for consultation in older printings. The first text is entitled *Naẓm al-farāʾiḍ wa-jamʿ al-fawāʾid fī bayān al-masāʾil allatī waqaʿa fīhā l-ikhtilāf bayna al-Māturīdīya wa-l-Ashʿarīya fī l-ʿaqāʾid*. This was composed around 1133/1721 by ʿAbd al-Raḥīm b. ʿAlī Shaykhzāde[39] and probably served as a handy and easily accessible compendium of theology. Its reader could find out, without too great an effort, which teachings, according to the knowledge of the author, the *mashāyikh al-Ḥanafīya* and the *mashāyikh al-Ashāʿira*, had specified as the forty pivotal questions of faith.[40] The second text is a more elaborate and challenging work, and was published in 1305/1887–8 in Istanbul. The title page bears the caption *K. al-Simṭ al-ʿabqarī fī sharḥ al-ʿiqd al-jawharī fī l-farq bayna kasbay al-Māturīdī wa-l-Ashʿarī*; and as the title indicates is a composite of the work of two Māturīdite scholars. The foundation must have been the *ʿIqd al-jawharī*, a book of Khālid Ḍiyāʾ al-Dīn, which cannot have appeared before the second half of the eleventh/seventeenth century.[41] The second layer is a commentary by ʿAbd al-Ḥamīd al-Kharpūtī (actually al-Khartabirtī) who we may assume was a prominent compiler and commentator of theological texts of the same era.[42]

It had thus become a prevalent practice to juxtapose the Sunnī *kalām* schools and to compare them with one another.[43] By this time theological

---

37 On him see *GAL*, vol. 2, 345ff. and suppl. vol. 2, 473ff.

38 Edward Badeen, *Sunnitische Theologie in osmanischer Zeit* (Würzburg, 2008). This contains the text (pp. 81–132 of the Arabic) as well as a short introduction on the author and his work (pp. 51–61 of the German).

39 On the author see *GAL*, suppl. vol. 2, 659.

40 ʿAbd al-Raḥīm b. ʿAlī Shaykhzāde, *Naẓm al-farāʾid wa-jamʿ al-fawāʾid fī bayān al-masāʾil allatī waqaʿa fīhā l-ikhtilāf bayna al-Māturīdīya wa-l-Ashʿarīya fī l-ʿaqāʾid* (Cairo, 1317/1899). This work was printed in Cairo 1317/1899 and is 60 printed pages; on this work see Daniel Gimaret, *Théories de l'acte humain en théologie musulmane* (Paris, 1980), 95f., 172f.

41 Brockelmann names him in *GAL*, suppl. vol. 2, 909, no. 39 as the unknown author of a work by the title of *ʿIqd al-jawhar*. It is permissible, despite this, to identify him with Khālid Ḍiyāʾ al-Dīn, mentioned in *GAL S* I 759 ß: This personage left behind annotations to Siyālkūti's (d. 1067/1656) super-gloss on Najm al-Dīn al-Nasafī's articulation of belief.

42 He wrote, for example, glosses on a commentary on a work of Birkawī (d. 981/1573); see *GAL*, suppl. vol. 2, 657, no. 21 d.α.

43 Besides the texts named here, an additional three texts have the same theme: 1) Kamālpashazāde (d. 940/1533), *Risāla fī ikhtilāf bayna al-Ashāʿira wa-l-Māturīdīya*;

standards had been so reinforced that such comparisons were not focused on differences, but rather with an eye toward harmonization. Regardless, not every scholar felt compelled to uphold the dictum of affinity between the doctrines of al-Ashʿarī and al-Māturīdī. Kamāl al-Dīn al-Bayāḍī (d. 1078/1687) for instance, who was mentioned earlier, deliberately dispensed with these generalizations and attempted, in spite of them, to present a new image based on the original sources. What he discovered was a cause for suspicion and led to the following, by no means euphoric, judgment: The reoccurring statement that the contradictions between al-Ashʿarī and al-Māturīdī are merely linguistic (*lafẓī*) is a complete delusion (*wahm*), and wishful thinking on the part of such commentators. In reality the disagreement is based on matters of content (*maʿnawī*)[44]—and indeed, as he pedantically documents, occurs not regarding a few issues, but actually fifty problems of the most diverse themes and types.[45] Ultimately, however, al-Bayāḍī does not wish to be a mischief-maker in the midst of all the willingness to compromise and reconcile. This is because, according to his conceptualization, civil order among the Sunnīs is more important than emphasizing respective particularities which could possibly lead to social strife. He thus abates himself, adding that these fifty problems still only deal with minutiae. This gives him the room to impart a maxim which is of decided import; namely, that both theological schools must mutually respect one another and do not have the right to dismiss or defame the other as heretical (*tabdīʿ*).[46]

4 The State of Research and Current Conceptualizations

The statements on al-Māturīdī that we have encountered in the Islamic sources thus combine and transmit certain concepts from their own particular theological history. Their origins lie partly in the fifth/eleventh century and partly in the eighth/fourteenth century. Their main tendencies depend on whether they are written from the perspective of a "Māturīdite," or a "Sunnī," or in the case of al-Bayāḍī, from a combination of various perspectives. It has not been

2) Yaḥyā b. ʿAlī b. Naṣūḥ Nawʿī (d. 1007/1598), *Risāla fī l-farq bayna madhhab al-Ashāʿira wa-l-Māturīdīya*; 3) Muḥammad al-Isbarī Qāḍizāde (c. 990/1582), *Risāla Mumayyiza* (or *Mumayyizat*) *madhhab al-Māturīdīya ʿan al-madhāhib al-ghayrīya.* These texts are also edited and briefly analyzed in Badeen.

44 Al-Bayāḍī, 23.13.

45 Ibid., 53.4–56 ult.

46 Ibid., 23.13f.

easy for modern researchers to discover these relations, since the texts mentioned were not always as readily available as they are today, but were procured bit by bit, through discoveries of manuscripts or through an acquaintance with unique oriental prints. Unfortunately, it was the most recently composed texts that were delved into first, i.e., those authored in Ottoman or Mamlūk times. After some time, Māturīdite texts from the fifth/eleventh century followed. Only afterwards did the works that al-Māturīdī himself left behind become available such that they came to the general foreground of interest.

As a result of this turn of events, one may regard the history of the research as non-linear, and actually divided into three greater stages. Each draws on a particular corpus of texts available to it, and thus reflects, consciously or unconsciously, the image presented in those texts.

The first stage, which continued until the middle of the twentieth century, was represented by the comparison of al-Ashʿarī and al-Māturīdī. It was initiated by Spitta (1876), who consulted the *Rawḍa al-bahīya* of Abū ʿUdhba for his book on al-Ashʿarī, and made it so well-known that it was henceforth accorded great importance. On the basis of Abū ʿUdhba, Spitta listed the thirteen known points of disagreement between the two theologians. Along with this list, he adopted the thesis that al-Māturīdī and al-Ashʿarī had, all in all, professed the same teachings, and differed from each other only in small details.[47] Spiro (1904) was then to discover shortly after the turn of the century that Abū ʿUdhba had merely been a later compiler. As he was able to prove, the idea of the analogy between the two systems went as far as al-Subkī, i.e., the eighth/fourteenth century.[48] However, this only accorded the idea more authority, and it was henceforth considered more or less proven that two nearly identical *kalām* schools had developed in Sunnī Islam. Even Goldziher (1910) somewhat tersely pronounced: "It is not worth addressing the small differences between these closely related doctrinal views in more detail."[49] And after him a number of authors pronounced similar verdicts, their evidence inevitably being the list of the thirteen points of difference. This is the case, to various degrees, for Horten (1912),[50] MacDonald (1936),[51] Klein (1940),[52] and Tritton (1947).[53] This

47 See Wilhelm Spitta, *Zur Geschichte Abū 'l-Ḥasan al-Aś'arî's* (Leipzig, 1876), 112ff.

48 Spiro, 294.

49 Goldziher, *Vorlesungen über den Islam*, 117f.

50 Max Horten, *Die philosophischen Systeme der spekulativen Theologen im Islam nach Originalquellen dargestellt* (Bonn, 1912), 531.

51 See D.B. MacDonald, *EI*^{1}, s.v. "Māturīdī" (vol. 3, 475–7); compare *Shorter EI* (1961), 362f.

52 In his introduction to the edition of al-Ashʿarī's *Ibāna*, trans. W.C. Klein as *Abū l-Ḥasan ʿAlī ibn Ismāʿīl al-Ashʿarī's al-Ibānah ʿan uṣūl al-diyānah* (*The Elucidation of Islam's Foundation*) (New Haven, 1940), 37.

53 Tritton, *Muslim Theology*, 174ff.

same tendency was, in a certain way, even represented in the generally more astute observations of Gardet and Anawati (1948).[54]

Al-Māturīdī's own works, in contrast, were not taken into account at that time, even though it was known that two very important texts of his were extant in manuscript form: the *Taʾwīlāt al-Qurʾān* or *Taʾwīlāt ahl al-sunna*, of which several manuscripts existed in Europe,[55] and the *K. al-Tawḥīd*, which Goldziher (1904)[56] and Browne (1922)[57] had already referred to. But these texts were left unexamined, which explains why the impression that one had of al-Māturīdī was completely dominated by the comparative approach—namely, by the concept of a "second al-Ashʿarī from the East."

This view changed only due to the fruits of the second stage of research, which took place during the 1950s and '60s. Its merit lay in its verification of the close relationship between the Māturīdite and the Ḥanafite tradition, and was chiefly accomplished by three researchers with respectively different emphases. Schacht (1953) drew attention to the previously overlooked "prehistory" of the conceptualization of al-Māturīdī. He explained that a popular Ḥanafite theology had already existed by the third/ninth century, and he emphasized the necessity of comparing it with the ideas of al-Māturīdī.[58] Tancî (1955), on his part, brought to light the later historical self-conception of Māturīdite theology. We have him to thank for the reference to the revealing passages in the *Tabṣirat al-adilla*, in which Abū l-Muʿīn al-Nasafī describes the Samarqand school and traces it all the way back to Abū Ḥanīfa.[59] This allowed for the discovery of another image of al-Māturīdī; one from within the Māturīdite school itself, which aimed at depicting the theologian as a mere exegete of his famous Kufan predecessor. At the same time, this discovery laid the groundwork for the possibility of dismantling the one-sided "Sunnī" approach of the late Middle Ages: the great extent to which al-Māturīdī's theology was bound to the early Ḥanafites was now realized, and one could now conclude that its spread and development was directly linked to the history of that legal school. This overview, greatly needed but demanding in its execution, was accomplished by Madelung (1968) in his previously mentioned breakthrough publication

54 Gardet and Anawati, 60f.

55 Observed by Brockelmann, *GAL* I 195 u. *SI* 346.

56 In an article found in the appendix of Spiro.

57 Edward Granville Browne, *A Supplementary Hand-List of the Muhammadan Manuscripts including all those written in the Arabic Character, Preserved in the Libraries of the University and Colleges of Cambridge* (Cambridge, 1922), 167 (no. 1015 (a)).

58 Joseph Schacht, "New Sources for the History of Muhammadan Theology," *SI* 1 (1953): 24f. and 36ff.

59 Muḥammad b. Tavît al-Tancî, "Abû Mansûr al-Mâturîdî," *Ankara Ilahiyat Fakültesi Dergisi* 4 (1955).

"The Spread of Māturīdism and the Turks."[60] There he demonstrated what was presented at the beginning of this work; that al-Māturīdī's influence had long been restricted to Transoxania until his theology finally made its way westward, traveling with the Turks to the central territories of Islam.

Even Madelung could not access an edition of the works of our scholar while developing his theses; these titles, though long known of, had not yet been made available in printed form. Their contents, however, had been partially made public and several authors had consulted the pertinent manuscripts in order to inform themselves firsthand about the theological views of al-Māturīdī. Götz (1965) for example, did so in his presentation of *Taʾwīlāt ahl al-sunna*, in which he described the Istanbul manuscripts and explained various doctrinal particularities of the work.[61] Schacht (1953) had already emphasized in his previously mentioned article the importance of the *K. al-Tawḥīd*, and expressed therein his intention to edit it himself.[62] Unfortunately, he was not able to actualize this plan. But interest in this text was widely awakened, such that several publications from the 1960s are to be found in which the *K. al-Tawḥīd* is discussed either as a whole (Allard 1965)[63] or examined with an eye toward specific topics and themes (Brunschvig 1965)[64] and Vajda (1966 and 1967).[65]

Al-Māturīdī's works themselves only emerged as the focus of interest in the third stage of research which began in 1970 and continues to this day. It commenced with the edition of *K. al-Tawḥīd* by Kholeif (1970), followed one year later by the first volume of the *Taʾwīlāt* published by Ibrāhīm and al-Sayyid ʿAwaḍayn (1971). Around the same time, the Qurʾān commentary was also the subject of a London dissertation (Rahman 1970). A critical edition was proposed therein, which, however, appeared only some years later—again, as a single incomplete volume (printed in 1982 in Dacca and in 1983 in Baghdad). After these first attempts to make al-Māturīdī's works accessible, more than twenty years passed before interest in editing his works regained its impetus. A great share of the responsibility for these renewed efforts belongs to Bekir

60 The lecture was held in 1968 and appeared in print in 1971.

61 Manfred Götz, "Māturīdī und sein Kitāb Ta'wīlāt al-Qurʾān," *Der Islam* 41 (1965): 27–70.

62 Schacht, "New Sources," 41f.

63 Michel Allard, *Le problème des attributs divins dans la doctrine d'al-Ašʿarī et de ses premiers grands disciples* (Beirut, 1965), 419–427.

64 Robert Brunschvig, "Devoir et Pouvoir: Histoire d'un Problème de Théologie musulmane," *SI* 20 (1964): 25f.

65 Georges Vajda, "Le témoignage d'al-Māturīdī sur la doctrine des Manichéens, des Dayṣānites et des Marcionites," *Arabica* 13 (1966): 1–38 and 113–128; and idem, "Autour de la théorie de la connaissance chez Saadia," *REJ* 126 (1967): 135–189 and 275–397.

Topaloğlu: In 2002, he published a Turkish translation of the *K. al-Tawḥīd*, and in collaboration with Muhammed Aruçi followed in 2003 with a new edition of the Arabic text.[66] After this, attention turned to the *Taʾwīlāt*: In 2004, a complete edition of this work appeared for the first time (in five volumes); however, it was based on the texts of only two later manuscripts (among the over thirty extant) and lacked the standards of a critical edition.[67] Thus, in 2005, publication began in Istanbul of a new, well documented, and critical edition of the *Taʾwīlāt al-Qurʾān* by the collaboration of several editors under the supervision of Bekir Topaloğlu. It has been arranged in eighteen volumes.[68]

Parallel to the initial activity in editing and publishing his texts, research on al-Māturīdī has intensified since 1970 as well, as scholars began to take a closer look at his theological views. In the process, the *Taʾwīlāt al-Qurʾān* received less attention; only two contributions were dedicated to it, those published by Rahman (1981)[69] and Galli (1982).[70] Besides these two, Gilliot (2004) made use of the text when he tried to explain an ambiguous Qurʾānic passage that has been the object of many debates.[71] In contrast, the *K. al-Tawḥīd*, which has a much greater significance for the study of *kalām*, has had a far greater reverberation. This much was evident from the extensive first reactions following the publication of the printed edition.[72] But it is even more clearly documented by the great number of contributions written since on specific

66 *Kitâbü't-Tevhîd*, ed. Bekir Topaloğlu and Muhammed Aruçi (Ankara, 2003). The new edition reads better than the Kholeif edition in some parts, but does not take into account the possibilities that a comparison of other testimonies (such as that of Abū Salama al-Samarqandī, Abū l-Muʿīn al-Nasafī, etc.) would provide for the constitution of the text. Thus the *K. al-Tawḥīd* here is cited from the Kholeif edition, which is more well-known and more readily accessible.

67 *Taʾwīlāt al-Qurʾān*, ed. Fāṭima Yūsuf al-Khaymī, 5 vols. (Beirut, 2004).

68 *Taʾwīlāt al-Qurʾān*, ed. Bekir Topaloğlu et al. 18 vols. (Istanbul, 2005–11).

69 Muḥammad Mustafizur Raḥman, *An Introduction to al-Maturidi's Taʾwilat Ahl al-Sunna* (Dacca, 1981).

70 Ahmad Mohamed Ahmad Galli, "Some Aspects of al-Māturīdī's Commentary on the Qurʾān," *IS* 21 (1982): 3–21.

71 Claude Gilliot, "L'embarras d'un exégète musulman face à un palimpseste. Māturīdī et la sourate de l'Abondance (*al-Kawthar*, sourate 108), avec une note savante sur le commentaire coranique d'Ibn al-Naqīb (m. 698/1298)" in *Words, Texts and Concepts Cruising the Mediterranean Sea: Studies on the Sources, Contents and Influences of Islamic Civilization and Arabic Philosophy and Science Dedicated to Gerhard Endress on his Sixty-fifth birthday*, ed. R. Arnzen and J. Thielmann (Leuven: Peeters, 2004), 33–69.

72 See in particular the reviews by Madelung in *ZDMG* 124 (1974): 149–151; Frank in *OLZ* 71 (1976): 54–56; Daiber in *Der Islam* 52 (1975): 299–313; and van Ess in *Oriens* 27–28 (1981): 556–565.

aspects of the work: Frank (1974) examined the role of "natures" (*ṭabāʾiʿ*) in al-Māturīdī's theology,[73] and Watt (1973 and 1974)[74] attempted a general presentation of the text, from which he also initiated a series of doctoral theses intended to describe the environment of our thinker more precisely.[75] A bit later we find Monnot (1977), whose interests lay in the *K. al-Tawḥīd*'s representation of dualism,[76] Gimaret (1980), who made a precise analysis of its theory of human agency,[77] and Ibrahim (1980), who summarized its proofs for God's existence.[78] At the same time, Pessagno translated the text completely into English[79] and examined it in a series of articles on intellect and faith (1979),[80] the concept of will (1984),[81] theodicy (1984),[82] and the reconstruction of Muḥammad b. Shabīb's teachings (1984).[83] In the meantime, the level of interest in the East was also significant. We must primarily mention the Turkish works of Kemal Işik (1980)[84] and M. Said Yazıcıoğlu (1985 and 1988),[85] as well as the summary presentation of Belqāsim al-Ghālī (1989)[86] in Arabic.

---

73 Frank, "Notes and Remarks," 137–149.

74 Watt, *Formative Period*, 312ff. as well as idem, "The Problem of al-Māturīdī."

75 Farouq ʿUmar ʿAbdallāh al-ʿOmar, "The Doctrines of the Māturīdite School with Special Reference to as-Sawād al-Aʿẓam of al-Ḥakīm as-Samarqandī" (PhD diss., Edinburgh, 1974); Ahmad Mohamed Ahmad Galli, "The Place of Reason in the Theology of al-Māturīdī and al-Ashʿarī" (PhD diss., Edinburgh, 1976); to the extended circle also belongs Joseph Givony, "The Murjiʾa and the Theological School of Abū Ḥanīfa: A Historical and Ideological Study" (PhD diss., Edinburgh, 1977).

76 Guy Monnot, "Mātorīdī et le manichéisme," *MIDEO* 13 (1977): 39–66.

77 Gimaret, *Théories*, 175ff.

78 Lutpi Ibrahim, "Al-Māturīdī's Arguments for the Existence of God," *Hamdard Islamicus* 3 (1980): 17–22.

79 Pessagno indicates in his publications (see references in footnotes 76–79) several times that he completed an English translation of the *K. al-Tawḥīd*. The publication of the text has not been possible thus far.

80 J. Meric Pessagno, "Intellect and Religious Assent: The View of Abū Manṣūr al-Māturīdī," *MW* 69 (1979): 18–27.

81 Idem, "Irāda, Ikhtiyār, Qudra, Kasb: The View of Abū Manṣūr al-Māturīdī," *JAOS* 104 (1984): 177–191.

82 Idem, "The Uses of Evil in Maturidian Thought," *SI* 60 (1984): 59–82.

83 Idem, "The Reconstruction of the Thought of Muḥammad ibn Shabīb," *JAOS* 104 (1984): 445–453.

84 Kemal Işik, *Mâtürîdînin Kelâm Sisteminde İman, Allah ve Peygamberlik* (Ankara, 1980).

85 M. Said Yazıcıoğlu, "Mâtürîdî Kelâm Ekolünün İki Bükük Simasi: Ebû Mansûr Mâtürîdî ve Ebu 'l-Muîn Nesefî," *Ankara Ilahiyat Fakültesi Dergisi* 127 (1985): 281–298 as well as idem, *Mâtürîdî ve Nesefî'ye Göre Insan Hürriyeti Kavrami* (Ankara, 1988).

86 Belqāsim al-Ghālī, *Abū Manṣūr al-Māturīdī: Ḥayātuhu wa-ārāʾuhu al-ʿaqdīya* (Tunis, 1989). See al-Ghālī's bibliography for further titles, ibid., 295ff. The *Arab Heritage Newsletter* 4,

In addition, there have been entries on "Māturīdī" and the "Māturīdīya" published in 1991 in the second edition of the *Encyclopaedia of Islam*, both written by Madelung.[87] Since this time, there have been two larger publications on al-Māturīdī worth mentioning. One is by Mustafa Cerić, who published a brief overview of al-Māturīdī's life and teachings in 1995.[88] The second is by Salim Daccache, who in 2008 published a revised version of his 1988 Paris dissertation, wherein he dealt with the issue of creation in al-Māturīdī's theology.[89]

All this demonstrates a persistent interest in the subject matter, and the research documented here undoubtedly allows us to be much better informed about al-Māturīdī than we were some decades ago. Nevertheless—and with the same emphasis—it must be said that the greater portion of necessary analysis and presentation work concerning al-Māturīdī's life, thought, or religious and cultural environment has yet to be achieved.[90] And by the same token, even if we were to set al-Māturīdī aside to focus on the Māturīdite theologians who came after him, not only do we find research on them lacking, but quite often an edition of the necessary texts is unavailable from the outset as well.[91]

Undertaking a study of al-Māturīdī still promises the opportunity to claim a unique beginning. But such an endeavor is also dependent to a great extent on the methodology with which one attempts it, since there are naturally many ways to approach the theology of the "man from Samarqand," and it is by no means predetermined at the onset which one will be the most successful based on the current state of affairs.

One point of access, for example, might be an attempt at describing al-Māturīdī's doctrine as thoroughly as possible by means of the *K. al-Tawḥīd*, in the way that Gimaret has done in a marvelously systematic manner with

---

nos. 42, 43 (Mar.–June 1989), 16, states that a masters thesis was written in the same year in Medina by the title of "Al-Māturīdīya wa-mawqifuhum min tawḥīd al-asmā' wa-l-ṣifāt" by Shams al-Dīn Muḥammad Ashraf.

87 See *EI*², vol. 6, 846f.; 847f.

88 Mustafa Cerić, *Roots of Synthetic Theology in Islam: A Study of the Theology of Abū Manṣūr al-Māturīdī (d. 333/944)* (Kuala Lumpur, 1995).

89 Salim Daccache, *Le problème de la création du monde et son contexte rationnel et historique dans la doctrine d'Abū Manṣūr al-Māturīdī (333/944)* (Beirut, 2008).

90 This is what Gimaret postulates in his "Pour un rééquilibrage des etudes de théologie musulmane," *Arabica* 38 (1991), 17—for a study entitled "Māturīdī, sa vie, son oeuvre, sa doctrine."

91 Madelung gives an overview of the published and unpublished texts in "Der Kalām," in *Grundriss der arabischen Philologie II*, ed. Helmut Gätje (Wiesbaden, 1987), 334–336. To this must be added an edition which has just appeared: Abū Isḥāq al-Ṣaffār al-Bukhārī, *Talkhīṣ al-adilla li-qawā'id al-tawḥīd*, ed. Angelika Brodersen (Beirut, 2011).

the doctrine of al-Ashʿarī.[92] Such an undertaking might seem feasible at first glance. But Gimaret's work shows us quite clearly that a study of this type in particular has certain prerequisites that are as yet unmet. In regard to al-Ashʿarī (and Iraq), we know his religious and theological milieu to a reasonable extent, and we can say with whom he studied, whose doctrines he drew nearer to, and whose doctrines he freed himself of. As a result, we can also say relatively precisely where in his doctrine he adopted or modified older concepts, and what his personal stance to them had been. In the case of al-Māturīdī, which involves the theology of Samarqand, we have no comparable background information nor criterion at our disposal. This has unavoidable consequences for any analysis of the *K. al-Tawḥīd*'s argumentation since any number of views therein could be ascribed to al-Māturīdī, but because of said deficiency we would not yet know whether we were actually dealing with the author' own views, or whether older concepts, current in Transoxania at the time, had in fact been adopted and repeated.

Another approach might have been the masterful way in which Allard undertook his studies on al-Ashʿarī.[93] Allard chose a certain focus in theology and traced first how it was treated by the Iraqi theologians of the third/ninth century, then by al-Ashʿarī, and then by his first important students. This approach also proved fruitful, but one must again admit that it is hardly feasible with al-Māturīdī in a comparable form. In contrast to the scholars of Iraq, so far we do not know the prominent theologians of Transoxania, and can hardly tell which of them should be viewed as a starting point of inquiry. Thus far, it is again the unknown nature of the milieu that places clear boundaries to our understanding.

If this is the case, then our first task can only be to overcome these obstacles. This is why another method of investigation has been selected for the work at hand. If our goal is to describe al-Māturīdī's theology as adequately as possible, we must first identify his intellectual premises, which means that we must precisely ascertain what the religious and theological world of northeastern Iran looked like before and during al-Māturīdī's lifetime. Such an undertaking will naturally make great demands on the patience of the reader, and is also accompanied by new incalculable factors which would have been avoided were the focus restricted to al-Māturīdī alone. But in light of the current state of research it appears to be indispensable, as only in this manner will we garner the necessary criteria for assessing our scholar and his unique intellectual profile.

---

92 Daniel Gimaret, *La doctrine d'al-Ashʿarī* (Paris, 1990).

93 Allard, *Le problème*.

In this spirit, the first section of this book will examine the Ḥanafite theology of Transoxania preceding al-Māturīdī's scholarly activity. This begins in the second/eighth century, as the ideas of Abū Ḥanīfa were redacted in the East, and move through a series of notable personages up to al-Ḥakīm al-Samarqandī (d. 342/953), a contemporary of our scholar, whose ideas were still extensively rooted in the traditional doctrines of faith circulating at that time. The goal of this overview is not to thoroughly summarize the scholarly world of the Ḥanafites from the second/eighth century to the beginning of the fourth/tenth century. That would be of little service to the understanding of al-Māturīdī, and moreover, van Ess has already done so within a larger contextualization.[94] Instead, the extant theological texts play a more prominent role here. They will be surveyed work by work, in chronological format, in order to better comprehend how doctrines of faith developed in the region, and thereby determine the basis upon which our theologian developed his argumentation.

This preliminary historical survey is followed in the second section by a synchronic treatment of the religious environment that al-Māturīdī encountered in Samarqand during his lifetime, and the manner in which he came to distinguish himself from it. The Ḥanafite school as a whole no longer occupies the main point of focus. Instead, al-Māturīdī himself, as well as his teachers, students, and works are called into examination. Other Muslim views present at that time will also be examined, as well as the "foreign" religions present in Samarqand that incited al-Māturīdī to debate from within his capacity as a Ḥanafite scholar. These were, as will be shown, numerous indeed, though not all of them presented a real theological challenge; often these were represented by social groups of limited constituency, and in some cases were embodied only in specific doctrines that were known and discussed in educated circles but were not necessarily represented by an actual group in the region at the time. Nonetheless, not all adversaries could be ignored or dismissed with a few words. On the contrary, at the beginning of the fourth/tenth century, it appears that new and unresolved issues arose in the Ḥanafite theology of Transoxania. Al-Māturīdī (as well as his colleagues) had to establish his position with regard to them, and this may have been the impetus for him to think over the traditional conceptualizations of his school, and lead them in a new direction.

How this process itself played out is demonstrated in the third section of our study. It takes us at last to al-Māturīdī's doctrine, which is presented from two vantage points. The first of these is a general overview of our theologian's ideas based on an analysis of the framework of the *K. al-Tawḥīd*; this will allow

94 Josef van Ess, *Theologie und Gesellschaft im 2. und 3. Jahrhundert Hidschra. Eine Geschichte des religiösen Denkens im frühen Islam* (Berlin/New York, 1991–96), vol. 2, 491ff.

us to determine how al-Māturīdī systematized his thought and which external stimuli he responded to. The second approach focuses on specific theological questions and problems addressed by al-Māturīdī. This cannot aim to be a comprehensive analysis; that might be achieved instead by another study fully dedicated to the elucidation of his doctrine in all of its details. What can be achieved, however, is a portrait of al-Māturīdī as a thinker, entailing his most characteristic methodologies and important doctrines. For this purpose, such themes will be chosen as occupy a central position in his theology and which likewise demonstrate the various methods utilized in his efforts to both defend Ḥanafite *kalām* from its emerging rivals, as well as (re)conceptualize it, when necessary, in an incontrovertible formulation.

Al-Māturīdī's distinctiveness, as revealed through this process, emerges from the fact that he did not advocate just any ideas, as it were, but was actually capable of erecting an intellectual edifice perceived by the mainstream of Islamic belief to be an adequate expression of its theological conceptualizations. This, first and foremost, is what gives his doctrines a dimension that transcends his own identity, and this phenomenon in turn obliges us to conclude with another examination of his position and its place in the entirety of Sunnī theology. Our concluding analysis tries, therefore, to come full circle in regard to our opening remarks, summarizing that which distinguishes al-Māturīdī's thought and examining how his actual relationship to Abū Ḥanīfa and al-Ashʿarī should be seen. By the end of our study, asking this question will have become meaningful again, because only after evaluating al-Māturīdī's thinking on its own merits can we obtain a criterion that allows us to evaluate whether or not and to what extent the Islamic imagery of his personage has been justified.

The book closes with yet a few more preliminary remarks concerning the Māturīdite school itself. These are not extensive, but are limited to the question of how the school developed, and why it happened to form as it did in the fifth/eleventh century. But there is still a long way to go until such considerations are permitted—and, as noted, these should not begin with al-Māturīdī himself, but rather with the origins of the doctrine of faith for which al-Māturīdī made his vocation.

PART 1

Preliminary History and Conditions: The Ḥanafite Tradition in Northeastern Iran

CHAPTER 1

The Foundation and Establishment of Ḥanafite Theology in the Second/Eighth and Early Third/Ninth Centuries

1.1 The Preparatory Role of the Murjiʾa

Abū Ḥanīfa's theological conceptions were adopted and studied in northeastern Iran like nowhere else. While the development of *kalām* elsewhere mostly skipped over his name, and only a few thinkers such as al-Najjār in Rayy remained indebted to his legacy, here on the eastern boundary of the Islamic Oecumene the Master's ideas were already known during his lifetime and rapidly formed the basis of an independent school that held its own ground.[1]

This might be surprising at first, if one considers that Abū Ḥanīfa was at home in centrally-located Kufa.[2] He was active there as a notable scholar and from there his reputation spread not just eastward but far and wide in the Muslim world. However, this general renown was not based on his practice of *kalām*, but rather on his contributions to the development of *fiqh*. He was known as *the* prominent representative of the Kufan legal school, both praised and reviled for the methodology which, through his efforts, found acceptance in the emerging science of jurisprudence.[3]

Abū Ḥanīfa's positions on theology were relatively less influential, and perhaps it could not have been any other way: His views in this field were not as original and groundbreaking as they had been in *fiqh*, being merely one voice among many that were already more keen than he was on grappling with newly emerging theological questions. Furthermore, there stands the incriminatory fact that Abū Ḥanīfa was infamous for being sympathetic to the doctrines of the Murjiʾa. The latter had long lost their good standing in Iraq,[4]

---

1 The theological positions that the Ḥanafites adhered to in the other regions of Islam are described by Madelung, "The Spread," 112ff.

2 On his biography, see the articles by U.F. ʿAbd-Allāh, "Abū Ḥanīfa," *EIr*, vol. 1, 295ff. and J. Schacht "Abū Ḥanīfa al-Nuʿmān," *EI*², vol. 1, 123f., as well as van Ess, *Theologie*, vol. 1, 186ff.

3 On Abū Ḥanīfa's methodology see Joseph Schacht, *The Origins of Muhammadan Jurisprudence* (Oxford: 1950), 269ff., 294ff., on the critique of it see van Ess, *Theologie*, vol. 1, 188ff.

4 Wilferd Madelung, *Der Imam al-Qāsim ibn Ibrāhīm und die Glaubenslehre der Zaiditen* (Berlin, 1965) 236ff.; van Ess, *Theologie*, vol. 1, 221ff.; on later polemics against the Murjiʾa see Watt, *Formative Period*, 119ff.

 | DOI 10.1163/9789004261846_003

so it is not surprising that his Murji'ite leanings were the basis of defamation against his person as well. He himself rejected this criticism and explained that the description "Murji'a" was only an invective used by spiteful opponents and ought to be replaced by *ahl al-ʿadl wa-l-sunna*.[5] But this did not change the fact that his teachings were rooted in the same outlook of that group and that such negative verdicts as came down on them were likewise applied to Abū Ḥanīfa's theology in the central regions of Islam.

Matters were conducted completely differently in Transoxania, where the stage was better set for his teachings. The reason for this was not a purposive mission or propaganda campaign carried out by Abū Ḥanīfa himself, but a set of local events that actually predate the period of his scholarly activity. In this regard, it was the very Murji'a themselves who played a key role in his Transoxanian success even as they were a cause for his disparagement in Iraq. They had already established themselves as a prominent religious movement in northeastern Iran by the first half of the second/eighth century, and became the deciding factor for the adoption of Abū Ḥanīfa's doctrinal views in the entire region over subsequent decades.

The historical events that led to Murji'ite dominance in Transoxania and its neighboring regions have already been presented and analyzed by Madelung several times.[6] Their starting point was an issue that was initially political, but soon took on theological dimensions. Those regions that had only recently been conquered by the Muslims at the beginning of the second/eighth century, were, as newly-conquered territories and borderlands, accessible by the "mission" to a considerable extent, and more likely than elsewhere to witness conversion of the indigenous population to Islam.[7] The numerous converts may have been welcome to the pious, but they presented a nuisance to governmental administration—the first concern of which was the treasury. Each new convert caused a decrease in the total income from tax collection, since he was remitted the *jizya* that he had paid as a non-Muslim.

In light of these circumstances it is not surprising that Transoxania witnessed significant disputes concerning the poll tax. The governors responsible

5 Cf. Abū Ḥanīfa, *Risāla ilā ʿUthmān al-Battī*, in al-Kawtharī, *al-ʿĀlim wa-l-mutaʿallim*, 37.19–38.4. This section of the book hereafter cited as *Risāla I*.

6 On the following see Wilferd Madelung, "The Early Murji'a in Khurāsān and Transoxania and the Spread of Ḥanafism," *Der Islam* 59 (1982): 32–39 and idem, *Religious Trends*, 14ff.; see also Gholam Hossein Sadighi, *Les mouvements religieux iraniens au IIe et au IIIe siècle de l'hégire* (Paris, 1938), 24ff., and van Ess, *Theologie*, vol. 2, 492f.

7 On this see Richard W. Bulliet, *Conversion to Islam in the Medieval Period: An Essay in Quantitative History* (Cambridge, MA/London, 1979), 16ff.

for Khurāsān were not well-disposed to relinquish this source of income, and seem to have nevertheless taken the *jizya* from many new converts. These converts on their part were aggrieved by this policy, and even tried to sue for their rights from the caliph in Damascus.[8]

The argumentation on both sides naturally revolved around the question of which prerequisites were necessary for recognition as a Muslim. This did not remain a question of political policy, however, but on a more abstract level could also entail deliberation on how the term "believer" ought to be defined. Consequently, this question led one, even unintentionally, into the domain of theology. The authorities, who aimed to set hurdles as high as possible for the recognition of converts, wanted first to test whether or not they were truly familiar with the new religion. They insisted that it was not sufficient, strictly speaking, to profess Islam, but that one had to be capable of practicing the religious obligations properly and of properly reciting a *sūra* of the Qurʾān[9]—knowing full well that this must have been difficult for some Sogdians or Turks, regardless of how earnestly their conversions had been intended.

Those affected by these policies were not ready to acquiesce to these demands. They of course expected that their conversion to Islam, i.e., a declaration of belief in God and His messenger, would allow them to be considered believers without any further qualifications. On this premise they could invoke a position that had already been developed in Islamic theology, represented in its classical form by the Murjiʾa. The Murjiʾa had defined belief as strictly a declaration of faith. They intended thereby to rule out from the concept of religious belief the incorporation of deeds beyond the basic creedal articulation of Islam.[10] It is not surprising then, that the Murjiʾites would come to take on

8 Abū Jaʿfar Muḥammad b. Jarīr al-Ṭabarī, *Taʾrīkh al-rusul wa-l-mulūk*, ed. M.J. de Goeje (Leiden, 1879–1901), vol. 2, 1353.15ff.

9 Ibid., vol. 2, 1354.9ff. and especially 1508.3ff. (translated by Madelung, *Religious Trends*, 16). It was of course required that one recite the Qurʾānic *sūra* in Arabic. Significantly, the Ḥanafites, when they later moved toward rapprochement with the Iranian converts, argued that the Qurʾān could be recited in Persian as well. On this, see van Ess, *Theologie*, vol. 2, 491f.

10 This definition of belief was not found at the start of Murjiʾite doctrines, but rapidly found admission from them, being in fact a necessary complement to the idea that no one could deny a sinner the status of a believer: on this see Madelung, *Der Imam al-Qāsim*, 229; Michael Cook, *Early Muslim Dogma: A Source-critical Study* (Cambridge, 1981), 29ff.; van Ess, *Theologie*, vol. 1, 169 and 176. In later heresiographies and polemics, this definition of belief is conventionally seen as the main doctrine of the Murjiʾa; on this see Wensinck, *Muslim Creed*, 131ff.; Toshihiko Izutsu, *The Concept of Belief in Islamic Theology: A Semantic Analysis of îmân and islâm* (Tokyo, 1965), 83ff.; Wilferd Madelung, "Early Sunnī Doctrine

the cause of the new converts. Through completely different motives, a contact point thus emerged in which the Murji'a became the natural allies of the Transoxanians in their fight against the poll tax, and consequently the ruling authorities as well.

The particular events in which this conflict of principles manifested itself all took place in the first half of the second/eighth century and are recorded in al-Ṭabarī's annals. Already by the year 100/718–9 he writes that members of the Murji'a had engaged in questioning the *jizya*,[11] and under 110/728–9 we hear of the first uprising led by Murji'ite leaders.[12] Only six years later began the great revolt under al-Ḥārith b. Surayj. His political goals were surely much more ambitious in scope, but this rebellion also had religious motivations distinctly Murji'ite in inspiration.[13] Its most prominent supporter, the famous theologian Jahm b. Ṣafwān,[14] modified the definition of belief to an even more extreme form. Being a Muslim, according to his view, did not even require an audible declaration professed in front of others. To him it was enough if one acknowledged God and the truth of His revelation in one's own heart.[15]

The revolt of al-Ḥārith b. Surayj ultimately fell through in 128/746, and over time the question of the poll tax lost its volatility. But the events of those years were not without consequence for the religious milieu of northeastern Iran. In fact, they brought about changes that were a determining force for the future development of theology in the area. The Murji'a had managed through their activism to establish themselves as the leading religious movement of

---

Concerning Faith as Reflected in the Kitāb al-īmān of Abū ʿUbayd al-Qāsim b. Sallām (d. 224/839)," *SI* 32 (1970): 233–254; Givony, 151ff.; J. Meric Pessagno, "The Murji'a, Īmān and Abū ʿUbayd," *JAOS* 95 (1975): 382–394. An overview of the relevant heresiographical accounts is now available in Daniel Gimaret and Guy Monnot, *Shahrastani. Livre des religions et des sects* (Peeters/Unesco, 1986), 421ff.

11 al-Ṭabarī, vol. 2, 1353–5; see also Madelung, "The Early Murji'a," 33, and idem, *Religious Trends*, 15f.; Sadighi, 33f.

12 al-Ṭabarī, vol. 2, 1507–10; see also Madelung, "The Early Murji'a," 33, and idem, *Religious Trends*, 16f.; Sadighi, 35f.

13 H.A.R. Gibb, *The Arab Conquests in Central Asia* (New York, 1923), 69ff.; Wilhelm Barthold, *Turkestan down to the Mongol Invasion* (London, 1977), 190ff.; M.J. Kister, "Al-Ḥārith b. Suraydj," *EI*², vol. 3, 223f.; Madelung, "The Early Murji'a," 33ff., and idem, *Religious Trends*, 17f.

14 See Richard M. Frank, "The Neoplatonism of Ğahm Ibn Ṣafwān," *Le Muséon* 78 (1965): 395–424; Watt, *Formative Period*, 143f.; van Ess, *Theologie* vol. 2, 493–507.

15 Abū l-Ḥasan ʿAlī b. Ismāʿīl al-Ashʿarī, *Maqālāt al-Islāmīyīn wa-ikhtilāf al-muṣallīn*, ed. H. Ritter (Wiesbaden, 1963), 132.9–11; Abū l-Fatḥ Muḥammad al-Shahrastānī, *al-Milal wa-l-niḥal*, ed. W. Cureton (London, 1942–46), 61.12ff.; also Gimaret and Monnot, *Shahrastānī*, 296; van Ess, *Theologie*, vol. 2, 496f.

the region, and they seem to have accomplished this so successfully that they apparently did not have any serious contenders. Their dominance in some places must have even been overwhelming, as is evident, for instance, in that the city of Balkh could even sardonically be described as "Murjiʾābād."[16]

Despite this great success, the movement nevertheless did not yet possess any inner autonomy in these same border regions of Islam. This was because it lacked its own scholarly tradition that could be passed on to its adherents without recourse to outside scholars; i.e., if a Murjiʾite sought instruction, he still had to journey to Iraq, and more precisely Kufa, which traditionally had been the stronghold of the Murjiʾa. Abū Ḥanīfa was that city's most prestigious scholar in his time, and did not hesitate to offer his instruction to these advice-seekers from the East, since he professed Murjiʾite views himself.[17]

The second foundational step for the religious milieu of Transoxania and its neighboring regions followed almost inevitably from this configuration. Many that studied in Kufa and returned to their homes brought back Abū Ḥanīfa's teachings as the fruit of their travels. Eastern Iran thus did not remain Murjiʾite in a general sense, but rather adopted Abū Ḥanīfa's particular doctrines almost immediately after their formulation. The aforementioned city of Balkh seems to have shaped the beginnings of this development:[18] By 142/759–60 a student of Abū Ḥanīfa's had been made *qāḍī* of the city,[19] and with the exception of a short interlude following his death (in the year 171/787–8) the Ḥanafites remained at the helm thereafter. Other cities like Bukhārā and Samarqand followed after a certain interval of time, but already by the early third/ninth century, when our reports become more substantiated, these cities show a thoroughly Ḥanafite visage.[20]

16 Wāʿiẓ-i Balkhī, *Faḍāʾil-i Balkh*, ed. ʿAbd al-Ḥayy Ḥabībī (Tehran, 1350/1972), 28 ult.

17 Ibid., 28f.; also Madelung, "The Early Murjiʾa," 36, and idem, *Religious Trends*, 18.

18 Indeed, one must add the qualification that we are also best informed about Balkh in the early period. The reason for this is the already cited city chronicle *Faḍāʾil-i Balkh* of Ṣafī al-Milla wa-l-Dīn Abū Bakr ʿAbdallāh b. ʿUmar b. Muḥammad b. Dāwūd Wāʿiẓ-i Balkhī, written up to the year 610/1213–4, that has only been published in a Persian version (translated 676/1278) edited in Tehran. On this work, see Bernd Radtke, "Theologen und Mystiker in Ḫurāsān und Transoxanien," *ZDMG* 136 (1986): 536/569; on the history and culture of Balkh in early Islamic times see also C. Bosworth, "Balḵ" (II.), *EIr*, vol. 3, 588–591, and van Ess, *Theologie*, vol. 2, 508f.

19 Namely ʿUmar b. Maymūn al-Rammāḥ (d. 171/787–8), see Wāʿiẓ-i Balkhī, 124–9; Radtke, 540; Ibn Abī l-Wafāʾ al-Qurashī, *al-Jawāhir al-muḍīʾa fī ṭabaqāt al-Ḥanafīya* (Hyderabad, 1332/1913), vol. 1, 399 (no. 1105).

20 Madelung, "The Early Murjiʾa," 38f. More details on the spread of the Ḥanafites in Samarqand will be available when the extant city chronicles have been evaluated, such as the *Kitāb*

Thus did a comparatively homogenous religious milieu develop in north-eastern Iran which possessed—already at an early stage—the foundations upon which a fully-fledged theological tradition could develop. Here, Abū Ḥanīfa's teachings spread widely, and not only was his legal methodology readily accepted, but so too were the doctrines that he propounded in the discipline of *kalām*.

1.2 Abū Ḥanīfa (d. 150/767) and the Letters to ʿUthmān al-Battī

1.2.1 *The First* Risāla

The above mentioned events demarcate our historical framework and make it seem plausible that a Ḥanafite *kalām* school indeed emerged in Transoxania and Tokharistan. Although this does not suffice to clarify what internal features this school possessed nor which main doctrines or even texts it based itself on. this too may be reconstructed with a degree of certainty, since we do possess pertinent information that is astoundingly strong and reliable for such an early period of Islamic history.

The real stroke of luck is that Abū Ḥanīfa himself seems to have left behind texts of theological significance. Unlike *fiqh*, for which we have no record whatsoever of his writings at our disposal, several works in the discipline of theology have been transmitted in his name. Some of them, like the *Waṣīya* or the so-called *Fiqh akbar II*, must be excluded at the outset as a source for Abū Ḥanīfa's theology, since Wensinck has detected a much later date of composition for them.[21] But there still remain four informative texts that must be imputed to the immediate circle of the "school founder": Two short letters, addressed to a certain ʿUthmān al-Battī, as well as the more elaborate *Kitāb al-ʿĀlim wa-l-mutaʿallim* and *Kitāb al-Fiqh al-absaṭ*.[22]

If we would attempt to gain insight into Abū Ḥanīfa's ideas from these texts, yet another distinction is in order: The two latter texts, the *K. al-ʿĀlim* and the *Fiqh absaṭ*, were very probably not written by his own hand. They are not presented as systematic treatises, but rather as teaching dialogues wherein a

---

al-qand fī maʿrifat ʿulamāʾ Samarqand of Najm al-Dīn Abū Ḥafṣ ʿUmar b. Muḥammad al-Nasafī (d. 537/1142) which has recently been edited. A preliminary review of these texts is given by J. Weinberger, "The Authorship of Two Twelfth-century Transoxanian Biographical Dictionaries," *Arabica* 33 (1986): 369–382.

21 Wensinck, *Muslim Creed*, 185–187 and 245–247.

22 See GAS, vol. 1, 409–419, nos. II, VIII, IX, and X as well as J. Schacht, "Abū Ḥanīfa al-Nuʿmān," *EI²*, vol. 1, 123bf., who only names one *Risāla*.

student queries the master in order to subsequently transmit questions and answers for posterity's sake. In both cases one can thus assume that the students mentioned are the actual authors. This in turn suggests the idea that the master's teachings are not always authentically represented, but are possibly presented from a later perspective, not to mention interpretation.[23]

In regard to the letters to ʿUthmān al-Battī, such concerns do not seem to be necessary. They actually take us back to Abū Ḥanīfa himself and thereby convey to us an adequate impression of which themes and features were characteristic of his thought. It should be pointed out that the issues which he addresses there are not ordered systematically, but apparently rise from the exigencies of an actual debate. In this respect, these texts cannot be described as *kalām* treatises in the strictest sense, but their content is nonetheless clearly theological and touches upon questions of such enduring relevance, that we may, despite such qualifications, describe them as "germ cells" of Ḥanafite theology.

The two epistles to ʿUthmān al-Battī have reached us in different conditions and up to now researchers have considered them differently. It is therefore advisable to initially examine them separately, especially since their contents do not complete each other or overlap, but are in each case devoted to a different thematic emphasis.

One of the two letters that I will henceforth refer to as the first, was published already by 1949,[24] and has been deemed an authentic document by consensus. J. Schacht affirmed its authenticity,[25] and his judgment has been reconfirmed several times since then.[26] The indications thereof are truly impressive and are adequate as a proof: For one thing, the later Muslim tradition knows that Abū Ḥanīfa wrote to ʿUthmān al-Battī.[27] Furthermore, and more importantly, the

23 See Fr. Kern, "Murǵitische und antimurǵitische Tendenztraditionen in Sujūtī's al la'āli al-maṣnūʿa fī l aḥādīt al mauḍūʿa." *ZA* 26 (1912): 169n1; J. Schacht, "Abū Ḥanīfa al-Nuʿmān," *EI*², vol. 1, 123b; Madelung, *Religious Trends*, 18f.; van Ess, *Theologie*, vol. 1, 193f. On *K. al-ʿĀlim wa-l-mutaʿallim* and *al-Fiqh al-absaṭ* see the present book, chapter 1, 1.3 and 1.4, where the so-called *Fiqh akbar I* is mentioned.

24 In al-Kawtharī, *al-ʿĀlim wa-l-mutaʿallim*, 34–38.

25 See J. Schacht, "Abū Ḥanīfa al-Nuʿmān," *EI*², vol. 1, 123bf., and idem, "An Early Murciʾite Treatise: The Kitāb al-ʿĀlim wa-l-mutaʿallim," *Oriens* 17 (1964), 100n4.

26 Madelung, *al-Imam al-Qāsim*, 235, and idem, *Religious Trends*, 19; Cook, *Early Muslim Dogma*, 30; van Ess, *Theologie*, vol. 1, 193; see also *GAS*, vol. 1, 418, no. VIII.

27 Ibn al-Nadīm, *al-Fihrist*, ed. G. Flügel (Leipzig, 1871–72), 202.11 and (in Eng. trans.) *The Fihrist of al-Nadīm: A Tenth-century Survey of Muslim Culture*, trans. Bayard Dodge (New York, 1970), vol. 1, 500; Ibn Abī l-Wafāʾ, vol. 1, 148.10 and Ibn Quṭlūbughā, *Tāj al-tarājim* (Baghdad, 1962), 18.4, where the redaction of the brief is attributed to Ismāʿīl b. Ḥammād, a grandson of Abū Ḥanīfa; Gustav Flügel, "Die Classen der hanefitischen Rechtsgelehrten,"

content of the extant text does not show any special features that would cause us to doubt its authenticity; it fits with what we know about Abū Ḥanīfa and the religious terminology and intellectual world of the middle of the second/eighth century.[28]

It can also be added that the exterior form confirms this impression; it seems free of literary stylizations and communicates from a personal perspective with a matter-of-fact style. Illustrative of this are the introductory and concluding remarks, which are completely extant. At the beginning of the letter, Abū Ḥanīfa appeals to the addressee by name (*Risāla I*, 34.14) and in visible solidarity (34.15–17 and 35.4f.), mentions his previous letter as a reason for writing himself (34.16), and even cites the words that ʿUthmān al-Battī must have used in addressing him (34 ult.). The same very personal tone is found again at the end, when Abū Ḥanīfa alludes to a possible continuation of the dialogue: He does not want to prolong his explanations at the moment, and therefore asks that ʿUthmān follow up with questions if something has remained unclear. In that case he would gladly explain in more detail, as he hopes that ʿUthmān will henceforth turn to him in any situation without reluctance (38.4–7). This sounds concrete and is characterized by curt speech as well as moderate friendliness. This does not necessarily rule out the possibility that a later forger could have affected such a tone, but if this were the case, one could argue that a different literary style would have been adopted along with a more extensive presentation of the content matter.

Besides the question of authenticity, it is also significant for our purposes whether or not Abū Ḥanīfa's letter was actually transmitted not only in Iraq but also in northeastern Iran, as well as if and when it could have been received by the latter's resident theologians. Thankfully, the edited text provides us with this information in the *riwāya* prefixed to the opening section.[29]

From this it follows that it must have first been known in Baghdad: Abū Yūsuf (d. 182/798)[30] the famous student of Abū Ḥanīfa, is supposed to have transmitted it, followed by Abū ʿAbdallāh Muḥammad b. Samāʿa (d. 233/847),[31] who followed him in the position of *qāḍī* of the capital city. But by the third name already we are no longer in Iraq, but rather in the northeast, where the *riwāya* would remain for generations. After Ibn Samāʿa, a certain Nuṣayr

in *Abhandl. d. Königl. Sächs. Ges. d. Wiss.*, VIII (Leipzig, 1860), 282; al-Bayāḍī, 18.7 and 19.7 mentions "the *Risāla*."

28 A summary of this is to be found in van Ess, *Theologie*, vol. 1, 200ff.

29 *Risāla I*, 34.3–12. In an Istanbul manuscript there is another *riwāya* preserved; see van Ess, *Theologie*, vol. 1, 193.

30 *Risāla I*, 34.10; al-Bayāḍī, 21.-1f. also names Abū Yūsuf as a transmitter of the *Risāla*, on him see GAS, vol. 1, 419ff.; J. Schacht, "Abū Yūsuf," EI^2, vol. 1 164f.; Flügel, 282ff.

31 *Risāla I*, 34.10; on him see Ibn Abī l-Wafāʾ, vol. 2, 58f.; Ibn Quṭlūbughā, 54f.; GAS, vol. 1, 435.

b. Yaḥyā l-Faqīh[32] is named as a transmitter, which can only mean Nuṣayr b. Yaḥyā l-Balkhī. Concerning him we not only know his death date (268/881–2)[33] with relative confidence, but also that he played a significant role in the eastern Ḥanafite tradition. He is vaunted in the city chronicle of Balkh as an ascetic scholar,[34] but must have also stood out for his contributions to *fiqh*, since about a century afterward, Abū l-Layth al-Samarqandī[35] has an entry on Nuṣayr's views[36] in his compilation on previous legal scholars, the *Nawāzil fī al-furūʿ*. The same is true for the fourth person in the chain, Abū l-Ḥasan ʿAlī b. Aḥmād al-Fārisī,[37] who is supposed to have died in the year 335/946–7. An entry is dedicated to him in the *Faḍāʾil-i Balkh*,[38] and he is also mentioned in the *Nawāzil* of Abū l-Layth.[39]

The rest of the *riwāya* can be sufficed by a short summary. Three names follow, on whom biographical works do not report, the *nisba*s of which however divulge where they presumably took up residence: Abū Saʿīd Muḥammad b. Abī Bakr al-Bustī, Abū Ṣāliḥ Muḥammad b. al-Ḥusayn al-Samarqandī, and Abū Zakarīyāʾ Yaḥyā b. Muṭarraf al-Balkhī.[40] Then we meet Abū l-Muʿīn Maymūn b. Muḥammad al-Makḥūlī l-Nasafī (d. 508/1114), the famous theologian and systematizer of the Māturīdite school[41] who is also supposed to have known the *Risāla*. After him the chain includes several more famous Ḥanafites, until it ends with Ḥusām al-Dīn al-Sighnāqī (d. 711/1311 or 714/1314).[42]

This is all very informative, since it shows that the letter to ʿUthmān al-Battī was read in scholarly circles all the way up to the later Māturīdites. What is pivotal for us is that the *riwāya* documents how early the text reached Balkh and from there made its way to Transoxania.

The contents of the letter are addressed in much more detail in part three of this chapter. For the time being, it is still important to describe the essential framework of the text, determining which themes it treats and how its

---

32 *Risāla I*, 34.10.

33 Ibn Abī l-Wafāʾ, vol. 2, 200.2; Wāʿiẓ-i Balkhī, 257 ult.; Muḥammad ʿAbd al-Ḥayy al-Laknawī, *al-Fawāʾid al-bahīya fī tarājim al-Ḥanafīya* (Cairo, 1324/1906), 221.4f.

34 Wāʿiẓ-i Balkhī, 257f.; see Radtke, 545f.

35 Died 373/983. See J. van Ess, "Abū ʾl-Layt as-Samarqandī," *EIr*, vol. 1, 332f.

36 *GAS*, vol. 1, 447, where the death date "around 250/864" is given. According to Abū l-Muʿīn al-Nasafī, *Tabṣira*, vol. 1, 130.4ff., Nuṣayr also transmitted Muḥammad al-Shaybānī's views from an intermediary link.

37 *Risāla I*, 34.9.

38 Wāʿiẓ-i Balkhī, 297–99 (death date on 297.3); also see Radtke, 547.

39 *GAS*, vol. 1, 447.

40 *Risāla I*, 34.8f.

41 Ibid., 34.7; on him see the introduction, section 2.

42 Ibid., 34.3; on al-Sighnāqī see Madelung, "The Spread," 125n39.

argumentation is structured. Both points of emphasis will be continuously revisited in regard to the texts we will be examining, taking us step by step to al-Māturīdī himself. From the development of the thematization and refinement of the structure and argumentation, it will be demonstrated how systematic *kalām* slowly emerged out of a nucleus of theological views found among the early eastern Ḥanafites.

Abū Ḥanīfa's *Risāla* was conceived as a defense and is apologetic in its aims. This was precipitated by two accusations which we come to understand were brought against the author and which he felt compelled to fend off. As he tells us himself, it was reported that he had become a Murji'ite, and furthermore, that he spoke of the "believer gone astray" (*mu'min ḍāll*).[43]

The two accusations can be interpreted very differently, depending on the point of view presumed for his critics. Given the various possibilities, a Khārijite or a Muʿtazilite could have expressed the same criticism, since an adherent of either of these groups would have certainly opposed the Murji'ites on the topic of a believer who had become a sinner. However, the few reports that we have about ʿUthmān al-Battī make his adherence to such positions improbable,[44] and suggest that we presume a different background for him. He was not prominent in theology, but rather in jurisprudence, and to later writers he was remembered above all else as a reliable transmitter (of *ḥadīth*).[45] This does not mean much in and of itself, since it is similar to what is reported about many scholars, but it does clear a path to a more probable hypothesis: We may presume that ʿUthmān al-Battī was from the circles of *ḥadīth* transmitters, where great emphasis was placed on devotional transmission and the Murji'ites were seen as a dangerous heresy.

---

43 *Risāla I*, 34 ult.; for a detailed analysis of the text see van Ess, *Theologie*, vol. 1, 194ff.

44 The fact that Abū Ḥanīfa keeps in mind that his views could be misunderstood as Muʿtazilite or Khārijite (cf. *Risāla I*, 36.9–19) also speaks against the possibility of such a background for ʿUthmān al-Battī.

45 On his schooling in *fiqh* see Ibn Qutayba, *K. al-Maʿārif*, ed. Tharwat ʿUkāsha (Cairo, 1960), 153.10; Ibn Ḥajar al-ʿAsqalānī, *Tahdhīb al-tahdhīb* (Hyderabad, 1325–27/repr. Beirut, 1968) vol. 7, 153 ult. f.; al-Dhahabī, *al-Mushtabih fī l-rijāl: asmā'ihim wa-ansābihim*, ed. ʿAlī Muḥammad al-Bajāwī (Cairo, 1962), 45.-2; his role as transmitter is described by Ibn Ḥajar, vol. 7, 153.-5ff.; on the name of his father there are different views: Ibn Qutayba, 596.16–18 names ʿUthmān b. Sulaymān b. Jurmūz, and Ibn Ḥajar, vol. 7, 153.6 (as well as idem, *Lisān al-mīzān* [Hyderabad, 1329–31/repr. Beirut 1390/1971], vol. 7, 303 [no. 4022]) names ʿUthmān b. Muslim b. Jurmūz; see also Muḥammad b. Khalaf Wakīʿ, *Akhbār al-quḍāh*, ed. ʿAbd al-ʿAzīz Muṣṭafā l-Marāghī (Cairo, 1366/1947), vol. 1, 323.5f. and al-Dhahabi, *Mīzān al-iʿtidāl fī naqd al-rijāl*, ed. ʿAlī Muḥammad al-Bajāwī (Cairo, 1381/1963), vol. 3, 53.

This criticism on the part of the *ḥadīth* transmitters was provoked by the question of "faith" or "belief" (*īmān*). They were not willing to exclude actions from its definition as the Murji'ites had done, but insisted that belief grew through good deeds and decreased through bad ones. This did not mean that sinners were excluded from the community of believers as the Khārijites claimed as did the Muʿtazilites (albeit inconsistently). But it meant, nevertheless, that according to the conceptualization of the *ḥadīth* transmitters, disobedience and misdeeds impacted belief, and that one who has gone astray could no longer be regarded as a believer in the full meaning of the word.[46]

As said before, it can no longer be determined with certainty whether ʿUthmān al-Battī wrote on the basis of these assumptions. But it is the way that Abū Ḥanīfa responds to him that strengthens such a conclusion, as he emphasizes precisely these two points which came to the foreground in disputes with the *ḥadīth* transmitters.

From the outset Abū Ḥanīfa concerns himself with a methodological principle always dear to the partisans of *ḥadīth* narration, and affirms, curtly and succinctly, that he is not carrying out any innovation (*bidʿa*) whatsoever, but that his statements are rooted solely in the Qur'ān and the *sunna* of the Prophet. What follows is essentially a detailed description of belief, characterized by a persistently defensive stance against a conception of belief that incorporates deeds. It looks like a panorama of Murji'ite opinions and is in principle, with certain repetitions and overlaps, concentrated on four interconnected themes: the definition of belief that excludes deeds, the equality of belief of all believers, the "pushing-back" of judgment about believing sinners, and the particular case of ʿUthmān and ʿAlī.

Although Abū Ḥanīfa here articulates the views of the Murji'ites in a more or less classical manner, he refuses, ultimately, to be labeled as a Murji'ite. His argument for this is not simply that he has unjustly been considered among this group. Rather he opines that he and those similarly oriented have only been given such a same out of malice and have earned another appellation instead. Since the term Murji'a had obviously become an invective, Abū Ḥanīfa was compelled to replace it, as already mentioned, with *ahl al-ʿadl wa-ahl al-sunna.*

When he later emphasizes adherence to the *sunna* as constitutive for his teachings, he is referring back to the beginning of his text and renews the affirmation that he is only propounding teachings that are in accordance with the

46 On the concept of belief according to the Sunnī *ḥadīth* transmitters, as later manifested in the *K. al-Īmān* of Abū ʿUbayd al-Qāsim b. Sallām (d. 224/839), see Madelung, "Early Sunnī Doctrine," and Pessagno, "The Murji'a."

foundational truths of Islam, i.e., the words of the Prophet. The description of *ahl al-ʿadl*, in contrast, is not as unequivocal, but allows a certain room for interpretation. Perhaps what was meant thereby was that each Muslim has the duty to speak out against every injustice.[47] Or perhaps it was only supposed to mean that one professed what was just and true and did not fall into error and injustice like so many others.[48]

In summary, the first *Risāla ilā ʿUthmān al-Battī* was in its time a thoroughly engaging text and promising for future exegesis. Important problems were addressed therein in a way that was appealing and surely comprehensible to readers of many backgrounds. At the same time, the door for further elaboration remained open, since Abū Ḥanīfa gave, as the concluding overview attests to, only general positions without establishing his theses in detail; thus later generations were left room for further inquiry and refinement.

THE STRUCTURE OF THE *RISĀLA I*[49]

34.13–35.5	[Introduction] therein:
34 ult.	**ʿUthmān al-Battī's Allegations** (a) ABŪ ḤANĪFA IS A MURJIʾITE (b) ABŪ ḤANĪFA TALKS OF A "BELIEVER WHO HAS GONE ASTRAY" (*MUʾMIN ḌĀLL*)
35.2–3	**Methodological Rebuttal** We are not practicing any innovation (*bidʿa*); rather we abide by the Qurʾān and the *sunna* of the Messenger of God.
35.5–38.4	[Main Section] **Rebuttal from Contents** On (b) JUSTIFICATION OF THE EXPRESSION *MUʾMIN ḌĀLL* 1. Rational Argumentation

47 According to Madelung, *Der Imam al-Qāsim*, 235, and idem, *Religious Trends*, 15.

48 Cf. Schacht, "An Early Murciʾite Treatise," 102; Josef van Ess, "Kritisches zum Fiqh akbar," *REI* 54 (1986): 336n31, and idem, *Theologie*, vol. 1, 199f.

49 The contents of the Arabic text are given in summary form. I have added the accompanying notes.

THE STRUCTURE OF THE *RISĀLA I*

35.5–11	1) *On the Definition of Belief* Muḥammad called the people at first only to testify to the one God (*yashhadū*) and affirm (*iqrār*) his prophethood. Whoever followed this call attained the status of a believer (*muslim/īmān*).
35.12–18	2) *On the Separation of Belief and Actions (I)* Duties (*farā'iḍ*) were only explained to the believers (*ahl al-taṣdīq*) at a later point and are thus considered deeds (*'amal*) that enlarge upon the actual act of affirmation (*taṣdīq*) of the Prophet's message. Whoever contravenes them, therefore, has not lost faith (*īmān*) itself.
35.18–22	3) *No Differentiated Ranking in Belief* People differ in carrying out duties. Belief, in contrast (here: religion/ *dīn*), is equal among all the angels (*ahl al-samā'*) and the people.
35.22–36.9	4) *On the Position of Sinners* A person can, without losing his belief, become disobedient (*'āṣin*) and make mistakes (sinful ones) if he is ignorant (*jāhil*) or astray (*ḍāll*). Even Moses and Jacob (in the Qur'ān) made these types of mistakes.
36.9–19	5) *On the Separation of Belief and Actions (II)* If duties really belonged to belief, then what would the first adherents to Islam be called before they were explained its duties? "Disbelievers"—reminiscent of the doctrine of the Khārijites? Or "neither believing nor disbelieving"—according to doctrines of the Mu'tazilites? In addition, even 'Alī himself described the adversaries whom he fought as believers!
36.19–ult.	6) *Judging 'Uthmān and 'Alī (I)* One of the two parties (which nevertheless remained believers!) must have been wrong. Saying which one of them it was we leave to God.
37.1–6	7) *The "Promise and Threat"* A believer without sins is awaited by Paradise; a disbeliever who sins is awaited by Hell. The decision concerning a believing sinner is left to God.

(*cont.*)

THE STRUCTURE OF THE *RISĀLA I*	
37.6–7	8) *Judging ʿUthmān and ʿAlī* (*II*) We leave it to God, since both were Companions of the Prophet and transmitters of his *sunna.*
	II. Proof from Tradition
37.7–18	Our doctrine corresponds to the views of many well-known authorities (which Abū Ḥanīfa lists by name): The first civil war had to do with a fight between Companions of the Prophet. They all remained—despite possible mistakes—believers nonetheless.
	On (a) REFUSING THE DESCRIPTION OF A MURJIʾITE
37.19–38.4	The name Murjiʾite is just the invention of spiteful opponents. In reality those so described stand for *ʿadl.* Thus they ought to be called *ahl al-ʿadl wa-ahl al-sunna.*
38.4–9	[Conclusion] Tentative qualifications to this explanation; offer to continue the correspondence; blessings.

1.2.2 *The Second* Risāla

As mentioned previously, the second letter that has been transmitted to us as correspondence from Abū Ḥanīfa to ʿUthmān al-Battī has not received as much notice in the research. It is not yet published, and in its manuscript form it has gone largely unnoticed.[50] As a result, it only recently became a document of interest when van Ess introduced it in his history of early Islamic theology and first undertook an analysis of it.[51]

50 The text is not mentioned in the relevant articles on Abū Ḥanīfa by Joseph Schacht, "Abū Ḥanīfa al-Nuʿmān," *EI*^{2}, vol. 1, 123f. nor by ʿUmar Farūq ʿAbd-Allāh, "Abū Ḥanīfa," *EIr*, vol. 1, 295ff. Sezgin, in *GAS*, vol. 1, 418, no. IX refers to a second *Risāla* to ʿUthmān al-Battī. However, the manuscript named by him (Selim Ağa 587/11, fols. 164a-176a) only gives a variant version of the first letter. On this manuscript see van Ess, *Theologie*, vol. 1, 193.

51 Ibid., vol. 1, 204–207.

Van Ess immediately took the opportunity to point out that the authenticity of this work is more questionable than that of the first *Risāla*. We do not possess clear indications as to its author, so ultimately it must remain an open question as to whether the letter can be traced back to Abū Ḥanīfa in its current form. What argues for his authorship is that the manuscript in which it is transmitted states explicitly that it is a *Risāla li-Abī Ḥanīfa al-Nuʿmān b. Thābit al-Kūfī ilā ʿUthmān al-Battī*.[52] But it should be emphasized that this is the only precise indication we have against a number of uncertainties and question marks.

First, it is problematic that the extant text is clearly incomplete. The opening statements and the closing formulas are missing, such that we cannot use the language of this part of the text for evaluative purposes as we could for the first *Risāla*.

Second, the Islamic tradition only knows of a single letter to ʿUthmān al-Battī. None of the authors who attribute such a work to Abū Ḥanīfa suggest that there might be two—which is not necessarily significant but still leaves us with certain doubts.

Regardless, the question of the authenticity of the *Risāla* cannot be answered by such external indicators. A clearer view can only be attained on the basis of its contents. This leads us, as will soon be shown, very close to Abū Ḥanīfa. Still, it seems most proper to admit that in this case no definitive judgment is possible.

The reason for this, above all others, is the fact that the subject matter of the letter is completely different from that of the first *Risāla*, which rules out any closer comparison between the two. Whereas the first letter dealt with the definition of belief and how a sinner ought to be categorized in relation to it, the second letter deals exclusively with the problem of human free will and responsibility. When dealing with this topic the author takes an approach whereby he differentiates between various hypothetical starting points and undertakes a separate treatment for each.

At first he is concerned with explaining that human beings are responsible to their Creator even before they have access to revelation. God has shown all created things (by way of natural cognition) that they should worship Him and how they should serve Him. As a consequence, human beings have always been obligated to obey God, which means, in another formulation, that no one can excuse himself of his sins by saying that he had no access to the religion.[53]

---

52 MS Tehran Majlis 8/31, 30. The text of the manuscript which is the basis of the following presentation was kindly made available to me by Professor van Ess.

53 See in regard to this the following structure of the *Risāla II*, summarized below. I cannot give more precise citations since I did not have access to a copy of the manuscript but

Complete knowledge of God's commandments and one's own responsibility, however, is only known through revelation, meaning the Qur'ān. Therein one learns more precisely how deeds come into existence, and learns that within them divine will and human responsibility are bound together.

The author elucidates in detail on how this latter theme must be conceptualized according to a specific model: At the beginning of every deed exists the intention (*nīya*) of the person to bring about something good or bad. God is not forced to react, but generally does—aiding the good with His divine assistance (*tawfīq*) and allowing the bad to happen with His abandonment (*khidhlān*). In each case, however, the person can only actualize his intention when God has bestowed on him the necessary capacity (*quwwa*). The upshot then is that both are operative in the origination of actions, and it would be wrong to view either God or people alone as their initiator. Or, in the formulation of the polemical words of the author: One may neither follow those who assign humans the entirety of the deed (*ahl al-tafwīḍ*), nor those who see God's influence and determination exclusively (*ahl al-ijbār*).

The image that appears here has some authentic aspects to it and does not lack a certain originality. But it is still questionable whether we can attribute the text to Abū Ḥanīfa himself or if it should be seen as a later forgery. Van Ess did not hesitate to point out that these ideas are not atypical for the second/eighth century.[54] The Shīʿites employed very similar concepts and likewise claimed that they adhered to a middle way between *jabr* and *tafwīḍ*.[55] Furthermore, they were, like Abū Ḥanīfa, primarily present in Kufa.

More important than this parallel in time and locale, however, is another conformity that van Ess has already pointed out: Many of the concepts that we encounter in the second *Risāla* are also found in later Ḥanafite theology. One can even say, without exaggeration, that these teachings can be seen as the common property of the Transoxanian Ḥanafites. This is certainly the case for the doctrine outlined at the beginning on the natural acquisition of the knowledge of God. Al-Māturīdī adhered to this position[56] as did his student one generation removed Abū Salama;[57] and we know from al-Pazdawī

only Professor van Ess' transcript.

54 Van Ess, *Theologie*, vol. 1, 205f.

55 Wilferd Madelung, "The Shiite and Khārijite Contribution to Pre-Ashʿarite Kalām," in *Islamic Philosophical Theology*, ed. Parviz Morewedge (Albany, NY, 1979), 124.

56 See Ulrich Rudolph, "Ratio und Überlieferung in der Erkenntnislehre al-Ašʿarī's und al-Māturīdī's," *ZDMG* 142 (1992): 72–89.

57 Abū Salama Muḥammad b. Muḥammad al-Samarqandī, *Jumal uṣūl al-dīn*, ed. Ahmet Saim Kılavuz as *Ebû Seleme es-Semerkandî ve Akâid Risâlesi* (Istanbul, 1989), 9.7 and 9.16ff.

that the *mutakallimūn* of Samarqand invoked Abū Ḥanīfa extensively to support this tenet.[58] The same measure of continuity within the school is found in regard to the topic of *qadar*, which took a central position in the *Risāla*. Its hallmark feature, the stated goal of providing a middle way between Qadarites and Jabrites, is precisely the guideline by which later Ḥanafites oriented themselves. We encounter it with al-Ḥakīm al-Samarqandī,[59] his somewhat older contemporary Makḥūl al-Nasafī,[60] and from al-Māturīdī onward in every work from the school.[61]

Certainly the exposition given by all the later authors indicates a considerably higher degree of systematization and differs in another notable manner: The later authors almost always use the same formulation: God creates all acts, while the role of the human being is to carry out what has been created by God.[62] This is to be contrasted with the alternative position constructed in the second *Risāla* where the "letting-occur" (*amḍā*) on the part of the Creator is juxtaposed with human intentionality; the emphasis of these two dimensions was seldom discussed in later argumentation.[63] In this respect the doctrines of the second *Risāla* are uncertain and vague, indeed semi-archaic. In addition to this, we can reiterate the peculiar fact that opponents are not yet described there with the later customary terminology such as "Qadarīya" and "Jabrīya," but instead as *ahl al-tafwīḍ*[64] and as *ahl al-ijbār*.

---

58 *Uṣūl*, 207.12–15 and 210.13–16. Al-Pazdawī himself is of the opinion that with this claim of Abū Ḥanīfa, injustice is being committed (ibid., 210.17ff.); he adheres to the view that there is no knowledge of God without revelation (ibid., 207.6ff.). Ibn al-Dāʿī, 91.9f., likewise imputes to Abū Ḥanīfa the argument for rational knowledge of God.

59 See below, 96ff., and in al-Ḥakīm al-Samarqandī, *K. al-Sawād al-aʿẓam* (Būlāq, 1253/1837–38) [hence referred to as *K. al-Sawād*], particularly sections 6 and 42.

60 See below, 81ff., as well as the overview of the content of the *K. al-Radd* below, especially Chapter B. III and IV, C III (beginning) and IV (beginning).

61 See Gimaret, *Théories*, 179ff. and here 300ff.

62 For example, *K. al-Sawād*, 11.10–13 (section 6)/Istanbul edition, 8.11–13; Marie Bernand, "Le Kitāb al-Radd ʿalā l-bidaʿ d'Abū Muṭīʿ Makḥūl al-Nasafī," *Annales Islamologiques* 16 (1980): 65.1 and 66.8f.; Abū Salama, 21 ult.ff.

63 The eminent role that intention is accorded in the conceptualization of the second *Risāla* was the argument that induced van Ess to ultimately accept Abū Ḥanīfa as the author (*Theologie*, vol. 1, 206f.).

64 The term "*fawwaḍa*," in contrast, is supported by Abū Ḥanīfa's student Abū Muṭīʿ al-Balkhī, cf. 42.7 of Abū Muṭīʿ al-Balkhī, *al-Fiqh al-absaṭ*, in al-Kawtharī, *al-ʿĀlim wa-l-mutaʿallim*, 39–60 [hence referred to as *Fiqh absaṭ*].

Notwithstanding, these considerations are not enough to prove that Abū Ḥanīfa was the author of the second *Risāla*.[65] Instead we must suffice with the above conclusions that the letter brings us into proximity with the great Kufan scholar and at least originates from his immediate surroundings. If this result can be abided by, then the purpose of our deliberations has, in principle, been fulfilled, since we also know that the author was an early Ḥanafite and we can moreover operate on the premise that he was also part of the particular tradition of northeastern Iran. Under these premises it is not illegitimate to conceptualize the *Risāla* as being between Abū Ḥanīfa and his first students, since regardless of how one answers the question of its authorship, the letter remains in one way or the other a component of the early history of eastern Ḥanafite theology.

THE STRUCTURE OF THE *RISĀLA II*

[Foreword]

Letter from Abū Ḥanīfa to ʿUthmān al-Battī on the various views held on *qadar*.

[Introduction]
DELINEATION OF HERESIES

We distance ourselves as much from the doctrines of the "people of delegation" (*ahl al-tafwīḍ*) as from those who represent the "people of coercion" (*ahl al-ijbār*).

[Main Section]
HIS OWN POSITION

1) *Responsibility of human beings before revelation*

God has created all people to worship Him and has shown them the way to obedience. Because of this He has enjoined the argument (*ḥujja*) upon them and given them initiative toward the (correct) course of action (*ḥamalahum ʿalā l-maḥajja*).

65 The later sources (al-Baghdādī, Ps.-Māturīdī) mentioned by van Ess, *Theologie*, vol. 1, 206nn6–8 that aim to associate similar concepts to Abū Ḥanīfa do not change anything. Their wording corresponds again to later terminology and if anything deviates from the formulation of the second *Risāla*.

2) *Responsibility of human beings after revelation*

Then He revealed to them the Qurʾān as a (final) proof and gave them limbs as a means for them to act (*yaʿmalūn*) and be taken to reckoning (*yuḥāsabūna wa-yusʾalūna*).

In any case, God has not just given them the capacity (*quwwa*) to fulfill his commands, but He has them clutched by the forelock (*akhadha bi-l-nawāṣī*; see Q 11:56): Nothing can be brought about by their wills but it is He that lets it occur through His will (*bi-irādatihi wa-mashīʾatihi*).

3) *The origin of good deeds*

If a person intends (*nawā*) something good, then God lets it happen if He wills (*amḍā lahu mā nawā*) with His power and His divine assistance (*tawfīq*) and rewards him for it, since God is exalted above preventing people from acts of obedience and depriving them of a reward.

4) *The origin of bad deeds*

If, in contrast, the person intends something bad, then God either forsakes him (*khadhalahu*) because of His justice, so that the sin can take place, or He prevents him from it, due to His grace (*faḍl*), even though he had been striving to commit the sin (*ḥāriṣ ʿalayhā*).

5) *God's mercy and justice*

God shows threefold mercy (when He gives his assistance, when He gives reward, and when He wards off sin) and justice once (when He allows the sin to happen).

6) *Human ability and duty*

Nothing can happen without God freeing the way (*takhlīya*) and deciding (*ḥukm*). Yet the basis for which people may be blamed comes from themselves, since God only demands of His servants those things that He has put them in a condition to do.

The example of prayer is given: If a person is sick and does not have the capacity (*quwwa*) to stand, then he may perform it sitting. If health comes back to him, this would be for him essentially a command to pray standing.

Such is the matter with all actions: God has given people a capacity to do all that He has made a duty (*kallafa*) upon them. Were He to take away this capacity, however, then the duty would also fall away.[66]

1.3 Abū Muqātil al-Samarqandī (d. 208/823) and the *Kitāb al-ʿĀlim wa-l-mutaʿallim*

The *Kitāb al-ʿĀlim wa-l-mutaʿallim* is much more elaborate in its presentation than the two texts studied above, and takes the first step, so to speak, on the path to a Ḥanafite tradition. Here we have for the first time a text not by Abū Ḥanīfa, but rather by an author from his circle of students. What he puts forth is not supposed to be new, and definitely not original, but rather the selfless effort to reproduce and explain the views of his teacher.

This meaningful process of authorship has long gone unrecognized by the Muslim tradition, which has always listed the text as one of Abū Ḥanīfa's works,[67] leading some current editions to still name him as the actual author of the text.[68] Yet all clues suggest otherwise and make clear that not Abū Ḥanīfa, but rather one of his followers, Abū Muqātil al-Samarqandī (d. 208/823) ought to be seen as the author of the *K. al-ʿĀlim*. True, in the majority of manuscripts and bibliographical citations he is merely named as the first transmitter of the text,[69] but the text makes its actual provenance clear and unmistakable. It conscientiously separates between the questions of the student and the answers that he receives from his teacher, yet quite evidently shows the same literary style in both elements of the dialogue.[70] Besides, Muslim tradition by no means completely forgot the original circumstances; an author as late as

66 This last point is a clear rebuff of the idea of *taklīf bimā lā yuṭāq*, which al-Māturīdī and his successors also spoke out against. On this theme see Brunschvig, "Devoir et pouvoir."

67 For example, Ibn al-Nadīm, *Fihrist* 202.12; *Uṣūl*, 4.4; Ḥājjī Khalīfa, *Kashf al-ẓunūn ʿan asāmī l-kutub wa-l-funūn*, ed. Mehmet Şerefettin Yaltkaya and Kilisli Rifat Bilge (Istanbul, 1941–43), 1437.4; al-Bayāḍī, 18.7.

68 Such as the edition by al-Kawtharī, and that edited by Muḥammad Rawās Qalʿajī and ʿAbd al-Wahhāb al-Hindī al-Nadwī, *al-ʿĀlim wa-l-mutaʿallim* (Aleppo, 1972). The latter edition provides the basis of our study and is hereafter cited as *K. al-ʿĀlim*. See also GAS, vol. 1, 418, no. IX.

69 For example, Ibn al-Nadīm, *Fihrist* 202.12: "*rawāhu ʿanhu Muqātil*"; Ḥājjī Khalīfa, 1437.7: "*rawāhu Muqātil ʿan al-imām*"; al-Bayāḍī, 21.-1f.; see also the *Manāqib* by Muwaffaq al-Dīn al-Makkī, cited by Schacht, "An Early Murciʾite Treatise," 98.

70 See Schacht, ibid., 100, who asserts that the *K. al-ʿĀlim* borrows stylistically from the *Risāla I* to ʿUthmān al-Battī as well as from the *Fiqh absaṭ*.

al-Dhahabī knew to report, in contrast to the mainstream, that Abū Muqātil had been the actual *ṣāḥib Kitāb al-ʿĀlim wa-l-mutaʿallim*.[71]

What role this Abū Muqātil could have played in Abū Ḥanīfa's circle is only ascertainable in its general contours from the available sources today. The Ḥanafite *ṭabaqāt* works pass over his name in silence, so we only have a few statements in the biographical compilations of the *ḥadīth* narrators to depend on.

They stress very strongly that Abū Muqātil was not reliable as a transmitter. He is supposed to have claimed things which were not true and have even been disposed in the case of certain narrations to invent *isnād*s for the sake of their beauty.[72] Yet he was known also to be pious, even possessed by ascetic zeal,[73] and what he accomplished in the field of *fiqh* seems to have been well recognized by his peers.[74] However, none of these testimonials tell us anything about his relationship to Abū Ḥanīfa, which seems to rule out the possibility of elaborating further on this critical point for the evaluation of the text. One anecdote suggests to us that Abū Muqātil cultivated a close relationship with the Master.[75] But this sounds more like a literary topos, especially since it does not explain why the Ḥanafite tradition so persistently overlooked his name.

There remain only two secure coordinates by which we can assess the possibility of a personal acquaintance between Abū Muqātil and Abū Ḥanīfa. The first is his death date, generally given as the year 208 (823).[76] Accordingly, he is supposed to have lived a long life. In this light a meeting with Abū Ḥanīfa is not ruled out, even though the student must have still been young.

The second significant piece of data is the report claiming that Abū Muqātil frequented Mecca.[77] This also argues for a meeting of the two, since a trip from eastern Iran to the Ḥijāz would not leave Kufa too far off the path. It is thus possible that Abū Muqātil knew the great Kufan and that his *K. al-ʿĀlim* is based on

71 Al-Dhahabī, *Mīzān*, vol. 1, 558.1 and after him Ibn Ḥajar, *Lisān*, vol. 2, 323.1f.

72 Ibn Ḥibbān al-Bustī, *K. al-Majrūḥīn*, ed. al-Ḥāfiẓ Begh (Hyderabad, 1390/1970), vol. 1, 257.2ff.; al-Dhahabī, *Mīzān*, vol. 1, 557f. (no. 2120); Ibn Ḥajar, *Lisān*, vol. 2, 322f. (no. 1322) and idem, *Tahdhīb*, vol. 2, 397ff. (no. 695); also Ibn Abī Ḥātim al-Rāzī, *K. al-Jarḥ wa-l-taʿdīl* (Hyderabad, 1371–73/1952–53), vol. 3, 174 (no. 748). On the *isnād* forgeries see Ibn Ḥajar, *Lisān*, vol. 2, 323.7 and 323.-2f. and idem, *Tahdhīb*, 397.-2f. and 399.1f.

73 Ibn Ḥibbān, vol. 1, 257.1; see van Ess, *Theologie*, vol. 2, 561n21.

74 Ibn Ḥajar, *Lisān*, vol. 2, 322.-3f. and 323.-7f. and idem, *Tahdhīb*, vol. 2, 398.-5; according to Jalāl al-Dīn al-Suyūṭī, *al-Laʾāliʾ al-maṣnūʿa fī l-aḥādīth al-mawḍūʿa* (Cairo, undated), vol. 1, 99.8, he was even a *qāḍī*.

75 Al-Dhahabī, *Mīzān*, vol. 1, 557.-5f.; Ibn Ḥajar, *Lisān*, vol. 2, 322.-5f.

76 Al-Dhahabī, *Mīzān*, vol. 1, 557.-8f.; Ibn Ḥajar, *Lisān*, vol. 2, 322.-7 (with typos) and idem, *Tahdhīb*, vol. 2, 398.-4.

77 Ibn Ḥibbān, vol. 1, 252.8f.

personal contact and conversation with him. This is not proven through these considerations, however—there still remains the possibility that the text, far from being a real conversation log, is merely a compilation of narrations from Abū Ḥanīfa presented in the form of a fictional dialogue.

In addition, Abū Muqātil's significance for the Ḥanafites in Samarqand remains questionable. His *nisba* suggests that he lived in that city,[78] but it is not clear what contributions he made in promoting the Ḥanafite school there nor even how long the city remained the base of his activity.[79] It is plausible to assume that Abū Muqātil did play a certain role in Samarqand in this regard. But even so, we would be reassured to find something more precise from the sources and not have to resort to so much speculation.

All in all the author of the *K. al-ʿĀlim* remains a ghostly figure in the Islamic tradition, whereupon one cannot quite resist the notion that this impression was, perhaps, intentional: the text was no doubt widely appreciated, but it was meant to be seen as a work of Abū Ḥanīfa, recognizing Abū Muqātil only as a transmitter who dutifully lent the Master his own voice. In order for this image to seem plausible, it was perhaps not a disadvantage if the student was not granted autonomy or his own profile by posterity.

The success of the *K. al-ʿĀlim* and its wide dissemination in northeastern Iran were not disrupted by issues of authorship whatsoever. On the contrary, we know that it was received there quite early and we can also determine that it played an important role as a source text for Transoxanian theology. The former is known through its *riwāya* that has remained extant. The latter may be inferred from the fact that the *kalām* works of the Māturīdites constantly borrow from and cite this work. Both facts are important and demonstrate the inner continuity of the Ḥanafite school. Thus it is fitting to examine the text a bit more closely.

The paths of transmission for the *K. al-ʿĀlim* have already been examined by Schacht.[80] As he has demonstrated, various false leads from the manuscripts and later traditions can be left aside in order to concentrate on a more noteworthy *isnād* preserved in the Cairo manuscript which al-Kawtharī included in his edition of the text.[81] This one clearly indicates that the *K. al-ʿĀlim* reached

78 The *nisba* al-Samarqandī is attributed to Abū Muqātil in all of the sources. In addition, Ibn Ḥajar, *Tahdhīb*, vol. 2, 397.9 also gives al-Khurāsānī.

79 Al-Suyūṭī's claim (*Laʾālīʾ*, vol. 1, 99.8) that he was the *qāḍī* of Samarqand is in principle the only report in this regard, and it is not just isolated, but also late. Besides this we do find out from yet another source that Abū Muqātil came to Nishapur (al-Khalīfa al-Naysābūrī, *Talkhīṣ-i Tārīkh-i Nīshābūr*, ed. Bahman Karīmī [Tehran, 1340] 15.-3).

80 Schacht, "An Early Murciʾite Treatise," 98ff.

81 For the *isnād* in the Aleppo edition used here, see Qalʿajī, 22.-6ff.

Balkh very quickly and from there was disseminated outward through the entire region.

This important finding is not set back by Schacht's view that the *isnād* was not reliable in its entirety;[82] his doubts only apply to its documentation of later centuries. Schacht considered the earlier part of the *riwāya* which follows directly from Abū Muqātil—the part most critical for us here—as authentic. This is so because the chronological intervals are reasonably short and we know from other sources that there were teacher-student relationships between all of the figures mentioned there. The names that follow Abū Muqātil are Abū Muṭīʿ al-Balkhī (d. 199/814)[83] and ʿIṣām b. Yūsuf al-Balkhī (d. 215/830);[84] Abū Sulaymān Mūsā l-Jūzjānī (d. after 200/815)[85] and Muḥammad b. Muqātil al-Rāzī (d. 248/862);[86] Abū Bakr Aḥmad b. Isḥāq al-Jūzjānī, a student of Abū Sulaymān and also teacher of al-Māturīdī;[87] and finally Abū Manṣūr al-Māturīdī (d. 333/944) himself.

The lower part of the *riwāya* starting from al-Māturīdī, moreover, is actually less doubtful than Schacht's skepticism makes it appear. Here, ʿAbd al-Karīm b. Mūsā l-Pazdawī, Muḥammad al-Nasafī, the latter's son the famous Abū l-Muʿīn al-Nasafī, Burhān al-Dīn ʿAlī b. al-Ḥusayn al-Balkhī, and Ibn Qāḍī l-ʿAskar (d. 651/1252) are all mentioned as transmitters. Schacht was most suspicious about this part of the chain because of the fact that almost 320 years are supposed to be spanned by only five transmitters. But we must ask ourselves where the gap actually is and whether or not the entire list of names actually becomes dubious as a result.

As for ʿAbd al-Karīm b. Mūsā l-Pazdawī (d. 390/999), the great-grandfather of the well-known Abū l-Yusr al-Pazdawī; we know that he studied with al-Māturīdī.[88] Thus the immediate continuation of the *riwāya* seems to be correct. Then the *isnād* reaches Abū l-Muʿīn (d. 508/1114) in two steps, which is rather a large leap, yet cannot be ruled out, since the above mentioned Abū Yusr al-Pazdawī (d. 493/1100), a contemporary of al-Nasafī, happens to report to us that he discovered particular details about al-Māturīdī

82 Schacht, "An Early Murciʾite Treatise," 99ff.

83 On him see the following chapter.

84 Wāʿiẓ-i Balkhī, 196–201; also see Radtke, 543; al-Dhahabī, *Mīzān*, vol. 3, 67 (no. 5628); Ibn Ḥajar, *Lisān*, vol. 4, 168 (no. 413); Ibn Abī l-Wafāʾ, vol. 1, 347f. (no. 961); al-Laknawī, 116.6ff.

85 Wāʿiẓ-i Balkhī, 210–214; Radtke, 543; Ibn Abī l-Wafāʾ, vol. 2, 186f. (no. 580); Ibn Quṭlubūghā, 74f. (no. 227); al-Laknawī, 216.2ff.; Flügel, 286f.

86 Ibn Abī l-Wafāʾ, vol. 2, 134 (no. 411); Ibn Ḥajar, *Lisān*, vol. 5, 388 (no. 1261) and idem, *Tahdhīb*, vol. 9, 469f. (no. 760); another death date, 242 AH, is given in Ḥājjī Khalīfa, 1457.17, and after him Ismāʿīl Bāshā l-Baghdādī, *Hadīyat al-ʿārifīn, asmāʾ al-muʾallifīn wa-āthār al-muṣannifīn*, ed. Kilisli Rifat Bilge and Ibnülemin Mahmut Kemal Inal (Istanbul, 1951–55), vol. 2, 13.-11.

87 Ibn Abī l-Wafāʾ, vol. 1, 60 (nos. 77 and 79); al-Laknawī, 14.10–14; Flügel, 293 and 295.

88 Ibn Abī l-Wafāʾ, vol. 1, 327 (no. 881); al-Laknawī, 101.88ff.

from his great-grandfather ʿAbd al-Karīm by means of his own father Muḥammad.[89] If this is the case with the al-Pazdawīs, then a parallel case with the Nasafīs, an equally learned family,[90] is just as possible.

Again, that Burhān al-Dīn al-Balkhī (d. 547/1152) is ultimately supposed to have received the text from Abū l-Muʿīn al-Nasafī is completely plausible. He was his student, as Ibn Abī l-Wafāʾ imparts to us.[91] Finally, there is a lengthy interval of time, which is unbridgeable, between him and the last name of the *isnād*, Ibn Qāḍī l-ʿAskar (d. 651/1252).[92] A name or two may be missing, but that is not sufficient grounds to doubt the credibility of the entire *riwāya*.

The significance of the *K. al-ʿĀlim* as a foundational text and source for the Māturīdites is evident first of all in the fact that the text, as mentioned, was read and cited over the course of centuries. We find allusions and references to the work time and time again in later *kalām* works, even if the precision of reproduction varies greatly among individual authors.

Al-Māturīdī, for example, was not very precise in his citations. Nowhere does he make the effort to reproduce citations verbatim from texts which he built on, and he also never mentions a source by its title. But from time to time, he invokes older authorities, stating only that a certain opinion is supposed to have been transmitted from a certain scholar. In such places Abū Ḥanīfa's name comes up more often than others (as one might expect), and where it does, we find numerous statements that can be juxtaposed with certain passages in the *K. al-ʿĀlim*.[93]

The testimony that Abū l-Yusr al-Pazdawī left behind is more unequivocal and exemplary for our purposes. He was distinguished by a generally well-developed sense of his own theological tradition, which he wanted to distinguish, not just from heretical views but also from other specifically named theological schools. This clearly ingrained in him such an appreciation for earlier authorities that he diligently reproduced sections of their works verbatim. This is particularly evident in the case of the *K. al-ʿĀlim*; he speaks of having read the work, and proves this claim more than once by giving a citation.

The *K. al-ʿĀlim* is mentioned early on, in *Uṣūl*, 4.4. This is followed by a passage (*Uṣūl*, 4.5–7) that is faithfully taken from the text of Abū Muqātil (*K. al-ʿĀlim*, 33.3–6), as well as a second passage (*Uṣūl*, 4.7–11) which, with one exception, also comes from

89 *Uṣūl*, 3.1ff.

90 On the genealogy of Abū l-Muʿīn al-Nasafī, see Josef van Ess, *Ungenützte Texte zur Karrāmīya. Eine Materialsammlung* (Heidelberg, 1980), 56f.

91 Ibn Abī l-Wafāʾ, vol. 1, 320 (no. 992); Flügel, 312.

92 Ibn Abī l-Wafāʾ, vol. 1, 362 (no. 998).

93 Compare, for example, al-Māturīdī, *Taʾwīlāt*, vol. 1, 81.8f. with *Kitāb al-ʿĀlim*, 93.7ff. (in section 28); for the *K. al-Tawḥīd* see below, 225n41.

the same (*K. al-ʿĀlim*, 34.2–ult.). In contrast, two other statements from al-Pazdawī are more problematic. First, he wants to attribute *Uṣūl*, 175.11–13 to the *Fiqh akbar* of Abū Ḥanīfa though this can actually only be done in the sense of its meaning (compare *Fiqh absaṭ*, 46.11–12); a more exact, though not verbatim parallel to this passage would have been *K. al-ʿĀlim* (97.2–3). Second, according to him *Uṣūl*, 233.13–15 is also supposed to be a citation from the *K. al-ʿĀlim*, but we lack the verification for this, even if the pertinent theme is treated thoroughly there (section 23, 81.8–85.4). Therefore al-Pazdawī must have either cited certain sections from memory, or, unsurprisingly, cited a version that is no longer accessible to us today.

Long after al-Pazdawī or Abū l-Muʿīn al-Nasafī, we encounter the Ottoman scholar Kamāl al-Dīn al-Bayāḍī (d. 1098/1687). Even he still refers to the *K. al-ʿĀlim*[94] (and the other texts attributed to Abū Ḥanīfa) and conceives of his own work, the *Ishārāt al-marām*, as an exegesis of these early and groundbreaking texts.

The fact that all of these authors only mention Abū Ḥanīfa's name, not Abū Muqātil, as author of the *K. al-ʿĀlim* needs no explanation. Neither the biographers nor the theologians from among the Ḥanafites concerned themselves with the details of how their canonical texts developed. As a consequence they retained the image that we have meanwhile become familiar with: Abū Ḥanīfa was instrumental in the development of theology, whereas Abū Muqātil merely recounted what he learned thereof for the sake of posterity.[95]

The evident success of the *K. al-ʿĀlim* can be explained not only because of its attribution to Abū Ḥanīfa, but also due to the appealing form in which the work was written. Linguistically easy to understand and without any terminological ballast, the schematization is so pedagogically constructed that even a simple listener or reader could access the text and grasp its contents.

The topics which it touches upon are equivalent in many respects to those dealt with in the first *Risāla* to ʿUthmān al-Battī. The main theme is still the definition of belief, the axiom of equality of belief among angels and people, and the concept that judgment about sinners ought to be "pushed back." But the schematization is much more differentiated and expands beyond the borders of the older set of questions. Thus we find that argumentation with those who think differently has intensified, especially when the opponents are from the Khārijite camp (*K. al-ʿĀlim*, sections 33–36 and 45–46). In a further novelty, we see that practical piety takes a more prominent position in the case where the question of worship (*ʿibāda*) of God is explained (ibid., sections 37–40).

---

94 Al-Bayāḍī, 18.7, 21.-1 and more; from al-Nasafī cf. *Tabṣira*, vol. 1, 25.2f.

95 Abū Muqātil appears as a transmitter of a saying of Abū Ḥanīfa in *K. al-Sawād*, 16 ult. (Istanbul edition, 11 ult.; ʿOmar, 115).

More important than these small additions is the thematic expansion which we encounter right at the beginning of the work. Here we find a lengthy justification of theological speculation, with claims that go far beyond the methodological observations that we remember from the first *Risāla*. There, Abū Ḥanīfa conclusively defended himself against possible accusations from *ḥadīth* transmitters and explained that he was not practicing any innovation, being bound to the Qur'ān and *sunna*.[96] Abū Muqātil, in contrast, has moved to a new position that is clearly on the offensive. Simple piety measured in terms of *ḥadīth* is not sufficient to determine what the exigencies of religion are, and when difficult issues arise it may not be sufficient. Truth and falsehood are only distinguishable by speculation, such that one is dependent on one's own considerations to be properly guided (*K. al-ʿĀlim*, sections 1–4, compare sections 30–31).

This is certainly an elementary plea for the human intellect and shows us by its lack of intricacy how early the *K. al-ʿĀlim* can be placed in the development of theology, since if one could reason undauntedly in this manner on such a delicate theme, then the arguments advanced by opposing parties on the subject cannot have been worked out in greater detail at the time.[97] But in two aspects this introductory section points us to the future and leads us one step closer to *kalām*: one is its emphasis on the distinctive function of the intellect; the other is the fact that the *K al-ʿĀlim* has an introductory section on epistemological questions which later became a hallmark of all later works in *kalām*.

THE STRUCTURE OF THE *KITĀB AL-ʿĀLIM WA-L-MUTAʿALLIM*[98]

Justification of theological speculation

1) Knowledge (*ʿilm*) is always our foundation. Deeds (*ʿamal*) can only be a consequence (*tabaʿ*) of knowledge and never compensate for deficient knowledge.

96 *Risāla I*, 35.2–3.

97 The same is true of the way that Abū Muqātil cites *ḥadīth*, and the form in which these *ḥadīth* are apparently available to him. These also allow one to make conclusions about the early composition of this text, as Schacht ("An Early Murciʾite Treatise," 105n3, 109f., 112n1, 116f.) and after him Cook (*Early Muslim Dogma*, 30) point out.

98 The Qalʿajī-Nadwī edition already cited forms the basis of this presentation, as it not only reproduces the Cairo manuscript as al-Kawtharī does, but also works off the other manuscripts (see the introduction to the edition, Qalʿajī and Nadwī, 20 and 25). The description of the Arabic text follows in summary; I have added the thematic titles. An overview on the *K. al-ʿĀlim* has already been given by Schacht, "An Early Murciʾite Treatise," 104ff.; starting in chapter 32 his paragraph enumeration deviates by a number from the enumeration in the Aleppo edition.

2) It is not sufficient to restrict oneself to *ḥadīth*. We must ourselves recognize what is true/right and what is wrong.
3) Distinguishing between truth and falsehood is obligatory.
4) This must always be carried out in a definitive way. Critique of the *ḥadīth* transmitters. Critique of the use of alleged *ḥadīth*. Distancing from Shiʿites, Khārijites, and Murjiʾites.

Definition of belief

5) Carrying out religious duties (*farāʾiḍ*) takes place in practicing the religious law (*sharīʿa*), but is not a part of belief (*īmān*) itself. Belief comes before deeds; the religion (*dīn*) was the same among all the prophets, but the religious laws that they brought differed.
6) Belief (*īmān*) is affirmation (*taṣdīq*), knowledge (*maʿrifa*), certainty (*yaqīn*), avowal (*iqrār*), and Islam.
7) The believer can practice *taqīya* without losing his belief. His continuous affirmation with the heart allows belief to carry on.
8) One ought not to hastily conclude that there is a plurality in the concept of "belief" because there are several descriptions for it (see 6).
9) In reality these are all various names with the same meaning.

No differentiation of rank in belief

10) The belief of common people is the same as the belief of angels and of prophets; only their obedience (i.e., deeds) differs.
11) Angels and prophets are more obedient because of their greater virtue (*makārim al-akhlāq*) and higher insight into God's actions. Whoever sins has not doubted God, but maintains his convictions and thus his belief as well.
12) Exemplification of 11) through an analogical example (*qiyās*). Merit of *qiyās* as an aid to knowledge: It is necessary because the ignorant deviate from truth through a lack of it.

Promise and threat

13) Despite the equality of belief, the prophets attain a "supplement" (*faḍl*) in otherworldly reward, just as they exceed us in all good things. Nevertheless, the believing person obtains his just reward, and even a "supplement" as well, since he may enter Paradise by the intercession of the prophet.

14) Disbelief (*shirk*) is punished in any case; some sins will surely be forgiven. Which they will be and whether it might be all of them except for disbelief, we do not know.
15) Thus there is hope and fear in regard to all sins except disbelief, according to their gravity in various degrees. A *qiyās* on this subject.
16) With all sins except disbelief it is more commendable to ask for forgiveness for those who commit them than to curse them. Just as disbelief is the worst sin, belief is the highest merit. From the former, one expects the harshest punishment and from the latter, the greatest reward.

Commanding the correct and forbidding the reprehensible

17) All of *ahl al-ʿadl* (= his own group) have the same view of sins that occur in the Muslim community. But the level of their insight and their political engagement vary. *Qiyās: ahl al-ʿadl* are like an army, the soldiers of which react cleverly and bravely, in varying degrees, in the face of the enemy.

Belief and sin

18) A believer can commit grave sins and still love God. Only a disbeliever is an enemy of God.
19) That he sins despite his love for God (being overcome by passions) is not an inherent contradiction. Human actions are often inconsistent.
20) Furthermore, the believing sinner does not necessarily expect to be punished, but hopes for God's forgiveness and hopes that he will repent in time.
21) Another example is that one often takes risks with dangerous things in one's life—but always in the hope of coming out unharmed from danger.

Definition of disbelief

22) Disbelief (*kufr*) is rejection (*inkār*), repudiation (*juḥūd*), and denial (*takdhīb*) of God, His revelation, and the revealed duties. Neglecting these duties does not make one a disbeliever, but a believing sinner.
23) If someone rejects the Prophet Muḥammad, then he is not an adherent to true *tawḥīd*. Disbelief always lurks behind denial of the Prophet as its real cause (as is the case with Christians and Jews).

Fighting off various polemics

24) It is absurd to ask the hypothetical questions of how to evaluate someone who believes in Muḥammad but wants to kill him (thus making an arbitrary distinction between belief and actions).
25) It is just as absurd to ask whether someone who believes in God can attribute a son to God (and imply that based on our definition of belief we ought to recognize Christians and Jews as believers).
26) Our definition of hypocrisy (*nifāq*) as "disbelief in the heart and belief on the tongue" is the original definition and is in accordance with the Qur'ān (and likewise excludes deeds).

Defense of the principle of irjā'*—promise and threat*

27) God alone knows people's hearts and knows who believes and disbelieves. People and even angels only see exteriors and are not capable of judging. Whoever claims to do so despite this, is committing disbelief.
28) The angels first "pushed back" their judgment (*irjā'* = *wuqūf*) and were a role model for everyone through this (see Qur'ān 2:31–32). In some situations (depicted in the form of an allusion to the situation of the community after the first civil war) one cannot do otherwise. In regard to reward and punishment, we only know that Hell comes to disbelievers and Paradise comes to prophets as well as all those to whom the prophets have promised it. For sinners, there is fear as well as hope.
29) Our ability to judge whether certain people go to heaven is not based on our insight, but only on statements from an authoritative text (*naṣṣ*).
30) Even if a *ḥadīth* says that a sinner is no longer a believer, this is not correct. The *ḥadīth* must be wrong, since it contradicts the Qur'ān, and its transmitter is blameworthy.
31) If a *ḥadīth* says that a sinner's prayer will not be accepted for forty days, this may be correct, but it is not certain. We only know that God takes account of all of people's actions, but how He evaluates them is unknown.
32) Only a few things bring good deeds to naught in any case: disbelief, seeking benefit under cover of good deeds, and ostentation (*murā'āt*).

Position on the Khārijites

33) Even if some describe us as disbelievers and slander us, we only call them liars and do not dispute their belief.

34) Even those who accuse themselves of disbelief are not necessarily disbelievers.
35) Disbelief is only committed by those who explicitly disassociate themselves from God.
36) Thus it is also wrong to claim that whoever sins obeys Satan and is therefore a disbeliever.

Worship (ʿibāda)

37) Worship consists of faith-based obedience as well as hope and fear.
38) It can only be directed to God, since everything else would be disbelief. If we fear something in everyday life (a *qiyās* on this), then our fear in reality also goes back to God as its cause.
39) The believer fears God much more than any worldly regime.
40) Worship of God and knowledge of Him suffice to be a believer. One does not have to first be able to specify and define belief and disbelief.

Promise and threat

41) Belief removes the believer from the worst punishment. But we cannot say more on the recompense of sins.

Arguing with disbelievers

42) There are many forms of disbelief, but disbelief is in itself (as rejection of God) always the same, even if disbelievers sometimes pretend to worship God. In contrast, belief is always the same (among angels and people), even if differences arise in carrying out duties.
43) Disbelievers might even say "God is our lord" but they are just jabbering words that they have heard without understanding them.
44) Although the Prophet called us to belief in God, we do not know God through the prophets, but we know the prophets through God. Only God can bestow us with the honor of belief.

Arguing with Khārijites

45) Association (*walāya*) is based on satisfaction with good deeds, disassociation (*barāʾa*) on aversion toward bad deeds. The sinless believer merits only *walāya*, the unbeliever merits only *barāʾa*. The believers who have become sinful merit them both.

46) *Kufr al-niʿam* means to deny that all benefaction comes from God. Whoever does this becomes a disbeliever (from God's perspective).

1.4 Abū Muṭīʿ al-Balkhī (d. 199/814) and the *Kitāb al-Fiqh al-absaṭ*

This series of early texts will close with the *K. al-Fiqh al-absaṭ*, which we owe to Abū Muṭīʿ al-Balkhī (d. 199/814). The author, also a student of Abū Ḥanīfa,[99] was a well-known man and made great efforts to spread Ḥanafite teachings in the East. For sixteen years he was active as a *qāḍī* in Balkh,[100] and though he occasionally traveled—in his youth to Mecca (and thus probably to Abū Ḥanīfa)[101] and later also to Abū Yūsuf in Baghdad[102]—his main place of activity was clearly in his hometown. There he instructed his own students in the discipline of *fiqh*,[103] and earned the reputation of being sagacious and well-versed in religious topics.[104] The anecdote relating his vehement protest against an improper use of a Qurʾānic citation (Q 18:12) in a letter of the caliph's (Hārūn al-Rashīd) clearly places him in Balkh. He is even supposed to have said to the governor of the city that one who committed such abuse of holy scripture became a disbeliever; and it is said that he later declared the same thing from the pulpit of the mosque.[105]

Perhaps this brought him the reputation of being especially intent on "commanding the correct and forbidding the reprehensible" (*al-amr bi-l-maʿrūf*

---

99 Al-Dhahabī, *Mīzān*, vol. 1, 574.3 and idem, *al-ʿIbar fī khabar man ghabar*, ed. Ṣalāḥ al-Dīn al-Munajjid (Kuwait, 1960–66), vol. 1, 330.2; then al-Laknawī, 68.18 and 21; Ibn Ḥajar, *Lisān*, vol. 2, 334.7f.; Ibn Abī l-Wafāʾ, vol. 2, 265.-2; Flügel, 285; also Abū l-Layth al-Samarqandī, *Tanbīh al-ghāfilīn* (Cairo, 1302), 12.-10; see also, in regard to this and what follows, L.A. Griffen, "Abū Moṭīʿ al-Balḵī," *EIr*, vol. 1, 344f.

100 Ibn Abū Ḥātim al-Rāzī, vol. 3, 122.6; al-Khaṭīb al-Baghdādī, *Taʾrīkh Baghdād* (Cairo, 1349/1931), vol. 8, 223.8; Wāʿiẓ-i Balkhī, 146 ult; al-Dhahabī, *Mīzān*, vol. 1, 575.-7 and idem, *ʿIbar*, vol. 1, 330.3; Ibn Ḥajar, *Lisān*, vol. 2, 335.14 and 336.2f.; Ibn Abī l-Wafāʾ, vol. 2, 266.3f.; Ibn Quṭlūbughā, 87.5; al-Laknawī, 69.19.

101 See Abū l-Qāsim al-Balkhī al-Kaʿbī, *Maqālāt al-Islāmīyīn*, in Sayyid, *Faḍl al-iʿtizāl*, 93.2, where Abū Muṭīʿ himself states that he had been in Mecca.

102 Al-Khaṭīb al-Baghdādī, vol. 8, 223.11f.; see also Wāʿiẓ-i Balkhī, 148.-3f.

103 Al-Dhahabī, *Mīzān*, vol. 1, 574.6; Ibn Ḥajar, *Lisān*, vol. 2, 334.9; Ibn Abī l-Wafāʾ, vol. 2, 262.2; al-Laknawī, 68.16 and 12.

104 Al-Khaṭīb al-Baghdādī, vol. 8, 223.7f.; al-Dhahabī, *Mīzān*, vol. 1, 574.6ff.; Ibn Ḥajar, *Lisān*, vol. 2, 334.9ff.; Ibn Abī l-Wafāʾ, vol. 2, 266.3; al-Laknawī, 68.16 and 22f.

105 Al-Khaṭīb al-Baghdādī, vol. 8, 224.3ff.; Wāʿiẓ-i Balkhī, 149.7ff. and also Radtke, 541; al-Dhahabī, *Mīzān*, vol. 1, 574.-4ff.; Ibn Ḥajar, *Lisān*, vol. 2, 334.-3ff.; Ibn Abī l-Wafāʾ, vol. 2, 266.4ff.; Ibn Quṭlūbughā, 87.5ff.

wa-l-nahy ʿan al-munkar).[106] Aside from this, it was said about him afterwards that he was a Jahmite, since he is supposed to have said that Paradise and Hell were temporary.[107] But this must have only been a polemical allegation, since Abū Muṭīʿ clearly distanced himself from Jahm and also this particular idea.[108]

It is more telling, however, that he is consistently characterized as a Murjiʾite, although here the point of view of the observer is pivotal. Within the Ḥanafite school tradition, with authors such as Ibn Abī l-Wafāʾ and Ibn Quṭlūbughā, one would have naturally avoided this epithet, since it placed a skewed light on the entirety of the Ḥanafites. The biographical notices penned by the *ḥadīth* transmitters on their part repeated it all the more assiduously,[109] because to them it seemed to be an unmistakable criterion for the probable unreliability of Abū Muṭīʿ. As a Ḥanafite, the famous *qāḍī* was already suspect, and it is not surprising if, in such circles, he was usually classified as a weak transmitter.[110]

There is consensus that Abū Muṭīʿ reached the considerable age of 84.[111] Precisely when he died, however, is disputed. The sources give different possibilities between 177 and 204 AH,[112] but there are good reasons to settle on the year 199/814 as a death date. This particular date is given by the majority of the authors, and the *Taʾrīkh Baghdād*, which we can thank for other valuable information as well, gives the precise date up to the day.[113]

106 Al-Dhahabī, *ʿIbar*, vol. 1, 330.5ff.; al-Laknawī, 68.20.

107 Al-Khaṭīb al-Baghdādī, vol. 8, 225.8ff.; al-Dhahabī, *Mīzān*, vol. 1, 574.16f. and idem, *ʿIbar*, vol. 1, 330.5; Ibn Ḥajar, *Lisān*, vol. 2, 334.-7 and -4f.; al-Laknawī, 68.20.

108 *Fiqh absaṭ*, 56.15–19; also 52.1–5. It is interesting, by contrast, to see that Abū Ḥanīfa himself supposedly stood close to Jahm's position on this question; see van Ess, *Theologie*, vol. 2, 505.

109 Ibn Abī Ḥātim al-Rāzī, vol. 3, 122.6; al-Khaṭīb al-Baghdādī, vol. 7, 225.5; al-Dhahabī, *Mīzān*, vol. 1, 574.15f.; Ibn Ḥajar, *Lisān*, vol. 2, 334.-6 and 335.-7f.; al-Laknawī, 68.-2f. (based on al-Dhahabī).

110 Ibn Abī Ḥātim al-Rāzī, vol. 3, 121 ult. ff.; al-Khaṭīb al-Baghdādī, vol. 8, 225.7ff.; al-Dhahabī, *Mīzān*, vol. 1, 574.8ff. and idem, *ʿIbar*, vol. 1, 330.5; Ibn Ḥajar, *Lisān*, vol. 2, 334.11ff. and 335.-7ff.; al-Laknawī, 68.19 and -6ff. (based on al-Dhahabī).

111 Al-Khaṭīb al-Baghdādī, vol. 8, 223.16; Wāʿiẓ-i Balkhī, 146.-3f.; al-Dhahabī, *Mīzān*, vol. 1, 575.-7ff. and idem, *ʿIbar*, vol. 1, 330.3; Ibn Ḥajar, *Lisān*, vol. 2, 335.14f.; Ibn Abī l-Wafāʾ, vol. 2, 266.4; Ibn Quṭlūbughā, 87.4f.; al-Laknawī, 69.1f.

112 The year 177 is given in Flügel, 285; the year 197 by Ibn Abī l-Wafāʾ, vol. 2, 266.4 and Ibn Quṭlūbughā, 87.4f.; the year 199 from al-Khaṭīb al-Baghdādī, vol. 8, 223.15f.; al-Dhahabī, *Mīzān*, vol. 1, 575.-7f. and idem, *ʿIbar*, where Abū Muṭīʿ is named under the year 199; Ibn Ḥajar, *Lisān*, vol. 2, 335.14f.; al-Laknawī, 68.17f. and 69.1f.; the year 204 is in Wāʿiẓ-i Balkhī, 146.-3.

113 According to al-Khaṭīb al-Baghdādī, vol. 8, 223.15f., Abū Muṭīʿ is supposed to have died on 12 Jumāda al-Ūla 199 (30 December 814) in Balkh.

According to the same source, Abū Muṭīʿ was a teacher and for a long time also a public figure. Fortunately his influence was not confined to his immediate circle, but disseminated in particular through the *Fiqh absaṭ*, the text which he left behind for us. Upon closer examination, it is clear (as in the case of the *K. al-ʿĀlim*) that the question of its authorship was determined with a specific purpose in mind, as Muslim tradition in this instance also downplayed the role of the student in the composition of the text. For this reason we again find the claim that Abū Ḥanīfa was the author and Abū Muṭīʿ was actually its first transmitter.[114] After the initial case of the *K. al-ʿĀlim*, this is hardly a problem, since here just as there, the clues present in *Fiqh absaṭ* clearly tell another story; and we may note again that al-Dhahabī also reassessed Abū Muṭīʿ as the actual *ṣāḥib* of the work.[115] The form, presentation, and the developed state of the thematization convincingly prove that we are not dealing with the words of Abū Ḥanīfa, but rather a text by one of his students.

It was almost inevitable that the *Fiqh absaṭ*, as well as the previously mentioned texts, spread widely in northeastern Iran, given the circumstances of Abū Muṭīʿ's life. If this does not suffice as proof, the following may also be adduced as supporting evidence: (a) A *riwāya* is available in the *Fiqh absaṭ* (40.3–7) which remains completely within the region in question; it even gives two names directly after Abū Muṭīʿ (*Fiqh absaṭ*, 40.6f.: Nuṣayr b. Yaḥyā and Abū l-Ḥasan b. Aḥmad al-Fārisī), names that we have already encountered in the *isnād* of the first *Risāla* to ʿUthmān al-Battī.[116] In addition (b), the *Fiqh absaṭ* is named in the texts of the Māturīdites and even the eastern Ashʿarites over and over again. It may suffice to mention the commentaries on it by Ps.-Māturīdī (see below), as well as al-Pazdawī (*Uṣūl*, 4.4.) and al-Juwaynī.[117] According to al-Juwaynī there is even supposed to have been a commentary by the pen of Abū Bakr b. Fūrak (d. 406/1015).[118]

The *K. al-Fiqh al-absaṭ* was thus a widely read text and it almost seems as if we are therewith definitively treading on solid ground of the eastern Ḥanafite school. But unfortunately this work is also knotted with difficulties and problems, of which at least two are of great import.

---

114 Ibn Abī l-Wafāʾ, vol. 2, 265 ult.; Ibn Quṭlūbughā, 87.1; al-Laknawī, 68.14f.; Flügel, 285; Ḥājjī Khalīfa, 1287; al-Bayāḍī, 21.-1f.; likewise the Cairo manuscript of the *Fiqh absaṭ* as well as al-Kawtharī's edition.

115 Al-Dhahabī, *ʿIbar*, vol. 1, 330.2 and afterward al-Laknawī, 68.18f.

116 Moreover we can assume that the *isnād* of the *Fiqh absaṭ* was transmitted incompletely. The interval between Abū Muṭīʿ (d. 199/814) and Nuṣayr al-Balkhī (d. 268/881–2) is clearly too large.

117 ʿAbd al-Mālik b. ʿAbdallāh al-Juwaynī, *al-Kāfiya fī l-jadal*, ed. Fawqiya Ḥusayn Maḥmūd (Cairo, 1399/1979), 27.8.

118 See also GAS, vol. 1, 611, no. 9, where a commentary of Ibn Fūrak's on *K. al-ʿĀlim* is noted.

The first concerns the nature of the relationship between the *Fiqh absaṭ* and the text that has come to be known as the *Fiqh akbar I* of Abū Ḥanīfa. The issue is of fundamental significance for our inquiry, since the *Fiqh akbar I* has long been considered an important milestone in the development of the Islamic creed.

The text, a collection of ten theological articles, was published by Wensinck in an English translation in 1932,[119] and to this day it holds an established position in the historiography of Muslim dogma. Pivotal to this was Wensinck's demonstration of the text's historically prominent position, which was widely accepted by his fellow scholars. He regarded it as the authentic creed of Abū Ḥanīfa,[120] which meant that one could regard it as the first Islamic articulation of faith and as a prototype for all later *ʿaqāʾid*.

Wensinck did not fail to mention, however, that the text was nowhere transmitted in Arabic in the form that he had presented—he had in fact reconstructed it from a later commentary (interestingly enough attributed to al-Māturīdī in some manuscripts), a text that was published some time ago, the *Sharḥ al-Fiqh al-akbar*.[121] Based on this he believed he was able to refer to a foundational text of Abū Ḥanīfa, which, according to his view, must have possessed the classical form of a decalogue.

Wensinck likewise pointed out that the *Fiqh absaṭ* of Abū Muṭīʿ had a noteworthy relationship to the supposed *Fiqh akbar*. He found there nine out of ten articles of the text he had reconstructed; the first six grouped at the beginning, and numbers eight to ten spread over the rest of the text. This did not permit him to doubt the independent existence of the *Fiqh akbar*, but was considered yet another proof of its independent existence and authenticity. Such was Wensinck's assumption, because Abū Muṭīʿ invoked the authority of Abū Ḥanīfa, and it seemed only natural to assume that the same views of the Master which he reproduced in the *Fiqh absaṭ* were to be found in more accurate form in the *Sharḥ al-Fiqh al-akbar*.[122]

Wensinck was ultimately undecided as to the literary form of the original *Fiqh akbar I*. Evidently he thought that it was not written by Abū Ḥanīfa himself, but rather based on what he had said. He may have supposed it to be a self-contained text, yet one that may not have existed independently outside of another work. This is the only way one can understand Wensinck's comments at key sections of the text which argue

---

119 Wensinck, *Muslim Creed*, 103f.; see also the German translation from Joseph Schacht, *Der Islām mit Ausschluss des Qorʾāns* (Tübingen, 1931), 35f. and van Ess, "Kritisches," 328.

120 Wensinck, *Muslim Creed*, 122ff.

121 Printed in the *Rasāʾil al-sabʿa fī l-ʿaqāʾid* (Hyderabad, 1980), section I. Hereafter referred to as *Sharḥ*.

122 Wensinck, *Muslim Creed*, 123; cf. ibid., 112 and 221.

that the "editor and commentator" of the *Fiqh akbar I* probably extracted the text that he commented upon (in the *Sharḥ*) from the *Fiqh absaṭ*.[123]

Wensinck's hypotheses were too complicated and perhaps too vague to remain persuasive, with all their open possibilities. His foundational conceptualization prevailed, however, as the quintessence of his considerations—namely, that the reconstructed *Fiqh akbar I* gives us access to a decalogue originating from the second/eighth century in precisely the same form, and thus refers us to the authentic creedal doctrines of Abū Ḥanīfa.[124]

This image was only questioned when van Ess examined the text again and revisited the method by which it had been reconstructed. He contrasted the *Sharḥ al-Fiqh al-akbar* with the *Fiqh absaṭ* anew and came thereby to a completely different result: The commentary (*Sharḥ*) does not take us back to a hypothetical *Fiqh akbar I* at all. Instead it may be viewed much more straightforwardly, and without any risky assumptions, as a commentary of the *Fiqh absaṭ* of Abū Muṭīʿ al-Balkhī.[125]

The key factor for this correction of the text's supposed provenance was not a new hypothesis, but a comparison of the words utilized in both texts. It led to the conclusion that the *Sharḥ* and *Fiqh absaṭ* not only corresponded to each other in nine citations attributed to Abū Ḥanīfa, but that the parallels went much further.[126] The *Sharḥ* reproduces numerous passages from the *Fiqh absaṭ* true to the letter and provides them with a theological commentary. Given this, it is misleading to presume the existence of a third text, e.g., a hypothetical decalogue that both authors are supposed to have had available to them. The *Fiqh absaṭ* itself is the sought-after original text, the commentary of which was found valuable by later generations.

Such a result not only gives occasion to reconsider seemingly certain ideas about Abū Ḥanīfa; it also invites an unexpected assessment particularly relevant to Abū Muṭīʿ's text, since only now has the significance and enduring influence of the *Fiqh absaṭ* become clear.

In any case this reappraisal of the text also poses a new problem—one that brings us to the second important question indicated above: If the *Fiqh absaṭ* was indeed read often and commented upon over the course of centuries, during which Ḥanafite theology did not remain static, then this engagement with the text could hardly have taken place without leaving a trace. In fact, a considerable danger arose that later generations might approach the text and try, to a

---

123 Ibid., 123.

124 Representative of many others are the articles by J. Schacht on Abū Ḥanīfa, "Abū Ḥanīfa al-Nuʿmān," *EI*², vol. 1, 124a and ʿUmar Farūq ʿAbd-Allāh, "Abū Ḥanīfa," *EIr*, vol. 1, 301a.

125 Van Ess, "Kritisches," 329ff.

126 See the table, ibid., 331.

certain degree, to make it correspond to the transforming theological conceptions of the times.

The first clue that this suspicion may be justified is the title itself, which apparently transformed from *K. al-Fiqh al-akbar* to *K. al-Fiqh al-absaṭ*.[127] This alone shows that the text was modified although this alteration can be explained easily.[128] The second indication definitely bears more import; namely the fact that the entire *Fiqh absaṭ* in its currrent form does not leave a definitive impression as a text. It does not seem nearly as deliberate in its construction as the *K. al-ʿĀlim*, for example. What is even more striking are the various jumps in its thematization and its stylistic inconsistency. This truly justifies the assumption that it was worked upon later and that its original form differed from the one extant today. But where precisely the differences are is difficult to determine in detail with the materials at our disposal and we must suffice with only cautious speculations.

Van Ess based his analysis on the idea that the modifications made on the text of the *Fiqh absaṭ* were considerable in scope.[129] The last third of the text seemed especially suspect to him, because there the theme changes often and because the *Sharḥ al-Fiqh al-akbar*, which cites the *Fiqh absaṭ* regularly, seems to completely ignore this section. The conformity that he noted between the two texts only applies to pages 40–52 of the Kawtharī edition of the *Fiqh absaṭ*, but not the pages that follow (53–58).

Van Ess himself emphasized that his comparison of the citations was only preliminary. Because of this, it is perhaps unsurprising if our renewed examination of the two texts leads to a change in perspective: What we learn is that the author of the *Sharḥ* copied from the *Fiqh absaṭ* to a much greater degree than was previously believed. The progression of citations is more dense than was supposed and actually extends beyond the first two-thirds of the work into the text as a whole. On the basis of these findings two observations can be maintained in regard to the original composition of the *Fiqh absaṭ*: The text cannot have originally been much shorter than the version transmitted to us

127 All of the sources named in note 114 only mention one *Fiqh akbar*, as do al-Pazdawī, al-Juwaynī (see above 55), Ibn al-Nadīm (202.11, Dodge trans. vol. 1, 500), as well as the *Sharḥ al-fiqh al-akbar*.

128 Later, several works circulated under the title *al-Fiqh al-akbar*, so that for the sake of differentiation, the longest of them was described as *al-absaṭ* ("the most comprehensive"); see van Ess, "Kritisches," 338 and idem, *Theologie*, vol. 1, 207f. The so-called *Fiqh akbar II* was influential, too (see Wensinck, *Muslim Creed*, 188ff.; also Hell, 29ff.).

129 Van Ess, "Kritisches," 330f.

right now, and it will not be possible to attain complete clarity about its original form solely from a comparison with the *Sharḥ*.[130]

As a matter of thoroughness, the known citations mentioned above, as well as new additions, are compiled once again in an overview. The edition of the *Sharḥ al-Fiqh al-akbar* utilized here is different than the one used as the basis of van Ess' work.

Fiqh absaṭ	*Sharḥ*
40.9 f.:	2.8 f.
40.10:	3 ult.
40.10 f.:	4.7 f.
40.11 f.:	5.-3
40.12:	6.3
40.12 f.:	6.5
40.14:	6.8
40.16 f.:	6.15–17
40.17:	see 7.3–6
41.3–13:	8.-2–9.10
41.17 f.:	9.11 f.
41.18–22:	9.16–ult.
41 ult.–42.5:	9 ult.–10.4
43.5–7:	11.4–7
44.10 f.:	14.7 f.
44.-5 f.:	15.3 f.
44.-4 ff.:	cf. reference in 15.8
45.16 f.:	15.8 f.
45.18 ff.:	cf. reference in 15.11 f.
45.21–46.11:	cf. reference in 16.12–14
46.12:	16.14 f.
46.13 f.:	16.16

130 It might be thought that the *Sharḥ al-Fiqh al-akbar* would be absolutely useless to the analysis of the *Fiqh absaṭ*, because all of the alterations in the text of the *Fiqh absaṭ* that took place before it reached the commentator. But there are two considerable arguments against this: 1) the fact that the commentator still knew the text as *Fiqh akbar*, and 2) the way in which the question of God's location is treated: The author of the *Sharḥ* takes issue at the *Fiqh absaṭ* 49.1–52.1, where God is spoken of as having a precise location (see *Sharḥ*, 17.13ff.), but he does not mention *Fiqh absaṭ* 57.1–3, where the presentation conforms exactly to his own ideas. This may only have been added later to the *Fiqh absaṭ*.

(*cont.*)

Fiqh absaṭ	*Sharḥ*
47.6 f.:	cf. 16.-3
47.7 f.:	17.10–12
47.8 f.:	cf. 16.-2 f.
47.15–48.1:	20.6–14
49.1:	17.13 f.
49.2:	17.15 f.
51.1–52.1:	20.1–6
52.1 f.:	21.4 f.
52.2:	22.2 f.
52.17–21:	22.9–13
53.7:	26.-5
53.8 f.:	26.-4
53.9–11:	cf. 26.-3
53.14 f.:	53.17–19
and 53 ult.–54.9:	summarized in 27.3–8
53.16 f.:	23.5
55.2 f.:	27.9 f.
56.15 f.:	31.9 f.
56.20:	33.11 f.
56.21 f.:	33.12
56.22:	33.15
57.3:	cf. 22.13 f.
57.9:	33.-2 f.
57.9 f.:	34.1
57.11 f.:	cf. 35.-5 f.

A second starting point for reevaluating the text and possibly reconstructing its oldest layer lies in its numerous repetitions. They suggest that some formulations were originally lacking and were only added later in order to stress certain points. But even in such cases, caution remains imperative, as can be demonstrated quite clearly. This is most evident in the case of divine will, which is discussed several times in the *Fiqh absaṭ*. At first its treatment seems to reach the point of redundancy and the impression arises that an entire chapter could merely be a belated addition to a similarly themed previous one.[131] But upon closer analysis it becomes clear that this second section, in some form or another, must have been considered part of the original composition of the work, since it was available to the author of the *Sharḥ*, who cites a complete sentence from it.[132]

Hence only a third criterion could be truly unequivocal, i.e. the existence of incongruities and internal contradictions related to content. These are not many, but nevertheless are scattered throughout, as is demonstrated here by an example to conclude our analysis of the text. The evidence provided here not only makes it clear that insertions were made precisely at the occasion of pivotal themes in the work, but also vividly illustrates the complex circumstances of its textual transmission.

Near the closing of his text, Abū Muṭīʿ comes to a discussion of the description of God, and expresses some views that one would describe with later terminology as doctrines of attributes (*Fiqh absaṭ*, 56.20–57.6). In this passage several expressions are present which surely cannot go back to the author in the form transmitted here:
(a) This is the case at the beginning of this excerpt, where what has been said is described as the teaching of the *ahl al-sunna wa-l-jamāʿa* (*Fiqh absaṭ*, 56.21)—a name that, in this sense, only emerged as the self-description of the eastern Ḥanafites at a later time.[133]

(b) Then follows a passage in which it is explained that God is not in a location, but is eternal, which means before all locations existed (*Fiqh absaṭ*, 57.1–3). This replicates the views of the Ḥanafite Māturīdites starting from the fourth/tenth century, but clearly contradicts the ideas that Abū Muṭīʿ presented only a few pages before this (*Fiqh absaṭ*, 49.1–53.1).[134]

---

131 *Fiqh absaṭ*, 55 (Bāb ākhar fī l-mashīʾa) as added to 53f. (Bāb al-mashīʾa).

132 *Fiqh absaṭ*, 55.2f.: *Sharḥ*, 27.9f.

133 Even in the *K. al-Sawād al-aʿẓam*, al-Ḥakīm al-Samarqandī describes his own group as the *ahl al-ʿadl* or the *ahl al-sunna* (section 42). Only later does the name *ahl al-sunna wa-l-jamāʿa* appear, and then as a self-description of the Māturīdīya, used often by Abū l-Layth al-Samarqandī (e.g., *Bustān al-ʿārifīn*, in Abū l-Layth, *Tanbīh al-ghāfilīn*, 206.1), Abū Shakūr al-Sālimī (see Madelung, "The Spread," 117) and Abū l-Yusr al-Pazdawī (*Uṣūl*, 235–7 = section 95).

134 For the later development see the representative example of al-Māturīdī, *Tawḥīd*, 67ff. The author of the *Sharḥ*, apparently Māturīdite, on his part takes issue with the idea of a precise location for God, which Abū Muṭīʿ (*Fiqh absaṭ*, 49.1ff.) advocated. He cites this spot, reinterprets it as absurd and thereby presumes that Abū Muṭīʿ did not assign a location to God (*Sharḥ*, 17.13ff.). The same is done by al-Kawtharī, who uses the *Sharḥ* as evidence for this in his edition (see *Fiqh absaṭ*, 49n1). The second passage in the *Fiqh absaṭ*, which then speaks against a location for God (57.1–3), conforms in intention exactly with the position advocated by the *Sharḥ*.

(c) Finally, there is yet another noteworthy phrase that suggests to the reader the interchangeability of divine attributes. The question is asked whether one may say that God has power through will and wants through knowledge. And without the problem being explained more precisely, the answer is straight to the point: "Yes!" (*Fiqh absaṭ*, 57.4–6). This has no point of origin among the ideas of the early Ḥanafites whatsoever, but is actually completely alien to the point of view on which the *Fiqh absaṭ* is based. This part of the text would make more sense in the context of the Muʿtazilite doctrine of attributes, or more precisely said, as a reflection of the concept of God professed by Abū l-Hudhayl (d. 226/840–1 or 235/849–50).[135] The latter died almost a century after Abū Ḥanīfa, however, and was also younger than his student Abū Muṭīʿ. We can thus rule out this section as being part of the original *Fiqh absaṭ*.

In view of this evidence, it would seem reasonable to view the entire passage on attribute teachings (56.20–57.6) as a later addition and completely eliminate it from the *Fiqh absaṭ*. But doing this would probably not be equitable to the text, since a comparison with the *Sharḥ* provides evidence that even here certain sentences may have belonged to the original form of the work (see the table above). It suffices to say that whoever reworked the *Fiqh absaṭ* did not make the analysis easy for us. His goal was not just to explain the work with complementary additions, but to take a much more active role in commentary, extracting certain sentences, breaking them up, and letting them merge together in his own new context of explication.

If one keeps all these difficulties in mind, it becomes clear that it is useless to try to reconstruct the original form of the text with the materials which are available to us at the moment. In order to gain a more precise image, we would need to evaluate the original manuscripts as well as the other commentaries[136] which so far have gone unexamined; even then certain questions would remain hard to answer. Despite all this, the text in its extant form is by no means unusable but it is actually rather valuable: The preceding observations show that the base material of the text in its essential features is from the original source, and though some uncertainty remains for purposes of citation, we can nevertheless affirm that we have an important testimonial of early Ḥanafite theology at hand.

This is even more meaningful since the *Fiqh absaṭ* does not just repeat statements that we know from other early Ḥanafite texts such as the *K. al-ʿĀlim*.

135 On this, see Richard M. Frank, "The Divine Attributes According to the Teaching of Abu 'l-Hudhayl al-ʿAllaf," *Le Muséon* 82 (1969): 451–506.

136 Sezgin names in GAS, vol. 1, 414 yet another commentary of a certain Ibrāhīm b. Ismāʿīl al-Malaṭī which is reportedly identical to the *Sharḥ* of Ps.-Māturīdī, as well as a commentary by ʿAṭāʾ b. ʿAlī l-Jūzjānī (seventh/thirteenth century).

Its thematization is much more expansive, and the premises that it offered for later theological explication were certainly more numerous than any text that preceded it. The questions of belief, the condition of the sinner, and the recompense in the afterlife are still given considerable attention; but besides these, other themes are touched on which in their level of detail enlarge upon and even surpass the classical emphases of Murji'ite doctrine.

This is especially true for the argumentation on the topic of predestination, which forms perhaps the central point of the entire text. We have some acquaintance with this subject from the second *Risāla* to 'Uthmān al-Battī, but here a much more detailed exposition awaits us, within which is a section that brings up the problem of human ability (*istiṭā'a*) for the first time. Another unprecedented aspect is what Abū Muṭī' has to say on God and His attributes. More novelties are found in various smaller themes, such as reflections on eschatology, and the fact that the principle of "commanding the correct and forbidding the reprehensible" is explicitly emphasized.

The beginning of the text, contrary to what has long been believed, is not as significant. There, Abū Ḥanīfa summarizes the quintessence of his view of belief, and names a series of principles which were the groundwork for Wensinck's reconstruction of the supposed *Fiqh akbar I*. The starting point for this list is a question that Abū Muṭī' is supposed to have asked his teacher: namely what, in his view, is "the greatest insight" (*Fiqh absaṭ*, 40.8f.: "*al-fiqh al-akbar*"). Abū Ḥanīfa's answer to this is short and of astonishing simplicity. First, five maxims are enumerated which should be understood as guiding principles for part of the *Fiqh absaṭ*, but not for the entire text.[137] Afterwards, an additional sixth statement follows which expresses his general outlook towards the practice of theology: Insight (*fiqh*) in the religion (*dīn*), is more excellent than insight into the legal rulings (*aḥkām*); and recognizing how one ought to serve one's Lord is better than collecting much knowledge (*'ilm*).[138]

This sounds sensational here at the beginning of the *Fiqh absaṭ*, especially since the text does not revisit this contrast between theological realization and the collection of (transmitted) knowledge. It is nevertheless not an isolated new position that throws a fundamentally different light on Abū Ḥanīfa's views. Similar considerations were also found, for example, at the beginning of the *K. al-'Ālim*, as we have seen, where the discussion went into even more detail.[139] If one takes this into consideration, then the six

137 *Fiqh absaṭ*, 40.7–13; see the description of the construction of the text below.

138 *Fiqh absaṭ*, 40.14–17.

139 *K. al-'Ālim*, sections 1–4.

principles presented at the beginning of the *Fiqh absaṭ* as the "greatest insight" of Abū Ḥanīfa do emphasize characteristic features of his religious orientation. However, they do not form the essence of his doctrine of belief, but are simply an incomplete repetition of what is treated elsewhere more clearly and in more detail.

In regard to the format of the work itself, ultimately only superficial comparisons can be made with the *K. al-ʿĀlim*. They are of course both unified by the fact that they are constructed as didactic dialogues. But while the *K. al-ʿĀlim* is literarily developed and exhibits a lucid outline such that it also warrants the description of a didactic dialogue, the *Fiqh absaṭ* seems more like a collection of ideas that are often only associationally connected with one other. Abū Muṭīʿ's questions are almost always short and abrupt; in contrast the answers of the teacher are differentiate themselves greatly in terms of style and elaborateness. In addition, the author often presents his argumentation through the use of *ḥadīth*, so that he does not always express himself explicitly, but within citations.[140]

This has certain consequences for the following outline. Although we have attempted here to provide a general exposition of the work, the sudden changes in the themes discussed in the text sometimes rule out a precise or straightforward summary. Furthermore, if one takes into consideration that the text as it is extant may deviate from Abū Muṭīʿ's original composition, then the description of its argumentation can only be tentative in some respects.

140 Cook (30) points out that the instructive usage of *ḥadīth* in the argumention of the *Fiqh absaṭ* lets one assume that the text was composed "distinctly later" than the *K. al-ʿĀlim*—based on the assumption of Schacht's hypothesis of the development and growing influence of *ḥadīth* on theology. The comparison between the *K. al-ʿĀlim* and the *Fiqh absaṭ* actually seems to attest to this, since the *Fiqh absaṭ* is the later work, this being indicated by its abundant themes and the state of the discussion. Nevertheless, in terms of the life spans of the two authors, the interval cannot have been very long. And one must also consider that the *K. al-ʿĀlim* was probably written in Iraq, and the *Fiqh absaṭ* certainly in Balkh, so it is possible that we are dealing with differing local developments.

THE STRUCTURE OF THE *KITĀB AL-FIQH AL-ABSAṬ*[141]	
40.7–13	*Description of the "greatest insight"*[142] 1) A believer does not lose his faith because of a sin. 2) One should call to what is correct and forbid the reprehensible. 3) What struck you could not have missed you, and what misses you could not have struck you. 4) All the Prophet's Companions are owed the same loyalty. 5) We leave judgment over ʿUthmān and ʿAlī to God.
40.14–17	*Elaboration on this description* 6) Insight in religion is more excellent than insight into the religious rulings (*aḥkām*). Clarification: The most excellent insight consists in understanding belief in God, and learning the religious commands (*sharāʾiʿ*), the prophetic practices (*sunan*), and punitive laws (*ḥudūd*), as well as the dissent and consensus of the community.
40.17–41.16	*Definition of belief (on the basis of the well-known īmān-ḥadīth)* Belief: Bear witness (*shahāda* to God, the prophets, the angels, books, messengers, the Last Judgment, and the decree (*qadar*) of good and bad by God). Religious commands (*sharāʾiʿ*): praying, alms, fasting, pilgrimage, ablution. Righteous action (*iḥsān*): Serve God[143] as if you see Him.
41.17–42.5	*Believer—Disbeliever* Believer: Whoever acknowledges what has been mentioned as well as the Qurʾān, even if he does not always understand them. Disbeliever: Whoever claims that he (despite the existence of the Qurʾān) does not know anything about these same commandments, or claims that something was not created by God. Exception: Outside of the domain of Islam (*fī arḍ al-shirk*) one is already a believer if one avows oneself to Islam, even without knowing the duties or the Qurʾān.

141 The page numbers refer to the edition of al-Kawtharī. Chapter headings are not given in italics since they come from the text. I have added the description of the themes in italics.

142 *Fiqh absaṭ*, 40.7–17, translated by van Ess, "Kritisches," 333f.

143 In the print of *Fiqh absaṭ* (41.13), this reads: *an taʿmala lillāhi ka-annaka* ... The *Sharḥ* (9.9f.), however, cites the sentence probably more correctly: *an taʿbuda lillāhi ka-annaka* ...

(*cont.*)

THE STRUCTURE OF THE *KITĀB AL-FIQH AL-ABSAṬ*	
42.5–8	*Again: Definition of belief* Belief: Bearing witness to the one God, His angels, books, messengers, Paradise, Hell, and the resurrection, that good and bad come from God, no one can have deeds delegated to them (*yufawwiḍ*), and people will receive what is decreed for them.
42.9–43.4	*Transition to predestination* Whoever recognizes this, but by reference to Q 18:29, is of the opinion that the will belongs to him, is still a believer. He misunderstands the Qurʾān, but is not denying it. The same is true for the one who, on the basis of Q 4:79, is of the opinion that misfortune that afflicts people comes from themselves. What is correct is for people to ascribe to themselves what is bad only insofar as it is what God afflicts them with as a punishment for their sins (see Q 42:30).
43.5–7	*Human capacity* (*istiṭāʿa*) God commands people to obedience, but creates for them the capacity by which they may be obedient and disobedient. If God punishes people, this is occasioned by the misapplication of this capacity.
43.7–24	*Discussion with a Qadarite* Everyone must realize that God is not just the creator of the good, but also the bad. Even if we apparently choose our actions (e.g., with an articulation of disbelief, or like Pharaoh in the Qurʾān), God is still behind them.
Chapter on the Decree (*Bāb fī al-qadar*)	
44.3–9	*Predestination* Citation of the famous *ḥadīth*:[144] Whether a person enters Heaven or Hell is already certain from the mother's womb and documented by an angel.

144 Mentioned by al-Bukhārī, Abū Dāwūd, al-Tirmidhī, Ibn Maja, and Ibn Ḥanbal—see the citations in Wensinck, *Concordance et indices de la tradition musulmane* (Leiden, 1936–88),

THE STRUCTURE OF THE *KITĀB AL-FIQH AL-ABSAṬ*

44.10–19	*Calling to what is correct* *Al-amr bi-l-maʿrūf wa-l-nahy ʿan al-munkar* is a correct principle, but cannot lead to fighting in the community (*jamāʿa*). If two groups fight against each other, they must reconcile with one another. Only if a group remains aggressive (*al-fiʾa al-bāghiya*) can one compel them toward submission for the sake of justice.
44.19–45.16	*On the Khārijites* We do not hold the Khārijites as disbelievers, but we fight against them as ʿAlī and ʿUmar b. ʿAbd al-ʿAzīz did, since ultimately they deny the beneficence of God (*kufr al-niʿam*). But if they do return to peace, then we will relent from persecuting them.
45.16–46.15	*Delimitation of belief as avowal without doubt / Against the manzila bayna al-manzilatayn* Disbeliever: Whoever claims that they are not able to distinguish between a believer and a disbeliever or claims not to know which punishment is decreed for a disbeliever. Having said that, one should not, as a Muslim, doubt one's belief, but should say about oneself that one is truly a believer (*anā muʾminun ḥaqqan*), since there are no other groups alongside believers other than disbelievers and hypocrites. Claiming to be a real believer is not based on entitlement to a place in Paradise. Only God decides this, even though one may certainly go to Hell for his sins and to Paradise for his faith.
46.15–16	*No differentiated ranking in belief* The belief of believing people is like the belief of angels.
46.16–23	*Belief and actions* The essence of belief is avowal. In view of this, belief can be complete even with deficient actions.

vol. 6, 235b, s.v. "*muḍgha*"; on the topic see Josef van Ess, *Zwischen Ḥadīt und Theologie. Studien zum Entstehen prädestinatianischer Überlieferung* (Berlin/New York, 1975), 1ff.

(*cont.*)

THE STRUCTURE OF THE *KITĀB AL-FIQH AL-ABSAṬ*	
46.23–47.12	*Promise and threat / On disbelief* The believing sinner will ultimately go to Paradise after a (temporary) punishment in Hell. Hell awaits the disbelievers. Disbeliever: Whoever believes in everything, but says that he does not know whether Moses or Jesus were really prophets;[145] or whoever says that he does not know whether disbelievers go to Paradise or Hell.
47.12–48.1	*Belief and actions* If one is heedless in one's actions, but is firm in belief in God and His revelation, one may expect punishment from God, but also reward. In contrast, whoever carries out all duties properly while doubting in God, is on the way to Hell.
48.2–12	*The preservation of the community*[146] One must fight wrongdoers without calling them unbelievers, and assist the righteous group (*al-fiʾa al-ʿādila*). Governance must be tolerated even if it commits violations, because there will always be good and bad people in the community (*jamāʿa*). If the entire community is unjust, emigration is the only thing to do.
49.1–52.1	*God is in heaven over us* Disbeliever: Whoever claims not to know whether God is in heaven or on earth,[147] or whoever declares that God is on the throne but that one cannot specify whether the throne is in heaven or earth, since God ought to be described with the high and not the low. Transition to a *ḥadīth*, in which a maidservant is considered a believer because she points to the sky when asked the question, "Where is God?"

145 Mentioned by Wensinck, *Muslim Creed*, 104 as article 8 of the *Fiqh akbar I*.

146 This section overlaps in part with *Fiqh absaṭ*, 44.10–19, which is the reason van Ess ("Kritisches," 337n37) proposed to view it as a later insertion. Here one must also, if possible, separate the real from the fake: the overlap only applies to the statement on the *fiʾa al-bāghiya*; what follows concerning governance is new.

147 Article 9 of the *Fiqh akbar* according to Wensinck, *Muslim Creed*, 104.

THE STRUCTURE OF THE *KITĀB AL-FIQH AL-ABSAṬ*

52.1–5	*The reality of the punishment of the grave* Whoever denies the punishment of the grave is a Jahmite and is doomed,[148] since this point is clearly in the Qurʾān and cannot be misunderstood.
52.5–14	*Promise and Threat* We humans do not know who will go to Paradise and who will go to Hell. Paradise is not assured even for a Muslim.
52.14–16	*Prayer behind sinners* Praying behind sinners is permissible since the person who is leading the prayer is solely responsible for their own actions.
52.16–53.5	*Against innovation and against fighting among Muslims* Armed fighting and error from innovations lead one to Hell. It is correct to learn the Qurʾān and take on transmitted truth. The *ḥadīth* of the 73 groups in the community, of which only one (*al-sawād al-aʿẓam*) will be saved.
Chapter on the Will (*Bāb al-mashīʾa*)	
53.6–54 ult.	*Will, satisfaction, and command of God* God wills everything (*mashīʾa*) that happens, since He has created everything. God is pleased (*raḍiya*) that He creates everything, but His approbation (*riḍā*) only applies to things that are good and not the bad. God only commands (*amr*) the good. This is why God may penalize on account of the bad.
A Further Chapter on the Will (*Bāb ākhar fī l-mashīʾa*)	
55.1–13	*Discussion with a Qadarite* If God willed, He could make all created beings obedient, including Iblīs. Therefore all actions of created beings, even the scandalous, happen by God's will. Nevertheless, God may punish disobedience, because it occurs against His command and against His satisfaction. Punishment applies to a sinner only for that which he himself does, e.g., for drinking wine.

148 Ibid., as article 10.

(*cont.*)

THE STRUCTURE OF THE *KITĀB AL-FIQH AL-ABSAṬ*	
Chapter on the Refutation of Those Who Call Another a Disbeliever Because of a Misdeed (*Bāb al-radd ʿalā man yukaffiru bi-l-dhānb*)	
55.15–56.2	*Position of the sinner* It is wrong to call a sinner a disbeliever. He remains a sinning believer, as the Qur'ān attests to numerous times.
56.2–14	*Belief as avowal without doubt* It is wrong to say, "I am a believer, if God wills," because with the *istithnā'* one expresses doubt concerning one's belief. And if one doubts, then one's good works come to naught before God. But if one believes and commits sins, then one must fear punishment, but may also hope for forgiveness.
56.15–19	*Paradise and Hell* Paradise and Hell are created, but everlasting. To deny this would be a denial of the Qur'ān and therefore disbelief in regard to God.
56.20–57.6	*God and His attributes*[149] God is not described with attributes of the creation. Anger (*ghaḍab*) and approbation (*riḍā*) are two of His attributes. [Insertion: (Which are to be understood) "without how". This is the teaching of *ahl al-sunna wa-l-jamāʿa.*] God is angry and content without one being able to say that His anger is His punishment and His approbation is His reward.[150] We describe God just as He has described Himself: Citation of Qur'ānic statements, among which are Q 112 and 2:255.

149 The reconstruction attempted here of later insertions into the text is based on the arguments mentioned above, 62.

150 This is alo cited by the author of the Sharḥ (33.15), who, however, reinterprets the text of the *Fiqh absaṭ*, and allows for the interpretation of God's anger as His punishment, and God's approbation as His reward (33.14–17).

THE STRUCTURE OF THE *KITĀB AL-FIQH AL-ABSAṬ*

[Insertion: God has a hand which is nonetheless not a body part (*jāriḥa*) and is not like the hand of His creation, but rather is above (*fawqa*) it, since He is the creator of hands.[151] The same is true for the face and the self (*nafs*). God is also not in a location, but has always been, before He created locations. Before, there was no "where," no creation and no thing (*shay'*).]

If one is asked what the One who is Willing wills by, the answer is: With the attribute (= the will). He is also powerful through power, and knows through knowledge.

[Insertion: Is He also powerful through the will and does He will with knowledge? Yes.]

Chapter on Belief (*Bāb fī l-īmān*)

57.8–10 *The seat of belief in humans*

The source and seat of belief is the heart, but it branches out throughout the body.

57.10–14 *Relationship between God and man*

God does not request (*ṭalaba*) anything from people, but has the right (*ḥaqq*) to be worshiped and have no one associated with Him. The right of people is to be given forgiveness and reward. In regard to the believers, God feels approbation (*riḍā*), and in regard to Iblīs He feels anger (*sukhṭ*).

57.14–58.13 *Predestination*

When God says, "Do what you want" (see Q 41:40), this is to be understood as a threat (not as a justification of free will). See also Q 41:17 and Q 18:29. People ought to worship God alone, but God determines (*qadar*) all things. Several Qur'ānic citations.

151 This too—as well as the following passage on the "location" of God—is an argument that is only found much later in the Ḥanafite and Māturīdite texts (e.g., *Uṣūl*, 28.3–5 and 244.12ff.). There it serves to explain the probably belated addition of *bi-lā kayfa*.

CHAPTER 2

Development in the Third/Ninth Century

2.1 Stagnation in Theology and a Lack of Sources: Abū Bakr al-Samarqandī (d. 268/881–2)

In the works described above we may observe a unity of creedal expression that laid the groundwork for a self-sufficient and internally coherent Ḥanafite theology. They evoke numerous themes of theological import and discuss them in detail, with some convictions so deeply ingrained that we encounter them regularly in these texts in the same classical formulations. If one were to ask about the essence of belief, the createdness of actions, or the consequences of sins, one would get the same characteristic Ḥanafite answer, and if later thinkers aimed at further elucidation on these central themes, they would find useful conceptual bases for their own considerations. In this sense, one may speak of the emergence of a distinct theological profile for eastern Ḥanafites as early as the beginning of the third/ninth century, and as such it only required the sustained elaboration of its doctrines for an autonomous and distinct school of *kalām* to come into existence.

This development, as we know, transpired in an impressive manner. But its first steps were rather unsure and faltering, since for the entire third/ninth century, which we must first account for before proceeding, one cannot say that theological disputation in northeastern Iran progressed to any notable extent. The period naturally had its share of Ḥanafite scholars of prestige and rank devoted to the tradition: the *isnād*s of the aforementioned works name an entire series of them;[1] and Abū l-Muʿīn al-Nasafī later—in part by citing these same names—would reconstruct a proper school of Samarqand, in which the tradition between Abū Ḥanīfa and al-Māturīdī apparently went uninterrupted.[2] Among them he names renowned Ḥanafites such as Abū Sulaymān al-Jūzjānī, Abū Bakr al-Jūzjānī, and Abū Naṣr al-ʿIyāḍī, who were al-Māturīdī's immediate teachers. However, they apparently did not develop the science of *kalām* very considerably, since we find no theological works written by them. What is more, even the Māturīdites of later centuries barely mention the texts from

---

1 In particular the *isnād* of *K. al-ʿĀlim*, but also the *isnād*s of the first *Risāla* and the *Fiqh absaṭ*.

2 *Tabṣira*, vol. 1, 356.6ff. = Tancî, 3ff.; and now van Ess, *Theologie*, vol. 2, 564. Compare the second chapter of the introduction above.

DOI 10.1163/9789004261846_004

this period, referring instead either to earlier texts (from the correspondence with ʿUthmān al-Battī up to the *Fiqh absaṭ*) or those works written after 900 CE.

Thus the theology of Transoxania can hardly have been influenced by any decisive factors from the middle to late third/ninth century,[3] which also means that a certain development was delayed there which elsewhere had taken place rather quickly. This was, after all, the same century during which Iraq experienced enormous developments in *kalām*. Heated theological discussions were commonplace there, and even led—especially in the aftermath of the *miḥna*[4]—into the arena of political dispute. Points of intellectual dispute became more distinct and each group came to know more precisely where its boundaries were to be drawn. By comparison, the theological topics that dominated Baghdad only arose with comparable virulence in Transoxania more than fifty years later; no issues seem to have arisen in the region which necessitated a resolution through theological discourse

This may not be all that surprising and is similarly true of other remote regions of the Islamic world. However, it instructively illustrates what a difference existed between the sociopolitical center of Baghdad and the periphery. This temporal lag between the two is also an important consideration for our understanding of the respective decisions taken by al-Ashʿarī and al-Māturīdī in the fourth/tenth century. In Iraq, al-Ashʿarī could look back at an entire century of dispute, dealing with systems of thought developed in detail and sharpened into numerous points of contention. Al-Māturīdī, by contrast, found himself in a theological milieu which was still only on the verge of establishing its borders and definitions.

The impression of a relative stagnation of eastern theology does not indicate, however, that the influence of the Ḥanafites had declined at that time. On the contrary, the Ḥanafīya were probably established there without any rivals, with no need to develop and defend their doctrines. All the important *qāḍī* positions of the region were occupied by Ḥanafites.[5] This dominance in judicial administration brought along with it many discussions on topics of *fiqh* and was likely yet another reason for not being held up with problems of

---

3 This assessment applies only to the narrower area of *kalām*. Other forms of religious expression such as mysticism and Qurʾānic exegesis went separate ways, so that their development in northeastern Iran is characterized by different phases and other regional emphases. For more detail on this, see van Ess, *Theologie*, vol. 2, 509ff. and 544ff.

4 On this see Martin Hinds, "Miḥna," *EI*², vol. 7, 2–6.

5 See Heinz Halm, *Die Ausbreitung der šāfiʿitischen Rechtsschule von den Anfängen bis zum 8./14./Jahrhundert* (Wiesbaden, 1974), 102ff. for Bukhārā, Nasaf, and Samarqand; ibid., 73ff., on Balkh and other cities in Khurāsān.

kalām. But ascertaining more than this in detail is a futile task as long as we cannot access the sources from which we might derive a more precise image. For now we may make the preliminary observation that there is an absence of theological texts from this period, and this is noteworthy because it underscores the true enormity of the upsurge in theology in the time period to follow.

However, there is at least one relatively useful entry point to third/ninth century Transoxanian scholarly activity which must be mentioned here to conclude our investigation. This is embodied in the historical reports on Abū Bakr Muḥammad b. al-Yamān al-Samarqandī, a scholar who may be considered representative of the period's general tendencies just described. He was by no means an influential theologian for the following generation, but if a Ḥanafite scholar from this time period were to be mentioned at all, then his name certainly ought to be mentioned first.

Abū Bakr died in the year 268/881–2 after presumably spending his entire life in his hometown of Samarqand.[6] What distinguishes him from his Samarqandian contemporaries, however, is not his biography, but rather the fact that several titles of his works have been transmitted. Two of them remain, for the time being, only titles: their contents cannot be ascertained. There is nothing more precise to be reported on the *K. al-Anwār*,[7] and the *K. al-I'tiṣām*[8] was simply dedicated to *ḥadīth*.

More can be said, however, in relation to two other works attributed to Abū Bakr. One of them, no longer extant, was apparently dedicated to theological speculation.[9] In this book al-Samarqandī set himself against the Karrāmīya, a religious group that arose during his lifetime. This allows us to infer that he argued in the style of *kalām*, and we can even conjecture that his exposition was rather appealing, since this refutation of the Karrāmīya was the only theological text from the late third/ninth century to be referenced again at a later time period.[10]

---

6 *Tabṣira*, vol. 1, 358.7ff. = Tancî, 7.4; Ibn Abī l-Wafā', vol. 2, 144 (no. 443); Ibn Quṭlūbughā, 68 (no. 205); al-Laknawī, 202; Ḥājjī Khalīfa, 119, 839, and 1726; 'Umar Riḍā al-Kaḥḥāla, *Mu'jam al-mu'allifīn* (Damascus, 1957–61), vol. 12, 120; *GAS*, vol. 1, 500; I. 'Abbās, "Abū Bakr Samarqandī," *EIr*, vol. 1, 264f.

7 Mentioned only in al-Kaḥḥāla, vol. 12, 120; afterward by 'Abbās in *EIr*, vol. 1, 264f.

8 Ibn Quṭlūbughā, 68 (no. 205) and Ḥājjī Khalīfa, 119; al-Nasafī, *Tabṣira*, vol. 1, 358.8 (= Tancî, 7.5) identifies it as a *kalām* text; he also incorrectly identifies the *K. Ma'ālim al-dīn* as a *kalām* text.

9 Namely, the *K. al-Radd 'alā l-Karrāmīya*; see al-Nasafī, Ibn Abī l-Wafā', Ibn Quṭlūbughā, and al-Laknawī as n6.; Ḥājjī Khalīfa, 839; on this see van Ess, *Ungenützte Texte*, 75 and Madelung, *Religious Trends*, 39.

10 Al-Nasafī, *Tabṣira*, vol. 1, 164.16f., see van Ess, *Ungenützte Texte*, 75.

In regard to the fourth of Abū Bakr's known compositions, we have more than just assumptions to work with, since it has been transmitted to us in a manuscript from Mashhad.[11] Its title, *Maʿālim al-dīn*, sounds promising, and would seem to present the possibility of directly accessing theological discussions. But a look at the manuscript shows that the theme of the text is completely different. It is confined strictly to argumentation on questions of law, without a single word on theology. Thus this text is useless as a source for our purposes as well, and only allows us to conclude that we have a text on *fiqh* from Samarqand of the third/ninth century, but none on theology.

2.2 Ḥanafite Elements in Ibn Karrām's Theology (d. 255–869)

If, despite these difficulties, it is still possible to attain a certain image of eastern Ḥanafite theology in the third/ninth century, it is thanks to a circumstance, the meaning and significance of which is not apparent at first sight; namely, the appearance of Muḥammad b. Karrām (d. 255/869) and the spread of the teachings connected with his name.

Ibn Karrām[12] was a formative figure in the religious history of eastern Iran. At the center of his work was the call to piety and a life of asceticism, but he also developed his own views on theology and law, and motivated the formation of a school of thought. Neither of these happened without antagonism; they actually produced severe reactions. Thus we find that Ibn Karrām led an unstable life characterized as much by great reverence as by distrust and adamant persecution on the part of the authorities.

---

11 Al-Nasafī, Ibn Abī l-Wafāʾ, Ibn Quṭlūbughā, and al-Laknawī as n6. Ḥājjī Khalīfa, 1726. On the manuscript, contained in 365 folios and dated 804 AH, see *GAS*, vol. 1, 600 and Kāẓim Mudīr-Shānačī, ʿAbdallāh Nūrānī, and Taqī Bīnīsh, *Fihrist-i nuskhahā-yi khaṭṭī-i du kitābkhāna-i Mashhad* (Tehran, 1351), 1020.

12 A detailed appraisal of Ibn Karrām's life and work is given by C. Bosworth, "Karrāmiyya," *EI*², vol. 4, 667–669; new and important material is in van Ess, *Ungenützte Texte*, 7f., which also collects the literature since Bosworth. In regard to the last years, one ought to mention Aron Zysow, "Two Unrecognized Karrāmī Texts," *JAOS* 108 (1988): 577–587, and Madelung's summary of Sufism and the Karrāmiyya in his *Religious Trends*, 39–53. We can also add van Ess, *Theologie*, vol. 2, 609f. In contrast, there is the rather one-sided and less rewarding work by Jean-Claude Vadet, "Le karramisme de la Haute-Asie au carrefour de trois sectes rivales," *REI* 48 (1980): 25–50.

Having grown up in Sīstān,[13] he must have headed northward to Khurāsān early on, in order to seek instruction on questions of faith and on proper moral conduct. He is supposed to have stayed in Nishapur, Marw, and Herat, and also in Balkh, where Ibrāhīm b. Yūsuf (d. 239/853–4 or 241/855–6),[14] a student of Abū Yūsuf, was his teacher. After that followed five years in Mecca, and finally a return home, with stops in Jerusalem and Nishapur on the way. Ibn Karrām must have found confidence in his own religious views by then, since the period of his public appearance as a preacher and ascetic began at that time. This soon brought him into conflict with the local government, which from that point on was to constantly plague him. To start with, he was expelled from Sīstān. Then he was thrown in jail by the governor of Nishapur after preaching in Khurāsān and its neighboring eastern regions. There he waited eight years to be freed (in 251/865). Because of this he spent the last part of his life again in Jerusalem, where he finally died in 255/869.

The dispute over Ibn Karrām's teachings did not come to an end when he died, though the emphasis of such criticisms must have changed over the course of its development. His public appearances, motivated by missionary claims and colored with expressions of dissent against the authorities, must have stood in the foreground. He called for a return to a lifestyle agreeable to God, and did so in a manner apparently characterized by an ostentatious display of self-sufficiency and an accusatory tone toward those with wealth and property. This had the consequence of imbuing his movement with both religious and social volatility.[15]

Later on, however, criticism was focused on certain of his theological views. Such examples as his "strongly anthropomorphic" view of God or his "incorrect" definition of belief soon became classical points of contention included in all the later Muslim heresiographies. On these topics several polemics were written dedicated solely to refuting his doctrines.[16]

---

13 Summarizing from the biographical material given by Bosworth in "Karrāmiyya," *EI*^{2}, vol. 4, 667. The most important sources on Ibn Karrām's life are al-Samʿānī, *K. al-Ansāb*, ed. Abd al-Rahman ibn Yahyā Muʿallimī (Hyderabad, 1962–82), vol. 11, 60–63 (no. 3417); al-Ṣafadī, *K. al-Wāfī bi-l-wafayāt*, ed. H. Ritter and S. Dedering (Istanbul/Damascus/Wiesbaden, 1949), vol. 4, 375–377 (no. 1921); al-Dhahabī, *Mīzān*, vol. 4, 21–22 (no. 8103); Ibn Ḥajar, *Lisān*, vol. 5, 353–356 (no. 1158).

14 Ibn Abī l-Wafāʾ, vol. 1, 52 (no. 62); al-Laknawī, 11–13; Wāʿiẓ-i Balkhī, 214–219; also see Radtke, 544.

15 C. Bosworth, "Karrāmiyya," *EI*^{2}, vol. 4, 667b; Madelung, *Religious Trends*, 43f.; van Ess, *Theologie*, vol. 2, 609f.

16 A compilation of these refutations appears in van Ess, *Ungenützte Texte*, 74ff., see also C. Bosworth, "Karrāmiyya," *EI*^{2}, vol. 4, 668b, and Madelung, *Religious Trends*, 39f.

The eastern Ḥanafites were first in line in the numerous list of his opponents. Their resistance began, as we saw above, immediately after the promulgation of these new ideas, when Abū Bakr al-Samarqandī (d. 268/881–2) published his refutation against them, possibly still during the lifetime of Ibn Karrām. After this precedent, the sequence of critics did not cease for a long time: al-Ḥakīm al-Samarqandī later took the Karrāmīya to task in his *K. al-Sawād al-aʿẓam*;[17] and al-Māturīdī attacked them in both of his main works, the *K. al-Tawḥīd* and the *Taʾwīlāt*.[18] Out of the numerous later examples, only the detailed argumentations of al-Pazdawī[19] and Abū l-Muʿīn al-Nasafī[20] need be mentioned here.

However, this antagonistic position on the part of the Ḥanafites entailed a particular element which distinguished it from other polemics: It can only have emerged as promptly and as sharply as it did because the issue had to do with quarantining a member of their own family, so to speak. Ibn Karrām had truly created his own intellectual edifice, which answered some questions in a fully new way that did not share key features with other schools. But despite the autonomy of his ideas, including those which were more eccentric in their details, one must not overlook the fact that, in many foundational positions, in law as well as theology, he built on views that had been developed by Abū Ḥanīfa, and by the eastern Ḥanafites in particular.

In regard to *fiqh*, this genuine relationship to the Ḥanafite school was noted by Muslim observers,[21] and has now been clearly proven by Zysow by means

17 *K. al-Sawād*, sections 31, 44, 45, and 47.

18 In al-Māturīdī's *Tawḥīd*, 38f. and 373.8 the Karrāmīya are anonymously criticized, and by name at ibid., 378.-2. They are also mentioned by name in *Taʾwīlāt*, vol. 1, 35.10; then at ibid., vol. 1, 91.8, the critique continues under the nickname of *al-mutaqashshifa* ("the self-mortifiers"); compare to Madelung, "The Spread," 121n32a.

19 See the index of al-Pazdawī's *Uṣūl al-dīn* under the names "al-Karrāmīya," "Muḥammad b. al-Hayṣam," and "*al-mujassima*." Al-Pazdawī mentions the *mujassima* at the beginning (*Uṣūl*, 1.14–16), "such as people like Muḥammad b. al-Hayṣam," as the worst heretics from which one may take any teachings.

20 See the compilation of pertinent passages from the *Tabṣirat al-adilla* in van Ess, *Ungenützte Texte*, 77f.

21 Muḥammad b. Aḥmad al-Muqaddasī, *K. Aḥsan al-taqāsīm fī maʿrifat al-aqālīm*, ed. M.J. de Goeje (Leiden, 1906), 365.11; Ibn al-Dāʿī, 76.3 and 91.4ff attributes a legal methodology to the Karrāmites, but goes on to explain that some of them essentially followed the teachings of Abū Ḥanīfa; ʿAbd al-Jalīl b. Abī l-Ḥusayn al-Qazwīnī al-Rāzī, in his *K. al-Naqḍ*, ed. Jalāl al-Dīn Ḥusaynī (ʿUrmawī, Tehran 1371/1952), 74.-5f., reveals that among the Ḥanafites were those who affiliated themselves with Ibn Karrām's theological positions. According to Ibn Shayba, *Muqaddima Kitāb al-taʿlīm*, ed. Muḥammad ʿAbd al-Rashīd al-Nuʿmānī (Hyderabad, 1384/1965), 205, Ibn Karrām combined anthropomorphic theology with Ḥanafite law. See also van Ess, *Ungenützte Texte*, 17 and 79, and Zysow, 583f.

of new sources.[22] Any similarity in the area of *kalām*, by contrast, has long been denied by Muslims; for this reason it has only slowly been ascertained by modern research. Massignon provided an initial impulse for this thesis, with his view that Ibn Karrām had taken it upon himself to skillfully defend Sunnī views against the Muʿtazila.[23] This clue was followed up most prominently by Madelung in a series of detailed analyses and the careful use of evidence.[24]

Madelung singled out three points in particular wherein the views of Ibn Karrām were recognizably derived from Ḥanafite doctrine: The definition of belief, which under closer scrutiny develops in other directions, but essentially aims to exclude people's actions from belief;[25] the description of God's attributes, which was discussed in a controversial manner but which possessed the common premise that God's attributes of action are to be seen as eternal (in the sense that He has been able to act from eternity); and finally, the view insisting on the recognition of God's existence by one's intellect, without the addition of revelation.[26]

The entire list of concurrences, however, is even longer and there seem to be at least three further contact points, which we will briefly mention here. The Ḥanafite tradition is at the basis, for example, of Ibn Karrām's view that Good as well as Evil in the world is willed and predetermined by God.[27] One can read the same thing in the *Fiqh absaṭ* and this is repeated later by all the Māturīdite theologians.[28]

22 Ibid., especially 583f. and 587.

23 Louis Massignon, *Essai sur les origines du lexique technique de la mystique musulmane* (Paris, 1954), 263ff.

24 Madelung, *Religious Trends*, 40ff.

25 Ibid., 40; on this same basis al-Ashʿarī counted the Karrāmīya among the Murji'a in his *Maqālāt*, 141.5ff.

26 On both, see Madelung, *Religious Trends*, 41f.

27 See the detailed examples in van Ess, *Ungenützte Texte*, 13–17. See also al-Shahrastānī, 84.12ff. on Ibn al-Hayṣam, as well as Gimaret and Monnot, 359.

28 *Fiqh absaṭ*, 43.7–24; 53.6–55.13; on the time after al-Māturīdī, see Abū l-Layth al-Samarqandī's *ʿAqīdat al-uṣūl*, edited by A.W.T. Juynboll with the title *Een Moslimsche Catechismus in het Arabish met eene Javaansche interlineaire vertaling in pegonschrfit uitgegeven en in het Nederlandsch vertaald*, in *Bijdragen tot de Taal-Land-en Volkenkunde van Nederlandsch-Indië*, ser. IV, vol. 5 (1881): 218.2f. and 226.4–227.5 [henceforth referred to as *ʿAqīda* I]. This corresponds to the pages in Juynboll's other edition, "Samarḳandī's Catechismus opnieuw besproken" in *Bijdragen tot de Taal-Land-en Volkenkunde van Nederlandsch-Indië*, ser. IV, vol. 5 (1881): 269.9f. and 273.7–14 respectively [henceforth referred to as *ʿAqīda* II]. See also Abū l-Layth, *Bustān*, 206.-12ff. and *Uṣūl*, 42.9–53.7.

Besides this, we have grounds for presuming that two of Ibn Karrām's most "erratic" doctrinal points are in fact not so far from the position of the eastern Ḥanafite school. His literary understanding of certain Qur'ānic verses, for instance, in which God sits on the throne, is described as being "up," or described in corporeal form,[29] is not irreconcilably different from that which the *Fiqh absaṭ* has transmitted to us as Abū Ḥanīfa's view, where it is said that the person who, when asked where God was to be found, replied "in heaven," and pointed their hand upward, and was to be considered a believer.[30]

Certain Ḥanafite parallels are even found in his idea of an original faith that the descendants of Adam (according to Q 7:172) had affirmed to God before their birth.[31] These are usually interpreted as mystical components of Ibn Karrām's theological conceptualizations. But according to al-Pazdawī's reports, most theologians of the *ahl al-sunna wa-l-jamāʿa*, including himself, also believed in such a covenant (*mīthāq*) between God and humanity.[32]

This will occupy us in further detail later on, but the short summary here sufficiently demonstrates Ibn Karrām's great dependence on the mainstream Ḥanafite tradition. It can be demonstrated that he owed the foundations of his own doctrine to it, and while his own particular views took took into consideration additional stimuli, they were also formed on its basis. If this is the case, then Ibn Karrām's doctrines thus reinterpreted can be an important source for us, since what he adopted of Ḥanafite theology was taken from around the middle of the third/ninth century. This means that the Ḥanafite elements of his doctrine reflect precisely the same intellectual stage which the school's theology had reached by that time.

Such backward shifts and projections must naturally be undertaken with great caution and are only truly valid if they can be verified through other sources. But this method does in fact furnish us with unexpected insights into the state of the discourse among eastern Ḥanafites of that time, since it is ultimately more reliable than it might seem in the face of possible doubts.

One could argue, for instance, that the validity of such a judgment is undermined by basic geography. Ibn Karrām was not originally from Transoxania, but from Sīstān, and he had been particularly active in Nishapur. As a result, he may not have known the Ḥanafite teachings of the northeast at all, but instead been familiar with the traditions of Sīstān and Khurāsān which were imbued with another regional hue.

29 al-Shahrastānī, 80ff.; on this see Gimaret and Monnot, 347ff., with similar references.

30 *Fiqh absaṭ*, 49.1–42.1.

31 al-Baghdādī, *K. al-Farq bayna al-firaq*, ed. Muḥammad Badr (Cairo, 1328/1910), 211.-4ff.

32 *Uṣūl*, 211.4ff.

Concerns such as this, however, are hardly tenable if one takes what the sources impart to us seriously, since we know that Ibn Karrām also received instruction in Balkh. Furthermore, his actual teachings speak against such an assumption. If his views converge to such a great extent with the Ḥanafites of Tocharistan and Transoxania, he can hardly have been the inheritor of a completely different regional tradition. Instead, Ibn Karrām ought to be viewed as an important witness who demonstrates to us that Ḥanafite doctrine as we have come to know it in *Fiqh absaṭ* and the other texts, had spread throughout the entirety of eastern Iran.

One could further argue that the transmission of Ibn Karrām's teachings is markedly problematic and uncertain.[33] Unfortunately, we cannot learn anything more about his works in their original form, except through a few citations, scattered among later authors' works.[34] In the meantime, we are dependent to a considerable extent on heresiographers like al-Baghdādī and al-Shahrastānī in order to reconstruct his ideas. Their reports ought to be treated with special caution in this case, however, since the Karrāmite teachings went through a radical change in the fourth/tenth century under Muḥammad b. al-Hayṣam (d. 409/1019).[35] Bearing this qualification in mind, it is not easy to know whether they reproduce the older or newer form of the Karrāmite teachings. As a consequence it seems downright improper to try to derive a Ḥanafite foundation from them for a very specific and early time period.

This second problem is a difficult one, and in this case would be impossible to resolve if we were actually dependent on the later heresiographies as the most important sources. Fortunately, despite the prevalence of this view, it is not true to the extent that might be suspected. We possess an early textual testimony of great consequence, which up to now has not been sufficiently evaluated. It was written in Transoxania shortly after 900 CE, and for that reason is quite valuable to us, because it reveals the form of Karrāmite doctrine for that time in clear detail. We are also dealing with a heresiography, but in this case, a type in which a creedal text is hidden: the *Kitāb al-Radd ʿalā ahl al-bidaʿ* of Abū Muṭīʿ Makḥūl al-Nasafī, the significance of which as a source will occupy us in the following section.

---

33 See van Ess, *Ungenützte Texte*, 80f.

34 Ibid., 11ff.

35 Ibid., 60ff.

CHAPTER 3

The State of Theology during Al-Māturīdī's Lifetime

3.1 Abū Muṭīʿ Makḥūl al-Nasafī (d. 318/930) and the *Kitāb al-Radd ʿalā ahl al-bidaʿ wa-l-ahwāʾ*

Abū Muṭīʿ Makḥūl b. Faḍl al-Nasafī (d. 318/930) was a prolific author and also the progenitor of a scholarly family of intellectual distinction. His son, Muḥammad b. Makḥūl, did not reach the prominence of his father, but still possessed enough standing among the Ḥanafites to be dignified by his own entry in Ibn Abī l-Wafāʾ's biographical dictionary.[1] The same was true of Aḥmad al-Makḥūlī, a grandson,[2] as well as Aḥmad's nephew Abū l-Maʿālī Muʿtamad, who also bore the *nisba* al-Nasafī al-Makḥūlī.[3] Three generations later, Abū l-Muʿīn al-Nasafī himself emerged from this family, a scholar who could certainly be described as the most brilliant and influential theologian of the early Māturīdīya.[4]

Makḥūl himself, however, despite this key position, hardly left a trace in the biographical literature. We know that he died in the year 318/930,[5] and we also find the name of one of his teachers, who is otherwise unknown.[6] The pertinent sources tell us no more,[7] and do not do justice to the prominence that he is supposed to have enjoyed in the religious development of northeastern Iran.

Makḥūl was certainly influential, as may be demonstrated by a look at the works that have been transmitted under his name. Two of them are extant in

1 Ibn Abī l-Wafāʾ, vol. 2, 134, no. 412.

2 Ibid., vol. 1, 121, no. 239. He died in 379/989 in Bukhārā.

3 Ibid., vol. 2, 177, no. 543.

4 The genealogy of the family is compiled by van Ess in *Ungenützte Texte*, 56f.

5 Ḥājjī Khalīfa, 1430 (see title *K. al-Shuʿāʿ*) and 1571 (see title *K. al-Luʾluʾīyāt*: has a typo here); cf. Flügel, 295.

6 ʿImrān b. al-ʿAbbās b. Mūsā l-Misnānī; cf. Yaʿqūb b. ʿAbdallāh Yāqūt, *K. Muʿjam al-buldān*, ed. F. Wüstenfeld (Leipzig, 1866–60 [Leipzig repr. 1924]), vol. 4, 533.13–15.

7 Ibn Abī al-Wafāʾ, vol. 2, 180, nos. 552 and 553, is confined to a short description of works. Further documentation (for example, al-Kaḥḥāla, vol. 12, 319, or Sezgin, *GAS*, vol. 1, 601f.) does not mention or contain additional material. However, we do find from Makḥūl himself in his *Radd* (Bernand, "Le Kitāb," *Annales Islamologiques* 16 (1980): 92.14f. [hereafter referred to as *Radd*]), that he was active in the city of Balkh. Based on this statement, Bernand (ibid., 41) apparently decided that he was also originally from there.

 | DOI 10.1163/9789004261846_005

complete form. Although the third is considered lost, enough information is known about it that we may incorporate it into our image of the author.

It is immediately apparent that these texts differ greatly in subject, being dedicated respectively to different disciplines of religious study. The *K. al-Shuʿāʿ*, for which we do not currently possess a manuscript, belongs to the discipline of Ḥanafite law. In this text, Makḥūl is supposed to have said that one's prayer is invalid if one raises one's hands during or while rising from *rukūʿ*.[8] With this statement, he touched on a delicate topic of contention among the legal schools, and spurred on a discussion that would continue on into the eighth/fourteenth century.[9]

In contrast, the *K. al-Luʾluʾīyāt*,[10] still extant in manuscript, has a more paranetic nature. It deals with piety and asceticism, and gives advice on how a pious life ought to be led.[11]

This finally brings us to a work of theology; the third of Makḥūl's works, and certainly the most well-known of them as well: the *Radd ʿalā ahl al-bidaʿ*. This is an exceedingly valuable source for our subject inquiry, but aside from our own particular interests, the *Radd* is also in and of itself an important heresiographical text, occupying a conspicuous position in the theological literature of Islam.

Chronologically speaking, it ought to be placed immediately beside al-Ashʿarī's *Maqālāt al-Islāmīyīn*. Both are supposed to have been composed at the beginning of the fourth/tenth century and describe in detail the theological ideas and trends of Islam at that time.[12] Thus the *Radd* is one of the earliest sources of its type which has remained extant in its entirety.

In regard to content and geographical orientation, however, it presents no competition to the *Maqālāt*, but rather serves as a useful and informative complement. Makḥūl al-Nasafī reports almost nothing about theology in Iraq, but instead describes those teachings that were dominant in his eastern homeland. Developments had run a different course there, as we have previously discussed, and were not as multi-layered and complex as they had long been in Basra and Baghdad. Thus it is also not surprising that the *Radd* is constructed more simply and does not possess the abundance of information and precision of detail that one finds again and again in the *Maqālāt*.

---

8 Ibn Abī l-Wafāʾ, vol. 2, 180.3ff.; Ḥājjī Khalīfa, 1430; see van Ess, *Ungenützte Texte*, 57.

9 Madelung, "The Spread," 125f. n39.

10 *Uṣūl*, 241.10; Ibn Abī l-Wafāʾ, vol. 2, 180.8 (see also vol. 1, 121.-6); Ḥājjī Khalīfa, 1572; Flügel, 295; for the manuscripts see Sezgin, *GAS*, vol. 1, 602.

11 Van Ess, *Ungenützte Texte*, 59f.

12 On the dating of the *Maqālāt al-Islāmīyīn* in detail, see Allard, 58ff.

Unlike al-Ashʿarī's approach in the *Maqālāt*, Makḥūl al-Nasafī placed great value on presenting his own views in complete detail. Each description of a "heretical" teaching is immediately followed by a refutation and an explanation of his own "orthodox" position, which is generally even longer than the heresiographical report. Hence the *Radd* also functions as an excellent source for the views of the religious group with which Makḥūl affiliates. Consequently, one has only to ascertain this particular affiliation in order to have at one's disposal a detailed self-representation of that group.

This brings us to a point of difficulty in describing the *Kitāb al-radd ʿalā ahl al-bidaʿ*. Makḥūl by no means discloses his theological identity, but instead encrypts it with great care and precaution. When he comes to speak of the views of his own religious orientation, he only describes it as the "collective" (*al-jamāʿa*). This represents a claim to dominance by numbers, which certainly rules out an association with a smaller group. But the question still remains as to which of the two presumably largest collectives of eastern Iran of his time he intended: the Ḥanafīya of the "mainstream," or the newly-formed camp of Ibn Karrām.[13]

As a consequence of this uncertainty and the ambivalent nature of the text, the research has already considered both possibilities. Marie Bernand, the editor of the *Radd*, clearly decided on the first, identifying Makḥūl al-Nasafī as a Ḥanafite along classical lines. According to her views, his text is essentially an important document from the beginnings of the *kalām* school that she calls Ḥanafite-Māturīdite.[14]

The arguments which Bernand presented to support this thesis are all based on a series of questions on free will and predestination. She sees Makḥūl's position on these as completely "Ḥanafite-Māturīdite," and seeks to demonstrate this on the basis of two sections in particular: the statement that God willingly creates people's bad deeds, even if He does not approve of them or command them (*Radd*, 43); and the middle position that Makḥūl has very consciously adopted on this theme. He clearly goes on the offensive against the Qadarīya (i.e., the Muʿtazila) as well as the Jabrīya (wrongly interpreted by Bernand as Ashʿarīya), and then explains that actions are created by God, but carried out by people (ibid., 43ff.).

Similar ideas are to be found, no doubt, in the writings of al-Māturīdī and many of those who would follow in his footsteps. In fact, they are sometimes presented in very

13 The Karrāmīya had already become widespread during the lifetime of their founder in Khurāsān and Transoxania, as emerges from the *K. Rawnaq al-qulūb* of ʿUmar al-Samarqandī—see van Ess, *Ungenützte Texte*, 31f.; cf. also Madelung, *Religious Trends*, 44f. and Bosworth, "Karrāmiyya," *EI*², vol. 4, 668bf.

14 *Radd*, 41–44 and 49.

similar formulations.[15] But despite such agreements, this observation does not quite make for a dependable argument, since al-Māturīdī did not develop these particular concepts, but rather inherited them from the Transoxanian tradition. In this context, they did not represent any unusual opinion, but had in principle always been present. Abū Ḥanīfa had already expressed himself in this manner,[16] and Abū Muṭīʿ did so after him in more detail.[17] More significant than this consensus among the Ḥanafites is the fact that Ibn Karrām expressed nothing contrary to this, as we have been able to prove, but in fact expressed very similar views.

Finally, one may conclude with another point that Bernand overlooked: Makḥūl says clearly that the capacity (*istiṭāʿa*) for action already exists with the person before the deed (*Radd*, 66.6f. and 97.17ff). The Ḥanafites look at this in a completely different way, and this view was also not shared later by the Māturīdites.[18] In contrast, there are clear indications that Ibn Karrām of all people advocated this very position which was out of favor in the East.[19]

The contention with Bernand's arguments has thus taken us to the Karrāmīya, who have already been noted in the context of the intellectual background for Makḥūl's *Radd*. Van Ess was the first to consider their relevance, though he argued cautiously, and never abandoned certain caveats. To him, a proximity to the Karrāmīya seemed attested to by the fact that Makḥūl al-Nasafī also showed himself in this text (as in the *Luʾluʾīyāt*) to have ascetic tendencies and to have adopted a life of asceticism. What argued against this association, however, was the author's criticism in the *Radd*, of the anthropomorphists (*mushabbiha*), which can always be regarded as a position against the theology of Ibn Karrām.[20] Thus van Ess ultimately left his assessment of the author open-ended, and limited himself to affirming a relationship to the Karrāmīya, without committing to Makḥūl's explicit affiliation with this school.[21]

15 Compare Gimaret, *Théories*, 179ff., on whose presentation of the Māturīdite position Bernand oriented herself (*Radd*, 43n2).

16 *Risāla II* introduction.

17 *Fiqh absaṭ*, 42.9–43.4, 43.7–24, 53.6–55.13.

18 For example, *Fiqh absaṭ*, 43.5–7; *K. al-Sawād*, section 42; on the development of this problem among the Māturīdīs, see 305ff.

19 *Uṣūl*, 116.7f.; Abū Shakūr al-Sālimī, *al-Tamhīd fī bayān al-tawḥīd*, MS Berlin 2456, fol. 122b ult. ff.; *Tabṣira*, vol. 2, 544; al-Ṣafadī, vol. 4, 376.4; see also van Ess, *Ungenützte Texte*, 24, 25n82, 79, as well as Gimaret and Monnot, 359f. n94.

20 Van Ess, *Ungenützte Texte*, 58.

21 Ibid., 60; Zysow, 577n3, comments on van Ess' exposition, also to the effect that the Karrāmite origins of the *Radd* appear "highly doubtful."

Such reserve seems appropriate, given the indeterminate resources available. Yet, the actual historical circumstances might allow for greater license, since it is not certain that the Karrāmīya ought to be conceived of as a definitively outlined group or sect, the views of which accorded with a predetermined opinion. Later authors in fact portrayed a distinctly different image. Ibn al-Dāʿī for instance (from the early seventh/thirteenth century),[22] claimed that some had the theology of a Karrāmite, but the legal views of a Ḥanafite. And ʿAbd al-Jalīl al-Rāzī (sixth/twelfth century)[23] was also careful, despite uncertainties in his presentation[24] to report on those Karrāmites who went beyond the "school boundaries." This may tell us very little about the circumstances of the year 900 CE, but it is unlikely that at such a time when the individual schools of thought were first forming that the rifts between them would have been wider and less traversable.

In any case, such a nuanced description does seem to apply to Makḥūl al-Nasafī's profile. He was certainly Ḥanafite in *fiqh*; this emerges from his *K. al-Shuʿāʿ* and it is clearly on this basis that he was included in the Ḥanafite *ṭabaqāt* literature. In theology, however, Makḥūl did not follow Abū Ḥanīfa, but rather Ibn Karrām, and did so to a much greater extent and in a more explicit manner than has been observed till now.

All of the specific questions on creed that can secure this judgment will occupy us again later; hence only the most important points will be listed here which may serve as characteristic features for understanding his theological outlook.

We have already discussed Makḥūl's view on free will. It reminds us of Ibn Karrām because it seeks a middle path between the Qadarīya and Jabrīya, but also grants people the capacity to act before the deed itself.

The position that he adopts as the definition of faith is also Karrāmite. He not only excludes deeds from faith as the Ḥanafites do, but also excludes perception of the heart, which for Abū Ḥanīfa had been an integral component of the same.[25] For Makḥūl it

---

22 *GAL*, suppl. vol. 1, 711 and 757; Helmut Ritter, "Philologika. III. Muhammedanische Häresiographien," *Der Islam* 18 (1929): 46; van Ess, *Ungenützte Texte*, 12.

23 Madelung, "The Spread," 110n3 and idem, "Imāmism and Muʿtazilite Theology," in *Le Shīʿisme imâmite*, ed. T. Fahd (Paris, 1979), 20f.; Jean Calmard, "Le chiisme imamite en Iran à l'époque seldjoukide, d'après le *Kitāb al-Naqḍ*," *Le monde iranien et l'Islam. Sociétés et cultures* 1 (1971): 44.

24 Van Ess, *Ungenützte Texte*, 79.

25 *Risāla I*, 35.7f. and 35.12; *K. al-ʿĀlim*, section 5 and 6; *Fiqh absaṭ*, 40.17ff. and 42.5ff.; *K. al-Sawād*, section 1 and 43. For later time periods compare e.g., al-Māturīdī's *Tawḥīd*, 373.88ff. (where the Karrāmīya are criticized); Abū l-Layth, *ʿAqīda II*, 274.13–15; Abū Salama, 26 ult. f.; *Uṣūl*, 149.5ff., 242.18, 244.6f.

is sufficient if one confesses belief with the tongue.[26] The only remaining function for the heart is to confirm that which has already been done.[27] Moreover, he is of the view that we cannot, in any case, be aware of what goes on inside a person.[28]

It is also notable that Makḥūl emphatically argues for a primordial covenant (*mīthāq*) by all people with God.[29] Such concepts were not completely foreign to the Māturīdites, as we have seen, but they must have been of central importance for Ibn Karrām and those who followed him.

The devaluation of the life of this world and repudiation of material possessions[30] is also unequivocally Karrāmite, as has been mentioned before. Makḥūl does not, however, go so far that an association with Ibn Karrām is immediately evident. Rather, he is keen to insert a moderate critique of Sufism, touching only on erratic and antinomian tendencies.[31] Asceticism itself is left untouched, such that one gets the impression from the wording of the text that the author is consciously served by an ambiguous strategy. By critiquing heterodox mysticism he puts himself above suspicion of speaking in favor of religious enthusiasm, and thus achieves space for his support of Sufism of the Karrāmite variety.

The same technique of argumentation, which stigmatizes the excesses of others in order to protect one's own unquestioned position, seems to be at hand when Makḥūl addresses the question of the image of God. Here, as we have seen before, he puts great value on distancing himself from "those who make similar" (the *mushabbiha*; he also does the same in regard to the Jahmites). This seems calculated, however, and suggests subtle purposes. What he accuses them of is exaggeration: attributing hair, fingernails, curls, eyebrows, flesh, blood, and more of the like to God.[32] Makḥūl al-Nasafī stigmatizes such ideas as absurd, but he says no word against the Karrāmite ideas that God is a body or possesses hands and a face.[33] Thus his depiction of God, which is explicitly

---

26 *Radd*, 62.17 (which with Bernand [n. 3] ought to complete *qawl*), 62.20, 70.3 and elsewhere (see below n41). For Ibn Karrām's position see al-Shahrastānī, 84.-2ff.; Gimaret and Monnot, 360 with further documentation in n97.

27 *Radd*, 62.17f., 71.16, 119.5 see also below n42.

28 Ibid., 69.7ff. and 70.5f.

29 Ibid., 70 ult.–71.10.

30 Ibid., 94.13ff. and 100.5.

31 Ibid., 102.6–103.6 (against the "Ḥubbīya"). The Karrāmīya were accused of antinomianism in the *Sawād al-aʿẓam* (*K. al-Sawād*, section 47), thus Makḥūl's sectioning-off of such currents must be understood as a conscious attempt to redeem the honor of the Karrāmites.

32 *Radd*, 120.-3f. The polemic applies well to Muqātil b. Sulaymān; see van Ess *Theologie*, vol. 2, 529.

33 See al-Shahrastānī, 80.11ff. and 83.-2f. Gimaret and Monnot, 349 and 358; see also *Tawḥīd*, 38f.; *Uṣūl* 28.15ff. and 30.1ff.; al-Nasafī's report in the *Tabṣirat al-adilla* in van Ess, *Ungenützte Texte*, 66; the description of Ḥakīm al-Jushamī, ibid., 25.

distinguished from that of the *mushabbiha*, is by no means incompatible with that of Ibn Karrām's doctrine. Makḥūl, in contrast, claims that God ought only to be described as He Himself has done in the Qur'ān;[34] he thereby asserts a maxim, which in this general form could of course also be shared by the ascetics of Sīstān.[35]

All this[36] makes clear that Makḥūl al-Nasafī is substantively indebted to Ibn Karrām in his theology. At the same time it is clear that he did not boast of this dependency, but actually gilded it over, or to some extent even consciously hid it. It was apparently unfavorable to conspicuously represent oneself as a Karrāmite in an environment so fundamentally oriented to the contrary. This is the reason Makḥūl did not deny his own positions, but chose to present them defensively rather than on the offensive.

The format of his work helped him in this pursuit, since despite all the assertions found there about his own *jamāʿa*, the text still remains a heresiography in its compositional form. The sequence by which he treats individual themes is therefore dictated by the succession of sects described; thus while the author draws on his own position while contending with an opponent, he does so within the context of a single selected problem and is never compelled to present his views all together.

Of course, Makḥūl did not just enumerate the various doctrines and religious sects of his time, but ordered them according to certain considerations, and refuted them in three separate sections: The work starts with an introductory section dedicated principally to methodological questions and gives the names of the sects that will be discussed (*Radd*, 54.13–62.10). Then the doctrines of the six main groups (Ḥarūrīya,[37] Rawāfiḍa,[38] Qadarīya, Jabrīya, Jahmīya, Murji'a) are presented and a detailed refutation is undertaken of each (ibid., 62.11–68.20). Only in the third and longest section of his work does the author take on his opponents in depth, dividing the main groups into twelve and then focusing on them one by one (ibid., 68.21–124.21). In this manner he reaches the oft-invoked number of the 72 sects that are supposed to have gone astray.

34 *Radd*, 121.4ff.

35 If one only thinks of such Qur'ānic verses as Q 3:73, 5:64, 57:29 ("*yad Allāh*") as well as Q 2:115, 2:272 among others ("*wajh Allāh*").

36 Two more views could be added, which were held by the Karrāmīya as well as the Ḥanafites: a) God's attributes are eternal (*Radd*, 67.3ff.) and b) God is knowable by the intellect (ibid., 72.1ff.).

37 I.e., the Khārijites.

38 I.e., the Imāmites.

This was in principle supported by the famous words of the Prophet and thus left its imprint on Islamic heresiography, not only here but overall.[39]

This sequence of polemics and detailed descriptions is quite interesting, but inconsequential for our purposes, since it does not belong to the specific history of Ḥanafite nor Karrāmite theology, but rather falls under the outline of the general religious development of Islam.

Much more illuminating, however, is what Makḥūl reports on the views of his own *jamāʿa* in the form of refutations of other groups. This is presented in the following overview of the text, though his argumentation cannot be studied in detail as with the previously examined works. Much of what Makḥūl repeats on various occasions need only be mentioned once; other particulars are not cited here, since they merely reflect stubborn argumentation with obscure particularities. Furthermore, one ought not to forget that the text, read against the grain in this manner, is being divested of its actual literary form and only serves us as a quarry for a very specific inquiry. Our intention, however, is not to appreciate it as a literary document, but only to attain as much information as possible on the theology of the Karrāmīya. In this respect, it reveals itself as a source that is fascinating in its great range of expression and its high precision.

THE THEOLOGY OF THE *KITĀB AL-RADD ʿALĀ AHL AL-BIDAʿ WA-L-AHWĀʾ*

	[Introduction]
54.13[40]–57.15	Defense of theological speculation: In order to determine the correct *sunna*, one cannot rely on contradictory traditions, but must reflect on one's own.
57.16–58.22	The tradition explicitly demands of us that we make (intellectual) combat against heresy and sectarianism.

39 On the *ḥadīth* see Wensinck, *Concordance*, vol. 1, 297a. It is also used as the introduction by al-Ḥakīm al-Samarqandī (*K. al-Sawād*, 2.5ff). Compare further *Fiqh absaṭ*, 52.19. On the meaning of the tradition for Islamic heresiography, see e.g., Ignaz Goldziher, "Le dénombrement des sects mahométanes," *RHR* 26 (1892): 129–137; Henri Laoust, "La classification des sectes dans le farq d'Al-Baghdâdî," *REI* 29 (1961): 22f.; Gimaret and Monnot, 31ff.

40 The two previous sections of the edited text (*Radd*, 53: Praise of God and the Prophet; ibid., 54.2–12: admonishment to reflect and hold fast to the religion) were probably added by another hand. The text itself ought to begin with the *isnād* (ibid., 54.13).

THE THEOLOGY OF THE *KITĀB AL-RADD ʿALĀ AHL AL-BIDAʿ WA-L-AHWĀʾ*	
58.23–59.20	It is wrong to even interact in a friendly way with heretics.
59.21–60.12	Branches of heretical sects and their subdivisions.
60.13–ult.	The names of the six main groups for whom Hell is certain: Ḥarūrīya, Rawāfiḍa, Qadarīya, Jabrīya, Jahmīya, Murjiʾa.
61.1–62.10	The names of the 72 subsidiary groups. Only the 73rd group will be saved, the *jamāʿa*.
	[Main section A] **Refutation of the Six Main Groups**
62.13–63.8	I. Refutation of the Ḥarūrīya *Definition of Belief* Belief is speech, actions are (only) in regard to His laws (*al-īmān qawl wa-l-ʿamal sharāʾiʿuhu*);[41] the affirmation of belief is cognizance in the heart (*wa taṣdīq al-īmān al-maʿrifa bi-l-qalb*)[42] (62.17f.). Belief is avowal to God (*wa huwa iqrār bi-rabbihi wa huwa al-īmān*) (62.20). *Position on ʿAlī* Even if the Ḥarūrīya consider ʿAlī's actions (*ʿamal*) to be deficient, he was not deficient in his avowal to God (*fī l-iqrār bi-llāh*), which is why he must be considered a believer (61.18f.).[43]
63.9–64.3	II. Refutation of the Rawāfiḍa *Position on ʿAlī* ʿAlī's rank is high, as is that of all Companions. But it stands clearly under that of the prophets (63.17–22).[44]

41 For similar, see ibid., 69.7, 70.3, 117.1, 117.4; 118.6, 118.10; cf. 108.12f., 119.10f.

42 Cf. ibid., 71.16 and 119.5. The formulation is not chosen by chance, but deliberately reminiscent of the Ḥanafite definition of belief (*al-īmān taṣdīq bi-l-qalb wa iqrār bi-l-lisān*), although its declaration is rather different. Compare *K. al-Sawād*, 7.12; *Taʾwīlāt*, vol. 1, 35.11f.

43 For similar, see *Radd* 77.16–78.2.

44 See critiques on the adoration of ʿAlī, ibid., 78.4–14, 79.19–80.5, 80.11–ult., 81.17–82.6.

(*cont.*)

THE THEOLOGY OF THE *KITĀB AL-RADD ʿALĀ AHL AL-BIDAʿ WA-L-AHWĀʾ*	
64.4–65.8	III. Refutation of the Qadarīya *Free will—Predestination* Everything that exists in the heavens and the earth was created and decided (*qaḍāʾ*) by God (64.11f.). As such, everything is subject to God's power and it is wrong to attribute to Him any aspect of impotence or weakness. He would, in that case, not be a perfect Creator and Lord (64.13–ult.). Because of this, one can also not say that God has delegated command to people (*fawwaḍa*), nor say that He has neither created nor willed what is bad (65.1).
65.9–66.16	IV. Refutation of the Jabrīya *Free will—Predestination* We attribute (*nasaba*) actions to people, but [we attribute] the decision (*qaḍāʾ*), power (*qudra*), and creation (*takhlīq*) of their actions to God (65.14f.; cf. 66.8f.). If this were not so, one would not need prophets nor judgment after death (65.15–18). We agree with the Jabrīya on the following points: (a) The good and the bad are predetermined (*qadar*) by God. (b) Both are written on the preserved tablet (65 ult. f.). With the Qadarīya we share views on: (a) God not exacting from anyone more than he can bear (see Q 2:286) (b) Capacity (*istiṭāʿa*) exists before actions (66.6f.).
66.17–67.18	V. Refutation of the Jahmīya *God as Existent* Since God is (see 66.-2 ff.), then He is a thing (*shayʾ*) though by no means like (other) things (*ashyāʾ*), since He is a Creator of things (67.3).[45]

45 Compare, ibid., 95.12–16; 105.17ff. *Shayʾ* here ought to be understood as "something/a being" and not in the concrete sense as "thing," although in theological discussion it is often (mis)understood as such. The dispute was provoked originally by a doctrine of Jahm b. Ṣafwān. On the topic, see van Ess, *Theologie*, vol. 2, 499.

THE THEOLOGY OF THE *KITĀB AL-RADD ʿALĀ AHL AL-BIDAʿ WA-L-AHWĀʾ*	
	Doctrine of Attributes God is an eternal Creator (*khāliq azalī*) with all of His attributes, and created things are created along with all of their attributes and actions (67.3–5). The Creator is not temporally limited but eternal without beginning and without end (*qadīm dāʾim*), even when He has not (always) created (67.7f.).[46] *Qurʾān* (Within *ḥadīth*:) To claim that the Qurʾān is created is disbelief (67.14f. and 67.16ff.).
67.19–68.20	VI. Refutation of the Murjiʾa *Promise and Threat* Carrying out God's commands (like prayers for example) is not based on the inclination of the believer, but it is his duty (68.3ff.). For this reason it is not right to assume that the believer will not be harmed by any sins. God's threat of punishment is meant seriously and mentioned often in the Qurʾān (68.9–14).
	[Main Section B] **Refutation of the 72 Sects**
69.1–78.19	I. Refutation of the 12 Sects of the Ḥarūrīya *Definition of Belief* Belief only consists of speech, not actions (69.7). God charged the Prophet with identifying people as believers as soon as they spoke the *shahāda*; i.e., he was supposed to accept their speech as testimony and leave the probing of hearts (*ḍamāʾir*) to God (69.10–17).[47] *Position of the Sinner* This is why no one can be viewed as an unbeliever due to a sin. We attribute belief to all of the "people of the *qibla*" and leave (the judgment of) people's hearts to God (69.7f.).

46 Compare *Radd*, 95.17 and 106.7ff.

47 Similar at ibid., 70.5f.

(*cont.*)

THE THEOLOGY OF THE *KITĀB AL-RADD ʿALĀ AHL AL-BIDAʿ WA-L-AHWĀʾ*
Free Will—Predestination God wills all of people's actions; He also creates them, as it is stated in the Qurʾān (Q 37:96) (70.21f.). *Primordial Covenant* All people, even children, must be either believers or disbelievers, since all of them acknowledged God on the Day of the Covenant (*yawm al-mīthāq*) and are born with the natural disposition (*fiṭra*) of a believer. If they later disbelieve, this is a departure from belief (70 ult.–71.10). *Rational Knowledge of God* No one is excused for their disbelief, since one could have known of God through the prophets; if not Muḥammad, then one of his predecessors. Furthermore, God has given us other proofs (*ḥujaj*), such as signs (*āyāt*) and examples (*ʿibar*) in the creation. Everyone can come to know of the Creator through these (71.17–72.4). *Necessity of the Imamate* It is wrong to say that the community may no longer have a commander (*amīr*) when it comes to disagreement. The Prophet has ordered us to adhere to the powerful and obey them. The community will thus always be in the right, because the greatest mass (*al-sawād al-aʿẓam*) does not go astray (77.1–10). *Calling to what is Good and Forbidding the Reprehensible* The Imam, who ought to be of Qurayshite lineage, should be given obedience.[48] Only if he fights the believers ought one defend oneself. Whoever draws their sword against the community, however, is to be killed (78.6–14).

48 Cf. ibid., 84.1–7.

THE THEOLOGY OF THE *KITĀB AL-RADD ʿALĀ AHL AL-BIDAʿ WA-L-AHWĀʾ*

78.20–87–87,13	II. Refutation of the 12 Sects of the Rawāfiḍa *Prayer behind Sinners* One should pray behind all believers, even if one is dealing with sinners, heretics, or hypocrites, since prayer is always of benefit to the one who prays (83.5–19).
87.14–96.2	III. Refutation of the 12 Sects of the Qadarīya *Free Will—Predestination* It is wrong to believe that God can only justly reward and punish people if He has made them the masters of their affairs (*an yumlikahum umūrahum*) and has no effect during their actions (cf. 87.16f.). The correct view is that He must only make them masters of their affairs in the sense of capacity (*ʿalā maʿnā l-istiṭāʿa*). I.e., He makes them capable (*yuṭawwiquhum*) of that which He has commanded them, and does not command them to do that for which they have no capacity (87.19f.). However, God is the sole master of actions in the sense of the will (*ʿalā maʿnā l-mashīʾa*), the decision (*qaḍāʾ*), the decree (*qadar*), and creation (*takhlīq*) (87.20–22). Not only the good, but also the bad is determined by God, who possesses power over all things (88.5–10; 88.19–89.1). The bad happens with God's will, decision, degree, knowledge, and creation, but not with His command (*amr*), His approbation (*riḍā*), His particularization (*takhṣīṣ*), His love (*ḥubb*), or His choice (*ikhtiyār*) (89.1f.). This is so because there are three types of actions: Sins that God determines and wills on account of which He can nevertheless punish; merits (*faḍāʾil*), for which He has approbation and which He rewards; and finally, duties that He commands and likewise rewards (89.2–7). Actions are never morally neutral, but are always either good or bad and one is rewarded or punished for them (89.16–90.3). *Createdness of Belief* Belief and disbelief are mentioned in the Qurʾān, but are not as a result part of the uncreated Qurʾān; they are created, which the Qurʾān indicates (90.19–91.12).

(*cont.*)

THE THEOLOGY OF THE *KITĀB AL-RADD ʿALĀ AHL AL-BIDAʿ WA-L-AHWĀʾ*	
	Ontology Everything that exists is something/existing (*shayʾ*), and thus possesses an essence (*dhāt*), since therein lies the verification (*ithbāt*) of its existence (91.16–92.6).[49] *Qurʾānic Exegesis* We should believe everything in the Qurʾān, as well as the abrogated and the ambiguous (*mutashābih*) (92.10–12). The interpretation of the ambiguous, however, is left to those who are knowledgeable about it (92.-1f.).[50] *Anthropology* Creatures are different according to their natures (*fī l-ṭabāʾiʿ*) (92.16f.). *Promise and Threat* Sincere repentance of a believer will be accepted by God (93.6–17). *Asceticism* The world is bad and cursed and along with it all human actions that are not in obedience to God. Striving for sustenance (*qūt*) diverts us from worship of God and takes us to Hell (94.13–15).
96.3–105.10	IV. Refutation of the 12 Sects of the Jabrīya *Free Will—Predestination* People carry out their own deeds (*yaʿmalūnahā*) (96.10). Otherwise, being taken to account for deeds would make no sense (96.13f.). God gives them power to act (*taṭwīq*), in that He plants (*gharaza*) a capacity (*istiṭāʿa*) in them (97.1f.). This capacity already exists before the action, since God does not oblige anyone to do something which they are incapable of doing (97.17f.).

49 Compare ibid., 95.17f.

50 Compare ibid., 95.3–7.

THE THEOLOGY OF THE *KITĀB AL-RADD ʿALĀ AHL AL-BIDAʿ WA-L-AHWĀʾ*

	Promise and Threat God rewards and punishes people as a consequence for their own deeds (99.8–11), i.e., for that which they earn (100.-2). One cannot claim that people are fortunate (= destined for Paradise) or unfortunate (= destined for Hell) independently of their deeds. Reward and punishment are measured according to deeds (101.12–102.5). *Against Antinomianism from the Ascetics* True love of God does not disregard religious laws, but fulfills them to the utmost (101.11–103.6). Love of God does not exempt people from punishment (103.11–104.2).
105.11–114.15	v. Refutation of the 12 Sects of the Jahmīya *Knowledge of God* God is conceivable to the creation, otherwise we would not know of His existence. He Himself has described Himself to us (105.17–19) and moreover is knowable through the signs of creation (108.21–109.6). *Vision of God* We cannot see Him in this world, but the pious will in the Afterlife (105.19). *God's Throne* Since God is one, He has a limit. He sits on the throne and is over us in heaven (107.1–17). *Doctrine of Attributes* All of God's attributes are eternal and uncreated, including His speech (106.7–16). *Qurʾān* Hence the Qurʾān is likewise uncreated (110.1–8; cf. 111.17–112.3), whereas the pronunciation and recitation of the Qurʾān—as a human act—certainly ought to be recognized as created (113.7–114.2).

(*cont.*)

THE THEOLOGY OF THE *KITĀB AL-RADD ʿALĀ AHL AL-BIDAʿ WA-L-AHWĀʾ*	
	Promise and Threat Believers also go to Hell because of their sins. But they will not stay there forever (108.1–9). *Paradise and Hell* Paradise and Hell are already created and will not pass away (110.13–ult.). *Prophethood* God cannot forsake His creation, but has sent them a messenger in order to commit them to worship and obedience (111.6–8). *Eschatology* The punishment of the grave and the intercession of the Prophet are real (112.8–ult.).
114.16–124.21	VI. Refutation of the 12 Sects of the Murjiʾa *Promise and Threat* God has not just enjoined belief upon us, but also duties, and threatened us with punishment if they are neglected (114.22–115.3). What we do in this world is by no means arbitrary, but has been prescribed exactly by prophets and their revelations (115.9–21). Obedience and disobedience are also clearly distinguishable for us (116.7–17). *Definition of Belief* Belief consists in pronouncing the *shahāda*, not knowledge or actions (117.1–7, 117.13–118.6, 118.10–119.5). *Further Conditions of Belief* Belief does not decrease or increase (119.10). The belief of a prophet is like the belief of the angels Gabriel and Michael (119.-3). One should have no doubt concerning one's own belief, and thus should not add the *istithnāʾ* to his profession of faith (120.5–19).

THE THEOLOGY OF THE *KITĀB AL-RADD ʿALĀ AHL AL-BIDAʿ WA-L-AHWĀʾ*	
	Significance of the Ḥadīth Among the *ḥadīth*, just as with Qurʾānic verses, are those that abrogate and are abrogated, and those that are clear and ambiguous. One must therefore examine them and understand their meaning (121.20–122.10). In addition, one must reflect on one's own, since there are no transmissions that answer all the questions of religion (122.17–123.16). *Calling to What is Good and Forbidding the Reprehensible* Calling to the good and forbidding the reprehensible is assumed of the believers and not the *amīr*s. One must obey righteous leaders and also put up with those that are unjust. But if they command people to sin, then there can be no obedience (123.22–124.14).
124.22–126.15	[Conclusion] All these sects adhere to false opinions and must be shunned by us. This is why we have demonstrated their heresy. For we desire to abide by the Prophet and his *sunna*.

3.2 Al-Ḥakīm al-Samarqandī (d. 342/953) and the *Kitāb al-Sawād al-aʿẓam*

Makḥūl al-Nasafī was a demonstrative example of how a Karrāmite of north-eastern Iran might express his views at the beginning of the fourth/tenth century; confident and clear in his theological argumentation, even subtle in regard to particular formulations, but also careful when it came to emphasizing the characteristic traits of his own position. However, the degree to which this type of reservation seems to be characteristic of the Karrāmīya becomes clearer when we compare it to a second text, one that can be considered contemporary to the *K. al-Radd*. This text represents the efforts of the Transoxanian Ḥanafīya to document their theological positions, and was written with no qualifications or provisos, but with a tone of apodeictic certainty.

That the Ḥanafites were able to assume such a different tone is not surprising, given their dominance at that time. Their position in the region had become more consolidated than ever before. As we have seen, the Ḥanafite school had long reached ascendancy in the region, and so traditionally possessed the wide approval of the population. Political patronage was soon to follow, which on its part was surely aware that a generally recognized and enduring religious orientation could only be useful for the stability of the polity.

This awaking official interest accompanied the rise of the Sāmānid dynasty.[51] Since the early third/ninth century, family members of the Sāmān-Khudā had already been active as governors in Samarqand, Shāsh (latter-day Tashkent), Fergana, and for a time, also Herat. However, this had only been under the order and suzerainty of the Ṭāhirids. Only when the leadership of the latter was broken by the attacks of Yaʿqūb al-Ṣaffār (259/873) did Sāmānid influence grow and then quickly break through into a lopsidedly more important position. In 261/875 Naṣr I b. Aḥmad was invested by the caliph with power over the province of Transoxania. Around the year 287/900, his brother Ismāʿīl b. Aḥmad, after a Ṣaffārid victory, even became governor of Transoxania and Khurāsān. The family maintained this prominence for almost a century, and this role also explains their interest and engagement in questions of theology.

Sāmānid religious policy was by no means conducted in such a way that it enforced a particular theology by military force, tantamount to the creation of a state dogma. No one, it seems, was compelled to follow Abū Ḥanīfa's teachings.[52] On the contrary, since 275/888–9, the Shāfiʿī *madhhab* was allowed to spread in Samarqand with official authorization. The scholar Muḥammad b. Naṣr al-Marwazī,[53] who supported the Shāfiʿī school, even came to receive Ismāʿīl b. Aḥmad's overt patronage.[54] All the same, governmental interest in

51 On the following, see Barthold, 209ff., esp. 210 and 225; Richard N. Frye, *Bukhara: The Medieval Achievement* (Norman, OK, 1965), 38ff. and idem, "The Sāmānids," in the *Cambridge History of Islam*, vol. 4 (Cambridge, 1975), 136ff.; C.E. Bosworth, *The Islamic Dynasties* (Edinburgh, 1967), 101f. Our main source for these events is Abū Bakr Muḥammad b. Jaʿfar Narshakhī, *Tārīkh-i Bukhārā*, ed. C. Shefer as *Description topographique et historique de Boukhara par Mohammed Nerchakhy suivie de textes relatifs à la Transoxanie* (Paris, 1892), 74ff./trans. Richard N. Frye, *The History of Bukhārā: Translated from a Persian Abridgement of the Arabic Original by Narshakhi* (Cambridge, 1954), 76ff.

52 At least, the sources do not indicate that compulsion in questions of religion was practiced. An exception might be the execution of the Ismāʿīlī missionary Muḥammad al-Nasafī (d. 332/943), whose background is not precisely known. What has been transmitted indicates that he converted the Sāmānid Naṣr b. Aḥmad (r. 301–31/914–43) and a few dignitaries at the court to Ismāʿīlīs. The *amīr*'s son, Nuḥ b. Naṣr, immediately after his accession, is supposed to have persecuted the Ismāʿīlīs and executed al-Nasafī. See Ismail K. Poonawala, *Biobibliography of Ismāʿīlī Literature* (Malibu, CA, 1977), 40ff. and Heinz Halm, *Die Schia* (Darmstadt, 1988), 276.

53 On him see al-Subkī, vol. 2, 246ff.; further documentation in Sezgin, *GAS*, vol. 1, 494.

54 Halm, *Ausbreitung*, 108; Madelung, *Religious Trends*, 26.

matters of religion was by no means impartial or neutral. Ḥanafite teaching was clearly preeminent over all other rival schools, and this manifested in a significant and consequential step taken for its recognition and unification.[55]

The abovementioned Ismāʿīl b. Aḥmad (r. 279–95/892–907), recognized as the actual founder of Sāmānid power, called the scholars of Samarqand, Bukhārā, and other cities of Transoxania together and requested that they compile the orthodox view of belief in a single creed.[56] The goal of this undertaking was to combat various heresies, which in the meanwhile had become native to the region. This also meant, de facto, that Ḥanafite theology was to receive a fixed catechism, the significance of which was compounded since it was issued by the double authority of the *ʿulamāʾ* and the political rulers.

In keeping with this ambitious goal, the scholar commissioned to author the text was of generally acknowledged rank. The choice fell on Abū l-Qāsim Isḥāq b. Muḥammad b. Ibrāhīm,[57] called al-Ḥakīm al-Samarqandī (d. 342/953),[58] who was identified as a religious authority in various subjects. In the area of *fiqh*, he was distinguished by his officiating position; he had studied with Muḥammad b. Khuzayma al-Qallās[59] in Balkh and apparently also with Abū Naṣr al-ʿIyāḍī[60] in Samarqand, and then was active for a long time in his home-

55 Besides the *K. al-Sawād al-aʿẓam*, the unbroken importance of the Ḥanafīya is evidenced for the same time period and also from Samarqand from a work we possess on Ḥanafite law: the *K. al-Furūq* of Abū l-Faḍl al-Karābīsī al-Samarqandī (d. 322/934), which is extant in two Istanbul manuscripts; see *GAL*, suppl. vol. 1, 295; *GAS*, vol. 1, 442f.; Joseph Schacht, "Aus zwei arabischen Furūq-Büchern," *Islamica* 2 (1926): 508. An examination of the text (according to MS Feyzullah 921/1 fol. 1–25b) shows that it gives us no information on questions of theology at all.

56 See the introduction on the Persian translation of the *K. al-Sawād*, ed. ʿAbd al-Ḥayy Ḥabībī (Tehran 1348/1969), 17.4ff.); on this see Madelung, "The Early Murjiʾa," 39 and idem, *Religious Trends*, 30.

57 *K. al-Sawād*, Persian trans. 18.6ff.

58 *GAL*, vol. 1, 174 and suppl. vol. 1, 295; *GAS*, vol. 1, 606; in detail see Wilferd Madelung, "Abū 'l-Qāsem Esḥāq Samarqandī," *EIr*, vol. 1, 358f., where the sources are compiled. In Ibn Abī l-Wafāʾ, vol. 1, 139 there are two erroneously separated entries on Isḥāq b. Muḥammad b. Ismāʿīl al-Ḥakīm al-Samarqandī. The first and more elaborate (no. 302), reproduced in Samʿānī's entries, must be the original. The second (no. 305), in contrast, consists of only one statement: that Isḥāq reportedly studied law and theology with al-Māturīdī, his presumably older contemporary. This functions as a later supplement, all the more, since we have no further inducement to see al-Māturīdī as Abū l-Qāsim's teacher.

59 al-Samʿānī, vol. 4, 208.3f.; on this as well as what follows see Madelung, "Abū 'l-Qāsem Eṣhāq Samarqandī," *EIr*, vol. 1, 358a; on al-Qallās see Ibn Abī l-Wafāʾ, vol. 2, 53, no. 171.

60 *Tabṣira*, vol. 1, 357.7f. = Tancî, 5.5–7; on Abū Naṣr al-ʿIyāḍī, cf. Ibn Abī l-Wafāʾ, vol. 1, 70f., no. 117.

town in the position of *qāḍī*.[61] Beyond that, Abū l-Qāsim garnered high acclaim as a Sufi, and is particularly remembered in this regard by posterity. His main teachers of Sufism were ʿAbdallāh b. Sahl al-Rāzī[62] as well as the famous Abū Bakr al-Warrāq,[63] whose memory was clearly cherished by his student.[64] More important still is that Abū l-Qāsim himself taught this discipline: Numerous mystical aphorisms (*ḥikam*) are transmitted from him on the basis of which he apparently earned the sobriquet "al-Ḥakīm";[65] these were also transmitted in later Sufi literature.[66]

The assignment handed to him was, in every sense, more theological than of a legal or Sufi-mystic nature; Abū l-Qāsim was supposed to author a creed that would reflect the most important theological doctrines of the Ḥanafīya on a popular level. He seems to have accomplished this, and to general acclaim at that. The text that he presented as the result of his efforts, the *Radd ʿalā aṣḥāb al-ahwāʾ al-musammā K. al-Sawād al-aʿẓam ʿalā madhhab al-imām al-aʿẓam Abī Ḥanīfa*, later came to be better known as the *K. al-Sawād al-aʿẓam*.[67] It found the endorsement of the other parties involved[68] and apparently served the function of an official catechism in Sāmānid territory.[69] Still in the same century, probably under the rule of Nūḥ b. Manṣūr (366–87/976–97), the text was translated into Persian.[70] After this it must have continued to be read and

61 al-Samʿānī, vol. 4, 208.1; Ibn Abī l-Wafāʾ, vol. 1, 139.5; al-Laknawī, 44.12. Abū l-Qāsim possibly wrote a work on *fiqh* as well, called *al-Mukhtaṣar fī l-ḥayḍ*, if the Ḥakīm al-Qāḍī mentioned in Ibn Quṭlūbughā, 26 (no. 69) is the same person.

62 He is likely the same ʿAbdallāh b. Sahl al-Zāhid mentioned by al-Samʿānī, vol. 4, 208.3 and Ibn Abī l-Wafāʾ, vol. 1, 139.3f. as Abū l-Qāsim's teacher. On him see al-Sulamī, *K. Ṭabaqāt al-ṣūfīya*, ed. J. Pedersen (Leiden, 1960), 82.3.

63 al-Anṣārī Harawī, *Ṭabaqāt al-ṣūfīya*, ed. ʿAbd al-Ḥayy Ḥabībī (Kabul 1341/1962), 263.2ff.; al-Laknawī, 44.9f. On al-Warrāq in detail, see Wāʿiẓ-i Balkhī, 261–273; Radtke, 546.

64 al-Sulamī, 219.5ff.

65 al-Samʿānī, vol. 4, 208.1ff.; Ibn Abī l-Wafāʾ, vol. 1, 139.5f.; al-Laknawī, 44.9 and 44.13; see also van Ess, *Theologie*, vol. 2, 565n51.

66 Maḥmūd b. ʿUthmān, *Firdaws al-murshidīya fī asrār al-ṣamardīya*, ed. F. Meier (Leipzig, 1948), 248 ult.ff.; Abū Naṣr Ṭāhir b. Muḥammad al-Khānaqāhī, *Guzīda dar akhlāq u taṣawwuf*, ed. Īrāgh Afshār (Tehran 1347/1968), *passim* (s.v., under Abū l-Qāsim); according to Abū Bakr Muḥammad al-Kalābādhī, *al-Taʿarruf li-madhhab ahl al-taṣawwuf*, ed. ʿAbd al-Ḥalīm Maḥmūd and Ṭāhā ʿAbd al-Bāqī Surūr (Cairo 1380/1960), 33.1f. al-Ḥakīm is supposed to have composed a work on the proper conduct (*muʿāmala*) for Sufis.

67 Ḥājjī Khalīfa, 1008; *GAL*, vol. 1, 174 and suppl. vol. 1, 295; *GAS*, vol. 1, 606.

68 *K. al-Sawād* (Pers. trans.), 19.2ff.

69 Madelung, "The Early Murjiʾa," 39; idem, *Religious Trends*, 30.

70 *K. al-Sawād* (Pers. trans.), 19.3f.; Madelung, "The Early Murjiʾa," 39; *Religious Trends*, 30; and idem, "Abū 'l-Qāsem Eṣḥāq Samarqandī," *EIr*, vol. 1, 358b; Frye (*Bukhara*, 102), asserts that Nuḥ b. Naṣr (r. 331–43/943–54) was the initiator of the Persian translation. The

taught often,[71] since the numerous extant manuscripts and prints show various departures from and additions to the text that are only explainable through its wide circulation and high estimation.

Given these circumstances it is clear how important the *K. al-Sawād al-aʿẓam* is for the sake of our becoming better acquainted with Transoxanian theology. This text is not merely the representation of a few scholars' teachings, but is, to a certain extent, a "public text" in which a wide theological consensus is expressed. If this is the case, then a particular question takes on considerable importance for us: What was the exact relationship between this popular text and al-Māturīdī's teachings? Answering this question is indispensable, but also difficult, given the challenging chronological framework that we are dealing with.

Al-Ḥakīm al-Samarqandī (d. 342/953) lived contemporaneously to al-Māturīdī (d. 333/944). Both resided in Samarqand, neither of them apparently leaving it for any long period of time. They also must have known each other more or less well, as the sources clearly indicate.[72] It only remains to be clarified

---

Persian translation of the *Sawād* is probably intended when Ḥājjī Khalīfa, 1157 speaks of a Persian *ʿaqīda* of Abū l-Qāsim.

71 The later pilgrim handbooks by Abū Ṭāhir Samarqandī (*Samarīya dar bayān-i awṣāf-i ṭabīʿī u mazārāt-i Samarqand*, ed. Īrāj Afshār (Tehran, 1343/1965), 106.10ff.) and Mullā ʿAbd al-Ḥakīm Tājir (*Qandīya dar bayān-i mazārāt-i Samarqand*, ed. Afshār (Tehran, 1334/1955), 3.1ff., 5.10ff., 20.9ff.) testify to the reverence enjoyed by Abū l-Qāsim as a fighter against heresy. On these two texts see Weinberger, 381. The persistency of interest in the *K. al-Sawād al-aʿẓam* is also demonstrated by the fact that it was printed repeatedly in the East, even in Ottoman times. However, in each case the number of prints was few, such that today, with some effort, one can only track down a few examples. In regard to the Arabic version, the following editions are known: Būlāq 1253/1837–8 (accessible in a copy located in the École des Langues Orientales); Istanbul, 1288; Istanbul, 1304/1886–7 (not mentioned in the GAL and GAS; available in the British Library); Istanbul (no date) (later than the previously mentioned edition, reproduced with some additional mistakes; not mentioned in the GAL and GAS; incomplete copy in Harvard University Library); Istanbul, 1313 (with commentary); Kazan, 1878; there is a Tatar translation of this, published in Kazan, 1881, also not mentioned in the GAL and GAS (available in the Moscow Lenin Library). A modern Turkish translation by ʿAini Efendi Bulghari was published in 1258/1842 in Būlāq. The medieval Persian version, certainly revised at the end of the eighth/fourteenth century (see Madelung, "Abū 'l-Qāsem Eṣḥāq Samarqandī," *EIr*, vol. 1, 359a), was edited by A. Ḥabībī in Tehran, 1969. The English translation finished by al-ʿOmar in his dissertation (79–218), refers to the manuscripts in the British Museum Or. 12781 and the Bibliothèque Nationale 824,1.

72 Of particular interest is the earliest biographical source for both, al-Nasafī's *Tabṣirat al-adilla*, where we even find that al-Ḥakīm al-Samarqandī honored the deceased al-Māturīdī with a eulogy (*Tabṣira*, vol. 1, 358.17–19 = Tancî, 8.2–4).

whether this personal contact was a cause for influence in theological views. Had the apparently older and subsequently more famous al-Māturīdī actually been Abū l-Qāsim's teacher, or was he simply a contemporaneous scholar from the same city? Or, with an eye to the text in discussion: Are we already encountering a "new," "Māturīdite" doctrine in the *K. al-Sawād al-aʿẓam*, or does the text still represent the "older" Ḥanafite theology? If the first is the case, then we may assume that al-Māturīdī had been an immediate authoritative influence on his contemporary. If the second is the case, then the *K. al-Sawād* still serves as a valuable documentation of traditional Ḥanafite teachings in a generally recognized formulation of the time; this can then function as a backdrop from which al-Māturīdī's uniqueness and originality may be more precisely and meaningfully brought out.

Both options are appealing, but the decision is not easy—especially since we must keep in mind that the answer to this question is the first important deliberation needed for a more comprehensive view of al-Māturīdī's thought. However, we are not compelled to formulate such a judgment without taking some preliminary steps. There have already been a number of attempts to more precisely determine the theological position of the *K. al-Sawād* from this context. For now we will discuss these in detail, in order that the entire extent of the problem may be known.

The older and still more prevalent view envisions al-Ḥakīm as al-Māturīdī's student, and also in some sense as one of the first Māturīdites. This was stated as the *Sawād* became more generally known, and has dominated in the pertinent literature until today. This was started with Goldziher (1904, 295), who described the text in 1902 as "the oldest Māturīdite handbook." Brockelmann in 1937 (*GAL*, suppl. vol. 1, 295) adopted Goldziher's characterization, and Sezgin in 1967 (*GAS*, vol. 1, 606) repeated Brockelmann's position verbatim. Tritton (1966, 96) went a step further, intending to draw the relationship between the two theologians even closer together. Al-Ḥakīm, according to him, had certainly studied *fiqh* and *kalām* with his famous contemporary; it was even possible that he was "a brother of the more celebrated al-Māturīdī who was the founder of the school." The traditional estimation of al-Ḥakīm as the first of the Māturīdites was found again in Watt's writing (1985, 243). Watt could refer there to a study by one of his students, completed in the meantime with his own encouragement: In this Edinburgh dissertation with the programmatic title "The Doctrines of the Māturīdite School with Special Reference to as-Sawād al-Aʿẓam of Al-Ḥakīm as-Samarqandī," F.O.A. al-ʿOmar translated the *K. al-Sawād* into English and undertook a theological analysis of the text. His results seemed to confirm on a wider basis that which had already long been presumed. Al-Ḥakīm, according to al-ʿOmar (1974, i., 1, and 60), had studied with al-Māturīdī and had even shared a bond of friendship with him. His formulated creed accordingly represents the early dogma of the Māturīdite school.

The other conceivable view of things has only seldom been propagated until now[73] and has only been emphasized most prominently by Madelung. In any case, his evaluations also reveal various nuances and thereby clearly reflect how complicated the debate concerning the text actually is. In his first statement on the work (Madelung 1968, 118f. n30) he still followed one of Tancî's suggestions and held that it was possible that the *Sawād* did not originate from al-Ḥakīm at all, but was written a century afterward. Later, however, Madelung relinquished this primary consideration (chiefly due to the Persian version of the text that had appeared since then) and described the *Sawād* as a traditional Ḥanafite document by the hand of Abū l-Qāsim (Madelung 1982, 39; idem, 1988, 30). He mentioned al-Māturīdī's name here in passing, but only for the purpose of chronology and not in order to establish a deeper connection. The grounds for this position were revisited in the article "Abū 'l-Qāsem Eṣḥāq Samarqandī" (*EIr*, 1985, 358a and 359a) in which Madelung examined the relationship between the two thinkers more closely. There he showed that the *Sawād* does not contain a single specifically Māturīdite doctrine; in fact, in certain points it even contradicts al-Māturīdī's theology. If later sources claimed that al-Ḥakīm had been his student, this can only have been a retrospective misjudgment of the text. The *K. al-Sawād al-aʿẓam* was thus evaluated in a considerably different manner, in what was intended as a conscious revision of previous positions. When the first of these articles by Madelung was republished in a 1985 anthology, it was expanded by a corrective appendix explaining this new verdict.[74]

Since then only van Ess (1991, vol. 2, 565) has briefly engaged in this debate again, when he presented al-Ḥakīm al-Samarqandī in his history of early Islamic theology. He

73 Ritter's position, for example, was a bit divergent, see his "Philologika. III," 41, where he chooses to refrain from judgment and only describes the text in a general manner. In contrast, Tancî (10n4) doubts whether the text was even written by al-Ḥakīm al-Samarqandī. He indicates that on page 32 (line 9) of the Istanbul print (= *K. al-Sawād*, 47.10f. [Būlāq]) al-Ḥakīm was cited as a dead authority, and on this basis concludes on a later date of composition. The argument does not hold weight because the entire section (30.-2–32.17 [Istanbul] = *K. al-Sawād*, 35.9–47.-3 [Būlāq]) is clearly a secondary addition. There an entire list of notable scholars are named (among whom is also the later Abū l-Layth al-Samarqandī: 31 ult. [Istanbul] = *K. al-Sawād*, 47 ult. [Būlāq]) as evidence for a particular view, which does not fit at all with the style of the work that is otherwise quite uniform. The same list of authories is found in the London and Paris manuscripts inserted in another part of the *Sawād* (cf. al-ʿOmar, 188ff.). We are apparently dealing with a list of authoritative names that has been integrated into the text by later scribes.

74 Madelung, *Religious Schools and Sects in Medieval Islam* (London, 1985), sec. II, Addenda et Corrigenda, 168a on page 118. However, Madelung clearly only stated his general stance on the topic, since he later went against his previous statements in an article "Sonstige religiöse Literatur," *Grundriss der arabischen Philologie II*, 380, where he stated that, "Das Glaubensbekenntnis steht der Māturīditischen Dogmatik nahe, macht aber Zugeständnisse an populäre traditionalistische Auffassungen."

also decided to separate the two theologians and was of the opinion that al-Ḥakīm had not been a student of al-Māturīdī, but rather ought to be classified as a straightforward Murji'ite in the general sense.

The abovementioned considerations and debates demonstrate a wide spectrum of positions, which is not out of the ordinary for academic discourse; after all, the nature of scholarly argumentation is driven by a variety of factors and it is only natural if we end up with contrary views here as well. But if the course of argumentation is observed more precisely, it becomes clear that something else is being expressed therein. We are not just observing a difference of opinion, but rather the disclosure of complications of the first order that lie in the subject matter itself and thus have long stood in the way of consensus. Priority must be given to dealing with them, since the attempt to resolve them has led to conclusions that determine the course for further considerations.

The first of these conclusions is that al-Māturīdī's views do not seem to represent an tremendous break in the theological tradition of Samarqand or even all of Transoxania. If, so far as can be seen, it can be reasonably argued that al-Ḥakīm had actually been al-Māturīdī's student but that his work had not been influenced by al-Māturīdī, then there cannot have been too deep a rift between al-Māturīdī's views and the Ḥanafite theology of previous generations. Instead, much of what was taught before al-Māturīdī was retained both in his own writings and in the writings of those after him. This means, however, that we still have no clear and indisputable criterion by which a pre-Māturīdite phase, so to speak, may be distinguished from a post-Māturīdite phase.

To then conclude that al-Māturīdī did not bring about any lasting changes would be erroneous, however, since differences between his views and those of other Ḥanafites, such as al-Ḥakīm al-Samarqandī, have already been established. How these differences ought to be evaluated nevertheless remains open to debate. And this leads us to a second foundational observation based on the scholarly views just presented.

Up to now, it was always assumed, by a more or less unspoken consensus, that Ḥanafite theology in Transoxania was only detectably changed once, namely at the moment when al-Māturīdī engaged in it. According to this view, two theological edifices were presumed; one was a guiding force for al-Māturīdī's work, while the other he is supposed to have established himself. Such an image, however, not only emphasizes—in a questionable manner at that—the authority of well-known figures; it also lacks a certain historical plausibility. This is so because it ought to happen only very seldomly that an entire system is supplanted by one which follows it. It is much more probable for development to play out over several stages through the contributions of successive generations, some adding more, some adding less. Changes in ideas should not be seen as the result of a single transformation of an intellectual edifice, but rather as the outcome of constant revision undergone by its individual parts.

If these modified expectations are abided by while we reexamine the relationship between the *K. al-Sawād al-aʿẓam* and the doctrines of al-Māturīdī, a perspective emerges that has not come up in the debate as yet. We obtain an image not of a two-layered, but three-layered structure, since the views found in al-Māturīdī's and al-Ḥakīm's works can ultimately be divided into three categories.

The first of these are those doctrines on which both thinkers agree, but which are also professed by earlier authors, such as Abū Muqātil al-Samarqandī or Abū Muṭīʿ al-Balkhī. In these cases, al-Māturīdī and al-Ḥakīm are only repeating that which had long been discussed among the eastern Ḥanafites. Because of this fact, such parallels only tell us about the continuity of doctrines in Transoxania, but nothing about the special relationship between the two theologians. A few examples may be named here: the definition of belief, disapproval of the *istithnāʾ*, the status of believing sinners, God's eternal attributes, as well as the recognition of the visio beatifica—at least in regard to what applies to the characteristic outlines of these themes.[75]

The second category consists of teachings for which a consensus between al-Māturīdī and al-Ḥakīm can be found, but which do not conform to the opinions of earlier Ḥanafites. These deal in particular with considerations of God's "concrete" characteristics, e.g., His satisfaction and anger, His sitting on the throne, or the question of whether the Creator can be attributed to a specific location at all.[76] These topics all deal with the greater problematization of how the seemingly anthropomorphic descriptions of God in the Qurʾān ought to be interpreted. On this basis one can assume that discussion on these particular topics had developed in the second half of the third/ninth century among the generality of the Transoxanian Ḥanafites. Here, al-Ḥakīm al-Samarqandī and al-Māturīdī were apparently not professing their own unique positions, but rather those generally widespread in their time, which differed, however, from older views dating to the time of Abū Ḥanīfa and his immediate students.

The sources at our disposal give us no indication as to who brought about this change in Ḥanafite theology, yet one can still imagine the occasion that provoked it.

---

75 These agreements are described in detail by al-ʿOmar, 62–67 (belief, sin); ibid., 69f. (God's attributes of action) and ibid., 71ff. (visio beatifica). Al-ʿOmar, however, does not see that the old Ḥanafite intellectual stock lies at hand. He defines the teachings as Māturīdite and concludes therefrom that al-Ḥakīm, in all of these points, had been a student of al-Māturīdī.

76 See especially paragraphs 29.45 and 46. Cf. for example *Tawḥīd*, 67ff. On the question of the throne, see al-ʿOmar, 73f.

The reason may have been disputation with Ibn Karrām, which began already in the middle of the third/ninth century (with Abū Bakr al-Samarqandī). His anthropomorphism had rather crude features and was vehemently criticized all around, suggesting that the Ḥanafites at this juncture visibly aimed to distance themselves from him and sought another profile. On this and the general topic see further below, 287ff.

We come finally to the third category, i.e., those topics that show no common ground between al-Ḥakīm and al-Māturīdī, but instead display serious differences. These are to be found in various central areas of belief and thus convincingly demonstrate the final verdict: There cannot have been a teacher-student relationship between the two theologians. These differences tell us that al-Ḥakīm stood closer to the traditional conceptualizations of the Ḥanafites,[77] while al-Māturīdī very clearly sought out new intellectual paths and ways of refining the doctrine. Particularly notable examples are the treatment of free will,[78] the createdness of belief, and after these the manner in which the ambiguous verses of the Qurʾān (*mutashābihāt*) ought to be handled.[79] It also ought to be mentioned that the entire method and style of argumentation that we encounter in the *K. al-Sawād al-aʿẓam* is evocative of the earlier discussed Ḥanafite texts, and not even remotely comparable to al-Māturīdī's elaborate dialectic.

All of this testifies to the effect that Abū l-Qāsim Isḥāq al-Ḥakīm al-Samarqandī cannot have been the disciple of his famous contemporary. Not only did he not profess the latter's unique and newly formulated theses; the format of his presentation stood completely in continuity with that of earlier Ḥanafites who had not yet become seriously involved with rationalistic theology. At the same time, our deliberations also demonstrate that it is not enough for al-Ḥakīm to merely be characterized in the general sense as a Murjiʾite or as

77 "Traditional" is meant here in two senses: a) First, he adheres to the older views of the Ḥanafites, especially in regard to the question of free will. b) Second, specific views are more strongly oriented toward tradition (and the Traditionists); this is true concerning the treatment of belief and ambiguous Qurʾānic verses. We lack detailed treatments for both themes in earlier Ḥanafite texts.

78 Al-ʿOmar also put these in his list of the agreements between al-Māturīdī and al-Ḥakīm (see 74ff.), but incorrectly, as a closer examination shows. One point of similarity is that both sought a middle path between the Qadarites and Jabrites. The eastern Ḥanafites had long done so: Abū Ḥanīfa shows this in his second *Risāla*, and even the Karrāmite Makḥūl al-Nasafī—not suspected of Māturīdite tendencies—attempted this in his *K. al-Radd*. In contrast, al-Māturīdī introduced new aspects in the discussion on free will (and the capacity of human beings). Not a trace of this is to be found in the *K. al-Sawād al-aʿẓam*.

79 Sections 10 and 46. Madelung has already shown these differences; "The Spread," 117ff. n30. They were noticed in part by al-ʿOmar, 60f., who chose not to attach any great significance to them.

a Ḥanafite of the older persuasion. This is true because he not only passed on received formulas, but actually possessed an outlook that went much farther than that, one which encompassed demonstrably newer topics of discussion that only arose in the second half of the third/ninth century. In this regard, he is closer to al-Māturīdī than the scholars of earlier generations such as Abū Muqātil or Abū Muṭīʿ.

Moreover, this conclusion is also affirmed through a few external factors which will briefly be explained here. First, one may presume that al-Māturīdī had not yet formulated his teachings by the beginning of the fourth/tenth century, but actually did so much later.[80] The *K. al-Tawḥīd* at least, which is our main source for his theology, can only have been composed long after the *Sawād*.

Furthermore, it is noteworthy that for one hundred years the biographical literature knows nothing about al-Ḥakīm being al-Māturīdī's student. Al-Nasafī knows both of them only as students of Abū Naṣr al-ʿIyāḍī (*Tabṣira*, 357.7f. = Tancî, 1955, 5.5–7), and Samʿānī does not go into the topic. Only for the first time with Ibn Abī l-Wafāʾ (1332/1913, vol. 1, 39 [no. 305]) and al-Laknawī (1324/1906, 44.8f.) do we find sources saying that al-Ḥakīm studied with al-Māturīdī; these cannot be considered old and authentic transmissions.[81]

And finally, a last consideration may be added: If al-Māturīdī had been the foremost teacher and theologian in Samarqand during the reign of Ismāʿīl b. Aḥmad, it would likely have had other consequences on the official creed being composed. He himself would have been commissioned to write this important document, and not one of his students, who would in any case just repeat the master's pronouncements.

To summarize, we may attest that the *K. al-Sawād al-aʿẓam* is exceptionally valuable and informative for our further investigations. It replicates what the Transoxanian Ḥanafites at the turn of the fourth/tenth century agreed upon, and thus describes the theological consensus upon which al-Māturīdī built his own views and from which he also made his departure. The value of the *Sawād* as a source is increased by its relative expansiveness on questions of theology; in addition to the themes which one might expect, such as the definition of belief, the status of the sinner, predestination, or recompense in the next life, al-Ḥakīm also covers numerous other questions. God and His attributes are discussed repeatedly, but he also examines the depiction of the Creator in the Qurʾān, the origins of the Qurʾān itself, eschatology and piety, asceticism and reverence for saints, respect for the Companions of the Prophet, political conduct in the community, as well as numerous points of contention from the domain of law.

80 Madelung has said as much in "Abū 'l-Qāsem Eṣhāq Samarqandī," *EIr*, vol. 1, 358a.

81 In particular since there is reason to believe that the entry in Ibn Abī l-Wafāʾ was only added later.

Religious opponents are cited repeatedly, but only in general terms, and never in a manner in which specific thinkers and their views are discussed.[82] The author is more concerned with his own teachings, which are presented extensively and in a detailed manner. However, a certain problem awaits the reader as well: al-Ḥakīm refrains from dealing with similar questions en bloc, i.e., in consecutive paragraphs and in a systematic organization. Presumably to heighten one's attentiveness, he jumps from theme to theme, so that an article of belief may be followed by two further ones on the community, and then another one on belief. As a result, the image that we obtain on specific complexes of interrelated questions only forms slowly over the course of reading, and sometimes receives an unexpected additional nuance only much later on in the reading.

Be that as it may, if his text is to be presented here to conclude this section, the order which he himself gave it must be preserved. A reordering of its paragraphs from the perspective of content might seem to make study of the text easier at first, but the original character of the teachings, integral for a correct impression of the work, would thereby be lost. Ultimately, al-Ḥakīm did not intend to compose a systematic *kalām* treatise, but rather an accessible and easily understood guide for the believers of Transoxania in his time.

One problem in describing the text, however, lies in the fact that despite all the existing printings, we do not yet have a reliable edition. The available versions diverge in wording and also vary in the number of paragraphs. According to the texts to which I have access, the prints from Būlāq and Istanbul have 60 paragraphs, the Persian translation has 61, and the English translation by ʿOmar, based on a London manuscript and a Paris manuscript, has 62 (which, if one may believe Ḥājjī Khalīfa, *Kashf*, 1008, ought to be the original number). The situation is additionally complicated by the fact that the actual text of the *Sawād* is preceded by an introductory list of articles of belief which was added later. These usually match the main text, but not in the Būlāq and Istanbul prints, where they actually list 61 instead of the 60 articles found there.

The indicated discrepancies cannot be sufficiently explained and compensated for based on the current state of research. When the text of the *Sawād* is cited below for paragraphs, pages, and line numbers, the Arabic editions are used (with differentiation between pagination for the Būlāq and Istanbul prints). In order to facilitate a comparison with the other versions, a concordance of the varying paragraph counts is added here as well. The abbreviations used therein are:

---

82 The Rawāfiḍ, Qadarites, Jabrites, Muʿtazilites, Khārijites, and Jahmites are mentioned as heretical groups, along with the Karrāmites (sections 31, 44, 45, and 47) and Murjiʾites (sections 44, 59, and 60), which is particularly interesting. Along with these are the Zoroastrians (section 41), and the "Dahrīya" (section 50).

B/I	= Būlāq 1253/1837–8 and Istanbul 1304/1886–7 and Istanbul (undated) (the numbering of the paragraphs, pages, and lines match in both Istanbul editions)
List B/I	= The introduction to B/I
O	= Edition in ʿOmar, "The Doctrines" (based on MSS Brit. Mus. Or. 12781 and Bibl. Nat. 824,1)
P	= Persian translation, edited by Ḥabībī.
x	= Not found

B/I	List B/I	O	P
1	1	1	1
2	2	2	2
3	3	3	3
4	4	4	4
5	5	5	5 (cf. 61)
6	6	6	6
7	7	7	7
8	8	9	8
9	9	8	7
10	10	10	9
11	11	11	10
12	12	12	11
13	13	13	12
14	14	14	13
15	15	15	14
16	16	16	15
17	17	17	16
18	18	18	17
19	19	19	18
x	20	20	19
20	21	21	20
21	22	22	21
22	23	23	22
23	24	24	23
24	25	25	x
25	26	26	x
26	26	27	x
27	26	28	x
28	27	29	x
29	28	30	24

(cont.)

B/I	= Būlāq 1253/1837–8 and Istanbul 1304/1886–7 and Istanbul (undated) (the numbering of the paragraphs, pages, and lines match in both Istanbul editions)
List B/I	= The introduction to B/I
O	= Edition in ʿOmar, "The Doctrines" (based on MSS Brit. Mus. Or. 12781 and Bibl. Nat. 824,1)
P	= Persian translation, edited by Ḥabībī.
x	= Not found

B/I	List B/I	O	P
30	29	31	25
31	30	32	26
32	31	33	27
33	32	34	x
34	33	35	28
35	34	36	29
36	35	37	30
37	36	38	31
38	37	39	32
39	38	40	33
40	39	41	34
41	40	42	35
42	41	43	36
43	42	44	37
44	43	45	37
45	45	46	38
46	44	47	39
47	46	48	40
48	47	49	41
49	48	50	42
50	49	51	43
50	50	52	44
51	51	53	45
52	52	54	46
53	53	56	47
54	54	55	48
55	56	58	50 (cf. 54)
56	55	57	49
57	57 & 58	59	x

B/I	= Būlāq 1253/1837–8 and Istanbul 1304/1886–7 and Istanbul (undated) (the numbering of the paragraphs, pages, and lines match in both Istanbul editions)
List B/I	= The introduction to B/I
O	= Edition in ʿOmar, "The Doctrines" (based on MSS Brit. Mus. Or. 12781 and Bibl. Nat. 824,1)
P	= Persian translation, edited by Ḥabībī.
x	= Not found

B/I	List B/I	O	P
58	59	60	51
59	61	61	52
60	60	62	53 (55–60 without correspondence)

THE STRUCTURE OF THE *KITĀB AL-SAWĀD AL-AʿẒAM*

Belief

1) A Muslim should not doubt his own belief by adding the *istithnāʾ* ("If God wills") to the words "I am a believer." Rather, it is more proper to describe oneself as a believer without doubts or restrictive clauses.

Belief consists of affirmation (*taṣdīq*) with the heart, and avowal (*iqrār*) with the tongue. Both acts happen with the will of God, since no human act comes to be without God's doing. Consequently it is superfluous to pronounce the *istithnāʾ*, and to a certain degree, even false and deceiving, since it carries the insinuation (though unspoken) that a person could carry out actions with his own will (*mashīʾa*) and free choice (*ikhtiyār*), without God willing them.

Thus the *istithnāʾ* is actually disbelief when it is applied to past or present deeds. And it is heretical innovation (*bidaʿ*) when one relates it to future actions.

This is also confirmed by the praxis of *fiqh*: All commitments are viewed as invalid if delegitimized by the addition of "if God wills."

Community

2) A believer ought not to pit himself against the community of Muslims, because the community (*jamāʿa*) as a whole is always with the truth. Muḥammad has pledged this to us through his *sunna*, and it is our duty to preserve and carry out the *sunna* of the Prophet.

Praying Behind Sinners

3) This is why praying behind sinners is always valid, whether they are pious or open sinners.

Position of the Sinner

4) A sinning Muslim remains a believer, unless he considers his offense to be permissible, by which he commits disbelief. One does not become a believer or disbeliever as the result of good or bad actions, but rather from belief or disbelief themselves.

Prayer for the Dead

5) One should pray for every dead believer, whether he was pious, sinning, young or old.

Free Will—Predestination

6) All good and bad is determined by God (*taqdīr*). Yet, it is done (*fiʿl*) by people who are then justly taken to account by God for their actions.

This circumvents the misguidance of the Jabrīya and the Qadarīya. The Jabrites attribute the entire action to God, saying that His predetermination is responsible for everything, and thus people can produce excuses for all their sins. But as a result they have attributed human characteristics and actions, and even disbelief to God—which is nothing but sheer disbelief on their part. The Qadarites, in contrast, attribute the entirety of human action to people, saying that they alone carry out their will, while God apparently has no will or determining influence on these actions. Thus have they given people godly attributes, which is also an expression of disbelief.

The correct position is that people's obedience comes from God's decision (*qaḍāʾ*), decree (*qadar*), will (*mashīʾa*), divine assistance (*tawfīq*), approbation (*riḍā*), and command (*amr*); disobedience, in contrast, comes from God's decision, decree, will, and abandonment (*khidhlān*), but without His approbation and His command. God knows humans have duties (*farāʾiḍ*) that He wills and likes, and sins (*maʿāṣin*) that He wills without liking or commanding them.

God has thus decided (*qaḍāʾ*) obedience and disobedience, well-being and misfortune. If one is involved in disobedience, then one should also consider it just, and make efforts to make penance for it. It would be wrong to not feel responsible for anything like a Jabrite; or to think, like a Qadarite, that the disobedience was not determined by God; or to believe, like a Muʿtazilite, that disobedience without penance must necessarily be punished by God.

Community/Promise and Threat

7) One may not raise the sword against any Muslim without just cause.

Whoever intentionally kills someone else must face the following consequence: Only if he repents will God forgive him. If he does not repent, then he is subject to God's decision. God may forgive him out of grace (*faḍl*) or justly (*ʿaḍl*) punish him with Hell. The punishment of Hell, however, will never be eternal for a believer, since entry to Paradise is certain on the basis of his belief. Only the Muʿtazilites argue against this, thereby committing heresy.

Law

8) Wiping shoes (in place of washing the feet) is permissible, both while traveling as well as at home (with differing conditions).[83]

Community

9) One should perform the Friday and Eid prayers under every commander (*amīr*), whether he is just or unjust. Obedience is a religious duty. The ruler receives reward and punishment from God.

Is Belief Created or Uncreated?

10) Belief is a bestowal (*ʿaṭāʾ*) from God, which is actualized by people. Consequently, it is partly uncreated, and partly created.

We describe belief as knowledge (*maʿrifa*) in the heart and avowal (*iqrār*) with the tongue. Knowledge, avowal, and movement of the tongue are actions on the part of the human being, and are thus created. But in addition to these components of belief, it remains that God gives us knowledge (*taʿrīf*) and divine assistance (*tawfīq*), and that in uttering our avowal we repeat God's speech (i.e., the *shahāda* articulated in the Qurʾān). These are attributes of God, which accordingly can only be uncreated.

This can be compared with the Qurʾān: as the speech of God it is an attribute of the Creator and thus uncreated. Its recitation, however, is performed by humans and thus must be considered created.

83 On the topic see Wensinck, *Muslim Creed*, 158ff. with references to other Ḥanafite texts.

Creator—Creation

11) All attributes and actions of the Creator are uncreated. The actions of the creation, in contrast, are not pre-eternal (*qadīm*), but rather created.

Uncreatedness of the Qur'ān

12) The Qur'ān is God's speech in actuality (*bi-l-ḥaqīqa*), not metaphorically (*bi-l-majāz*). Thus it is an uncreated attribute of the Creator (as are all 104 revelatory texts since Seth, the son of Adam). Whoever disputes this and claims that even one word of the Qur'ān is created, is a Jahmite and Muʿtazilite. Even worse than these are those who refrain (*waqafa*) from passing judgment on this issue.

Eschatology

13) The punishment of the grave is real. Only Muʿtazilites dispute this.

14) The interrogation by Munkar and Nakīr is likewise a reality. Only the Qadarites deny this.

Praying for the Dead

15) The prayers and alms of the living benefit the dead. The Muʿtazilites are also wrong about this.

Intercession of the Prophet

16) The Prophet Muḥammad (but not the other prophets) will intercede with God on behalf of the great sinners of his community. All Muslims will ultimately arrive in Paradise thanks to this intercession. The sinless reach Paradise without reckoning (*ḥisāb*), those with minor sins do so after a slight (*yasīr*) reckoning, and those with major sins do so after being punished in Hell and being given reprieve by Muḥammad's intercession.

Honoring the Prophet

17) The Prophet's voyage to Heaven (*miʿrāj*) is a reality, because the Qur'ān tells us about it. Whoever denies the relevant verses is a disbeliever, and whoever interprets them incorrectly is a heretic.

Eschatology

18) On the Day of Resurrection, the book (with descriptions of the actions of each person) will actually be read out loud.
19) The reckoning (*ḥisāb*) on the Day of Resurrection is real.
19a) The scale (for people's deeds) is real.[84]
20) The bridge (*ṣirāṭ*) over Hell is real.

Paradise and Hell

21) Paradise and Hell are created, but everlasting. Whoever says they are uncreated is a disbeliever; whoever says they are transitory is a Jahmite.

Eschatology

22) On the Day of Resurrection, God will take people directly to account without an intermediary.

Companions of the Prophet and the First Caliphs

23) The ten Companions whom Muḥammad promised Paradise are already there.
24) After the death of the Prophet there was no one more excellent (*afḍal*) than Abū Bakr. He was rightfully caliph.
25) After Abū Bakr's death the same was true of ʿUmar.
26) After ʿUmar's death it was true of ʿUthmān.
27) After ʿUthmān's death it was true of ʿAlī.
28) None of the Prophet's Companions ought to be disparaged or slandered.

God's Attributes

29) God is angry through His anger (*ghaḍab*) and pleased through His approbation (*riḍā*). Both attributes are uncreated and unchangeable. Thus they ought not to be compared with human attributes of the same name, nor interpreted metaphorically. God's anger does not mean Hell, and God's approbation does not mean Paradise. Rather, one goes to Hell through God's anger, and to Paradise through God's approbation.

---

84 This article is not found in texts B and I, but rather in the pre-appended list (as no. 20) and in the Persian translation (as no. 19).

Beatific Vision

30) The inhabitants of Paradise will see God, but we cannot say how and we have no clear comparison for it (*bi-lā mithāl wa lā kayfa*). However, with certainty we can say that the vision of God may not be interpreted (in the metaphorical sense) and we may not claim, for example, that God will be seen with the eyes of the heart instead of the eyes of the head.

Piety—Reverence for the Saints

31) The rank of the prophets is higher with God than the rank of the saints (*awliyāʾ*). Only heretics such as the Karrāmites claim the contrary.
32) Yet one must believe in the miracle working (*karāma*) of the saints, since these are affirmed in the Qurʾān itself through numerous examples.

Predestination

33) It is wrong to claim that whether each person will go to Paradise or Hell is determined without regard for their deeds. The *ḥadīth* on one's destiny being determined in the mother's womb[85] only relates to their life (*ḥayāt*), sustenance (*rizq*), and lifespan (*ajal*). Everyone earns misfortune through bad deeds or earns good fortune through good deeds. However, God can make the fortunate person unfortunate (at any time) with His justice (*ʿadl*), and make the unfortunate person fortunate (at any time) with His grace (*faḍl*). This is so because God alone determines His own decisions; furthermore, obedience and disobedience from human beings make no sense without a corresponding reward/punishment.

Types and Ranks of Intellect

34) There are five types of intellect (*ʿaql*): (a) one from natural disposition (*gharīzī*), which all people possess; (b) one sharpened by effort (*takallufī*), which everyone can acquire; (c) one bestowed from God (*ʿaṭāʾī*), which only believers possess;[86] (d) a prophetic intellect (*min jihat al-nubuwwa*), which is reserved for the prophets; and (e) an intellect of nobility (*min jihat al-sharaf*) endowed solely to Muḥammad, who has been given a unique character (*khuluq*) and level of understanding.

85 Cf. *Fiqh absaṭ*, 44.3–9.

86 Cf. the Definition of Belief as a Bestowal from God, section 10.

God's Attributes

35) God has always been the Creator, even before He created the creation, since God is unchanging.
36) God, in and of Himself (*bi-dhātihi*), is actually (*bi-l-ḥaqīqa*) knowing and powerful and thus possesses (the attributes) knowledge and power. To claim that He does not possess such (an attribute of) knowledge, would mean that God only knows in a metaphorical sense (*bi-l-majāz*) or in an untrue manner (*bi-l-kadhib*).

Promise and Threat

37) In regard to judgment in the afterlife, there are five categories of people: (a) disbelievers, (b) hypocrites, (c) believers without sins, (d) believers who have atoned (*tawba*) for their sins in this world, and (e) sinful believers without atonement. The first two groups go to Hell, the third and fourth go to Paradise. The fifth is subject to the will of God; He may either forgive them immediately or send them to Hell first and then let them into Paradise on the basis of His grace (*faḍl*), their belief, or the intercession of the Prophet.

God's Omnipotence and Justice

38) God always does what He wills, and what He does is always just. Whether or not people understand His actions or consider them good or bad is immaterial, since their judgment can be wrong.

Qur'ān

39) What we recite and write is actually the Qur'ān, the uncreated speech of God, and not just the Qur'ān in a figurative sense, since the Qur'ān was actually revealed (not in a metaphorical sense), and not in a manner which is partly real and partly metaphorical. Otherwise, there would be several Qur'āns, in which case God would be keeping the real Qur'ān from us.

Nevertheless one must observe a differentiation: God speaks His speech without letters, without inflection, without a voice, without temporal sequence, without how, when, where, and how much. However, Gabriel, and then Muḥammad, transmitted the Qur'ān with their voices and with letters, just as it is now pronounced and written by the people.

Thus the recitation, paper, ink, and pen are also created; what is not created is that which is recited and written down, i.e., the speech of God, the revealed Qur'ān. Whoever disputes this can only be a disbeliever.

Belief and Sin

40) Belief exists always in actuality and never in a figurative sense. There is only actual belief, actual disbelief, and even worse, hypocrisy.

Whoever wishes to attribute belief to the sinner in the mere metaphorical sense, is either asserting that one becomes a disbeliever through sins (thus being a Khārijite), or that belief is decreased through sins (which is also false, since actions are not part of belief).

When a believer sins and subsequently repents, God will forgive him. If he does not repent, then he is subject to the will of God, who may either punish or forgive him.

Promise and Threat

41) If one must satisfy the legal claims of an opponent, but dies without doing so and without having repented from his sin, then God takes the corresponding amount away from his good deeds and transfers them to his opponent.

Free Will—Predestination—Capacity to Act

42) God's divine assistance (*tawfīq*) and abandonment (*khidhlān*), as well as human capacity to act (*quwwat al-ʿamal/istiṭāʿa*) happen at the same time as the human act, neither before nor after. This is the teaching of the *ahl al-ʿadl* (O: *ahl al-sunna*).

Since humans possess a capacity to act, they are also given responsibility (*kullifa*) for their actions, and on its account they must justify themselves (*yulzamu ʿalayhi al-ḥujja*).

Only God has the capacity to assist and support. He gives this assistance to those who obey and want to gain God's approbation. In contrast, God forsakes the disobedient.

What the Qadarites and Jabrites say concerning this same question is wrong for other reasons: The Qadarites are wrong because according to their view divine assistance (and capacity) already exist before the act; the Jabrites are wrong because according to their opinion both only occur afterward.

Belief

43) Belief must always be consummated by the heart and tongue. If done with the tongue alone, it is hypocrisy. If done with the heart alone, it is disbelief, unless the excuse of a speech impediment or the like applies.

44) However, numerous heretics deviate from the correct view of belief (as affirmation with the heart and avowal with the tongue). For the Karrāmites, belief is complete with the tongue and not the heart; for the Jahmites, belief is complete either with the tongue and not the heart, or even as knowledge in the heart without (simultaneous) affirmation in the heart or avowal of the tongue. The last is also true for the People of the Book (*ahl al-kitāb*). The Murji'ites restrict themselves to the tongue without knowledge in the heart. Finally, the innovators (*mubtadiʿ*, what is described is the view of belief professed by the Traditionists) call for the avowal with the tongue, knowledge in the heart, and actions from the rest of the body parts.

Image of God and Interpretation of the Qur'ān

45) God is not similar to anything else, since the Creator and the created are completely incomparable; even in this world one cannot compare a person and a thing he makes. Thus it is disbelief to impute anthropomorphic features to God.

46) God is not in any place, nor does He come and go, nor has He any other attribute in the manner of the characteristics of created things. The complete form of belief is thus to acknowledge God without wanting to say "how" He is.

God is the Lord of all places, but He Himself is not in any place. He is on (*ʿalā*) the throne, but not above (*fawqa*) it, since spatial boundaries would result from the latter.

Coming and going likewise cannot be said about Him, since this implies circumstances (such as coming near, and others) which do not apply to God.

Such things are only mentioned in the ambiguous verses (*mutashābihāt*) and *ḥadīth*. One must believe in them, but not try to explain them, since an explanation (*tafsīr*) would lead to a denial (*taʿṭīl*) (of the depiction of God), and a literal understanding, by contrast, would lead to assimilation (*tashbīh*) (of God) (with human beings).

Piety and Acquisition

47) Earning a livelihood (*kasb*) at some times (*fī baʿḍ al-awqāt*) is a religious duty, as shown in the Qur'ān and *ḥadīth*. Refraining from doing so can only be through a concession (*rukhṣa*) (from God). If one denies the ability to earn, then one becomes a heretic and Karrāmite. It is also wrong to claim that sustenance (*rizq*) comes through earnings (*kasb*), since *rizq* is given by God at all times and to all people.

Belief

48) Belief and actions are to be separated. Belief is an act of obedience to God, but not every act of obedience is belief. The prophets, to whom were revealed different religious laws, have always had one and the same belief.
49) Belief is the same among all pious people, sinners, angels, and prophets. The angels may surpass us in good works, but not in belief.

Eschatology

50) Resurrection after death and the hour of judgment are realities. Who denies them, is an unbeliever, whoever disputes them fundamentally is a "Dahri".

Law

51) The *witr* (i.e., *ṣalāt al-witr*, the odd-numbered prayer)[87] consists of three *rakʿa*s (bending at the torso) and one *taslīma* (greeting of peace).
52) Ritual impurity of the one who leads prayer leads to the ritual impurity of the congregation, otherwise one could just as well pray behind a Jew, Christian, or Zoroastrian. If a Muslim rules differently on this, then praying behind him is also invalid.
53) Ritual washing with a small amount of stationary water is invalid.
54) It is permissible to wipe shoes (as seen above in article 8). After taking off the shoes, however, one subsequently needs to do the complete ritual washing.

Belief—Qurʾānic Exegesis

55) Belief does neither grow nor decrease. Some people cite Q 48:4 for their opposing view ("So that they grow in their belief"). But what is meant there is not belief itself, but rather certainty (*yaqīn*), affirmation (*taṣdīq*), or persistence (*baqāʾ*), as we know through reliable exegetes. This shows us, however, that one cannot just interpret the Qurʾān with their opinion (*bi-l-raʾy*), since many verses not only have an outwardly (*ẓāhir*) recognizable meaning, but also an inner (*bāṭin*) meaning, which does not open itself up to everyone. Thus, reliable Qurʾānic exegesis (*tafsīr*) only comes from following the transmitted interpretations of the Prophet's Companions and those who possess knowledge.[88]

87 On which see Welch in W. Montgomery Watt and Alford T. Welch, *Der Islam I* (Stuttgart, 1980), 276–278.

88 For details on this exegetical principle, see Ignaz Goldziher, *Die Richtungen der islamischen Koranauslegung* (Leiden, 1920), 61ff.

Law

56) When blood, pus, and similar come out of the body, the ritual washing is invalidated and must be done again.

Predestination

57) Belief and unbelief have not been determined from eternity, but may change through the turn of convictions. Iblīs was a believer as long as he still honored God, and Abū Bakr and ʿUmar were in disbelief during the time of their idolatry. Whoever is of the view that belief or disbelief is predetermined without the possibility of conversion is a Jabrite.

Love of God—No Antinomianism

58) No one who loves God can take his love of God as a pretext to disregard the Creator's commands in this world, since the love of God actually means observing all commands and prohibitions and fulfilling one's duties. This is exemplified best with Abraham and Muḥammad.

Fear of God—Promise and Threat

59) Every believer must fear God in regard to his own destiny. As many examples show, no one can be sure whether he will die as a Muslim or a disbeliever. Whoever does not fear God is either a Jabrite (who believes that he does not bear responsibility for anything), or a Murji'ite (who believes that he is saved from any punishment because of his belief).

60) By contrast, no believer may doubt God's mercy, even when having committed many major sins (with the exception of disbelief), since if he repents God will certainly forgive him. Even if he does not repent from it, God can either punish or forgive him.

Only heretics view things differently: the Khārijite, who labels the sinner as a disbeliever; the Muʿtazilite, who claims that a sinner who does not repent goes eternally to Hell; and likewise the Murji'ite, who believes that he does not even depend on God's forgiveness.

PART 2

The Emergence of al-Māturīdī

CHAPTER 4

Life and Activity

4.1 Biographical Reports

Abū Manṣūr Muḥammad b. Muḥammad b. Maḥmūd al-Māturīdī,[1] if we may believe the few transmitted reports concerning him, did not lead a life that was notable in any way nor different from that of his scholarly contemporaries in Samarqand. Nothing indicates that he held any public office, nor that he possessed more disciples, popularity or even associations with the Sāmānid court of Bukhārā than anyone else. The decisive personal experiences of the type that have been transmitted concerning other theologians such as al-Ashʿarī[2] are also not mentioned. On the contrary, after al-Māturīdī became famous, his biographers were evidently in a predicament to find any noteworthy reports about him, and had nothing sensational to say. Thus the relevant sources do not read as biographies, but rather as lists of works that have been enlarged upon by brief statements on his personage and a few words of praise.

We owe the first and also most important of these to Abū l-Muʿīn al-Nasafī (d. 508/1114). As noted earlier, he described the Samarqand school in his *Tabṣirat al-adilla*. There he accorded al-Māturīdī a rather detailed passage, distinguished by its various biographical details, but in particular by its comprehensive knowledge of his theological works.[3] Al-Nasafī's efforts must clearly be viewed with a sense of hindsight toward al-Māturīdī as the outstanding figure of eastern Ḥanafite theology; at almost the same time, Abū l-Yusr al-Pazdawī (d. 493/1100) commemorated our scholar in his *Uṣūl al-dīn* in much the same manner. He praised him there with a short eulogy, focusing more on his theological accomplishments than the events of his life.[4]

These testimonies are the material for the generally short entries on al-Māturīdī in the later Ḥanafite *ṭabaqāt* works, or more generally speaking, the bibliographies written in Ottoman times. These add little to al-Nasafī's

1 *GAL*, vol. 1, 195 and suppl. vol. 1, 346; *GAS*, vol. 1, 604–606; al-Baghdādī, *Hadīya*, vol. 2, 36–37; Khayr al-Dīn al-Ziriklī, *al-Aʿlām* (Beirut, 1984), vol. 7, 242; al-Kaḥḥāla, vol. 11, 300. The most detailed representations of al-Māturīdī's biography are found in D.B. MacDonald, "Māturīdī," *EI*[1], vol. 3, 475–477, esp. 476a; Götz, 27–29; Kholeif (Arabic introduction to the *K. al-Tawḥīd*, 1–3); al-ʿOmar, 18–21; Madelung, "al-Māturīdī," *EI*[2], vol. 6, 846–847, esp. 846a.

2 For the most detail on al-Ashʿarī's famous conversion, see Allard, 37ff.

3 *Tabṣira*, vol. 1, 358.15–359 ult.; cf. 357.7 and 360.11.

4 *Uṣūl*, 2.-2–3.5.

 | DOI 10.1163/9789004261846_006

entry, and are mostly dependent, whether directly or indirectly, on his presentation in the *Tabṣira*. The list of these authors is as follows: Ibn Abī l-Wafāʾ (d. 775/1373),[5] Ibn Quṭlūbughā (d. 879/1474),[6] Kamālpashazāde (d. 940/1533),[7] Ṭashköprüzāde (d. 968/1560),[8] Ḥājjī Khalīfa (d. 1067/1657),[9] Kamāl al-Dīn al-Bayāḍī (d. 1078/1687),[10] al-Sayyid al-Murtaḍā l-Zabīdī (d. 1205/1791),[11] and finally, Muḥammad ʿAbd al-Ḥayy al-Laknawī (d. 1304/1886).[12]

These sources all tell us that al-Māturīdī very probably died in the year 333/944. Al-Nasafī does not name this date, but only says, by way of comparison, that the Master passed away a short time after al-Ashʿarī (d. 324/935).[13] This does not argue against the more precise death date given by the later authors, but only shows that his particular interest was theological and not biographical.[14] Al-Nasafī had in mind certain attacks made by the Ashʿarites, who spread the idea that Transoxanian theology did not adhere to the teachings of the early predecessors, but rather introduced heretical innovations that

5 Ibn Abī l-Wafāʾ, vol. 2, 130f. (no. 397); cf. vol. 2, 267 (no. 177).

6 Ibn Quṭlūbughā, 59.1–7 (no. 173).

7 *Ṭabaqāt al-mujtahidīn*; not accessible to me, however, cf. Flügel, 274, 293, 295, 298, and 313, which bases itself particularly on Kamālpashazāde.

8 Aḥmad b Muṣṭafā Ṭāshköprüzāde, *Miftāḥ al-saʿāda wa-miṣbāḥ al-siyāda* (Hyderabad, 1356), vol. 2, 21–22; a passage on al-Māturīdī also appears in Ṭāshköprüzāde's still unpublished *Ṭabaqāt al-Ḥanafiya*, which I can only refer to from Kholeif's descriptions; he used a manuscript of the work.

9 Ḥājjī Khalīfa, 262, 335f., 518, 751, 1406, 1408, 1573, 1782.

10 al-Bayāḍī, 23.55ff.

11 (Al-Sayyid Muḥammad b. Muḥammad al-Ḥusaynī) al-Murtaḍā l-Zabīdī, *K. Itḥāf al-sāda al-muttaqīn bi-sharḥ asrār Iḥyāʾ ʿulūm al-dīn* (Cairo, 1311/1893–94), vol. 2, 5.3ff.; al-Murtaḍā l-Zabīdī also says explicitly that he owes his biographical reports to two sources (ibid., vol. 2, 5.5–7): a) *Al-Jawāhir al-muḍīʾa* by Ibn Abī l-Wafāʾ and b) the *K. al-Ansāb* by Majd al-Dīn Ismāʿīl b. Ibrāhim b. Muḥammad al-Kinānī al-Bilbaysī (d. 802/1399). The latter is not available in print, but clearly available in manuscript. On this see *GAL*, suppl. vol. 2, 69, where the author's name is not given completely or correctly. The author of the *K. al-Ansāb* ought to be the same as the "Majd al-Dīn Ism. B. Ibr. M. al-Kinānī al-Ḥanafī" mentioned by Brockelmann in *GAL*, suppl. vol. 1, 469 (on 266n2). He also wrote an adaptation of al-Buṣīrī's *Burda*.

12 al-Laknawī, 195.4–11.

13 *Tabṣira*, vol. 1, 360.11; taken from Ibn Abī l-Wafāʾ, vol. 2, 130 ult. and al-Murtaḍā l-Zabīdī, vol. 2, 5.12.

14 Moreover, al-Nasafī is not quite precise in his biographical details. In the following sentence, for example (*Tabṣira*, vol. 1, 360.11f.), he claims that al-Ḥakīm al-Samarqandī died in the year 335, while all other sources are in consensus on 342 as the death date.

only arose one hundred years after al-Ashʿarī.[15] This claim naturally had to be repudiated, which is why he made this comparison in al-Māturīdī's biographical entry. To him, the exact date of al-Māturīdī death is not as meaningful as the fact that he belonged to the same generation as al-Ashʿarī. Al-Nasafī's intention here is to present the school of Samarqand as a venerable institution. By contrast, all other sources that impart information on his death date do not reflect such considerations and motives. They concern themselves merely with determining the year in question, agreeing unanimously (two mistakes aside) on the year 333/944.[16]

In comparison, it is considerably harder to ascertain al-Māturīdī's age, and accordingly, his birthdate. The sources tell us nothing, and thus we would be advised to assess the lifespans of his teachers in order to deduce his age. But even this method—already imprecise enough—is even more uncertain in the case of al-Māturīdī than with others, since the sources are by no means united on who his teachers were.

Al-Nasafī only states that Abū Naṣr Aḥmad al-ʿIyāḍī was his teacher,[17] and so do Ibn Abī l-Wafāʾ,[18] Ibn Quṭlūbughā,[19] and Ṭāshköprüzāde.[20] Another possible teacher is mentioned, however, in an unexpected location of Ibn Abī l-Wafāʾ's *Jawāhir*: Abū Bakr Aḥmad b. Isḥāq al-Juzjānī.[21] Both al-ʿIyāḍī and al-Juzjānī

15 These reproaches are reported by al-Nasafī in his *Tabṣira*, vol. 1, 310.8ff. The following fifty pages are then dedicated to a refutation of these criticisms. Al-Pazdawī also dealt with this topic. He explicitly defends the priority of al-Māturīdī (and Abū Ḥanīfa) against al-Ashʿarī and reproaches the Ashʿarites for spreading false notions on the topic (cf. *Uṣūl* 70.4–12).

16 Ibn Abī l-Wafāʾ, vol. 2, 130.-2f. and 131.1f.; Ibn Quṭlūbūghā, 59.3; Ṭāshköprüzāde's *Tabaqāt* in Flügel, 274 and 295. In regard to the errors, Ḥājjī Khalīfa names the year 332/943 (1406.-11) and Ṭāshköprüzāde the year 336/947 (in the *Ṭabaqāt*; cited by Kholeif, Arabic introduction to *Kitāb al-Tawḥīd*, 3n1), contradicting their earlier entries. It is furthermore noteworthy that both theologians, according to the later authors al-Bayāḍī and al-Murtaḍā l-Zabīdī, are again taken up from al-Pazdawī and al-Nasafī's perspective to emphasize that al-Māturīdī was not a successor to al-Ashʿarī, but in a way was even his predecessor (al-Bayāḍī, 23.11f.; al-Murtaḍā l-Zabīdī, vol. 2, 5.29ff.). Thus competition did persist between the two schools.

17 *Tabṣira*, vol. 1, 357.7f. and 359.14–16.

18 Ibn Abī l-Wafāʾ, vol. 2, 130.-6f.; see also vol. 1, 70 ult. f. and 4.1f.

19 Ibn Quṭlūbughā, 59.4.

20 Ṭāshköprüzāde, vol. 2, 22.2f.

21 Ibn Abī l-Wafāʾ, 246 (no. 45). The second name is not Abū Sulaymān al-Jūzjānī, whom Madelung erroneously mentions in "al-Māturīdī," *EI*², vol. 6, 846a. Abū Bakr was a student of the more famous Abū Sulaymān (cf. *Tabṣira*, vol. 1, 356.11f. and Ibn Abī l-Wafāʾ, vol. 1, 60.-7f.).

are also mentioned by Kamālpashazāde.[22] Al-Bayāḍī and Murtaḍā l-Zabīdī on their part give us four names, mentioned in two pairs: al-Māturīdī is supposed to have transmitted knowledge from Abū Bakr al-Jūzjānī and Abū Naṣr al-ʿIyāḍī as well as from Nuṣayr b. Yaḥyā l-Balkhī and Muḥammad b. Muqātil al-Rāzī.[23] Our final source, al-Laknawī, only knows one teacher, and not al-ʿIyāḍī as one might expect, but Abū Bakr al-Jūzjānī.[24]

Now it is immediately suspicious when names are mentioned in the sixteenth and seventeenth centuries which had never been mentioned before. No reliable information can be suggested by these reports, but rather the development of a legend that must have been nurtured on the idea that such a great thinker as al-Māturīdī cannot have been inspired by a single teacher. However, these premises alone do not suffice to exclude all three of these *fuqahāʾ* who were only mentioned later as al-Māturīdī's teachers; a more dependable criterion is needed. The second pair that al-Bayāḍī and Murtaḍā l-Zabīdī mentioned, Nuṣayr b. Yaḥyā l-Balkhī (d. 268/881–2)[25] and Muḥammad b. Muqātil al-Rāzī (d. 248/862),[26] cannot be seriously considered for a connection with al-Māturīdī. Both were renowned scholars, but they did not live in Samarqand[27] and are nowhere else mentioned in association with our theologian. Moreover, in the case of al-Rāzī at least, we are presented with an untraversable temporal distance, since al-Māturīdī would have had to have lived one hundred years in order to have even had the chance to hear from him.

The case is different in regard to Abū Bakr al-Jūzjānī, who is mentioned along with al-ʿIyāḍī as al-Māturīdī's second teacher. We not only find numerous references in the literature to his role, but two further indications that suggest a genuine relationship between him and al-Māturīdī. First, we know that he actually taught in Samarqand, and with scholarly acclaim at that, since, according to

22 *Ṭabaqāt* in Flügel, 293 and 295.

23 Al-Bayāḍī, 23.6ff.; al-Murtaḍā l-Zabīdī, vol. 2, 5.17–24, where al-Murtaḍā l-Zabīdī may very well be dependent on al-Bayāḍī (cf. ibid., vol. 2, 3.18). Al-Murtaḍā is generally distinguished by his tendency to construct numerous teacher-student relationships among the early Transoxanian Ḥanafites. If one were to believe his entry at vol. 2, 5.25ff., then almost all scholars of a certain generation studied with almost all the scholars of the previous generation (and beyond).

24 al-Laknawī, 195.4f.

25 Wāʿiẓ-i Balkhī, 257 ult.; Ibn Abī l-Wafāʾ, vol. 2, 200.2; al-Laknawī, 221.4f.

26 Ibn Ḥajar, *Lisān*, vol. 5, 388.-6f. and idem, *Tahdhīb*, vol. 9, 470.5; Ḥājjī Khalīfa, 1457.17 and after him al-Baghdādī, *Hadīya* 13.-11 all give 242 AH as the death date.

27 *Tabṣira*, vol. 1, 356ff., names neither of them in his list of Samarqand theologians. Furthermore, we know for certain that Nuṣayr al-Balkhī lived in Balkh: cf. Wāʿiẓ-i Balkhī, 257f. and also Radtke, 545f.

al-Nasafī's characterization, the local theological tradition actually first began with al-Jūzjānī.[28] The second indication—which takes us back to an earlier point in our inquiry—is provided by the transmission of older Ḥanafite texts, and is very useful. Here we refer to the *isnād* of the *K. al-ʿĀlim wa-l-mutaʿallim*, of which there are good justifications to argue for its authenticity. According to this piece of information, the text was narrated by Muḥammad b. Muqātil al-Rāzī (and Abū Sulaymān al-Jūzjānī) to Abū Bakr al-Jūzjānī, who transmitted it to Abū Manṣūr al-Māturīdī.[29] These indications still do not prove that there was a teacher-student relationship between the last two, but they do make it highly probable, such that it ultimately seems sensible to presume two teachers for al-Māturīdī; namely Abū Bakr al-Jūzjānī and Abū Naṣr al-ʿIyāḍī, the latter of whom is named by all the sources.

This can only garner us a very general orientation in our search for al-Māturīdī's birth date, since the death dates for both of his teachers are unknown. We only know that al-ʿIyāḍī died in a military campaign of the Sāmānid *amīr* Naṣr b. Aḥmad (r. 261–79/874–92) against the Turks,[30] whereas the biographical dictionaries do not give us certainty concerning al-Jūzjānī's death date.[31] Still, the information on al-ʿIyāḍī's death tells us more than it would seem to at first glance. It can be confidently said that the military campaign happened only in the last years of Naṣr b. Aḥmad's rule, i.e., shortly before or after 890 CE.[32] One may further assume that al-Māturīdī did not learn from al-ʿIyāḍī as a youth, but rather as a student with mature judgment and a certain degree of independence, since according to the reports—assuming this is not another topos—al-ʿIyāḍī thought very highly of his student and used

28 *Tabṣira*, vol. 1, 356.11 and 356.16f.; see also van Ess, *Theologie*, vol. 2, 564.

29 See the *K. al-ʿĀlim*, 22.-2f.

30 *Tabṣira*, vol. 1, 356.-2; Ibn Abī l-Wafāʾ, vol. 1, 70 ult. f.; cf. Flügel, 295.

31 *Tabṣira*, vol. 1, 356.11–15; Ibn Abī l-Wafāʾ, vol. 1, 60 (nos. 77, 79). al-Laknawī, 14.10–14; cf. Flügel, 294. There was in fact a death date in Ḥājjī Khalīfa, 1406 (see *K. al-Tawba*) originally, but it is unfortunately unreadable now. Al-Baghdādī's entry (*Hadīya*, vol. 1, 46) that Abū Bakr died after 200 is worthless; the same is said concerning his teacher Abū Sulaymān (Ibn Abī l-Wafāʾ, vol. 2, 186.-6). One could venture to say that Abū Bakr al-Jūzjānī, as al-ʿIyāḍī's teacher, evidently died before his student. But this is not necessarily the case, since al-ʿIyāḍī died a premature death.

32 Al-ʿIyāḍī must have held the position of *qāḍī* (of Samarqand) before his death (cf. Ḥājjī Khalīfa, 1018.13; see also van Ess, *Theologie*, vol. 2, 564), which could only have been possible in the last few years of Naṣr b. Aḥmad's reign. The first *qāḍī* of the Sāmānids was Abū ʿAbdallāh Muḥammad b. Aslama al-Azdī, who died in 268/881 (*Tabṣira*, vol. 1, 358.1–3; Ibn Abī l-Wafāʾ, vol. 2, 33 (no. 100); see Halm, *Ausbreitung*, 110). He is also supposed to have been followed immediately in that position by his son Ismāʿīl (*Tabṣira*, vol. 1, 358.5f.).

to start his theological lessons only when al-Māturīdī had arrived to class.[33] These clues justify at least a tentative hypothesis: al-Māturīdī can be reckoned not to have been much younger than twenty when he learned from al-ʿIyāḍī and thus was born around the year 870 CE if not shortly before.

Such theoretical detours and hypotheses are fortunately not necessary when it comes to determining the location of our theologian. All the available information points to the city of Samarqand. He was born there, as shown by his *nisba*, derived from Māturīd (or Māturīt), a district located somewhat at the edge of the city.[34] He also died there, according to the consensus of the sources.[35] One tries in vain to find any further indication that al-Māturīdī ever left his native city for any reason. His tomb, in any case, lies in Jākardīzā, the scholars' graveyard of the city, where it is supposed to have been visited and held in honor for a long time.[36] Al-Ḥakīm al-Samarqandī, the author of the *Sawād*, apparently arranged for it to be adorned with an epitaph.[37] But even this report may belong to the stuff of legend, since in another place we read that al-Māturīdī was buried in a certain Turbat al-Muḥammadīn, where more than 400 believers with the name Muḥammad found their final resting place.[38]

Such indications at least give a certain understanding of the external conditions of al-Māturīdī's life. But this alone must suffice us, since to write a biography in the actual meaning of the word is, as said before, impossible, as the sources do not recount to us any major occurrences or in fact any single event from his life.[39]

Only a single report deserves mention here. It is found in al-Pazdawī's entry, as one of our earliest testimonies, and what is more, it explicitly refers back to

33 *Tabṣira*, vol. 1, 459.14f.

34 al-Samʿānī, vol. 12, 2–3 (no. 3568); al-Murtaḍā l-Zabīdī, vol. 2, 5.4; al-Laknawī, 195.9–11.

35 Ibn Abī l-Wafāʾ, vol. 2, 130 ult. f.; Ibn Quṭlūbughā, 59.3; Ṭāshköprüzāde, vol. 2, 22.2; al-Murtaḍā l-Zabīdī, vol. 2, 5.13; Flügel, 274 and 295.

36 Ibn Abī l-Wafāʾ, vol. 1, 4.5 (where *bi-Jākardīzā* is miswritten as *bi-Mākardīn*); Abū Ṭāhir, 78.4ff.; Mullā ʿAbd al-Ḥakīm, 5.10.

37 *Tabṣira*, vol. 1, 358.17–19.

38 Ibn Abī l-Wafāʾ, vol. 1, 4.4f.

39 Al-Bayāḍī, 23.5, also gives al-Māturīdī the *nisba* al-Anṣārī, giving rise to the speculation that he could be of distinguished Medinan heritage (cf. Kholeif, Arabic introduction to *K. al-Tawḥīd*, 2; al-ʿOmar, 18). But al-Bayāḍī's claim is based on a misunderstood sentence from al-Samʿānī, vol. 12, 3.10ff., which deals with a grandson of al-Māturīdī (through the son-in-law), as Madelung has already clarified in "al-Māturīdī," *EI*², vol. 6, 846a. Al-Murtaḍā l-Zabīdī, who probably found the *nisba* in al-Bayāḍī, explains it by saying that al-Māturīdī aided the *sunna* to victory (*nāṣir*) (vol. 2, 5.14f.).

his great-grandfather, who had been a student of al-Māturīdī.[40] According to him, our theologian was an ascetic (*zāhid*), and according to a Pazdawī family tradition had even produced several beneficial miracles (*karāmāt*).[41]

The report is brief, but highly significant, since it brings al-Māturīdī in connection with the circles of the pious friends of God (*awliyāʾ*) and ascetics, and thus poses the question of his relationship to Sufism. This question will occupy us later, since there are in fact signs of such a connection, as has been demonstrated early on in the research.[42] But one ought to evaluate these signs cautiously, and determine from the outset in what sense a relationship between our theologian and Islamic mysticism truly merits discussion.

We ought to exclude the possibility that al-Māturīdī viewed himself as a Sufi and preached the path of mysticism to others. We have no indications of this at all. Quite the opposite: There are noteworthy indications that make this particular idea seem improbable and out of place. None of al-Māturīdī's extant works address any themes that were particular to Sufism (e.g., trust in God, scrupulousness, etc.). None of the lost works indicate such a theme from their titles.[43] And finally, al-Māturīdī's name is not mentioned in any of the later biographical compilations of the Sufis; this can only mean that they did not consider him from among their ranks.[44]

It is another question altogether whether al-Māturīdī's theology was at all influenced by Sufi concepts. This would not be surprising for a Transoxanian scholar of the fourth/tenth century, since we have already seen that Ḥanafite theology in the region could not always be sharply separated from mystical tendencies. Ibn Karrām bound the two together, with an emphasis on asceticism. Al-Ḥakīm al-Samarqandī, al-Māturīdī's contemporary, was known as a judge and Sufi. And when only a few centuries later, al-Kalābādhī (d. 380/990) from Bukhārā wrote his handbook on Sufi teachings and practice (*K. al-Taʿarruf*

40 On ʿAbd al-Karīm the great-grandfather, cf. below, 144f.

41 *Uṣūl*, 2.-2ff.

42 Tilman Nagel, *Geschichte der islamischen Theologie* (Munich, 1994) 137ff.; Nagel even treats al-Māturīdī directly alongside authors such as al-Ḥārith al-Muḥāsibī under the title "Sufism and Rationalism."

43 Cf. below, 180ff.

44 This also relativizes al-Pazdawī's claim that al-Māturīdī performed miracles, seen in a parallel report in al-Nasafī, *Tabṣira*, vol. 1, 359.11–14. According to this latter source, al-Māturīdī's knowledge and spiritual abilities were immeasurably plentiful. Whoever grasps his accomplishments can only come to the conclusion that God singled him out with miracles (*karāmāt*), gifts of grace (*mawāhib*), divine assistance (*tawfīq*), and guidance (*irshād, tasdīd*). This is so because in the normal course of things (*fī l-ʿādāt al-jāriya*) many scholars combined do not possess the knowledge that was assembled in him alone.

bi-madhhab ahl al-taṣawwuf), he showed himself well acquainted with the teachings of the theologians.[45]

Al-Māturīdī is not really comparable to these other authors. He expresses himself in a completely different way. and unlike them is at home in the intellectual discipline of *kalām*. But this does not negate the possibility that since he lived in a milieu generally open to Sufism he may have received inspiration from that type of orientation; what we have learned from al-Pazdawī's remarks then is to keep this in mind during our future investigations.

4.2 Teachers

4.2.1 *Abū Bakr al-Jūzjānī*

Until now, not much has been achieved in regard to establishing al-Māturīdī's actual biography. We still barely know more about him than we do about other Islamic scholars whose location and death date is known. Fortunately, we have not exhausted all the conceivable ways to approach our subject based on the preceding information. Even now we may court the possibility of departing from the reports on al-Māturīdī himself and instead focus on describing his environment, i.e., all the people with whom he interacted in theological discussions and who certainly must have had an effect on his personal development.

The previous section has shown that al-Māturīdī was taught by two scholars, Abū Bakr al-Jūzjānī and Abū Naṣr al-ʿIyāḍī. Next we ought to ask what he could have learned from them, or, to formulate it differently, how we should conceive of their intellectual orientations and theological profiles. The sources do tell us something about this, although of course no complete picture can be assembled.

Abū Bakr al-Jūzjānī[46] clearly played a great role in the development of the Ḥanafite theological school of Samarqand. And if al-Nasafī is to be believed, the school even had its proper beginnings with him,[47] since he describes Abū Bakr

45 On this see Madelung, "The Spread," 121n32a; cf. also on al-Kalābādhī the article by P. Nwyia, "al-Kalābādhī," *EI*², vol. 4, 467; the particularly interesting theological parts in the *K. al-Taʿarruf* are in chapters 5–28 (al-Kalābādhī, 33–84).

46 See *Tabṣira*, vol. 1, 356.11–14; Ibn Abī l-Wafāʾ, vol. 1, 60 (nos. 77 and 79), as well as ibid. vol. 2, 246 (no. 45); Ḥājjī Khalīfa, 1406 (s.v. *K. al-Tawba*); al-Laknawī, 14.10–14; al-Baghdādī, *Hadīya*, vol. 1, 46; Flügel, 293 and 295. Cf. also Ibn Quṭlūbughā (13.2), whose entry on al-Jūzjānī, however, is clearly contaminated with the entry on the much later Aḥmad b. ʿUthmān b. Shabīḥ al-Jūzjānī.

47 *Tabṣira*, vol. 1, 356.11ff.; see van Ess, *Theologie*, vol. 2, 564.

as a student of Abū Sulaymān al-Jūzjānī,[48] i.e., a non-Samarqandian scholar, which implies a non-local source for the teachings which he later disseminated in the Transoxanian metropolis. However, such an image, which places the beginnings of Samarqand theology in the middle of the third/ninth century, clearly overemphasizes al-Jūzjānī's role, since as we know, the Ḥanafites had long been established in that city. Abū Muqātil al-Samarqandī presumably wrote his *K. al-ʿĀlim* here, and Abū Bakr al-Samarqandī, the opponent of the Karrāmīya, was also active there as a jurist and defender of the true faith.[49] Given this, we cannot say that al-Jūzjānī represented a wholly new beginning for that city; rather, we may presume that he established a distinct approach on the basis of different strands of past tradition, which was to be cultivated and developed by subsequent generations.[50]

As previously mentioned, Abū Bakr al-Jūzjānī's chronology cannot be known precisely from the extant reports.[51] He was probably born in the third/ninth century, but this is not stated explicitly by our sources. However, all authors do report that he was a versatile scholar. He is supposed to have been well versed in the various disciplines of study and been equally competent in the principles (*uṣūl*) as well as the branches (*furuʿ*),[52] which surely means that he enjoyed great prestige as a jurist. This apparently found expression in several compositions, which are, however, no longer extant. We do know of two titles from which his various interests can be gleaned. The first, *K. al-Farq wa-l-tamyīz* (The Book of Differentiation and Specification),[53] is not clearly dedicated to a specific discipline of knowledge, but we can assume with a fair degree of probability that it was a juristic work.

Al-Jūzjānī's second work, however, was more well-known: the *K. al-Tawba* (The Book of Repentance). Ḥājjī Khalīfa reports of it to us, but unfortunately

48 Abū Sulaymān apparently came from the area of Balkh, but is also supposed to have spent some time in Baghdad. On him see al-Khaṭīb al-Baghdādī, vol. 13, 35f. (no. 6993); Ibn Abī l-Wafāʾ, vol. 2, 186f. (no. 580); al-Laknawī, 216.1–3; Flügel, 286f.; GAS, vol. 1, 433.

49 He is also mentioned later in the *Tabṣira*, vol. 1, 358.7ff. as a contemporary of Jūzjānī.

50 Abū Bakr apparently transmitted the *K. al-ʿĀlim wa-l-mutaʿallim* from both Abū Sulaymān al-Juzjānī as well as Muḥammad b. Muqātil al-Rāzī. He thus had several teachers and can be said to have brought with him to Samarqand several avenues of influence for the development of religious thought there.

51 Cf. above, 129n31.

52 *Tabṣira*, vol. 1, 356.13; Ibn Abī l-Wafāʾ, vol. 1, 60.6f.; al-Laknawī, 14.10f. The explanation that a scholar is familiar with the *uṣūl* as well as the *furūʿ* is a literary topos by which his rank as *faqīh* is supposed to be expressed. For al-Nasafī the entire school of Samarqand is distinguished by having bound together the *uṣūl* and *furūʿ* (*Tabṣira*, vol. 1, 356.8).

53 Ibid., vol. 1, 356.14; Ibn Abī l-Wafāʾ, vol. 1, 60.7; al-Murtaḍā l-Zabīdī, vol. 2, 5.17; al-Laknawī, 14.11; cf. Ibn Quṭlūbughā, 13.2.

without a closer characterization of its content.[54] Based on the title alone, we can assume that it must have been a work on piety, which fits well with the image of a scholar connected with popular religion as well as Sufism. One is reminded, for example, of the famous *K. Tanbīh al-ghāfilīn* (Book of Admonition to the Heedless) which Abū l-Layth al-Samarqandī wrote a century later.[55] Yet such analogies are largely speculative. We can only determine that the book was not about *kalām*, and that one could hardly describe Abū Bakr al-Jūzjānī as a *mutakallim*. Thus, al-Māturīdī likely did not learn speculative theology from him, but rather Ḥanafite jurisprudence, as well as traditional Ḥanafite teachings on piety and faith.

4.2.2 *Abū Naṣr al-ʿIyāḍī*

The case differs in regard to al-Māturīdī's second teacher, Abū Naṣr al-ʿIyāḍī,[56] who does bring us much closer to the discipline of *kalām*. He was also a student of Abū Bakr al-Jūzjānī,[57] but as a theologian he clearly possessed a profile completely of his own.

Muslim tradition was not overly concerned with his accomplishment as a *mutakallim*, but was more impressed with the fact that he died as a martyr. Al-ʿIyāḍī had indeed, as we saw earlier, followed the Sāmānid ruler Naṣr b. Aḥmad into battle against the Turks. There he was taken prisoner and died at the hand of a disbeliever. This made him forever a hero of the faith, and he is thus always appraised as such. He is described as having been especially brave and uncompromising,[58] and it is also emphasized that he was a man of knowledge as well as a man of battle.[59] The further the biographers are from al-ʿIyāḍī's time, the more clearly the circumstances of his ideal martyrdom are known. Eventually, one knows that it took place in the vicinity of the city of Isfijāb,[60] and a further source even knows the events of his final hour and imparts to us al-ʿIyāḍī's words at the moment of his death and his last bequest.[61]

The statements on his scholarship also sound similarly histrionic, presenting many topoi which are to be found in descriptions of other scholars. He was,

---

54 See sources from previous note. Also see Ḥājjī Khalīfa, 1406.

55 On the oft-read and still often printed *Tanbīh al-ghāfilīn*, cf. van Ess, *EIr*, vol. 1, 333a.

56 Cf. *Tabṣira*, vol. 1, 356.16–357.8; Ibn Abī l-Wafāʾ, vol. 1, 70f. (no. 117); Ḥājjī Khalīfa, 1018; al-Laknawī, 23.7–12; Flügel, 295. See also a short entry in van Ess, *Theologie*, vol. 2, 564, and a very imprecise description by al-ʿOmar (15–17).

57 al-Nasafī, *Tabṣira*, vol. 1, 356.16; Ibn Abī l-Wafāʾ, vol. 1, 70.12f.; al-Laknawī, 23.8f.; Flügel, 295.

58 *Tabṣira*, vol. 1, 356 ult. f.

59 Ibn Abī l-Wafāʾ, vol. 1, 70.14; al-Murtaḍā l-Zabīdī, vol. 2, 5.20.

60 al-Laknawī, 23.10f.; on Isfijāb, cf. Barthold, 175ff.

61 al-ʿOmar, 16f., clearly, according to Muḥammad b. Sulaymān al-Kaffawī, *Ṭabaqāt katāʾib aʿlām al-akhyār min fuqahāʾ madhhab al-Nuʿmān al-mukhtār*.

in regard to knowledge (*ʿilm*), an ocean of unattainable depths[62] and by the age of twenty had already far surpassed his contemporaries.[63] Besides this he was distinguished not only by his astuteness, but also his tenacity and scrupulous observation of religious duties (*waraʿ*).[64] If one is to believe a transmission from al-Ḥakīm al-Samarqandī, Abū Naṣr al-ʿIyāḍī was able to silence, by means of only a few words, every heretic and disputant who wished to provoke him with deliberately misinterpreted Qurʾānic verses.[65]

These are, of course, rhetorical exaggerations, but the message they impart certainly has its kernel of truth, since al-ʿIyāḍī must have been an esteemed scholar whose influence was felt in the following generation. He is supposed to have left behind forty students upon his death,[66] which again, seems too precise. But one may believe without difficulty that he did have many students, given that at least four of them are known to us by name: besides al-Māturīdī in particular, we find the already mentioned al-Ḥakīm al-Samarqandī, but also two sons of the master: Abū Aḥmad Naṣr al-ʿIyāḍī and Abū Bakr Muḥammad al-ʿIyāḍī, who emerged later as scholars in their own right.[67]

In regard to what ultimately can be said of Abū Naṣr al-ʿIyāḍī's theological orientation, three relevant points may be further described here. First, we may assume that he had reservations in regard to the Traditionist circles and their religious views. In fact, we hear that he had not transmitted a single report nor a single *ḥadīth*.[68] Elsewhere, we also learn that he spoke disparagingly of Muḥammad al-Shāfiʿī.[69] The latter's conception of the principles of law had, however, been welcomed by the Traditionists of eastern Iran and adopted as a guide[70]—thus we can see that al-ʿIyāḍī's position on those who saw the measure of things in pietistic transmission of reports alone was rather dismissive.[71]

62 *Tabṣira*, vol. 1, 357.1f.

63 Ibid., 357.6f.

64 Ibn Abī l-Wafāʾ, vol. 1, 70.-5f.; al-Murtaḍā l-Zabīdī, vol. 2, 5.20.

65 *Tabṣira*, vol. 1, 357.3–6.

66 Ibid., 357.7f.; Ibn Abī l-Wafāʾ, vol. 1, 70 ult. f.; al-Murtaḍā l-Zabīdī, vol. 2, 5.21; Flügel, 295.

67 *Tabṣira*, vol. 1, 357.8ff.; Ibn Abī l-Wafāʾ, vol. 1, 70.13ff. and ult.ff.; al-Laknawī, 23.9f.

68 Ibn Abī l-Wafāʾ, vol. 1, 70.15f.

69 Flügel, 295.

70 Cf. *Uṣūl*, 146.17–19, 153.7, 153.13–17 on the shared positions of the Shāfiʿites and the Traditionists. On the acceptance of the Shāfiʿite school in the Traditionist circles of East Iran, cf. Madelung, *Religious Trends*, 27f.

71 At the bottom of this is merely the old opposition between the Murjiʾites and the Traditionists. Cf. Schacht, "An Early Murciʾite Treatise," 101f.; Madelung, "The Origins of the Controversy Concerning the Creation of the Koran," in *Orientalia Hispanica sive studia F.M. Pareja octogenario dedicatea*, ed. J.M. Barral (Leiden, 1974; repr. in idem, *Religious Schools*), 519; idem, "Early Sunni Doctrine," 239 and 247f. and idem, *Religious Trends*, 21ff.

This is not to say that he was not suitably respectful of the early community. On the contrary, we find, as the second important aspect of his thought, that al-ʿIyāḍī explicitly honored the Companions of the Prophet and defended them against denigration. He authored a book in this spirit with the title *al-Sayf al-maslūl ʿalā man sabba aṣḥāb al-rasūl* (The Drawn Sword Against Those who Insult the Companions of the Prophet), which was known to Ḥājjī Khalīfa.[72] He may have been prompted to write this by the fact that he traced his own lineage back to Companions from Medina.[73] But such a particular motive is not necessary. The Ḥanafites had always placed value on honoring the entirety of the members of Muḥammad's original community without exception, which also meant that ʿUthmān and ʿAlī are shown great respect.[74] In this respect al-ʿIyāḍī was only taking up a traditional theme, though he may have been the first to dedicate a specific treatment to it.

The third point we ought to mention is clearly a departure from the Ḥanafite praxis of northeastern Iran encountered so far. It also provides us with a clue that holds the greatest significance for speculation on al-ʿIyāḍī's religious orientation. We learn that Abū Naṣr had composed another text, the general content of which may be ascertained. It dealt with the topic of God's attributes, and it is explicitly reported that he disputed therein with the doctrines of the Muʿtazila and al-Najjār.[75] This means that al-ʿIyāḍī practiced *kalām*; and this is noteworthy for the Transoxanian Ḥanafites that we have come to know so far. All of the texts of the second/eighth and third/ninth centuries that we have seen till now have dealt with the question of creed, not in the systematic manner of a theological treatise, but rather as didactic dialogues, refutations, and creedal statements, i.e., in a literary form tailored to a larger and less specialized public.

Al-ʿIyāḍī's book on God's attributes could thus be an early, if not the first example of eastern Ḥanafite *kalām*. One may very well deduce that he was an inspirational or formative influence on and role model for al-Māturīdī. The latter learned from al-ʿIyāḍī that it was not sufficient to base his religious views on tradition, and learned from him how to utilize reason in theological dis-

---

Cf. also Makḥūl al-Nasafī (*Radd*, 121.13–122.10) who portrays and attacks the Ḥashwīya in a piquant manner as a subgroup of the Murjiʾa. In any case there were also opponents of *kalām* and its rationalist methods among the Ḥanafite traditionalists. On this see Madelung, "The Spread," 112ff. and idem, *Religious Trends*, 29.

72 Ḥājjī Khalīfa, 1018.12f.; Flügel, 295.

73 *Tabṣira*, vol. 1, 356.16f.; Ibn Abī l-Wafāʾ, vol. 1, 70.10–12; al-Laknawī, 23.7f. and 23.12.

74 *Risāla I* 36.18–25 and 37.6–18; *K. al-ʿĀlim*, section 28; *Fiqh absaṭ* 40.11–13; *K. al-Sawād*, sections 26–28; cf. also *Radd* 77.16–78.2.

75 *Tabṣira*, vol. 1, 357.2f.

cussion and polemic. This consideration helps us to somewhat better appreciate the circumstances of the remarkable fact that after all our readings of the older Ḥanafite texts,we will quite suddenly and unprecedentedly encounter in al-Māturīdī's work a technically refined and stupendously developed articulation of *kalām*.

4.3 Students

4.3.1 *Abū Aḥmad al-ʿIyāḍī*

The image that we set out to obtain of al-Māturīdī's field of activity can be rounded out by incorporating information on his direct students and their theological developments. Here we also come across certain reports of interest, which again must be examined to see if such transmissions can be trusted in their details. Al-Māturīdī had long been famous when the reports at hand were written. Because of this, their authors not only show the tendency to attribute to him the greatest possible number of teachers, but also the desire to extend the circle of his students further than was practically feasible.

Clearly, the more prominent scholars of Samarqand in the fourth/tenth century represented a special case for the biographers. Whoever lived in the city at this time and gained a reputation in later Islamic theology was inevitably portrayed as a pupil of the great master. This is the reason why we find renowned *ʿulamāʾ* depicted as al-Māturīdī's disciples, even though the historical basis for this is lacking upon closer scrutiny.

One example of these is al-Ḥakīm al-Samarqandī, the author of the *K. al-Sawād al-aʿẓam*, whom we have already discussed. Later isolated reports describe him as a student of al-Māturīdī, though an examination of the earlier sources, in particular the texts of both authors, shows that there is no basis for such speculation.[76] A similar case can be found with an even more famous scholar, Abū l-Layth (d. 373/983).[77] His works represent perhaps the most extensive collection of fourth/tenth-century juristic and theological texts that we possess from Samarqand, and thus he has come to be portrayed as a first generation Māturīdite.[78] The indications clearly speak against this, however, as will be shown in more detail below.[79]

76 Cf. above, 101ff.

77 Cf. J. Schacht, "Abū ʾl-Layth al-Samarḳandī," *EI*², vol. 1, 137a and J. van Ess, "Abū l-Layt Samarqandī," *EIr*, vol. 1, 332f.

78 Interestingly enough, not by Muslim tradition, but rather in modern research: cf. for example Watt, *Der Islam II*, 424, and al-ʿOmar, 35–50.

79 Cf. below, 320 and 326ff.

If one sets aside these prominent figures and leaves aside the name of Abū ʿIsma al-Bukhārī, who only appears late and in a single isolated source,[80] no more than three people remain who—convincingly in our view—studied with al-Māturīdī. They may have actually formed our theologian's inner circle, and each embodies a certain aspect that is informative about the nature of his scholarly activity.

The first, Abū Aḥmad Naṣr b. Aḥmad al-ʿIyāḍī,[81] shows us at once that the ʿIyāḍī family remained connected with al-Māturīdī and worked with him in the following generation in the discipline of theology. Abū Aḥmad was the eldest son of the previously mentioned Abū Naṣr and had studied under his father along with al-Māturīdī before eventually studying under his former colleague. His own reputation is also notable, at least if one can believe the later reports about him. They contain encomiums as usual, in this case drawn with particularly broad brushstrokes, without consideration for rhetorical subtlety. His contemporary, Abū Ḥafṣ al-Bukhārī, is supposed to have said that the Ḥanafite teachings must be correct simply because Abū Aḥmad believed in them, since his sincerity would not permit this to be a fallacy.[82] And al-Ḥakīm al-Samarqandī, whom we have already encountered several times as a composer of panegyrics, apparently had a striking formulation ready: al-ʿIyāḍī's son was the greatest scholar of all of Khurāsān and Transoxania for the past two hundred years, or if one really thought about it, ever.[83]

What are missing in these examples of enthusiastic praise are concrete statements on whether or not Abū Aḥmad composed theological works. In regard to his brother Abū Bakr, it is narrated that he had written against the Muʿtazila in his so-called "Ten Issues" (*al-Masāʾil al-ʿashr al-ʿiyāḍīya*), a title which up to now fits very well with the reports on his father and in particular al-Māturīdī's work.[84] In contrast, Abū Aḥmad does not seem to have left behind anything comparable, or in fact any text still read centuries later when his biography was composed.

Still, he was doubtlessly important as a theologian, which brings us to the point for which he becomes informative in regard to al-Māturīdī's influence. A

80 Only al-Laknawī, 116.-7f.

81 *Tabṣira*, vol. 1, 357.9–17 and 359.1; Ibn Abī l-Wafāʾ, vol. 2, 192f. (no. 599) and vol. 2, 237 (no. 2); al-Laknawī, 220.15–20.

82 *Tabṣira*, vol. 1, 357.10–13; Ibn Abī l-Wafāʾ, vol. 2, 192.-2ff.; al-Laknawī, 220.17f.; Abū Ḥafṣ al-Bukhārī (see Flügel, 292) was clearly the grandson of the more famous Abū Ḥafṣ al-Kabīr who is described by Ibn Abī l-Wafāʾ (vol. 2, 249 (no. 66)) and which Flügel (290) counts among only the second generation of Ḥanafites.

83 *Tabṣira*, vol. 1, 357.13–17; Ibn Abī l-Wafāʾ, vol. 2, 237.-8ff.; al-Laknawī, 220.18–20.

84 *Tabṣira*, vol. 1, 357.18–20.

student of al-ʿIyāḍī himself wrote a theological work that has been transmitted to us in manuscript form. The author, Abū Salama Muḥammad b. Muḥammad al-Samarqandī, is little known, and at the moment a lack of reports prevents us from placing him chronologically with more precision;[85] if it is true that he is a "grand-student" of al-Māturīdī, then we may place him in the middle and late fourth/tenth century.[86]

His work, the *Jumal uṣūl al-dīn*, is more unequivocal than the scanty information on its author. As noted, it remains extant in an Istanbul manuscript and has recently been made available in a Turkish edition.[87] A closer look quickly shows its contents to be quite rewarding. The text not only represents the earliest theological summary still extant written after al-Māturīdī's rise to prominence in Samarqand; its content also stands particularly close to the conceptualizations of our theologian. Abū Salama did not present the Ḥanafite creed in the style of older works such as the *K. al-Sawād al-aʿẓam*—which his contemporary Abū l-Layth al-Samarqandī certainly did.[88] Rather, he maintained all the essential details of al-Māturīdī's teachings, often even in their intricate formulations, such that his *Jumal uṣūl al-dīn*—as no other work known till now—can be viewed as the earliest extant testimony for a specifically Māturīdite tradition.[89]

---

85 Sezgin correctly suspects Abū Salama to be in the second half of the fourth/tenth century (GAS, vol. 1, 607); also cf. Madelung, "The Spread," 118n20 and idem, "Der Kalām," 334. Van Ess wishes to see him as a contemporary of al-Māturīdī (*Theologie*, vol. 2, 564).

86 Abū Salama's studies with Abū Aḥmad al-ʿIyāḍī are confirmed through two sources: al-Nasafī's statements (*Tabṣira*, vol. 1, 358.11f.) as well as the colophon to the manuscript (see the following footnote) of *Jumal uṣūl al-dīn*, where this is also asserted (in the printed edition see Abū Salama, 38.10–12).

87 MS Şehid Ali Paşa 1648/1, fols. 1–17 (in the copy available to me fol. 1a as well as 16b f. are missing). The edition is by A.S. Kılavuz, Istanbul, 1989. Fols. 19–168 of the same manuscript which Götz (28n8) states to contain a text on the *Uṣūl al-dīn* (without naming the author) was not available to me.

88 Cf. generally van Ess' evaluation, *Theologie*, vol. 2, 565.

89 There was not a school that followed al-Māturīdī in the fourth/tenth century. Abū Salama is a unique case; he took notes of what was taught in al-Māturīdī's circle (just as disciples of other theologians such as al-Ḥakīm al-Samarqandī had done). Nevertheless his work is by and large an easily understandable and abbreviated summary of al-Māturīdī's *K. al-Tawḥīd*. The construction of both texts is similar, the doctrine nearly identical (cf. in detail Section III B of this book), and the formulation is often the same. What follows is an overview of the chapter titles of the *Jumal uṣūl al-dīn* (cf. also Götz). The page numbering is based on the Kılavuz edition.

1) *al-qawl fī jumal min uṣūl al-dīn* (7–11)
2) *al-qawl fī ithbāt ḥadath al-ʿālam wa-anna lahu muḥdith* (11–12)
3) *al-qawl fī ithbāt al-tawḥīd* (13–14)

But, as stated, Abū Salama was not a direct student of the great master. He was probably only indirectly acquainted with his thought, through Abū Aḥmad al-ʿIyāḍī. It may thus be concluded that the latter was the intermediary point in question, adopting his teacher's new ideas and passing them on with precision to the following generation.

4.3.2 *Abū l-Ḥasan al-Rustughfanī*

The second of al-Māturīdī's students to be named here is Abū l-Ḥasan ʿAlī b. Saʿīd al-Rustughfanī (d. ca. 350/961), whose *nisba* tells us that his home was a village near Samarqand.[90] Surprisingly many later authors have something to report about him,[91] which also shows that he did not just stand in the shadow of his famous teacher, but was remembered as a scholar in his own right.

---

4) *al-qawl fī ithbāt al-ṣifāt* (14)
5) *al-qawl fī maʿrifat al-waḥdānīya* (14–15)
6) *al-qawl fī maʿrifat ṣifātihi* (15–17)
7) *al-qawl fī l-takwīn annahu ghayr al-mukawwan* (18)
8) *al-qawl fī nafy al-makān* (text is missing in the manuscript; title completed by Kılavuz based on a commentary)
9) *al-qawl fī l-qurʾān* (19)
10) *al-qawl fī l-muḥāl wa-l-kadhib* (19–20)
11) *al-qawl fī l-qadar* (20–22)
12) *al-qawl fī l-aṣlaḥ* (23–25)
13) *al-qawl fī l-istiṭāʿa* (25–26)
14) *al-qawl fī l-īmān wa-l-maʿrifa* (26–28)
15) *al-qawl fī l-amr wa-l-nahy wa-l-waʿd wa-l-waʿīd* (28–30)
16) *al-qawl fī l-ruʾya* (31)
17) *al-qawl fī l-risāla* (31–33)
18) *al-qawl fī l-imāma* (33–35)
19) *al-qawl fī l-waqf fī l-qurʾān* (35–36)
20) *al-qawl fī mutashābih al-qurʾān* (36–37)
21) *al-qawl fī l-maʿdūm* (38).

90 On him see Tancî, 7n8; *GAS*, vol. 1, 606f.; Götz, 28f. (who wrongly holds him as a teacher of al-Māturīdī); al-ʿOmar, 32ff. It is not completely clear how the name of his home and *nisba* are to be correctly vocalized. By far the greater part of the sources give the *nisba* as Rustughfānī (cf. sources in the following footnote). The form Rustufghānī is also to be found (al-Samʿānī, vol. 6, 117.5f., which al-ʿOmar wishes to adopt) and Rustufghanī as well as Rustufghan (Ṭāshköprüzāde, vol. 2, 143.-2 and Ibn Abī l-Wafāʾ, vol. 2, 310.8, the latter going against his own *Usus*). Rustughfannī, as Götz proposes, has no support in the sources.

91 *Tabṣira*, vol. 1, 27.2f., 28.12ff., 91.2ff., 358.12–14; ibid., vol. 2, 688.16f.; 764.15f.; al-Samʿānī, vol. 6, 117f. (no. 1779); Ibn al-Athīr, *al-Lubāb fī tahdhīb al-ansāb* (Cairo, 1357–69), vol. 1, 466.12–14; Ibn Abī l-Wafāʾ, vol. 1, 363.5–7 and vol. 2, 310.7ff. (no. 436); Ibn Quṭlūbughā, 41

Al-Rustughfanī's independence clearly began in the area of law. His personal views were usually brought up regarding two well-known issues of this subject matter. The first was a practical problem that a Muslim might occasionally face in daily life: did it count as a ritual washing if one stepped into a small water basin from one side and stepped out from the other? We are not told his answer to this, but we do discover that he gave an influential ruling, since it was taken into account even centuries later when the problem was discussed.[92]

The second question was of a more theoretical nature and according to the statements of our sources even led to a controversy between al-Rustughfanī and his teacher al-Māturīdī. It touched upon *ijtihād*, or to be more precise, whether a *mujtāhid* was invariably wrong in his *ijtihād*, if when trying to determine the true circumstances of an issue a (logical) mistake was inadvertently made.[93] Here we also do not know which position al-Rustughfanī advocated, just as al-Māturīdī's position is also kept from us.[94] But one can still point out the noteworthy fact that the old saying, *kullu mujtahid muṣīb*, which was attributed to Abū Ḥanīfa among others,[95] gave rise to debate and was very openly discussed among the Ḥanafites.

In the meantime, al-Rustughfanī not only shows himself to have attained his own profile in *fiqh*, but in theology as well, which is more meaningful for us. Here we have several indications to this effect that certainly deserve closer

---

(no. 121); Ṭāshköprüzāde, vol. 2, 143.-2ff.; al-Bayāḍī, 214.1f.; Ḥājjī Khalīfa, 67.70, 1223 and 1422; al-Laknawī, 65.-7ff.

92 Ibn Abī l-Wafāʾ, vol. 2, 310.9–11.

93 Ibn Abī l-Wafāʾ (vol. 2, 310.12–13) states that this dissent between al-Māturīdī and his student was generally well known (*maʿrūf*).

94 Götz purports to know which views al-Māturīdī and Rustughfanī represented, but the citation from Ibn Abī l-Wafāʾ is not informative in this regard. The information in al-ʿOmar (33) is based on Götz.

95 Ibn Abī l-Wafāʾ hastens to comment on the argument, mentioning Abū Ḥanīfa's solution, who is supposed to have advocated the motto *kullu mujtahid muṣīb*, with the qualification, however, that the *mujtahid* is only right in relation to the search (*fī l-ṭalab*), whereas he can miss that which is sought after (*maṭlūb*) (vol. 2, 310.14–15). On the problem in general, see J. Schacht, "Khaṭaʾ," *EI*², vol. 4, 1100ff.; van Ess, "Kullu muğtahid muṣīb," in *Dirāsāt islāmīya*, ed. F. Jadʿan (Irbid, 1983), 123–141 and idem, *Theologie*, vol. 2, 161ff., as well as Halm, *Die Schia*, 88f., who explains the application of the principle in Shīʿite jurisprudence. Among the Māturīdites, one adds to the maxim that the *mujtahid* can also be wrong. Cf. the classical formulation by Najm al-Dīn al-Nasafī (*al-ʿAqāʾid*, ed. W. Cureton as *Pillar of the Creed of the Sunnites* [London, 1843], 5.-3) to which should be added a detailed elaboration of this theme in its commentary by al-Taftazānī (*Sharḥ al-ʿaqāʾid al-nasafīya*, ed. C. Salamé [Damascus, 1974], 202.-4ff.; trans. Edgar Elder, *A Commentary on the Creed of Islam: Saʿd al-Dīn al-Taftāzānī on the Creed of Najm al-Dīn al-Nasafī* [New York, 1950], 166ff.).

study. The first bit of evidence is, strictly speaking, nothing more than the literary illustration of a thesis. Al-Rustughfanī is said to have reported a dream in which he discussed the forgiving of sins with al-Māturīdī. The master apparently advocated the idea that God can forgive any believer, even someone who has never prayed. The student, in contrast, does not seem convinced of such trust in God and believes he has uncovered the weakness of this argument with the command to pray found in the Qur'ān.[96]

The animated presentation of such a narration naturally suggests fiction, but the theme as such may have been a topic of real discussions between al-Māturīdī and al-Rustughfanī. It is true that the Murji'ite-Ḥanafite circles always professed an optimistic viewpoint in regard to God's judgment on human sins.[97] This had long stood in the crossfire of criticism,[98] such that it is not surprising if disputation among the Ḥanafites themselves resulted over this point.[99]

The second report, in contrast, is considerably more cut-and-dry in tone. It is found in the *Ishārāt al-marām* of al-Bayāḍī, where it is said word for word which view Abū l-Ḥasan professed in regard to the process of creation (*takwīn*) and created actions (*af'āl*).[100] What al-Bayāḍī notes there is quite short and on the whole does not deviate from mainstream Ḥanafite-Māturīdite theology. But the mere fact that he still cites al-Rustughfanī is a proof of his importance and shows that he was still read in the seventeenth century.

People had, in fact, been reading him five centuries earlier, as a look in al-Nasafī's *Tabṣira* shows us. There, al-Rustughfanī is mentioned several times

96 Ibn Abī l-Wafā', vol. 2, 310.15–17; Ibn Quṭlūbughā, 41 (no. 121), in which see lines 3–5.

97 *Risāla I*, 37.1–6; *K. al-'Ālim*, sections 14, 15, 28; *Fiqh absaṭ* 46.23–47.12; *K. al-Sawād*, sections 7, 16, 37, 40, 60; Abū l-Layth, *Bustān*, 125–127 (= section 81) and idem, *'Aqīda* I, 225.-2ff. = *'Aqīda* II, 273.2ff. The tenor of the statements says that a believing sinner undergoes divine judgment. God can punish as well as forgive all things.

98 The critique accused the Murji'ites of claiming that a believer is not harmed by any grave sins. These views were attributed now and then to the entirety of the Murji'a (*Radd*, 67.20–68.2; for later times cf. al-Shahrastānī, 33.4ff. and 103.4ff.; see Gimaret and Monnot, 186f. and 419f.). For the most part, however, it was acknowledged that there were rather particular opinions held by specific Murji'ites (al-Ash'arī, *Maqālāt*, 147.14–16; *Radd* 114.18–21 and 115.5–8; and al-Shahrastānī, 104.-6f.).

99 The Ḥanafites clearly reacted very early to the polemic. Al-Ḥakīm al-Samarqandī had undoubtedly already distanced himself from the Murji'a, who, according to his assertions, all believed that the sins of believers do not affect them (*K. al-Sawād*, sections 59 and 60). Al-Pazdawī knows, however, that this was only the case with a specific group of the Murji'a (*Uṣūl*, 132.7–9). The most famous Murji'ite to actually profess this doctrine (with nuance) may have been Muqātil b. Sulaymān (see van Ess, *Theologie*, vol. 2, 531).

100 al-Bayāḍī, 214.1f.

and always in relation to a clearly outlined theological position. In one place we read that he shared al-Māturīdī's view that faith based solely on revelation and faith based on reflection on the signs found in creation were of the same rank.[101] Elsewhere we read how al-Rustughfanī dealt with dualists in his debates with them.[102] We also see that, according to his opinion, there was no difference between the question concerning one's lifespan (*ajal*) and life's provision (*rizq*).[103] Finally, al-Nasafī shows us that al-Rustughfanī wrote on the problematic question of the extent to which "life" ought to be attributed to the deceased at the moment of the punishment of the grave (in order to ensure his ability to feel pain).[104]

Unfortunately, we cannot read the texts being cited here, as they are no longer extant.[105] There were originally at least four of them, which in regard to our own inquiry can perhaps be divided into two groups. The *Fatāwā l-Rustughfanī*,[106] or Abū l-Ḥasan's collection of legal rulings, are probably of less interest to us. The *K. al-Khilāf*[107] remains completely closed to us—nothing is reported on its contents. However, the other two texts are much more informative since they did happen to be devoted to a particularly interesting theme.

The *K. Irshād al-muhtadī* deals with *kalām* and may also have been al-Rustughfanī's main work. All of the later biographies mention this title first;[108] al-Bayāḍī also explicitly cites this text as a source when he mentions Abū l-Ḥasan's views on the doctrine of God's attributes.[109] In contrast, the fourth text, the *K. al-Zawāʾid wa-l-fawāʾid*, does not belong to the discipline of theol-

101 *Tabṣira*, vol. 1, 27.2f. and 28.12ff.; Ṣābūnī also cites Rustughfanī in his *Kifāya* on the question of the faith of a *muqallid*; on this theme, cf. Josef van Ess, *Die Erkenntnislehre des ʿAḍudaddīn al-Īcī. Übersetzung und Kommentar des ersten Buches seiner Mawāqif* (Wiesbaden, 1966), 47ff.

102 *Tabṣira*, vol. 1, 91.2ff.

103 Ibid., vol. 2, 688.16f.

104 Ibid., vol. 2, 13ff.

105 Sezgin says in GAS, vol. 1, 607 that a text of Rustughfanī's by the title *al-Asʾila wa-l-ajwiba* exists in a manuscript, but the reference seems to be mistaken. The manuscript (Murad Molla 1829, fols. 154a–176b) contains a different text at the cited pages (see al-ʿOmar, 33f.). Otherwise the title mentioned is not verifiable anywhere else in the bio-bibliographical literature.

106 Ṭāshköprüzāde, vol. 2, 143.-2; Ḥājjī Khalīfa, 1223.

107 al-Laknawī, 65.-7ff.

108 *Tabṣira*, vol. 1, 358.13 and 91.2; Ibn Quṭlūbughā, 41 (no. 121, l. 2); Ṭāshköprüzāde, vol. 2, 143 ult. f.; Ḥājjī Khalīfa, 67; al-Laknawī, 65.-6 and 65.-3f. The same work (possibly an abridgement) may also be meant when Ḥājjī Khalīfa (70) mentions a texts named *al-Irshād fī uṣūl al-dīn*.

109 Al-Bayāḍī, 214.1.

ogy, but could possibly be more interesting because it was more unusual: It is unanimously described by the sources as a work dealing with categories of knowledge (*aṣnāf al-ʿulūm* or *anwāʿ al-ʿulūm*).[110]

As we possess no manuscript of this work, we naturally cannot say precisely what is meant by this. But it is worth keeping in mind that in northeastern Iran there was a tradition of works on the classification of sciences. The most famous of these was the *Mafātīḥ al-ʿulūm* by al-Khwārizmī, who was active toward the end of the fourth/tenth century in the Sāmānid court at Bukhārā.[111] But al-Khwārizmī was not a unique case, since already, about fifty years before him, Ibn Farīghūn had written his *Jawāmiʿ al-ʿulūm*, and a generation before that Abū Zayd al-Balkhī had written his *Aqsām al-ʿulūm*.[112] The *K. al-Zawāʾid* of al-Rustughfanī might then be a very comparable classification of knowledge and its scholarly methods, and it would have been immensely informative to possess a work of this type from the pen of a Ḥanafite, let alone a student of al-Māturīdī. But as long as we lack a copy of the text, we may only speculate about its contents. For now, we only know the title, and it confirms for us what has already become clear from several indications; namely, that Abū l-Ḥasan al-Rustughfanī must have been a versatile and original scholar who played an important role in the reception of al-Māturīdī's teachings, as well as for the overall development of the Transoxanian Ḥanafite school of the fourth/tenth century.

4.3.3 *ʿAbd al-Karīm al-Pazdawī*

Abū Muḥammad ʿAbd al-Karīm b. Mūsā l-Pazdawī (d. 390/999),[113] who must be mentioned here as al-Māturīdī's third student to conclude, did not possess

---

110 *Tabṣira*, vol. 1, 358.13f.; Ibn Quṭlūbughā, 41 (no. 121, l. 2f.); Ṭāshköprüzāde, vol. 2, 144.1; Ḥājjī Khalīfa, 1422; al-Laknawī, 65.-6 and 65.-2.

111 Cf. A.I. Sabra, "al-Khʷārazmī," *EI*², vol. 4, 1068f.; the theological section of the work is discussed by Bosworth, "Al-Ḫwārazmī on Theology and Sects: The Chapter on Kalām in the Mafātīḥ al-ʿulūm," *BEO* 29 (1977): 85–95.

112 See Hans-Hinrich Biesterfeldt, "Die Zweige des Wissens: Theorie und Klassifikation der Wissenschaften im mittelalterlichen Islam in der Darstellung des Ibn Farīghūn" (unpublished Habilitationsschrift, Bochum, 1985). See also idem, "Ibn Farīghūn's Chapter on Arabic Grammar in his Compendium of the Sciences," in *Studies in the History of Arabic Grammar II*, ed. Kees Versteegh and Michael G. Carter (Amsterdam/Philadelphia 1990), 49–56; on the general tradition see Gerhard Endreß, "Die wissenschaftliche Literatur," *Grundriss der arabischen Philologie II*, ed. Helmut Gätje (Wiesbaden, 1987), 450f.

113 This is the year of his death cited in Ibn Abī l-Wafāʾ, vol. 1, 327.7f., who bases this on *Taʾrīkh Nasaf*; also later in al-Laknawī, 101.10. The *nisba* is based on Pazda/Bazda, a fortified area

a comparable stature as a jurist nor a *mutakallim*. We do not hear of any teaching connected with his name, nor are there any indications that he wrote any works. That he is mentioned here, however, is due to the special way in which he was bound to the work or rather the influence of al-Māturīdī, his teacher. He quite clearly played a role in disseminating theological ideas and works. We have already encountered him earlier in this regard. His name is found in the *riwāya* of the *K. al-ʿĀlim wa-l-mutaʿallim*, which he is supposed to have transmitted to Muḥammad al-Nasafī; as we recall, he had in fact transmitted the text from Abū Manṣūr al-Māturīdī. To this we can immediately add that the biographers do not just describe him generally as a transmitter, but also explicitly as a student of al-Māturīdī,[114] from which we can conclude that he also passed on the latter's teachings.

This unremarkable fact in and of itself has a special importance in al-Pazdawī's case, since he was the ancestor of a family from which such famous Māturīdite theologians as Abū l-Yusr al-Pazdawī (d. 493/1100) and Fakhr al-Islām Abū l-Ḥasan al-Pazdawī (d. 482/1089) would emerge.[115] They thus founded an unbroken theological tradition and were certainly conscious of this continuity: Abū l-Yusr mentions his great-grandfather explicitly in the *Uṣūl al-dīn*, as we have seen earlier, and indicates there that his reports on al-Māturīdī have been passed down in the family over generations.[116]

Thus a certain current of influence proceeded from ʿAbd al-Karīm onward, albeit in a narrow and definable circle. At that time in a scholarly community such as Transoxania, which clearly possessed a certain stability, such influences may have been more significant and weightier than elsewhere. In the discipline of *kalām*, in any case, one ought to keep such continuities in mind; we already saw such a genealogical lineage from Makḥūl al-Nasafī (d. 318/930) to Abū l-Muʿīn al-Nasafī (d. 508/1115). Likewise in the Pazdawī family there was a tradition of transmitting knowledge over several generations. What this means in detail for the development of the Māturīdites is yet to be made clear.

---

six parasangs from Nasaf on the road from Nasaf to Bukhārā: cf. al-Samʿānī, vol. 2, 201.5f.; Ibn Abī l-Wafāʾ, vol. 2, 288.-8; al-Laknawī, 101.8f.

114 Ibn Abī l-Wafāʾ, vol. 1, 327.6f.; al-Laknawī, 101.9.

115 ʿAbd al-Karīm is sometimes described in the literature as the grandfather of both famous Māturīdites, though apparently the term *jadd* (in Samʿānī, vol. 2, 203.8) is understood too narrowly. He was really the great-grandfather, as by a) the testimony of Abū l-Yusr al-Pazdawī and b) the genealogy of both brothers in al-Samʿānī, vol. 2, 201.7 and 202.2.

116 *Uṣūl*, 3.1–3.

But one may nevertheless assert that an ancestor of the famous Pazdawī brothers of the fifth/eleventh century was an immediate student of al-Māturīdī.

1. The chart does not represent the entirety of early Ḥanafites in the East, but only sketches out the paths of transmission in their developing theology. The biographical reports and *isnād*s of the early Ḥanafite texts that we have analyzed up to this point were used as the basis for this chart. Ḥanafite scholars who, according to the sources, had no relation to these scholars (as their teacher, student, transmitter) are omitted. Thus, such names such as Abū Bakr al-Samarqandī (d. 268/881) do not appear in the diagram. The page numbers in the following notes refer to pages in the preceding text, in which their biographies and intermediary roles are discussed.
2. Cf. above, 5, 28ff., 42f., and 55.
3. Cf. above, 30n30.
4. Cf. above, 5.
5. Cf. above, 42ff.
6. Cf. above, 45 and 53ff.
7. Cf. above, 45n84.
8. Cf. above, 30n31.
9. Cf. above, 45n86, and 128.
10. Cf. above, 45n85, 72, and 133n48.
11. Cf. above, 30f., 55, and 128.
12. Cf. above, 45, 72, 128, and 132ff.
13. Cf. above, 72, 99, and 134ff.
14. Cf. above, 31 and 55.
15. Cf. above, 45 and 125ff.
16. Cf. above, 135 and 137ff.
17. Cf. above, 135 and 138.
18. Cf. above, 97ff. and 135.
19. Cf. above, 140ff.
20. Cf. above, 138.
21. Cf. above, 45f. and 144f.
22. Cf. above, 139f.

CHART *Theological Transmission among the Eastern Ḥanafites up to al-Māturīdī and his Students*

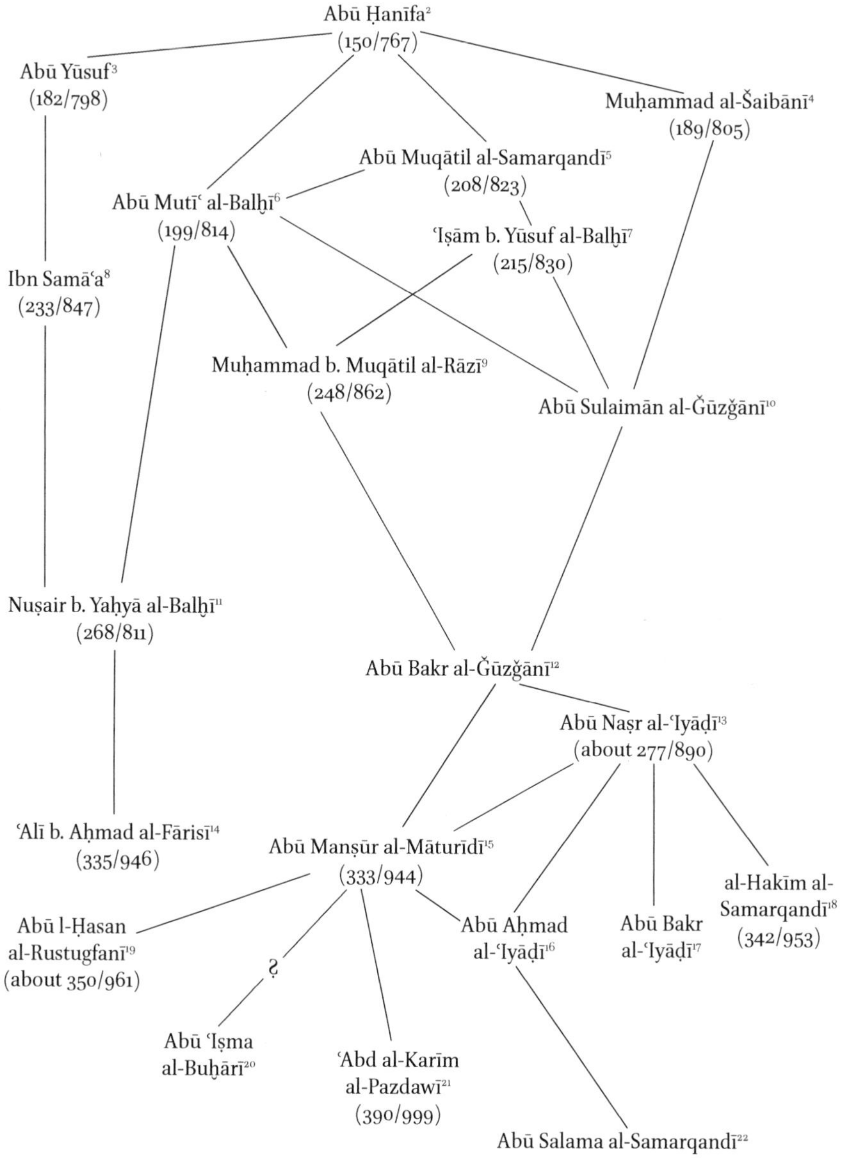

CHAPTER 5

Theological Opponents

5.1 The Wide Spectrum of Polemic

With the theologians named up to now, from Abū Ḥanīfa to ʿAbd al-Karīm al-Pazdawī, we have described a milieu that may rightly be characterized as Abū Manṣūr's religious and intellectual background. All these names belonged to the Ḥanafite tradition he called his own, and their texts which we have examined display an understanding of faith which is supposed to have guided him and formed the basis which he used for his own deeper theological reflections.

When it comes to speculative theology, however, both for al-Māturīdī as well as *mutakallimūn* from other regions of the Islamic world, we are not dealing with the mere refinement and development of one's own doctrine. Religious apology played a significant formative role here as well, since fending off and refuting other views usually gave cause for reflecting on one's own understanding, whether in debate with adherents of other religions, or even worse, with disagreeable representatives of rival Islamic sects.

The overview of the Ḥanafite tradition attained thus far has not told us everything that there is to know about al-Māturīdī's social and intellectual environment. The impression we now have must be broadened and expanded upon. Despite the dominance that the Ḥanafites had achieved in Transoxania by al-Māturīdī's time, other groups had also appeared in Samarqand, or at least their religious teachings had reached there. They also deserve some brief examination, since this can help us to assess which challenges al-Māturīdī faced and to analyze what incited him to change, perpetuate, or reformulate the traditional Ḥanafite doctrine he inherited.

How this theological argumentation itself was undertaken will occupy us in the third section of this study. For now, we will only shed light on the identities of al-Māturīdī's interlocutors; i.e., the religious groups that a Ḥanafite in Samarqand had to confront in the early fourth/tenth century. Fortunately, these are not too difficult to establish, since we have a dependable source for the task: al-Māturīdī himself names them explicitly in his main work, the *K. al-Tawḥīd*, our primary source for all our subsequent inquiries. Although he does not grace his theological predecessors with even a single mention—except Abū Ḥanīfa—he tells us precisely who his opponents are and why their views are unsatisfactory, if not outright dangerous.

 | DOI 10.1163/9789004261846_007

The list of opponents that may be compiled from such remarks is long and will be given here in its entirety. It encompasses several non-Islamic religions and worldviews, as well as a number of "sects" and thinkers of Islam. Among the former are Jews,[1] Christians,[2] Dualists[3] of different types (Zoroastrians,[4] Manichaeans,[5] Marcionites,[6] and followers of Bardesanes[7]), the Hellenistic philosophical legacy summed up in the word "Dahrīya"[8] (in detail, the *aṣḥāb al-hayūlā*,[9] *aṣḥāb al-ṭabāʾiʿ*,[10] "the philosophers,"[11] Aristotle[12]), and finally individuated groups such as the "Sumanīya,"[13] the "Sophists,"[14] and the Sabians.[15] Among the latter group (i.e, Muslims) we see the Khārijites,[16] Muʿtazilites,[17] Karrāmites,[18] and Ismāʿīlīs,[19] as well as explicitly named theologians: Jahm b. Ṣafwān,[20] Muqātil b. Sulaymān,[21] al-Najjār,[22] al-Burghūth,[23] al-Naẓẓām,[24] Jaʿfar b. Ḥarb,[25] al-Aṣamm,[26] Muḥammad b. Shabīb,[27] Abū ʿĪsā l-Warrāq,[28] Ibn

1 *Tawḥīd*, 102.5, 119.20f., 209.16–210.10.
2 Ibid., 119 ult.ff., 209.16–212 ult.
3 Cf., in a general sense, ibid., 34.4ff., 35.5ff., 87.12ff., 90.7ff., 91.-1ff., 113.1ff., 115.21ff.
4 Ibid., 88.16ff., 172.12ff., 235.19ff.
5 Ibid., 34.9ff., 157.1ff., 171.8ff.
6 Ibid., 171.1ff.
7 Ibid., 163.12ff.
8 Ibid., 82.13ff., 111.19ff., 121.5ff., 141,8ff.
9 Ibid., 24.1, 82.15f., 112.3, 147.4ff.
10 Ibid., 89.8ff., 112.2, 112.6, 116.23ff., 141.12ff.
11 Ibid., 25.9ff.
12 Ibid., 147.12ff.
13 Ibid., 153.4–153.5 and 155.12ff.
14 Ibid., 153.6–155.11.
15 Ibid., 171.7f.
16 Ibid., 323.-3ff., 332.18, 342.5ff., 352.16ff.
17 Ibid., 16.7ff., 86–92, 97.8f., 120.5ff.
18 Ibid., 378.1, 378.17f.
19 Ibid., 63 ult.ff., 93–96.
20 Ibid., 66.11f., 102.8ff., 103.11, 248.15f.
21 Ibid., 346.15.
22 Ibid., 99.7ff. (as "al-Ḥusayn"), 100.3ff., 120.13ff., 263.14ff.
23 Ibid., 120.13ff.
24 Ibid., 150.9ff., 152.8ff., 155.12ff.
25 Ibid., 169.4ff.
26 *Taʾwīlāt*, vol. 1, 48, 80, 8f., and 83.4.
27 *Tawḥīd*, 123.12ff., 126–135, 137–141
28 Ibid., 186.10ff., 191.16ff., 195.17ff., 199.17ff., 200.13ff., 284.16ff.

al-Rawāndī,[29] and Abū l-Qāsim al-Kaʿbī al-Balkhī.[30] Along with these are other polemical descriptions that do not outline a determinable group, but must be examined on a case by case basis in order to see whom the author wishes to apply them to. Among these are the "Ḥashwīya,"[31] "Mushabbiha,"[32] "Qadarīya,"[33] "Jabrīya,"[34] and finally the "Murji'a" as well.[35]

As one passes over these names in such a condensed form, a superficial image emerges that is quite surprising at first sight. It would appear to a certain extent that Samarqand was a meeting place of vastly different religious creeds, and that al-Māturīdī was the prevailing grandmaster of criticism there. Both notions, however, are imprecise in their accuracy and degree, since these lists ought to be interpreted first. There are in fact large disparities as to what each of these individual names personally meant for al-Māturīdī.

Some of the listed personages and creeds may have been anything but a pressing and direct challenge to our theologian. Although he mentions their views, comments on, and critiques them, this is only done in a derivative manner. He had heard of them and possibly read of them, but he was not personally confronted by them, and when he took them on in his work, he was not describing any actual discussion that took place in Samarqand. Rather, he was participating in a general form of argumentation against certain notorious opponents which was ubiquitous in Islamic *kalām*, and which even centuries later could be found in similar formulations in the writings of the most varied authors.

The refutation of the "Sumanīya" and the "Sophists" belongs to this first category of purely literary disputation. The comments on the Sabians and on Muqātil b. Sulaymān may also be included.

In the case of Muqātil b. Sulaymān, the famous Qur'ān commentator from Balkh, who is probably being referred to as "Muqātil" (*Tawḥīd*, 346.15), al-Māturīdī himself admits that he is merely reproducing a citation of the Muʿtazilite al-Kaʿbī. He then uses this to judge al-Kaʿbī (ibid., 346.16ff.), though he never mentions Muqātil's own views again.[36]

---

29 Ibid., 187.9ff., 193–202.

30 Ibid., 49.15ff., 60.3ff., 75.2ff., 236.11ff.

31 Ibid., 318.3ff., 331.2ff., 332.18ff., 378.17ff.

32 Ibid., 23.21, 92.13, 100.7, 120.16ff.

33 Ibid., 227.9ff., 228 ult. f., 314.6ff.

34 Ibid., 225.2ff., 229.1ff., 319.18ff., 384 ult.ff.

35 Ibid., 229.1f., 318.12ff., 332.8ff., 342.6ff.

36 This is the case in the discipline of systematic theology. Muqātil's Qur'ān exegesis was naturally of interest to al-Māturīdī; one can infer this from his mention in the *Ta'wīlāt al-Qur'ān*; see e.g., *Ta'wīlāt*, vol. 1, 197.1 and 227.11, vol. 2, 285.8 and 392.1. On Muqātil, see

The report on the Sabians is likewise clearly secondary, again only consisting of a single sentence. It does not deal with the Sabians of Ḥarrān, but rather the Mandaeans from southern Iraq who are often referred to with this name (cf. Gimaret 1969, 279f.). It is also clear here that al-Māturīdī is only citing another author, this time not al-Kaʿbī, but rather Muḥammad b. Shabīb.[37]

The same Ibn Shabīb is also al-Māturīdī's source for the "Sophists" (*Tawḥīd*, 153.12, 154.4, 154.-2), i.e., the infamous skeptics who, according to the statements of many Islamic theologians, questioned the possibility of sure knowledge (ibid., 153.6–155.11; trans. Vajda, "Autour," 183–187). They were also to be found in Iraq; ʿAbbād b. Sulaymān, for instance, is supposed to have debated them there (see, in general, van Ess, 1966, 231ff.). But even there, by the fourth/tenth century, the name was not bound with any specific group, but was rather a label affixed to a collection of propositions. See Saʿadyā Gaon (1881, 65.3ff./trans. [Rosenblatt 1948], 78ff.), who happens to distinguish between three groups of "Sophists."

Finally, the same is true of the "Sumanīya," whom al-Māturīdī mentions in two places in conjunction with the "Sophists" (on the "Sumanites" in general, see van Ess 1966, 257ff. and Gimaret 1969, 288ff.). First he describes them as a part of the "Dahrīya" (*Tawḥīd*, 152f.) and attributes to them the thesis that the world sinks unceasingly downward; this idea is found in a similar form in al-Khwārizmī's *Mafātīḥ al-ʿulūm* (1895, 35.2ff./trans. Bosworth 1977, 93); on this theme see Gimaret (1969, 295–297).

Claude Gilliot, "Muqātil, grand exegete, traditionniste et théologien maudit," *JA* 279 (1991): 39–92; van Ess, *Theologie*, vol. 2, 516ff.

37 The sentence reads: "The teaching of the Sabians is the same as the teaching of the Manichaeans, except that—according to Ibn Shabīb—there is a slight difference which he does not define (more closely)" (*Tawḥīd*, 171.7f.). Here al-Māturīdī makes a mistake without realizing it. Ibn Shabīb, who was from Iraq, was probably thinking about the Mandaeans when he was speaking of the Sabians, and drew certain parallels between their teachings and Manichaeism. To al-Māturīdī, there was no difference between Sabians and Manichaeans. However, the Manichaeans of his native city called themselves Sabians, as al-Birūnī tells us (*al-Āthār al-bāqiya ʿan al-qurūn al-khāliya*, ed. E. Sachau [Leipzig, 1878], 209.2; trans. E. Sachau, *The Chronology of Ancient Nations* [London, 1879], 191). Moreover, it is known that the term "Sabian" was often used on account of its Qurʾānic basis, causing confusion in Arabic literature. Dāwūd b. Marwān al-Muqammiṣ, the Jewish philosopher of religion of the third/ninth century, named them and the Manichaeans together in his *ʿIshrūn maqāla* (ed. and trans. S. Stroumsa [Leiden, 1989], 131.4f.). Muḥammad b. Aḥmad al-Nasafī, Transoxanian Ismāʿīlī and contemporary of al-Māturīdī, considers not only Mani, but also Marcion and Bardesanes from among the Sabians. See "Abū Ḥātim al-Rāzī on Persian Religion," in Samuel M. Stern, *Studies in Early Ismāʿīlism* (Jerusalem, 1983), 33f. It should also be taken into account that the simple concept of "heathens" can also be understood from the term Sabian (cf. Dimitri Gutas, "Plato's Symposion in the Arabic Tradition," *Oriens* 31 [1988]: 43f.).

He then describes them as skeptics who apparently only wish to acknowledge sensory perception—if that—as a means of knowledge (*Tawḥīd*, 155.12ff.; trans. Vajda 1967, "Autour," 187–189). In both cases it is clear, however, that al-Māturīdī is reproducing the fruits of his own reading: He does not merely refer to the theses of the "Sumanīya" but immediately follows with a reply from al-Naẓẓām. Then he again acknowledges (*Tawḥīd*, 155.12) that he found the entire passage from Ibn Shabīb's writings.

In regard to the "Sumanīya" in particular, this dependency on an Iraqi source is definitely surprising, since what is meant by them is Buddhists (on their identification in detail see Gimaret 1969, 288–291). The adherents of Buddha's teachings did not first encounter Muslim conquests in the Fertile Crescent, but rather in eastern Iran. They were especially numerous in old Bactria, where Balkh is supposed to have been their most important center. Buddhist preaching also enjoyed a certain degree of success in Transoxania, including Samarqand (though there only slightly) (Emmerick 1983, 949ff. [esp. 960], and idem, "Buddhism I. In Pre-Islamic Times," *EIr*, vol. 4, 492ff.; Haussig 1983, 187ff.). Thus it is odd that we do not find, with al-Māturīdī or the early Ḥanafite authors of the region, traces of direct argumentation with Buddhists. The only pertinent report is a dispute between them and Jahm b. Ṣafwān, but even this seems, based on its general characteristics, to merely have been spread on polemical grounds (Pines 1936, 132f.; Madelung 1965, 20 and 242; Gimaret 1969, 299ff.; for possible Indian influences on Jahm, see van Ess 1991–96, vol. 2, 504).

Given the silence on the part of the sources, we must definitely conclude that Buddhism barely left a trace on *kalām* (apart from the stereotyped reports on the "Sumanīya"). There are probably two reasons for this, which though entirely dissimilar are ultimately complementary. First, Buddhism must have lost its significance as a religion in eastern Iran rather quickly (according to Melikian-Chirvani, "Buddhism II. In Islamic Times," *EIr*, vol. 4, 498a, already shortly after the Islamic conquest), even though later Muslim authors are still informed about its previous widespread presence in this area (e.g., Ibn al-Nadīm 1871–2, 337.14 and 345.13f./trans. Dodge 1970, 801 and 824; and Malaṭī 1388/1968, 99.9). The other reason is that Transoxanian theology, despite its distance, was quite indebted to the forerunning themes of Iraqi theology. Attention was not necessarily given to the cultural and historical particularities of the region itself as points of emphasis. Instead the discussion was carried out with a view toward the core regions of Islam; thus views on the "Sumanīya" were informed by Iraqi scholars, even though the group was clearly a genuinely eastern phenomenon.

From al-Māturīdī's list of opponents we can distinguish a second category of religious groupings. They too cannot have played too great a role in regard to his theological reflections. But in contrast with the first category, it can be assumed that he personally came into contact with them in some form or another, since not only were they present in northeastern Iran, but they had already been addressed in the earlier eastern Ḥanafite texts that preceded his own work. These are the Khārijites, Jahmites, and Karrāmites, as well as the Jews and Christians from among the non-Muslims.

The Khārijites and Jahmites had been enemies of the eastern Ḥanafites from the beginning, so the dispute with them during al-Māturīdī's lifetime had long been carried out along specific paths of reasoning. The former were discussed by Abū Muqātil al-Samarqandī (*K. al-ʿĀlim*, sections 4 and 33–36), Abū Muṭīʿ al-Balkhī (*Fiqh absaṭ*, 44.19–45.16 and elsewhere), and in the *K. al-Sawād* (sections 9 and 60); and the followers of Jahm b. Ṣafwān were heavily criticized in the *Fiqh absaṭ* and in the *K. al-Sawād* (52.1–5, and sections 12, 21, and 44, respectively). If the critique of (the Karrāmite scholar) Makḥūl al-Nasafī is incorporated, it becomes quite clear that both groups must have had a significant influence, since he names them in his *K. al-Radd* as two of the six prominent and dangerous instigators of heresy (60.13ff., 61.1ff. and elsewhere).

This traditional offensive on the part of the Ḥanafites is not surprising. There had been Khārijites in eastern Persia since the early second/eighth century; they were found in appreciable numbers in Khurāsān and even to the point of domination in Sīstān which came under their rule for a time (Madelung 1988, 58ff.; van Ess 1991, vol. 2, 3.1). Jahmites were certainly present in eastern Iran; they had their roots in the region, where their presence continued (despite some conjectures to the contrary) without interruption after the death of their "founder" (van Ess 1991–96, vol. 2, 507f.).

The Karrāmites too had their home in the East, and were met there with disdain on the part of the Ḥanafite theologians, as we have already seen. In this case the Ḥanafite resistance is just as old as the "sect" itself and can be seamlessly traced from Abū Bakr al-Samarqandī through al-Ḥakīm al-Samarqandī (*K. al-Sawād*, sections 31, 44, 45, and 47) up to al-Māturīdī.

The case is somewhat different in regard to the polemic against Jews and Christians. As is known, both religious communities had long been settled in northeastern Iran. Christians met the Islamic conquerors there; these were mostly Nestorians whose mission had enjoyed great success in Central Asia (Haussig 1983, 218ff.; Spuler 1961, 139ff.; and Hage 1969). Jews, for their part, were represented in much fewer numbers. But there are traces of their presence from pre-Islamic times (cf. M. Zand, "Bukhārā VII. Bukharan Jews," *EIr*, vol. 4, 532 and 534) and in Balkh in the third/ninth century we even encounter a prominent and original representative of Jewish theology (on him see Rosenthal 1949, and Simon and Simon 1984, 43f).

Such details as the views of Ḥīwī or the detectable Nestorian dominance were not observed by the Ḥanafite theologians, or at least they were not thematized.[38] They

38 Ḥīwī al-Balkhī seems, however, to have been an interesting parallel for another Muslim thinker; van Ess (*Une lecture à rebours de l'histoire du muʿtazilisme* [Paris, 1984], 12) has shown that his claims of numerous contradictions in the Old Testament can be meaningfully be compared with certain views of Ibn al-Rāwandī.

polemicized in a very general way against both of the rival religions, the most prominent accusation being that neither the Jews nor the Christians had remained true to *tawḥīd*. We read this already from Abū Muqātil al-Samarqandī (*K. al-ʿĀlim*, sections 23 and 42), and in a very similar way from al-Māturīdī (*Tawḥīd*, 102.6 and 119.20ff.).[39]

Having taken a look at the aforementioned Jahmites and Karrāmites, we are now led to examine in more depth the purely polemical descriptions used by al-Māturīdī: i.e., "Murji'a," "Mushabbiha," "Qadarīya," "Jabrīya," and "Ḥashwīya." These groups are also found widely in the earlier Ḥanafite texts. But there, just as with al-Māturīdī's work, it can be determined very quickly that the usage of such labels is not necessarily associated with an actual report on the spread of a religious school. Only in the case of the "Ḥashwīya" does the usage of the label impart new information; we learn that a certain group existed in Transoxania which is nowhere mentioned in the Ḥanafī literature with another, more neutral name. In all other cases, these polemical terms describe groups and people whom we have already encountered by other names. Our task here is only to decipher these catchwords by determining which specific groups or people they are applied to.

The term "Mushabbiha" was already used by Makḥūl al-Nasafī (*Radd*, 120.20–121.12), by which he clearly implied an unusual meaning. He restricted it to a single thinker like Muqātil b. Sulaymān, in order to avoid any association between this label and the Karrāmites. Al-Māturīdī's usage is much wider and more conventional. To him, "Mushabbiha" applies to all those who attribute any type of bodily attributes to God; he was primarily thinking of Jews (*Tawḥīd*, 120.16–18) and the followers of Ibn Karrām (ibid., 23.21, 92.13, 100.7).

Use of the juxtaposition of "Qadarīya" and "Jabrīya" is an even older custom and was common among the Ḥanafites from the beginning. They all wished to tread the middle path in the question of human acts, as is clear in their emphasis of the contrary positions of "Qadarite" and "Jabrite" (cf. the *Risāla II; Fiqh absaṭ*, 43.7ff. and 55.2ff.; *Radd*, 64.4ff.; *K. al-Sawād*, sections 6, 10, and 42). Al-Māturīdī was merely taking up an old custom, and this is also clear in his intentions for using these terms: A "Qadarite" for him was always a Muʿtazilite (*Tawḥīd*, 314.6–316.15), which one may also assume for the earlier texts; as for the "Jabrites," whom he occasionally equates with "Murji'ites" (ibid., 229.1f., 384.11ff.), Jahm b. Ṣafwān and his followers seem to be intended (but not al-Najjār however, whom al-Māturīdī explicitly seeks to defend from this accusation) (ibid., 312.17ff.).

39 This proximity to Abū Muqātil does not rule out the possibility that al-Māturīdī also utilized an Iraqi source for his description of Jewish and Christian teachings; namely Ibn Shabīb—he names him again as his authority (*Tawḥīd*, 210.18) for at least one Christological teaching: Adoptionism

And thus we arrive at the term "Murji'a," whose presence among the names on the list is quite significant in some aspects; the term had for a long time been the source of a rather irksome problem for the Ḥanafites. They professed, in regard to the definition of belief, what many clearly considered to be the principle of *irjāʾ*, and given that this label was permeated with the smell of heresy, the Ḥanafites had been compelled since the time of Abū Ḥanīfa himself to ward off being labelled "Murji'ites" by their opponents (*Risāla I*, 37.19ff.; cf. *K. al-ʿĀlim*, section 4; *K. al-Sawād*, sections 44, 59, and 60). This issue, which had long been dodged by early authors, was taken up by al-Māturīdī with a rather elegant solution. He distanced himself at once from certain "Murji'ites" in whom he saw "Jabrite" tendencies (*Tawḥīd*, 229.1f., 318.12ff., 384.12ff.), but at the same time he rehabilitated the "Murji'ites" as long as the term was understood to refer to the adherents of the true understanding of *irjāʾ* (ibid., 332.8ff., 342.6ff., 381.13ff.). In this way, he participates in the general anti-Murji'ite critique, but unlike his predecessors he finds a way, despite his probable unease, to acknowledge this characteristic in his own tradition.

More informative than the four terms just mentioned is al-Māturīdī's repeated usage of the term "Ḥashwīya." Only Makḥūl al-Nasafī precedes him in this usage among the earlier Ḥanafites we have reviewed, and the statements of both theologians together give a fully coherent image. For Makḥūl, the "Ḥashwīya" are people who only think of *ḥadīth*, without, as he smugly adds, understanding the deeper meanings of these highly treasured holy texts (*Radd*, 121.13ff.). On his part al-Māturīdī reproaches them for three fundamental errors: they apparently insisted on equating deeds with faith (*Tawḥīd*, 331.2ff.), held faith itself to be uncreated (ibid., 385.12.), and furthermore, were convinced that the *istithnāʾ* ought to be appended to the statement "I am a believer" (ibid., 390.12ff.).

All these characterize the particularities of the Traditionists very well, and one can thus assume that they were also present in Transoxania. He was probably referring to the Shāfiʿite *madhhab*. In comparison to the Ḥanafī *madhhab*, it cannot have played a very significant role, but did find its adherents in various cities. In Samarqand itself, there were presumably a few.[40] In Bukhārā, however, and also in Shāsh (Tashkent) there had been more openness to al-Shāfiʿī's teachings.[41] Bukhārā was also the home of the theologian al-Ḥalīmī;

40 Madelung, *Religious Trends*, 26.

41 Madelung, "The Spread," 124n38.

he was active at the end of the fourth/tenth century and although a Shāfiʿite,[42] he enjoyed great renown among the Ḥanafites.[43]

But that is a discussion of a later generation. As for al-Māturīdī's time proper, the presence of the Traditionists in Transoxania cannot have been overly large. It must have been noticable, for otherwise our theologian would probably not have remarked on their views while discussing certain topics. From an overview of the *K. al-Tawḥīd*, however, these comments are limited in scope, such that one cannot count the *ḥadīth* scholars and the Shāfiʿites among his main opponents.

There remains one more religious school to discuss, the name of which is not found in the *K. al-Tawḥīd* at all; namely the Imāmīya. We know that at the turn of the fourth/tenth century they had entered Samarqand through the efforts of Muḥammad b. Masʿūd al-Ayyāshī (Madelung 1988, 84f.; van Ess 1991–96, vol. 2, 566f.), who instructed the more famous Muḥammad al-Kashshī. The Ḥanafites reacted to this; Makḥūl al-Nasafī combats the Shīʿites as the sixth group of the "Rawāfiḍ" (*Radd*, 82.7–ult.), and later Abū l-Layth al-Samarqandī compiled narrations in the *Bustān al-ghāfilīn* against the Imāmīya (in Abū l-Layth 1302 AH, section 28, 207f.). We do not have a clear picture of al-Māturīdī in regard to them, but he is supposed to have written a *Radd Kitāb al-imāma li-baʿḍ al-Rawāfiḍ* (cf. *Tabṣira*, vol. 1, 395.5f.), which was very probably a polemical epistle written against Twelver Shīʿites. Furthermore, al-Nasafī tells us his views on the imamate in detail (ibid., vol. 2, 829.8ff.; cf. 832.9ff. and 834.3ff.). But in the *K. al-Tawḥīd*, the question is left out completely, such that we possess no direct evidence of al-Māturīdī's polemic against the Imāmites.

5.2 The Muʿtazilite Challenge

Through our studies so far it has become clear that al-Māturīdī's long list of opponents must be relativized. Some groups, such as the "Sumanīya" or the "Sophists" were clearly only known in Samarqand of the fourth/tenth century through hearsay. Others, like the Jahmites, were more well known, such that disputes with them had long been conceptually definied and taken established formats. Others, such as the Traditionists and Shāfiʿites became noteworthy in the city or in the wider region only slowly over time and did not give rise to serious and challenging debates.

42 *GAS*, vol. 1, 607f. On al-Ḥalīmī's juristic views cf. Nagel, *Festung des Glaubens*, 261 and 319. His dogmatic work, the *K. al-Minhāj fī shuʿab al-īmān*, was published in Beirut (1399/1979) in three volumes.

43 *Uṣūl*, 203.8.

At the same time, this insight does not mean that all of the groups that al-Māturīdī attacked can be viewed as being of secondary importance for one reason or another. On the contrary, de-emphasizing some names logically leads to the accentuation of others, since there were certainly theologians whom al-Māturīdī persistently confronted. These must now be distinguished from the abovementioned.

The most noteworthy without a doubt are the practitioners of Muʿtazilite *kalām*. We encountered them earlier as opponents of the eastern Ḥanafites, beginning with the first *Risāla* to ʿUthmān al-Battī up to the *K. al-Sawād al-aʿẓam*. But in all these texts the discussion was quite schematic and limited by two identifiable aspects. The first of these was in regard to content, emphasis being given to notorious issues such as free will or the classification of extreme sinners. The second is that the Muʿtazila were always referred to as a definitive "sect," without the perception that they were made up of individual thinkers who, to varying degrees, had rather different teachings.[44] This meant that the view of the Muʿtazila held by the Transoxanian Ḥanafites bore archaic features and for quite some time was not necessarily up-to-date.[45] There was also a lack of opportunities to keep abreast of new developments: None of the famous Muʿtazilites of the third/ninth century managed to find their way East, nor did their students who had moved from eastern Iran to Iraq and become acquainted with the current state of the debate there attain a high profile; they also remained, for their part, in Baghdad or Basra.[46]

Al-Māturīdī's *K. al-Tawḥīd*, on the other hand, offers us something completely unprecedented. He does not suffice with mentioning the Muʿtazila now and then in order to repeat the same well-known theses, but actually discusses

44 *Risāla I*, 36.12–14 (without naming them explicitly) and *Risāla II* (s.v. *ahl al-tafwīḍ*); *Fiqh absaṭ*, 43.7ff. and 55.2ff. (as "Qadarīya"); *K. al-Sawād*, sections 6, 12, 13, 14, 15, and 60 (as "Muʿtazila") as well as sections 6, 10, 14, and 42 (as "Qadarīya"); *Radd*, 77.11ff. and 88.15ff. Makḥūl has, in addition, a vague representation of al-Naẓẓām (*Radd*, 95.8ff.)

45 This is explicitly true only of Transoxania. In Khurāsān, for instance, the situation was certainly different. Muʿtazilites had been present during al-Ma'mūn's residence there (cf. van Ess, *Une lecture*, 9); and at a later point inhabitants displayed a greater familiarity with the Muʿtazilite teachings there. Ibn Karrām's theses, for example, are based on an intimate knowledge of Muʿtazilite teachings. Our image in regard to Transoxania could change, however, if Abū Naṣr al-ʿIyāḍī's work on the question of God's attributes were still extant.

46 Al-Kaʿbī gives two names in his *Maqālāt al-Islāmīyīn*: Abū l-Ṭayyib al-Balkhī, who is supposed to have studied with Jaʿfar b. Ḥarb, and Ibrāhīm al-Balkhī, who is also from among the generation before al-Khayyāṭ (see al-Kaʿbī, *Maqālāt al-Islāmīyīn*, 74.15f. and 103.8 respectively). The latter is probably not identical with Ibrāhīm b. Yūsuf al-Balkhī.

their views frequently and in unprecedented detail.[47] For almost every topic he provides details on the corresponding Muʿtazilite position and never fails to explain the inadequacy of these ideas in detail. The result is that the phantom image of a cohesive Muʿtazilite "sect" gives way to a representation that is much more detailed and realistic. Al-Māturīdī knew specific thinkers and did not hesitate to name them repeatedly; in fact his own statements allow us to deduce which representatives of Muʿtazilite theology were most significant to his development.

5.2.1 *Abū l-Qāsim al-Balkhī al-Kaʿbī and the Baghdad School*

The first and most important of them was an immediate contemporary of al-Māturīdī; namely, Abū l-Qāsim al-Balkhī al-Kaʿbī. His teachings are discussed in the *K. al-Tawḥīd* in great detail;[48] one could even say without exaggeration, that no other thinker is dedicated nearly as much attention to any other thinker. The reason for these persistent attacks on al-Balkhī has to do with a rivalry that was largely geographically determined. Abū l-Qāsim was from Balkh, and after his studies in Baghdad and other periods of residence elsewhere, he returned to spend the greater part of his life in his hometown. In the year 307/919, he took the position of vizier for the governor Aḥmad b. Sahl and somewhat later he was offered a teaching position in Nasaf, not far from Samarqand. When he died in 319/931, he enjoyed the highest prestige in the region. Even al-Māturīdī grudgingly acknowledged this when he sarcastically remarked that the Muʿtazilites seemed to consider Abū l-Qāsim "Imam of the world's inhabitants" (*imām ahl al-arḍ*).[49]

The man from Balkh brought Muʿtazilite rivalry to northeastern Iran, not timidly but with an unsettling confidence and even vehemence. Al-Kaʿbī was undoubtedly among the prominent theologians of the epoch; this is recognizable from his large oeuvre and his preeminent intellectual activities. From the perspective of the Muʿtazilite tradition, he was of the Baghdad persuasion; he had studied with al-Khayyāṭ in the capital, and sometimes borrowed from al-Naẓẓām's writings. In regard to his systematization, however, al-Kaʿbī went beyond these older layers, drawing up a refined dogmatic system which even now is not known in all of its details; thereby influencing many sub-categories of *kalām* (e.g., theories of cognition and physics) with his own distinctive

47 *Tawḥīd*, 16.7ff., 86–92, 120.5ff., 169.12ff., 215.4ff., 230–236, 264–286, 320–323, 365–368, 390.12ff. and elsewhere.

48 Ibid., 16.17, 49.15ff., 60.3ff., 75.2ff., 82–85, 236–256, 266–286, 294–303, 307–314, 316–319, 343.12ff. and elsewhere.

49 Ibid., 49.17.

imprint. In addition to this he had a strong interest in philosophy: This led him to a major dispute with the famous Muḥammad b. Zakarīyā' al-Rāzī (d. 313/925); but it also led to friendly encounters, as with his compatriot Abū Zayd al-Balkhī (d. 322/934) who had studied with al-Kindī, and these encounters provided a basis for the fruitful dissemination of the latter's philosophy in eastern Iran. Contact with Abū Zayd seems to have had its influence on al-Kaʿbī, who even adopted several philosophical ideas (e.g., the denial of a vacuum). As we shall see, al-Māturīdī himself adopted genuinely philosophical concepts. This too might be dependent on Abū Zayd al-Balkhī's influence, or possibly come from al-Kaʿbī's mediation of the former's ideas.

For al-Kaʿbī's biography and teachings, see the dissertation of Racha Moujir el Omari entitled, "The Theology of Abū l-Qāsim al-Balḫī/al-Kaʿbī (d. 319/931): A Study of its Sources and Reception" (Yale University, 2006). Before this dissertation, the most detailed effort had been by van Ess, "Abū 'l-Qāsem Kaʿbī," *EIr*, vol. 1, 359–362. Cf. Albert Nader, *Le système philosophique des Mu'tazila* (Beirut, 1956), see index; Watt 1973, 300–302; idem 1985, 300–302; Madelung 1965, 159; Frank 1978, see index; Gimaret and Monnot 1986, see index. For an overview of al-Kaʿbī's numerous works, mostly lost today, see Sayyid 1974, 46ff., which also reproduces (on 63ff.) a part of al-Kaʿbī's *K. Maqālāt al-Islāmīyīn* (on this text see Ritter 1929, 39). Besides this text there seems to be only a single other book available, in manuscript form (cf. *GAS*, vol. 1, 622f.). On his dispute with al-Rāzī, cf. the latter's *Rasā'il falsafīya*, in the edition by P. Kraus (1939, 167f.); on the role of Abū Zayd al-Balkhī in spreading al-Kindī's teachings, cf. Endreß (1987, 449f.), with further bibliographical information.

5.2.2 *The Basran School*

The confrontation with al-Kaʿbī led al-Māturīdī to focus on the doctrines of the Baghdad school when disputing with the Muʿtazila. The Basran school, in contrast, which had a greater influence on al-Ashʿarī, is not named explicitly in *K. al-Tawḥīd* and thus retreats to the background. All the same, it would be hasty to therefore preclude it any influence. There are convincing indications to the effect that al-Māturīdī also knew Basran Muʿtazilite teachings and referenced them in his writings; we can even say with some probability which sources his ideas go back to in this regard.

We are most likely dealing with the *K. al-Uṣūl al-khamsa* ("Book of the Five Principles") by Abū ʿUmar Saʿīd b. Muḥammad al-Bāhilī (d. 300/912). Several later authors report that al-Māturīdī had read his work and refuted it with a work of his own.[50] Unfortunately, al-Bāhilī's text and al-Māturīdī's refutation are both lost. Although al-Bāhilī was definitely not a prominent scholar among

50 Cf. below, 180n2.

the Iraqi Muʿtazilites, that being said, he was a close confidant of Abū ʿAlī al-Jubbāʾī,[51] and it was even said that he transcribed all of al-Jubbāʾī's texts.[52] Consequently, al-Bāhilī's *Uṣūl al-khamsa* must have been an authentic representation of al-Jubbāʾī's theology, one on which al-Māturīdī could rely.

Al-Māturīdī's interest in such newer Iraqi intellectual trends is impressive and shows how carefully he oriented himself and kept in tune with the times as a theologian. He did not suffice by merely replicating the stock arguments and debates long cultivated in Transoxania in other forms.[53] Al-Māturīdī wanted to keep up with the newest developments in *kalām*, and was able to do so, because his disputes with al-Kaʿbī and al-Jubbāʾī brought him to possess the knowledge base and discursive capacity of an Iraqi *mutakallim*.

5.2.3 *Ibn al-Rāwandī*

In other aspects, however, perspectives in Samarqand and Baghdad differed greatly. This becomes clear when al-Māturīdī mentions other Muʿtazilites and describes them rather differently from how they were usually described by writers in the capital. The most striking example of this can be seen in his discussion of the elusive figure of Ibn al-Rāwandī. He is discussed in relatively extensive detail in the *K. al-Tawḥīd*, which in and of itself is not out of the ordinary, but his ideas here are actually acknowledged and respectfully accepted—which would hardly have been the case for a contemporary text from Baghdad.

In Iraq, Ibn al-Rāwandī had long been considered a full-blown heretic. He was accused of defecting from the teachings of the Muʿtazila, leaving the fold of Islam, and plunging into a whirlpool of heresy. The background for these accusations, as is known, was an internal conflict among the Baghdad Muʿtazilites. The effect of the polemic, however, went far beyond their inner circle. Ibn al-Rāwandī was presented, essentially, as a monster—a dangerous renegade—and he could not clear himself of these labels because the Iraqi sources were followed to a great extent by the rest of the Islamic community.

---

51 ʿAbd al-Jabbār al-Qāḍī, *K. Faḍl al-iʿtizāl*, in Sayyid, *Faḍl al-iʿtizāl*, 310.4ff.

52 Ibn al-Murtaḍā, *Ṭabaqāt al-Muʿtazila*, ed. S. Diwald-Wilzer (Beirut/Wiesbaden, 1961), 97.3ff.

53 The high degree to which al-Māturīdī is informed on the details of contemporary Muʿtazilite theology is accentuated by the fact that later Transoxanian authors fall far short of him in this regard. Both Samarqandian theologians Abū Salama and Abū l-Layth, who follow him on "the Muʿtazilites," do so in an abbreviated form. Al-Khwārizmī names only the older authorities of the school (such as Abū l-Hudhayl, al-Naẓẓām or Muʿammar) in his *Mafātīḥ*, the teachings of whom had long been overtaken by the Jubbāʾites and al-Kaʿbī.

However, this was not the case in eastern Iran, where people saw things differently. As al-Māturīdī's comments testify to, Ibn al-Rāwandī was not viewed as a heretic in Samarqand, but actually as a defender of Islam. He earned this reputation for having confronted Abū ʿĪsā l-Warrāq in theological disputation. To al-Māturīdī, the latter was (as per the common view) a real disbeliever, since he claimed that there had never been prophethood, because such an institution was superfluous and irrational.[54] Ibn al-Rāwandī, for his part, had distanced himself from such monstrous heresies, and according to the *K. al-Tawḥīd*, he exposed al-Warrāq as a Manichean[55] and refuted him with shrewd argumentation.[56] In turn, Ibn al-Rāwandī is supposed to have given a positive set of explanations for the necessity of prophethood. The main thrust of their argument asserted that prophets did not just institute religion, but were also beneficial for the cultural development of mankind.[57]

All this apparently affected al-Māturīdī deeply, since he stands more or less under Ibn al-Rāwandī's spell in regard to his critique of al-Warrāq as well as the structure of thought underlying it. Even more surprising is al-Māturīdī's adoption of Ibn al-Rāwandī's systematic arguments, whereby he justifies prophethood on a very rational basis,[58] understanding it in the broader sense as a culturally-productive force. This fits well with his own theology, but one ought not to forget that the origin of this idea was Ibn al-Rāwandī, the Muʿtazilite whose own school condemned him but whom al-Māturīdī took inspiration from without reservation.

The different assessments of Ibn al-Rāwandī found in the Islamic sources are also reflected in modern research. These were initially based on the testimonies from Iraq and concluded therefrom that he was a heretic who turned away from the Muʿtazila and bound himself in an unholy alliance with Abū ʿĪsā l-Warrāq. An essay by Paul Kraus from 1934 was critical for the advancement of this point of view (Kraus, "Beiträge zur islamischen Ketzergeschichte," 1933–34; repr. 1994). This image persisted for a long time and was still the basis of Vajda's article ("Ibn al-Rāwandī," *EI*², vol. 3, 905f.).

A revision of this assessment only became possible when awareness of al-Māturīdī's remarks grew, since they showed that Ibn al-Rāwandī ought to be distinguished from al-Warrāq. The way was thus cleared for a more thoughtful reevaluation of this thinker

---

54 *Tawḥīd*, 186.10ff. (on prophetic miracles); 191.16ff. and 196.17ff. (on Muḥammad and the Qurʾān); 200.13ff. (on the irrationality of prophethood).

55 Ibid., 197.2, 199.18, 201.21ff.

56 Ibid., 187.9ff. and in detail 193–201.

57 Ibid., 193.15f.; he was probably provoked to say this because of Ibn al-Rāwandī's comments starting at 179.11.

58 Cf. ibid., 179.11f.

of such terrible disrepute, and consideration was taken of his intellectual independence and his significance as symptomatic of the internal crisis which the Muʿtazila underwent in the second half of the third/ninth century. Van Ess' contributions led the way, and he has applied himself to this topic repeatedly (cf. van Ess 1978; idem 1984, 2ff.; idem 1980, "Al-Fārābī"; idem 1991–96, vol. 4, 8.2.2 and also the references in ibid., vol. 6, 433ff.).

5.2.4 *Muḥammad b. Shabīb*

The last Muʿtazilite mentioned in detail in the *K. al-Tawḥīd* is Muḥammad b. Shabīb. He is also appreciated by al-Māturīdī in a way different from the norm in Baghdad, but in this case, the differences are less grave, and relate more to theological views than personal integrity.

The truth is that Ibn Shabīb did not have a significant role in Iraq. He was known there as a student of al-Naẓẓām, of whom he was a contemporary,[59] but was not known to have developed any other ideas that might give him a distinctive profile. Ibn Shabīb was probably only remembered because he professed "Murjiʾite" theses in response to some theological questions. This compromised him in the eyes of his Muʿtazilite colleagues and led to some confusion on the part of some later commentators in their evaluations of him. Observers from the outside (al-Ashʿarī, al-Khwārizmī, al-Baghdādī, al-Shahrastānī) usually classified him as a "Murjiʾite." The Muʿtazilite tradition differed on how to deal with him: Some played down Ibn Shabīb's Murjiʾite inclinations and counted him as one of their own.[60] Others, however, who were less accommodating, were of the opinion that the Muʿtazila were better off without his membership.[61]

In al-Māturīdī's eyes, it may have been just this tendency toward the Murjiʾa that made Ibn Shabīb stand out. That is not to say that this made him a comrade, but it did put him in a more favorable light. This being so, al-Māturīdī by no means overlooked the fact that Ibn Shabīb really belonged to the Muʿtazila. He mentions it explicitly,[62] and does not spare him straightforward criticism when he finds it necessary.[63] But the tone with which he does so is significant; it is never injurious, but rather moderate in choice of words and departs

---

59 Al-Shahrastānī, 18.13; al-Masʿūdī, *K. al-Tanbīh wa-l-ishrāf*, ed. M.J. de Goeje (Leiden, 1894), 395.-2.

60 ʿAbd al-Jabbār, 279.11ff.; Ibn al-Murtaḍā, 79.9ff.

61 Abū l-Ḥusayn b. ʿUthmān al-Khayyāṭ, *K. al-Intiṣār wa-l-radd ʿalā Ibn al-Rāwandī al-mulḥid*, ed. Albert Nader (Beirut, 1957), 93.11f.

62 *Tawḥīd*, 131.11.

63 E.g., ibid., 149 ult.ff.

clearly from the cutting sort of attacks which al-Kaʿbī is subjected to in the *K. al-Tawḥīd*.

Their points of disagreement operate on several levels, starting with the question of the description of God and the concept of the creation.[64] But the format of Ibn Shabīb's work must have interested al-Māturīdī even more; later we will see how the construction and literary style of the *K. al-Tawḥīd* essentially owes itself to his example.[65] Part of this is due to the fact that al-Māturīdī uses the Muʿtazilite thinker to a great extent as a doxographical source: Much that he reports on other sects he owes not to his own studies, but rather, as he himself admits, to Ibn Shabīb's books. He informed himself on the teachings of al-Naẓẓām and Jaʿfar b. Ḥarb by this means, for example,[66] but he was also especially indebted to him for his informative presentations in the *K. al-Tawḥīd* on non-Islamic groups and foreign religions. This has already been demonstrated in the case of the "Sophists" and "Sumanites;" the same applies for the "Dahrīya"[67] and might as well be the case for others, especially the dualistic religions.[68]

Since the discovery of these detailed citations in the *K. al-Tawḥīd*, two attempts have been made to reconstruct the theological views of Ibn Shabīb. The first was by Pessagno (1984, "The Reconstruction"), who drew upon entries from al-Ashʿarī, al-Baghdādī, al-Shahrastānī, and Ibn al-Murtaḍā, in addition to al-Māturīdī's reports. The second attempt was made by van Ess, taking Pessagno as a starting point and adding further material, including previously unknown references from Dāwūd al-Muqammiṣ, Tawḥīdī, ʿAbd al-Jabbār, and Ibn Mattawayh (1991–96, vol. 4, 124ff. and vol. 6, 338ff.; cf. as well Gimaret and Monnot, 1986, index).

5.3 The Ḥanafite Rivals: al-Najjār and the School of Rayy

The Muʿtazila were thus the greatest of al-Māturīdī's opponents from among the Muslim theologians. But they were not his only challenge on that front; al-Māturīdī was concerned with yet another *mutakallim* whom he closely

64 Ibid., 126.1ff.

65 Cf. below, 228ff.

66 On al-Naẓẓām cf. *Tawḥīd*, 155.12; the short statement on Jaʿfar b. Ḥarb (ibid., 169.4ff.) is also dependant on Muḥammad b. Shabīb; this is reason to conclude that the entire context (the dispute with the Ḍaysānīya) goes back to him.

67 *Tawḥīd*, 123.12ff. and 137.21ff.

68 On this see Wilferd Madelung, "Abū ʿĪsā l-Warrāq über die Bardesaniten, Marcioniten und Kantäer," in *Studien zur Geschichte und Kultur des Vorderen Orients. Festschrift für Bertold Spuler zum siebzigsten Geburtstag*, ed. Hans R. Roemer and Albrecht Noth (Leiden, 1981), 219n31.

associated with them, one whose teachings repeatedly gave rise to discussion in the *K. al-Tawḥīd*—Abū ʿAbdallāh al-Najjār, or al-Ḥusayn as al-Māturīdī simply refers to him.[69]

Al-Najjār lived in Rayy and was active there in the first third of the third/ninth century. His teachings were widely taken note of in Iraq as the detailed entry in al-Ashʿarī's *Maqālāt* attests to. But in Transoxania he had been a concern for even longer. Makḥūl al-Nasafī, for example, criticized him in his *Radd*,[70] and al-Māturīdī's own teacher, Abū Naṣr al-ʿIyāḍī, as we saw earlier, is supposed to have written a book on the divine attributes in which he apparently disputed with the Muʿtazila and the Najjārīya. This work is lost, however, and Makḥūl al-Nasafī's remarks are restricted to a single topic that is handled very briefly.[71] Consequently, both reports only establish that al-Najjār's teaching had been received in the East before al-Māturīdī's time. How he had been viewed on specific details, however, is first documented in the *K. al-Tawḥīd*. This source convincingly shows us that the Transoxanians took the theologian of Rayy seriously and were intent on refuting him and his successors (such as al-Burghūth).

There was certainly good cause to do so. Al-Najjār's school represented a formidable rival to them in two aspects: First, it was geographically close to the Transoxanians. The greater part of its adherents did not live in Iraq, but Iran; this was attested to for Rayy until the sixth/twelfth century,[72] and a similar case is reported of Jibāl and Jurjān.[73] The presence of the Najjārīya had to be reckoned with even farther East, in fact; as Ibn al-Dāʿī (presumably in the early seventh/thirteenth century) reported, they were to be found (among other places) in the region of Bukhārā, i.e., central Transoxanian territory.[74]

Along with this geographically determined competition came a more significant form of rivalry. Al-Najjār did not belong to the Muʿtazila as al-Māturīdī claimed,[75] nor could he be classified like Ibn Shabīb as a thinker with a Muʿtazilite foundation and Murjiʾite tendencies. In reality, his doctrines were

69 Cf., for example, *Tawḥīd*, 99.7, 100.4, 120.13 (together with al-Burghūth). Al-Māturīdī also calls al-Najjār's followers the "Ḥusaynīya" (321.17).

70 *Radd*, 99.5ff.

71 Makḥūl attributes two theses to al-Najjār which are polemical in tone and are supposed to characterize him as a "Jabrite": God punishes people for His own actions; and God will punish or reward (dead) children according to the extent of the belief or disbelief of their parents (*Radd*, 99.6f.).

72 Calmard, 46.

73 Muqaddasī, 384.14 and 365.9. Muqaddasī wrote in the later fourth/tenth century.

74 *Tabṣira*, 91.6f.

75 *Tawḥīd*, 263.14; cf. ibid., 120.13.

actually much closer to Transoxanian teachings in their general aims, since they represented a noteworthy parallel attempt to formulate a specifically Ḥanafite theology.

Be that as it may, the man from Rayy never achieved the reception he desired. This might be because he did not base himself on the foundational texts of Abū Ḥanīfa and his first students, who as we have seen, played a great formative role in Balkh and Samarqand. Instead, he grounded himself on other, alternative intellectual edifices already characterized by more elaborate forms of systematization: One of his sources was the Ḥanafite Bishr al-Marīsī, who was also his link to a group called the "Murji'a from Baghdad," and Ḍirār b. 'Amr is usually mentioned as his second teacher. Abū Ḥanīfa's ideas thus only form the greater sphere of al-Najjār's thought, such that it is not surprising if the latter's teachings were only partly consistent with eastern Iranian theology.

Al-Najjār's thought shows similarities to points of doctrine found in the classical Murji'ism of the Ḥanafites. Some examples are the description of belief, the punishment of sins, as well as the imperative to command that which is correct and forbid the reprehensible. But differences in regard to several other important questions are undeniable: Al-Najjār was closer to the Muʿtazila in his teachings on the divine attributes. As for human agency, he was known to have opinions on this topic which he shared with neither the Muʿtazila nor the eastern Ḥanafites; in this respect he was regarded with suspicion as being a determinist.

Al-Māturīdī's reaction to him thus changes accordingly over the course of the *K. al-Tawḥīd*. On some questions, such as the description of God, for example, he accuses al-Najjār and his student al-Burghūth of making the same mistakes as the Muʿtazila.[76] In the chapter on the human capacity to act he also berates him as a Muʿtazilite, although the accusations that follow are very different from those made elsewhere against the Muʿtazila.[77] In total, however, al-Najjār's image in the *K. al-Tawḥīd* is not entirely negative, since there are several points on which al-Māturīdī shows himself to be led by a feeling of commonality. The agreement on *irjāʾ* is, of course, such an example,[78] the calling toward the correct and forbidding of the reprehensible is another.[79] The same is also true of the passage in which al-Najjār is defended against the Muʿtazilite attribution of him being a "Jabrite."[80] Even more informative than

76 Ibid., 120.13–15.
77 Ibid., 263.14ff. and 265.15ff.
78 Ibid., 341.17f.; also 323.9ff.
79 Ibid., 100.3ff.
80 Ibid., 321.17ff.

this, however, is a discussion on the divine providence, in which al-Māturīdī clearly developed his ideas in close conversation with the views of the theologian from Rayy.[81]

The number of these passages in proportion to the entirety of the *K. al-Tawḥīd* is admittedly unimpressive. This might prompt the objection that al-Najjār did not actually play a critical role for al-Māturīdī, since he is mentioned in the *K. al-Tawḥīd* briefly and infrequently. However, this impression is deceptive, as will be shown later. It must be kept in mind that our theologian incorporated al-Najjār's teachings even when omitting mention of his name; his treatment of ontology and his doctrines on attributes may be mentioned for now as examples. What follows from this, however, is that al-Māturīdī did not emphasize al-Najjār's role, but rather played it down; it seems he thought much more about his colleague in Rayy than he wished to impart to us. This too is best explained as an indication of rivalry between two schools that were competing for a similar audience. The goal of each school was not to bring attention to its competitor through argumentation, but rather to make itself more significant in the eyes of the reading public.

Al-Najjār's works are unfortunately lost, but his teachings can be adequately reconstructed from the plentiful entries in the heresiographical literature. The most important of these reports we owe to al-Ashʿarī (summarized by Watt [1973, 199ff.; idem 1985, 203f.]) and al-Shahrastanī (Gimaret and Monnot, 1986, 298ff.). Al-Najjār's theology was reconstructed by van Ess, who initially discussed it in an essay on Ḍirār b. ʿAmr and the Jahmīya (1968, 56ff.), and then again with a somewhat different evaluation (1991–96, vol. 4, 149ff.]. An additional perspective emerges from the interesting parallels with the Ibāḍites, which Madelung has brought attention to in "The Shiite and Khārijite Contribution," 1979, 127f. (idem 1965, 242f.; idem 1971, 113f.; idem 1988, 29f.). See further material by Gimaret (1980, 69ff.) on the question of human actions (and idem 1990, index).

5.4 The Focal Point of the Discussion: Refutation of the Dualists and the "Dahrīya"

There are two further examples which demonstrate that the frequency with which al-Māturīdī mentions certain opponents does not necessarily reflect their immediate significance. These are the dualistic religions, as well as the various intellectual currents summed up under the catchword "Dahrīya" which

81 Ibid., 96–101; by name 99.7ff. and 100.3ff.

are mentioned (at least in the first half of the *K. al-Tawḥīd*) time and time again. This insistent mention requires evaluation as well, though in this case the result differs from the case of al-Najjār, as the frequency of these citations is certainly disproportionate to their actual significance for al-Māturīdī.

This is not discernible at first glance, however; al-Māturīdī's tremendous expenditure of energy in his campaign against these groups is remarkable. The argumentation with dualists is visibly preponderant, being extensive in its detail and laced with biting criticisms. One by one we learn what the Manichaeans,[82] Bardesanes' followers,[83] the Marcionites,[84] and the Zoroastrians[85] are supposed to have thought, and each system of thought is refuted in full detail.[86] Manichaeism and Zoroastrianism also play an important role; the latter is brought into comparison when other teachings—because of their apparent proximity to Zoroaster's ideas—are labeled as dangerous.[87] The religion of Mani, however, is the most ubiquitous of all the foreign systems mentioned in the *K. al-Tawḥīd*. We encounter it repeatedly under its own name,[88] but it might also be what al-Māturīdī is referring to when he speaks generally of Dualists (*thanawīya*)[89] or Zindīqs.[90]

Al-Māturīdī's image of the "Dahrīya," in comparison, is recognizably less detailed, but this can hardly be surprising given the origins of the term. This, again, is not a name for a clearly outlined "sect," but rather a polemical label often used in *kalām*. "Dahrīya" is derived from *dahr* (in the sense of "beginningless time") and as a general term was supposed to describe all people and schools that profess the eternality of material in one way or another.[91] Figuring

82 Ibid., 157.1–16; trans. Vajda, "Le témoignage," 4ff. and Guy Monnot, *Penseurs musulmans et religions iraniennes. ʿAbd al-Jabbār et ses devanciers* (Paris, 1974), 303f. as well as idem, "Mātorīdī et le manchéisme," 147f.

83 *Tawḥīd*, 163.12–164.5; Vajda, "Le témoignage," 23ff.

84 *Tawḥīd*, 171.1–6; Vajda, "Le témoinage," 31ff.

85 *Tawḥīd*, 172.12–17; Monnot, *Penseurs musulmans*, 305.

86 *Tawḥīd*, 157.17–163.11 (against the Manicheans); 164.6–170 ult. (against Bardesanes); 171.10–172,11 (against Marcion); 172.18–174.9 (against the Zoroastrians; cf. Monnot, *Penseurs musulmans*, 305ff.).

87 *Tawḥīd*, 88.16ff., 91.5, 113.17f., 119.18, 235.19ff., 314.8ff., 386.15ff.

88 Ibid., 34.9ff., 119.18, 171.7ff.

89 Ibid., 34,4ff., 35.5ff., 67.6, 87.12ff. and elsewhere.

90 Ibid., 89.7, 90.16, 91.2f., 92.12f. and elsewhere. On the image of Manichaeism in the *K. al-Tawḥīd*, cf. in general Monnot, "Mātorīdī et le manichéisme."

91 Goldziher's comments are still foundational to this theme: see his entry "Dahrīya," *EI*[1], vol. 1, 932f., which shows that very different personages and teachings were described

out whom al-Māturīdī specifically had in mind requires still more consideration. This is not always an easy task, however, since the longer such simplifying labels are used, the more they tend to develop their own sway and end up as inexact representations of reality.

By al-Māturīdī's time the term had long since reached the stage of generalization and abstraction. This has consequences when we ask ourselves which historically concrete group of people and teachings are meant when he speaks of the "Dahrīya." The answer we reach is by no means clear. Al-Māturīdī does not cite names or geographical locations, instead he draws up broad theoretical tableaus in which all the conceivable offshoots of the heresy are described. Even these are useful no doubt, but one must be aware that they do not deal with concrete historical information. Rather they represent the entire sum of possible characteristics which at that time might have caused one to be categorized among the dreaded "Dahrīya."

This being understood, it suffices us to describe the most detailed of these overviews as a representative example,[92] which will also clearly confirm how the author's drive to classify preponderated over his attention given to historical foundations: The initial assumption of al-Māturīdī's presentation here is that this heresy is best understood by first acquainting ourselves with an essential dichotomy. We are not dealing with one, but actually two competing views, he explains. One group of the "Dahrīya" actually believes that the world has eternally possessed its current form; in contrast, the other group claims that there has always existed a primordial material principle (*aṣl*), but they believe that it only came to realize its actual form over the course of time, thanks to a creative influence on our world. Even this schematic lacks comprehensiveness and certainty, however, since there were additional debates on what the primordial material substrate of all things actually was. Thus our Muslim observer is again compelled to arrange both sections of the "Dahrīya" into several subgroups.

In the first case, i.e., those who profess the eternality of the world, this differentiation plays out rather subtly. We first hear of two factions, one which believes that the cosmos regulates itself with complete autonomy, while the

with this term. In his view it seems most adequate to translate it as "Materialists" or "Naturalists." Cf. Goldziher-Goichon, "Dahriyya," *EI*², vol. 2, 95ff., which is expanded based on an overview of the usage of the term in theological literature up to the twentieth century. A short overview is also given by Martin J. McDermott, "Abū ʿĪsā l-Warrāq on the Dahriyya," *MUSJ* 50 (1984): 387f.

92 *Tawḥīd*, 111.19–113.6; cf. also 30.1ff., 121.5ff., 141.8ff.

other assumes pre-existing elements of nature alongside a creator whose creative act has already occurred in pre-eternity. In addition, a further distinction is made within the first, godless faction, in regard to which primordial principle its members speak of. Some profess the eternal elements of nature (the *aṣḥāb al-ṭabāʾiʿ*), some an eternal material substance (the *aṣḥāb al-hayūlā*), and a third group was of the view that the four elements in particular (*al-arbaʿ min al-ṭabāʾiʿ*) were the origins of all existence.

The subdivisions of the second main branch of "Dahrites" are, in comparison, not as complex. Each is characterized by the belief that an eternal material principle could be combined with a temporal origin to the world. They too are not unified in their teachings, but may be divided into four groups each with its own doctrines: The first believe that God created from a pre-existing substance (*ṭīna*). The second (namely the *aṣḥāb al-nujūm*) view the stars as the starting point of the world and believe that they caused the emergence of the world when they started to move. The third exclusively glorify primordial material (*hayūlā*), which is supposed to have always existed and been unformed, and then at some time become differentiated through the emergence of accidents. The fourth group, to conclude, brings us back again to the Dualists, this time viewed from a different perspective, since they too are none other than a group of "Dahrīya" who believe in (two) primordial principles and believe that the world emerged from their mixing.

Even leaving the rather casually subsumed group of Dualists aside, the entire overview might seem a bit tendentious and conspicuously constructed. We hear of theses, not people. Even when a group happens to be mentioned by name, this is usually done by means of an abbreviation of their doctrine, with descriptions such as *aṣḥāb al-ṭabāʾiʿ* or *aṣḥāb al-nujūm*. Nevertheless, al-Māturīdī does not suffice with the mere theoretical view of things; in two other places in the *K. al-Tawḥīd* the image of the "Dahrīya" is enlarged upon in a more informative manner. Here, we finally find names, and ones that furthermore have a prominent position in Islamic heresiography.

One of these names is Aristotle. This might seem a bit unexpected, but there is good reason for it from the point of view of a *mutakallim*, since the ancient philosopher of course professed views that accorded with the *kalām* image of the "Dahrīya." He taught the eternality of the world, described an eternal elemental cycle, and assumed there to be a certain autonomy at work in nature, an autonomy that Islamic theology widely rejected. Al-Māturīdī thus sees him as the intellectual father of Materialism. But he was doubtless aware of the fame of the man that he was criticizing. This is probably why he makes an effort not only to appear as an opponent of Aristotle, but also as someone well acquainted with his work, citing his book *al-Manṭiq* ('Logic') and explaining, without it being contextually necessary, the meaning of the ten Aristotelian categories.[93]

The second name he mentions was of more pressing concern for a Transoxanian of the fourth/tenth century. These were the Ismāʿīlīs, whom al-Māturīdī mentions once as Qarmatians[94] and another time as Bāṭinites.[95] He also accuses them of being "Dahrites," but for a different reason: they are supposed to have professed the doctrine that the entire world was already structurally contained in the first existent (the Intellect).[96]

The little al-Māturīdī reports on the Ismāʿīlīs is very informative, showing him again to be quite up to date: the idea of the Intellect as the origin of ideas was a part of the Neoplatonic doctrines that had just arisen among the Sevener Shīʿites at that time. Muḥammad b. Aḥmad al-Nasafī (i.e., a Transoxanian) had introduced them; he was said to have occasionally had associations with the Sāmānid court. He was eventually executed in Bukhārā in 332/943,[97] but his teachings must have been noticed and discussed in Samarqand even during his lifetime, as al-Māturīdī's descriptions of them would suggest. It is a remarkable observation that the Neoplatonic beginnings of Ismāʿīlism, which had such a far-reaching legacy over the course of history, are referred to doxographically for the first time in *K. al-Tawḥīd*.

Still, the comments on the Ismāʿīlīs are only an aside within a greater argument that al-Māturīdī was carrying on with the "Dahrīya" and in particular the Dualists. The emphasis of the dispute lay elsewhere altogether, as we

---

93 Ibid., 147.12ff., where Aristotle is described as the *ṣāḥib* of the Dahrite teachings. Philosophical views are elsewhere treated as heresies in *kalām*, similarly to the views of the Dualists, Christians, etc. They raise questions (*masāʾil*) and put forward doubtful arguments (*shubah*), which a *mutakallim* must discuss in order to defend the truth (cf. on the Basran Muʿtazilites, Richard M. Frank, "Reason and Revealed Law: A Sample of Parallels and Divergences in kalâm and falsafa," in *Recherches d'Islamologie. Recueil d'articles offert à Georges C. Anawati et Louis Gardet par leurs collègues et amis* [Louvain, 1977], 134f.). Still, occasionally there were more precise responses to the ancient philosophers, as by Ḍirār b. ʿAmr, who is supposed to have written a "Refutation of Aristotle in Regards to Substances and Accidents" (van Ess, *Theologie*, vol. 3, 37 and ibid., vol. 5, 229).

94 *Tawḥīd*, 63 ult.

95 Ibid., 94.19.

96 Ibid., 63 ult.ff.

97 Presentations of his teachings are found in Heinz Halm, *Kosmologie und Heilslehre der frühen Ismāʿīlīya. Eine Studie zur islamischen Gnosis* (Wiesbaden, 1978), 12ff.; Paul E. Walker, *Early Philosophical Shiism* (Cambridge, 1993), 55ff.; W. Madelung, "Ismāʿiliyya," *EI*², vol. 4, 203b. On the transmission of his texts, cf. Rudolph, *Doxographie des Pseudo-Ammonios* (Stuttgart, 1989), 24ff.; on his teachings that the Intellect is the origin of all ideas, ibid., 130.

saw before, and to such a degree of involvement that one ultimately must ask what it was that provoked al-Māturīdī to maintain such an insistent polemic. Were there really so many Manicheans, Zoroastrians, and adherents to other dualistic systems in Samarqand that he was compelled to this form of argumentation? Did he really meet so many adherents of various "Dahrite" groups, among them Aristotelians, worshipers of the stars and elements, and "Materialists," such that Transoxania can virtually be made out to be an enduring sanctuary of the Hellenistic intellectual tradition?

The answer in both cases is probably in the negative, but a distinction is to be made between the "Dahrites" and the various groups of Dualists. The adherents of the dualistic religions were certainly present in Samarqand, even if not in proportion to the criticism they received in the *K. al-Tawḥīd*. The Zoroastrians had an appreciable presence, and likely were widespread throughout Iran in the third/ninth and fourth/tenth century. We even know that there was a Zoroastrian community in Samarqand in particular, since they were addressed by a letter written around 830 CE, the text of which is still extant.[98]

Even more numerous were the Manicheans, who could look back on a long and successful mission in Central Asia. Sogdiana, in fact, had even developed into a second important center for them along with their base in Iraq. They experienced centuries of a blossoming, though tumultuous history there; and al-Māturīdī, as well as later authors, encountered them there as a well-organized and defined group.

The spread of Manichaeism in Transoxania began from the lifetime of its founder and by the fifth century had already reached Central Asia (Lieu 1985, 178ff.; Haussig 1983, 232ff.; and Widengren 1961, 132ff.). Shortly before 600 there arose a schism of momentous consequence: the East, under the leadership of Samarqand, broke off from their leadership in Mesopotamia and developed their own unique doctrines as well as their own church order (Ibn al-Nadīm, 1871–72, 334.3ff.; Klimkeit 1987, 62f.; idem 1989, 22ff.; idem 1991, 7ff.; Lieu 1985, 179). This is the condition in which the Manichaeans encountered the Muslim conquerors, who certainly had no closer contact than that, at least initially. The clergy left Samarqand only shortly before the occupation by the Arab armies in the year 712 and turned further eastward to Turkish lands (Haussig, 237f.).

A Manichean community must have remained in the city, however, because two hundred years later it came to have great significance again. At that time the Caliph al-Muqtadir (r. 295–320/908–32) put great pressure on the Manichaeans of Iraq,

98 Mary Boyce, *Zoroastrians: Their Religious Beliefs and Practices* (London, 1979), 152ff.; on the letter, ibid., 157f.; cf. also Moshe A. Shaban, "Khurāsān at the Time of the Arab Conquest," in *Iran and Islam* (*Festschrift Minorsky*), ed. C.E. Bosworth (Edinburgh, 1971), 488.

causing them to leave the area; the Archegos of the Mesopotamian church was able to find refuge in Transoxania and set up camp in Samarqand where he spent his life in exile (Ibn al-Nadīm, 337.20ff. and 338.25f.; Monnot 1974, 97 (reprinted: idem 1986, 130); van Ess 1991–96, vol. 1, 420f.). He was probably not unwelcome there, since good relations with him must have been useful for foreign relations with the Uigurs and Turks, and Manicheans in the region came to be granted *dhimmī* status (Ibn al-Nadīm, 337.26.). Thus the community in Samarqand experienced a new upswing during al-Māturīdī's lifetime, and a few decades later was still strong. In the anonymous *Ḥudūd al-ʿālam* (written 372/982–83) we find out, in fact, that there was a Manichean convent (*khānqāh*) in the city (Minorsky 1937, 113). According to al-Bīrūnī (d. after 442/1050), the community of Manichaeans in Samarqand was the largest in the Islamic world (al-Bīrūnī 1878, 209.2/trans. Sachau 1879, 191).[99]

By contrast, it is much less plausible to assume that al-Māturīdī also engaged with the teachings of Marcion and Bardesanes in as much detail. Both were associated in some form or another with Transoxania, but the available reports do not give us a reliable picture and are not in accordance at all with the views referred to in the *K. al-Tawḥīd.*

The more complicated case is that of the Marcionites. We have an excellent doxographical reference that only recently came to be well known. It is from the *K. al-Maqālāt* of Abū ʿĪsā l-Warrāq and is transmitted to us in the *Kitāb al-Muʿtamad fī uṣūl al-dīn* from Ibn al-Malāḥimī (writing after 436/1044), a Muʿtazilite from Khwārizm (cf. Madelung 1981, 210f.). This sources show al-Warrāq to have been well informed on the Marcionites; his report is not only more detailed than any other reference in Islamic heresiography, but is also clearly nuanced. The (second) section sketches out Marcionite teachings as decidedly dualistic and thus corresponds with the image found in the rest of the Islamic sources. The much greater part, however, is without parallel in the Arabic literature according to the current state of research. There Marcion's doctrines are not interpreted as dualistic, but are presented in their authentic form, or at least in the way that we recognize them from much earlier Christian sources (translated completely by Madelung, ibid., 216ff., and afterwards, van Ess 1991–96, vol. 1, 432f.).

The conclusion to be drawn from the stupendous wealth of knowledge which Abū ʿĪsā l-Warrāq presents has certain consequences for our view of the Transoxanian milieu. It may be presumed that al-Warrāq used two very different sources. The second, shorter section of his entry is supposed to be based on the statements of the *mutakallimūn*, who, as is known, came up against a dualistically influenced form of Marcionite teaching (ibid., 431.). The longer, authentic report goes back to the "original" Marcionites, whom al-Warrāq must have also met personally. In this case

99 Under the name of Sabians, cf. van Ess, *Theologie*, vol. 2, 560n5.

they must have come from northeastern Iran; there are two other clues to this effect as well: Ibn al-Nadīm, who says in the *Fihrist* (339.18f./trans. 807) that the Marcionites in Khurāsān were numerous; and several reports on the so-called "Māhānīya," who apparently were present in Transoxania and were usually grouped together as a branch of the Marcionites (see Madelung 1981, 217ff.; idem 1988, 6; van Ess 1991–96, vol. 1, 433f.).

The hypothesis that would secure the Marcionites a firm place in the intellectual life of Central Asia has something to argue for it, but requires yet more proof, since both strands of evidence brought to support it are too problematic to be really sound. In regard to the "Māhānīya," our sources are contradictory. Also, Ibn al-Nadīm's reports on different religious conditions in the East need to be reverified: He overestimates the role of Buddhism in Transoxania,[100] and not only is he prepared to accord the Marcionites a large number of followers in Khurāsān, but he also states that there were many followers of Bardesanes in the area (and on into China!),[101] which is definitely no longer tenable.

The role of the Marcionites in Samarqand thus remains unclear. But our evaluation of al-Māturīdī's entry on them remains in principle unaffected. What he reports on their doctrine is not the apparently authentic Marcionite teaching as we know it from older Christian testimonies and Abū ʿĪsā l-Warrāq, which can likewise be associated with the "Māhānīya" of Transoxania. His discussions are based instead on Islamic interpretations of his time that developed in Iraq which classified Marcion as a dualist. Al-Māturīdī does not serve in this case as a witness to a particular regional development of the religion in Transoxania. He does not know the Marcionites better than others, and does not debate them in the manner of an actual flesh and blood opponent. He represents them very conventionally in a doxographical report which moreover is dependent on an Iraqi source (probably Ibn Shabīb).[102]

The same can be said without any reservations on his debate with the Dayṣanites. Their core lay demonstrably in Iraq,[103] and this is where all the information found in Muslim heresiographies originates. What al-Māturīdī himself writes probably goes back again to Ibn Shabīb. Even when Abū ʿĪsā l-Warrāq turns to a discussion of the Dayṣanites, he is also apparently dependent on a Mesopotamian source.[104] If, as just mentioned, Ibn al-Nadīm nevertheless states that there were Bardesanites in the East, this cannot have

100 Ibn al-Nadīm, 345.13f.; trans. Dodge, 824.
101 Ibn al-Nadīm, 339.6; trans. Dodge, 806.
102 On Ibn Shabīb, cf. Madelung, "Abū ʿĪsā l-Warrāq," 219.
103 Van Ess, *Theologie*, vol. 1, 426ff.
104 Madelung, "Abū ʿĪsā l-Warrāq," 214f.; van Ess, *Theologie*, vol. 1, 429.

been too significant, since this report is completely restricted to the Arabic sources and is not confirmed by any others, whether Sogdian or Chinese.[105]

Ultimately, al-Māturīdī's argumentation with the "Dahrīya" does not belie any noteworthy regional context. Nothing indicates that there was a special tradition of Hellenistic thought in Samarqand. There were of course a few meeting points: the Ismāʿīlīs for example, who had just opened themselves up to Neoplatonism; and al-Kindī's philosophy, which thanks to Abū Zayd al-Balkhī had found adherents in the East. Al-Māturīdī is quite conscious of them and they are mentioned to some extent in the *K. al-Tawḥīd.* But when he argues against the "Dahrīya," these newer trends of thought do not stand in the foreground, focus is given instead to older conceptual models more characteristically "materialistic" or Aristotelian, in a manner of speaking. In any case, our theologian never reports more than snippets of information; too little to have been informed by actual opponents. It is more probable that he depended on a literary source instead. This brings us one final time to Iraq, to Ibn Shabīb in fact, whom al-Māturīdī occasionally refers to as his source for the teachings of the "Dahrīya."[106]

There have of course been hypotheses that in eastern Iran a particular form of Hellenism had remained, but these are vague and have not lead to clear results. Their basis was the Graeco-Bactrian kingdom, which blossomed in the third and second century BC and has been brilliantly described by Tarn (1951). The archaeological find of Ai Khānum, excavated in the 1960s in Afghanistan also dates to this period (in summary, Bivar 1983, 188ff.). A fragment of a Greek text was even discovered there in which Platonic teachings of the Ideas and *methexis* are treated in dialogue form (Hadot and Rapin 1987, 224ff., esp. 244ff.).

Still, one ought not to formulate a hypothesis with this type of scattered historical data,[107] even when incorporating the Arabic sources, since they are also marginal, and moreover pose particular problems of their own. This is the case with regard to

---

105 H.J.W. Drijvers, *Bardaisan of Edessa* (Assen, 1966), 203, knows no parallels. It is also interesting that Īshoʿdād from Marw, a Nestorian from the ninth century, critiques Mani and Marcion but not Bardesanes.

106 *Tawḥīd,* 123.12, 126.1, 137.21, 141.9 and elsewhere; on the Ismāʿīlīs cf. above, 170, on Abū Zayd al-Balkhī, see above, 159.

107 Even more daring, but seemingly without basis, are theories that not only postulate a continuity between the time of the Diadochoi and Islam, but between the Greek settlement in Bactria and northwestern India and the religious views found there in the present day. This is focused especially in the Hindukush, but as it turns out, it is increasingly untenable in its entirety. Cf. the summarizing remarks by Karl Jettmar, *Die Religionen des Hindukusch* (Stuttgart, 1975), 18f., 33, 174 and 472f.

the discussion on whether the theology of Jahm b. Ṣafwān, a Transoxanian, may have had a Neoplatonic background (set off by Frank 1965; see in particular Zimmermann 1986, 135f. and van Ess, 1991–96, vol. 2, 499f.) or also the occasionally expressed hypothesis that early east Iranian mysticism was influenced by Neoplatonism and Gnosticism (see e.g., Schimmel 1975, 56f. on al-Ḥakīm al-Tirmidhī; in contrast see Radtke 1986, 551ff.). But another question, also pertinent at this juncture, has not yet been asked; namely, the reason the Ismāʿīlīs in Transoxania of all places embraced Plotinus' philosophy.

These are all open questions, the answers to which still have no consensus. Furthermore, they relate to the Platonic legacy and not the "Dahrite" teachings that are so conspicuously dominant in the *K. al-Tawḥīd*. Even when addressing the question of Neoplatonism some caution is in order. Even if its existence is demonstrable in eastern Iran, it could still have come from the West—meaning Iraq. Furthermore, it would be of interest to reexamine whether, alongside the oft-mentioned Ḥarrānians (Tardieu 1986 and idem 1987; on his thesis, see e.g., Hadot 1987, 10ff., but also the various critical reactions, e.g., by Concetta Luna 2001), the Christians (such as the Nestorians) should be considered possible transmitters of these teachings.

Such considerations go far beyond al-Māturīdī and so there is no reason to follow them further. His argumentation with the "Dahrites" and the Dualists in the *K. al-Tawḥīd* has been shown to not depend essentially on his particular religious milieu of Samaraqand, but rather on his incorporation of discussions that took place in other regions of the Muslim world. This is not really surprising in regard to these two non-monotheistic challenges, since in the East they had long been the target of the most serious criticism. This began, leaving Greek texts aside, with the Syrian Christian theologians. Their great teacher, Ephraem Syrus (d. 373),[108] set the tone, and other authors, such as

108 The most important text is Ephraem's *Hymnen Contra haereses*, which is exclusively dedicated to refutations of Mani, Marcion, and Bardesanes. It was published and translated by Edmund Beck (CSCO 169 and 170), and ought to be compared with the older edition of A. Rücker (BKC 61). On an evaluation of Ephraem's critique, cf. Edmund Beck, *Ephräms Polemik gegen Mani und die Manichäer im Rahmen der zeitgenössichen griechischen Polemik and der des Augustinus* (Louvain, 1978). On Ephraem in general, see Anton Baumstark, *Geschichte der syrischen Literatur mit Ausschluß der christlichpalästinenischen Texte* (Bonn, 1922), 31ff.; Ignatius Ortiz de Urbina, *Patrologia Syriaca* (Rome, 1965), 56ff.; Carsten Colpe, "Literatur im Jüdischen and Christlichen Orient," in *Orientalisches Mittelalter*, ed. W. Heinrichs (Wiesbaden, 1990), 101ff.

Theodor bar Kōnī (fl. 791/2),[109] Īshoʿdād from Marw (ca. 850)[110] and Moses bar Kepha (d. 903) followed his lead.[111] Muslims increased their criticism substantially in regard to scope and intensity. The most detailed example we have is the *Mughnī* of the Qāḍī ʿAbd al-Jabbār (d. 415/1025).[112] But the foundational

---

109 On the author see Baumstark, 218f. and Ortiz de Urbina, 216f., where the rather plentiful secondary literature is outlined. The book, the *Liber scholiorum*, is extant in two different versions, the recension of Seert (ed. Addaï Scher [Louvain, 1954], and French trans., Robert Hespel and René Draguet, *Théodore bar Koni, Livre des scolies* (*recension de Séert*) [Louvain, 1981–82], and the recension of Urmiah (ed. and trans. Robert Hespel), to which ought to be added the supplement of Silvan von Qardu (cf. Ortiz de Urbina, 143), edited and translated by Hespel as well. Overall, one achieves an image with hardly any rival in later Islamic polemic, in regard to its scope. Theodor bar Kōnī criticized all the dualistic groups named by al-Māturīdī: the Zoroastrians (Mimrā XI, 12 [Seert recension]), the Manichaeans (Mimrā XI, 58 and 59 [Seert recension] and Mimrā IX, 10 [Urmiah recension]), the Marcionites (Mimrā XI, 36 [Seert recension]), and Bardesanes (Mimrā XI, 49 [Seert recension]). But he also incorporates views into his polemic which the *K. al-Tawḥīd* judges as "Dahrite." Among these are the "Naturalists," whom he accuses of replacing God with the four elements (Mimrā XI, 12 [Seert recension]), and which correspond to the *aṣḥāb al-ṭabāʾiʿ* in Arabic. And in particular is Aristotle, who he mentions several times, in order to close in on points which are also of concern to al-Māturīdī: the teaching of eternal material (Mimrā XI, 9 [Seert recension]) and the ten categories (Mimrā VI, 17 and 18 [Seert recension]; 2nd collection, section 24ff. [Silvan von Qardu supplement]; cf. Mimrā VI. 73 and 76 [Seert recension]).

110 Baumstark, 234; Ortiz de Urbina, 217f., including further literature. The text in question is Īshoʿdād's commentary on Genesis (*Commentaire d'Išoʿdad de Merv sur l-Ancien Testament. I: Genèse*, ed. J.M. Vosté and C. van den Eynde [Louvain, 1950], trans. C. van den Eynde as *Commentaire d'Išoʿdad de Merv sur l'Ancien Testament. I: Genèse* [Louvain, 1955]), which has been edited by von Vosté and van den Eynde and translated by the latter. There one finds criticisms of Mani (14.16 and 116.24 Syrian text) and Marcion (116.24). Additionally the (meteorological) views of Aristotle are also described several times (31.20, 32.1, 39.12).

111 On this author see Baumstark, 281f. and in particular Schlimme, Der Hexaemeronkommentar des Moses bar Kepha, 1ff. Schlimme undertook a study of the long-unpublished text and translated it into German (ibid., 91ff.). The following citations are from his chapter and page count. Moses bar Kepha again criticizes the Dualists and the "Dahrites" in detail, in particular Mani (I, 15), Bardesanes (I, 14), Aristotle (I, 12), the "Materialists" (I, 13 and 46; cf. IV, A 18) and even the "Sophists" (I, 22). The tone of his polemic, for its own particular reasons, is decidedly "Islamic."

112 See ʿAbd al-Jabbār, *al-Mughnī fī abwāb al-tawḥīd wa-l-ʿadl*, ed. A.H. Maḥmūd and S. Dunyā (Cairo, 1960–65), vol. 5, 9ff., where among others, the teachings of the Manichaeans (10ff.), Dayṣanites (16f.), Marcionites (17f.), Zoroastrians (71ff.), Christians (80ff.), Sabians (152ff.), and idolaters (155ff.) are described. The representation of Iranian religions by ʿAbd al-Jabbār has been treated in detail by Monnot, *Penseurs musulmans*, 149ff.

argumentation had taken place earlier, in the latter half of the second/eighth century,[113] although unfortunately, hardly any extant literary examples are available. A certain impression can be formed, however, from the *K. al-Intiṣār* of al-Khayyāṭ (d. ca. 300/912).[114] Even more informative than this work, however, because of their more systematic approach, are the relevant works extant from Islam's "neighbor-religions" such as Judaism, the theology of which detectably came under the influence of Muslim *kalām* in the third/ninth century. There the format and argumentation of Islamic theology are reflected quite clearly, for example in the writings of the Iraqi Dāwūd b. Marwān al-Muqammiṣ[115] or the famous Saʿadyā Gaon.[116] A Zoroastrian text comes to mind as well, namely the *Shkānd-gumānīg wizār*, a unique Pahlavi work from the ninth century, left behind by Mardānfarrukh-ī Ohrmazddād. The Manichaeans and the "Dahrīya"

113 Ibid., 91ff.; van Ess, *Theologie*, vol. 1, 416ff.; Lieu, 83ff.

114 In the *K. al-Intiṣār* the Dayṣanites and Zoroastrians play a particular role. The "Dahrites" are mentioned often, the Manichaeans regularly. Examples are found in the indexes of Nader's edition and translation. Another interesting text from the early third/ninth century is the *Mīmar fī wujūd al-khāliq* by the Melkite bishop of Ḥarrān, Theodor Abū Qurra (d. between 825 and 830), published by L. Cheikho, "Mimar li Tadurus Abi Qurrah fi Wugud al-Haliq wa d-Din al-Qawim," *al-Machriq*, 15 (1912): 757–774, 825–842; trans. Georg Graf, *Die Arabischen Schriften des Theodor Abû Qurra* (Paderborn, 1910); and meanwhile republished by Ignace Dick, *Mīmar fī wujūd al-khāliq wa al-dīn al-qawīm* (Jūniya, 1982), the edition referenced here. There one also finds detailed polemics against Dualists—the Zoroastrians (201.2ff./trans. 24f.), the Manichaeans (205.-7ff./trans. 27ff.), the Marcionites (208.-3ff./trans. 29) and the followers of Bardesanes (209.10ff./trans. 30).

115 On this author, see Vajda, "Autour," *REJ* 126 (1967): 135–189 and 275–397. Cf. Simon and Simon, 45f. Al-Muqammiṣ left behind a religious-philosophical work (not completely extant), the *ʿIshrūn maqāla*, which was published and translated by S. Stroumsa. Its layout and content are heavily influenced in orientation by Islamic *kalām* (see al-Muqammiṣ, 23ff.). Also in polemic one can recognize numerous parallels: the Marcionites (chap. XIV.1) and the Manichaeans (see index) are refuted, but also the "Dahrīya," the *aṣḥāb al-hayūlā* (numerous citations found in the index), and the "Sophists" (here called *mutajāhila*, i.e., the skeptics; ibid., 25). In addition, there is an extensive entry on Aristotle, particularly his logic (chapters I and II).

116 The literature on Saʿadyā is plentiful and early on was compiled in a monograph (Jacob Guttmann, *Die Religionsphilosophie des Saadia* [Göttingen, 1882]). For an introduction see Simon and Simon, 46ff. Saʿadyā's major philosophical work, the *Kitāb al-Amānāt* likewise reflects Muʿtazilite *kalām*, both in regard to his arrangement as well as its religious criticism. The Dualists are named (especially in Saʿadyā, 48.12ff. [Arabic text]), the "Dahrīya" (ibid., 63.6ff.; cf. 55.7ff. and 57.-8ff.) and the skeptics (ibid., 65.-3ff.; see van Ess, *Erkenntnislehre*, 231ff.).

were both contended with there, which surely has to do with the influence of *kalām*.[117]

Seen in this light, al-Māturīdī stands in a long tradition of critique, and we must keep this in mind for our final evaluation. Our examination shows that his argument with the Dualists and the "Dahrites" in the *K. al-Tawḥīd* is a multi-layered structure. One can, in principle, maintain that al-Māturīdī, when attacking these two groups, does not differ from his Iraqi colleagues. He is defending Islam against a fundamental challenge and fighting in order for belief in the one God, *tawḥīd*, to triumph over its adversaries.[118] At the same time, his critique is different from comparable polemics, since it is not only based on this general goal, but also had certain motives, at least two of which ought to be emphasized again.

First, it ought to be clear by now that our theologian did not always debate the same opponents as a *mutakallim* in Baghdad or Basra might have. Though both were concerned with refuting the Dualists and "Dahrites," there were nevertheless key differences, especially in the degree of urgency given to the debate with them. One of the particularities of Transoxania, for example, was the Neoplatonic orientation of the Ismāʿīlīs; another was the significant presence of Manichaeans and Zoroastrians in the area. Although the historical presence of these latter groups had long since dwindled in Iraq, they held their ground in Samarqand, and maintained a strong position. Thus al-Māturīdī had good reasons to dwell on these religions more than others, since he was thereby laying the foundations for Muslims to claim supremacy for Islamic theology in a region where it had not been permanently established yet.

His thoroughness is only really explainable by considering his second motive, which is certainly of altogether greater significance. This can be evinced from the literary topos that al-Māturīdī relies upon, or to be precise, the manner and style with which he follows his exemplary literary model.

117 The text has been translated by P.J. de Menasce. On the text see Boyce, 155 and Carsten Colpe, "Iranische Traditionen," in *Orientalisches Mittelalter*, ed. W. Heinrichs (Wiesbaden, 1990), 83. The *Shkānd-gumānīg wizār* of course is not comparable to a systematic *kalām* work in its layout. Its purpose is to defend Zoroastrianism against Islam, Judaism, Christianity, and Manichaeism. It is interesting, however, that the "Dahrīya" and "Sophists" are attacked here (Mardānfarrūkh-i Ohrmazdād, *Škand-gumānīg wizār*, ed. and trans. by P.J. de Menasce [Fribourg en Suisse, 1945], chap. VI, 77ff.). The parallels here to the Arabic texts are unmistakable, such that the Islamic influence cannot be doubted.

118 It has long been known that the principles of Islamic theology show an anti-dualistic streak because they were formed in a dualistically imprinted environment. Nyberg described this phenomenon for the early period, and Nagel gives important remarks on the later periods (see his *Geschichte*, index, see "Dualismus," "Gnosis").

The work in discussion, as we have seen repeatedly, is a work of the Muʿtazilite Ibn Shabīb. But al-Māturīdī does not merely cite this text as is without commentary; in fact he makes his own additions, along with very telling remarks. According to him, Ibn Shabīb, generally speaking, or even the Muʿtazilites as a whole, dealt with both of these heretical groups, but the result of their efforts can only be described as lacking, since this ultimately did not lead to a refutation of the Dualists[119] or the "Dahrites,"[120] but merely to confusion in the minds of the Muʿtazilites.

Thus, to al-Māturīdī, the fight with disbelievers had more than just one battle front. It served not only to defend Islam, but at the same time to demonstrate the incompetence of inter-Islamic rivals. These reasons together explain why our theologian conspicuously expended so much effort with the Dualists and the "Dahrites," and so we can maintain that the upshot of his exposition is as follows: Islamic theology is doubtlessly superior against such disbelieving adversaries. But it will only conclusively triumph when it adheres to the arguments put forth by al-Māturīdī and dismisses the unfounded views and sophistry of the Muʿtazilites.

119 *Tawḥīd*, 86–92; 192.12ff., 235.19ff., 314.6ff. and elsewhere.

120 Ibid., 86–92, 120.5ff., 149–152 and elsewhere.

CHAPTER 6

Works

6.1 Lost Works

This argumentation with the Dualists and the "Dahrīya" has thus brought us back again to the Muʿtazila, and there can be no doubt that we have been led back once more to the core of al-Māturīdī's theology. The Muʿtazilites not only demanded the greatest amount of attention in the *K. al-Tawḥīd*, but the rest of what we find in our theologian's other works confirms this impression and convincingly demonstrates that he did not contend with any other Islamic sect with comparable intensity or tenacity.

Of course, the image that we can sketch of al-Māturīdī's other works is incomplete. Like most Islamic theologians of the first centuries, his texts seem to be lost to a great extent. Only the manuscripts of the *K. al-Tawḥīd* and the *Taʾwīlāt al-Qurʾān* or *Taʾwīlāt ahl al-sunna* are accessible to us. His other works are not even known through fragmentary quotations, but only as titles listed in the bio-bibliographical literature. In the case of al-Māturīdī these are likely to have been reliably transmitted, and we may profitably turn to them to gain some insight into his theological orientation.

As already mentioned, the most striking impression one gets from these titles is al-Māturīdī's permanent offensive stance against the Muʿtazilites. Refuting them clearly took up the greater part of his works, though a differentiation is certainly to be made between generalized argumentations and engagement with specific contemporaries of his: Presumably only the *K. Bayān wahm al-Muʿtazila*[1] is directed against the school itself. Many sources report this book to us and we may presume that it was a general disputation against the main theses of the Muʿtazilites. Aside from this work, al-Māturīdī seems to have generally taken on specific individuals and their works that circulated in his hometown of Samarqand, singling them out with special refutations. This is probably how his *Radd al-Uṣūl al-khamsa*[2] came about, as a text that took on a work by the Muʿtazilite *mutakallim* Abū ʿUmar al-Bāhilī. His numerous polemics against al-Kaʿbī were developed in the same way; they were not restricted

1 *Tabṣira*, vol. 1, 359.4; Ibn Abī l-Wafāʾ, vol. 2, 130.-4 (as *K. Bayān awhām al-Muʿtazila*); Ibn Quṭlūbughā, 59.2f.; Ḥājjī Khalīfa, 262; al-Murtaḍā l-Zabīdī, vol. 2, 5.11; al-Laknawī, 195.7 (as *K. Awhām al-Muʿtazila*); al-Baghdādī, *Hadīya*, vol. 2, 36.-3.

2 *Tabṣira*, vol. 1, 395.5; Ibn Quṭlūbughā, 59.5; al-Laknawī, 195.7f.

 | DOI 10.1163/9789004261846_008

to the topics already mentioned in the *K. al-Tawḥīd*, but clearly engaged with entire books of his. One of these, the *K. Radd awāʾil al-adilla li-l-Kaʿbī*,[3] was a polemic against a major work of this famous Muʿtazilite, namely the *Awāʾil al-adilla fī uṣūl al-dīn*,[4] also critiqued elsewhere in Arabic literature.[5] The two others focused on more specialized issues: in the *Radd Kitāb al-Kaʿbī fī waʿīd al-fussāq*,[6] al-Māturīdī articulated the old Murjiʾite theme on the judgment of sins; and in the *K. Radd tahdhīb al-jadal li-l-Kaʿbī* he appears, as we will see shortly, to have focused on matters of dispute concerning principles of jurisprudence.

The Muʿtazilites were certainly not the only people who evoked al-Māturīdī's protest. He wrote specific polemics against the Ismāʿīlīs (likely Muḥammad b. Aḥmad al-Nasafī); and against the Imāmites. In the case of the Ismāʿīlīs, the entry in the *Tabṣirat al-adilla* informs us that there were two parts to his fundamental refutation against them.[7] As for the Imāmites, they were addressed in the book, *Radd Kitāb al-imāma li-baʿḍ al-Rawāfiḍ*,[8] which was probably a response to the scholarly activity of Muḥammad b. Masʿūd al-Ayyāshī in Samarqand.

In both cases it is not difficult to determine where al-Māturīdī's critiques may have lay, and thus we lose no conceptual perspective by the loss of the texts themselves. This is not the case with the next text, the title of which shows that it was conceived in a much more multi-layered manner: al-Māturrīdī's *K. al-Maqālāt*.[9] A *K. al-Maqālāt* was likely to have been a doxography of various Islamic and possibly also non-Islamic religious opinions, and would have been quite handy for our purposes, promising not only additional insight into the religious milieu of Transoxania, but also the author's starting premises. There are,

3 *Tabṣira*, vol. 1, 359.3f. and vol. 2, 567.14f.; Ibn Abī l-Wafāʾ, vol. 2, 130.-4; Ibn Quṭlūbughā, 59.2; al-Murtaḍā l-Zabīdī, vol. 2, 5.11.

4 On this work see Sayyid, 49f.; van Ess, "Abū ʿl-Qāsem Kaʿbī," *EIr*, vol. 1, 360b; el Omari, 98.

5 Cf. Muṭahhar b. Ṭāhir al-Maqdisī, *al-Badʾ wa-l-tārīkh*, ed. Clément Huart (Leroux, 1899–1919), vol. 1, 135.5f. and Ibn Zurʿa (d. 398/1008), who refuted the chapter on Christians in al-Kaʿbī's *Awāʾil al-adilla*. Cf. Paul Sbath, *Vingt traités philosophiques et apologétiques d'auteurs arabes chrétiens du IXème au XIVème siècle* (Cairo, 1925), 52ff.

6 *Tabṣira*, vol. 1, 359.4f.; Ibn Quṭlūbughā, 59.4f.

7 Ibn Quṭlūbughā, 59.6 and al-Laknawī, 195.8 speak of a *Radd ʿalā l-Qarāmiṭa*; cf. Flügel, 274. Al-Nasafī (*Tabṣira*, vol. 1, 359.7f.) distinguishes between two books against the Ismāʿīlīs; one refutes the principles (*uṣūl*) of their doctrines, and one refutes the branches (*furūʿ*).

8 *Tabṣira*, vol. 1, 359.5f.; Ibn Quṭlūbughā, 59.5.; al-Laknawī, 195.8; cf. Flügel, 274.

9 *Tabṣira*, vol. 1, 52.9, 162.3ff., 359.3, 405.6ff., vol. 2, 829.1f.; 834.4; Ibn Abī l-Wafāʾ, vol. 2, 130.-5f.; Ibn Quṭlūbughā, 59.2; Ṭāshköprüzāde, vol. 2, 21.-2; Ḥājjī Khalīfa, 1782; al-Murtaḍā l-Zabīdī, vol. 2, 5.11; al-Laknawī, 195.7; al-Baghdādī, *Hadīya*, vol. 2, 37.1.

furthermore, two more indications of the particular significance of this book: Muslim readers seem to have particularly esteemed it, since it is usually listed directly after the *K. al-Tawḥīd* as the second book in their lists of al-Māturīdī's works. We also know that al-Kaʿbī penned a *K. Maqālāt al-Islāmīyīn* himself, a work that was often used as a source by later heresiographers;[10] it would be useful to know what relationship al-Māturīdī's *K. al-Maqālāt* bore to al-Kaʿbī's work.

We may end our discussion of his lost works here. Apart from those mentioned, we only know of two other titles,[11] which are not on theology, but law. Even these works point to al-Māturīdī's distinctive theoretical interests: They were not collections of rulings or explanations of juridical cases, but rather considerations on the foundations (*uṣūl*) of *fiqh*. His *Maʾkhadh al-sharāʾiʿ*[12] certainly dealt with the sources from which religious laws could be derived. The second text, the *K. al-Jadal*,[13] was probably dedicated to the methodological procedures of jurisprudence.

Apparently al-Kaʿbī responded to this second book with a refutation. We know that he was concerned with questions of hermeneutics and methodology,[14] and a *K. al-Tahdhīb fī l-jadal* is named among his works.[15] Al-Kaʿbī's reply also does not seem to have gone unanswered, since, as we saw earlier, there is a *K. Radd tahdhīb al-jadal li-l-Kaʿbī*[16] counted among al-Māturīdī's works. If appearances do not deceive us, the argument went back and forth, and it is highly regrettable that we cannot date this exchange with more precision. Both

10 It was used by al-Ashʿarī, ʿAbd al-Jabbār, and al-Shahrastānī among others; see van Ess, "Abū ʾl-Qāsem Kaʿbī," *EIr*, vol. 1, 360b. For a partial edition of the text see Sayyid, 63ff.

11 Another title, namely the *K. al-Durar fī uṣul al-dīn*, only emerges later in the sources, and may not refer to an authentic work. Ḥājjī Khalīfa (751) names it first without describing it further; al-Baghdādī, *Hadīya*, vol. 2, 36.2 and Flügel, 295 are based on Ḥājjī Khalīfa. One may assume al-Māturīdī's opus to have been more prolific than the titles mentioned here. Al-Nasafī, to whom we owe the first and most detailed list of works says at the end that he knew of other books attributed to al-Māturīdī (*Tabṣira*, vol. 1, 359.7f.).

12 *Tabṣira*, vol. 1, 146.8, 359.7, vol. 2, 784.16; Ibn Quṭlūbughā, 59.6f.; Ṭāshköprüzāde, vol. 2, 22.1; Ḥājjī Khalīfa, 1573; al-Laknawī, 195.8; al-Baghdādī, *Hadīya*, vol. 2, 37.1; cf. Flügel, 274.

13 *Tabṣira*, vol. 1, 395.7; Ibn Quṭlūbughā, 59.7; Ṭāshköprüzāde, vol. 2, 22.1f.; Ḥājjī Khalīfa, 1408; al-Laknawī, 195.9; al-Baghdādī, *Hadīya*, vol. 2, 36 ult. f.; cf. Flügel, 274.

14 Van Ess, "Abū ʾl-Qāsem Kaʿbī," *EIr*, vol. 1, 360b f. and idem, *Erkenntnislehre*, see index under "Kaʿbī."

15 E.g., Ḥājjī Khalīfa, 518; see Sayyid, 47, from which the suggestion comes to see al-Kaʿbī's *K. al-Tahdhīb fī l-jadal* as a refutation of al-Māturīdī's *K. al-Jadal*; cf. el Omari, 105.

16 *Tabṣira*, vol. 1, 359.4; Ibn Quṭlūbughā, 59.4; Ḥājjī Khalīfa, 518; al-Baghdādī, *Hadīya*, vol. 2, 36.-2.

contenders were of course Ḥanafite by *madhhab*. That which divided them most was their theology, and it would be particularly interesting if we could determine how far this difference played out, not only in creed but also in their respective jurisprudential methodologies.

6.2 Extant Texts

6.2.1 *The* Taʾwīlāt al-Qurʾān *or* Taʾwīlāt ahl al-sunna

We are justified in our complaints over the loss of so many texts, but the situation is not too dire. Al-Māturīdī's texts have been transmitted more successfully than those of the other major theologians of his time. Unfortunately, it is quite common for their texts to be lost, this being the case with al-Jubbāʾī, Abū Hāshim, al-Kaʿbī, and al-Ashʿarī. With regard to our man from Samarqand, however, more fortunate circumstances are at hand which cannot be said of his peers—not even al-Ashʿarī—since the few texts by al-Māturīdī that have remained extant are his main works, and thus provide us with an amenable starting point for reconstructing his ideas.[17]

Leaving the different pseudepigrapha aside,[18] we are dealing with two books to be precise. The one best attested to is the *Kitāb Taʾwīlāt al-Qurʾān* or *Taʾwīlāt ahl al-sunna*, al-Māturīdī's extensive commentary on the Qurʾān. Numerous

17 We only possess a few fragments from Abū ʿAlī al-Jubbāʾī and Abū Hāshim, and no single completely extant work (cf. Gardet, "al-Djubbāʾī," *EI*², vol. 2, 569f. In al-Kaʿbī's case, some texts have been found (cf. el Omari, 97), but there is no text among them in which he displays his theology systematically (as presumably in the lost *K. Awāʾil al-adilla fī uṣūl al-dīn* and his *ʿUyūn al-masāʾil*). Of course the state is better in regard to al-Ashʿarī, but not as favorable as one might assume on the basis of the various extant treatises and the *K. Maqālāt al-Islāmīyīn*. Gimaret, on the contrary, shows us multiple times that it is precisely his large systematic works such as the *K. al-Mūjiz* (which al-Pazdawī [*Uṣūl*, 2.1f.] presents as being particularly important) that are missing; see his "Un document majeur pour l'histoire du kalām: le Muǧarrad maqālāt al-Aŝʿarī d'Ibn Fūrak," *Arabica* 32 (1985): 188ff.; idem, "Bibliographie d'Ashʿarī: un réexamen," *JA* 273 (1985): 229ff.; idem, *La doctrine*, 18f. This is why his exposition of al-Ashʿarī's teachings (*La doctrine*) is essentially constructed on the basis of Ibn Fūrak's *Mujarrad maqālāt al-Ashʿarī*, and only secondarily on al-Ashʿarī's own extant works.

18 What is meant are the pseudo-Māturīdite treatises long recognized as forgeries, such as the *ʿAqīda*, the *Sharḥ al-Fiqh al-akbar* and others. These texts are completely unknown to bibliographers such as al-Nasafī, and are not from the pen of our theologian, but rather were compiled by adherents of his school. As such they do not belong to al-Māturīdī's work, but show instead how he was received. This is why they are not examined here, but rather in an appendix at the end of the study.

manuscripts are extant,[19] and there are several indications that this text, precisely, has always garnered attention and general admiration. His biographers made visible efforts to emphasize this book among the list of his works, and it is a noteworthy fact that the *Taʾwīlāt al-Qurʾān*, as far as we know, is the only work of al-Māturīdī's to be graced with an extensive commentary.

But before we turn our attention to this work of Qurʾānic exegesis, some words are due on the biographers' descriptions of it. The first instance is found not with Abū l-Muʿīn al-Nasafī, but with Abū l-Yusr al-Pazdawī; in his *Uṣūl al-dīn* he names al-Māturīdī's *K. al-Tawḥīd* and *K. al-Taʾwīlāt* by name, emphasizing them over others.[20] Al-Nasafī subsequently adopted al-Pazdawī's commendation and added to it, saying that the *Taʾwīlāt* was a book unrivaled in its domain (*lā yuwāzīhi fī fannihi kitābun*), since nothing which earlier authors wrote in this discipline comes close to it (*lā yudānīhi shayʾun min taṣānīfi man sabaqahu fī dhālika al-fann*).[21] Thus the exceptional nature of this book was proclaimed by the highest authority, and it is no wonder that it henceforth remained acknowledged as such; al-Nasafī's words are to be found later in several works by figures such as Ibn Abī l-Wafāʾ,[22] Ḥājjī Khalīfa,[23] and Murtaḍā l-Zabīdī.[24] Only a few authors diverged from this emphasis of the *Taʾwīlāt* and listed it as just one book of al-Māturīdī's among many.[25]

Additional information is offered by the already mentioned commentary (*Sharḥ*) written on the *Taʾwīlāt*. It was written by ʿAlāʾ al-Dīn Muḥammad b. Aḥmad al-Samarqandī (d. 539/1144), stepfather of the famous ʿAlāʾ al-Dīn al-Kāsānī (d. 587/1191),[26] himself a well-known Ḥanafite theologian and jurist who had the good fortune to have learned from Abū l-Muʿīn al-Nasafī and Abū l-Ḥasan al-Pazdawī (Abū l-Yusr's brother).[27] His *Sharḥ* is also to be found in several manuscripts, mostly from Istanbul;[28] but as of yet its theological content has not been published or studied. One passage from its introduc-

19 Listed in GAS, vol. 1, 605; for a closer description, see Götz, 63ff.
20 *Uṣūl*, 3.3.
21 *Tabṣira*, vol. 1, 359.16–18.
22 Ibn Abī l-Wafāʾ, vol. 2, 130.-3f.
23 Ḥājjī Khalīfa, 335f.; cf. Flügel, 295.
24 al-Murtaḍā l-Zabīdī, vol. 2, 5.11f.
25 Ibn Quṭlūbughā, 59.3; Ṭāshköpruzāde, vol. 2, 21 ult.; al-Baghdādī, *Hadīya*, vol. 2, 36.-3.
26 On Kāsānī cf. GAL, vol. 1, 375f. and suppl. vol. 1, 643; Heffening, "al-Kāsānī," *EI*[1], suppl., 115f.; Heffening-Linant de Bellefonds, "al-Kāsānī," *EI*[2], vol. 4, 690; Madelung, "The Spread," 154f. with further sources.
27 On him and his work cf. GAL, vol. 1, 374 and suppl. vol. 1, 640; Flügel, 312f.
28 GAS, vol. 1, 605; Götz, 69f.

tion is noteworthy because it characterizes al-Māturīdī's original work in an interesting manner; there Samarqandī says that the *Taʾwīlāt al-Qurʾān* was not one of the books that al-Māturīdī wrote himself, such as the *K. al-Tawḥīd*, the *Maqālāt*, the *Maʾkhadh al-sharāʾiʿ* or other texts. Instead, his most prominent students wrote it from his lectures. This is why it is much easier to understand than the works that he wrote himself, albeit that the *Taʾwīlāt* is not completely free of a certain obscurity in expression (*ighlāq fī l-lafẓ*) and vagueness in meaning (*ibhām fī l-maʿnā*).[29]

This means two things. First, al-Samarqandī has assured us that the content of the *Taʾwīlāt al-Qurʾān* actually goes back to al-Māturīdī, since what he describes of its contents correspond to his doctrine. This has since been confirmed by various researchers as well who focused on finding correspondences between the *Taʾwīlāt* and the *K. al-Tawḥīd*.[30]

In contrast, the wording of the *Taʾwīlāt* does not necessarily go back to al-Māturīdī, since its style appears too polished and articulate to be from the master himself. Al-Samarqandī thus emphasizes that the work was compiled by several students on the basis of their lecture notes; and since al-Samarqandī was a student of al-Nasafī and Abū l-Ḥasan al-Pazdawī, one may conclude that this understanding was the general view of the Transoxanian Māturīdites. This explanation moreover sounds quite convincing. The most varied works of the master were still at hand and could be compared easily; the other texts revealed a peculiar, quite obviously poor style of Arabic diction, while the Qurʾān commentary was largely free of such shortcomings. A comprehensive comparison such as this is no longer possible, since we only possess the *K. al-Tawḥīd* in addition to the *Taʾwīlāt*. However, a comparison between these two texts alone argues for the higher stylistic merit of the Qurʾān commentary, since despite many similar expressions and idiosyncratic phrases,[31] it is more

29 The Arabic text is cited in the introduction to ʿAwaḍayn's edition of the *Taʾwīlāt* (*Taʾwīlāt ahl al-sunna*, Cairo, 1971), 19.2ff.; German translation in Götz, 30, and van Ess, Review of *Kitāb al-Tawḥīd*, 556f.

30 ʿAwaḍayn, introduction to *Taʾwīlāt*, 20; Götz, 31.

31 For example, the opening words of the sentence: *wa-l-aṣl* (*ʿindanā* [among others]) *anna*... (*Taʾwīlāt*, vol. 1, 7.9, 28.8, 35.1 and elsewhere; *Tawḥīd*, 29.11, 37.4, 42.14 and elsewhere) for "At the basis (of our view) is..."; or another sentence opener: *wa ʿalā dhālika*... (followed directly by a substantive; *Taʾwīlāt*, vol. 1, 12.8, 19.7, 45.5 and elsewhere; *Tawḥīd*, 12.15, 42.5 and elsewhere) for "The exact same goes for..."; compare the linguistic parallels which Kholeif mentions in the introduction to his edition of the *K. al-Tawḥīd* (Ar. text, 57).

fluently expressed and adheres more closely to the norms of classical Arabic grammar.[32]

Despite the work's relative elegance and accessibility, it has received little attention until recently because for a long time the text could only be consulted from the manuscript and was not available in print. The attempt to edit it began in the 1970s; it is only now that the project to make the *Taʾwīlāt* accessible in its entirety and satisfy the requirements of a critical edition has been completed.

The first attempt was the edition begun in 1971 by Ibrāhīm and al-Sayyid ʿAwaḍayn in Cairo, but it was not completed. Only the first volume, which includes commentary on Q 1–2:141, was released. Around the same time, M.M. Rahman edited the beginning of the *Taʾwīlāt* (Q 1–2:161). His work was apparently finished in 1970, but only published in 1982 in Dacca and again in 1983, this time in Baghdad. The next attempt was the five-volume edition produced in 2004 by Fāṭima Yūsuf al-Khaymī in Beirut. She presented the text of the *Taʾwīlāt* in print for the first time in its entirety. However, this edition was only based on two of the numerous extant manuscripts (as well as the older, incomplete editions by ʿAwaḍayn and Rahman), and thus cannot be considered a critical edition. The Istanbul edition, in publication since 2005, is the work of various editors under the direction of Bekir Topaloğlu and is in another league altogether. It is based on six manuscripts which were selected out of a review of the entire number available (see introduction to vol. 1, 45–46). Moreover, it cites excerpts from al-Samarqandī's *Sharḥ* of the *Taʾwīlāt* in its critical apparatus. The edition was completed just recently and is arranged in eighteen volumes (including the index volume).

Given the trudging pace of the text's publication over the years, it is not surprising that the *Taʾwīlāt* has hardly been studied till now. What has been published on the text is small in scope and very general in its conclusions, such that a more precise image of al-Māturīdī's exegetical work is lacking to this day.

Rahman has written the only somewhat detailed study on the work. Originally part of his PhD thesis, it appeared in 1981 (in Dacca), under the title *An Introduction to al-Māturīdī's Taʾwīlāt Ahl al-Sunna*. He offered no further insights on the particularities of the text, but only general observations on the author and the *tafsīr* genre in the Islamic tradition. The same must be said about the article by Galli entitled "Some Aspects of al-Māturīdī's Commentary on the Qurʾān" (1982). Gilliot's article (2004) is, of course, much more informed but only touches on a very small and particular question. The contribution by Götz, "Māturīdī und sein Kitāb Taʾwīlāt al-Qurʾān," written as early as 1965,on the basis of the manuscripts, is still the best informed general introduction to the text.

32 On the linguistic irregularities in the *K. al-Tawḥīd*, see the following chapter.

There can be no doubt that the *Ta'wīlāt al-Qur'ān* is an exceptionally interesting and noteworthy Qur'ān commentary. The text contains an abundance of earlier exegetical material,[33] and what is more, also provides valuable information on many details of al-Māturīdī's own theological positions. Our study can only incorporate elements of this latter component, and not provide the comprehensive analysis which the entire work deserves. We not only lack substantial preparatory research; the task also requires more precise notions of the history of Qur'ānic interpretation in the eastern Islamic Oecumene before and contemporaneous to al-Māturīdī. The series of texts that we surveyed in the first part of our study, from Abū Ḥanīfa's correspondence up to the *K. al-Sawād al-a'ẓam*, was only intended to sketch out the development of the discipline of systematic theology. Different principles and categories apply in regard to Qur'ānic exegesis, and they must likewise be culled from the variety of transmitted texts available.

It is to be expected by now that the general categories that Goldziher put forth in his pioneering work *Die Richtungen der islamischen Koranauslegung* (1920), though theoretically still applicable today, are not relevant to al-Māturīdī's work. In the time period we are concerned with, Goldziher distinguished between essentially two types of exegesis: "traditional Qur'ānic interpretation" (ibid., 55ff.), and "dogmatic Qur'ānic interpretation" (ibid., 99ff.). The first of these began with the explanations of the Companions and culminated with al-Ṭabarī (d. 310/923), a contemporary of al-Māturīdī's, whose monumental *Tafsīr* Goldziher regarded as the high point and conclusion of traditional exegesis (ibid., 86ff.). Dogmatic interpretation, according to Goldziher's conceptualization, had only just begun to take its contours at this time; this began with the Qur'ānic interpretations of the Mu'tazilites of the third/ninth century (ibid., 99ff.), but ostensibly went a long time before finding an expression comparable to al-Ṭabarī's work in stature or acclaim. Only with the famous *Kashshāf* of Zamakhsharī (d. 539/1144) is this genre supposed to have developed an outstanding exemplar on par with its traditionalist counterpart.

This thesis suggests two successive phases with a similar course of development; the "traditional," then "dogmatic" types of exegesis, each only haltingly developed, the results of which, in principle, were fixed in adequate textual form after the zenith of their development. Goldziher himself never said this explicitly, indicating instead that various works had been lost which could change this image (ibid., 113f.). But this is how he was to be understood; thus it is not surprising that later summaries of his conclusions are characterized by exactly this tendency. Gätje, for instance, surveyed

33 Partly on the authority of well-known earlier authorities like Ibn 'Abbās or Ḥasan al-Baṣrī (see Götz, 39), and in part based the theological interpretations of the Mu'tazila, al-Najjār, Muqātil b. Sulaymān and others (cf. the indexes of the different volumes of the *Ta'wīlāt*).

the history of exegesis in this sense (1971, 53ff.) and formulates there, as a matter of fact, that "in the first centuries after al-Ṭabarī no Qur'ān commentary has been written which was more important" (ibid., 54f.; cf. also Neuwirth 1987, 119f.).

It is obvious that Goldziher's framework does not apply to al-Māturīdī's *Ta'wīlāt al-Qur'ān*. His view of things is not only complicated by al-Māturīdī's work, but also by the existence of a number of other commentaries that also ought to be reckoned into the circumstances of al-Māturīdī's time and place. These must all be consulted for comparison in order to categorize and understand the *Ta'wīlāt* more precisely. As noted earlier, this is not a feasible addendum to our study on his systematic theology, but calls for an entire study of its own with a different approach altogether. Thus, to close this discussion, only the most important authors will be listed, those who—along with the later commentator ʿAlā' al-Dīn al-Samarqandī—must be incorporated into this analysis, because they promise to be quite informative for future evaluations of the *Ta'wīlāt*:

a) Muqātil b. Ḥayyān (d. 135/753), active in Balkh; though he left behind no complete *tafsīr* work,[34] he had a number of exegetical views.[35]
b) Muqātil b. Sulaymān (d. 150/767 or 158/775), also from Balkh, from whom we possess several texts, available in modern editions, which in the past years have repeatedly been a topic of special research.[36]
c) Abū l-Qāsim al-Kaʿbī (d. 319/931), the Muʿtazilite and great opponent of al-Māturīdī. He also wrote a copious, apparently twelve-volume *Tafsīr*[37] that seems to be lost, but is found in fragments in later works.[38]
d) Muḥammad b. Masʿūd al-Ayyāshī (beginning of the fourth/tenth century), the Shīʿite teacher (but Sunnī before his "conversion"!), who appeared in Samarqand during al-Māturīdī's lifetime. His Qur'ān commentary remains partially extant, and has been published in Qum.[39]
e) Finally, Abū l-Layth al-Samarqandī (d. 373/983), the most noteworthy person to appear among the Ḥanafite scholars of the city in the decades

34 According to *GAS*, vol. 1, 36.

35 Van Ess, *Theologie*, vol. 2, 510ff.

36 Cf. especially John Wansbrough, *Quranic Studies: Sources and Methods of Scriptural Interpretation* (Oxford, 1977), 122ff.; Kees Versteegh, "Grammar and Exegesis: The Origins of Kufan Grammar and the Tafsīr Muqātil," *Der Islam* 67 (1990), 206ff.; Gilliot, 39ff.; van Ess, *Theologie*, vol. 2, 516ff.

37 Ḥājjī Khalīfa, 441.

38 Van Ess, "Abū 'l-Qāsem Kaʿbī," *EIr*, vol. 1, 360b; cf. el Omari, 104f.

39 *GAS*, vol. 1, 42; van Ess, *Theologie*, vol. 2, 567n67.

after al-Māturīdī. We also have a *Tafsīr* of his, which, as with many of his texts, is well attested to from the manuscripts[40] and was edited not long ago.[41] Since Abū l-Layth had a generally conservative attitude on questions of creed, his work is particularly fruitful for insights into early Ḥanafite exegesis in the East.

6.2.2 *The* Kitāb al-Tawḥīd

The *Taʾwīlāt al-Qurʾān* may be a very promising Qurʾān commentary, but it is not the most important theological text al-Māturīdī left behind. His main work is, of course, his second text still extant today: the *Kitāb al-Tawḥīd*, which has already been discussed several times and from now on will occupy the absolute center point of our study.

The eminent significance of this book for our knowledge of early *kalām* is often emphasized in the literature,[42] and no further emphatic phrases are needed to underscore the importance of this text. Nonetheless, it is helpful to once again consider the reasons for its special role. These help to distinguish the text from others and accentuate its unique and characteristic features.

The first important detail is the fact that the *K. al-Tawḥīd* is the oldest theological summa extant from Islamic civilization. It is true, as numerous sources tell us, that the Muʿtazilites wrote systematic treatises earlier than this on the entire repertoire of *kalām* topics,[43] and the *K. al-Tawḥīd* also shows us that al-Māturīdī knew such works and was dependent on them in many respects.[44] But this does not change the circumstance that these works were not successfully transmitted to us. Al-Māturīdī's text is thus the first of its type that we can access, and on the merit of this alone it occupies a special position.[45] Furthermore, in order to properly understand what this book accomplishes, one must also take into consideration the relevant geographical factors:

40 *GAS*, vol. 1, 445f.

41 Edited by ʿAbd al-Raḥīm Aḥmad al-Ziqqa (Baghdad, 1985) in three volumes (*sūras* 1–6); unfortunately I have been unable to examine the other three-volume edition which appeared in Beirut in 1993.

42 One has only to compare Schacht, "New Sources," 24 and 41; and the following reviews by Madelung, Review of *Kitāb al-Tawḥīd*, 150; Daiber, Review of *Kitāb al-Tawḥīd*, 302; Frank, Review of *Kitāb al-Tawḥīd*, 54.

43 An overview of their early theological literature is given by Madelung, "Der Kalām," 326ff.

44 Cf. in particular below, 214ff.

45 One can include in this generalization al-Ashʿarī, whose great systematic work, the *K. al-Mūjiz*, is missing. From among al-Ashʿarī's extant works, the *K. al-Lumaʿ*, ed. Robert J. McCarthy as *The Theology of al-Ashʿarī* (Beirut, 1953), has perhaps the most systematic character, but from the outset it is clear that it is not comparable to the *K. al-Tawḥīd*.

al-Māturīdī was not a Muʿtazilite nor did he engage in the Iraqi tradition of developed *kalām* sciences. He lived in Samarqand, and in accordance with its theological tradition, was a Ḥanafite. Up to that time the well-known theological texts in that region were of the type seen in the first part of our study, such as the *Fiqh absaṭ* or the *K. al-Sawād al-aʿẓam*. Juxtaposing these with the *K. al-Tawḥīd*, it becomes stunningly clear what a qualitative leap al-Māturīdī's work achieved in regard to the extent of the thematization, the formalized manner of its layout, and the technique of its argumentations.

A second aspect ought to be considered, one which bolsters the first. The *K. al-Tawḥīd*, as viewed from the perspective of its author's intellectual development, does not represent a preliminary rough draft nor a random snapshot. Everything points instead to it being a later work of the master's, a large-scale summary of his teachings that could only have been so systematically conceptualized because it was based on much preparatory work. The entire layout of the text argues for this, as does the wide range of the polemic that al-Māturīdī presents, as seen above.

In addition, there are two further indications that may help us to more precisely determine the time of composition. As we saw in our examination of his theological opponents, al-Māturīdī wrote critiques of, among others, the Muʿtazilite theologian Abū l-Qāsim al-Kaʿbī and the Ismāʿīlī philosopher al-Nasafī. It is not possible for this critique to have been formulated in the last third of his life as both the Muʿtazilite and the Ismāʿīlī can only have come to Transoxania when al-Māturīdī had already reached a ripe age: Al-Kaʿbī's return East is first detectable in 307/919 when he appeared in Balkh and was appointed vizier to Aḥmad b. Sahl. The period of al-Nasafī's activity may take us to an even later date, although in his case only approximate chronological statements are possible. He went to Transoxania when the leader of the Ismāʿīlī *daʿwa* in Khurāsān, al-Ḥusayn b. ʿAlī al-Marwazī, apparently (on his deathbed) sent him there to spread the mission further. Al-Marwazī himself became the leader of the Ismāʿīlī mission in northeastern Iran relatively late. The sources do not determine a specific date, but indications point to the 320s AH.[46] Thus al-Nasafī's activity in the region can hardly have been before 320/932. Leaving aside the unlikely possibility that al-Māturīdī argued against al-Kaʿbī and al-Nasafī from hearsay before they came into his line of sight, it would then follow that the *K. al-Tawḥīd* was written only after 320/932.[47]

46 See the relevant passage in the article "The Early Ismāʿīlī Missionaries in North-West Persia and in Khurāsān and Tranxoxania," Stern, 218ff.

47 This is, at the same time, the last argument for saying that the *K. al-Sawād al-aʿẓam* cannot have been written under al-Māturīdī's influence. The *Sawād* was written during the

Our third major insight into the text is owed to the later Māturīdite tradition. The reactions and commentaries we find there unequivocally show that the *K. al-Tawḥīd* had, for a long time, been the literary basis, if not the catechism of the Māturīdites. Al-Pazdawī said this explicitly. "One could be sufficed with it (= the *K. al-Tawḥīd*),"[48] he proclaimed, by which he meant that the remaining entirety of theological literature was of a lower rank. Other authors also demonstrate to us what incomparable importance was attributed to this text: They always named the text first in the lists of al-Māturīdī's works,[49] and when they wrote their own works of theology, it was usually done with reference to the work of their master, in paraphrases and glosses.[50]

The *K. al-Tawḥīd* is rightly seen as an indispensable text, and there can be no doubt that it deserves to be studied. At the same time, it ought to be made clear that an analysis of it is no simple undertaking. The work bars immediate understanding and presents a series of difficulties, characteristic to it in particular, which now must be briefly discussed.

The reader's problems begin early, first of all with the language al-Māturīdī uses. It is so intentionally abrupt and unrelenting that everyone who has occupied himself with the study of the text has remarked upon this fact. Vajda long ago mentioned "l'imperfection trop évidente de son style,"[51] and since then a series of authors have also mentioned this irritating characteristic.[52] As it would happen, al-Māturīdī's form of expression is not only strange to modern readers: Muslim theologians even from among his own students, also shared this sentiment. We have already mentioned ʿAlāʾ al-Dīn al-Samarqandī's statements to that effect. He compared the style of al-Māturīdī's Qurʾān commentary with the *K. al-Tawḥīd* and therewith concluded that the *Taʾwīlāt al-Qurʾān* could not have come from al-Māturīdī's own pen, since it was much more lucid and comprehensible than the *kalām* work that he wrote himself. But such a *sottise* is not

reign of the Sāmānid Ismāʿīl b. Aḥmad (r. 279–95/892–907), or about thirty years before al-Māturīdī assembled his theology in a decisive manner.

48 *Uṣūl*, 3.5.

49 *Tabṣira*, vol. 1, 359.3; Ibn Abī l-Wafāʾ, vol. 2, 130.-5; Ibn Quṭlūbughā, 59.1f.; Ṭāshköprüzāde, vol. 2, 21.-2; al-Murtaḍā l-Zabīdī, vol. 2, 5.10; al-Laknawī, 195.6; cf. Ḥājjī Khalīfa, 1406. One also ought to incorporate the testimony of the Bosnian theologian Āqḥiṣārī (d. 1025/1616), described below.

50 Consequently, these same texts can also contribute to the restoration of the original diction of the *K. al-Tawḥīd*, such as the *Jumal uṣūl al-dīn* by Abū Salama al-Samarqandī or the *Tabṣirat al-adilla* of Abū l-Muʿīn al-Nasafī.

51 Vajda, "Autour," 174.

52 Madelung, Review of *Kitāb al-Tawḥīd*, 150; Frank, Review of *Kitāb al-Tawḥīd*, 54; Gimaret, *Théories*, 178f.; van Ess, Review of *Kitāb al-Tawḥīd*, 556 and 560f.

all there is to mention. Even al-Pazdawī, who had particularly strong praise for the *K. al-Tawḥīd*, added the unavoidable qualification that "nevertheless, there is in the *K. al-Tawḥīd* a little obscurity and long-windedness, and the organization is somewhat taxing (*illā anna fī kitāb al-tawḥīd… qalīla inghilāqin wa taṭwīlin wa-fī tartībihi naw'a ta'sīrin*); if this were not the case, we could suffice with it alone."[53] These linguistic obstacles, long recognized as characteristic of the work, do not make our reading any easier, nor does it spare al-Māturīdī the accusation of not being quite at home with the Arabic language.

His mother tongue was certainly Persian, which happened to be undergoing a renaissance during the fourth/tenth century in the Sāmānid kingdom. This is also recognizable from certain lexical idiosyncrasies that are most likely explained on the basis of a Persian background. "Yes" for example, is always *balā* for al-Māturīdī (e.g., *Tawḥīd*, 253.21 and 284.-3). The concept of "being" is seldom expressed as *wujūd*, but almost always with *hastīya*; (e.g., ibid., 7.8, 24.2, 24.18, 41.18, 79.10, 104.8, 176.15 and elsewhere, cf. the pleonasm of *al-wujūd wa-l-hastīya* [in 42.8]) al-Nasafī notices this, explaining that in al-Māturīdī's view the (active and passive) verbal noun *wujūd* was ambiguous (*Tabṣira*, vol. 1, 162.9ff.). In addition, van Ess indicates (1981, 561) that his construction of interrogative clauses occasionally shows an analogy to Persian syntax, since al-Māturīdī occasionally begins the clause with a superfluous *an*, as for example in *na'rifu an kayfa…* for "we know how" (*Tawḥīd*, 138.11). This is in accordance with the rule in Persian that *ke* is supposed to precede interrogative clauses.

In any case, it is not only the dependency on Persian that makes al-Māturīdī's style appear so unusual. His Arabic also shows specific idiosyncrasies which do not correspond to the norms of classical grammar or to the theological discourse of his time.

In regards to word choice, his deviations from the norm are not too serious, as there were not many suitable alternatives. It suffices us to say as a general observation that al-Māturīdī preferred abstract terms, which is evident through such expressions as *ulūhīya* (ibid., 20.6, 132.19), *awwalīya* (ibid., 139.18, 147.7), *jismīya* (ibid., 120.16, 139.7), *ḥadathīya* (ibid., 103.8), *ḥaqīqīya* (ibid., 13 ult.), *shay'īya* (ibid., 86.4, 104.10ff., 238.14f. and elsewhere), *'araḍīya* (ibid., 150.5), *ghayrīya* (ibid., 138.12), *huwīya* (ibid., 105.1, 132.16f.), and *hastīya*. Allard saw in this coinage of new words a proximity to philosophical terminology (1965, 422f.). But in the context of the East one must also think of the influence of Karrāmite theology, which also distinguished itself by introducing abstract terminology into religious language (as noted above).

53 *Uṣūl*, 3.4f. The manner of articulation, moreover, shows that al-Pazdawī's Arabic is also not free of Persian influence. "*Qalīlu inghilāqin*" is actually closer to "without obscurity" in Arabic, but is certainly to be understood here as "a bit of obscurity."

In contrast, the syntactical problems are more serious. They are quite conspicuous, and are to blame if the overall style is considered generally awkward and unpolished. Nouns, for example, are sometimes strung together in a manner uncommon to abstract intellectual discourse (such as *Tawḥīd*, 4.14: *wa ammā l-ʿaql, fa huwa anna kawna hādhā l-ʿālami li-l-fanāʾ khāṣṣatan laysa bi-ḥikmatin* for "Reason tells us that it is not in accordance with wisdom for the world to come into existence only for it to go into non-existence"). This same example shows how the stylistic device of ellipsis may lead to incomprehensibility. Furthermore, al-Māturīdī does not hesitate to repeat words several times in a sentence, even if the result is quite awkward (e.g., ibid., 206.3f., *innahu la-ashaddu taʿaṣṣuban min qulūb al-rijāl min al-naʿami min ʿuqūlihā* for "He [has become] because of the [hardened] hearts of the people more stubborn than the pasture animal because of its binding ropes"). And finally, he often, noticeably, chooses abrupt transitions between main and secondary clauses (examples in van Ess 1981, 560f.).

The general impression of the *K. al-Tawḥīd* so far is that of a clumsily, if not poorly written text. But the author must be given credit for one factor which has not been touched upon yet. The same reason for his terseness is precisely what makes his prose so dense and concentrated. Both reveal just how unremittingly he wrestled with the state of theology in his times, and reflect his unique profile as a striving and innovative thinker. This must have often driven him to use the shortest and most direct form of communication possible.

At the same time, the *K. al-Tawḥīd*'s opaque language is not the sole cause for its decreased readability. Sometimes the problem lies in the defective transmission of the text. Until now we only have a single manuscript, presumably written relatively recently, in which the text has been copied—with many obvious mistakes.[54] The copyist did have the opportunity to refer to a second manuscript during the copying process; several times he puts a *kh* on the margin, to be understood as *nuskha ukhra*.[55] But this, too, did not enable him to transmit the text to us in a reliable form. In fact, the manuscript shows signs that it was often misunderstood by the copyist.

The editor of the text was thus dealt a difficult task; unfortunately, we must add that he did not exhaust all the available resources to ameliorate the

54 MS Cambridge University Library Add. 3651. Mentioned by Browne, 167. References to Goldziher's remarks in Spiro, 295 and Schacht, "New Sources," 24. Description by Kholeif, introduction to the edition, *Tawḥīd*, 57 (Arabic) as well as xiv (Eng.). The manuscript has two date entries, the first 1191/1777 and the second 15 Shaʿbān 1150/8 December 1737. The latter is thus the terminus ante quem for the writing of the manuscript.

55 For example, in fol. 57b. below, 59a above, 97a center, 110a center, 154b above, and elsewhere.

situation. In this respect, the *K. al-Tawḥīd* is not only burdened by language difficulties and a poor mode of transmission, but also problems in its published edition. Kholeif makes frequent suggestions for emendations in the text, and these in fact do help and facilitate understanding; but he occasionally also reproduces the manuscript incorrectly or intervenes when there is not much benefit in doing so. A great number of these mistakes have since been corrected by the thorough remarks of Daiber[56] and van Ess.[57] But even taking into account all of these suggestions for improvement, the text still remains problematic in its current form and seems to have been less reliably transmitted than most other theological works which we know.[58]

This is why it is even more regrettable that Kholeif neglected an important source of help for the restoration of the text; namely, citations of the *K. al-Tawḥīd* from later theological works. These have not always been recognized, since the texts of the later Māturīdites, as our most important sources for them, were, until recently, not easily accessible. However, we now know that a whole series of citations or paraphrases of the *K. al-Tawḥīd* can be found, and in light of the manuscript's unreliable transmission, these may be instructive for establishing a stronger foundation for the text.

The earliest text which is significant in this regard is a work that until now has hardly been studied: the *Jumal uṣūl al-dīn* by Abū Salama al-Samarqandī, which is fortunately extant in a manuscript (MS Şehid Ali 1648/1, fols. 1–18; edited by Kılavuz in Istanbul). Abū Salama lived in the later fourth/tenth century and was a "grand-student" of al-Māturīdī. As a theologian he was hardly eminent, but as a transmitter of his master's ideas, his role cannot have been paltry. The *Jumal uṣūl al-dīn* is more or less a brief summary of al-Māturīdī's teachings from the *K. al-Tawḥīd*. This is clear even from the outward structure of the text, but the correspondence between the two works can even be seen in the details, i.e., in its wording, as well as its ideas. Abū Salama's work consists in paraphrasing the main views of the *K. al-Tawḥīd* and thus gives us numerous bases to reconstruct its original form more precisely.

From later times we have references of varying quality. Al-Pazdawī, for example, cites al-Māturīdī occasionally (*Uṣūl*, 34.10–12, cf. 70.9, 87.14–17, 123.1–3, 203.7) and by

56 Daiber, Review of *Kitāb al-Tawḥīd*, 303–312.

57 Van Ess, Review of *Kitāb al-Tawḥīd*, 561–565.

58 The same is true *mutatis mutandis* for the new edition published by Topaloğlu/Aruçi in 2003. It does adopt a few corrections proposed by Daiber and van Ess, but nevertheless remains limited to the text of the Cambridge manuscript, without incorporating the secondary quotations of the *K. al-Tawḥīd* from later sources (on which see more below). For this reason, the references to the *K. al-Tawḥīd* here are given according to the older and more well known edition by Kholeif.

no means always in agreement (cf. ibid., 207.12f., 211.16f.). But his remarks are short and not rewarding, and thus offer us no real benefit for the text of the *K. al-Tawḥīd*.

Al-Nasafī's statements in the *Tabṣirat al-adilla*, however, are much more informative. Al-Nasafī mentions al-Māturīdī by name (cf. *Tabṣīra*, index) and repeatedly cites certain sentences from his texts (especially the *K. al-Tawḥīd*, but also from the *Ta'wīlāt* and the *Maqālāt*). We may also observe that the *Tabṣira*, even when not mentioning al-Māturīdī, has no more than one point of dispute with the *K. al-Tawḥīd*; after all, the full title of the work is the *Tabṣirat al-adilla fī uṣūl al-dīn ʿalā ṭarīqat al-imām Abī Manṣūr al-Māturīdī*, and rightly so. Often parallel formulations and arguments can be followed for pages at a time, in which al-Nasafī's words are, in general, more intelligible.[59] Thus his text not only helps us to interpret al-Māturīdī's theology, but can also be very useful in the philosophical reconstruction of the *K. al-Tawḥīd*.

The extent to which this is true of later texts has not been surveyed till now. In any case, one ought to look at the *K. al-Kifāya fī l-hidāya* by Nūr al-Dīn al-Ṣābūnī (d. 580/1184), in which our theologian is cited (see e.g., fol. 63a on the definition of knowledge, 110a on God's speech; 120a on the possibility of seeing God, and more). One also ought to take into account the various pseudepigraphal works that have been attributed to al-Māturīdī, especially the *ʿAqīda* and the shorter *K. al-Tawḥīd*.[60] They are a product of his school and, thus do not originate from his own hand. However, their authors made the effort to correctly cite al-Māturīdī's works, and in doing so borrowed much from his main work.[61]

---

59 If one compares, for example, *Tabṣira*, vol. 1, 448–467 with *Tawḥīd*, 176–186 or *Tabṣira*, vol. 2, 715–718 with *Tawḥīd*, 305–310 and many other places.

60 For a description and evaluation of these texts see the appendix below.

61 However, the hypothesis that Daiber put forth (in his Review of *Kitāb al-Tawḥīd*, 302f.) is not confirmed. He points to the Bosnian scholar al-Āqḥiṣārī (d. 1025/1616; on him see *GAL*, vol. 2, 443 and suppl. vol. 2, 659), who in the introduction to his book *Rawḍāt al-jannāt fī uṣūl al-iʿtiqādāt* claims to have seen a copy of the *K. al-Tawḥīd* in Mecca, and closes the work by expressing a desire to write a compendium on the science of *tawḥīd* (MS Berlin 1841, fol. 91b 1–5; the text has meanwhile been edited by Badeen, *Sunnitische Theologie*, 31–60 of Arabic text). Daiber concludes, not unreasonably, that Āqḥiṣārī's work is a summary of al-Māturīdī's teachings. Unfortunately, this is not the case: Āqḥiṣārī is clearly recognizable as a theologian of the Ḥanafite-Māturīdite persuasion, but what he wrote is no *kalām* work, but merely a devotional catechism (MS Berlin 1841, fols. 92 a–107b). He begins with an explanation on the essence of belief, starting with an interpretation of the famous *ḥadīth* in which Muḥammad lays out the specifics of belief to the angel Gabriel. This does not relate to the *K. al-Tawḥīd*, but more with the popular *ʿAqīda* of Abū l-Layth al-Samarqandī or other creedal works that Āqḥiṣārī himself names as forerunners (fol. 92b 1f.): the *Fiqh akbar* of Abū Ḥanīfa (what is probably meant is the so-called *Fiqh akbar II*) as well as the *ʿAqāʾid* of al-Ṭaḥāwī, ʿUmar al-Nasafī, al-Sanūsī, and al-Suyūṭī. Al-Māturīdī, however, is mentioned only once in passing, to say that he believed in the

Besides the inadequacy of the printed edition, the faulty nature of the manuscript, and the above mentioned linguistic problems, there remains only one final problem; namely, the final redaction of the text, which brings to bear on the focal point of our interest, i.e., the content of the work itself. It does seem as if the *K. al-Tawḥīd*'s present form cannot be described as the final or authorized one—if there had ever been such a form. Palpable indications point to the likelihood that we possess a version that is incomplete, and possibly not the original. Two reasons in particular may be mentioned here: First, Gimaret has already shown that al-Nasafī claims several times to quote the *K. al-Tawḥīd* word for word in his *Tabṣira*, while no corresponding passage can be found in the transmitted form of the work.[62] The text available to al-Nasafī then, must have been more extensive, or at least formulated in a manner that departs from the version we have. Second, the text as it is transmitted in the manuscript does not give the impression that it was given its final redaction by al-Māturīdī. On the contrary, the author never writes in the first person, but always in the third, imparting what the *shaykh* Abū Manṣūr or *faqīh* Abū Manṣūr is supposed to have taught. Furthermore, the name is mentioned in both cases followed by the formula *raḥimahu Allāh*. This is, by itself, not out of the ordinary, but indicates the often observed practice that the work was not written out by the scholar himself, but by one of his students.[63] This being considered together with the relevant observations regarding to al-Nasafī's *Tabṣira*, there is good reason to be skeptical of the transmission of the manuscript.

The text of the *K. al-Tawḥīd* that we must work with then, has its pitfalls and impasses.[64] It will only become more reliable when another manuscript

true teachings of Abū Ḥanīfa (fol. 93b 8f). Comments on Mālik b. Anas, Shāfiʿī, Awzāʿī (all on fol. 93b 9f.), Bishr al-Marīsī, Ibn al-Rāwandī (both on fol. 94b 1) and Jahm b. Ṣafwān (fol. 94b 2) are all found in this brief doxographical form.

62 Gimaret, *Théories*, 176ff.

63 This view is supported by the fact that the *K. al-Tawḥīd* occasionally gives the impression that heterogeneous statements are being transmitted in the form of a compilation, e.g. where two answers are provided to the same question (see van Ess, Review of *Kitāb al-Tawḥīd*, 557). This should not be over emphasized, however.If al-Māturīdī occasionally repeats himself, that does not necessarily mean that the text was compiled by his students from their notes. The main reason is more likely chalked up to his theological methods: al-Māturīdī was working on the basis of various textual models which he also discussed and commented on, and it was thus necessary that he speak several times on the same or similar themes.

64 A further example is offered by the last chapter of the edited text (*Tawḥīd*, 393–401; on the relationship between *islām* and *īmān*). The scribe clearly found this passage in only one of the copies available to him, since he notes at the beginning of the section that this is

is found and a better edition exploits the available material. The conclusion to be drawn from our findings is not that the text is unusable in its current form, but merely that it ought to be read carefully and that the final world cannot be given on some finer details of its contents. In principle, the available text reproduces the original *K. al-Tawḥīd* in its essentials, as the numerous parallels in the *Jumal uṣūl al-dīn*, the *Tabṣirat al-adilla*, and other works indicate. On this premise, then, it can serve as the basis for our study of al-Māturīdī's theology.

"an issue which was added to the text in one manuscript" (*mas'alatun ulḥiqat bi-l-matn fī nuskhatin*; ibid., 393.1 = fol. 202a4f. of MS Cambridge). One could also ask about the authenticity of this section, for which an affirmative answer seems reasonable, since the section fits with the text, in terms of content and theological position. The language also shows the same lexical particularities as before (see the beginning of the final paragraph at *Tawḥīd*, 401.5: *wa-l-aṣl 'indanā anna* ...; cf. above, 185n31).

PART 3

Al-Māturīdī's Theology

CHAPTER 7

Structures and Their Forerunning Models

7.1 The Structure of the *Kitāb al-Tawḥīd*

As we have already established, the *K. al-Tawḥīd* overshadows all previous theological texts from Transoxania in its scope, intellectual breadth, and methodology. It does not restrict itself to merely presenting a few important creedal statements in appealing formulations. Its goal is rather to provide a summa of Islamic theology as a whole, presented within a veritable edifice of incontestable proofs.

The themes upon which al-Māturīdī elaborates in this pursuit clearly do not all possess the same importance in his view, since his investigations vary in detail and length. His introduction, for example, wherein he presents the epistemological foundations of his teachings (*Tawḥīd*, 3–11), is relatively short. The pages that follow immediately thereafter, wherein he deals with the first significant *kalām* issue—the temporality and the ontological structure of the world—is even more compact (ibid., 11–17). Later the mode of presentation becomes noticeably more expansive. This is most evident in the next section, which is centered on a description and defense of monotheism (ibid., 17–176). His argumentation remains similarly meticulous and explicit when going on to discuss prophethood (ibid., 176–215), the question of God's influence on human actions (ibid., 215–323), sin and punishment (ibid., 323–373), and the proper understanding of belief (ibid., 373–401).

The ordering of these topics in precisely this manner is not particular to this text, but corresponds more or less to the customary organization of Islamic theological treatises.[1] Al-Māturīdī's development of the argumentation within

1 Details on the structure and composition of the work are discussed in following sections. The issue is also discussed by Daccache, 49–67. On the structure of *kalām* works and their thematic arrangement, cf. in general Gardet and Anawati, 136ff., esp. 152ff. The layout of the texts varies a great deal in some respects, but the sequence of main themes shows a certain consistency. Their unifying principle, which one can also see in the *K. al-Tawḥīd*, has been summarized succinctly by al-Ashʿarī (cf. his *Risāla ilā ahl al-thaghr*, ed. Muḥammad al-Sayyid al-Julaynid as *Uṣūl ahl al-sunna wa-l-jamāʿa al-musammāh bi-risālat ahl al-thaghr* [Cairo, 1987], 34.3ff.): According to this, a) it must first be explained that the world is not eternal, but created (= part A of *K. al-Tawḥīd*, cf. the outline below); b) then it should be shown that the world is the work of a single Creator (= part B); c) third, it must be shown that Muḥammad is

 | DOI 10.1163/9789004261846_009

each thematic discussion is likewise based on well-known systematic principles of *kalām*. If one nevertheless gets the impression that the author's presentation is not free of repetition and digressions, this may be chalked up to two further elements of the work's internal composition which interrupt the progress of its exposition.

The first and more common of these two elements consists of passages in which an issue that has just been discussed is taken up again in deliberate argumentation with explicitly named opponents. This means that the solution which al-Māturīdī favors is already long familiar to the reader, but is now being defended against objections and refortified, while the mistakes and contradictions of competing solutions are pointed out.[2] Such discussions show the dialectic structure of Islamic theology quite clearly and are not a stylistic peculiarity to our author, but are well known elsewhere in *kalām* literature.[3]

The second element that occasionally checks the development of ideas in the *K. al-Tawḥīd* is entirely characteristic to the text itself; namely, al-Māturīdī's many reiterations of his theses and their expositions throughout the work.[4] The reason for this is not any negligence on his part, but rather the fact that the backstory of the text's composition is not entirely straightforward. Focusing on these repetitions alone is not sufficient to familiarize us with this story; this first requires a more comprehensive overview of the *K. al-Tawḥīd* in order to understand how al-Māturīdī conceived of and worked out its organization.

---

truly God's prophet (= part C); this is to be followed, finally, by what Muḥammad taught on belief and religious duties (= themes of parts D to F).

2 Cf., for example, the discussions on epistemology in *Tawḥīd*, 25.17ff.; al-Kaʿbī's doctrine of God's attributes (ibid., 49.14ff.); God's *ikhtiyār* (ibid., 60.1ff.). See more below in the description of the text's structure.

3 On the format of dialectics in Islamic theology, cf. van Ess, "The Logical Structure of Islamic Theology," in *Logic in Classical Islamic Culture*, ed. G.E. von Grunebaum (Wiesbaden, 1970), 23ff.; on a distinction between topical examination proper and the treatment of debated issues (*masāʾil*) and doubtful arguments (*shubah*) cf. also Frank, "Reason and Revealed Law," 128, and elsewhere.

4 Examples of repetition include the refutation of those who profess the eternity of the world (*Tawḥīd*, 30.1ff., 121.5ff. and elsewhere); the proof that Muʿtazilite teachings correspond to the views of non-Islamic religions (ibid., 86.1ff., 120.5ff. and elsewhere); the discussion on whether or not God may be described as a "thing" (*shayʾ*) (ibid., 39.19ff. and 104.6ff.); and the discussion of whether God may be localized to a place (ibid., 67.9ff. and 105.7ff.).

THE STRUCTURE OF THE *KITĀB AL-TAWḤĪD*[5]

(3–11)	**Prolegomena: Epistemology**
3.6–4.4	1. Religion may not be based on the belief in authority (*taqlīd*), but must be based on proofs.
4.5–6 ult.	2. Knowledge of the religion is acquired through transmission (*samʿ*) and the intellect (*ʿaql*).
7.1–11.4	3. Humans have essentially three means of acquiring knowledge: a) the senses, b) transmission, c) intellect.
(11–17)	A. THE WORLD
11.5–17.4	**Proof for the createdness of the material world**
therein:	
11.14ff.	1. The ontological structure of the world
13.20ff.	2. That which is created may henceforth exist eternally despite its temporal origins.
(17–176)	B. GOD
	I. **General assertions**
17.5–19.5	1. The existence of the Creator
19.6–23.7	2. The unity of the Creator
	3. The "otherness" of the Creator
23.8–24.16	3.1. God's difference from all created things
24.17–25.16	3.2. The meaning of our statements about God
	Discussion:
25.17–27.17	a. Refutation of those who dispute our teachings on epistemology
27.18–29 ult.	b. Deducing that which is unseen from that which is seen
30.1–37 ult.	c. Refutation of those who profess the eternity of the world
	II. **God's names and attributes**
	Discussion:
38.1–39.18	a. God may not be described as a body (*jism*).
39.19–43 ult.	b. God may not be described as a "thing" (*shayʾ*).

5 Page and line numbers correspond to Kholeif's edition. The chapter headings and thematic descriptions are based solely on the inner development of the text. Section headings from the manuscript that occasionally come up in the text or in the margins, or those which Kholeif added to his edition, are not taken into consideration, even if some parallels naturally result.

(*cont.*)

	THE STRUCTURE OF THE *KITĀB AL-TAWḤĪD*
	1. God's essential attributes, in particular:
44.1–45.9	1.1 Free choice (*ikhtiyār*)
45.10–13	1.2. Power (*qudra*) and will (*irāda*)
45.14–46.2	1.3. Knowledge (*ʿilm*)
	2. God's attributes of action
	2.1. Creating (*takwīn*)
46.3–ult.	2.1.1. Proof of the existence of the attribute: against the (Muʿtazilite) equation of creating with the created
47.1–49.13	2.1.2. Creating is just as eternal as knowledge and power.
	Discussion:
49.14–59 ult.	Presentation and refutation of al-Kaʿbī's doctrine on the attributes
therein:	
53.12–55.2 &	2.2. Speech (*kalām*)
57.10–59 ult.	Discussion:
	a. The correct understanding of God's free choice (*ikhtiyār*)
60.1–14	a.a. Against al-Kaʿbī
60.15–62.22	a.b. Against those who profess an autonomous process of nature
62 ult.–63.14	a.c. Against those who profess an eternal material substance (*ṭīna*)
63 ult.–64.2	a.d. Against the Ismāʿīlīs
64.3–65.5	a.e. Fundamental critique against the "Dahrite" groups mentioned from a.b. to a.d.
	b. The correct understanding of God's names (*asmāʾ*)
65.6–66.3	b.a. Origins and meaning
66.4–67.8	b.b. All names apply to God eternally (with a critique of Jahm b. Ṣafwān)
	III. Anthropomorphic descriptions of God in the Qurʾān
	1. God's sitting on the throne (*al-istiwāʾ ʿalā l-ʿarsh*)—is God in a place?
67.9–70.19	1.1. The differing views of the throne as well as the possibility of a localization for God
70.19–74.3	1.2. The differing views of the "sitting"

THE STRUCTURE OF THE *KITĀB AL-TAWḤĪD*

74.4–75.2	1.3. Summary of his own teachings
75.2–22	1.4. Disputation with al-Kaʿbī
75 ult.–76.11	1.5. Against the idea that God is in the sky above us
76.12–77.11	1.6. The meaning of the terms "near," "coming," "going," and "sitting" in regard to God
	2. The vision of God (*ruʾyat Allāh*) in Paradise
77.12–81.2	2.1. Proofs for the reality of the vision of God
81.3–82.5	2.2. Seeing God does not mean comprehending (*idrāk*) Him
82.6–85.14	2.3. Disputation with al-Kaʿbī
85.15–ult.	2.4. In sum: The vision of God is indisputable, but takes place in a way that is not knowable to us (*bi-lā kayfa*)
	IV. Dispute with Muslim opponents
86.1–92 ult.	1. Against the Muʿtazila: Proof that their main teachings are close to the ideas of foreign religions (especially the Dualists and the "Dahrīya")
therein:	
e.g., 86.4ff.	1.1. Against the thesis: that which is non-existent (*maʿdūm*) has always existed
e.g., 86.16ff.	1.2. Against the thesis: God has not eternally been the Creator
e.g., 86.20ff.	1.3. Against the thesis: God's act of creation is not different from that which is created, God's will is not other than that which is willed
89.2ff.	1.4. Against the thesis: Accidents function in the material world according to their own sets of laws
90.12ff.	1.5. Against the thesis: Humans, based on their freedom, can act in a way that God did not know previously
92.15ff.	1.6. Against the thesis: God always does that which is best (*al-aṣlaḥ*)
	2. Against the Ismāʿīlīs: It is permissible to attribute names to God.
93.1–94.18	2.1. The Ismāʿīlīs' accusation that one would consequently commit assimilationism (*tashbīh*) is wrong.
94.19–96.16	2.2. The Ismāʿīlīs' attribution of God's names to the Intellect and Soul leads one astray.
	3. Dispute with al-Najjār on God's wisdom and providence
96.17–100.2	3.1. The question of why God created the world (against al-Najjār, the Muʿtazilites, and the Ismāʿīlīs)

(*cont.*)

THE STRUCTURE OF THE *KITĀB AL-TAWḤĪD*	
therein:	
97.16 f.	The definition of wisdom
100.2–7 & 100.13–20	3.2. God's command and prohibition (in agreement with al-Najjār)
100.7–12 & 100.20–101 ult.	3.3. God's promise and threat (in agreement with al-Najjār)
102.1–104–5	4. On the correct understanding of the maxim "Whoever knows himself, knows his Lord" (against Jahm b. Ṣafwān, the Mushabbiha, Jews, and Dualists)
104.6–105.7	5. Again: On the use of the terms "thing" (*shay'*), body (*jism*) and being (*huwīya*) with God
105.7–106 ult.	6. Again: Is God in a place (due to His sitting on the throne)?
107.1–108.13	7. On the application of the categories: what (*mā*), how (*kayfīya*), where (*ayna*), and action (*fiʿl*) in the teaching on God's attributes
108.14–110.7	8. Theodicy: God's wisdom and providence in the creation of harmful creatures and substances (with a critique of the Muʿtazilite teaching of the optimum)
	V. Refutation of the disbelievers
	1. General considerations
110.8–111.12	1.1. Summary of the arguments for his own doctrines
	1.2. The reasons for the emergence of false doctrines:
111.13–18	1.2.1. Belief in authority (*taqlīd*)
111.18–113.6	1.2.2. The incapacity of many people to think abstractly from the sensorily perceived world and their current condition (with a classification of the "Dahrīya")
113.7–18	1.2.3. The false assumption (of the Dualists) that evil cannot come forth from a good principle
113.19–118.13	1.3. General refutation of these views (especially against the Dualists and the *aṣḥāb al-ṭabāʾiʿ*)
118.14–121.4	1.4. On the correct conception of *tawḥīd* and its distortion by the "Dahrīya," Dualists, Jews, Christians, Muʿtazilites (who come close to the "Dahrīya" and the Dualists), al-Najjār and al-Burghūth, the Mushabbiha, and the Ismāʿīlīs

THE STRUCTURE OF THE *KITĀB AL-TAWḤĪD*

	2. The “Dahrīya”
121.5–123.11	2.1. Classification and refutation of the teachings of the “Dahrīya” (and the Dualists)
123.12–125 ult.	2.2. Arguments from Muḥammad b. Shabīb against the eternity of the world and for the temporal nature of the creation (with a critical commentary by al-Māturīdī)
126.1–135.4	2.3. Theses and arguments by Muḥammad b. Shabīb on the question of God as the Creator (with critical commentary by al-Māturīdī): What, where, and how is God to be qualified? How, from what, why, and when did God create? How does one describe His attributes of “power” and “creating?”
	Discussion:
135.5–137.19	Defense of the necessity of rational speculation (*naẓar*) in theology.
137.20–139 ult.	2.4. Arguments from Muḥammad b. Shabīb for the temporal and created nature of material bodies (with favorable commentary by al-Māturīdī)
139 ult.–141.7	2.5. Proof that the assumption of various creators is absurd (with an argument by Ibn Shabīb and more detailed argumentation by al-Māturīdī)
141.8–149.21	2.6. Presentation (based on Ibn Shabīb and others) and refutation of the teachings of the “Dahrīya”
therein:	
147.12ff.	The categories of Aristotle
149 ult.–152.3	2.7. Ibn Shabīb’s and al-Naẓẓām’s arguments against the teachings of the “Dahrīya” (with a commentary by al-Māturīdī)
152.4–153.5	2.8. Against the Sumanīya’s thesis that the world is with no beginning and incessantly sinks downward: al-Naẓẓām’s arguments with a commentary by al-Māturīdī
	3. The Skeptics
153.6–155.11	3.1. Against the Sophists: Ibn Shabīb’s argumentation with a commentary by al-Māturīdī
155.12–156 ult.	3.2. Against the Sumanīya: Ibn Shabīb’s report of a discussion between al-Naẓẓām and the Sumanīya; commentary by al-Māturīdī

(*cont.*)

	THE STRUCTURE OF THE *KITĀB AL-TAWḤĪD*
	4. The Dualists
	4.1. The Manichaeans
157.1–16	4.1.1. Presentation of their teachings
157.17–163.11	4.1.2. Refutation (23 arguments)
	4.2. The Dayṣānīya
163.12–164.5	4.2.1. Presentation of their teachings
164.6–170 ult.	4.2.2. Refutation (17 arguments)
therein:	
169.4ff.	A report on a discussion between Jaʿfar b. Ḥarb and a Dualist
169.12ff.	An accusation against the Muʿtazila as being incapable of convincingly refuting the Dualists
	4.3. The Marcionites
171.1–6	4.3.1. Presentation of their teachings
171.7–10	4.3.2. Remarks on the Sabians and Manichaeans
171.10–172.11	4.3.3. Refutation of the Marcionites (four arguments)
	4.4. The Zoroastrians
172.12–17	4.4.1. Presentation of their teachings
172.18–174.9	4.4.2. Refutation (ten arguments)
	4.5. Summary of his own position
174.10–18	4.5.1. Defense of creatio ex nihilo
174.19–175.9	4.5.2. Defense of the wisdom of God which does not forbid the Creator from creating evil as well
175.10–176.5	4.5.3. Reproach against the disbelievers for making limited human imagination the sole standard of knowledge
(176–215)	C. PROPHETHOOD
	I. Existence and necessity of prophethood
176.8–13	1. Three reasons why heretics deny prophethood: – they do not believe in God – they believe in God but not in God's commands – they believe in God and His commands, but not in revelation, because they wrongly assume that the intellect suffices as a means of attaining knowledge
176.14–ult.	2. Refutation of the first view
177.1–179.8	3. Refutation of the second view
179.9–186.9	4. Refutation of the third view

THE STRUCTURE OF THE *KITĀB AL-TAWḤĪD*

therein:	
183.5–184.2	4.1. The three ways to knowledge (the senses, intellect, transmission): – where they apply – possible impediments – God's command is only known through transmission
184.3–7	4.2. The three categories of things: necessary, possible, impossible. In order to judge what is possible we require transmission.
	II. Argumentation with Abū ʿĪsā l-Warrāq and Ibn al-Rāwandī
	1. Abū ʿĪsā l-Warrāq
186.10–188.13	1.1. Refutation of al-Warrāq's objections to prophethood (by means of two teachings from Ibn al-Rāwandī)
188.14–190.15	1.2. Summary of the arguments for prophethood
190.15–191.15	1.3. Application of these arguments in the special case of Muḥammad
191.16–192.2	1.4. Al-Warrāq's objections to Muḥammad's prophethood
192.3–193.13	1.5. Refutation of these objections
	2. Ibn al-Rāwandī
193.14–202.8	Detailed discussion of his views with the following elements: – Ibn al-Rāwandī's arguments for prophethood – thirteen objections by al-Warrāq – Ibn al-Rāwandī's answers – al-Māturīdī's commentary
	III. The Prophet Muḥammad
202.9–209.15	1. Proof of Muḥammad's prophethood by means of four indications: – his unique qualities – signs (*āyāt*), sensibly perceivable, brought about by him – signs accessible to human understanding – the special configuration of outward circumstances of his life and his time
209.16–210.10	2. Critique of the Jews and Christians who denied Muḥammad and only desired to acknowledge certain prophets
	3. Refutation of the Christian teaching of Jesus as son of God
210.11–19	3.1. Presentation of several christological views (from Ibn Shabīb)

(*cont.*)

THE STRUCTURE OF THE *KITĀB AL-TAWḤĪD*	
210.20–215.3	3.2. Refutation of the Christian position, and proof that Jesus is only a prophet
(215–323)	D. GOD AND HUMAN ACTIONS
	I. God's actions
	1. The heretical teachings of the Muʿtazila
215.4–216.2	1.1. Their view: God's actions must follow a rationally knowable benefit
216.2–10	1.2. The reason for their error: their disputation with the Dualists was carried out in the wrong way
216.11–15	1.3. Dissent within the Muʿtazilites on the creation of harmful things
216.16–221.5	2. The correct view: God's omnipotence, wisdom, and providence
	II. Human actions
	1. The basic conditions of human action
221.13–221.10	1.1. The human being is created for testing (*miḥna*). His natural disposition (*ṭabāʾiʿ*/*ṭibāʿ*) wishes to lead him astray, but he is given all the means (senses, intellect, transmission) to pass this test.
222.10–223.4	1.2. The transmission has that which is unambiguous (*muḥkam*) and that which is ambiguous (*mutashābih*) but it is nevertheless clear and not contradictory in and of itself.
223.4–224 ult.	1.3. Possible causes for mistakes and wrong interpretations (natural disposition, belief based on authority…) and their elimination by use of reason.
	2. The status of human acts: createdness and/or self-determination
	2.1. The concept of the Jabrīya (which is identified here with the Murjiʾa; cf. 229.1)
225.2–16	2.1.1. Their teachings: actions are completely attributed to God. Humans only act metaphorically.
225.17–227.8	2.1.2. Refutation of the Jabrīya: humans actually act.
	2.2. Views of the Qadarīya (i.e., the Muʿtazilites)
227.9–228.6	2.2.1. Actions are completely attributed to humans. They act autonomously.

THE STRUCTURE OF THE *KITĀB AL-TAWḤĪD*

between them both:	
228.7–229 ult.	2.3. al-Māturīdī's concept: Actions are attributed to God and also to human beings. They are created (*khalq*) by God, but chosen (*ikhtiyār*), acquired (*kasb*), and done (*fiʿl*) by humans.
230.1–236.10	2.2.2. Refutation of the Qadarīya: twenty-one arguments against the autonomy of human acts (with the accusation that Muʿtazilite teachings come close to Dualist teachings).
	Discussion:
236.11–256.6	Explanation and refutation of certain arguments of the Muʿtazila (esp. al-Kaʿbī's); proof that "the Muʿtazilites are the Zoroastrians of this community."
therein:	
254.13–255.7	Exegesis of the Qur'ānic verses from which one can deduce the createdness of actions.
	3. Capacity to act (*istiṭāʿa* and *qudra*)
256.8–ult.	3.1. Distinction between two types of capacity: – the availability of physical and material prerequisites for such an action – the capacity for the action itself
257.1–258.14	3.2. The necessity for this distinction
258.15–259.20	3.3. The duty of humans to fulfill divine commands is founded on their always being equipped with the first type of capacity, i.e., before the action (*qabla al-fiʿl*).
259.21–262 ult.	3.4. The second type of capacity is only given to people during the action (*maʿa al-fiʿl*) itself. Without this empowerment from God they are incapable of doing anything (as opposed to what the Muʿtazila say).
	3.5. What does the capacity to act entail?
263.1–13	3.5.1. According to al-Māturīdī, Abū Ḥanīfa, the Muʿtazilites: two opposing actions.
263.14–264.7	3.5.2. According to al-Najjār: only one action.
[lacuna]	
264.7–12	3.5.3. Refutation of al-Najjār's theses
	Discussion:
264.13–286.7	Explanation and refutation of various theses on the capacity to act, being charged with more than one can bear (*al-taklīf bi-mā lā yuṭāq*), the two actor model, the origin of evil, and

(*cont.*)

	THE STRUCTURE OF THE *KITĀB AL-TAWḤĪD*
	the foreknowledge of God (against al-Najjār, the Muʿtazilites in general, and especially al-Kaʿbī)
	III. God's all-encompassing activity
	1. God's will (*irāda*)
286.8–294.10	1.1. Al-Māturīdī's position: God wills all actions, even if He neither orders the bad ones nor deems them good. Nevertheless, His will is no compulsion (proved by numerous Qurʾānic verses).
294.11–303.15	1.2. Explanation and refutation of al-Kaʿbī's views
303.15–305.12	1.3. Abū Ḥanīfa's arguments against the Qadarīya Defense of his own position
	2. God's decision (*qaḍāʾ*) and decree (*qadar*)
	2.1. al-Māturīdī's position
305.13–ult.	2.1.1. God has decided and decreed all that happens.
306.1–307.15	2.1.2. The meaning of the terms *qaḍāʾ* and *qadar*
307.16–314.3	2.2. Explanation and refutation of al-Kaʿbī's views. Justification: Human beings, despite God's decree, are responsible for their actions.
	Discussion:
	a. Meaning and usage of the name al-Qadarīya
314.4–316.15	a.a. It applies to the Muʿtazilites, since they are the Zoroastrians of this community.
316.16–319.3	a.b. Wrong interpretation of the name by al-Kaʿbī
319.3–17	b. Refutation of Qadarite (i.e., Muʿtazilite) arguments for the thesis that the capacity to act exists before the act (with an exegesis of the pertinent Qurʾān verses)
319.18–320.12	c. Refutation of the Jabrite denial of the human capacity to act
320.13–321.16	d. Refutation of the Muʿtazilite claim that we (i.e., the Transoxanian Ḥanafites) are Jabrites. They themselves are Jabrites when understood properly.
321.17–323.13	e. Refutation of the Muʿtazilite claim that al-Najjār is a Jabrite. His teaching is not correct, but their teaching is much worse and is actually Jabrite.
(323–373)	E. SIN AND PUNISHMENT
	I. An axiomatic evaluation of sinners and their destiny
323.14–325.12	1. The Khārijite's incorrect teaching: Every sin excludes people from belief and brings them eternally to hell.

THE STRUCTURE OF THE *KITĀB AL-TAWḤĪD*

325.13–329.5	2. The correct teaching is that one must distinguish between major and minor sins. According to all other Muslims (except the Khārijites), small sins do not make one a disbeliever or cause one to go to Hell eternally.
	II. The problem of major sins
329.6–332.5	1. Mention of various teachings on the status of the person who commits a major sin (as a disbeliever, polytheist, hypocrite . . .); the corresponding punishment, and the basic relationship of actions to belief.
332.6–343.11	2. Al-Māturīdī's position: The person who commits major sins remains a believer but is not exempt from punishment, since one must take seriously both the threat (argumentation against the Murji'a) as well as God's promise (argumentation against the Muʿtazila and Khārijites).
	Discussion:
343.12–360.9	Explanation and refutation of al-Kaʿbī's teachings on how works belong to belief, the status of the person who commits major sins, and the meaning of repentance.
360.10–364.2	3. Elaboration on al-Māturīdī's position: only disbelievers will be in Hell eternally.
	Discussion:
364.3–365.8	Proof that the Muʿtazilites, according to their own teachings, cannot deny belief to a sinner.
	III. The intercession of the Prophet
365.9–368 ult.	1. Against the Muʿtazilite teaching that there can be no intercession for major sins: both major and minor sins may be the subject of intercession and God's forgiveness.
369.1–370.22	2. Against the Khārijite teaching that sin is obedience to the Devil: sin is an offense, but not an intentional following of someone else. God Himself does not accuse sinners of the same.
370.23–373.5	3. Summary of his own teaching: the main differences are between believers and disbelievers, not between believers and sinners. God's threat relates to disbelievers and sinning disbelievers in different ways. This is why the one who commits major sins may still receive the intercession of the Prophet (with exegesis of a relevant Qur'ān verse).

(*cont.*)

THE STRUCTURE OF THE *KITĀB AL-TAWḤĪD*	
(373–401)	F. BELIEF
	I. **The essence of belief: Affirmation in the heart**
373.8	1. The Karrāmites' thesis: belief is avowal (*iqrār*) with the tongue.
373.9–378.16	2. Refutation: belief with the tongue alone is hypocrisy. The essence of belief is the act of affirmation in the heart. Presentation of proofs from transmission (373.10–377.9) and the intellect (377.10–378.16).
378.17–379 ult.	3. Exegesis of Qur'ānic verses that refute the views of the Muʿtazilites, Khārijites, Karrāmites, and Ḥashwīya.
	Discussion:
380.1–381.10	a. Against the thesis that belief is only knowledge (*maʿrifa*). Belief can in a certain sense be described as knowledge, but in its essence it is affirmation.
381.11–385.10	b. On the proper meaning of the term *irjāʾ/al-Murjiʾa* (against the Ḥashwīya in particular). If the description Murjiʾa is legitimately used as a derogatory word (e.g., in *ḥadīth*), then it applies to the Jabrīya, Ḥashwīya or Muʿtazila.
	II. **The createdness of belief**
385.11–388.9	Belief is a human action, and all human actions are, as already proven, created (against "a group of the Ḥashwīya").
	III. **Against the *istithnāʾ***
388.10–392 ult.	No believer should add "if God wills" to the declaration of faith (against the Ḥashwīya, Muʿtazila, and Khārijites).
	IV. **The relationship between belief (*īmān*) and *islām***
393.1–394.10	1. Different views which separate the two concepts
394.11–401 ult.	2. Al-Māturīdī's position: Both terms mean the same thing, but explain its characteristics with different emphases.

7.2 The Bipartite Nature of the Work

A study of the *K. al-Tawḥīd* on the basis of this outline confirms the aforementioned impression: Its text is not entirely uniform; it is awkward at times and also labored in its composition. This is a result of its combination of two different structural features in one text.

The first of these features is the repetitions already listed above. They are particularly noticeable in the first quarter of the text (until page 110), the section in which teachings on God and creation are discussed. Even later, the presentation is not completely free of repetition, which often leads to the impression of a lack of continuity or at least a lack of redaction.

The second feature is just as obvious, or perhaps even more so. The *K. al-Tawḥīd* as a whole, despite some small quirks, is not confusing or disorganized by any means, but seems to be well-thought out from beginning to end and follow a unified plan: the larger thematic divisions (sections A-F) each occupy a specific place determined by their own inner logic, and are constructed in an internally consistent way such that they can be understood independently of one another.

Both structural elements (i.e., the book's uneven attention to detail and its confident general organization) seem incongruous at first sight, which is precisely why they may be of key significance for our evaluation of the text. It stands to reason that the concurrence of these two features can help us draw conclusions about the nature of the text's composition, and it would be well-founded to conclude that these two features correspond to two distinct phases in the genesis of the text.

The unified schema of the *K. al-Tawḥīd* attests to the fact that we are dealing with a single text, and not a conglomerate of various treatises possibly compiled by a student of al-Māturīdī's at a later time. This assertion might seem obvious, since the work has been transmitted as a fixed unity in its manuscript form, but given the various frictions present in the text, it must be emphasized again, especially since modern research has seen the thesis proposed that a later redactor was responsible for compiling the work.[6]

The repetitions in the text point to a different conclusion. They permit the hypothesis that the *K. al-Tawḥīd* was planned as a single work, but was not written in a single period. It is more probable that al-Māturīdī worked for a long period of time on this comprehensive summa of his theological views. It is even likely that he was able to refer back to preparatory works that he had already written on different occasions (ones dealing with a particular theme or refuting a specific idea); such works then found a space in the comprehensive system of the finished product. This is a more plausible explanation as to why the book's systematic layout nevertheless contains a number of repetitions and sections that are not quite related to one another.

6 Cf. esp. Pessagno, "The Uses of Evil," 60ff.

Such an idea is, of course, nothing more than a hypothesis, but a number of other features would seem to make it more compelling: The text does in fact contain other indications that also suggest that it was composed in several drafts and stages.

The most important criterion is the unusual use of introductory religious formulas, or doxologies. In Arabic books, standardized phrases such as the *basmala* or the *ḥamdala* are generally used only once as a prologue for the entire work. Al-Māturīdī opens his *K. al-Tawḥīd* in this way as well,[7] but this is not the only opening phrase in the book; later, three subchapters of the text open with such doxologies, contrary to custom. The first occurrence is in the transition to the question of whether it is sinful for humans to reflect on why God created the world.[8] Such introductory formulas appear again at the commencement of argumentation against the "Dahrites" and Dualists.[9] And finally, there is a last doxology that opens the analysis of human actions.[10]

This would suggest that al-Māturīdī is starting anew each time he makes such a transition to another topic. If our hypothesis so far is true, then each of these insertions marks the spot where one of his preparatory works (i.e., a smaller treatment of the topic written earlier), was incorporated into the layout of the *K. al-Tawḥīd*. The most interesting is the last of these breaks (i.e., the doxology on page 221), which not only signals a transition to the next theological topic at hand, but also signals the most important change in perspective for the entire text, effectively dividing the *K. al-Tawḥīd* into two "halves" of quite divergent characteristics.

Up to page 221 of Kholeif's edition, al-Māturīdī handles the subject of God with all of its concomitants (A: God's creation; B: God's being; C: God's revelation; D.I: God's actions). After page 221, however, he turns to the topic of human beings (D.II–III: human actions; E: people's sins; F: people's belief). This suffices to demonstrate the presence of a decisive break in the text, since its most significant thematic change takes place there.

The difference between the two sections of the *K. al-Tawḥīd* can also be illustrated in other ways. One has only to compare them with the texts written by the older Ḥanafite theologians of Transoxania. Such a comparison strengthens our newly-won impressions, and makes visible how the doxology on page 221 also represents a turning point in regard to al-Māturīdī's bond to the Ḥanafite tradition: All the topics discussed from that point on are

7 *Tawḥīd*, 3.1–5 with an introductory *basmala* and *ḥamdala*; a single concluding encomium is found on 401.8.

8 Ibid., 96.17–20.

9 Ibid., 110.9–12, where the section even begins with the word *nabtadi'u* ("we begin")

10 Ibid., 221.7–12.

common to older texts, from the letters to ʿUthmān al-Battī up to the *K. al-Sawād al-aʿẓam*.[11] This holds true as regards the description of human actions (with some restrictions), but it is even more evident in the parts where sin, punishment, and belief are discussed. All of these topics had already been discussed extensively in earlier texts, and formed the basis of long-standing doctrines that were more or less binding on a Ḥanafite theologian. Thus it cannot be surprising if al-Māturīdī's teachings in this second section do not sound new or original. Instead, they show how he based his positions on the ideas of his predecessors and took their views as a model.

A survey of the first half of the *K. al-Tawḥīd*, however, gives a completely different impression. Although we find instances now and then of themes that have meeting points with older doctrinal works, e.g., the explanation of the Qurʾānic representation of God[12] or certain aspects of how the attributes of the Creator should be conceived and interpreted,[13] these do not change the general perception that al-Māturīdī is taking up thoroughly new questions here. Neither epistemological theory (in the book's prolegomena) nor the createdness of the world, nor even theology or prophethood were ever dealt with by the earlier Transoxanian Ḥanafites in a way which was systematic or that can even be closely compared to al-Māturīdī's exposition in the *K. al-Tawḥīd*.

The *K. al-Tawḥīd* is thus divided into two sections that are situated differently in the religious tradition of Transoxania. In the first, al-Māturīdī embarked on new territory and was unique among his Ḥanafite colleagues in doing so; he elaborated on issues that had barely been discussed, and thus he needed to offer solutions where it seems no conceptual framework had been secured before him. In the second section, however, the theological terrain had long been established. It had guidelines on the basis of which Ḥanafites could orient themselves—indeed they had to, if they cared to be accepted at all within the school of Samarqand. Here al-Māturīdī acted primarily to defend the prevailing positions of his school and only developed them further when it seemed appropriate to the circumstances.

If this observation is correct, then it has even further consequences for the composition of the text. In a technical sense, each half of the *K. al-Tawḥīd* was likely to have been individually planned and worked out: As long as al-Māturīdī

11 It is interesting that the doxology does not come at the beginning of part D (i.e., on page 215), but instead on page 221, after God's actions and the themes of wisdom and providence have been explained. This brings the second half of the *K. al-Tawḥīd* even closer to the earlier Ḥanafite texts since they do not discuss God's actions, but do deal with every topic discussed starting from page 221 onward.

12 *Tawḥīd*, 67.9ff.

13 Ibid., 44.1ff.

was dealing with classical Ḥanafite themes, he could rely on a number of well-known older texts. When elaborating on newer themes, however, these sources helped little or not at all. In such cases he was compelled to forge new paths or seek out models from other theological schools. In fact, it can even be demonstrated that the entire first half of the *K. al-Tawḥīd* was conceived according to the formal models of treatises written by representatives of other sectarian affiliations.

Such an idea might sound a bit bold, but it is actually not difficult to ascertain the type of text which our theologian must have had at hand while writing his work. The sequence by which he proceeds in the book's first half, from epistemology (the prolegomena), to discussion on the world (part A), to God (part B), and then prophethood (part C), corresponds precisely to a schema that we know from earlier *kalām*. It is the method by which the Muʿtazilites articulated the first principle (*aṣl*) of their theology, the doctrine of *tawḥīd*, in regard to its choice of themes, sequence, and internal logic.[14] It may therefore be assumed with great deal of likelihood that al-Māturīdī had such a Muʿtazilite text in mind as he conceptualized his own exposition. It is even tempting to add yet another conclusion: that the possible text in discussion may not have only left an imprint on the format of the *K. al-Tawḥīd*, but even gave it its name, because it also bore the title *K. al-Tawḥīd* itself.

The similarity in the layout used by al-Māturīdī and the Muʿtazilites is clearest if the view is restricted to the first part of the *K. al-Tawḥīd*, (pages 3 to 221). The later discussions that follow are much less precise in their layout and can only be juxtaposed with the four remaining Muʿtazilite *uṣūl* with great effort. This is most achievable with the passage on the acts of human beings, where the second Muʿtazilite principle of *ʿadl* can be seen. Part E ("sins and punishment") and F ("belief") mix talking points that belong to the third (*al-waʿd wa-l-waʿīd*) and fourth *aṣl* (*al-manzila bayna al-manzilatayn*). As for the fifth principle (*al-amr bi-l-maʿrūf wa-l-nahy ʿan al-munkar*), which treats the issue of political leadership and the nature of community, one may only look for it in vain in the *K. al-Tawḥīd*. Hence al-Māturīdī did not construct his entire work according to the schema of the *uṣūl al-khamsa*, although there can be no doubt that he knew the schema quite well.

The idea that the textual model which al-Māturīdī followed also had the term *tawḥīd* in its title is merely a hypothesis. But what speaks in favor of this idea is the fact that the title *K. al-Tawḥīd* was often used by the early Muʿtazila. Ḍirār b. ʿAmr wrote a book with this name, as did Muʿammar, and al-Naẓẓām (van Ess 1991–96, vol. 3, 261 and 270), and Muḥammad b. Shabīb, to whom al-Māturīdī is certainly indebted.

14 The most informative overview of what the Muʿtazilites discussed under the term "*tawḥid*," as well as their other four principles is still Nyberg, *EI*¹, "Muʿtazila," vol. 3, 854ff. Cf. also Gardet and Anawati, 152f. and D. Gimaret, "Muʿtazila," *EI*², vol. 7, 787ff.

Now the objection could certainly be made that we know too little about the treatment of *tawḥīd* by the Muʿtazilites to come to these far-reaching types of conclusions. Such a hypothesis of literary dependency certainly entails significant imponderables; the early Muʿtazilite texts that would enable us to assert the same schema are all lost, and thus our image of the *uṣūl al-khamsa* is based primarily on texts written after al-Māturīdī's lifetime.[15] Another problem also faces us: later Muʿtazilite authors evidently altered their original literary model such that the form which we presuppose for al-Māturīdī's time had already gone out of use.[16]

Such considerations are worrying but they can be assuaged to a great extent. Fortunately, we have access to theological works from other religions which can be referred to for comparison. Written in Iraq in the ninth and early tenth century CE, they are also imprinted by Muʿtazilite *kalām* to such an extent that they can serve as a mirror of their themes and polemics[17] as well as their conceptual framework.

Two of the pertinent texts for this purpose are from Jewish theology, which is long known to have come under the influence of the Muʿtazilites early on.[18] We are dealing here with the famous *K. al-Amānāt wa-l-iʿtiqādāt* by Saʿadyā Gaon (d. 942 CE) and the *ʿIshrūn maqāla* by Dāwūd b. Marwān al-Muqammiṣ (ca. 900 CE), which have only recently been published and studied. Both have already proven useful for us in categorizing al-Māturīdī's critique of the

15 This is also true for the presentation given by Nyberg. It must be kept in mind that this was not a study of a specifically dated text, but rather a summary of the general understanding of the five principles.

16 See the examples in Gardet and Anawati (153ff.). A decisive change that took place over time relates to the place where prophethood was discussed in the sequence of topics. In early texts (from the third/ninth century), prophethood still constitutively belonged to the *aṣl* on *tawḥīd*, as the fourth theme after epistemology, the structure of the world, and the description of God. The parallels in Jewish and Christian theology, which are discussed presently, show this clearly and this schema is repeated in al-Māturīdī's *K. al-Tawḥīd*. This method was already archaic by al-Māturīdī's time; by his time, prophethood seems to have been separated from theology and to have been discussed only much later in an ancillary section. Cf., for example, al-Ashʿarī's *K. al-Lumaʿ* or the *Mujarrad maqālāt al-Ashʿarī* by Ibn Fūrak. We lack corresponding contemporary sources of the Muʿtazila, but in their later works from the fifth/eleventh century we also no longer find prophethood in the context of *tawḥīd*: cf., for example, the *Mughnī* of ʿAbd al-Jabbār or the *K. al-Majmūʿ fī l-muḥīṭ bi-l-taklīf* of Ibn Mattawayh. Thus al-Māturīdī stands within an earlier tradition; this further demonstrates his dependence on earlier models.

17 Cf. above, 177f.

18 For a general discussion, see Simon and Simon, 37ff., and Julius Guttmann, *Die Philosophie des Judentums* (Munich, 1933), 69ff.

Dualists and "Dahrīya;" they likewise help us now in our attempts to historically contextualize the first half of the *K. al-Tawḥīd*.

In brief, the decisive point afforded by such a comparison is that the first four main themes which al-Muqammiṣ and Saʿadyā discuss correspond precisely with the issues that al-Māturīdī discusses in the *K. al-Tawḥīd* from page 3 to 211 (i.e., till the end of part C). In addition, these themes are conceptually unified; this may be explained by the fact that they are a reflection of the first *aṣl* of the Muʿtazila, the teaching of *tawḥīd*, with all of its implications.

	Division of the *ʿIshrūn maqāla* (Beginning of the text up to section 14)[19]
Sections 1–2	Epistemology
Sections 3–6	Composition of the world
Sections 7–12 (start)	God
Section 12 (end–14)	Prophethood and transmission

	Division of the *Kitāb al-Amānāt wa-l-iʿtiqādāt* (Beginning of the text up to section 3)[20]
Introduction	Epistemology
Section 1	Createdness of the world
Section 2	God
Section 3	Revelation and prophethood

A third text adds to this comparison. This one is not by a Jewish author, but from a Jacobite Christian, Moses bar Kepha (d. 903 CE). Moses also lived in Iraq and was a longtime bishop of Mosul. We have a whole series of his books, all written in Syriac. One of these works is an extensive Hexaemeron commentary in five volumes,[21] where Moses uses all the scientific facts of his time to explain the Bible's description of creation. He does not restrict himself to this alone; the text also contains a prologue (described as Book I) in which an outline of Christian dogma is given. This section is highly interesting for our purposes, since the manner in which Moses bar Kepha explains epistemology, the createdness of the world, the Creator, and prophethood clearly shows that, in regard to doctrinal exposition, he was deeply influenced by the Muʿtazilite theology of his time.

19 Cf. al-Muqammiṣ, 44–271.

20 Cf. Saʿadyā Gaon, 1–145/3–179 of Rosenblatt's translation.

21 Cf. Baumstark, 281f. The text, as already mentioned, has not been edited, but is only available in a German translation by Lorenz Schlimme (*Der Hexaemeronkommentar*).

I have discussed the text elsewhere in more detail;[22] there more information can be found on the author, his works, and the relationship between Christian and Islamic theology in his time. However, it is appropriate to present the structure of the first book of the Hexaemeron commentary here because it contains, as can be seen, striking parallels to the layout of our *K. al-Tawḥīd*. This similarity, as indicated earlier, can most likely be explained by assuming that both al-Māturīdī and Moses bar Kepha were dependent on a Muʿtazilite model.

	THE STRUCTURE OF THE HEXAEMERON COMMENTARY BY MOSES BAR KEPHA (BOOK I)[23]
	Prolegomena: Epistemology
I 1	The sources of knowledge: belief in revealed transmission; the senses, rational distinction, and examination.
	A. THE WORLD
I 2(a)	The temporality and createdness of the material world
	B. GOD
I 2(b)	God's existence
I 3	God's unity
I 4	God's eternality
I 5	God's unlimited nature (i.e., God is not in a place)
I 6	God's unknowability[24]
I 7	The immutability of God; therein: allegorical interpretation of anthropomorphic descriptions from the Old Testament, e.g., "God sits," "God's throne," "God sees"
	[I 8–10: Considerations on the trinity and the Bible]
I 11	Different theoretical theses on the origins of the world
I 12	Against those who profess the eternity of the world (Aristotle and Proclus)[25]

22 See Rudolph, "Christliche Bibelexegese und muʿtazilitische Theologie. Der Fall des Moses bar Kepha (gest. 903 n. Chr.)," *Oriens* 34 (1994): 299–313.

23 My summary is based on the translation which Schlimme published as *Der Hexaemeronkommentar*, 92–182. The chapter division (I 1–50) is his, I added the division in the prolegomena.

24 Cf. *Tawḥīd*, B.I.1.: the "otherness" of the Creator.

25 Cf. B.v.2.: the "Dahrīya," especially B.V.2.6., where Aristotle is also refuted.

(*cont.*)

STRUCTURE OF THE HEXAEMERON COMMENTARY BY MOSES BAR KEPHA (BOOK I)	
I 13	Against those who profess the eternity of material ("old pagans")[26]
I 14	Against those who profess the five primordial principles (Bardesanes)
I 15	Against those who profess the two primordial principles (Mani)
I 16	Conclusion: The one God is the originator of creation
	[I 17–18: On the necessity and significance of names]
I 19	What does the creation point toward? The existence of God and some of His attributes such as omnipotence, wisdom, and providence.[27]
	[I 20–21: Meaning and origin of the word "world"]
I 22	Refutation of the Sophists and their objections to the view of creatio ex nihilo
	[I 23: How could God create the world so quickly?]
I 24	Why did God create the world as something sensory and transitory? So that people could draw their own conclusions from the world which was created in this way.[28]
I 25	Why did God create the world in time? Because He freely created it.[29]
I 26	Did God create the world in the way which His power allowed? No, because His power is immeasurable.[30]
I 27	Did God possess power and knowledge before the creation? Yes, since He possesses them eternally.[31]
	[I 28–29: Did God create in time?]
I 30	God's eternal foreknowledge

26 Cf. the *aṣḥāb al-hayūlā* in the *K. al-Tawḥīd* (as above, 149n9).

27 Cf. B.I. discussion b.: deducing that which is unseen from that which is seen.

28 Cf. B.IV.3. argument with al-Najjār on God's wisdom and providence, especially B.IV.3.1.: on the question of why God created the world.

29 Cf. B.II.1.1.: God's unrestricted choice.

30 Cf. B.II.1.2.: God's power.

31 Cf. B.II.1.2. and 1.3.: God's power and knowledge.

STRUCTURE OF THE HEXAEMERON COMMENTARY
BY MOSES BAR KEPHA (BOOK I)

	C. PROPHETHOOD
	[I 31–33: The circumstances of the revelation to Moses]
I 34	Proofs for Moses' prophethood
I 35–37	Definition and description of prophethood in general
I 38	Proofs for Moses' prophethood
	[I 39: Why Moses did not speak on the reason for creation]
	D. GOD
I 40	Why did God create the creation?
	[I 41–45: On the Pentateuch of Moses, the translation of the Old Testament, and the sequence of creation]
I 46	Against the philosophers: God is also the creator of the four elements.[32]
	[I 47–50: Questions on the Old Testament, especially the Book of Genesis]

7 Possible Sources

On the basis of our considerations so far a few conclusions can be established in order to properly assess al-Māturīdī's theology. It has been demonstrated that he referred to various older models in organizing his concepts, especially in the first part of the *K. al-Tawḥīd*, which is recognizably dependent on a Muʿtazilite textual model. This last insight, however, certainly has its limits. Although we may say with a great deal of confidence which type of text al-Māturīdī must have worked with, we still do not know the specific work to which he owes such essential directives for the organization of his own book.

In order to approach this question, or indeed the sources of the *K. al-Tawḥīd* at all, yet another further consideration is in order. But from the beginning we must bear in mind a rather large qualification. Whatever we would like to presume of al-Māturīdī's sources, and regardless of the type of acquaintance

32 Cf. the *aṣḥāb al-ṭabāʾiʿ* in the *K. al-Tawḥīd*.

we might presume him to have with the theological literature of the time, most of our speculations cannot be proven; almost all *kalām* texts of the third/ninth century are lost to us, as is unfortunately also the case with the majority of the texts that we will presently discuss. In the face of such conditions, our prospects are limited. We can only attempt to demonstrate a relationship between certain parts of the *K. al-Tawḥīd* and the ideas of earlier authors and see whether book titles have been attributed to them on themes relevant to our study. Actual proof, only to be had by a comparative study of the texts themselves, is ruled out; thus almost all conclusions that we may formulate on the sources of the *K. al-Tawḥīd* are hypothetical in nature.

Nevertheless, the book's last chapter is a notable exception, as previously mentioned. We do have access to the earlier Ḥanafite texts from Transoxania, and we have depended on them to recognize the bipartite foundations of al-Māturīdī's work. Our theologian clearly used these as sources for his presentation, and this can be proved for several parts of the *K. al-Tawḥīd*.

Although limited in extent, the influence of these texts in the passages is detectable where the divine attributes are explained[33] or those where the Qur'ān's depiction of God, i.e., "God's sitting on the throne" and the visio beatifica are discussed;[34] the early Ḥanafites did not have elaborate theories about these, but had definitive views of the type found in the *K. al-Sawād al-aʿẓam* in particular, the tenor of which was replicated by al-Māturīdī.[35]

His dependence on this Ḥanafite tradition becomes much more prevalent in the second half of the *K. al-Tawḥīd*.[36] There we find a series of classical themes dealt with extensively over the preceding centuries by that school, so it is entirely understandable if we discover that al-Māturīdī was indebted to the teachings of his predecessors. Moreover, he has no intention of denying his dependence on that tradition; he explicitly cites Abū Ḥanīfa several times when discussing human capacity to act,[37] the origin of *irjāʾ*,[38] as well as argumentation with the Qadarites[39] and the Khārijites.[40] He gives no detail about the great Kufan, only indicating what Abū Ḥanīfa is supposed to have thought,

---

33 *Tawḥīd*, 38.1–49.13, i.e., chapter B.II.1. and B.II.2 of our outline.

34 Ibid., 67.9–85 ult., i.e., B.III.

35 Cf. *K. al-Sawād* sections 11, 35 and 36 on the divine attributes, section 46 on God's throne, and section 30 on the visio beatifica.

36 I.e., in sections D-F.

37 *Tawḥīd*, 263.4f.

38 Ibid., 382.19ff.

39 Ibid., 303.15ff.

40 Ibid., 369.21ff.

but the little there is still allows us to recognize that he is citing the *K. al-ʿĀlim*[41] of Abū Muqātil al-Samarqandī as well as the *Fiqh absaṭ*[42] of Abū Muṭīʿ.

Al-Māturīdī thus knew the texts analyzed in the first part of our study first-hand. Although this sheds light on the literary models he acquainted himself with for particular topics, the broader question of his textual sources is still not solved, and has only just been asked. We still lack clues on large sections of the *K. al-Tawḥīd* for which we must assume he was working with sources from outside the Ḥanafite tradition.

The next step then leads us beyond the Transoxanian tradition. It is appropriate now to consider once more how great the influence that al-Māturīdī's theological opponents had on him. So far we have only discussed those theologians who were explicitly named in the *K. al-Tawḥīd* and specified which among them can be seen as actual adversaries of our *mutakallim*. Any such argumentation, however, did not occur on an abstract and inconceivable plane; these were disagreements on specific theses advocated in specific works. It is reasonable then to seek out the reverberations of such works in the *K. al-Tawḥīd*. This in turn raises the question of whether or not certain parts of al-Māturīdī's book were planned and elaborated in conscious argumentation with a specific "adversarial" work—which may also have been one of the sources he relied on.

One exemplary instance of such a case is the discussion with Ibn al-Rāwandī. Its thematic structure is clearly lineated and it is situated very conspicuously in the *K. al-Tawḥīd:* Ibn al-Rāwandī is mentioned for the first time on page 187,[43] and from that point on, he accompanies al-Māturīdī's discussions continuously up to page 202, where a final discussion of one of his doctrines occurs.[44] This suffices to make the described passage (186.10–202; i.e., chapter C.II. in our outline) appear as a textual unit, but two further indications, also strengthen this impression. First, the author does not mention any other theologian in this section as an authority. Second, the entire presentation is closed and revolves around a single problem; the demonstration of the necessity of prophethood, or (in another formulation) the credibility of those who affirm it. Al-Māturīdī achieves this by recapitulating Ibn al-Rāwandī's arguments point by point (in his argumentation against Abū ʿĪsā l-Warrāq) on this theme.

41 Cf. ibid., 369.21ff. with *K. al-ʿĀlim*, section 36 (discussion with Khārijites on the understanding of sins) and *Tawḥīd*, 382.19ff. with *K. al-ʿĀlim*, section 28 (on the origin of *irjāʾ*).

42 Cf. *Tawḥīd*, 263.4f. with *Fiqh absaṭ*, 43.5–7 (on the capacity to act) and *Tawḥīd*, 303.15ff. with *Fiqh absaṭ*, 43.7ff. (discussion with a Qadarite).

43 *Tawḥid*, 187.9.

44 The name is cited for the last time on *Tawḥid*, 199.17, but the teaching presented there ends at 202.8.

In brief, we can conclude that this is nothing other than the reworking of a text by Ibn al-Rāwandī. This thesis is also strengthened by the existence of other sources that inform us that Ibn al-Rāwandī occupied himself with this issue. He wrote a *K. Ithbāt al-rusul* as well as a *K. al-Akhbār wa-l-radd ʿalā man abṭala al-tawātur*.[45] Even the more well-known *K. al-Zumurrud*, also available in fragments, may have been dedicated to the same issue.[46] It is probable then, that al-Māturīdī had one of these works in front of him as he wrote this section of his *K. al-Tawḥīd*. And what he wrote himself was indebted to his choice of model to such a great extent that we can still discern it behind his own teachings.

The example of Ibn al-Rāwandī is not an isolated case. The manner in which al-Māturīdī draws from the writings of Muḥammad b. Shabīb also suggests that he was familiar with a specific work of his and utilized it, to a certain extent, en bloc. In his case we find the same phenomenon as mentioned above: He is cited in the *K. al-Tawḥīd* in a well delineated section where his name is regularly mentioned (121–176, with an addition at 210),[47] and what is cited consistently deals with the same theological issues. These passages where al-Māturīdī refers to Ibn Shabīb are predominantly dedicated to the refutation of disbelievers, starting with the "Dahrites," then the Skeptics and the Dualists (Manichaeans, Dayṣanites, Marcionites, Zoroastrians) in a comprehensive presentation,[48] and ending with a critique of Christianity.[49] It thus follows that Ibn Shabīb was likely the doxographic source on all these groups. An impression like the one we garnered of Ibn al-Rāwandī's influence on al-Māturīdī is again at hand: namely, that an entire section of the *K. al-Tawḥīd* can chiefly be seen as a theological contention dependent on a specific literary model (110.8–176.4; i.e., chapter B.V. of our outline; as well as 210.11–215; i.e., chapter C.III.3).

There is a distinction to be made between these two examples, however. In this case we cannot point to a relevant title of Ibn Shabīb's works dealing with the teachings of other religions. The tradition only knows one of his books, a

45 Both titles are named in Ibn al-Nadīm, *Fihrist*; cf. Johann Fück, "Some hitherto Unpublished Texts on the Muʿtazilite Movement from Ibn al-Nadīms Kitāb al-Fihrist," in *Professor Muhammad Shafiʿ Presentation Volume*, ed. S.M. Abdallah (Lahore, 1955), 72, as well as the translation of the *Fihrist* by Dodge, 422f. See also Madelung, Review of *Kitāb al-Tawḥīd*, 150, and Frank, Review of *Kitāb al-Tawḥīd*, 55. On his list of works see van Ess, *Theologie*, vol. 6, 433ff.

46 This is van Ess' view in particular, *Une lecture*, 16n3.

47 Specifically *Ṭawḥīd*, 123.12ff., 126–135, 137–141 and so on till 171.7; along with these is 210.18, which is actually related thematically to the previous citations.

48 Ibid., 121.5–176.7.

49 Ibid., 210.11–215.3; the indebtedness to Ibn Shabīb is indicated on 210.18.

Kitāb al-Tawḥīd, which seems to have been highly acclaimed.[50] This does not argue against our hypothesis, since a detailed refutation of disbelievers could certainly fit into the scope of a book entitled *K. al-Tawḥīd*, as al-Māturīdī's own text proves well enough. Even if this is not the case, the postulated source in question nevertheless must have been written by Ibn Shabīb.

Both examples allow for a comparison, in that they indicate the same working method: In both cases, an older text was integrated into the *K. al-Tawḥīd*, al-Māturīdī partly summarizing the ideas of its author, but more so commenting on and reworking them into his own paradigm. If this holds true in the case of Ibn Shabīb as well as Ibn al-Rāwandī, then it is reasonable to presume that the same process was undertaken with other theological opponents. And there are in fact signs that all his major adversaries whom we listed above can be brought in connection with one (or several) clearly delineated passages from the *K. al-Tawḥīd*.

Muḥammad b. Aḥmad al-Nasafī for instance, the Ismāʿīlī Neoplatonist, must be behind pages 93.1 to 96.16 (chap. B.IV.2.). There the Ismāʿīlī doctrine is described and vehemently attacked. Al-Māturīdī's acquaintance with the doctrine is so exact and so surprisingly up to date that only an original work, presumably al-Nasafī's *K. al-Maḥṣūl*,[51] can have been his point of reference.

The case is comparable to that of al-Najjār, the Ḥanafite from Rayy. His name is repeated continually throughout the *K. al-Tawḥīd*;[52] however, two sections may be identified as being specifically dedicated to his views: The first of these is in pages 96.17–101 ult., where God's wisdom and providence are explained by means of various examples and for which al-Najjār's *K. al-Luṭf wa-l-taʾyīd* may have been the basis.[53] After this come pages 263.14–264.12 (cf. also 265.15–18), where the human capacity to act (*istiṭāʿa*) is the focus; al-Najjār was well known to have had his own stance on this issue,[54] and this is reflected in such works as the *K. al-Istiṭāʿa* as well as the *K. al-ʿIlal fī l-istiṭāʿa*.[55]

This brings us finally to al-Kaʿbī, the great Muʿtazilite and al-Māturīdī's chief opponent. His case is naturally somewhat different, since al-Māturīdī did not

50 Ibn al-Murtaḍā, 71.9; van Ess, *Theologie*, vol. 6, 338, also names treatises on other themes. But he himself grants that these treatises may have been parts of a more extensive *K. al-Tawḥīd* (*Theologie*, vol. 4, 125).

51 On the *K. al-Maḥṣūl* cf. Poonawala, 42f.

52 Besides the places named here, he is also mentioned in *Tawḥīd*, 120.13ff. (as one name among others) and in 321–324, where al-Najjār is defended against attacks from the Muʿtazilites; furthermore his doctrine sometimes also plays a role even when his name is not explicitly given.

53 Ibn al-Nadīm, 179.-2; van Ess, *Theologie*, vol. 6, 377 (no. 12).

54 Cf. van Ess, "Ḍirār b. ʿAmr," 58.

55 Ibn al-Nadīm, 179.22f. and 179.26; van Ess, *Theologie*, vol. 6, 377 (nos. 14 and 15).

argue with him on individual themes, but on a foundational level. However, the many places in which we find his name in the *K. al-Tawḥīd*, are not just scattered throughout the book, but can actually be described as units dedicated to specific issues. In the first half of the text, al-Kaʿbī is only mentioned in the sections on the world (11.5–17.4; i.e., section A),[56] and the section on God's attributes and the description of God in the Qurʾān (38.1–85 ult.; i.e., B.II. and B.III).[57] In the second half, however, his figure becomes a considerable stumbling block. This is true in regard to all teachings on human actions (215–323; i.e., part D) as well as the issue of sin and punishment (323–373; i.e., part E).[58] It is evident that al-Māturīdī had to defend his own Ḥanafite convictions on these topics against the incisive objections of this Muʿtazilite theologian, and his persistent discussion with al-Kaʿbī can only be the result of a detailed acquaintance with his adversary's texts. It follows that this likely took place in conversation with one of al-Kaʿbī's main works, such as the famous *ʿUyūn al-masāʾil*,[59] if not as a refutation of several works altogether.

All this demonstrates that al-Māturīdī was steeped in the theological literature of the time, but it also shows that he was dependent to a considerable extent on the textual models in front of him. In this respect we are justified in returning to an earlier question (this time slightly modified); namely, which of the authors just mentioned (or more precisely, which text) could have been the formal model that al-Māturīdī followed in the first half of his *K. al-Tawḥīd*? Aside from specific discussions with opponents (such as al-Najjār, Ibn al-Rāwandī, etc.) this section does display formal unity. It must then—in regard to its structure and layout—also have had a unified model from which it worked. After all that has been said about the dependency on a Muʿtazilite *tawḥīd* schema, the original can only have been a Muʿtazilite text.

The answer to this question is again only speculative, but it stands to reason given our considerations up till now. If one of the texts named above, then the *K. al-Tawḥīd* by Muḥammad b. Shabīb deserves to be mentioned. Ibn Shabīb's book was the only book cited above with *tawḥīd* explicitly mentioned as a theme. Furthermore it enjoyed the reputation in its time as "an excellent book" on *tawḥīd*.[60] It is thus reasonable to presume that it was the formal model for the first half of al-Māturīdī's *K. al-Tawḥīd*. This means that Ibn Shabīb served al-Māturīdī in two ways: as a doxographical source for his argumentation with

56 Cf. *Tawḥīd*, 16.17.

57 In detail, ibid., 49.15ff., 60.3ff., 75.2ff., 82–85.

58 In detail, ibid., 236–256, 266–286, 294–303, 307–314, 316–319, 343–360.

59 Cf. Sayyid, 48 (no. 20).

60 Ibn al-Murtaḍā, 71.9.

disbelievers (110ff.), and as a formal model from which the entire structure of theology was treated, in its sequencing and main themes.

This relationship, as said, cannot be proven, but there are two indications that support this view:

a) As we saw above, the first half of the *K. al-Tawḥīd* does not follow just any model (i.e., one irrespective of chronology) in order to answer questions on *tawḥīd*, but a model that must have been older. This requirement is best satisfied by Ibn Shabīb since, as al-Naẓẓām's student, he fits into the milieu of the first half of the third/ninth century.
b) The epistemology section that al-Māturīdī presents at the beginning of his teachings (*Tawḥīd*, 4.5–11.4) reveals certain archaic traits. It is based exclusively on the tripartite nature of knowledge acquisition (senses/transmission/reason) and does not mention the later distinction between "necessary" and "acquired" knowledge, which had long been present among the Muʿtazilites of his generation, such as al-Jubbāʾī (see Frank 1974, 142n26, and my own, "Ratio und Überlieferung" [1992], n37). Furthermore, al-Kaʿbī's definition of knowledge (*ʿilm*) and deduction (*istidlāl*), which were of general interest in *kalām* (cf. van Ess 1966, 72 and 244), are not yet mentioned by al-Māturīdī. This again suggests an older Muʿtazilite source, and Ibn Shabīb is, again, a reasonable choice.

In sum, our considerations on al-Māturīdī's possible sources give the following image:

PART I (BEGINNING–215.3; 221.5)[61]

Structure	Ibn Shabīb, *K. al-Tawḥīd*
11.5–17.4	al-Kaʿbī, *ʿUyūn al-masāʾil* (?)
38.1–49.13	Older Ḥanafite texts (esp. the *K. al-Sawād al-aʿẓam*)
38.1–85 ult.	al-Kaʿbī, *ʿUyūn al-masāʾil* (?)
67.9–85 ult.	Older Ḥanafite texts (esp. the *K. al-Sawād al-aʿẓam*)
93.1–96.16	Muḥammad b. Aḥmad al-Nasafī, *K. al-Maḥṣūl* (?)

61 The first part, strictly speaking, ends at Tawḥīd, 215 (with the conclusion on the teachings of prophethood), the second begins at page 221 (with an explanation of human actions, and in particular with the doxology on that page). The section of text in between is a transition in which al-Māturīdī's conception of God's actions is summarized again. If much in this passage reminds us of previous discussions (esp. ibid., 96.17–101 ult.), it can be seen as a summary of part I, which is primarily a discussion of God.

(*cont.*)

96.17–101 ult.	al-Najjār, *K. al-Luṭf wa-l-ta'yīd* (?)
110.8–176.5	Ibn Shabīb, *K. al-Tawḥīd*
186.10–202.5	Ibn al-Rāwandī, *K. Ithbāt al-rusul* or *K. al-Akhbār wa-l-radd ʿalā man abṭala al-tawātur* or *K. al-Zumurrud*
210.11–215.3	Ibn Shabīb, *K. al-Tawḥīd*
	PART II (221.6–END)
221.6–END	Older Ḥanafite texts (esp. the *K. al-ʿĀlim wa-l-mutaʿallim* and the *K. al-Fiqh al-absaṭ*)
221.6–373.5	al-Kaʿbī, *ʿUyūn al-masā'il* (?)
263.14–264.12	al-Najjār, *K. al-Istiṭāʿa* or *K. al-ʿIlal fī l-istiṭāʿa* (cf. 265.15–18)

The results assembled here are not conclusive in nature, but must remain hypothetical as long as further verification on a wider textual basis is not possible. At the same time, the principle behind these hypotheses remains valid, since, regardless of which sources al-Māturīdī actually used in each case, it is still true that he remained extraordinarily committed to the literary models at hand.

This is the most important result of the present section. It illustrates to us al-Māturīdī's methods and how he worked on the basis of older texts for each distinct theme. This conclusion also helps us in another way; it enables us to answer a series of questions that have often been posed in regard to the redaction of the *K. al-Tawḥīd.*

For instance, the noteworthy fact that the text contains several doxological sections may now be explained; these elements of the text point to reworkings of other original sources. We can also explain why al-Māturīdī takes up and discusses several themes repeatedly; this is to be expected if one considers that the textual substrata of his discussion changes while he allows himself to depend heavily on their development of ideas. What is more, this understanding of his methodology allows us to reach another conclusion concerning the content of al-Māturīdī's theology, which in turn leads us to the subject of the following chapter. As we will show there, al-Māturīdī was reoccurringly indebted to different models while working out theological doctrine. Sometimes his theology bears the unmistakable imprint of his contentions with al-Kaʿbī; in other cases it is clearly under the influence of Ibn al-Rāwandī or al-Najjār. This is not surprising, given our previous considerations; it is in fact a logical outcome of al-Māturīdī's methods, further underlining his formulation of positions on particular theological topics in contention with specific antecedents.

CHAPTER 8

An Outline of al-Māturīdī's Teachings

Prolegomena: Epistemology

The *K. al-Tawḥīd* begins, as we have seen, with an discussion of epistemological questions.[1] Therein, al-Māturīdī explains why people follow numerous false beliefs and heresies and then clarifies which pathways of knowledge should be tread instead so that all the correct insights of religion can ultimately be attained. He presents his alternatives confidently, and as expected, displays an optimistic perspective on what can possibly be known. He does not discuss, for example, whether or not there are, in fact, proofs for the truth of a particular religion; that they exist is supposed to be certain.[2] It is only a matter of how they are to be found and what can prevent people from knowing them.

Al-Māturīdī arrives at the latter—i.e., the cause of all error—very quickly. It is the widespread phenomenon of belief based on authority (*taqlīd*), the inclination of so many to latch onto one or another intellectual or religious figure without actually understanding or even fathoming the bases of their views. The consequence of this is that by now every sect and orientation has found its adherents. This is also to blame for the persistence of these devotees in their adoption of deviant teachings and their belief that they are in the sole possession of the truth.[3]

Whoever frees himself of *taqlīd*, however, recognizes the criteria that will help him arrive at the proper doctrine. Such a person knows, namely, that among the many preachers who purport to possess religious truths, one must be located who does not merely make claims but also proves his teachings with convincing arguments.[4] We have the means at our disposal to carry out this rather difficult task because humans have access to three methods that make them capable of differentiating between truth and falsehood: the senses (*ʿiyān* as a pars pro toto) which we share with all living beings; inquiry (*naẓar*) with

1 *Tawḥīd*, 3.6–11.4; cf. the French paraphrase by Vajda, "Autour," 174–179; for a detailed discussion of al-Māturīdī's epistemology cf. Cerić, 63–106, and Daccache, 81–179.

2 Cf. *Tawḥīd*, 3.12f.: *illā an yakūna li-aḥadin … ḥujjatu ʿaqlin … wa burhānun … fa huwa al-muḥiqqu.*

3 Ibid., 3.6–11; on the critique of *taqlīd*, cf. also 59.13, 95.6, 111.14, 123.8, 168.8, 168.15, 197.2, 223.5, 363.19.

4 Ibid., 3.11–4.4.

 | DOI 10.1163/9789004261846_010

our own intellect (*ʿaql*); and transmission (*samʿ/akhbār*), in as much as it can be secured.[5] These never cease to help us find the answers to secular questions, and as such can also be of use in matters of religion, though certainly the importance of the senses retreats somewhat while rational inquiry and transmission carry a weightier role.[6]

What al-Māturīdī presents here is not conceptually new, and I have treated it in more detail elsewhere.[7] Thus it suffices at this point to emphasize again what can be described as the two characteristic features of his epistemology. First, al-Māturīdī is dependent on older Muʿtazilite models, since he knows a tripartite schemata for obtaining knowledge, but not the bipartite classification of necessary (*ḍarūrī*) and acquired (*muktasab*) knowledge which came to prominence with al-Jubbāʾī. Second, our theologian distinguishes himself by leaving people a relatively large degree of freedom for rational speculation to act. The intellect is said to be capable of proving the existence of God from His creation and of knowing what good and bad acts are. This greatly distinguishes al-Māturīdī's epistemology from that of al-Ashʿarī, who did not give human thought a comparable type of autonomy and fundamentally restricted the priority of the intellect in favor of transmission.

The consequences that follow from this epistemological framework are important for our subsequent examinations because they essentially determine the form in which al-Māturīdī argues and demonstrates his arguments. Indeed, he does not restrict himself to mentioning his epistemological foundations only once, as in the introduction to the *K. al-Tawḥīd*. On the contrary, he is concerned with reiterating these principles explicitly when he states that a certain argument is based on the impressions of the senses, rational inferences, or statements of transmission (especially the Qurʾān, seldom the *ḥadīth*).

This makes his discourse admittedly cumbersome at times. Furthermore, as we will soon see, his categorization of arguments into one of three categories does not work in all cases. But this resolute application of method creates a noticeable result overall: It leads al-Māturīdī to secure his theological views, when possible, on multiple epistemological grounds. This means that in regard to almost all the details of his theological doctrine, we are told why they are acceptable from the intellect as well as from transmission, and if possible also from the perspective of the senses.[8] Our theologian thus adheres to the principles of his introductory statements throughout the course of his work,

5 Ibid., 7.1–11.4.

6 Ibid., 4.5–6 ult.

7 Rudolph, "Ratio und Überlieferung."

8 For specific examples, cf. Rudolph, "Ratio und Überlieferung," 84f.

which is advantageous to the reader, since a clearly organized argumentation awaits—even if the premises upon which the demonstration of proofs operate are not always proven, but taken for granted.

8.1 The World

8.1.1 *The Contingency of the World*

8.1.1.1 Al-Māturīdī's Proofs

The first litmus test for the method just mentioned is a theme which always acts as an opener for the presentation of *kalām* texts: the proof that the sensible world that surrounds us may not be conceived of as an eternal universe, but rather as a contingent product of a Creator, created in time.[9] It was commonplace for a *mutakallim* to claim this, but al-Māturīdī nevertheless makes the effort to secure it intellectually and prove it painstakingly, since all of his further views on the role of the Creator and the role of humanity are based on these premises. Furthermore, he also needed to irrefutably prove the createdness of the world in order to be well-prepared for the confrontation with the "Dahrīya," i.e., those who taught that the universe was eternal.

The repertoire of arguments he presents is accordingly wide in scope. It incorporates all three of the mentioned epistemological pathways, a fact that al-Māturīdī himself points out with visible satisfaction.[10] Transmission says clearly that the world must be created;[11] the senses confirm it,[12] and the intellect can demonstrate it with irrefutable arguments.[13] Whoever claims in the face of these findings that this thesis is doubtful or unproven must then either be obstinate or a fool.

The series of arguments that our theologian assembles is not exactly linear, but is interrupted at times by opponents' objections, and in turn, his refutations against said objections. Nevertheless, the manner in which he proves his theses displays a largely coherent and internally consistent approach. In order to navigate our way through al-Māturīdī's thought, we will present these theses

9 This topic is at the focus of Daccache's book on al-Māturīdī (cf. especially 181–334); cf. also Cerić, 108–141.

10 *Tawḥīd*, 11.6f.: *al-dalīl … huwa shahādat al-wujūhi al-thalāthati allatī dhakarnā min subul al-ʿilm bi-l-ashyāʾ*.

11 Ibid., 11.7: *fa-ammā al-khabar …*

12 Ibid., 11.17: *wa ʿilm al-ḥiss …*

13 Ibid., 12.16: *wa ʿalā dhālika ṭarīq ʿilm al-istidlāl …*

here fully, illustrating his procedures step-by-step as he simultaneously tackles issues from multiple perspectives.

First argument: God Himself has revealed to us (in the Qurʾān) that He is the Creator of all things (*khāliqu kulli shayʾin*). This revelation has been transmitted to us in reliable ways (*Tawḥīd*, 11.7–9).

Second argument: No person ever claimed that they eternally (*qidam*) existed. Rather, everyone knows that they were born and grew up slowly over time. Thus our own experiences and the general transmission of people show us that living beings in the world are not eternal, but come into existence in time (*Tawḥīd*, 11.10–13).

Third argument: As our senses show us, all corporeal substances (*aʿyān*) are subject to necessity (*ḍarūra*) and need (*ḥāja*) of something else. It is a characteristic of that which is temporal to be dependent on something else, since that which is eternal possesses sufficiency (*ghinan* or *ghanāʾ*) in and of itself, i.e., autarky (*Tawḥīd*, 11.14–16).

Fourth argument: The same can be derived from the observation that existence of the living and the dead are mutually conditional. Neither of them is conceivable without the other, and that which is dependent on something else can only be created and temporal (*Tawḥīd*, 11.16–12.2).

Fifth argument: All sensible things unify in themselves varying and opposing natures (*ṭabāʾiʿ mukhtalifa wa-mutaḍādda*) the specific property (*ḥaqq*) of which would cause them to repel (*tanāfur*) and disperse (*tabāʿud*) from one another. As things nevertheless remain together, this can only be the work of an external Creator. Thus things are created and temporal (*Tawḥīd*, 12.3f.).

Sixth argument: The world consists of parts (*ajzāʾ wa-abʿād*). We know that these individual parts come into existence after they did not exist (*ḥādith baʿda an lam yakun*) and that they grow and become larger. This must then apply for the entire world, since the sum of finite pieces cannot be infinite (*ghayr mutanāhin*) (*Tawḥīd*, 12.5–7).

Seventh argument: The world contains both good and bad, small and large, beauty and ugliness, light and darkness. Opposites are signs of change and decay. What decays cannot possibly come into existence by itself (*Tawḥīd*, 12.8–11).

Eighth argument: As the intellect recognizes, a body (*jism*) is either at rest (*sukūn*) or in movement (*ḥaraka*). These cannot both occur in a body at the same time, and thus also cannot apply to a body in pre-eternity. Rest and movement, accordingly, have an origin, and thus exist temporally. If no body is conceivable without rest or movement, then all bodies, i.e., the entire world, must come into existence in time (*Tawḥīd*, 12.16–20).

Ninth argument: Unliving bodies do not remain still nor move by themselves alone; rather, another influence affects them and in this manner they are useful for the needs (*ḥawāʾij*) and benefits (*manāfiʿ*) of others. What serves others, however, is not self-sufficient and is thus created. Living bodies that then derive benefit from such unliving bodies can thus only be created (*Tawḥīd*, 12.21–13.2).

Tenth argument: The change which material things are subject to proves that they, as well as their various conditions, are created in time. Even if one were to (falsely) assume the existence of eternal and primordial matter, nothing would change. It would only mean that this material had become nonexistent when the world was created, while the world came into existence at that (temporally conceivable) moment (*Tawḥīd*, 13.3–19).

Eleventh argument: It is actually false to contest our arguments by presupposing that corporeal substances (*aʿyān*) always continue to exist in changing states (i.e., movement or rest, connection or separation, etc.). This contestation mixes up two concepts that need to be differentiated. "Temporal" (*ḥadath*) means that something exists after it did not exist (*al-kawn baʿda an lam yakun*). Thus, "temporality" and "preeternality" are mutually exclusive by definition. Continuous "perpetuity" (*baqāʾ*), in contrast, means that something (further) exists in constantly renewed time (*al-kawn fī mustaʾnaf al-waqt*) and this can definitely be the case in something temporal (*Tawḥīd*, 13.20–14.1).[14]

Twelfth argument: Furthermore, transmission tells us about the unlimited temporal perpetuation of created things, such that we merely have to ask ourselves whether we believe the transmission or not (*Tawḥīd*, 14.1–4).

Thirteenth argument: We also know that each series (e.g., of numbers or a causal chain) must have a beginning, but does not necessarily need an end. Otherwise nothing would exist (*Tawḥīd*, 14.5–16).

Fourteenth argument: Every movement marks the end of the previous movement; every connection marks the end of something previous to it. The same is true for other accidents, such that they both comprise a beginning and an end. Thus they can only exist in time (*Tawḥīd*, 14.17f.).

Fifteenth argument: A body can continuously exist because it is always bestowed the accident of "perpetuation" (*baqāʾ*). In order to be pre-eternal, it would need to be given a corresponding accident. This is contradictory in

14 This is perhaps an answer to the thesis that new temporal accidents could constantly occur in an eternal material substance. This is usually attributed to Ibn al-Rāwandī (cf. Gimaret, *La doctrine*, 225).

and of itself, since accidents (*aʿrāḍ*) are by definition temporal and the act of bestowal can also only be temporal (*Tawḥīd*, 14.19–15.2).

Sixteenth argument: We know no writing without someone who writes, and no division without someone who divides. The same may be said of connection, movement, rest, and everything else in the world. Thus, behind every occurrence is one who brings it about, such that the world itself is caused, which means created (*Tawḥīd*, 15.15–19).

Seventeenth argument: Every single piece of the sensible material world will cause the one who reflects to understand that he is not eternal but was brought forth in time. Reflecting on this cannot be wrong, for we would not have been given the capacity to do so otherwise (*Tawḥīd*, 15.20–ult.).

8.1.1.2 The Background of the Argument

Reading his exposition in this compact sequence is astounding at first, given the multifaceted argumentation on which he bases the temporal creation of the world. Al-Māturīdī is not just trying to combat and refute the views of the "Dahrites," who, in all of their varieties, worked on the assumption of an eternal material substance (cf. the tenth argument). He is trying to advance his own position; and in order to achieve this goal he went far beyond what *kalām* treatises usually dedicated to the theme of creation.[15]

There is a second factor in his series of proofs just as pronounced as its extensiveness. Namely, the fact that it contains several overlaps and repetitions. Often his arguments do not introduce a new train of thought to the one that preceded it. Rather, they enlarge upon the previous one with an additional aspect. This is why, in order to do justice to his exposition, one must first consider which foundational propositions the greater number of arguments can ultimately be reduced to.

This task is rather tricky in some regards. We nevertheless possess a rather secure starting point. Al-Māturīdī himself summarizes his arguments as concrete units when he states which of the three modes of knowledge mentioned in his prolegomena they are to be categorized in. Accordingly, the first part of the explanation is based on statements of transmission (argument 1 and 2; also argument 12). The second part is supposed to be built on the findings of the senses (arguments 3 to 7). The intellect is ostensibly the medium to which we owe our knowledge of the rest (arguments 8 to 17 with the exception of 12).

One's first impulse might be to object that this classification is imprecise, even incoherent: What is described here as "knowledge by the senses" (*Tawḥīd*,

15 One may compare, for instance, al-Ashʿarī's brief exposition in *K. al-Lumaʿ*, sections 3–6, or in the *Mujarrad* (Ibn Fūrak, 37f.), but also the pertinent passages of later Māturīdite works.

11.14: *'ilm al-ḥiss*) is not without rational consideration. And what is considered the "inference" of the intellect (*Tawḥīd*, 12.16: *'ilm al-istidlāl*) also requires premises that come from other sources, particularly from the senses (e.g., in the eighth argument, the first "intellect-based" argument).

But this objection does not apply in principle to the intentions that guide al-Māturīdī, as obvious as it may seem from the perspective of methodological clarity.[16] In fact, al-Māturīdī does not seek to claim that "knowledge from the senses" comes solely and directly from the senses, or that a proof from the intellect is solely based on the intellect. His criteria are different. He defines the distinction between the pathways of knowledge not according to purely subjective epistemological considerations, but in conjunction with the object of knowledge (i.e., the physical world) as well.

Our theologian describes "knowledge from the senses" as an insight ultimately derived from sensible parameters. This means, in regard to the specific case of arguments 3 to 7, that rational considerations are of course at hand. But the premises from which they start are sensible as well, since we are dealing with corporeal substances (*a'yān*) and the fact that they are finite, dependent, and imbued with inner contradictions. According to al-Māturīdī we know all of this by sense perception, such that he can categorize the foundation of the entire argument as based on the senses (*Tawḥīd*, 12.3: *maḥsūs*).

An intellectual proof in contrast is based on (among other things) at least one premise that is only known by the intellect. In the arguments named (after number 8) this would usually be the existence (presumed by al-Māturīdī) of accidents (e.g., *Tawḥīd*, 15.1: *'araḍ*) such as movement, rest, connection, etc., the knowledge of which we owe to abstraction. The rule is as follows: we sense, with our eyes, that a body moves, but this movement, which occurs through an accident called "movement" (*ḥaraka*), can only be determined by the intellect. The intellect also determines which characteristics this accident possesses and why one can derive the temporality of bodies therefrom, and by extension the temporality of the entire world.

---

16 It may have been precisely this methodological problem that led Islamic theologians to refine their epistemology and to introduce the bipartite classification already mentioned several times. This did not differentiate primarily between the media of knowledge, but rather between the character of knowledges, as "necessary" (*ḍarūrī*) or acquired (*muktasab*). Necessary knowledge was supposed to be indisputable and appeared to be directly understandable to everyone. It was well attested to by transmission and the data that we owe to the senses. All knowledge of the intellect, in contrast, was considered acquired, i.e., derivative. The intellect can only begin to draw conclusions when the senses or transmission have provided it with a secured starting point from the outset. On the development and elaboration of this concept, cf. Gardet and Anawati, 374ff.; van Ess, *Erkenntnislehre*, 113ff.; Gimaret, *La doctrine*, 160ff.

Applying this distinction that al-Māturīdī always kept in mind quickly allows us to see that his extensive exposition is based on a few main considerations. The arguments he gives vary considerably in length, since he deals with transmission only briefly, the senses in more detail, and then the intellect with the most comprehensive detail. In principle, however, his arguments based on each medium of acquiring knowledge can be reduced to two expository statements, elaborated with varying nuances and facets.

Transmission tells us

a) that God Himself speaks in the Qurʾān of creating the world in time (arguments 1 and 12), and
b) that all people have always known that they came to exist at a certain time and then slowly developed, which must be true for everything (argument 2).

With the senses, however, we realize

c) that in all sensible bodies (*aʿyān*) opposing natures (*ṭabāʾiʿ*) are united and are subject to an external compulsion, which shows that they cannot be autonomous, but are subordinate to a Creator and Guider (argument 3, 4, 5, and 7); and
d) that the individual parts of this world (i.e., the bodies) are finite (in regard to space and time), from which it can be concluded that the entirety cannot be infinite (argument 6).

Finally, our intellect knows

e) that corporeal substances (*aʿyān*) can only exist thanks to accidents (*aʿrāḍ*) such as movement and rest, which are bestowed on them. On their part, these accidents are temporal and can be bound endlessly to a body, but not in pre-eternity. Thus it is ruled out that a body has always existed (arguments 8, 9, 10, 11, 14, 15, and 17).
f) that everything which exists in the world must have a cause (argument 16) and that the causal chain cannot be ad infinitum without a beginning (argument 13).[17]

17 In this last case two arguments are thus bound together; strictly speaking, these do not prove the createdness of the world, but rather the existence of a creator. This is done by inferring the originator from the creation and thereby denying the possibility of a regressus ad infinitum.

The number of arguments may thus be reduced to six. This not only makes his approach more transparent, but now that these have been reduced to their essential principles, we can also see the relationship between al-Māturīdī's line of thought and the views of other Muslim theologians more clearly. He naturally did not come up with the arguments presented here from the ground up; he found much to base them on in the works of earlier authors who also reflected on the createdness of the world. However, we may also note that from the outset al-Māturīdī's manner of appropriating this *kalām* tradition conclusively shows his own personal imprint. He does not suffice with sifting through the opinions of his predecessors, but alters them in accordance with the context of his own theology, thereby giving the entire line of argumentation a new appearance.

That being said, the origins of the proofs presented may be outlined as follows:

On a) The first argument for transmission is clearly taken from the Qur'ān, since al-Māturīdī explicitly says that God Himself has informed us about His role as the Creator (*Tawḥīd*, 11.8: *akhbara*). And even though he does not quote a complete verse of the Qur'ān, the wording of his statements is so clearly derived from the holy text that there can be no doubt of the intentional association between the two.[18]

On b) The second argument, in contrast, appeals in general to human experience, i.e., the knowledge that has been transmitted among people for ages. Everyone, he says, recognizes by themselves and from others that one has not existed eternally, but rather was born and then brought in various steps to maturity. This immediately shows us that al-Māturīdī does not understand the term "transmission" to mean solely the Qur'ān or *ḥadīth*, but also other mundane traditions, so far as they are sufficiently attested to and trustworthy.[19] This by no means makes his argument "secular" or alien to the reasoning of Islamic theology: Other parallels can be found for this in *kalām*, the most interesting and chronologically closest of which is the teaching with which al-Ashʿarī begins his *K. al-Lumaʿ*.[20] Al-Ashʿarī there also talks about how the human being goes through different stages of development: he names the stages of *nuṭfa* (sperm), *ʿalaqa* (embryo), and *muḍgha* (fetus) explicitly because they emphasize the dependent nature of human beings and moreover are

18 Cf. the references to Qur'ānic verses Kholeif gives in the notes on the text (*Tawḥīd*, 11nn3–5).

19 On this tendency in al-Māturīdī and in early *kalām* in general, cf. van Ess, *Erkenntnislehre*, 411f., and Rudolph, "Ratio and Überlieferung," chapter III.

20 Al-Ashʿarī, *K. al-Lumaʿ*, sections 3–6; see Gimaret, *La doctrine*, 230ff.

supported by Qurʾānic verses.[21] Altogether his argumentation is much more detailed and does not have the same goal in mind, since al-Ashʿarī wishes to prove the existence of God while al-Māturīdī wants to prove the createdness of the world. But the basic idea is still comparable, since both theologians explain that human beings are invariably transformed without their own doing, from which they also conclude that humans are not autonomous but in need of one who is in control.

On d) The denial of the possibility of the infinite has a much longer backstory. Al-Māturīdī bases his work on this thesis when he states that the parts of the world that came to exist in time cannot form an infinite (and thus eternal) series. The principle of the argument comes from Aristotle. The Greek philosopher, however, did not profess the contingency of the world, but rather its eternity; he believed that time as well as movement were without beginning. But with regard to space, Aristotle was of the view that the supposition of infinite extension (or here, an infinitely extended body) was impossible.[22] John Philoponus, the Christian Aristotelian of the sixth century, carried this argument over to the temporal dimension. He also ruled out infinitude, or to be precise, an unending series of past temporal points and events. His argumentation, which influenced numerous Jewish and Muslim thinkers,[23] has become especially well known for its influence on the philosophical tradition that formed around al-Kindī (d. after 250/864).[24] But comparable ideas can also be found in early *kalām*, which is to say, among the Muʿtazilites; this can be shown, for example, of al-Naẓẓām (d. 232/847).[25] Al-Māturīdī's statements then are likely to have been influenced by this school.

On f) The view that a chain of causes cannot be conceived of without a beginning also goes back to antiquity. This, of course, again reminds us of

---

21 Q 23:13–14.

22 Hellmut Flashar, "Aristoteles," in *Grundriss der Geschichte der Philosophie. III: Ältere Akademie—Aristotles—Peripatos*, ed. H. Flashar (Basel/Stuttgart, 1983), 393ff.

23 See Herbert A. Davidson, "John Philoponus as a Source of Medieval Islamic and Jewish Proofs of Creation," *JAOS* 89 (1969): 357–391; idem., *Proofs for Eternity, Creation and the Existence of God in Medieval Islamic and Jewish Philosophy* (New York/Oxford, 1987), 86ff.

24 Cf. al-Kindī's *Fī l-falsafa al-ūlā*, in al-Kindī, *Rasāʾil al-Kindī al-falsafiya*, ed. Muḥammad ʿAbd al-Hādī Abū Riḍā (Cairo, 1369–72/1950–53), vol. 1, 114.11ff.; see in translation Alfred L. Ivry, *Al-Kindi's Metaphysics* (Albany, NY, 1974), 68ff. and 147ff. Similar views are found in several of al-Kindī's treatises, such as the *Risāla* "On God's oneness and the finitude of bodies in the world" which was edited in al-Kindī, *Rāsāʾil*, vol. 1, 202ff. and translated into French in idem, *Cinq Epîtres*, ed. Daniel Gimaret (Paris, 1976), 93ff. On all these see Davidson, *Proofs*, 106ff.

25 Al-Khayyāṭ, sections 19 and 20; see Davidson, *Proofs*, 117f.

Aristotle, who not only utilized this principle in the famous teaching of the First Mover, but also established it as a general axiom.[26] But Aristotle only marks the beginning of a long tradition. The idea became independent thereafter and we encounter it regularly in texts of late antiquity or of Arabic philosophy, when God is discussed as "the First Cause" (*al-ʿilla al-ūlā*).[27] In *kalām*, this idea found acceptance in different wording but again with the same intention. The argument may be referenced for the first time in the work of the Muʿtazilite al-Iskāfī (d. 240/853).[28] There the relevant ideas are shortened and reduced to their quintessence, but this does not speak against their belonging to this tradition; instead it only shows that the author was solely interested in the final inference or immediate proof therefrom of the existence of the Creator. The same is basically true of al-Māturīdī, since he only briefly repeats the conclusion that each chain of events must be caused by a first cause (argument 13). Moreover, he enlarges on this idea with a completely different argument, adding that if a (created) work exists, then an active Creator may be presumed to exist as well (argument 16).[29]

On e) The proof by means of accidents, in contrast, has no forerunner from antiquity. It takes us directly to Islamic theology, since it is based on premises that were developed and recognized there. Abū l-Hudhayl (d. 226/840–1 or 235/849–50) probably stands at its origins, as he also formulated the ontological basis for the same. But it was spread by a great number of theologians, since in later centuries it became the classical standard argument for the createdness of the world, as well as for the necessity of a Creator.[30]

On c) One unique contribution of early Islamic theology is the proof from the supposed antithetical nature of bodies and their subjection to an omnipotent Creator. It is found, for example, in the ideas of Ibn Shabīb, who may even have been the immediate source used by al-Māturīdī.[31] Ibn Shabīb himself was dependent on al-Naẓẓām, who is cited as the earliest authority in *kalām* for this idea: According to al-Khayyāṭ, he said

26 On the unmoved mover, cf. *The Metaphysics* XII; on the principle of the necessity of a first cause, see *The Metaphysics* II, 2.

27 For references, cf. Endreß, *Proclus Arabus: Zwanzig Abschnitte aus der Institutio theologica* (Beirut, 1973), 142 and 206ff. as well as Rudolph, *Doxographie*, 177 and 246.

28 Al-Khayyāṭ [section 5], 19.6ff.; trans., 12.

29 On this proof of God used often in theology, cf. Davidson, *Proofs*, 154ff.

30 On the history of this proof, see ibid., 134ff.; a precise analysis of its application by al-Ashʿarī is given by Gimaret, *La doctrine*, 219ff.

31 Cf. van Ess, *Theologie*, vol. 4, 128f.

> I found hot and cold united (*mujtamiʿayn*) in a single body although they are opposed to one another and repelled from one another (… *min al-taḍādd wa-l-tanāfur*). Then I realized that they could not unite by themselves, since their polarity is their own, while that which unifies them has created them (already) unified (*ikhtaraʿahumā*) and (in doing so) subjugated them (*qaharahumā*) to something that contradicts their essence (*jawhar*). Thus this fact that they can be unified despite their polarity shows that the one who unified them also created them.[32]

The proximity to al-Māturīdī's views is obvious, and shows that our theologian, on the merit of his use of proof by contradiction (c) and accidents (e) stands rather close to the Muʿtazilite tradition. But this is not the only thing that makes these last two ideas stand out among the list of different arguments seen above. They are, furthermore, accorded the greatest significance from al-Māturīdī's perspective, since, for one thing he developed these two proofs—and none of the others—extensively and over the course of several pages (with arguments 3, 4, 5, and 7, as well as 8, 9, 10, 11, 14, 15, and 17). In addition, he limits himself there to a formulation based on "corporeal substances" (*aʿyān*), "accidents" (*aʿrāḍ*), and "natures" (*ṭabāʾiʿ*): this means that he does not argue from generally understood premises that an author from antiquity or early Christianity could share in, but rather from premises that were constitutive for his own ontology. These concepts will bring us closer to al-Māturīdī's particular worldview and his analysis of the creation. Our next step, then, is to establish how he understood them.

8.1.2 *The Ontological Structure of the World*

8.1.2.1 Bodies and Accidents

As it would happen, determining al-Māturīdī's view of created existence is anything but easy, since we face an unexpected problem in regard to precisely this theme in his work. The *K. al-Tawḥīd* lacks clear and comprehensive statements on the topic, and has no outline that takes up the question systematically. Instead, all we have are individual statements strung together and partly scattered throughout the work. Al-Māturīdī neither explains his ontology nor presents it formally. We must reconstruct it ourselves, and on a textual basis that remains fragmentary and leaves key questions open-ended.

---

32 Al-Khayyāṭ (section 26), 40.10–14; cf. ibid., 40.-4ff.; see also Kholeif's English introduction to the edition of the *K. al-Tawḥīd* (*Tawḥīd*, xxiif.). Before *kalām* this proof certainly did have antecedents (though in a different formulation) in Christian theology, with Athanasius, ʿAmmār al-Baṣri, Hiob of Edessa and others, see van Ess, *Theologie*, vol. 3, 367.

This situation is surprising to a certain extent for an author of the early fourth/tenth century, since at this time in *kalām* the framework in which Muslim theologians contemplated the structure of created being had long been demarcated. Consequently, al-Māturīdī did not have to develop a new theory of his own, but was free to choose from among the various theories available to him, the selection primarily coming down to three different models.

The first of these came from the second/eighth century and can be traced back to Ḍirār b. ʿAmr, but found a number of adherents in the third/ninth century, in particular al-Najjār, and (with some qualifications) al-Burghūth. According to this model,[33] the world is made up of individual components, so-called accidents (*ʿaraḍ*, pl. *aʿrāḍ*). Ḍirār understands them as all qualitative phenomena, i.e., that which he considers to be perceivable to the senses. As for bodies, they play only a secondary role in his system. They have no self-subsistence, being nothing more than clusters of accidents. If they change, this is explained consequently as the reconfiguration of one or more constitutive accidents. In order to explain the continuity of the body's existence, however, Ḍirār was compelled to a type of concession. He had to distinguish between qualities that form bodies, and those which only emerge in previously existing bodies. To the first kind, such as heat and cold, dryness and moisture, lightness and heaviness, he attributed a certain independence, and also called them "parts" (*abʿāḍ*). The second type, such as lust and pain, in his opinion, were not able to persist independently. They are not constitutive of bodies and thus are only named "accidents" (*ʿaraḍ*, pl. *aʿrāḍ*), in a more restricted sense.

The second model is diametrically opposed to this idea.[34] It had various advocates (e.g., Hishām b. al-Ḥakam and al-Aṣamm), among whom al-Naẓẓām was a leading figure. According to the latter, the material world was not constituted of accidents, but bodies. This means, then, that all the qualities that Ḍirār characterizes as merely accidental were defined by al-Naẓẓām as corporeal. They are not static, however, and can actually change, because bodies are constantly in a state of mixing. They penetrate each other (*mudākhala* or *tadākhul*), and may be concealed in one another (*kāmin*). These can become visible, however, as soon as a physical process effects a change. To illustrate this, al-Naẓẓām liked to name wood as an example. When wood burns, fire is freed from within, and in fire the previously latent substances of heat and light show themselves. Thus the world is presented as a single commixture of bodies that are outwardly perceivable in various proportions.

33 Cf. van Ess, "Ḍirār b. ʿAmr [1]," 251ff.; idem, *Une lecture*, 89ff.; idem, *Theologie*, vol. 3, 37ff.; on al-Najjār and al-Burghūth cf. ibid., vol. 4, 150f. and 143f.

34 Van Ess, "Ḍirār b. ʿAmr [1]," 246ff.; idem, *Une lecture*, 43ff.; idem, *Theologie*, vol. 3, 331ff.

The third available model functions at first like a synthesis of the first two, since it classifies both bodies and accidents as the foundational components of the created world. But in reality a more radical change in perspective is at hand. This is because corporeal parts are conceived of here as the smallest indivisible pieces (*al-juzʾ alladhī lā yatajazzaʾ* or *al-jawhar*) that exist.[35] We have now reached atomism, which has long been known as characteristic of Islamic theology.

Atomistic teachings were professed by various thinkers of the third/ninth century (Muʿammar, Bishr b. al-Muʿtamir). The model created by Abū l-Hudhayl prevailed because it was adopted by al-Jubbāʾī (d. 303/915–6) with a few modifications and through him found acceptance in later *kalām*. According to this conceptualization,[36] every created thing (*shayʾ*) that possesses existence (*wujūd*) must either be corporeal or an accident. The corporeal is defined as whatever occupies space (*mutaḥayyiz*), carries accidents (*ḥāmil* or *muḥtamil li-l-aʿrāḍ*), and occasionally also, though a bit more problematically formulated,[37] as that which can subsist through itself (*qāʾim bi-nafsihi*). Accidents were described with the opposite qualities. They cannot occupy space and can only reside in something else (*qāʾim bi-ghayrihi*). Thus they constantly require a substrate (*maḥall*), and this substrate by definition can only be a corporeal substance (*jism*). The structure of the corporeal was conceived of atomically as noted earlier; this raised the question of how many atoms were necessary for the formation of a *jism*. Abū l-Hudhayl said six, while Muʿammar said eight, both thinking three-dimensionally and representing the pioneers of the later dominant Muʿtazilite view that a body was long (*ṭawīl*), wide (*ʿarīḍ*), and deep (*ʿamīq*). Already by the third/ninth century there were dissenting voices, however, such as al-Iskāfī, for whom two-dimensionality sufficed and who advocated a minimum of two atoms. Al-Ashʿarī followed him as well, also preferring the alternative definition of a body as that which was composed (*muʾallaf/al-muʾtalif* or *al-mujtamiʿ*) of two parts.[38]

---

35 On the terminology see Pines, 3f.

36 Arthur Biram, *Die atomistische Substanzenlehre aus dem Buch der Streitfragen zwischen Basrensern und Bagdadensern* (Berlin, 1902), 10ff.; Otto Pretzl, "Die frühislamische Atomenlehre. Ein Beitrag zur Frage über die Beziehungen der frühislamischen Theologie zur griechischen Philosophie," *Der Islam* 19 (1931): 118ff.; Pines, 1ff.; Frank, *Beings and Their Attributes*, 39f.; Gimaret, *La doctrine*, 43ff.; Dhanani, 38ff.

37 On the problem see Gimaret, *La doctrine*, 36ff.

38 Pines, 4ff.; Hans Daiber, *Das theologisch-philosophische System des Muʿammar ibn ʿAbbād al Sulamī* (*gest. 830 n. Chr.*) (Beirut, 1975), 322ff.; Gimaret, *La doctrine*, 67ff.

Atomism, as is known, was able to supplant the other two models previously mentioned. It began its way to dominance around the turn of the third/ninth to the fourth/tenth century and from that point on left its long imprint (with certain variations) on the physical worldview of *kalām*. However, this is undoubtedly true only for the Muʿtazilite and Ashʿarite schools; as noted earlier, the case of al-Māturīdī is more complex. Our task now is to determine what he thought concerning the ontological structure of creation in order that his position in regard to the three models just described be elucidated.

During the process of reconstructing al-Māturīdī's position, it is noticable at once that he does not refer to atomism in his entire conceptual framework. He neither affirms the theory nor criticizes it, but quite simply excludes it from his deliberations.[39] Thus, one seeks in vain in the *K. al-Tawḥīd* for the term *al-juzʾ alladhī lā yatajazzaʾ* as well as the corollary question of how many pieces are required for the formation of a body.

This fact relates to a second feature of the work which is terminological in nature. Namely, the term that al-Māturīdī uses to describe an atom throughout the work; *jawhar* or *jawhar wāḥid*. Here the word takes on different meanings, two to be precise, which must always be distinguished from one another. Sometimes what is meant is a body or a corporeal entity.[40] In these cases one could replace *jawhar/jawāhir* with *ʿayn/aʿyān* (individual, concrete entities), which our theologian usually uses in such places. *Jawhar*, however, more often is intended to specifically describe the material substance or essence of a thing, or the sum total of properties which it possesses by nature. This is why al-Māturīdī speaks of the essence of good and evil[41] while debating the Manichaeans as well as the essence of light and darkness.[42] Or, we hear him say that every person,[43] the Prophet Muḥammad,[44] or the world as a whole,[45] possesses a *jawhar*. Along with this it may be added that occasionally the

39 Though the concept as such must have been known to him, since he surely knew al-Jubbāʾī's theology through Abū ʿUmar al-Bāhilī and since al-Kaʿbī also thought atomistically (though in a modified form). Khwārizmī also indicates indirectly that atomism did not play a role among the Ḥanafites of Transoxania of the fourth/tenth century; he names atomism in his *Mafātīḥ* as a theological concept, but ascribes it exclusively to the Muʿtazila (cf. Bosworth, "Al-Ḫwārazmī," 88).

40 Cf. especially *Tawḥīd*, 142.15ff., where al-Māturīdī distinguishes between *jawāhir* and *aʿrāḍ*; see also ibid., 12.-2ff. in regard to unliving bodies.

41 Ibid., 170.4.

42 Ibid., 170.18f.

43 Ibid., 187.1.

44 Ibid., 202.12ff.

45 Ibid., 186.16f.

terms *jawhar* and *khilqa* (natural disposition, created nature) are collocated in a complementary and explanatory fashion.[46]

Our theologian is not forging a new path with this interpretation. He is merely ignoring the particular meaning that *jawhar* had acquired in *kalām*, and using the word according to general linguistic usage (as well as the terminology of peripatetic philosophy).[47] But this ultimately only raises new issues. If bodies possess a natural material constitution, something must be described as the bearer of this disposition. If it is, moreover, clear that bodies are not constituted of atoms as their smallest components, then what takes the place of atoms?

Al-Māturīdī's answer is given in several steps. First it is established that the world consists of bodies and accidents (cf. arguments 3, 8, and 15 above). This is brought up again later when two types (*nawʿān*) of created things (*ashyāʾ*) are discussed: corporeal substances (*ʿayn*), i.e., bodies (*jism*); and qualities (*ṣifa*), i.e., accidents (*aʿrāḍ*).[48] In a third part of the book al-Māturīdī is even more precise, telling us something that will assist us in our analysis; namely, the necessity of distinguishing between "the simple elements" (*al-arkān*[49] *al-basīṭa*), i.e., accidents and qualities, and "composed corporeal substances" (*al-aʿyān al-murakkaba*), i.e., bodies.[50]

Bodies are defined more precisely in other contexts. They have limits (*nihāyāt*)[51] and are thus limited (*maḥdūd*).[52] They also have sides (*jihāt*),[53] the number of which is set at six.[54] Consequentially we learn that they have three dimensions (*abʿād thalātha*)[55] and are also extended and composite.[56] Finally,

46 Ibid., 395.10; cf. 214.4f.

47 In Arabic philosophical terminology *jawhar* replicates the Greek word "ousia," which Aristotle also associated with two meanings: the concrete individual thing that cannot be predicated of anything else, and the essence or form of a thing; cf. *Metaphysics* V 8 1017b23 and also Andreas Graeser, *Die Philosophie der Antike 2. Sophistik und Sokratik, Plato und Aristoteles* (Munich, 1993), 223ff.

48 *Tawḥīd*, 40.18.

49 This part of the manuscript (fol. 45a-9) ought to be read as "*arkān*" (see Daiber, Review of *Kitāb al-Tawḥīd*, 305) and not "*idrākāt*" as Kholeif puts in the edition.

50 *Tawḥīd*, 94.9f.

51 Ibid., 38.4f., 42.10, 43.17 (read: *muḥtamilatun*).

52 Ibid., 104.13.

53 Ibid., 38.4, 42.10, 104.-1f.

54 Ibid., 165.6.

55 Ibid., 43.2, 38.5, 42.10.

56 Ibid., 104 ult.; cf. 39.14.

the natural assumption that bodies accept (*qabila*) accidents[57] and thus form their substrate (*maḥall*)[58] may also be added. Indeed, all of this does not exactly give the impression of a very meticulous theory, but it suffices to make an important observation, namely that al-Māturīdī conceived corporeal substances as three-dimensional and is thus building on a Muʿtazilite tradition.

The text tells us even less about accidents. We only hear that they are indivisible.[59] Besides this, we see only a few typical examples for this category of being, such as action, movement, and rest.[60] Otherwise, al-Māturīdī merely explains that the Muʿtazilites gave accidents too much autonomy.[61] This scant amount of information fits with another observation of al-Māturīdī's, from which one can infer his attitude toward the topic. It was directed against Ibn Shabīb (i.e., a Muʿtazilite), but our theologian is not really reproaching him for saying something wrong on the subject of accidents; rather, he is simply disturbed by the fact that Ibn Shabīb philosophizes in detail on the subject. Such long-winded talk (*iṭnāb*), he tells us quite tersely, is superfluous and has no serious use (*manfaʿa*) for a theologian.[62]

Al-Māturīdī does not hesitate to admit to the reader his disinterest in the finer details of ontology. Thus, we can hardly be surprised that he does not exactly treat this theme with exemplary stringency and definitive clarity. Nevertheless, the compilation of individual observations and hints does indeed bring us a bit farther along. We now know that, according to our theologian, bodies are three-dimensionally constructed structures. It is also known that in his view accidents are merely simple irreducible foundational elements of the universe. The only problem is that the theoretical nature of the relationship between the two remains as open as it was before; one could thus far conceivably conclude that a body is only constructed of accidents, for example. But al-Māturīdī never states this decisive idea anywhere in the *K. al-Tawḥīd*. Thus, it is advisable to not simply presume so, but rather to verify whether or not we can find, in the works of his students, statements that offer some clarity on this point.

As is immediately apparent, however, examining the sources is no easy and direct task, since the theologians who can be considered successors or even students of al-Māturīdī are by no means unified on this topic. Abū Salama

57 Ibid., 42.10.
58 Ibid., 43.17.
59 Ibid., 39.12f.
60 Ibid., 39.13f.
61 Ibid., 89.2ff.
62 Ibid., 137.-1ff., esp. 138.15f., 139.6f., and 139.11.

(d. second half of the fourth/tenth century) for instance, who, as we already saw, was directly dependent on al-Māturīdī, did not mention the theme at all. He repeats his master's individual arguments for the createdness of the world and existence of a Creator, and of course, in doing so addresses the phenomena of bodies and accidents.[63] But he does not provide a single statement that might offer more precision to our observations up to now.

Abū l-Layth al-Samarqandī (d. 373/983) is even less informative. He does not discuss the problematics of the ontology of created being anywhere,[64] which again confirms that he may have been an influential Ḥanafite scholar, but cannot be reckoned from among the narrower circle of *mutakallimūn* of Transoxania.

However, in the writings of Abū Shakūr al-Sālimī, the next relevant theologian in chronological order (from the second half of the fifth/eleventh century), a slight surprise awaits us. He actually presents an elaborate system of physics in his *K. al-Tamhīd fī bayān al-tawḥīd*. It does not follow in al-Māturīdī's footsteps, however, but is clearly conceived among Ashʿarite lines: Abū Shakūr definitely knows atoms (*jawāhir*),[65] and he assumes the world to be constructed out of them and accidents (*aʿrāḍ*)[66] in their role as the two foundational elements of created existence. Bodies (*ajsām*), in contrast, seem to be secondary for him because on their part they are already formed of atoms. He also does not consider them three-dimensional as the Muʿtazilites do (he criticizes them for this), or as al-Māturīdī does, whose name he omits. Rather, to him bodies are that which is characterized by composition (*tarkīb*) and unity (*taʾlīf*)[67]—an idea which ought to demonstrate to us direct dependence on al-Ashʿarī's ideas.

Abū l-Yusr al-Pazdawī (d. 493/1100) then follows the trail set out by Abū Shakūr. He also depicts the world as constructed of accidents (*ṣifa*/*aʿrāḍ*), bodies (*jism*), and atoms (*jawhar*/*al-juzʾ alladhī lā yatajazzaʾ*).[68] As for bodies, two atoms are enough to form them.[69] Al-Pazdawī does not offer more detail, but the little he does give us is enough to determine that we have once again come upon the teachings of al-Ashʿarī.

63 Abū Salama (section 2), 11.2–12 ult.

64 Abū l-Layth's creed (*ʿAqīda*), his Qurʾān commentary, as well as the texts *Bustān al-ʿārifīn*, *Tanbīh al-ghāfilīn*, and *Waḥy al-asrār* were all examined.

65 *Tamhīd*, fol. 24b8–10, 25b10–ult., 26a10–b2.

66 Fol. 24b12–25a1, 25b10–ult., 25b ult.–26a10.

67 Fol. 24b10–12.

68 *Uṣūl*, 11.15ff. and 12.3f.

69 Ibid., 14.2–7.

After these first impressions it seems as if al-Māturīdī's ontological conceptualizations were marginalized in his own school from its beginning. And as a matter of fact, they were, and with such ease as can only be called astonishing. Nevertheless, we have yet another opportunity to discover something more precise on al-Māturīdī's description of the world, since there is a later author who finally took up this theme with interest, and with a sharper historical consciousness; namely, the next theologian of the group, Abū l-Muʿīn al-Nasafī (d. 508/1114). We have three extant expositions by him on the question of ontology: one in the form of generalizations, the *Baḥr al-kalām*; a more precise kind in *Tamhīd li-qawāʿid al-tawḥīd*; and finally, a detailed reference in the *Tabṣirat al-adilla*, which has already served us often as a source. In this last work, al-Nasafī not only lays out his own views, but actually cites excerpts from al-Māturīdī's writings. We thus have access to an exceptionally interesting overview that may be very helpful to us on the issue at hand.

In regard to al-Nasafī's own views, his position must be described as an attempt at compromise. He is, as soon becomes clear, an atomist. He nevertheless does not wish to follow al-Ashʿarī, but seeks instead to maintain his autonomy and distance from him. The world, according to Abū l-Muʿīn, consists of material substances (*aʿyān*) and accidents.[70] The category of substances must also be partitioned; they may occur as compounds and thus be bodies (*ajsām*), but they can also be simple, such that one must also speak of atoms (*jawāhir*).[71] The definition of an atom and accident are basically familiar: the first is described as that which subsists through itself (*al-qāʾim bi-dhātihi*) and can take on opposing forces (*al-qābil li-l-mutaḍāddāt*).[72] The second is supposed to be a description of those qualities that apply to created things (*ism li-l-ṣifāt al-thābita li-l-muḥdathāt*),[73] such as colors, flavors, smells, or whatever else can apply to that which has variation. When defining a body, al-Nasafī gives more background information. He is particularly concerned with showing that al-Ashʿarī's conception of the body as the unification of two atoms is misleading.[74] Al-Nasafī, on his part, asserts that bodies are three-dimensional,

70 Abū l-Muʿīn al-Nasafī, *K. al-Tamhīd li-qawāʿid al-tawḥīd*, ed. Jīb Allāh Ḥasan Aḥmad (Cairo, 1986), 123.3f.

71 Ibid., 123.4ff.; *Tabṣira*, vol. 1, 44.11f. and 45.16–18; cf. Abū l-Muʿīn al-Nasafī, *K. Baḥr al-kalām* (Cairo, 1329/1911), 20.5f.; trans. Arthur Jeffery, in *A Reader on Islam: Passages from Standard Arabic Writings Illustrative of the Beliefs and Practices of Muslims* (S-Gravenhage, 1962), 388.

72 *Tabṣira*, vol. 1, 46.1f.; cf. al-Nasafī, *Tamhīd*, 124.1f.: *wa huwa al-juzʾ alladhī lā yatajazzaʾ*.

73 *Tabṣira*, vol. 1, 49.-1f.; cf. al-Nasafī, *Tamhīd*, 124.3ff.; on "*thabata li-*" cf. van Ess, *Erkenntnislehre*, 437.

74 *Tabṣira*, vol. 1, 48.5–49.15.

but he does not prove it. Instead, Abū l-Muʿīn characterizes this thesis as a view recognized long ago, which had been professed by his predecessors (*awāʾil aṣḥābinā*), and had well served the Muʿtazilites[75] and mathematicians (*ḥussāb*)[76] because it was a more adequate description of the physical world.

In this particularly lucid presentation of his own position, al-Nasafī, as said before, incorporates several comments on al-Māturīdī's positions. They are thoroughly straightforward and doxographical, but there is a deeper reason for their appearance here. The decisive impulse again seems to have been the importance in Islam of showing respect for tradition. Abū l-Muʿīn clearly wanted to avoid the impression that the concept he was presenting—which was surely his own original synthesis—was actually his own, and thus a new approach. Instead, it was supposed to represent a direct path back to al-Māturīdī. In order to achieve this appearance, al-Nasafī cites our theologian selectively, and in doing so discretely reinterprets him as an authority who supports his own views.

This tendency reveals itself in the first explicit mention of his name. According to this reference, al-Māturīdī divided the world into *aʿyān* and *aʿrāḍ*—which is correct. But then we hear that by *aʿyān* he means composite bodies as well as simple atoms,[77] and this does not accord with the facts. Thus we can already see how citations and interpretations are brought together in al-Nasafī's presentation.

The same situation faces us in the case of the next topic; i.e., the definition of bodies. Here Abū l-Muʿīn explains that al-Māturīdī was uncommitted on the topic, since he sometimes presumed the three-dimensionality of bodies, but sometimes affirmed two-dimensional structures as well.[78] This also, as we have come to know, is not quite correct, because our theologian very certainly favored three-dimensionality. But here the wrong interpretation is less important than the justification that al-Nasafī gives for it. He indicates that such (apparent) vacillations were actually typical of our theologian's thought. Al-Māturīdī did not really interest himself in these types of issues, because of "his custom of not busying himself with knowledge of the reality (*ḥaqīqa*) of a thing, if to him there was no need (*ḥāja*) for it in regard to his religion (*dīn*)."[79]

Al-Māturīdī is thus accused of a lack of precision in his analysis of the world, and we cannot really claim that this is unwarranted. But even this is not said

75 Ibid., 47.15f.
76 Ibid., 47.8.
77 Ibid., 44.13–15.
78 Ibid., 47.17ff.
79 Ibid., 48.1f.

by al-Nasafī without a deeper purpose, since a bit later he shows how valuable such an allegation can be as an instrument for the interpretation of so-called "doxographical" reports.

This time it is provoked by the doctrine of Ḍirār b. ʿAmr and al-Najjār. They both, as mentioned earlier, professed the thesis that only accidents exist, and that bodies result from the unification of accidents.[80] This is wrong of course, al-Nasafī immediately stresses.[81] But their teaching still concerns him greatly since it not only embodies a simple error in the history of theology, but apparently continues to present a certain danger. The reason for this is found in the next passage, which is of such great significance that it deserves to be reproduced here fully:

> Even though the master and guide Abū Manṣūr (al-Māturīdī) hardly settled (*rakina*) on this teaching, he still decided that it was more probable (*fa-qaḍā li-hādhā l-raʾy bi-ḍarbi rujḥānin*) because the leading advocates of this doctrine were of the opinion that the senses were incapable of proving the existence of a subsistent thing in the visible world (*shayʾin qāʾimin bi-l-dhāti fī l-shāhid*) not composed of these accidents just mentioned—because not a single thing can be perceived with the senses other than these accidents. At the same time he did not want to accept this teaching and expressed in his *K. al-Maqālāt* the following point of view: "This is a thing from which one ought to refrain since one can find no religious duty (*farḍ*) in it which one would be neglectful for not knowing." And (he could say) this because it is well known of the teachings of our school's representatives (*aṣḥābinā*) that they do not concern themselves with investigation into the reality (*ḥaqāʾiq*) of things, if there is no necessity for them to do so in order to affirm the principles of religion (*uṣūl al-dīn*).[82]

The particular characteristics of accidents, al-Nasafī adds explanatorily, are so decisive that the createdness of the world could be deduced from their existence alone. The question, however, of whether one can presume anything other than them to be primary (i.e., atoms) has no relevance whatsoever for one's faith.[83]

---

80 Ibid., 51.10ff.

81 Ibid., 52.3f.

82 Ibid., 52.5–11.

83 Ibid., 52.11–15.

The approach taken here is ambiguous and suggestive at the same time. Abū l-Muʿīn duly praises our theologian as a sensitive religious thinker, but in the same breath he tells us that because of this religious aspect of his character al-Māturīdī was not entirely reliable on a more "profane" aspect of theology such as the nature of the world. He was thus liable to leave let certain uncertainties creep in or even neglect apparent gaps in his presentation. Fortunately, al-Nasafī intervenes, thinks out what was left open-ended, and corrects that which has failed. The school founder's system has thus been renewed and also won additional status.

This strategy was doubtlessly intentional and to be sure was extremely successful: al-Nasafī's ontological model, which had been intended to appear to later thinkers as al-Māturīdī's position, prevailed among the later Māturīdites. We find it again almost unchanged with al-Ṣābūnī (d. 580/1184).[84] And even more importantly, it found acceptance, word for word, in the creed of Najm al-Dīn al-Nasafī (d. 537/1142)[85] which came to have a decisive role for the spread of Māturīdite ideas.

Still, al-Nasafī's new interpretation does not quite conceal al-Māturīdī's original ideas, since he himself must admit that his thesis on the structure of the world was not really based on his views. Al-Māturīdī had actually taken a different position. We can now attempt to summarize that position, since Abū l-Muʿīn has confirmed to us its most significant features (those which earlier drew our attention in the *K. al-Tawḥīd*), though he did not necessarily agree with them.

---

84 In his *K. al-Kifāya fī l-hidāya* (MS Yale Univ. Library 849, fols. 55b–259), Nūr al-Dīn Aḥmad b. Maḥmūd al-Ṣābūnī essentially follows the presentation given by al-Nasafī in the *Tabṣira* (cf. *Kifāya*, fols. 66a–69b), albeit with two exceptions: the critical passage in which al-Māturīdī's proximity to the "accidentalists" is made clear is completely lacking (it ought to be on fol. 68); furthermore, he takes al-Ashʿarī's side in regard to the definition of a body and explains that a structure of two atoms is enough (fol. 67a–b).

85 The decisive section reads: "The world in all of its parts is created in time (*muḥdath*), since it consists of corporeal substances (*aʿyān*) and accidents. Substances are that which does not subsist in and of itself and is either composed (and thus a body [*jism*]), or not composed (and thus an indivisible little piece, i.e., an atom [*jawhar*]). An accident is that which does not subsist in and of itself, but occurs in bodies and atoms, such as colors, ways of being (*akwān*), flavors, and smells" (al-Nasafī, *ʿAqāʾid*, 1.-4–ult.; trans. Schacht, 82; cf. al-Taftāzānī, *Sharḥ*, 24 ult.–31.13; trans. Elder, 28–35). It is interesting that Najm al-Dīn al-Nasafī not only replicated the doctrine of Abū l-Muʿīn extensively, as we have seen, but he also cited it verbatim and with only a few abridgements based on the *Tamhīd li-qawāʿid al-tawḥīd* (cf. al-Nasafī, *Tamhīd*, 123.3–125.1).

First, our theologian treated the questions of ontology as a secondary problem. He was not interested in the world as a phenomenon, as a structure to be explained in and of itself. It interested him only in as much as it was created and thus pointed toward its Creator. This, one could interject, is a reasonable perspective for a theologian. But it was by no means an obvious one, as al-Nasafī's reaction proves. Rather this attitude shows a particular feature of al-Māturīdī's thought; it demonstrates that he focused on questions of religion (*dīn*) in regard to one's personal relationship with God, while largely putting aside other themes that were otherwise discussed more extensively in *kalām*.

These pious tendencies did not relieve al-Māturīdī from making ontological distinctions in his theological work; and in fact he did so, as we showed with al-Nasafī's help. The critical piece of information was al-Nasafī's indication that our theologian sympathized with the ideas of Ḍirār b. ʿAmr and al-Najjār. This was, of course, a faux pas in his view, and Abū l-Muʿīn immediately made the effort to undo its effect, but this does not change the fact that it is precisely this inclination toward Ḍirār and his doctrines on accidents that fits with the statements of the *K. al-Tawḥīd*. We did see, after all, that al-Māturīdī ignored atomistic conceptualizations. We can also assert that he never took al-Naẓẓām's teaching of the mixing of bodies seriously.[86] Instead he only knows accidents as "simple elements" (*arkān basīṭa*); whereas bodies he viewed as "composed" (*murakkab*),[87] which only leaves one to presume that accidents are their primary components. And if al-Māturīdī states elsewhere that the world consists of "pieces" (*ajzāʾ wa-abʿād*),[88] this also does not contradict our thesis here, because these "parts" (*abʿāḍ*) were also found in the work of Ḍirār, who described accidents as constituting bodies in precisely the same manner.[89] Our theologian is thus following a predetermined terminology, which we may conclude preliminarily to be indebted—at least in regard to its foundational ontological conceptualization—to a model first formulated by Ḍirār b. ʿAmr.

8.1.2.2 Natures

This finding certainly leads us to a new problem: Our theologian not only mentions *aʿyān* and *aʿrāḍ*; he also speaks of the *jawhar*, i.e., the natural disposition of bodies, as well as the *ṭabāʾiʿ*, or natures, which clearly have a relationship

86 The teaching is criticized explicitly; cf. *Tawḥīd*, 138.17ff.

87 *Tawḥīd*, 94.9f.

88 Cf. the sixth argument for the createdness of the world, and *Tawḥīd*, 12.5ff.

89 Cf. above, 243.

with this *jawhar*. The latter also form an integral component of his view of physicality, and thus demand further clarity.

It is clear from the outset that this task does not pose the same level of difficulty as our previous inquiry, since al-Māturīdī discusses them in detail and his views on the subject have already been partly examined in an article written by Richard Frank some time ago.[90]

As our theologian always emphasizes, the *ṭabāʾiʿ* in his view are omnipresent. Every corporeal substance (*ʿayn*), i.e., that which is perceivable by the senses (*maḥsūs*), is composed of them.[91] This means that they are not only the structural basis of the world (*kāna al-ʿālam bi-aṣlihi mabnīyan ʿalā ṭabāʾiʿa mukhtalifatin wa-wujūhin mutaḍāddatin*),[92] but also of the microcosm (*al-ʿālam al-ṣaghīr*), i.e., the human being, in which the most varying passions (*ahwāʾ*), natures, and desires (*shahawāt*) arise.[93] His views here even take on the character of a definition, since he tells us that people may be described in two ways, either as "the rational mortal being" (*al-ḥayy al-nāṭiq al-mayyit*),[94] as they are usually described, or with another formulation which al-Māturīdī uses more often, when he says that they are composed of an intellect (*ʿaql*) and natures.[95]

The unification of natures into bodies is by no means the result of their own properties. To the contrary, the specificity (*ḥaqq*) to which they are obligated (*bi-l-ṭabʿ*) dictates mutual repulsion (*tanāfur*) and being separated and distanced (*tabāʿud*).[96] This is why the "natural philosophers" (*aṣḥāb al-ṭabāʾiʿ*) who believe that the *tabāʾiʿ* order the entire existence of the world through an eternal and autonomous process are wrong.[97] The correct view, in fact, is that they are not capable of such a constructive work; if they were left to themselves they would necessarily destroy the universe, because every nature necessarily opposes the others.[98]

---

90 Frank, "Notes and Remarks"; cf. also Marie Bernand, "La critique de la notion de nature (Ṭabʿ) par le Kalām," *SI* 51 (1980): 73f.

91 *Tawḥīd*, 18.1 and 12.3.

92 Ibid., 5.2.

93 Ibid., 5.2–5.

94 Ibid., 43.3; the resonance with Aristotle's definition ("animal rationale") is unmistakable. Al-Ashʿarī explicitly derived this formulation on this basis (Gimaret, *La doctrine*, 69).

95 *Tawḥīd*, 10 ult. f., 201.12ff., 218.20ff., 221.18ff., 223.10ff., 224.15ff.

96 Ibid., 12.3f., 18.1, 117.10, 143.3f.

97 E.g., ibid., 142.12ff.; on the *aṣḥāb al-ṭabāʾiʿ*, cf. van Ess, *Theologie*, vol. 2, 39ff.

98 *Tawḥīd*, 143.9ff.

Order and harmony, our theologian explains, are consequences of an external cause, namely the omnipotent Creator.[99] He created natures and bound them into bodies, although their essence actually works against unification.[100] Al-Māturīdī is also concerned with the fact that created beings continue to exist despite this inner opposition and tension,[101] and that if they do change, then this happens in an ordered and sensible way.[102]

In contrast, what natures specifically are seems to be less important for al-Māturīdī. He never defines them in greater detail. But we do have some indications from which we can deduce with a great deal of confidence that they are none other than the four primary qualities of heat, cold, moisture, and dryness. These are discussed in al-Māturīdī's arguments against the Dualists. He accuses them of being positively obdurate in their line of reasoning by which they conclude that the number of primordial principles are two: If one really argues that Good and Bad form an irreconcilable opposition and consequently must exist in and of themselves without beginning, then one could just as well make the claim that natures are also mutually opposed and thus eternal entities, which would make the number of primordial principles four.[103] Or, just to heighten the absurdity of the idea, one could just as legitimately argue for the number five, since the *tabāʾiʿ* ultimately unify through a fifth principle (i.e., the body), which also represents something different, since for its part it is not describable as hot or cold.[104]

Al-Māturīdī's position here is quite clear, but further observations on his view of the *ṭabāʾiʿ* can still be made for a fuller picture: In another section we learn that heat (*ḥarāra*) rises up according to its nature (*bi-ṭabʿihā*), while cold (*burūda*) sinks down for the same reason.[105] Elsewhere, we read that cooling and heating are natural effects.[106] In a third context, burning and cooling off are named as consequences of the nature of fire and snow respectively.[107] Throughout all of this, al-Māturīdī continues to emphasize that all natural processes ultimately go back to God as their Creator. This differentiates him fundamentally from the *aṣḥāb al-ṭabāʾiʿ*, whom he considers part of the "Dahrīya"

99 Ibid., 116.-2ff.

100 Ibid., 18.1f., 12.4, 122.12ff., 94.12ff., 29.15ff.

101 Ibid., 143.3ff., 117.10ff.

102 Ibid., 151.12ff.

103 Ibid., 165.4f.

104 Ibid., 165.7f.

105 Ibid., 117.13f.

106 Ibid., 146.20ff.

107 Ibid., 264.9f.

and whose teachings he clearly juxtaposes with his own understanding of nature:

> As regards the *ṭabāʾiʿ*, it should be said of (their) existence (*wujūd*) that when things strike together (*iḍṭirāb*) and move, they bring forth (*tuwallidu*) heat in that which is struck and moved, while stillness (*sukūn*) and stability (*qarār*) bring forth cold. Thus natures are that which emerges from the (changing) states of the world (*al-ḥāditha*), while the world does not emerge (*al-mutawallid*) from natures.[108]

Accordingly, we can immediately assert that the primary qualities play an important role in the physical worldview of our theologian. These are the prime components of bodies both large and small, and are also set loose when such bodies act, e.g., when heat comes from that which is struck together or cold comes from stillness. Through all of this it must not be forgotten, however, that the *ṭabāʾiʿ* in and of themselves possess no creative power. They can only follow their "nature," which avoids other "natures." Consequently they never merge together as bodies by themselves because this necessitates a (partial) resignation of their natural effect, which causes them to resist. Given that bodies nevertheless exist then proves the existence of an overruling principle, the all-powerful Creator. He not only created the *ṭabāʾiʿ*, He also controls them and thus guarantees the continuance of an ordered world.

However, there is yet another question that remains unanswered, one which takes us back to the starting point of our observations. If natures actually form the constituents of the material world, and if not a single body is conceivable without them—then how do they fit into al-Māturīdī's rigid ontological conceptualization? Until now we had started from the premise that he only admitted two types of created being, namely accidents as simple elements, and bodies, which he says are composed of the same.

According to Frank, the *ṭabāʾiʿ* here belong to the category of bodies. He believed that al-Māturīdī saw colors, flavors, and the like as corporeal,[109] and

108 Ibid., 145.7–9.

109 Frank, "Notes and Remarks," 139, with reference to *Tawḥīd*, 81.11f. The selection which Frank bases his views on (*Tawḥīd*, 81.7ff.), however, is very problematic. It deals with God having no limit (*ḥadd*) by which one can grasp Him, while all created things must be surrounded by limits. In this context we read the two important statements: "Every thing (*shayʾ*) has a limit by which it is grasped (*yudraku*) such as taste (*ṭaʿm* and *dhawq*), color (*lawn*), smell (*rāʾiḥa*) and other limits (*ḥudūd*) for the specificity (*khāṣṣīya*) of things. (For) God gave them all an external form (*wajh*) through which they are grasped (*yudraku*)

underlined this thesis with the observation that other theologians who also attributed an active role to natures in physics, such as al-Naẓẓām for instance, also started from the premise of corporeal *ṭabāʾiʿ*.[110]

It seems, however, that such a comparison does not do al-Māturīdī justice, since we have already determined that he clearly kept his distance from al-Naẓẓām on ontological matters. This, of course, does not rule out certain meeting points between the two, e.g., the (fifth) argument for the contingency of the world,which was based on the oppositional natures of things, and was taught by both al-Māturīdī and al-Naẓẓām (and the latter's student Ibn Shabīb). Nevertheless, common word choices are not as conclusive as a specific ontological framework, and al-Māturīdī's particular understanding of natures still requires more investigation. This we will now undertake, being helped again by consulting the writings of his successors, the later theologians of Transoxania.

First we must take into account that his concept of natures—much like his doctrine on accidents—ultimately did not receive the approval of the Māturīdites. The thought of Abū l-Yusr al-Pazdawī[111] and Abū l-Muʿīn al-Nasafī[112] is representative of this tendency. They completely ignored the concept, which

---

and encompassed (*yuḥāṭu*), even (*ḥattā*) (i.e., including) intellect(s) and accidents," ibid., 81.10–12. From the context, Frank clearly interprets al-Māturīdī as distinguishing between taste, color, etc. on one side, and accidents on the other. The former are supposed to be natures, possess limits, and indicate corporality, while the latter are incorporeal and thus have no external limits. This actually corresponds with (atomist) theologians' common understanding of accidents, but not with al-Māturīdī's views, which are based on other premises. Al-Māturīdī is merely trying to say here that everything which is created, up to the smallest components (i.e., accidents), has a form and is perceivable by the senses. Ḍirār also saw things that way, and al-Māturīdī explicitly agrees with this axiom (though cf. below, 260n119) as al-Nasafī shows (*Tabṣira*, vol. 1, 52.7). Al-Māturīdī mentions the intellect and accidents together in this excerpt, thus showing the same orientation. It is evocative of his definition of the human being as being composed of an intellect and natures. As such, natures are just a special category of accidents, which are all considered perceivable by the senses.

110 Frank, "Notes and Remarks," 139.

111 Al-Pazdawī emphasizes that fire does not function by nature (*bi-l-ṭabʿ*), because God creates the effect of fire in it (*Uṣūl*, 20.15–19). Furthermore, God does not have to create the exact same effects in the same things. If He does this, He is only following a habit (*Uṣūl*, 121.10–13 and 206.1–3). This also shows al-Pazdawī's proximity to the Ashʿarites.

112 Al-Nasafī does not mention the *ṭabāʾiʿ* in the *Baḥr al-kalām* or in the *Tamhīd*. The term comes up in the *Tabṣirat al-adilla*, but only in conjunction with a proof for the createdness of the world, which is adapted from al-Māturīdī (*Tabṣira*, vol. 1, 79.12–14). In al-Nasafī's own physics, natures play no role.

had the effect of effacing its role in Māturīdite theology from the later fifth/eleventh century to posterity.[113] In earlier times, however, perceptions seem to have been different, since we have the testimony of two authors who deal with the concept of the *ṭabāʾiʿ* in a relatively unprejudiced manner, and whose testimonies are very informative for us.

The first, but least important of the two is Abū l-Layth. He mentions natures among the various themes he addresses in his *Bustān al-ʿārifīn*, and confirms two theses that one may consider key features of the doctrine: that God created the world out of natures, and that they are considered to be the four primary qualities of all things.[114]

Abū Shakūr is much more informative, and approaches the theme on a foundational level. He is especially concerned with refuting the "natural philosophers" (here: *al-Ṭabāʾiʿīya*), which compels him to articulate himself very precisely. His first and most important accusation against them is by now long familiar: the *Ṭabāʾiʿīya* falsely consider natures to be autonomous and eternal entities, and thus they conclude that everything in the world came to exist through them.[115] Abū Shakūr has an additional critique to make which is novel in its formulation, and what is more, touches upon all the points that are important for our inquiry: He reproaches them for considering natures (*ṭabʿ*) to be fine corporeal substances (*jawhar laṭīf*), by which he means to make clear that their doctrine has proceeded incorrectly from the outset.[116]

One can already guess what Abū Shakūr would like to juxtapose with this idea. And he does say it—with much-appreciated clarity, in fact. According to him, a "nature" must be described as "an accident created in time which is compelled (*ʿaraḍ muḥdath majbūr*), and does not subsist in itself (*lā yaqūmu bi-dhātihi*), but rather inheres (*yaḥullu*) in all members (*jawāriḥ*), corporeal substances (*jawāhir*), and organs (*ālāt*/of the body)."[117] Al-Sālimī thus produces an actual definition and achieves a clarity which was painfully missing in al-Māturīdī's observations on ontology. But that aside, the parallels between his work and the *K. al-Tawḥīd* are unmistakable, and only shortly afterwards, al-Sālimī states an opinion that corresponds to what we have discovered in

113 At least, this is how one ought to interpret Najm al-Dīn's and al-Ṣābūnī's silence in his creed on the topic. We do find a reference to it in the *Lāmīya* of Ushī (ca. 569/1173), which is not that significant, however, since questions of ontology are left out there.

114 Abū l-Layth, *Bustān*, section 116, 191–193.

115 Abū Shakūr, *Tamhīd*, fol. 17a2ff.

116 Ibid., fols. 16b ult.–17a2.

117 Ibid., fol. 16b–2f.; cf. also ibid., 17b ult., where *ṭabʿ* is again defined as an accident, and 19a ult.ff., where the hypothesis that it could be a substance is refuted.

the meantime to be al-Māturīdī's own point of view: The foundation (*aṣl*) of nature (*ṭabīʿa*) is such that humans (*banī Ādam*), all living beings (*ḥayawānāt*), and corporeal substances (*jawāhir*) are composed of cold, heat, moisture, and dryness. Each of these natures is opposed to the others (*ḍiddun li-ṣāḥibihi*). These oppositions would never unify (*yajtamiʿu*) for a single moment in a (single) substrate (*maḥall*) if it were not for the compulsion (*jabr*) of a compelling (*jabbār*), wise, powerful, and knowing being, who was consequently also the Creator of all things.[118]

One could of course now object that Abū Shakūr was actually an atomist and thus could hardly be in a position to reproduce al-Māturīdī's ideas reliably. It is also true that the concepts of the two theologians are not comparable in many aspects. Yet their difference does not lie in the classification of natures as accidents, but rather in the extent of the role accidents are given in their respective frameworks. In this regard, al-Māturīdī professed a unique position within his school; and now, after many considerations, it has become clear enough to be summarized in its essential features.

Al-Māturīdī professed what might be called a monistic ontology. He viewed all phenomena of the material world as either emerging or being formed in some manner by accidents. Nevertheless, it is critical that we establish an essential dichotomy here, since our theologian ultimately distinguishes between two types of accidents, even if they can be generally unified under the label of qualities or properties.

He calls the first of these "natures," by which he means that which we know as the four primary qualities from the elemental doctrines of antiquity. To a certain extent they represent the material out of which God may form bodies at any time. But these cannot be seen solely as an object and mirror of divine actions, since they additionally function independently, "out of inner obligation." Consequently, they still distantly reflect the conception of nature found in antiquity even though al-Māturīdī fundamentally depends on showing that these powers are subject to the divine will.

In contrast, we recognize his second category of accidents as the classical phenomenon defined by Islamic theology. According to al-Māturīdī they do not contribute to the formation of bodies, but rather describe their changing states, such as stillness, movement, and color, or whatever else can change. We also learn that their number is much larger than four and that only some of

118 Ibid., fol. 17b 4–7.

them may inhere in a body at a given time. These accidents are also necessarily contingent, such that one can also infer a Creator from their existence.[119]

8.1.2.3 Informing Factors and Exemplary Models

This small number of axiomatic principles naturally do not add up to a complete and convincing ontological theory. They simply leave open too many questions which must be discussed but which our theologian does not answer. Bearing this in mind, it must be acknowledged that al-Māturīdī's doctrine does display its own distinctive profile: it not only combines various older concepts, but also follows its own internal logic; one which we may presume took into account the particular religious environment of Samarqand.

A few examples can be given here: Al-Māturīdī's minimal concern for the nature of the world's composition because of his concentration on personal piety and a relationship to God might be related to the strong presence of Sufis in Transoxania. His emphasis on all things ultimately consisting of accidents sounds like a reaction to the teachings of the Dualists (especially the Manichaeans), who were present in Samarqand and also claimed that the world was composed of bodies.[120] Finally, his assignment of a special role to the primary qualities shows his lack of prejudice toward the philosophers; we have already seen this type of attitude in northeastern Iran, with Abū Zayd al-Balkhī spreading al-Kindī's teachings and the Ismāʿīlīs riding on the wake of a new interest in Neoplatonism. At the same time, al-Māturīdī's thought contrasts sharply with certain theological models that were in vogue in Iraq in his time. The most striking example is atomism, which clearly did not interest him at all. Neither did occasionalism, which was professed by the Basran Muʿtazilites, by al-Ashʿarī, and by many later *mutakallimūn*,[121] yet it played no role with our theologian.

In any case, it is also true that al-Māturīdī's views were embedded in earlier theological traditions and he did not develop everything he presented completely from scratch. Rather, he worked to compile ideas and combine them

119 One can thus classify the arguments that we have been dealing with for the createdness of the world based on the type of accident that is presumed: If we are dealing with bodies perceivable to the senses (arguments 3, 4, 5, and 7), then naturally natures that are perceivable to the senses come to the fore. If, on the other hand, al-Māturīdī talks about movement, etc. (arguments 8, 9, 10, 11, 14, 15, and 17), then he is thinking about the second category of qualities. These too are perceivable by the senses (e.g., that something moves), but only the intellect can recognize the role of accidents in this context, which is why these arguments are classified as proofs based on the intellect.

120 Van Ess, *Theologie*, vol. 3, 335ff.; Dhanani, 182ff.

121 Gimaret, *La doctrine*, 58f. and 408.

anew. Thus we can also posit certain forerunning models for particular ideas from older *kalām*, with the qualification that the synthesis that al-Māturīdī formulated therefrom was his own.

The stimuli to which our theologian responded were certainly not from the Ḥanafite tradition of Transoxania; as far as we are able to determine, none of his predecessors—from Abū Ḥanīfa up to al-Ḥakīm al-Samarqandī—ever discussed questions of ontology. If one were to name an early author from the East at all, it would be Makḥūl al-Nasafī, the Karrāmite. But his remarks were also vague and from the outset decidedly too sparse to derive a comprehensive worldview from.[122]

Al-Māturīdī therefore had to improvise, and, given the circumstances, did the only thing possible: He based himself on the contributions of those theologians whom we have come to know as his adversaries and tested the theoretical premises which they presented. The results of the test,were apparently positive, since there is a lot to argue for al-Māturīdī taking inspiration from at least two thinkers whose theology he was actually arguing against.

The most important stimulus—as al-Nasafī unwillingly saw as well[123]—certainly came from al-Najjār. Al-Najjār followed the ontological model of Ḍirār b. ʿAmr and likely played the role of its medium to al-Māturīdī.[124] We may thus posit al-Najjār's historical influence in regard to two critical aspects of al-Māturīdī's ontology; namely his thesis that the world only consists of accidents, and his dichotomous categorization of these accidents. To al-Najjār this dichotomy consisted of 1) those accidents which consistently change in a body, and 2) those accidents which essentially constitute the body and to which he attributed a certain degree of spatiality (*taḥayyuz*).[125]

The paths of the two theologians do part significantly in regard to one important aspect, however: al-Māturīdī taught that there were only four constitutive accidents which he called natures, and identified them with heat, cold, dryness, and moisture. This does not correspond to al-Najjār's ideas at all,

122 It is only of interest for us that Makḥūl al-Nasafī also presumed the existence of natures. Unfortunately he does not describe their features more precisely, but only states that people can bear differing burdens because God creates them differently in respect to their natures (*fī l-ṭabāʾiʿ*); see *Radd*, 92.16f.

123 *Tabṣira*, vol. 1, 51.10ff. and 52.5ff.

124 Al-Ashʿarī, *Maqālāt*, 317.13ff. and 359 ult.ff.; *Uṣūl*, 12.2 and 250.16; al-Baghdādī, *Farq*, 196.11ff.; see van Ess, "Ḍirār b. ʿAmr [II]," 57 as well as *Theologie*, vol. 4, 150f.; Madelung, "The Shiite and Khārijite," 128.

125 Dhanani, 91f.

as the latter did not operate with the concept of natures; this then raises the question of whether we have another influence to reckon with here.

The presumption of natures in the late third/ninth century was by no means obsolete. Al-Burghūth, whom al-Māturīdī was aware of, did so;[126] Ibn Shabīb, who was much more familiar to him, did so as well.[127] Yet in both cases, the little that we know of their worldview does not fit with the statements of our theologian, and thus it is necessary to speculate about other possible contact points.

This makes another intellectual parallel which we initially did not even consider even more interesting. It leads us to back again to al-Kaʿbī, the Muʿtazilite, the man whom we know as al-Māturīdī's main opponent. Al-Kaʿbī was of course an atomist, but as a theologian standing in the Baghdad tradition, he maintained the concept of natures.[128] He even interpreted them in a manner that was comparable to al-Māturīdī's formulations; he was of the view that there were four *ṭabāʾiʿ*, the four primary qualities precisely. Al-Kaʿbī's theory of atoms, moreover, did not define natures as corporeal (as al-Naẓẓām had), which means he must have considered them to be either powers or characteristics, i.e., accidents.[129] Hence his doctrine displays a series of characteristics that also distinguish al-Māturīdī's thought, and the possibility cannot be ruled out that our Ḥanafite theologian was prompted, in regard to these points, by the disagreeable Muʿtazilite.[130]

8.2 God

8.2.1 *God's Existence*

Al-Māturīdī's discussions on the structure of the world cannot help simultaneously addressing the topic of God's existence. He not only described what he viewed as the constitutional components of material things, but also emphasized their lack of autonomy and their obvious contingency, thus postulating that they were all the work of an omnipotent Creator.

126 Van Ess, *Theologie*, vol. 4, 163f.

127 Ibid., vol. 4, 128f.

128 Van Ess., "Abū 'l-Qāsem Kaʿbī," *EIr*, vol. 1, 361af.

129 Abū Rashīd al-Nīsābūrī, *al-Masāʾil fī l-khilāf bayna al-Baṣrīyīn wa-l-Baghdādīyīn*, ed. M. Ziyāda and R. al-Sayyid (Beirut, 1979), 133.7ff. and 149.10ff.; Biram, 16.

130 A further indication of al-Kaʿbī's influence might also be al-Māturīdī's claim that a body only continues to exist when the accident *baqāʾ* is bestowed on it (cf. above, argument 15). The Muʿtazilite theologian also taught the same (Gimaret, *La doctrine*, 40, 66, and 125f.)

This postulate is secured and consolidated again at the beginning of his discussions on God. Before our theologian actually presents the details of his theology, he first repeats the proof for the existence of a Creator (*muḥdith*).[131] The arguments he enumerates are in essence the same that he produced for the createdness (*ḥadath*) of the world. He explains again that our experience shows that all the things we know go back to a creator (e.g., buildings go back to builders or writing goes back to writers).[132] Also, the world must be the work of a creator, because it could not have subsisted eternally, since its distinguishing feature is a plurality of opposites (e.g., the unified and separated;[133] good and bad;[134] living and dead;[135] accidents and bodies;[136] mutually opposing natures).[137]

However, al-Māturīdī does not allow for the existence of a higher principle to be simply inferred from the given facts of the world in an abrupt manner. Instead, he reflects on this notion and considers its unspoken premises: If one actually thinks that it is possible to validly infer an eternal Creator from the manifold nature of contingent things, one must accept a fundamental assumption. One must assume that God is not completely transcendent and unfathomable, but is actually connected in some way to His creation, such that He can be inferred therefrom. Al-Māturīdī knows as much, and says so in the *K. al-Tawḥīd* with the following words:

> The basis (*aṣl*) of these (arguments) consists in that nothing is accomplished by Him (i.e., God) without a wisdom so astounding (*ḥikma ʿajība*) and a sign so wondrous (*dalāla badīʿa*) becoming (visible), such that scholars are not capable of comprehending its (i.e., the creation's) being (*māʾīya*) and its type of existence. They all know that they are incapable of comprehending the true nature (*kunh*) of this (i.e., the creation) due to the wisdom and knowledge that are enclosed therein. This limitation, as well as others, are signs (*dalāla*) of the wisdom (*ḥikma*) of their Causer and Creator.[138]

131 *Tawḥīd*, 17.5–19.5; on al-Māturīdī's arguments and doctrines concerning God's existence and attributes, cf. also Cerić, 141–199.

132 Ibid., 18.10–12.

133 Ibid., 17.6–8.

134 Ibid., 17.9–13.

135 Ibid., 17.14–16.

136 Ibid., 17.17–20.

137 Ibid., 18.1–2. On the use of these proofs of God in arguing with unbelievers, cf. Ibrahim, "Al-Māturīdī's Arguments."

138 *Tawḥīd*, 18.13–16.

In the *Ta'wīlāt* he expands on this point:

> We have established previously that God is known in two ways: a) through the creation, since He has made signs (*dalā'il*) in the creation of every single (created thing), and [these signs] point (us) to His knowledge, His unity, and the fact that He neither created it in vain nor will He (one day) leave it to naught; and b) through the prophets ...[139]

Both citations substantiate that al-Māturīdī was aware of the epistemological premises of his proofs for God since he says there explicitly that we know the Creator because our world contains clues everywhere that point to Him. At the same time he expands on this idea with the implicit addition of a second premise; namely that human beings have also been endowed with the means to decipher and understand these clues that have been laid out by God.

8.2.2 *God's Knowability*

8.2.2.1 The Rationalistic Position of the Ḥanafites

The first premise was natural for a Muslim theologian. That the creation contains signs of its Creator was known from a source above all doubts. It was in the Qur'ān, and to be found in many verses such as Q 16:11–13:

> With (water) He grows for you grain, olives, palms, vines, and all kinds of other crops. There truly is a sign in this for those who reflect. By His command He has made the night and day, the sun, moon, and stars all of benefit to you. There truly are signs in this for those who use their reason. He has made of benefit to you the many-colored things He has multiplied on the earth. There truly are signs in this for those who take heed.

The second premise was more questionable, however, and was by no means a necessary result of the first. Even if one assumed that the world was filled with signs of its Creator, the question still remained as to the way in which these signs are accessible to us. Does the human being need divine assistance to understand them, i.e., the guidance of revelation? Or can he interpret them with his intellect on the basis of his own ability—which would mean admitting the possibility of naturalistic cognition of God?

---

139 *Ta'wīlāt*, vol. 1, 110.3–5; cf. ibid. 66.5f. and 125 ult. f.

Both views had been professed in Islam. As is known, Muʿtazilite theologians argued most strongly for the autonomy of the intellect in this regard.[140] Traditionist circles, however, were quite skeptical, and emphasized the dependence of the human being on revelation.[141] This also became characteristic of the Ashʿarite school; al-Ashʿarī did believe that there were clear signs for the existence of God, but in general he insisted that human beings first needed the stimulus of revelation in order to even become conscious of the pressing question of the existence of a Creator.[142]

Such considerations were foreign to al-Māturīdī, as we have already attested to. He stated unequivocally that there were two ways to knowledge of God; by the prophets and by rational observation of the creation.[143] Furthermore, in the course of explaining his epistemology he also stated that the intellect was capable of distinguishing between good and bad as well as proving the existence of a Creator.[144]

This optimistic position, however, should not be explained as a concession to the Muʿtazilites' views. It is actually rooted in a tradition that al-Māturīdī found in his own school. The Ḥanafites had always held a rationalistic position on this issue and claimed that God was knowable by natural means.

This is attested to by the school founder himself in the second *Risāla* to ʿUthmān al-Battī. There it says that God created all people so that they would worship Him and that He showed them all (already before the revelation of the Qurʾān) the way to obedience.[145] Al-Pazdawī further confirms for us that Abū Ḥanīfa thought this way; he reports that the latter held belief in God to be necessary even without recourse to revelation. This report is particularly credible because al-Pazdawī transmits it although he personally adhered to another opinion.[146]

---

140 Van Ess, *Erkenntnislehre*, 16ff. and 326; Madelung, *Der Imam al-Qāsim*, 20ff.; Frank, "Reason and Revealed Law," 124ff.

141 Van Ess, *Erkenntnislehre*, 21ff. with reference to the Ḥanbalites.

142 Richard M. Frank, "Al-Ashʿarī's Conception of the Nature and Role of Speculative Reasoning in Theology," in *Proceedings of the VIth Congress of Arabic and Islamic Studies (Visby-Stockholm 1972)*, ed. Frithiof Rundgren (Stockholm, 1975), 136–164; idem, "Reason and Revealed Law," 135ff.; Gimaret, *La doctrine*, 211ff.; also cf. Rudolph, "Ratio und Überlieferung," 73ff.

143 *Taʾwīlāt*, vol. 1, 110.3–5.

144 *Tawḥīd*, 9.16–18; 10.8–10; cf. 110.13ff.

145 Cf. van Ess, *Theologie*, vol. 1, 205.

146 *Uṣūl*, 207.14f. and 210.13ff. Al-Pazdawī's own view is clearly laid out (ibid., 207.6–8 and 209 ult.ff.). He shows himself to be united with al-Ashʿarī on this issue (ibid., 207.8) as well as with the Ḥanafite theologians of Bukhārā (ibid., 207.15f.). In contrast he explicitly

In the generation of Abū Ḥanīfa's first students, we find very few relevant statements on the theme. One can only mention the *K. al-ʿĀlim*, in which Abū Muqātil warns of restricting oneself to the guidelines of tradition and emphasizes that an individual must know for himself what is right and wrong.[147] Ibn Karrām's position, however, is much clearer. In regard to these issues, he adhered to strictly Ḥanafite lines and argued that rational knowledge of God was possible. The best testimony to this is from Makḥūl, i.e., an older contemporary of al-Māturīdī's. In his *Radd* we read that no person can justify their disbelief by pointing to their lack of knowledge of revelation: God did not just send us prophets to teach us, but also other proofs (*ḥujaj*) for His existence, such as signs (*āyāt*), examples (*ʿibar*), our own weaknesses (*ḍaʿf*) and inabilities (*ʿajz*), as well as the fact that we (as contingent beings) continually change from one state to another (*al-taḥwīl min ḥāl ilā ḥāl*).[148] This does not mean that we can perceive God with the senses, but rather that each person endowed with intellect is capable of recognizing Him through the creation.[149]

8.2.2.2 Inferring the Unseen from that which is Seen

Al-Māturīdī could thus look back on a long tradition of relevant positions on this topic. But at the same time it must have quickly become clear to him that what he read there was methodologically lacking. All the earlier authors had simply claimed that one could make rational inferences of the Creator's existence from the creation. None of them said how this inference ought to take place, and none of them specified the dangers associated with presuming a rationally traversable relationship between God and the world. Al-Māturīdī had to make up for this omission, and he did so in the style of a trained *mutakallim*, by dedicating an individual chapter to the topic of "inferring the unseen from that which is seen" (*dalālat al-shāhid ʿalā l-ghāʾib*).[150]

There we learn first of all that making inferences of hidden things is particularly tricky and susceptible to mistakes. Many people who carry out such inferences believe quite erroneously that that which is visible always indicates something which is the same (*mithl*) or similar (*naẓīr*) in the unseen domain. They thus believe that they can establish an analogy (*qiyās*) between the two

---

disagrees with al-Māturīdī and the scholars of Samarqand (ibid., 207.12f. and 207.20f.). On this conflict among the Ḥanafites of Transoxania, cf. Madelung, "The Spread," 117n30.

147 *K. al-ʿĀlim*, sections 2–4.

148 *Radd*, 71.17–72.4.

149 Ibid., 108.-3–109.6; on the topic, cf. Gimaret and Monnot, 360; Madelung, *Religious Trends*, 41; van Ess, *Ungenützte Texte*, 17n2.

150 *Tawḥīd*, 27.18–29 ult.

spheres. But this is a grave mistake, because they thereby make the obvious and sensibly perceivable into the foundation (*aṣl*), and turn the unseen into something derivative (*farʿ*) of it.[151]

This critique is directed first and foremost against the "Dahrites." This is seen in al-Māturīdī's expository critique of their fallacy that the world must have always existed eternally in the same form (*mithl*) as it is now visible.[152] In the background, however, lies a polemic against the Muʿtazilites as well. They also permitted the same standards to be applied to God and the creation when they claimed, for example, that God must always do the optimum (*al-aṣlaḥ*) and always be just.[153]

Our theologian sought to avoid such errors. This incited him to produce another axiom as the basis for his own doctrines: The visible is an indication of something which is alike (*mithl*) in the domain of the unseen, as well as something which is different (*khilāf*), in such a manner that the indication of difference is actually the more evident (*awḍaḥ*) of the two.[154]

This means that the cases in which such inferences are carried out must be examined more closely. Such scrupulousness is called for because the conclusions we draw from such thought processes are dependent on the given circumstances; or, to be precise, it is only in certain exceptional cases that a similarity between the seen and unseen can be legitimately inferred. It seldom happens that the relationships which we perceive from our own perspective can be directly applied to things which are not present.

As al-Māturīdī clarifies, this is only possible in principle if the inference is carried out within a soundly defined domain, i.e., within a type or species. In this case we can make a statement on something which we have not perceived with the senses but the nature of which is known through encounters with other similar cases. For example, everyone who has seen a fire at least once can speak about the features of other fires even if they happen to be out of their field of vision.[155]

In all other cases, however, such simple translations are not possible. This is especially evident when one tries to deduce a cause from an effect and thus

---

151 Ibid., 27 ult.–28.1.

152 Ibid., 28.1ff.; cf. ibid., 111.18ff., where the question of the proper inference of the unseen is connected with the polemic against the "Dahrīya."

153 On the critique of the principle of the *aṣlaḥ*, cf. ibid., 92.15ff. and 108.14ff.; on the application of the inference of the unseen by the Muʿtazila, cf. Nagel, *Festung des Glaubens*, 157f.

154 *Tawḥīd*, 28.6.

155 Ibid., 28.12–15 with the example of fire and bodies. Al-Māturīdī does not work out the theoretical basis of his argumentation in more detail.

crosses the boundaries between distinct genera. A building, for example, is completely different from its builder, and a text is completely different from the one who writes it.[156] How much more must this be true of the relationship between the creation and the Creator, since the world shows itself to be a dependent and non-autonomous structure, and precisely because of this we conclude that its principle (*aṣl*) is radically different, i.e., independent and autonomous.[157]

Thus, in the case of the divine Creator we may only come to conclusions in regard to disparity: We conclude from the given conditions of this world that He exists and commands it, but in principle our knowledge of God consists in our knowing His distance from created beings. Al-Māturīdī names further examples in this sense: our ignorance indicates God's knowledge,[158] our variety indicates His unity,[159] and our temporality His eternality.[160] And the fact that opposing things in this world have no power over themselves also shows that their Creator is all-powerful.[161]

In sum, al-Māturīdī teaches the possibility of rational knowledge of God. He thus positions himself contrary to other Sunnī doctrines such as those of the Ashʿarites, and outwardly would seem to take his place alongside the Muʿtazilite theologians. But the manner in which he describes his inferences of God's existence shows how carefully he utilizes this tool. He tries to avoid any comparability between "principle" and "derivative," i.e., the Creator and the world; in other words, he objects to there being any type of *analogia entis* conceivable. Instead, the relationship between the invisible God and His visible creation is determined inversely, since the various considerations mentioned are conclusive in that the Creator unifies in His perfect being that which the world is known to be deficient in.[162]

8.2.3 *God's Oneness*

One of the inferences we have mentioned is that the plurality of created things indicates the oneness of the Creator. This expresses another tenet that plays a

156 Ibid., 28.12–20; 29.4–6.

157 Cf. ibid., 29.6–10 and 29.19–21, as well as the arguments above for the createdness of the world.

158 Ibid., 29.15f. and 29.17f.

159 Ibid., 29.14f.

160 Ibid., 28 ult.–29.3.

161 Ibid., 29.15f.

162 The Ashʿarites, given their formulations, are compelled to be even more reserved in regard to the inference of the unseen; on this issue cf. Nagel, *Festung des Glaubens*, 158f.

central role in al-Māturīdī's theology. The thesis itself is neither unusual nor remarkable; it belongs to the very core of the Islamic faith and is repeated and explained by every *mutakallim*. It is striking, however, how often our theologian presents it in his *K. al-Tawḥīd*.[163] This might be related to the fact that the opponents of God's oneness, presumably the Dualists, were more strongly represented in Samarqand than elsewhere in the Islamic world.

The arguments al-Māturīdī uses to conduct this discussion are numerous, and as was the case earlier, are divided according to their relationship with the three modes of obtaining knowledge. Thus he begins with the evidences of transmission (*samʿ*);[164] follows them with the indications of the intellect (*dalālat al-ʿaql*);[165] and ends with that which can be inferred from the impressions of the senses or, as he calls it, "the creation" (*dalālat al-istidlāl bi-l-khalq*).[166] From this emerges an altogether imposing tableau of considerations that accomplishes two things for our theologian: It refutes the Dualists much more precisely and explicitly than the earlier Ḥanafite texts did, and at the same time it successfully aims to speak for all Muslims, because it offers an adequate expository proof for both schools of theology (i.e., the rationally arguing *mutakallimūn* as well as the Traditionists). Its outline takes the following course:

First argument: Transmission tells us that the One (*al-wāḥid*) has always had a prominent role among humanity. It is not just the description of majesty (*ʿaẓama*), dominion (*sulṭān*), high rank (*rifʿa*), and excellence (*faḍl*). It is also recognized as the principle of all things, because it is the principle (*ibtidāʾ*) of numbers and hence multiplicity, without itself being a number (*Tawḥīd*, 19.9–ult.).

Second argument: Furthermore, we learn through transmission that only a single God has imparted revelation. There are no prophets, nor signs in the creation that proclaim the existence of a second God (*Tawḥīd*, 20.1–4).

Third argument: A second God would have prevented a revelation which speaks of a single God. Consequently one can conclude from the existence of such a revelation that there is only one Creator (*Tawḥīd*, 20.5–10).

Fourth argument: The intellect tells us, in fact, that two (or more) gods would mutually prevent one another's activity (*tamānuʿ*). Just as kings always strive for dominance, the gods would also try to implement their power everywhere, and would consequently conflict with each other's plans. None could

163 The main proof is present in *Tawḥīd*, 19.6–23.7, cf. 110.13ff. and 139 ult.ff., but also 157.17ff.
164 Ibid., 19.9ff.
165 Ibid., 20.11ff.
166 Ibid., 21.15ff.

complete a creative work such as our world—unless they came to a compromise (*iṣṭilāḥ*). This is ruled out for an omnipotent and all-knowing God, because such a compromise is always a sign of ignorance (*jahl*) and weakness (*ʿajz*) (*Tawḥīd*, 20.11–21.6).

Fifth argument: It can thus be asserted that our conception of God only permits the existence of a single god. All the other configurations in which two gods would be conceivable—one ruling the other; one concealing its acts from the other; each of them having power over the other one's actions, etc.—are ultimately untenable. They lead to a situation in which none of them, or only one of them, deserves the name of God (*Tawḥīd*, 21.7–14).

Sixth argument: Observing the creation shows, furthermore, that the natural processes of the world (e.g., winter and summer; sun, moon, and earth) follow a unified course of direction (*tadbīr*). This direction can only be unified under the responsibility of a single administrator (*Tawḥīd*, 21.15–20).

Seventh argument: It is a feature of the world overall to consist of many different and mutually opposing things. Yet these are all arranged in harmony with one another without exception, and this allows us to recognize the will of the one God at work (*Tawḥīd*, 21.21–22.7).

Eighth argument: Opposing forces are even unified in specific individuals. No man (and also no other created being) is either only good or only bad, such that one might presume the existence of a good and bad creator as the Dualists do. Everyone encompasses both tendencies. Consequently the Creator must also be an all-powerful and encompassing principle (*Tawḥīd*, 22.8–15).

Ninth argument: Additionally, all concrete entities (*aʿyān*) that we can perceive are bodies (*ajsām*). All bodies consist of natures (*ṭabāʾiʿ*) that are characterized by repulsion and conflict. That they are nevertheless unified in a harmonic whole shows that they are directed by a God who possesses complete power, good will (*luṭf*), and wisdom (*ḥikma*) (*Tawḥīd*, 22.16–21).

The catalogue of arguments presented here is extensive, but may again be reduced to a few basic principles. Aside from al-Māturīdī revisiting points that are already familiar to us, he also develops his considerations by focusing on additional recurring motifs. One of these is the concept of *tadbīr*, the direction and providence of God (arguments 6 to 9). This is inferred from observing the creation, or, as al-Māturīdī formulates it, the observation of the acts of lordship (*afʿāl al-rubūbīya*).[167] These acts show themselves to be meticulously ordered and attest to the highest order of meaningfulness. From this it may be concluded that there can only be a single God at their origin, and not a number of competing principles.

---

167 Ibid., 22 ult. and 23.2ff.

The second motif (arguments 3 to 5) is the concept that the existence of two or three gods would lead to their mutual incapacitation (*tamānuʿ*). Al-Māturīdī derives this from the essence of the Creator, or, as he expresses himself here, "the states of divinity" (*aḥwāl al-rubūbīya*).[168] According to this conception, God may only be conceivable as all-powerful and all-knowing, i.e., a universal master. Consequently, no two gods may co-exist which earn this description, as one will prevent the self-realization of the other, there would never be a creation, and in essence there would also be no God, because neither of the two would possess universal lordship.

These two concepts were not new, nor were they developed by al-Māturīdī. In fact, they had long been used in theological argumentation and ultimately go back to antiquity. This is particularly the case in regard to the divine providence. This was a form of the cosmological or teleological proof for God that was particularly developed by the Stoics, but was also common among the Church Fathers.[169] It is also used in the Qurʾān, for example, in Q 27:59–63,

> Say, Praise be to God and peace on the servants He has chosen. Who is better: God, or those they set up as partners with Him? Who created the heavens and earth? Who sends down water from the sky for you—with which We cause gardens of delight to grow: you have no power to make the trees grow in them—is it another god beside God? No! But they are people who take others to be equal with God. Who is it that made the earth a stable place to live? Who made rivers flow through it? Who set immovable mountains on it and created a barrier between the fresh and salt water? Is it another god beside God? No! But most of them do not know. Who is it that answers the distressed when they call upon Him? Who removes their suffering? Who makes you successors in the earth? Is it another god beside God? Little notice you take! Who is it that guides you through the darkness on land and sea? Who sends the winds as

---

168 Ibid., 22 ult. ff.

169 On the Stoics and Church Fathers, see cf. Davidson, *Proofs*, 216ff. and 151f., as well as Josef van Ess, *Die Gedankenwelt des Ḥārit al-Muḥāsibī* (Bonn, 1961), 168f.; the Church Fathers held it to be possible in principle to infer the existence of a God from the signs present in this world (cf. Richard Heinzmann, *Philosophie des Mittelalters* (Stuttgart, 1992), 34ff. and 74 on Augustine). The basis for this was a statement by Paul in Romans 1:18–20, "The wrath of God is being revealed from heaven against all the godlessness and wickedness of people who suppress the truth by their wickedness, since what may be known about God is plain to them, because God has made it plain to them. For since the creation of the world God's invisible qualities—his eternal power and divine nature—have been clearly seen, being understood from what has been made, so that people are without excuse."

heralds of good news before His mercy? Is it another god beside God? God is far above the partners they put beside him!

It is thus unsurprising that this form of proof very soon found its way into *kalām*. There, it is attested to by the third/ninth century at the latest. One such instance can be found in the *K. al-Dalāʾil wa-l-iʿtibār ʿalā l-khalq wa-l-tadbīr* (The Book of Indications and Contemplation on Creation and Guidance), which is sometimes falsely attributed to Jāḥiẓ. There, the meaningful ordering of things is described in detail, from which the existence of a Creator is inferred.[170] A further example may be note which is more interesting for us, written by al-Muḥāsibī. In his *K. al-ʿAẓama* (Book on the Greatness of God) he also explains the idea of *tadbīr* in an equally detailed manner, but does not use it as proof for the existence of a Creator; instead, like al-Māturīdī, he infers God's oneness from it.[171]

The argument of mutual impediment is relatively younger. It can also be found in a Greek text, but this time a later Patristic work;[172] this is probably explained by the fact that debate with Dualists only became prominent at this later time. The Qurʾān is even more eloquent on this point. The classic argument that is always cited is found in Q 21:22: "If there had been in the heavens or earth any gods but Him, both heavens and earth would be in ruins: God, Lord of the Throne, is far above the things they say."[173] But there are further citations, for instance Q 17:42, "Say, If there were other gods along with Him, as they say there are, then they would have tried to find a way to the Lord of the Throne." Or, in Q 23:91, one reads "God has never had a child. Nor is there any god beside Him—if there were, each god would have taken his creation aside and tried to overcome the others. May God be exalted above what they describe!"[174]

The argument of *tamānuʿ* was developed in *kalām* on the basis of such Qurʾānic verses. It quickly became a classical weapon of choice in clashes with the Dualists and is found in variations in numerous texts: in the third/ninth

170 Davidson, *Proofs*, 219ff.; van Ess, *Gedankenwelt*, 170ff.; the text has since appeared in an English translation by M.A.S. Abdel Haleem under the title *Chance or Creation? God's Design in the Universe* (Reading, UK, 1995).

171 Translated by van Ess, *Gedankenwelt*, 163ff.

172 See John of Damascus [Johannes Damascenus], *Die Schriften des Johannes von Damaskos II: Expositio fidei*, ed. B. Kotter (Berlin/New York, 1973), "De fide orthodoxa" I, 5; Davidson names yet another reference from the Corpus Hermeticum (*Proofs*, 166).

173 Cf. *Tawḥīd*, 20.20.

174 Ibid., 20.19f. and 21.2f.

century, for instance, with Abū l-Hudhayl[175] and al-Muḥāsibī;[176] in the early fourth/tenth century not just with our theologian but also by al-Ashʿarī[177] and al-Ṭabarī;[178] and in following times in almost every theological treatise.[179]

Thus al-Māturīdī was able to look back at a tradition of such ideas even as he wrote his doctrines on the oneness of God. These did not come from the earlier Ḥanafite texts of his home region, but from a common theological heritage developed by Muslims in Iraq to fend off Manichaeism. At the same time it would be wrong to say that he merely repeated what his contemporaries said elsewhere. His argumentation also has its own special features, of which at least two ought to be emphasized.

The first is that al-Māturīdī greatly emphasizes the idea of divine direction and the ordered command of the world. This connects him with earlier Islamic theology, as we have seen, and in a certain way even with the cosmological thought of antiquity. But it distinguishes his thought from the formulations adhered to in his time by al-Ashʿarī, his great Sunnī scholarly counterpart. Al-Ashʿarī also knew the argument of *tadbīr*,[180] but it did not have a comparable role in his thought, and took a backseat to the argument of *tamānuʿ*. This is because in his worldview there was no place for the idea of autonomous natures that must be supervised. Al-Māturīdī's assessment was different: He definitely emphasized that the world was dependent on its Creator in every regard, but in his view, it still consisted of natures (*ṭabāʾiʿ*) which have independent effects that God must order and organize by His act of direction.

The second unique feature of al-Māturīdī's argumentation is not related to *tadbīr* or *tamānuʿ*, but takes us back to the beginning of the discussion (argument 1), where he reflects on the prominent role of the One (*al-wāḥid*) in human understanding. He is not concerned here with trying to prove that there is only one Creator. Instead, he wants to explore and determine the sense in which God is to be spoken of as One. These are speculations that do not just differentiate al-Māturīdī from al-Ashʿarī and other Sunnī authors; they are uncommon to classical *kalām* in general and thus deserve to be examined separately once more.

175 Van Ess, *Theologie*, vol. 3, 271.

176 Translated by van Ess, *Gedankenwelt*, 166f.

177 Gimaret, *La doctrine*, 252ff.

178 Al-Ṭabarī, vol. 1, 26.17ff.

179 Examples in Davidson, *Proofs*, 167ff. and Gimaret, *La doctrine*, 252; on the theological problems that were raised by this method of proof, cf. Nagel, *Festung des Glaubens*, 122ff.

180 According to a report from Ibn Fūrak, *Mujarrad*, 55.9f. Al-Ashʿarī believed that God must be named One in regard to His being (*fī nafsihi*), His description (*fī naʿtihi*), and His supervision (*fī tadbīrihi*); see Gimaret, *La doctrine*, 252.

8.2.4 *The Otherness of the One*

Investigating the meaning of the statement that God is One (*al-wāḥid*) clearly occupied our theologian considerably, since he made repeated efforts to explain it on a foundational level. In two such instances he attempted to develop the issue systematically.[181] A third instance is more polemical and serves to refute and fend off wrong conceptions of *tawḥīd*.[182]

As might be expected, this latter instance was more easily executed. Al-Māturīdī happened to possess an excellent tool for this purpose from his earlier discussions on epistemology. There, he claimed that God could be known by the intellect, meaning without the indications of revelation.[183] What this meant was that, in principle, each person could know, by the natural pathways of knowledge, that there was only one God. This assertion is taken up again here and formulated emphatically: "All people that are capable of rational inquiry have been given *tawḥīd* in its entirety."[184] Al-Māturīdī concludes therefrom that in fact all religious groups must have originally had a correct conceptualization of the oneness of God, but this was unfortunately no longer the case. The "Dahrites" negated (*naqaḍa*) this God-given insight,[185] as did the Dualists,[186] Jews,[187] Christians,[188] and natural philosophers.[189] Even most Islamic schools such as the Muʿtazila,[190] the followers of al-Najjār,[191] or the Anthropomorphists[192] went astray in regard to this issue. Only one group preserved the proper understanding of *tawḥīd*, namely his own;[193] this group

181 *Tawḥīd*, 23.8–26.16 and 43.10–15.

182 Ibid., 118.14–121.4.

183 Ibid., 10.8–10; cf. 110.13ff.

184 Ibid., 119.10: *uʿṭiya jamīʿu al-bashari mimman lahu naẓarun al-tawḥīda fī l-jumlati.*

185 Ibid., 119.13ff., *naqaḍa* in 119.11.

186 Ibid., 119.17ff.

187 Ibid., 195.20f.

188 Ibid., 119 ult.ff.

189 Ibid., 120.3f. as *aṣḥāb al-ṭabāʾiʿ*.

190 Ibid., 120.5ff. The Muʿtazilites are accused of two violations of *tawḥīd*: a) They permit that something else eternally exists with God (the *maʿdūm*). b) They claim that God only becomes a creator through the act of creation and becomes merciful through an act of mercy, and so forth, thus assuming change in the one, unchanging God.

191 Ibid., 120.13ff. Al-Najjār and al-Burghūth are also supposed to have said of God that He changes, since they believe that He exists in a place and say at the same time that God originally exists alone (i.e., without a place).

192 Ibid., 120.16ff. The Karrāmites are meant first and foremost.

193 Ibid., 119.11f.; cf. ibid., 121.1

teaches correctly that God is One in regard to His exaltedness (*ʿulūw*) and might (*jalāl*), His essence (*dhāt*), and His attributes (*ṣifāt*).[194]

What this means certainly needs further explanation, and al-Māturīdī tries to provide us some in the two other sections where he takes on the issue more systematically. This was not done without difficulty, however, since God ultimately evades every description being incomparable to anything nor having likenesses (*ashbāh*) or opposites (*aḍdād*).[195] The Qur'ān itself says the same, in the famous eleventh verse of *sūra* 42: "There is no likeness to Him" (*laysa ka-mithlihi shay'*). This is cited by al-Māturīdī to explain that the Creator has no counterpart, because everything that possesses a likeness (*mithl*) can be ordered under the category of numbers.[196] God, however, although being One, is not countable.[197] His unity is not a numerical quantity, but rather symbolizes His majesty (*ʿaẓama*), glory (*kibriyā'*), lordship (*sulṭān*) and power (*qudra*). It indicates His singularity (*tawaḥḥud*), in contrast to that which bears comparison and has an opposite.[198] It shows that He alone is always the same, while everything else, including the fixed stars (*thawābit*), is subject to change.[199] This means that God is one in a completely different way from all other things to which we otherwise attribute oneness. This brings al-Māturīdī to formulate the quintessence of his considerations in the following expression:

> Someone was asked for the meaning of (the expression) "the One" (*al-wāḥid*), and answered that it is used to describe four things:
> 1) a totality (*kull*) that cannot be doubled;
> 2) a part (*juz'*), that cannot be halved;
> 3) something between these two that allows both operations, larger than that which cannot be halved and smaller than that which cannot be doubled, since there is nothing beyond a totality;
> 4) and (finally) the fourth: That through which the (first) three exist (*qāma bihi*), (i.e.,) He and the other.[200] He has concealed who He is.

194 Ibid., 119.5ff.

195 Ibid., 23.9ff.

196 Ibid., 23.13ff.

197 Ibid., 23.8f., 25.5f., 121.1f.

198 Ibid., 23.16ff.

199 Ibid., 24.1ff.

200 The form of the text is not confirmed. According to the transmitted words, the entire sentence (ibid., 43.13f.) is *wa-l-rābiʿ huwa alladhī qāma bihi al-thalāthu, huwa wa lā huwa huwa akhfā man huwa.*

> (He is) the one before whom the tongue (*lisān*) falls silent and whom no exposition (*bayān*) may grasp, the one before whom the imagination (*awhām*) fails, and the intellect (*afhām*) is at a loss. This is God, Lord of the Worlds.[201]

The end of this passage almost has the character of a meditation. It is possible that al-Māturīdī was inspired here by Islamic mysticism,[202] and the same observation may be applied to the literary style he chose. The basic concept that he presents, however, is not from the teachings of the Sufis, but rather Neoplatonic philosophy. Our theologian himself acknowledges this in a certain manner, when he admits that in his speculations on the One he is also disputing the ideas of the philosophers.[203]

Neoplatonism had, in fact, developed the exact same views on transcendence and the incomparability of the highest principle. This holds true in regard to the statement that the One may not be equivocated with the "one" from among numbers, as well as the assertion that the One alone is absolute and one in every respect, while other things which are dependent on it, only have oneness attributed to them in a derivative form. This sectioning-off from the numerical one is already found in Plotinus. He stated this explicitly in Ennead VI 9,[204] but also mentioned it in other places, among which are two sections that were inserted into the Arabic paraphrasing of his works.[205] The distinction between absolute and relative oneness also goes back to Plotinus, but is found in even more detail with Proclus. Proclus opens his compendium

---

201 Ibid., 43.10–15. At the end al-Māturīdī makes an association with Q 1:2.

202 The eastern Sufis of course also reflected on the oneness of God, but their speculations went other ways. This can be seen by comparing him to the most famous author before al-Māturīdī, namely al-Ḥakīm al-Tirmidhī (cf. al-Ḥakīm al-Tirmidhī, *Drei Schriften des Theosophen von Tirmid*, ed. B. Radtke (Beirut, 1992), index, s.v. *waḥdānīya, tawḥīd*) and the most important author in the following generation, namely al-Kalābādhī (see al-Kalābādhī, 33–35: *Sharḥ qawlihim fī l-tawḥīd*). However, some parallels can be found in the wording. For example, the end of the section just cited from the *K. al-Tawḥīd* may be compared with al-Kalābādhī (135.1f.), which also states that God can neither be grasped by tongue (*lisān*) nor by exposition (*bayān*).

203 *Tawḥīd*, 25.9.

204 Enn. VI 9:5.38–43; references are from the Plotinus edition by Henry/Schwyzer.

205 Enn. VI 6:9.10–11; Enn. V 1:5.3–9, which was incorporated into the Theology of Aristotle (VIII 130–131 in Lewis' English translation, *Opera*, vol. 2. which corresponds to the Arabic edition of ʿAbd al-Raḥmān Badawī, *Aflūṭīn ʿinda al-ʿArab* (Cairo, 1966), 112.15–113.1); Enn. V 5:4.12–18, reproduced by the *Risāla fī l-ʿilm al-ilāhī* (Lewis edition, 182–183 = Badawī, 180.5–6).

of Neoplatonic metaphysics, the *Institutio theologica*, with it. And this text was also accessible in the Islamic world, where it was circulated starting from the third/ninth century in two paraphrased Arabic summaries.[206]

A Muslim reader, however, did not have to refer to such redactions of the Greek texts in order to become acquainted with Neoplatonic speculation on the One. Such ideas were also found in the works of al-Kindī, who likewise investigated the question of the being of the "true One" in his metaphysical writings. What he says there also displays Neoplatonic features and is strongly evocative of the ideas that we found with al-Māturīdī: The concept of "one" is applied to many things, including types and individuals,[207] and parts and their sums;[208] again, absolute oneness is only applied to the highest principle, which is furthermore strictly separated from the category of numbers.[209]

We can no longer ascertain how al-Māturīdī came to know of such concepts. Perhaps he owed them to Abū Zayd al-Balkhī, al-Kindī's student,[210] or some other contemporary medium of the philosopher's thought. After all, Neoplatonism was absorbed by the Transoxanian Ismāʿīlīs at the same time, which argues for a wider scope of reception.

It is certain, however, that al-Māturīdī knew and used Neoplatonic metaphysics. It helped him to deepen his concept of the oneness of God. This was unusual for a theologian of his generation, and distinguished him from the Transoxanian Ḥanafites as well as other contemporary *mutakallimūn*, whether the Muʿtazilites or al-Ashʿarī.[211]

---

206 Namely the so-called *Liber de Causis* and the *Propositiones* transmitted separately therefrom, which G. Endreß has edited and published in *Proclus Arabus*. The *Propositiones* 1–3 which interest us are found in the corpus of the *Proclus Arabus*; see Endreß, 253ff. and 3ff. (Arabic text).

207 Al-Kindī, *Rasāʾil*, vol. 1, 126.13ff.; trans. Ivry, 79.

208 Al-Kindī, *Rasāʾil*, vol. 1, 139.12ff.; trans. Ivry, 91. Al-Kindī's views are much more extensive and illuminate the relationship between the one and the many from many aspects, but one can still say that the above-cited section of *K. al-Tawḥīd* functions as a simplified summary of such lines of thought.

209 Al-Kindī, vol. 1, 146.15ff.; trans. Ivry, 98; cf. also Rudolph, *Doxographie*, 45 and 86 (no. XI, 6).

210 The possibility that Abū Zayd al-Balkhī brought al-Kindī's ideas East is always given, but can hardly be proved, since we no longer have access to al-Balkhī's philosophical works, with the exception of the *K. Maṣāliḥ al-abdān wa-l-anfus*, which, however, is more a mix of popular philosophical ideas and medical teachings.

211 There was, of course, Neoplatonic influence on *kalām*, but generally at a much earlier time. In eastern Iran this was particularly the case with Jahm b. Ṣafwān, who lived approximately 200 years before al-Māturīdī; cf. Frank, "The Neoplatonism," 395–424; van Ess, *Theologie*, vol. 2, 499f., cites newer literature.

8.2.5 *God's Attributes*

8.2.5.1 Earlier Ḥanafite Views

The preceding discussion should not be taken to mean that al-Māturīdī brought his theology completely in line with the concepts of Neoplatonism. It merely demonstrates that he elaborated his views on this point and contemplated the divine name of "the One" more so than other theologians.[212] That aside, al-Māturīdī generally described the Creator within the categories familiar to *kalām*. In doing so, he took up, one by one, all the main topics that were discussed among the theological schools of his time, and as representative of the Ḥanafites, stated which position he upheld.

One of these positions is that God may not be described, under any circumstances, as a body (*jism*).[213] This is directed against any form of anthropomorphism, but probably against the followers of Ibn Karrām specifically.[214] The Karrāmites were, as we have seen, the immediate rivals of the Ḥanafites in the East. In this respect, our theologian had every reason to treat this topic in more detail. But ultimately, he does not present any discussion which is specific to Transoxania. The Karrāmīya were also known in Iraq, as elsewhere, and their anthropomorphism was likewise decidedly rejected there.[215]

It is more significant, however, that al-Māturīdī calls God a "being" (*shay*ʾ).[216] Here, he is also following a consensus that had developed among the schools, this time in dispute with a teaching of Jahm b. Ṣafwān. Jahm had claimed that God was not a being but must instead be placed above beings, and he taught this thesis in eastern Iran.[217] But in his case as well, the discussion may be presumed to have long overstepped the boundaries of the region, since indepen-

212 For the statements of the Muʿtazilites and the Ashʿarites on the name *al-wāḥid*, cf. Daniel Gimaret, *Les noms divins en Islam. Exégèse lexicographique et théologique* (Paris, 1988), 191ff. Gimaret mentions (ibid., 196) that ʿAbbād b. Sulaymān had already refrained from describing God as one in the sense of a number. That position does show certain parallels to the views presented by al-Māturīdī, but the context is different and the idea did not catch on among the Muʿtazilites or the Ashʿarites. Al-Ashʿarī even says explicitly (as Gimaret also shows) that God may also be described as one in the sense of numbers (*min ṭarīq al-ʿadad ayḍan*), Ibn Fūrak, 58.8.

213 *Tawḥīd*, 38.1–39.18.

214 Al-Māturīdī refrains here from naming his opponents explicitly (however cf. *Tawḥīd*, 378.-2 and *Taʾwīlāt*, 44.6). But within his school, the discussion on the incorporeality of God is always targeted against the Karrāmīya. Cf. for example *Uṣūl*, 21.12ff. and *Tabṣira*, vol. 1, 119.6ff.; before al-Māturīdī, cf. *K. al-Sawād*, section 45.

215 Gimaret and Monnot, 349f. with numerous parallels.

216 *Tawḥīd*, 39.19–43 ult.

217 Van Ess, *Theologie*, vol. 2, 499.

dently of whether or not there were still Jahmites to be reckoned with in Iran during al-Māturīdī's time,[218] Jahm's teaching had, in the meantime, become known everywhere as a scandalous falsehood.[219]

Consequently, no distinctive profile for al-Māturīdī's theology can be derived from these two sections of the text. This only changes when we look at how he dealt with a third theme; namely, the question of how descriptions attributed to God are to be understood. The discussion here is divided into considerations on how the essence of the Creator and the actions He does may be adequately described. This is, in fact, the famous topic of the divine attributes, and brings us to one of the main points of disputation in *kalām*.

The theme had been heavily debated and demanded a painstaking treatment by al-Māturīdī, but he was not taken unawares nor was he unprepared for it. He certainly found precedents on this topic in the teachings of earlier generations of Ḥanafites. These did not form an elaborate theory, but by this time had reached a level of extensiveness and precision that provided him an adequate guide for his approach to the issue. This tradition, however, did not quite reach back to Abū Ḥanīfa; at least, the two texts that we possess from him, i.e., the letters to ʿUthmān al-Battī, do not mention a word on the question of attributes. The *K. al-ʿĀlim wa-l-mutaʿallim* also skips the theme. It is in the *Fiqh absaṭ* of Abū Muṭīʿ that we find the first relevant remarks of interest to us.

The critical passage there is unfortunately not quite confirmed in its textual form, since, as we were prompted to conclude earlier in our description of the work, we are dealing with a section for which we must consider the possibility that later changes and insertions were made. Nevertheless, certain foundational ideas may be reconstructed which are likely to have belonged to the text in its original form. They make clear that Abū Muṭīʿ maintained that God possesses distinct attributes not identical with His being. To the question of what the Willer (God) willed with (*shāʾa*), he lets Abū Ḥanīfa answer, "With the attribute (*bi-l-ṣifa*)," which means the will. We also find out that God is powerful (*qadīr*) through power (*qudra*), knowing (*ʿalīm*) through knowledge (*ʿilm*), and rules (*mālik*) through rulership (*mulk*).[220] Besides these, anger (*ghaḍab*) and approbation (*riḍā*) are also named as divine attributes.[221] The axiom upon which these statements are based is: "We describe Him as He has described Himself."[222] This means that God is to have those attributes attributed to Him

218 Van Ess thinks it possible, ibid., vol. 2, 507f.

219 Citations in Gimaret and Monnot, 292n6.

220 *Fiqh absaṭ*, 57.3–5.

221 Ibid., 56.20f.

222 Ibid., 56.22: *wa naṣifuhu kamā waṣafa nafsahu.*

(and only those) that He mentioned in the Qur'ān. But one must avoid two mutually exclusive fallacies as much as possible: One may not believe that the attributes in God's case have the same sense as the attributes of the same name in human beings.[223] Nor should one strip them completely of their meaning; it is equally wrong to allegorically interpret our statements about God, by, for example, claiming that His "anger" means nothing other than His punishment, and His "approbation" means nothing other than an act of recompense.[224]

More important details for Ḥanafite attribute-doctrines of the period can be seen among the Karrāmīya. They, too, maintained the axiom that God possesses distinct attributes, but they emphasized another point more strongly, one which previously had not been given so much attention; namely, that these attributes are eternal without exception. As later sources report to us, a very detailed Karrāmite theory developed therefrom. A distinction was made between those attributes that describe God's essence, and those that describe His actions. The former, such as knowledge or power, were all considered eternal, without exception. The latter, such as the creative act, for example, introduced a differentiation: The capacity to act by creating (labeled *khāliqīya* or *khāliqūqīya*) is a divine attribute (*ṣifa*) and thus eternal; hence it is also correct to eternally name God a creator (*khāliq*). In contrast, the actual act of creation (*khalq*) is described differently; it is accomplished in time (*ḥādith*). Thus it is not an eternal attribute of God, but rather an accident (*ʿaraḍ*) that first exists at the moment of the act.[225]

We can no longer determine whether this theory was professed by Ibn Karrām in this polished form.[226] The attestations thereto in our possession from the fourth/tenth century are certainly articulated in much less detail, such as those from Makḥūl al-Nasafī, the author of the *K. al-Radd ʿalā ahl al-bidaʿ*. Here we find several statements on the theme, but they only explicitly convey the axiomatic conviction that all of God's attributes are eternal.

This emerges for the first time in a section where Makḥūl takes on the Jahmīya. There he stresses that God is a pre-eternal Creator with all of His attributes (*wa huwa bi-jamīʿ ṣifātihi khāliqun azalīyun*), because His actions (*afʿāl*) and attributes (*ṣifāt*) are uncreated, while human actions and attributes

223 Ibid., 56.20.

224 Ibid., 56.21f.

225 Cf. Gimaret and Monnot, 351ff. and the summary of the doctrine by Bosworth, "Karrāmiyya," *EI*^{2}, vol. 4, 667f. and Madelung, *Religious Trends*, 42.

226 Van Ess in particular raises arguments against this (*Ungenützte Texte*, 80). He shows that the relationship between the Karrāmite doctrine of attributes and the methodology of Abū Hāshim must be explained first.

can only be created.[227] That is, one ought to say: "The Creator does not exist in time, but is pre-eternal and perpetual, even though He has not (always) been creating."[228] This maxim is repeated later several times. In the chapter on al-Naẓẓām we read the formulaic statement that God, with all of His attributes, has no beginning (*azalī*).[229] We see something similar in the dispute with Bishr al-Marīsī as well, where it is emphasized that not just some, but all of God's attributes are uncreated.[230] Al-Marīsī also professed the thesis of the createdness of the Qur'ān, which was an unforgiveable error in Makḥūl's eyes. This was the subject of a sharp rebuttal on the part of the latter, not just in the above-mentioned citation, but also within a critique of the so-called "Makḥlūqīya," where he once again reinforced the eternality of God's attributes and all of His actions, inclusive of the Qur'ān.[231]

With such statements Makḥūl is not far from the official position of the Ḥanafites. They also explicitly emphasized that all of the divine attributes have no beginning and are uncreated. This was affirmed in an illustrious and authoritative source: the *K. al-Sawād al-aʿẓam* by al-Ḥakīm al-Samarqandī, which, as we have seen, was written as the official Ḥanafite creed at the beginning of the fourth/tenth century.

There we immediately find a number of ideas that are now familiar to us. Several times we are told about the importance of distinguishing between the attributes and actions of God and man: the former are unchanging, eternal, have always been present; the latter, in contrast, came into existence only through a divine act of creation in time.[232] Al-Ḥakīm al-Samarqandī was also keen to avoid stripping statements about God of their meaning, and forbade their allegorical interpretation, giving as examples divine anger (*ghaḍab*) and divine approbation (*riḍā*),[233] as we saw earlier in the *Fiqh absaṭ*. His statements go even further in the 35th and 36th article of the creed, exclusively dedicated to the doctrine of attributes. In article 35, he writes:

> ... God was always a Creator (*lam yazal khāliqan*) before He created the creation. His state (*ḥāl*) does not change. Whoever claims that He was not

227 *Radd*, 67.3–5.

228 Ibid., 67.7f.: *inna al-khāliq laysa bi-muḥdathin wa innamā huwa qadīmun qā'imun wa-in lam yakun li-l-takhlīq.*

229 Ibid., 95.17.

230 Ibid., 106.12.

231 Ibid., 110.1ff.

232 *K. al-Sawād*, sections 10, 11, and 29.

233 Ibid., section 29.

> a creator before the creation, but instead became (*ṣāra*) a creator afterward (*baʿd*), speaks like someone who claims that God (*Allāh*) was not a god (*ilāh*) and then became God. To claim this, however, is disbelief…[234]

And in article 36, we read:

> God is knowing and powerful in and of Himself (*bi-dhātihi*). He has (*lahu*) knowledge (*ʿilm*) and power (*qudra*)… The real knower (*al-ʿālim bi-l-ḥaqīqa*) is someone who possesses knowledge. Whoever does not have knowledge is a "knower" either in the metaphorical sense (*bi-l-majāz*) or as a title (*bi-l-laqab*) or by deception (*bi-l-khadhib*). The real knower and powerful one is God. It is impossible to claim that He is knowing metaphorically or by a title or deception, because such a claim is disbelief…[235]

8.2.5.2 Al-Māturīdī's Contribution

The doctrine of attributes professed in Transoxania became more detailed from one author to the next, but it nevertheless maintained certain principles that gave it a stable framework. Summarized into three points they read as follows:

1) God has attributes such as knowledge or power, which are clearly conceived of as distinct entities not identical with His existence.
2) These attributes must be differentiated from the attributes of the same name applied to human beings, but must not be robbed of their meaning through allegorical interpretation.
3) They are beginningless and eternal, whether they describe God's essence or His actions.

These axioms afforded the Ḥanafite doctrine its own distinctive character. Although there were other groups that shared one or the other principle with them, no theological school other than the Ḥanafīya affirmed all three. This is especially pronounced in compparison with the Muʿtazilites. Of course, the latter did not address the question of attributes as a collective, but rather as individual thinkers with differences both large and small among them.[236] Still,

234 *K. al-Sawād*, 31.14–17 [21.18–21 Istanbul edition].

235 *K. al-Sawād*, 31.20–32.1 [21.23–26 Istanbul edition].

236 For more detail, see van Ess, *Theologie*, vol. 3, 272ff. (on Abū l-Hudhayl) and ibid., vol. 3, 399ff. (on al-Naẓẓām) as well as ibid., vol. 4, 130 (on Ibn Shabīb). It is also interesting to compare the views of al-Najjār alongside them (ibid., vol. 4, 157ff.).

they possessed a common set of principles that were noticeably different from the fundamentals of the Ḥanafite doctrine.

The main concern of the Muʿtazilites was that nothing be considered eternal along with God. They thus concluded that nothing with even minimal self-distinctness ought to be conceived of as an eternal complement to God's self. This means that they denied the existence of discrete essential attributes. These were not to be affirmed as distinct entities, but rather as aspects of the one divine essence. This means, by way of an example, that one can say that God has always been knowing, but this does not imply that He possesses a complementary attribute called knowledge. God does not know through something which makes Him knowing. He knows through Himself or through an act of knowing which is identical with Him.

Divine actions, in contrast, are radically distinct from His eternal essence. They are subject to change because God carries out various actions. This means they are temporal and cannot inhere in His unchangeable essence. Their location must be other than God; thus they are usually shifted instead to the objects of divine actions. To give an example: the act of creation (*khalq*) does not take place in God, but is identified by most Muʿtazilites with its result, i.e., temporally originated creation (*makhlūq*).[237]

It had long been known in Transoxania that the Muʿtazilites thought this way.[238] But disputes on such attribute-doctrines seems to have first flared up there in the early fourth/tenth century, i.e., during al-Māturīdī's lifetime. The catalyst for this was no doubt the emergence of al-Kaʿbī, who taught his school's doctrines in eastern Iran, claiming that only their teachings could truthfully uphold the tenet that nothing eternal co-exist with God.[239] He therewith put all of the Ḥanafites' tenets into question: the insistence on distinct attributes; the prohibition of allegorical interpretation; and the idea that all of God's attributes are eternal.

This situation naturally presented al-Māturīdī with the task of repudiating al-Kaʿbī's accusations and demonstrating that the conceptualization of the Muʿtazilites was wrong. His presentation on the divine attributes in the *K. al-Tawḥīd* is the product of his efforts for this cause. It chiefly consists of

237 Cf. the summary by D. Gimaret, "Muʿtazila," *EI*², vol. 7, 787ff., along with Madelung, *Religious Trends*, 41ff. and idem, "The Origins," 516ff.

238 Abū Naṣr al-ʿIyāḍī, one of al-Māturīdī's teachers, wrote a text on the issue of attributes in which he disputed the views of the Muʿtazilites and al-Najjār (cf. *Tabṣira*, vol. 1, 357.2f.). The text is unfortunately lost.

239 We know from al-Māturīdī that al-Kaʿbī put this principle forward as his main thesis. He even cites it as a saying of the Muʿtazilites: *lā yathbutu thammata ghayrun* (*Tawḥīd*, 55.15; cf. ibid., 55.11).

polemical statements against al-Kaʿbī, whom al-Māturīdī accuses of distorting the image of God Almighty in various ways.[240] The most important critique throughout is that it is actually the Muʿtazilite who wants to permit God to change; first because he presumes God to have only become the Creator through the act of creation;[241] and second, because he claims that God's speech (i.e., the Qurʾān) only came to exist in time.[242] Al-Kaʿbī himself ultimately shows how ridiculous his own aims are: He set out with the principle that nothing eternal exists other than God, and ends by saying that God Himself is brought down into the sphere of temporality and change.

Yet before al-Māturīdī could go about disputing with this Muʿtazilite point by point, he had to clarify his own position. This he did by introducing his extensive refutation with a relatively short outline of Ḥanafite attribute-doctrines.[243] There we find many statements which are familiar to us from earlier texts. Their format is different, however, because al-Māturīdī does not suffice by merely repeating the teachings of his school. He refines them, and above all, he proves them. This serves as an excellent example of how a long enduring religious conviction became a theoretically founded doctrine of *kalām*.

His exposition begins, as we have come to expect, with a reference to the different pathways of knowledge. Al-Māturīdī explains that the existence of the divine attributes is suggested by transmission as well as by the intellect.[244] Transmission plays no major part in his presentation: he merely states that it is accessible to everyone, because everything that is necessary is found in the Qurʾān and the other books of God.[245] It is the intellect that takes the foreground of al-Māturīdī's presentation; this enables our theologian to lay out the doctrines which follow within his own systematic framework wherein attributes of particular importance can be duly emphasized.

The first of these attributes is freedom, or to be more precise, God's free choice (*ikhtiyār*). For al-Māturīdī, this may be known by our observation of the world and our inference of the existence of the Creator: To begin with, it has already been proven that the world was created from nothing. The

240 *Tawḥīd*, 49.14–59 ult. The chapter is worthy of its own analysis. It begins with al-Māturīdī placing al-Kaʿbī's interpretation quite clearly in the doctrines of the Muʿtazila (ibid., 49.16f.), and it shows through numerous arguments and citations from al-Kaʿbī's texts how seriously al-Māturīdī took his opponent.

241 Ibid., 53.3ff.

242 Ibid., 53.12ff.

243 Ibid., 44.1–49.13.

244 Ibid., 44.3f.

245 Ibid., 44.4f.

world, furthermore, has the characteristic of consisting of many things which change and are in part contrary to one other. Neither of these two facts can be explained by a principle that acts solely as dictated by nature (*bi-l-ṭabʿ*) and by compulsion. Thus, it may be considered proven that the Creator is a freely and sovereignly acting God.[246]

Al-Māturīdī draws further conclusions from this foundational insight. A God who can create everything freely must also be endowed with other attributes. He must possess power (*qudra*) to have everything at His disposal. He must have the will (*irāda*) to create the world, by which He avails Himself of His complete discretionary power.[247] Moreover, God must possess complete knowledge (*ʿilm*), because His creation does not consist of randomly clustered things. The creation is deliberately and harmoniously organized as a whole, which shows that its creator is a knowing God.[248]

Up to this point the argumentation has been relatively simple. Al-Māturīdī has only occupied himself with the essential attributes and could claim, without explicit proofs, that they are eternal with God. In contrast, his subsequent discussion on attributes of action is more controversial. These were also described by the Ḥanafīya as eternal, but no other theological school followed them in this, and what is more, the gap between their views and those of the Muʿtazilites was particularly wide.

Because of this, al-Māturīdī tries, from this point on, to prove his views in detail. He does so for various attributes of action, such as hearing (*samʿ*), seeing (*baṣar*), magnanimity (*karam*), and generosity (*jūd*).[249] But the act of creation, or *takwīn*, stands very clearly at the focal point of his exposition. This is because the act of creation, in particular, brings God's action to expression in such an exemplary way that it is reasonable to center the theological discussion on this one point.[250]

Al-Māturīdī begins his exposition by stating again that God brought the world forth in complete freedom. Accordingly, the act of creation is neither a manifestation nor an attribute of His essence.[251] It is an action that God

246 Ibid., 44.10–45.9; *ikhtiyār* plays a foundational role in al-Māturīdī's theory, as is also seen in his defense of the doctrine later in discussion with al-Kaʿbī, the "Dahrites," and the Ismāʿīlīs (ibid., 60.1–65.5).

247 Ibid., 45.10–13.

248 Ibid., 45.14–46.2.

249 Ibid., 47.21–ult.

250 The evaluation of *takwīn* will, as a result, become a central point of dispute between the Māturīdites and the Ashʿarites. Cf. Rudolph, "Das Entstehen der Māturīdiya."

251 *Tawḥīd*, 46.11–15.

accomplishes, not necessarily so, but only if He wills it to be. But God has certainly always been capable of this act, and thus it is a delusion (*wahm*) to think that the act of creation does not subsist in Him but is only identified with the created result.[252] In fact, the correct view is that God is described with the act of creation eternally (*wuṣifa Allāhu bi-l-takwīn fī l-azal*),[253] even if created things have not existed eternally. This is so, al-Māturīdī explains, because "God has created so that things (at some point) exist as they are" (*kawwana li-tukawwana al-ashyāʾu ʿalā mā takūnu*).[254] This means that He is always the Creator of things which will one day exist in the world as the creation.

Our theologian justifies this statement by comparing *takwīn* with the rest of God's attributes, such as His knowledge or will. They are also considered eternal, and their objects likewise emerge only in time. We say that God has always known that something will come to exist at a certain point in time, and we say, likewise, that He has always wanted this existence. It follows that He has always been the Creator of the things that have come into existence at the moment that was known and wanted by Him.[255]

At the same time, al-Māturīdī grants that such considerations are possibly beyond our conceptions.[256] God's actions are different than the actions of humans, such that they ultimately elude our understanding. But this is precisely the reason that compels us to assert the eternality of *takwīn*: God does not function as we humans do, i.e., at certain points in time or by means of tools.[257] His actions are achieved without aids or restrictions. They are completely free in every aspect. This is because God acts by Himself (*bi-nafsihi*) just as He also possesses knowledge and power in and of Himself (*bi-dhātihi*).[258] It is only because of this that He can bring the creation into existence out of nothing.[259] It costs Him no effort.[260] He merely speaks the word "Be!" (*kun*).[261] Thus God's actions are not dependent on any condition, temporal or otherwise. They were always perfect. Consequently, God is eternally the Creator.

252 Ibid., 46.16–ult.
253 Ibid., 47.1.
254 Ibid., 47.2.
255 Ibid., 47.2–7, 47.11–13, 47.18–21, 48.9, 49.4f.
256 Ibid., 49.10f. and 49.6.
257 Ibid., 48.5f., cf. ibid., 48.10ff.
258 Ibid., 48.6.
259 Ibid., 48.7f.
260 Ibid., 49.11.
261 Ibid., 49.6f.

8.2.6 *The Ambiguous Descriptions of God in the Qurʾān*

8.2.6.1 Earlier Ḥanafite Views

The topic of divine attributes had been settled: al-Māturīdī established a formula that was not just applicable to *takwīn*, but could also be applied to other cases without difficulty. God was always perfect, and always the same, regardless of the essential attribute or act in discussion. His attributes were thus unchangeable perfections that befitted Him perfectly. This meant that they could not be compared to human features: they were never temporally bound, but all eternal; they could not be questioned in regard to their existence, but were real to the highest degree.

Still, this formula did not solve all possible issues. There were characterizations of God in the Qurʾān that were impossible to reconcile with such doctrines, i.e., those statements that were regarded as ambiguous (*mutashābih*) because they attributed more or less clearly anthropomorphic features to God. These still required special treatment, particularly as they had long fanned the flames of considerable discord among theologians.

The pertinent verses of the Qurʾān contained a number of issues (God's hand, God's face, God's coming and going, etc.). But Islamic theological discourse had, in the meantime, concentrated on two topics that were regarded as particularly important, albeit obscure. The first was the visio beatifica, the idea of the vision of God (*ruʾyat Allāh*) in the afterlife. This was asserted through Qurʾānic verses such as, "Some bright faces, on that day, will be happy, looking at their Lord" (*wujūh … ilā rabbihā nāẓiratun*);[262] initially, this might seem to be one of the more obvious, if not necessary components of the promised joys of Paradise. But this blissful idea was, possibly bound up with an uneasy consequence: If God can actually be seen, then He must possess clearly defined limits and an essence perceivable by the senses. But no one could really claim that of the Creator, because the Qurʾān seemed to preclude that very thing by expressing, in another verse, "No visions can encompass Him, but He encompasses all visions."[263]

The second topic of controversy arose due to the Qurʾānic mention of God's throne (*ʿarsh*). It says, matter-of-factly, that the angels carry it and surround it,[264] while other verses say that "The Merciful sat on the throne" (*al-raḥmān ʿalā l-ʿarsh istawā*)[265] or "then He sat on the throne" (*thumma istawā ʿalā l-ʿarsh*).[266]

262 Q 75:22–23.

263 Q 6:1–3.

264 Q 69:17, 39:75, 40:7, and more.

265 Q 20:5.

266 Q 7:54.

This presented a delicate challenge to exegetes. A God who can sit, has—one would think—a form and a limit. And a God who sits Himself on the throne exists in a certain location, which may be distinguished and spatially delineated from others. These again seemed to be features particular to the creation, and caused concern that anthropomorphisms would creep into theology in association with the throne.

The Transoxanian Ḥanafites did not always discuss these two topics, and were not always conscious of the pressing and prickly nature of the entire problem. Most of what we know about the time before al-Māturīdī indicates that the theme developed slowly and received detailed treatment only at a later point in time. The unselfconscious but still tentative beginnings are to be found once again with Abū Muṭīʿ. He formulated the first theses on the topic in the *Fiqh absaṭ*, but what he said there did not persist for long. The topic was soon deliberated and discussed by Ibn Karrām, who went about the issue in his own unique manner. This prompted the eastern Ḥanafites to react again, and undertake a revision of their own position, which is quite evident in the *K. Sawād al-aʿẓam*.

In regard to Abū Muṭīʿ, it can be said that such considerations centered on a single point. He asked the question of where God and the throne are to be found. The answer was, "in heaven," which clearly meant the direction above us. This is expressed in two sentences attributed to Abū Ḥanīfa in the *Fiqh absaṭ*: "Whoever says: 'I do not know if my Lord is in heaven or on earth,' is a disbeliever."[267] And, "The same is true for the one who claims: 'He is on the throne, but I do not know if the throne is found in heaven or on earth.' "[268] Abū Muṭīʿ subsequently explains that God, of course, may be described as that which is high (*aʿlā*), because the low (*asfal*) is not a characteristic of the divine by any means.[269] He then presents a *ḥadīth* that affirms his view explicitly and reinforces it. According to this narration, a man with a black female servant once came to the Prophet and explained that he had to set a believing slave girl free, and wanted to know whether the black girl fulfilled the conditions. "At that, the Prophet said to her: 'Are you a believer?', and she answered: 'Yes.' Then he asked her: 'Where is God?' and she pointed up to heaven. He then turned (to the man), saying, 'Let her free, for she is a believer!' "[270]

267 *Fiqh absaṭ*, 49.1; cf. *Sharḥ*, 17.13f.; Wensinck (*Muslim Creed*, 104) incorporated this sentence as article 9 in his hypothetical *Fiqh akbar* I.

268 *Fiqh absaṭ*, 49.2; cf. *Sharḥ*, 17.15f.

269 *Fiqh absaṭ*, 51.1f.; cf. *Sharḥ*, 20.1f.

270 *Fiqh absaṭ*, 51.3–52.1; cf. *Sharḥ*, 20.3–6; on the context of this citation cf. above, 68.

Abū Muṭīʿ thus localized the Creator in reality "above us in heaven," and it can therefore be assumed that he was expressing the current views of the eastern Ḥanafites at the time.[271] First, it is striking how matter-of-factly he could refer to Abū Ḥanīfa for this claim.[272] Second, we do not possess any proof that any eastern thinker of the early third/ninth century professed a different opinion.

Our next witness, Ibn Karrām, confirms that at least in this part of Iran "realistic" conceptions of God were dominant. As is known, he accepted Qurʾānic statements without interpretation, i.e., according to their exact wording. With this he seems, as shown, not to have followed any specific opinion, but merely adhered determinedly to that which was generally acknowledged in the region.[273]

The way that later authors, such as al-Shahrastānī or al-Nasafī, depicted the views of the scandalous ascetic from Sīstān has long been known. According to them, he described God as a body, which dictated the following consequences: God was supposed to be actually sitting on the throne, and thus touching it. This meant that he was limited on one side, from below. Moreover, no doxographer ever forgot to mention that according to Ibn Karrām's naïve understanding, God was localized "up" (*fawqu*), i.e., above us in heaven.[274]

It is notable that we can also find documentation for these views in a text from the late third/ninth century. Makḥūl al-Nasafī professed them, which again confirms that he was a true follower of the scholarly ascetic. In his text, the focus has shifted a bit as we mentioned earlier: in one section Makḥūl criticizes anthropomorphic exaggerations ("God has hair, fingernails, etc.") and by this consciously tries to distance himself from those thinkers who are criticized collectively as *mushabbiha*. But his sectarian identity becomes clearer in

---

271 One does find differing views in the *Fiqh absaṭ* on the same theme (56.20–57.6), but this passage seems to have been added in its essential components to the text only later (see above, 61f.).

272 Abū Ḥanīfa later had other views attributed to him (cf. van Ess, *Theologie*, vol. 1, 192), but this does not argue against this presumption. The Ḥanafites revised this "realistic" image of God over the course of time, and thus had to reclaim the "school founder" for the new view.

273 Accordingly, it seems as if Ibn Karrām's anthropomorphism cannot necessarily be seen as a concession to the circles of *ḥadīth* narrators, which up till now seemed reasonable to conclude.

274 *Tabṣira*, vol. 1, 120.6ff. and 121.3ff.; al-Shahrastānī, 80.3ff.; as well as Gimaret and Monnot, 347ff. with citations of parallels. Presentations of Ibn Karrām's pertinent views are given by van Ess, *Ungenützte Texte*, 20f., 24, 66, and 76f. (with further sources); C. Bosworth, "Karrāmiyya," *EI*², vol. 4, 667b f.; Madelung, *Religious Trends*, 41f.

another chapter; there he deals with the issue of the divine throne, and we find the same theses that the Karrāmīya were noted for in the later sources: God has a limit (*ḥadd*), sits on the throne, and is found above (*fawqa*) us in heaven (*fī l-samāʾ*).[275]

Ibn Karrām was certainly anything but a naïve thinker. That which distinguished him must have been the seriousness with which he approached the words of the holy text. In precisely this manner he arrived at an image of God that resembled human beings in a striking manner. This certainly not only provoked general irritation, but stimulated the eastern Hanafites in particular to reconsider and then modify their own conceptualizations in order to preserve a distance between themselves and such exaggerations.

The result of this revision can be encountered, as noted, in the *K. al-Sawād al-aʿẓam*. Here al-Ḥakīm al-Samarqandī criticizes the anthropomorphism of the Karrāmīya. But he also turns against views that would still have been reasonable in his own school a century earlier. Moreover, the thematic presentation takes on a decisive expansion: now both issues are explicitly discussed—the visio beatifica, the reality of which was clearly presumed for a long time without commentary; and the throne of God, the problematics of which had now surely become visible.

The section on the throne shows us most clearly how the exegetical approach had changed. Here al-Ḥakīm adheres to positions which, according to all appearances, would have been unthinkable for a Transoxanian Ḥanafite at an earlier time. In regard to the throne, he explains, it is by no means connected with the idea of a location, because the Qurʾān merely says that God sits beyond (*ʿalā*) it—which does not imply spatial boundaries—not that God sits above (*fawqa*) it. The Creator is positively not in a location. He does not need (*muḥtāj*) one. As such, His relation to the throne can be described only in the sense that the throne, like everything else, exists through God's power (*qāʾim bi-qudratihi*).[276]

The tenor of this interpretation is clear. Al-Ḥakīm acknowledges the words which are in the Qurʾān, but he contests the meaning that is normally presumed for them. Moreover, this method is not only valid for the throne, but is the exegetical principle used for all similarly difficult passages in the Qurʾān. This general rule is explained explicitly at the end of the paragraph, namely,

275 *Radd*, 107.1–17.

276 *K. al-Sawād*, section 46, 39.15ff.; Istanbul edition, 27.3ff. However, the printed edition of the *Sawād* seems not to reproduce this paragraph completely. Al-ʿOmar (167f. (in section 47)), who refers to two manuscripts, is more detailed and has possibly retained the original text.

that as soon as one comes across ambiguous statements (*mutashābihāt*) in the Qur'ān, caution must be taken. The reader should be clear on two things: First, that he must of course believe (*tu'min*) the divine words. But second, al-Ḥakīm also warns against interpretation (*tafsīr*), because in the first place, no person is obligated to do it (*li-annahu laysa farḍan ʿalayhi*), and furthermore, one knows where it will lead: namely to a negation (*taʿṭīl*) of the depiction of God—from which it follows that the interpreter will have become a heretic (*mubtadiʿ*).[277]

The principle is simple but versatile. Thus, it is not surprising that al-Ḥakīm applies it in the case of the visio beatifica as well which represented a similar case. A way had to be found by which a Qur'ānic statement could be acknowledged without facing unwanted consequences. And the same conceptual methods were useful again.

The inhabitants of Paradise, in al-Ḥakīm's view, actually see their Lord (*ru'yatan ḥaqqan*), because this is promised to us in scripture. However, we do not know how this happens and have no comparison in our mind for this vision (*bi-lā mithāl wa-lā kayfa*). But one thing is certain: one may not allegorically interpret the visio beatifica in any way, for example by saying that God can only be seen by the eye of the heart (*bi-ʿayn al-qalb*). This clearly contradicts the Qur'ān, and whoever claims this has automatically become a heretic (*mubtadiʿ*).[278]

8.2.6.2 Al-Māturīdī's Contribution

When al-Māturīdī entered the discussion, the foundational talking points had already been set. The Ḥanafites had come to agreement on a new position which was both conservative yet sufficiently flexible in its formulation that no critical changes needed to be made. Nevertheless, the pertinent chapter in the *K. al-Tawḥīd* cannot exactly be compared with the views just cited from the *K. al-Sawād al-aʿẓam*. Al-Māturīdī would not have been a systematizing thinker nor a *mutakallim* if he had not once again taken the opportunity to establish the views of his own school more precisely, and to demonstrate the errors of those who thought otherwise.

The visio beatifica was certainly the easier theme for him to handle. In this regard, he did not have problematic statements to deal with from his own school, but only the straightforward assertions from the *K. al-Sawād al-aʿẓam*. Furthermore, the front lines were clear and unambiguous. The Muʿtazilites had to be opposed, as they vehemently opposed the reality of the vision of

277 *K. al-Sawād*, section 46, 40.3ff.; Istanbul edition, 27.11ff.; al-ʿOmar, 168f.

278 *K. al-Sawād*, section 30, 26.19ff.; Istanbul edition, 18.14ff.; al-ʿOmar, 137ff.

God. This meant that al-Māturīdī had to dispute with al-Kaʿbī again, and the latter's arguments are accordingly refuted in detail in the *K. al-Tawḥīd.*

Before our theologian became involved in such debates, he clarified his own doctrine once more. It is based on the undeniable affirmation that the belief in the visio beatifica is necessary (*lāzim*) and true (*ḥaqq*).[279] First, God has promised us this vision, and not just once in passing, but in numerous parts of the Qur'ān.[280] Moreover, the intellect also tells us that the expectation of the divine vision is by no means irrational, but actually very well founded.

According to al-Māturīdī there are two reasons for this. The first is that God has promised us that He will reward the most beautiful of people's deeds (*aḥsana mimmā ʿamilū fī l-dunyā*), i.e., the true faith, with the most beautiful reward; and this most beautiful reward can be nothing other than bliss-inducing theophany.[281] The second argument supports and enlarges upon the first. It says that everyone agrees that we will know (*ʿalima*) God in the afterlife. The surest form of knowledge comes from the senses, and above all else, the certainty attained through seeing.[282]

At the outset a Muʿtazilite might seem powerless against such justifications. But al-Māturīdī takes his position so seriously that he dedicates several pages to it. In doing so he distinguishes again between proofs of transmission and arguments based on intellect; it may thus be presumed that al-Kaʿbī likewise undertook his considerations based on these two approaches.

Qur'ānic proofs in this context are not of great importance for us; a compilation of sections from al-Kaʿbī's great *Tafsīr* is presented, in order to become the target of our theologian's philological and exegetical finesse.[283] In contrast, al-Kaʿbī's arguments based on the intellect deserve particular attention. These naturally played a prominent role in the thinking of this Muʿazilite theologian, who based his views on two main points: The first was derived from the definition of "seeing." According to al-Kaʿbī, seeing is always characterized by certain physical processes, no matter where it takes place and what the object of vision is. These processes presume the corporeality of all participants, such that the word "vision" can never be said in relation to God in its common lexical sense.[284] The second argument he made was that "seeing" always means

279 *Tawḥīd*, 77.14.

280 Ibid., 77.15–80.7; the following verses are given Q 6:103, 7:143, 6:76, 75:22–23, 10:26, 5:101 as well as a *ḥadīth*.

281 *Tawḥīd*, 80.8ff.

282 Ibid., 80.16ff.

283 Ibid., 83.20ff.

284 Ibid., 82.6–9.

comprehension (*idrāk*) of an object, but this is also ruled out in relation to God.[285] To fully comprehend God contradicts the intellect and moreover is rejected by the Qur'ān.[286]

Both views are wrong, according to al-Māturīdī, and he mentions good reasons why this is so. He starts by refuting the second argument, saying that the equivocation of *ru'ya* and *idrāk* is contradictory. Seeing, as is known, is possible in different ways (*ʿalā wujūh*). In contrast, comprehension means "grasping the limits of a thing" (*al-wuqūf ʿalā ḥudūd al-shay'*).[287] To equivocate the two is thus a serious error—as we know from our own experience. Often we perceive things with our eyes without knowing exactly what they are. In such cases we have seen objects but not comprehended them, because they were too small, too far, or too poorly lit.[288]

Al-Māturīdī finds al-Kaʿbī's first argument to be even weaker. He comes to the conclusion that the Muʿtazilite defines vision absolutely, i.e., independently of whether it is discussed from the perspective of this life or the next. As a result, he has ultimately exposed himself, whether he means to or not, as an assimilationist (*mushabbih*),[289] because he ends up transposing the measure of the creation onto the Creator. This is always wrong, and consequently also wrong in regard to the visio beatifica.[290]

This essentially brings us to the result already formulated in the *Sawād*; thus it is only a matter of consequence that al-Māturīdī, like al-Ḥakīm, ultimately speaks of the matter of the vision of God "without how" (*bi-lā kayfa*).[291] Yet his manner of presentation is rather different, because various principles which were still constitutive for the author of the *Sawād* were pushed aside.

An important change can be observed in his attitude toward the ambiguous verses (*mutashābihāt*). They are now not merely accepted without commentary, but actually discussed in detail. Here, al-Māturīdī is quite willing to interpret the statements of the Qur'ān, even though by doing so he was running counter to the prohibition issued by al-Ḥakīm al-Samarqandī. A second innovation can be seen in the method our theologian uses to establish the necessity of the visio beatifica. He does not restrict himself to merely citing Qur'ān verses, but actually puts forth arguments by the intellect as well. This,

285 Ibid., 82.6.

286 Q 6:103.

287 *Tawḥīd*, 81.15ff.

288 Ibid., 81.18ff., 83.1f., 83.7f., 83.11ff.

289 Ibid., 85.5ff.

290 Ibid., 79.7ff. and 85.16ff.

291 Ibid., 85.16.

of course, is in accordance with his principle of demonstrating all doctrines, if possible, by more than one epistemological method. But it also runs counter to the example of al-Ḥakīm al-Samarqandī, which al-Māturīdī again consequently dismisses.

The same free manner of dealing with the views of his predecessors is also seen in a second theme: the question of whether God sits on the throne or is located in a place at all. Here, al-Māturīdī again affirms the position of the *Sawād*, but he also approaches it with his own methods, given his need to consider the fact that widely varying views have also been expounded on this issue.

According to his testimony in the *K. al-Tawḥīd*, the Muslims of his time were, in fact, quarreling on exactly this point.[292] Some of them thought that the throne (*ʿarsh*) was actually a bed (*sarīr*) carried by angels; God had sat Himself on it, which meant that He was found in a specific place.[293] A second group asserted that God, the All-powerful and All-present, was found in all places at the same time.[294] For others, this was also too concrete; for their part this third group claimed that He is currently in all places, but only in the sense that he preserves and knows all things.[295] And then there is yet another position, whose advocates al-Māturīdī leaves nameless and mentions with some reservation; this group points out that hands are raised up in prayer, which can only mean that God is above us in heaven.[296]

The intended targets of these doxographical references are not named explicitly. But for al-Māturīdī's contemporaries, the identity of those being referred to was certainly obvious, and even according to our current state of knowledge it can still be determined that in the order of this list, we are reading a description of Ibn Karrām, al-Najjār,[297] al-Kaʿbī[298] and the traditionally-minded Ḥanafites such as Abū Muṭīʿ, respectively. They must all be refuted in the following section, and as one can clearly see, the critiques al-Māturīdī advances differ greatly in respect to each of the four adversaries.

He deals with Ibn Karrām and al-Najjār relatively quickly. They both thought that they could localize God; the former in a particular place, and the latter in all places equally. These are both wrong, al-Māturīdī explains, since they

---

292 Ibid., 67.11.

293 Ibid., 67.12ff.

294 Ibid., 68.3ff.

295 Ibid., 68.11f.; cf. ibid., 75.3ff.

296 Ibid., 75 ult.

297 Al-Shahrastānī, 62.-4f. following al-Kaʿbī; see Gimaret and Monnot, 301f.; *Uṣūl*, 28 ult.f.; *Tabṣira*, vol. 1, 167.3ff.

298 *Tawḥīd*, 75.3ff.

presume for the Creator two features that are characteristic of the creation: a spatial limit and scope, and the need of a location at all.[299]

Al-Kaʿbī had evaded this pitfall, and thus refuting him was more difficult. He believed that God, in reality, was not in any place, such that the most that one could assert was that He was the Knower and Preserver of all places. But even this goes too far for al-Māturīdī, because the knowledge of God is an attribute of His essence, and the essence of our Lord can hardly be bound to any type of spatiality.[300] Furthermore, he adds with calculation, al-Kaʿbī this time professes a thesis that is almost acceptable, but at the price of contradicting his other teachings: al-Kaʿbī now says that God existed before all locations, and is thus exalted above all locations because He is absolutely not subject to change. But shortly before, he had said that God originally did not create, and only later became the Creator—which clearly presumes a change of God's essence.[301]

And finally, the fourth group that views God as "above in heaven" proving this with the position of the believers as they pray, is cautiously reprimanded by al-Māturīdī. He explains to them that one may also pray toward the East or West without presuming the Creator to be there; this is only done because these positions in the prayers are prescribed by God.[302] Despite this critique, his words carry a certain undertone of sympathy, otherwise he would not have ended the discussion with just these few words. He also would not have added at the end that one, of course, must take into account that heaven is the location and cradle of revelation (*maḥall wa-mahbaṭ al-waḥy*).[303]

Al-Māturīdī's own position is, however, quite different, since he is committed to the same principles as al-Ḥakīm al-Samarqandī on all the relevant issues. Accordingly, he believes that God is certainly not in any location, but one ought to still believe the Qur'ān, in that He sits on the throne in some kind of incomprehensible way.[304] Our theologian differs only in his more precise explanation of these positions and by proceeding in part with rational proofs and in part with proofs of transmission.

According to al-Māturīdī, the intellect shows us that God cannot be in any location. God created everything, including places. Thus if He already

299 *Tawḥīd*, 69.13–70.11.

300 Ibid., 75.16ff.

301 Ibid., 75.7ff.

302 Ibid., 76.1ff.

303 Ibid., 77.10, which is another attestation to the nature of al-Māturīdī's Arabic, which was not classical.

304 Ibid., 69.6 and 76.6f.

existed before them, He will always remain independent of them.[305] We nevertheless say that the Creator sits on the throne, and this we owe to the message of the Qur'ān. God imparts to us this unshakable fact, of which we can know nothing more precisely, because everything divine is beyond human conceptualization.[306] Only one other point may be added—and here al-Māturīdī's views become particularly rational: If God is mentioned in connection with the throne, then this is certainly not in order to bring out His exaltedness and might. It may be that a human would be honored by such a reference, but the Creator is entirely above all such things and in His case He receives no additional honor; instead it is only the throne that is praised and glorified through mention of this relationship to Him.[307]

8.2.7 *God's Wisdom*

One final addition is necessary in order to conclude the section on theology in the *K. al-Tawḥīd*. It also relates to God's actions, but from a perspective that has hardly been mentioned until now. We are not addressing the eternality or the individuated existence of God's actions. Instead, the discussion centers on whether they follow an inner set of laws, or, to formulate it at the human level of perception, whether God carries out His actions such that they can be comprehended by our intellect. This question occupied al-Māturīdī considerably, and he answered with an exposition of his concept of the Creator's divine wisdom (*ḥikma*).

The fact that God cannot be other than wise (*ḥakīm*) was obvious to every Islamic theologian. Every *kalām* school emphasized the principle that God always acts wisely and is always just.[308] The question remained only as to how to define these characteristics, since there were certainly different views on this topic, and these at times greatly diverged from one another.

If a Muʿtazilite spoke of justice and wisdom, he thought of rationally comprehensible norms. These norms were supposed to be independent of God's commands and prohibitions, and objectively reflect the good and the bad, the wise and the just. This means that humans can understand the good and the bad with their intellect. As life forms endowed with intellects, they are thus subject to moral duties. But this concept is also not without its consequences for the Creator; the deity must also act in accordance with these norms in order

305 Ibid., 69.6ff. and 71.6ff.

306 Ibid., 74.4ff., with reference to Q 42:11: "nothing is alike to Him."

307 Ibid., 70.16ff.

308 On the divine name *al-Ḥakīm*, cf. Gimaret, *Les noms divins*, 271f.; on *al-ʿĀdil* or *al-ʿAdl* see ibid., 341–347.

to be a wise and just God. His actions are thus rationally calculable and follow an unchanging criterion. This is why a great proportion of the Muʿtazilites, including Ibn Shabīb and al-Kaʿbī, professed the doctrine of the "Optimum"; namely, that God does not do any kind of unforeseeable actions, but instead always does that which is the "most beneficial" (*al-aṣlaḥ*) for the subjects of His actions.[309]

The formulation of the Ashʿarites was completely opposed to this. They rejected any idea of an objective norm or even a rationally comprehensible criterion. God Himself determines what wisdom and justice is, and this is determined in a way that does not admit justification. This is true because God can do or permit what He wants. Each of His acts is just and wise solely because it issues from Him. He could very well have done the opposite. There is no intelligible structure in what He does, or in what He commands or forbids. Humans thus cannot know their duties by rational means. Instead, they are directed to revelation in order to ascertain what is good and bad.[310]

These positions could hardly have been more contrary. Nevertheless, each laid claim to ensure an essential feature of God's identity. Al-Ashʿarī emphasized divine omnipotence and divine freedom. He wanted to avoid God being bound by anything, and thus willingly risked the impression that in his view the acts of the Creator are arbitrary. The Muʿtazilites, however, sought a God who was just and imparted this justice in understandable ways. Thus they postulated a criterion that applied to the acts of the Creator as well as the acts of man. But this entailed the danger of binding God to an external law and thus stripping Him of his inalienable omnipotence and freedom.

Such ideas must have played a role in al-Māturīdī's considerations[311] because he tried on his part to develop a conceptualization that sufficiently took into account both aspects—the divine sovereignty and the transparency of divine acts. The central concept that he applied therein was, as noted, wisdom; this being, in his understanding, an absolute, inscrutable attribute of the divine essence. This meant then, first, that for al-Māturīdī as for al-Ashʿarī, God acts

309 Robert Brunschvig, "Muʿtazilisme et optimum," *SI* 39 (1974): 5–23; Frank, "Reason and Revealed Law," 124ff.; Gimaret, *La doctrine*, 433–435.

310 Frank, "Reason and Revealed Law," 135ff.; Gimaret, *La doctrine*, 435ff.

311 Al-Māturīdī's main opponents in this issue are the Muʿtazilites. He constantly reproaches them for supporting the principle of the *aṣlaḥ* (*Tawḥīd*, 52.7, 92.15ff., 97.7ff., 124.9ff. and elsewhere) without recognizing its consequences. The concept is only supposed to have come about because the Muʿtazilites fell victim to the model of the God of good according to the teaching of the Dualists (ibid., 216.2ff.). Though al-Ashʿarī's views were unknown to al-Māturīdī, he certainly knew the Traditionists' view of God, which bore quite similar features and were also a decisive motivating factor for al-Ashʿarī.

in complete freedom. He does not do what is merely good or bad, but actually issues commands and prohibitions that determine what is good or bad. In distinction to al-Ashʿarī however, al-Māturīdī believed that these truths in fact did produce a stable and intelligible system of norms. This is because God always acts in wisdom. He holds Himself to norms that He has conclusively established. Thus humans may also attain the possibility of understanding the divine order of the creation, and can recognize the good and bad with their intellects—as the Muʿtazilites advocated.

Here the qualification must be added that al-Māturīdī nowhere completely justifies this conceptualization or handles it with the scrupulousness necessary. Instead, he utilizes it as an argument and sets it as a premise in numerous debates (with the Muʿtazila and the Dualists). However, the different elements in the *K. al-Tawḥīd* from which the concept is developed may be explained here. We will mention three in particular, each of which occur repeatedly and play a constitutive role in his exposition.

The first idea is that God is all-knowing and wise in an absolute sense.[312] Al-Māturīdī always emphasizes this theme when taking on the Muʿtazilite *aṣlaḥ* theory. He aims thereby to assert that there is no criterion by which God's wisdom can be measured. Its justification is only within itself. For who could venture to take the all-knowing Creator to account?[313]

The second idea is that indicators of wisdom are in fact found everywhere in the world. God did not hide His decisions, but actually imparted them in a form understandable to all humans. This is evident on numerous levels: in the harmonious direction (*tadbīr*) of the creation;[314] in the rationality of ethical norms;[315] and even in the way in which God creates harmful life forms and sub-

---

312 *Tawḥīd*, 216.16ff., 217.17ff., 220.5ff.

313 Ibid., 220.12ff. in relation to Q 21:23; this is why al-Māturīdī emphasizes as well that the innermost being (*kunh*) of divine wisdom is not conceivable to us (*Tawḥīd*, 108.16f. and 217.8f.).

314 *Tawḥīd*, 18.13–16 and elsewhere.

315 *Tawḥīd*, 10.17–20. However, al-Māturīdī does add the qualification that the intellect cannot distinguish the good from the bad in every case. It only knows the basic guidelines and knows, for example, that injustice and ignorance are ugly (*qabīḥ*), while justice and wisdom are beautiful (*ḥasan*). In many individual cases, however, good and bad emerge at the same time (which escaped the Dualists' notice); here humans often need divine instruction to implement the proper evaluation. This is why they also need the *sharīʿa*, because its detailed specifications are not rationally derivable (*Tawḥīd*, 217.13ff.). Thus the intellect does not have quite the same role for al-Māturīdī as it does for the Muʿtazilites; he acknowledges ethical norms only as far as they are due to God. Thus al-Maḥbūbī, a Māturīdite from the eighth/fourteenth century, is correct when he summarizes the

stances (*al-ḥayyāt wa-l-jawāhir al-ḍārra*) for specific reasons.[316] In all of these cases, divine wisdom is at work, and it manifests itself systematically so that human beings can perceive the clues of its existence.

It must then be asked, however, wherein the principle of divine wisdom consists. If it is reflected in all things, then a characteristic must also be found everywhere that can be described as "wise." Al-Māturīdī tries to name this principle. This is the third and last idea which will be mentioned here, and it is also, perhaps, the most interesting among them.

We learn that divine wisdom (*ḥikma*) expresses itself in two ways (*ṭarīqān*). One is the way of grace (*faḍl*), and the other is the way of justice (*ʿadl*).[317] Al-Māturīdī considers God's goodness to be immeasurable. It has no end (*nihāya*). Thus, one can also never assert that the maximally good (*al-afḍal*) has ever been expressed in a divine act.[318] Justice, on the other hand, can be fixed to a guiding principle. This, again, does not consist of God doing something supposedly maximal, e.g., the most beneficial (*al-aṣlaḥ*). Rather, God is Just because He treats everything in a way that befits it. Al-Māturīdī has two formulas for this. One, simply stated, is that being wise is to "hit the mark" (*al-iṣāba*).[319] The other almost takes the form of a definition, in the expression that God is wise because He "puts everything in its (proper) place" (*waḍʿu kulli shay'in mawḍiʿahu*).[320]

With these considerations, al-Māturīdī addressed the critical points of the issue, and managed to unify the two poles around which it revolved. He described God as the principle which "sets" (*waḍaʿa*) and determines everything according to its guidelines. But at the same time, he allowed for created things to receive their due; they were not positioned arbitrarily, but are instead part of an order in which everything has "its place" (*mawḍiʿuhu*). This holds true for all of God's actions, and thus every act of His that has some relation to His creation, because these actions are all "wise." To our theologian this

---

difference in the following way: to the Muʿtazilites, the intellect is the judge (*ḥākim*) of good and bad; for the Māturīdites, however, it is an instrument (*āla*) by which God permits us to distinguish the good from the bad (Gimaret, *Théories*, 214).

316 *Tawḥīd*, 108.14–110.7; an interesting chapter which merits study and should also be compared with Muʿtazilite theodicy, as well as with al-Ghazālī's doctrine of the "best of all possible worlds."

317 Ibid., 125.10.

318 Ibid., 125.10–12.

319 Ibid., 97.16 and 306.4.

320 Ibid., 125.14; cf. ibid., 97.16f., 110.16, 117.9, 306.4, and 307.5f.

means that they are freely chosen, yet are nevertheless accessible to rational understanding.[321]

8.3 Human Beings

8.3.1 *Human Rationality*

Al-Māturīdī managed to combine his view of God and the composition of the world through the concept of wisdom. In the process, wisdom was granted a key role in his general thought process, thus imbuing his distinct observations on various topics with the coherence of a systematic theory. This impression becomes even stronger when al-Māturīdī's doctrines on human beings are taken into account: The human being is the only created being who perceives all signs based on *ḥikma*; the only one in this world who reflects on and understands their indications and specifications. From this perspective, human activity constantly relates to divine wisdom because wherever the latter manifests, human intellect is called upon to know and understand what has been manifested.

Human rational knowledge, as we have come to know, extends over various domains. It encompasses ethical norms, analysis of the creation, as well as the proof that there is an omnipotent and omniscient Creator. This is the cornerstone of al-Māturīdī's entire intellectual edifice and it is no surprise that rational capacity occupies a central position in his definition of the human being.

We have come across this definition earlier.[322] It appears in two sentences that are formulated from entirely different perspectives. The first is based on theological tradition and explains that human beings consist of an intellect and natures.[323] This refers back to al-Māturīdī's ontological model, according to which a body consists of *ṭabāʾiʿ*, here incorporating the intellect as an additional accident as well.[324] The second definition, however, states that the human being is "a rational mortal being."[325] This comes of course from the

321 The concept al-Māturīdī presents is original and is developed from the premises of his own system. But this does not rule out his consideration of other influences. A related point that al-Māturīdī himself brings into play (*Tawḥīd*, 96.17ff.) is al-Najjār's teachings; another point, the significance of which can only be estimated with difficulty, is that Ibn Farīghūn (mid-fourth/tenth century) similarly defined wisdom in his *Jawāmiʿ al-ʿulūm* (cf. Biesterfeldt, "Die Zweige des Wissens," 157 and 37 of the Arabic text).

322 Cf. above, 254.

323 *Tawḥīd*, 10 ult. f.; cf. ibid., 201.12ff., 218.20ff., 221.18ff., 223.10ff., 224.15ff.

324 Cf. above, 254ff.

325 *Tawḥīd*, 43.3

Aristotelian tradition, which was known through translation from the Greek and was familiar to educated Muslims from the time of al-Kindī at the latest.

It is revealing that al-Māturīdī uses this philosophical formula without commentary. It demonstrates once more how open he was to stimuli from these quarters.[326] This is even more evident in another philosophical citation that he introduces rather casually into the discussion; his mention that the philosophers (*al-ḥukamāʾ*) had also claimed that the human being was describable as a microcosm (*ʿālam ṣaghīr*).[327] Admittedly, al-Māturīdī does not use this comparison between man and the world again; he only mentions it here, in this single instance, and does not even say whether it can be accepted or must be rejected. Precisely this, however, confirms his casual attitude to philosophical concepts. Moreover, a parallelism between man and the world is not out of place if one is of the view, as al-Māturīdī is, that both consist of natures that were put together and structured by divine wisdom.

Such definitions and analogies, in any case, only represent one part of his concept of man. They indicate the rank of the human being and show how he is to be categorized theoretically among other created beings. They say little, however, of his duties or his actual relationship to God. But a believer would ask about precisely that, and with more urgency than about theoretical contemplations. Al-Māturīdī must provide an answer to this, and he does so in the second half of the *K. al-Tawḥīd*.

The second section of the book is occupied with three themes, as stated. These are the issues of human agency, the constitution of belief, and the destiny of a sinner. The presentation is detailed and elaborated through numerous discussions, in contention with al-Kaʿbī in particular. In this respect al-Māturīdī remains completely loyal to the style of argumentation that he developed in the first half of his work. But the situation which he presumes is different this time: As noted earlier, here he was no longer on theological territory considered new for the Ḥanafites. On the contrary, these were topics for which there were long-standing Ḥanafite positions. Consequently, there are few unexpected or original theses to be found in the second half of the *K. al-Tawḥīd*; it was no longer al-Māturīdī's task to develop new perspectives, but rather to explain and defend that which had been taught by his predecessors.

326 In contrast, al-Ashʿarī explicitly rejected this definition; cf. Ibn Fūrak, 217.17–20.

327 *Tawḥīd*, 5.4.

8.3.2 *Human Actions*

8.3.2.1 The Conceptualization of the Ḥanafites and the Karrāmites

As indicated, the first of the older themes that al-Māturīdī preserved in this new undertaking was the topic of human agency. This had been discussed in detail before him by a series of earlier authors now familiar to us: The beginning was marked by Abū Ḥanīfa with his second *Risāla* to ʿUthmān al-Battī (on the presumption that this is in fact an authentic document).[328] Abū Muṭīʿ followed him, as did al-Ḥakīm al-Samarqandī. We may also add the Karrāmite Makḥūl al-Nasafī, who expressed similar views.

These authors' positions were by no means identical on all points, but they all followed a certain axiom that had been established by Abū Ḥanīfa. Namely, he had said that the correct position on the question of human agency was the one in the middle. Adhering to the middle position allowed for the avoidance of two extremist attitudes, which in Islam were usually associated with those called Qadarites and Jabrites. More often than not, this took the expression of repudiating both heretical groups and claiming to be equally far from both of their exaggerations.

The Ḥanafites accused the Jabrites of completely stripping human influence from their actions and attributing them solely to God: Because the latter concentrated entirely on the aspect of God in the creation of human actions, they thus erroneously concluded that He was the only doer, responsible for everything, while the human being was absolved of all occurrences. This can only be described as disbelief (*kufr*), because it would mean associating God with the most disgraceful things, and it would depict a completely human image of him.

As for the Qadarites, they apparently fell victim to the exact opposite problem. Their teaching denied God His part in human acts, and ascribed all aspects of actions (the originating will, cause, and execution) to humans. This divinizes the creation, and is likewise another variant of disbelief.

The correct path consequently lay in the middle, between these two. It was only attainable by redeeming the noble aspects of both heretical views: the Jabrites were right when they said that good and bad actions must be created, because other than God, there are, by definition, only created things. But at the same time, the approach of the Qadarites was also convincing; it said that humans had to undertake actions themselves in order to be responsible for them. Both principles ought to be combined then. In this manner a synergistic model emerged for Abū Ḥanīfa's followers, according to which God wills (*mashīʾa*), decrees (*qadar*), decides (*qaḍāʾ*), and creates (*khalq*) all human

328 On the question of authenticity, cf. above, 36ff.

actions, but the human is the only one who does (*fiʿl*) them. If it is a good deed he can count on God's assistance (*tawfīq*), but at the moment of a bad deed he has been forsaken (*khidhlān*) by God.

This model is only found in all of its facets with al-Ḥakīm al-Samarqandī (*K. al-Sawād*, section 6; cf. sections 33, 57, and 59) and Makḥūl al-Nasafī (*Radd*, 64.11–65.8, 65.14–66.16; cf. ibid., 70.21f., 87.18ff. and 99.19ff.), but the essential features are already prominent in the second *Risāla* to ʿUthmān al-Battī (cf. above, 40 for the juxtaposition of the *ahl al-tafwīḍ* and the *ahl al-ijbār*). In the *Fiqh absaṭ* the emphasis lay in criticizing the Qadarites (43.7ff. and 55.1ff.) and in the statement that everything is created and determined by God. Still, Abū Muṭīʿ is no predestinarian; he added the qualification that God only determines the bad as a punishment for previous sins (ibid., 42.14ff.).

Despite the general harmony conveyed by these Ḥanafite texts, an important problem still remained. This relates to the human capacity to act, the *istiṭāʿa*, which had also been oft-discussed and therefore had be incorporated in some form or another into al-Māturīdī's exposition. In principle there was unity to be found on the actual definition of "capacity," since all authors professed the view that it was not simply confined to a specific act, but also had to entail the possibility of two contrary acts.[329] Otherwise, the leeway attributed to humans in the execution of an act would be restricted from the outset.

Yet the issue of when humans were supposed to receive this God-given capacity to act was still up for debate. This could either be with the act (*maʿa al-fiʿl*), or before it (*qabla al-fiʿl*). Abū Ḥanīfa did not say anything precise on the matter, but only said in a general manner that humans were given the power (*quwwa*) to fulfill God's commands.[330] This gave rise to debate in the third/ninth century: The Ḥanafites decided on the first solution, and claimed that *istiṭāʿa* only came to exist with the action (*maʿa al-fiʿl*).[331] They aimed thereby to emphasize that in their view, the entire procedure of action stood under the sovereignty of the creator. The Karrāmites saw things differently, however; they claimed that God could not demand any (good) deeds from the creation as long as He had not made them capable (*taṭwīq*).[332] Accordingly, the *istiṭāʿa* had to be present in the human being already before the action.[333] If our understanding of Makḥūl al-Nasafī is correct, then he went so far as to hold the capacity

329 Even Abū Muṭīʿ, who inclined the most to predestination, thought this way (*Fiqh absaṭ*, 43.5–7). Abū Ḥanīfa also attested to this view (*Uṣūl*, 115 ult. f.).

330 See the second *Risāla* to ʿUthmān al-Battī, sections 2 and 6 of the main section, above, 40f.

331 *K. al-Sawād*, section 42.

332 *Radd*, 97.1ff. with the correction of "*al-taṭwīq*" for "*al-taṭrīq*"; cf. ibid., 97.17ff.

333 *Radd*, 66.4ff.; cf. 87.18f. and 97.17ff. On this view of the Karrāmites, see also *Uṣūl*, 116.7f.; van Ess, *Ungenützte Texte*, 24f. and 78f.; Gimaret and Monnot, 359f.n94.

to act as a constant, natural human ability, since he names as examples for this the ability to hear, see, or make use of one's healthy limbs (in the *ḥajj*),[334] saying furthermore that this capacity is implanted (*gharaza*) in the creation.[335]

8.3.2.2 Al-Māturīdī's Contribution

The theory of human agency that al-Māturīdī inherited was consequently not a closed system, but consisted of several elements.[336] Its contours were clear at the core, but at the same time, a significant degree of uncertainty prevailed on an aspect which was not insignificant. This unresolved problem was compounded by factors that al-Māturīdī's predecessors could not have foreseen; namely, that the entire theory came to be called into question by an outsider. Al-Kaʿbī had come to Transoxania, and it seems he attacked the Ḥanafites for their description of human actions more seriously than any other topic.[337]

Al-Māturīdī's response was not long in coming, and is found in all the necessary detail in his *K. al-Tawḥīd*. In fact, much that he says there on human agency only serves to parry al-Kaʿbī's accusations.[338] We learn from our scholar again that the Muʿtazilites not only spread nonsensical teachings, but were entrenched dangerously closely to heretics and foreign religions.[339]

Throughout the polemic, however, al-Māturīdī did not neglect to present his own view. He did this as his predecessors had, by declaring the proper position as lying in the middle between two extremes. The Jabrites had falsely assessed human actions, but the Qadarites had done so as well.[340] Consequently, the correct position could only be reached by treading a different path and seeking to contrast oneself from both heretical views.

---

334 *Radd*, 97.17ff.

335 *Radd*, 97.2.

336 On al-Māturīdī's ideas concerning free will and predestination, cf. also Cerić, 208–233.

337 Al-Kaʿbī's main accusation is that the Transoxanian Ḥanafites (and al-Najjār's followers) are actually Jabrites. In any case, that is what al-Māturīdī indignantly states (*Tawḥīd*, 320.13–323.13). Yet, the Ḥanafites were to blame for the seriousness of the disputes, since they had always claimed to possess the right doctrine based on evading the errors of the Qadarites (= the Muʿtazilites) and the Jabrites.

338 *Tawḥīd*, 227.9–228.6, 230.1–256.6, 294.11–303.15, 307.16–323.13.

339 Al-Māturīdī particularly wants to establish a proximity between the Muʿtazilites and the Dualists (ibid., 235.19ff. and 314.4ff.) and uses the famous *ḥadīth*, according to which the Qadarites are "the Zoroastrians of this community" (ibid., 244.3, 244.20, and 314.8). Furthermore, he insinuates almost ironically that the Muʿtazilites are the real Jabrites (ibid., 321.14 and 322.4f.).

340 Ibid., 225.2ff. against the Jabrites; 227.9ff. against the Qadarites (read on line 227.9 *ʿanhu*—in relation to God—instead of *ʿanhum*); 228 ult. for the juxtaposition.

The basic tendency of al-Māturīdī's doctrine itself, as he teaches it, is not surprising. Its main principle is the idea of cooperation between the Creator and His creation. God creates (*khalq*) actions,[341] and human beings do them (*fiʿl*).[342] This is explained more precisely here than in earlier texts, in that each act comprises several aspects (*jihāt*), some of which are attributed (*iḍāfa*) to God, and some of which are attributed to man.[343]

Besides this, al-Māturīdī adopts a concept from earlier authors which becomes a characteristic of his own teachings: the idea that a person, when acting, always possesses the capacity to do two contrary actions (*al-istiṭāʿa li-l-ḍiddayn*). Abū Ḥanīfa had already asserted this, as the *K. al-Tawḥīd* explicitly confirms.[344] In this regard the doctrine was not original, but actually a part of what the Ḥanafites traditionally professed.[345] Al-Māturīdī was to bestow the concept with a new and enduring terminological form, however, when he spoke in this context of human free choice, or *ikhtiyār*.[346] This term, which he first brought to prominence, was to catch on as a leitmotif of later theological discussions.[347]

Nevertheless, not all problems had been solved. There still remained the question of when the capacity to act was operative: during the act, as the earlier Ḥanafites said, or before it, as both the Karrāmites and the Muʿtazilites claimed. Al-Māturīdī sought an answer for this, but interestingly enough, he did not answer by merely repeating the Ḥanafite view. He answered like a true scholastic, taking both positions into consideration, and consequently arriving at a subtle distinction between them.

---

341 Ibid., 226.3f., 228.7f., 228.15, 235.10, 242.22f. and elsewhere; here the idea of predetermination (*qadar*) retreats into the background.

342 Ibid., 225.17, 227.9, 228.7, and 243.10.

343 Ibid., 228.8, 229.8ff., 237.15, and 240.22f.; on all in detail, see Gimaret, *Théories*, 179ff.

344 *Tawḥīd*, 263.4f.; cf. *Fiqh absaṭ*, 43.5–7.

345 This is not true for al-Najjār, the other Ḥanafite theologian. He believed that capacity is suited for only one act, and he is criticized by al-Māturīdī for this (*Tawḥīd*, 263.14ff.).

346 *Tawḥīd*, 103.14, 206 ult. and elsewhere. The opposing term to this is *ṭabʿ*, natural compulsion (ibid., 44.11, 103.16, 146.8ff., 152.1 and elsewhere). Both terms were, of course, already used by the Muʿtazilites. It is interesting that al-Māturīdī attributes *ikhtiyār* to God (ibid., 44.10ff.) as well as humans. This is not supposed to imply that humans are similar to God, but rather that both possess complete freedom as rational beings.

347 For references among the Māturīdites, cf. Gimaret, *Théories*, index on page 407. In the modern discussion on the freedom of mankind, the term is also used completely in the sense that al-Māturīdī used it (with authors such as Muḥammad ʿAbduh or the contemporary Muḥammad al-Shaʿrāwī).

According to al-Māturīdī, there is not one, but rather, two capacities to act (*qudra* or *istiṭāʿa*).[348] Humans possess the first by nature, since what is meant in this case is soundness (*salāma*) and health (*ṣiḥḥa*) available to the body and the intellect.[349] Al-Māturīdī says this is the precondition of every intentional act, which is why he describes it as "the capacity of means and states" (*istiṭāʿat al-asbāb wa-l-aḥwāl*).[350] It must always be available to humans, by which our theologian avoids saying "before the action" (*qabla l-fiʿl*), but in principle he means precisely that.

The second form of capacity is only granted to humans during the action itself (*maʿa l-fiʿl*). It puts them in the condition to make use of the means available to them.[351] It also represents the ability to do two contrary acts, such as obey or sin, for example.[352] This way, the individual receives the possibility of free choice (*ikhtiyār*),[353] but is still dependent on his Creator. He cannot choose anything and cannot use a single one of his limbs as long as he has not been given this second *istiṭāʿa*.

The solution al-Māturīdī suggests is complicated, without a doubt. Furthermore, we might very well accuse him of not taking his own path, but merely restricting himself to accepting the Ḥanafite and Karrāmite positions side by side. Yet in reality this is not the case at all. Al-Māturīdī ultimately frees himself of both paradigms and tries to incorporate only those approaches which he considers justified. This is not the mark of a compromise, but a synthesis. He was repeating, in his own way, that which other scholars in Transoxiana had tried in principle to do before him; namely, to find a higher understanding between the two opposing views of the Jabrites and the Qadarites.

Al-Māturīdī shared the Karrāmites' view that God may not oblige humans to do anything that He has not given them the ability to do. In order to argue this position he gave various examples of religious obligations, such as the *ḥajj*, giving alms, and *jihād*. He emphasized that it made no sense to burden believers with these duties if they were not fundamentally capable (*istaṭāʿa*) of carrying them out.[354] They all require a perpetual natural capacity, and this is what is meant by the first *istiṭāʿa*.

348 *Tawḥīd*, 256.6: *ʿalā qismayn*.

349 Ibid., 256.9ff. The *istiṭāʿa* is also understood in this sense by the Karrāmites and by al-Kaʿbī (cf. Gimaret, *La doctrine*, 132).

350 Ibid., 257.3.

351 Ibid., 256.16ff.

352 Ibid., 263.3–5.

353 Ibid., 263.12; cf. 146.8ff., 226 ult., 309.6ff.; on the theme, see Pessagno, "Irāda," 181ff.

354 *Tawḥīd*, 257.1ff. and 258.15ff.

Al-Māturīdī adopted another perspective from the Ḥanafites as well, one which argues that man cannot be empowered to act in complete independence, otherwise he would ultimately take on the role of a second Creator.[355] In order to counter this, a secondary, temporally-restricted capacity was presumed, one which guarantees that God retains direct influence in all human actions.

The doctrine that al-Māturīdī formulated aimed at striking a balance and was intended to consolidate the middle position that his school aspired to. But this does not change the fact that it did not exactly correspond to the views of the earlier generation of Ḥanafites. This probably explains why the school reacted to it with a certain reserve. Later theologians took note of al-Māturīdī's teachings on the topic, but for a long time they could not agree on whether this teaching ought to be followed or not.

Abū Salama followed al-Māturīdī without reservations, once more confirming his close bond to the master.[356] Abū l-Layth completely left out the sensitive theme of *istiṭaʿa*, which shows again that he is not to be ascribed to the Māturīdite school, or associated with the history of *kalām* in general.[357] Abū Shakūr clearly wanted to outdo al-Māturīdī in finesse, not stopping at just two capacities to act, but actually including up to three.[358] On his part, Abū l-Yusr al-Pazdawī went a step back and based himself on the older tradition that affirmed only one *istiṭāʿa*; according to al-Pazdawī this capacity only arises together with the act, and not before.[359]

That al-Māturīdī's conceptualization prevailed in the end, however, is thanks to the efforts of Abū l-Muʿīn al-Nasafī. He, like the master, also presumed there to be two capacities to act—the essential availability of the limbs, and a direct

355 Ibid., 259.21ff.

356 Abū Salama, 25.7ff.

357 Cf. Abū l-Layth, *Bustān*, section 23, 206.10ff.; idem, *ʿAqīda* I, 218.2 = *ʿAqīda* II, 269.9f. Cf. *ʿAqīda* I, 226.4ff. = *ʿAqīda* II, 273.7ff. In all of these, only *qadar* is discussed.

358 Abū Shakūr, *Tamhīd*, 123 a8ff.

359 Al-Pazdawī quite clearly has difficulty in hitting the right tone for his teachings on human capacity. In *Uṣūl* 109.5–9 he writes that humans must have intact limbs before the act, but he is careful not to speak of an *istiṭāʿa*. Then he speaks of a single momentary capacity (ibid., 109.17ff., as well as in 115.13ff.), he says explicitly that it only comes to exist with the action. Then he criticizes (ibid., 116.11ff.) scholars from his own school, who presumed a capacity before the act. Here al-Pazdawī reproaches them for having incorrectly understood Q 3:97, which al-Māturīdī himself actually used to prove the existence of his first *istiṭāʿa* (*Tawḥīd*, 257 ult. f.). Nevertheless, al-Pazdawī cannot dispense with humans having healthy organs at their disposal in order to act at all. He emphasizes, however, that this is a power (*qūwa*) and not a capacity (*Uṣūl*, 117 ult. ff.).

ability to act.[360] Through his influence, the idea found acceptance in the creed of Najm al-Dīn al-Nasafī.[361] Thus, the doctrine's place was secured in the memory of the school, such that al-Māturīdī's most important contribution to the theory of human action was in fact preserved and ultimately passed on.

8.3.3 *Belief and Sin*

Al-Māturīdī's respect for the older Ḥanafite tradition is also evident in the two last themes he discusses in the *K. al-Tawḥīd*. These relate to faith and the evaluation of the sinner, two questions that had been discussed since the beginning of the school. Ḥanafite teaching in this regard originated from an early Murji'ite legacy;[362] Abū Ḥanīfa had oriented himself on this basis when he gave his definitive answers in the first *Risāla* to ʿUthmān al-Battī on how belief and human sin were to be assessed.[363] His statements remained decisive in the times to follow and became the nucleus of all theology within his school. It is thus understandable that both themes were consistently presented in similar formulations in the *K. al-ʿĀlim*, the *Fiqh absaṭ*, and *K. al-Sawād*, as well as all later works of the Ḥanafite-Māturīdites.

The *K. al-Tawḥīd* is no exception to this. Al-Māturīdī advocates the same theses as the theologians before (and after) him did. This means that we already know the characteristics of his teachings from the earlier texts we have seen. Only the form of the presentation differs, because he does not restrict himself to repeating received doctrine; as usual he goes about proving it through detailed argumentation in engagement with his theological opponents.[364]

We learn that three principles must be abided by in regard to the evaluation of a sinner. The first is that a believer is still a believer even if he has committed a grave sin.[365] This is directed, as always within the Murji'ite-Ḥanafite tradition, against the Khārijites and Muʿtazilites, since the former believed that a

---

360 *Tabṣira*, vol. 2, 541.5ff.

361 Al-Nasafī, *ʿAqāʾid*, 2.-4ff./German trans. Schacht, *Der Islām*, 83; al-Taftāzānī, 90.4ff.; trans. Elder, 88ff.

362 Cf. above, 25f.

363 Cf. above, 33ff.

364 This is true for the entire course of argumentation, but especially for the inserted "discussions," conceived as refutations against the Muʿtazilites (*Tawḥīd*, 364.3–365.8), especially al-Kaʿbī (ibid., 343.12–360.9); on al-Māturīdī's concept of faith, cf. also Cerić, 201–205.

365 Ibid., 332.20 and 370.1ff.; cf. *Risāla I*, 35.12–18 and 36.9–19; *K. al-ʿĀlim*, section 5; *Fiqh absaṭ*, 40.17–41.16, 46.16–22, 47.12–48.1; *K. al-Sawād*, section 48.

sinner automatically became a disbeliever,[366] while the others claimed that a grave sinner took a middle position between belief and disbelief.[367]

A second thesis emerges from this foundational assertion. It concerns the destiny of humans in the afterlife, and says that a sinning believer is not awaited by eternal punishment in Hell. The worst punishment will be reserved for the worst evildoers; these are the disbelievers for whom al-Māturīdī also anticipates eternal damnation. Whoever is a believer, on the other hand, will at some point be rewarded with entrance to Paradise. He may expect punishment for his sins in Hell before this, but this will be temporally limited, and not endless.[368]

Because this promise of paradise stands, one may also hope for the Prophet's intercession for sinners that have passed away. This is the third principle that our theologian enumerates in good accordance with Ḥanafite tradition.[369] This also goes against the views of the Muʿtazilites and Khārijites, since they believed the Prophet would either only intercede for small sins,[370] or, they said, that there was no hope of intercession for sinners at all.[371]

Having explained the issue of sin, al-Māturīdī could now move on to the final part of his *K. al-Tawḥīd*, where he addressed the characteristics of religious belief. Here he likewise found himself in charted territory, since his school's definition of belief had been determined since the days of Abū Ḥanīfa. This definition states that belief consists of affirmation with the heart (*al-taṣdīq bi-l-qalb*) and avowal with the tongue (*al-iqrār bi-l-lisān*).[372] Thus, a believer is someone who testifies with sincere conviction that there is one God and that Muḥammad is His messenger. This also means that deeds cannot be included in actual belief; this position had long pitted the Ḥanafites against the concept of belief upheld by the Traditionists ("Ḥashwīya"), the Khārijites, and the Muʿtazilites.[373] This formulation furthermore stipulates that it is not sufficient to simply affirm God by words (*al-iqrār bi-l-lisān*), as the Karrāmīya

---

366 *Tawḥīd*, 323.17ff. and 328.3ff.

367 Ibid., 329.11, 331.7ff., and 336.1ff.

368 Ibid., 334.13ff., 339.1ff., 360.10ff.; cf. *Risāla I*, 37.1–6; *K. al-ʿĀlim*, sections 14, 15, and 41; *Fiqh absaṭ*, 46.23–47.12; *K. al-Sawād*, sections 7, 37, 40, and 60; also *Radd*, 108.1–9 and 114.22–115.3.

369 *Tawḥīd*, 365.12ff.; cf. *K. al-ʿĀlim* section 16; *K. al-Sawād*, sections 5, 15, and esp. 16.

370 *Tawḥīd*, 365.10f.

371 Ibid., 369.1ff.

372 *Risāla I*, 35.5–11; *K. al-ʿĀlim*, section 6; *Fiqh absaṭ*, 40.17–41.16 and 42.5–8; *K. al-Sawād*, sections 1 and 43.

373 Already in the *Risāla I*, 36.9–19.

claimed in the late third/ninth century, thus presenting a new challenge for the Ḥanafites.[374]

Al-Māturīdī's exposition takes all these perspectives into consideration.[375] In addition, he upholds Ḥanafite tradition by arguing against the addition of the *istithnāʾ* ("if God wills") to the statement "I am a believer.[376] From this perspective it can be said that he was in full accordance with the doctrine of his school. The principles on the basis of which he presented the concept of Islamic belief are precisely those common to his predecessors.

However, there still remained one problem, and al-Māturīdī did not hesitate to address it. This was the question of whether human belief was created or uncreated. The Ḥanafites in the second/eighth or early third/ninth century probably did not address the topic; we find no such indication in Abū Ḥanīfa's *Risāla*[377] or the writings of Abū Muqātil and Abū Muṭīʿ. Somewhat later, however, this does seem to have developed into a discussion in Transoxania; this is not surprising given that the theme had become a subject of debate in other Islamic regions.

In principle, a distinction can be made between two camps in the discussion on the status of belief. The Traditionists inclined toward saying that belief was uncreated, while the *mutakallimūn* usually said that it was created by God.[378] This general rule, however, does not always apply in individual cases,

374 For the Karrāmite doctrine, cf. *Radd*, 62.13–63.8, 69.10–17, 117.1–7, 117.13–118.6, and 118.10–119.5; the first transmitted refutation is found in the *K. al-Sawād*, section 43. As Madelung explains (*Religious Trends*, 40, with reference to al-Shahrastānī's *Milal*), the Ḥanafite polemic against the Karrāmites is unfair. The Karrāmites only said that someone who makes the avowal must be considered a *muʾmin* in regard to his legal status. Whether he is actually a believer and will be rewarded with entrance to Paradise for this, is only decided by God on the Last Day.

375 In *Tawḥīd*, 373.8ff., al-Māturīdī's own doctrine is developed in contention with Karrāmites' doctrine; he then follows (ibid., 378.17ff.) with a refutation of the Traditionists, Khārijites, and Muʿtazilites. Afterward (ibid., 380.11ff.) is yet another short polemic against the thesis that belief is only knowledge (*maʿrifa*). This is probably directed against the position of Jahm b. Ṣafwān (cf. al-Nasafī, *Tamhīd*, 390.6ff.).

376 *Tawḥīd*, 388.10ff. Cf. *Fiqh absaṭ*, 45.16–46.15; *K. al-Sawād*, section 1; cf. *Radd*, 120.5–19, as well as Abū l-Layth, *Bustān*, 196f. The chapter on the relation between *īmān* and *islām* added to the *K. al-Tawḥīd* (393.1ff.) also reproduces a classical Ḥanafite position. Cf. *K. al-ʿĀlim*, section 6 and the later *Uṣūl*, 154.1ff. and 221.3ff.

377 However, al-Pazdawī later tries to cite Abū Ḥanīfa as testimony for his own voice (*Uṣūl*, 155.8ff.), for which the reliability of his information is not verifiable.

378 Madelung, "The Spread," 117n30, with numerous examples which will be mentioned shortly.

since there were often controversial positions within a school,[379] the situation in Transoxania being a particularly illustrative example.

It seems that the Karrāmites held belief to be created, according, at least, to the views evinced in the *Radd* of Makḥūl al-Nasafī.[380] The Ḥanafites, however, were not unified on the topic. They held very different views, which even prompted al-Pazdawī to later claim that the origin of a scholar could be known (whether from Samarqand, Bukhārā, or the Ferghana Valley) by the position he held on the issue.[381]

There was an attempt, however, to find a compromise between the different factions. At least, this is how the doctrine formulated in the *K. al-Sawād al-aʿẓam*, the official creed of the Sāmānids, can be understood. There it says that belief is partly created and partly uncreated, because it comprises several aspects that are influenced by people as well as by God. It is to the human's merit that he acknowledges and bears witness to God and moves his tongue to do so. But at the same time, the knowledge, the assistance, and even the content of the testimony (the *shahāda*) must be given to him by God. Accordingly, divine attributes and human actions are working synergistically, and from this follows the result that belief is partly created and partly uncreated.[382]

Al-Māturīdī did not endorse this compromise. In fact, he does not acknowledge anywhere that the Ḥanafites disputed on the status of belief,[383] and what he himself says on the topic departs clearly from the formulation of the *K. al-Sawād al-aʿẓam*. For al-Māturīdī, belief is unquestionably created,[384] since

379 This was the case with the Muʿtazilites for example. Earlier representatives such as Ḍirār b. ʿAmr or Bishr b. al-Muʿtamir thought it was obvious that belief was created (van Ess, *Theologie*, vol. 3, 54 and 127). Abū l-Hudayhl did not because he wanted to set himself apart from thinkers who considered all human actions to be created (ibid., 283).

380 *Radd*, 90.19–91.12.

381 According to al-Pazdawī, the scholars of Samarqand thought that belief was created (*Uṣūl*, 155.3ff.); the Ḥanafites in Bukhārā, however, were of the view that one ought not say that belief was created in every aspect (*muṭlaqan*) (ibid., 154.15ff.); the theologians of Ferghana went a step further and completely prohibited talking about createdness in connection with belief (ibid., 155.1f.). Al-Pazdawī does not specify precisely for which time period this division was valid, but we must ask about the reliability of this schematic classification. We know that in Samarqand at least views different from these were held, as the examples of al-Ḥakīm al-Samarqandī, al-Māturīdī, and Abū l-Layth show.

382 *K. al-Sawād*, section 10.

383 He only names as opponents in this regard "a group of Traditionists" (*farīq min al-ḥashwīya; Tawḥīd*, 385.12).

384 Ibid., 385.12ff.

it is merely a human action (*fiʿl*),[385] and such actions must, as the Ḥanafite school tirelessly emphasized, be created without exception. Inconsistency in this is inadmissable; one ought to strictly abide by the principle that God is the Creator of all things (*khāliq kulli shay'in*).[386] This position was clearly was important to our theologian, since he defended it by constructing yet another framework of arguments based on transmission, the senses, and the intellect.[387]

What al-Māturīdī presents here is merely consistent with his other views as he laid them out in the *K. al-Tawḥīd*. Consequently, this last observation also confirms to us the systematic manner in which he carried out his theological contemplations. This particular position of his, however, which was no doubt too rationalistic for other Ḥanafites, was not maintained in his school. The question of the status of belief did not play a significant role in later times,[388] but if a Transoxanian theologian discussed the issue, he would not follow al-Māturīdī's lead, but instead would come back to the formula of compromise already laid out in the *K. al-Sawād al-aʿẓam*.[389]

385 Ibid., 386.9ff.

386 Q 6:102, 40:62; cf. *Tawḥīd*, 386.21f.

387 On the senses, cf. ibid., 385.17ff.; on transmission, ibid., 386.20ff.; on the intellect, ibid., 387.8ff.

388 The theme is skipped in a series of important texts. It is missing in the *Jumal* of Abū Salama, in the larger works of Abū l-Muʿīn al-Nasafī (i.e., the *Tabṣira* and *Tamhīd*) and thus also in the creed of Najm al-Dīn al-Nasafī which was important for the time to follow.

389 Abū l-Layth, *ʿAqīda* II, 274.12–16; idem, *Bustān*, 201; cf. Ps.-Abū l-Layth, *Hal al-īmān makhlūq*, in al-ʿOmar, 242.6–8; *Uṣūl*, 155.17ff.; al-Nasafī, *Baḥr al-kalām* (trans. Jeffery), 379f.

CHAPTER 9

Concluding Observations

1 Al-Māturīdī's Position in Islamic Theology

The *K. al-Tawḥīd* finds an appropriate conclusion with the description of belief. A complete circle is thus drawn from the capacity of human beings to know things (cf. p. 231ff.) up to their final achievement of perfection—by knowing God and being upright believers. The topics that al-Māturīdī discusses along the way were numerous and we have not examined them in all of their details. For some points, the general outline given in our overview of the work (cf. p. 201ff.) must suffice. The main themes that stimulated al-Māturīdī have been discussed in more detail, however, permitting us to detect various trends in his thought. Thus, it is possible to conclude our study by presenting a general characterization of his theology and determining what role he performed in the historical development of *kalām*.

Such an evaluation is of course a delicate procedure and always entails the danger of emphasizing certain aspects while neglecting others no less significant. But perhaps one can presume this risk to be less in al-Māturīdī's case than with other theologians. His thought has certainly presented itself as a unique attempt to formulate a new synthesis from various forerunning models. It follows that it ought to be all the easier to distinguish him from his contemporary theologians so as to ascertain what made him a leading representative of Sunnī *kalām*.

The first and most striking feature we must mention in this respect is the fact that al-Māturīdī marks a turning point in the theology of eastern Iran. He stood, as we have continually reaffirmed, in a certain tradition which he thoroughly respected. But by operating within this tradition, he actually changed it, and not in the sense of a gradual development, but so drastically in fact that a completely new quality took root.

Before the emergence of al-Māturīdī, theology in Transoxania was written in a relatively unembellished manner, as is evident from our analysis of its early development in the first part of this study. This started with the adoption of Abū Ḥanīfa's ideas, which means, more precisely, that his correspondence to ʿUthmān al-Battī was studied and transmitted. Shortly thereafter followed his pupils' texts, such as the *K. al-ʿĀlim* and the *Fiqh absaṭ*. And thus a particular religious orientation was established, which over the course of the third/ninth century came to embark on two rather different trajectories: one quite

 | DOI 10.1163/9789004261846_011

plainly within Abū Ḥanīfa's own school, embodied most prominently in the *K. al-Sawād al-aʿẓam*; and one marked more strongly by asceticism and the drive to piety from Ibn Karrām, whose theological views were held, to a large degree, by Makḥūl al-Nasafī.

All of these Ḥanafite texts are comparable in regard to their relatively simple and straightforward expository style. This distinguishes the entire tradition from the *K. al-Tawḥīd* that was to follow. The latter was not a work concerned solely with the delineation and affirmation of an already well-established creed, but a real work of speculative theology. And this means that Transoxania by and large entered the history of *kalām* thanks to al-Māturīdī and his work.

The difference is immediately clear from the methods al-Māturīdī utilized. He did not restrict himself to repeating transmitted doctrines in their traditional formulations. He tried to prove what he taught, and he derived new theses from others whenever possible. None of his predecessors in Transoxania had done so before him, and he was only able to do so because of a new medium at his disposal. This was his clearly structured epistemology, by which he revealed his thought processes and provided accountability on the basis of the various pathways of knowledge acquisition.

The doctrine that resulted from this new method was no longer the old one, though the extent to which this is true differs according to the topic at hand. Al-Māturīdī by no means rejected the teachings of his school, but only sought new pathways if there was no reliable earlier method available. In the second half of the *K. al-Tawḥīd*, where he discussed the qualities of human beings, he almost always taught the same doctrines as his predecessors. This was possible for him because the themes dealt with there were ones for which decidedly Ḥanafite positions had already been established. Be that as it may, a completely different situation was at hand for long stretches of the first half of the book; many issues were broached there which no earlier Ḥanafite had addressed. Consequently al-Māturīdī could not afford to be a conservative thinker when taking them up. He needed to address these new challenges, and as the horizon of problems broadened, he had to expand beyond his own school tradition.

At this point the different theological opponents and rivals who faced him in Transoxania come into play. Their presence is detectable everywhere in the *K. al-Tawḥīd*, but their respective significance depends on whether the pertinent theme had already been discussed in Ḥanafite tradition. That is to say, whenever al-Māturīdī could determine the answer to a question by referring back to a doctrine of his school, then argumentation with his opponents only served him as a critical foil. But wherever he entered theological virgin soil, he verified whether or not the ideas of other schools were possibly acceptable. There are plenty of examples of this. The most striking of them is the first part of the *K. al-Tawḥīd*, which relies on a Muʿtazilite model for its entire formal layout. But even specific ideas that al-Māturīdī presents can be brought in connection with various other thinkers. Sometimes he is indebted to al-Najjār (e.g., on the analysis of the world); other times to Ibn al-Rāwandī (cf. on the justification of prophethood); other things he learns from Ibn Shabīb, or authors whom the latter cites (cf. on the critique of foreign religions; for proof of the createdness of the world). The dispute with al-Kaʿbī was even more important, and though it seldom led al-Māturīdī to adopt a specific doctrine (cf. on the natures), its significance can hardly be overestimated, because so much that our theologian presents is owed to his theoretical assessment of the encounter with that Muʿtazilite thinker.

It was the Muʿtazila who challenged the Transoxanian Ḥanafites most during the lifetime of our theologian. Al-Kaʿbī was a chief representative of this challenge, as a scholar from Balkh who emerged in northeast Iran as a celebrated scholar. But this does not mean that al-Māturīdī's deliberations revolved exclusively around him and the other representatives of his school. There were other regional trends as well which influenced him and also left their impact on the *K. al-Tawḥīd*.

One of these, without a doubt, was the presence of the dualistic religions. At the time, they still played a greater role in northeastern Iran than they did in Iraq. This is why al-Māturīdī dealt with them in such detail. But he did this in a twofold manner, because his polemic likewise contained a critique against the Muʿtazila. The latter are accused of failing Islam in this very important religious debate as they were apparently unable to effectively refute the dualists. On the contrary, opines our theologian; the Muʿtazilites' disputes with these dangerous opponents had not led to a victory for the Muslims, but instead had the consequence of causing their theology to succumb to the pernicious influence of dualism.

Another trend that can be detected in the *K. al-Tawḥīd* is al-Māturīdī's interest in philosophical concepts. It begins with his inclination to adopt philosophical terminology (e.g., *māʾīya*, or *jawhar* in the sense of the Greek *ousia*), but also includes conceptual incorporations such as the definition of a human or speculations on the "oneness" of God. All this does not argue for a philosophical orientation in the conceptual framework of his thought; we can only maintain that al-Māturīdī took up individual stimuli and augmentations from such a milieu. But even this is noteworthy, because it was by no means an obvious choice for a *mutakallim*, particularly seeing as his theology was to represent a Sunnī theological school.

Al-Māturīdī's relation to the Sufis is less clear. It can only be said that he was known as a pious man whose main interest was the religious practice (*dīn*) of individuals. A particular inclination to the concepts of Islamic mysticism cannot be deduced on this basis; such a profile is actually more demonstrable in the case of other Ḥanafites who emerged shortly before and after him. It makes more sense not to bring his personage in proximity to Sufism, but rather to generally state that there were no conscious demarcations among the Transoxanian Ḥanafites vis-à-vis Sufism.

All of these observations show al-Māturīdī to be an open and attentive thinker. He was ready to examine foreign views and incorporate concepts from them which seemed suitable to him in his own synthesis. The exact nature of this synthesis itself has yet to be explained, however. Until now we have only come to know its different constitutive elements. The question remains as to whether there is a guideline according to which al-Māturīdī integrated these elements, or in other words, whether we can determine a conceptual framework for his entire system of theology.

The answer to this question is undoubtedly difficult in light of the material we have assembled, since it is not enough to simply maintain that al-Māturīdī updated the Ḥanafite theology that preceded him. However, the argument can be made that al-Māturīdī was attempting to apply a certain principle in his theology, one which he presumably held to be the quintessence of Ḥanafite thought: The seeking of a middle path between opposing theological views, and the preservation of a sensible balance between the differing exigencies of revelation and intellect, God and man, and God and the world.

Originally, this idea was only applied in the domain of human actions. In this topic the Ḥanafites had always called for both parties involved, i.e., God and man, to both be sufficiently taken into account. Al-Māturīdī, however, extended this principle and made it a foundational feature of his thought. Whenever a theological decision arose, he always evoked this ideal of equilibrium in its different aspects.

In his epistemology this was embodied in his constant efforts to equally emphasize the three pathways of knowledge acquisition (the senses, transmission, and the intellect). In his description of the world, we noted how he combined the independence of bodies (as natures) on one hand, together with their dependency on God (as accidents) on the other. As for humans, al-Māturīdī laid out the model of two capacities for action in order to more subtly explain the interplay between the Creator and His creation. And finally, in regard to God, he likewise strove for a balance of different aspects: on one side al-Māturīdī depicted the Creator as sovereign and unrestricted as the Traditionists called for; but on the other side, he allowed for God to act in a comprehensible manner, which corresponded moreso to the rationalistic understanding of the Muʿtazilites. This, too, was a balancing act of different theological demands and concepts. Nowhere is this as clear as in his concept of divine wisdom, which may be understood as the key to a theology of synthesis.

2 The Relationship to Abū Ḥanīfa

Given the complexity of his thought, the description of al-Māturīdī in numerous sources as a mere interpreter of Abū Ḥanīfa's thought is clearly a misleading simplification. This characterization not only makes an unreliable shift in emphasis, but also disregards al-Māturīdī's own achievements, consciously playing down those new elements that he introduced to Transoxanian theology.

That is not to say that there is no internal relationship between him and Abū Ḥanīfa. Quite the contrary, our entire study demonstrates how much the scholars of Samarqand in general were dedicated to cultivating the legacy of the Kufan master. This was also true of al-Māturīdī, who surely would have confirmed that he was merely concerned with perpetuating Abū Ḥanīfa's ideas. Yet the texts themselves tell another story, not simply displaying a pledge to continuity, but also showing how far developments had progressed from their origins. Demonstrating this is as simple as comparing the correspondence to ʿUthmān al-Battī with the *K. al-Tawḥīd.*

The qualification must be added, however, that later Māturīdites made an effort to accord Abū Ḥanīfa a different stature in his capacity as author and theologian. They not only attributed to him the early correspondence with ʿUthmān al-Battī; they also alleged that he wrote the *K. al-ʿĀlim*, the *Fiqh absaṭ*, as well as the much later *Fiqh akbar II*, and other various inauthentic "testaments." In such texts, the creed was naturally much more elaborate, such that many parallels could be seen between them and the work of al-Māturīdī. But even these texts are far from the *K. al-Tawḥīd.* And what is more, they do not demonstrate that al-Māturīdī and Abū Ḥanīfa thought similarly, but only that both of their images had shifted and been reinterpreted, thus creating the impression of proximity.

3 The Relationship to al-Ashʿarī

The second image of al-Māturīdī, which aims to present him as an eastern counterpart to al-Ashʿarī, is not as easy to evaluate. Much depends on the perspective emphasized, because each focus gives rise to a different judgment.

On one hand, parallels can naturally be found between the two theologians, and an adequate number of these have already been mentioned. These sometimes create the appearance of a deeper harmony, which most likely relates to the fact that al-Ashʿarī and al-Māturīdī were contemporaries. But on the other hand, the differences between the two are just as evident, and ultimately relate to more important issues. This is why it makes sense not to speak of an inner relationship between the thinkers, but only of specific views held in common.

They may be compared, for example, in their dealings with similar opponents in their theology; they both held their ground against the Muʿtazilites, for example. Yet it must immediately be added that this was not exclusive to them, but actually characteristic of a larger discussion that was taking place at that time everywhere.

One can likewise compare their foundation in the *sunna*. But this also does not quite make them birds of a feather, because their situation is by no means identical. Al-Ashʿarī had been an accomplished Muʿtazilite, and later tried to conspicuously procure, if not outright apply for, Ḥanbalite recognition. Al-Māturīdī grew up as an adherent of the eastern Ḥanafites, and remained known as such his entire life. In this respect he could argue with the Muʿtazilites from a secure position, and was never compelled to publicly prove his Sunnī identity.

But all of these are just external perspectives and evaluations. The question as to the relation between the two men's theologies remains critical. In that regard, it can only be soberly stated that there are no real deep consensuses between the two. The differences are actually vast. And this means that the view that both professed related teachings is essentially an illusion.

This is not the place to justify this assessment in detail. That would call for a number of new considerations and a comprehensive comparison. However, it may be asserted that the two theologians went about their intellectual approaches in completely different ways. This is true of all important themes discussed here, i.e., epistemology, the structure of the world, the being and acts of God, as well as the sphere of freedom granted to human beings.

This suggests that the enumeration of differences between the two which later Muslim authors have presented is insufficient, and misses the heart of the matter. This is especially true of al-Subkī, who wanted to limit the number of their differences to thirteen; he essentially concentrates on trivial matters and disregards those of greater significance. Al-Bayāḍī's descriptions are more precise, but also incorrect. He intended to present the differences between al-Ashʿarī and al-Māturīdī, for which he assembled a list of up to fifty points of contention; however he does not actually describe the teachings of the two theologians, but rather talking points that came up later between their two eponymically named schools. This is clear right from the beginning, when he shows no knowledge of any difference between the two scholars in regard to the physical world.

Characterizing al-Ashʿarī's theology in general, it might be said that he often asserted his theories in a manner that was terse, perhaps even to the point of abruptness. This is what Gimaret means when he ascribes to him an "esprit vigoreux, hardi," an "esprit brutalement simplificateur," and a "doctrine ... fortement typée."[1] Al-Māturīdī, by contrast, aims for something slightly different. Radicalism is precisely that which he wishes to avoid. His intention is to reach a synthesis that does justice to as many differing aspects as possible.

It is nevertheless appropriate that both doctrines are put together under the rubric of Sunnī *kalām*. One simply must be aware that the claim associated with this term is to be interpreted differently in each case. Al-Ashʿarī interprets it in such a manner that he divides between content and methodology. He knows *kalām* and its rational form of argumentation excellently, but he makes use of it to defend a position which, in its basis, corresponds to Sunnī Traditionism. Al-Māturīdī has a different interpretation. He does not merely adopt the methods developed by the *mutakallimūn*. He also tries to find a doctrinal balance, a meeting point between the religious ideas of the Traditionists and a type of thinking characterized by rationality.

4 The Formation of the Māturīdīya

The notion that both theologians are similar thinkers thus did not come from an objective examination of their teachings. It was rooted in the search for harmony that arose in the Ashʿarite and Māturīdite schools in the late Middle Ages. Before this could occur, the schools naturally had to come into their own first. In the case of the Māturīdites, this did not happen in direct connection with the activity of their master. It was instead the result of a longer process, which is sketched out here by way of conclusion.[2]

Its trajectory may be broken up into three relatively clear and distinct phases. The first, which continued until the end of the fourth/tenth century, is largely characterized by the fact that nothing of importance happened for the development of the school. Al-Māturīdī had followers, as had every prestigious

1 Gimaret, *La doctrine*, 22, 155, and 23 respectively.

2 The following considerations are presented in more detail in Rudolph, "Das Entstehen der Māturīdīya."

shaykh. The most important of them was Abū Salama al-Samarqandī, to whom we owe a summary of the *K. al-Tawḥīd*, namely the *Jumal uṣūl al-dīn*. But this does not change the fact that most of the Transoxanian Ḥanafites did not really take note of al-Māturīdī. On the contrary, they continued to follow the traditional understanding of religion that had been cultivated earlier in the region.

The best example of this is Abū l-Layth al-Samarqandī (d. 373/983), who can be described as the dominant Ḥanafite figure in the generation after al-Māturīdī. We still possess quite a few of his works, which shows how popular he was as an author. Among these are a creedal work, an extensive Qurʾān commentary, devotional texts such as the *Tanbīh al-ghāfilīn* and the *Waḥy al-asrār*, but also texts such as the famous *Bustān al-ʿārifīn*, in which religious instruction is combined with the literary devices of *adab* literature. Abū l-Layth often wrote on theological topics; thus the opportunities for him to debate al-Māturīdī's ideas were plentiful. But he did not seek them out; he does not mention al-Māturīdī anywhere in his works. Instead, Abū l-Layth merely abided by a creed in accordance with the standard found in the *K. al-Sawād al-aʿẓam*. This shows that the new form of theology that al-Māturīdī developed still had not found wide recognition. It was even possible to do without it in Transoxania, probably because no serious theological challenge presented itself in the late fourth/tenth century, whether on the part of the Muʿtazilites or the Ashʿarites.

Things changed only at the turn of the fifth/eleventh century, which marks the second phase in the process of the school's formation. This was marked by the detection of an Ashʿarite presence in northeastern Iran; a presence that had become unavoidable by this time, since the Ashʿarites had established themselves at their doorstep, so to speak. Their new center was set up in Nishapur around the end of the fourth/tenth century, and with scholars such as Ibn Fūrak (d. 406/1015) and al-Isfarāyīnī (d. 418/1027) it could boast of two important spokesmen. It was only a matter of time before the two schools took note of one another. If the sources do not mislead us, this happened at the latest by the middle of the fifth/eleventh century. At that time, the Ashʿarite author Abū Bakr al-Fūrakī (d. 478/1085) emerged as the first Ashʿarite of Transoxania. Contemporaneously, the Ashʿarites were also mentioned by name in a work by a Transoxanian theologian, namely Abū Shakūr al-Sālimī.[3] The outlook between the two groups was grim from the very beginning. There were serious criticisms on both sides and a clearly defined argument was even developed. The problem, mentioned earlier in the introduction, was regarding whether God's attributes of action are to be seen as eternal or temporal. This matter

3 *Tamhīd*, fol. 41a1ff.

came to a head on the question of whether God really is the Creator eternally. The Transoxanians naturally affirmed this; the Ashʿarites in Khurāsān opposed it. But both parties still had something in common as far as we are concerned: neither of them referred to al-Māturīdī when they argued; his name is not mentioned by al-Fūrakī nor by al-Sālimī in any context.

The revival of his name was reserved for the third phase of the process, which can be placed at the end of the fifth/eleventh century. This period was quite eventful: the dispute with the Ashʿarites became a dominant motif in the theology of the Transoxanian Ḥanafites, and finally led them to consider Abū Manṣūr al-Māturīdī as their decisive authority.

How this happened is reported to us by two Ḥanafite authors, Abū l-Yusr al-Pazdawī and Abū l-Muʿīn al-Nasafī, who are already known to us as distinguished sources. Between the two of them, al-Pazdawī strikes a more conciliatory tone. He believes that the debate on the attribute of "creating" was somewhat overblown, especially in the Ashʿarite camp. This made people unnecessarily emphasize the differences between the two groups, and quickly overlook the fact that al-Ashʿarī, despite some erroneous views, was a respectable theologian. Be that as it may, al-Pazdawī remains firm on the issue. He holds the Transoxanian position that God is to be described eternally as Creator. In order to substantiate this he presents a further argument that is decisive for us; namely, that the eternity of the attribute of creating had been professed by Abū Manṣūr al-Māturīdī. In his time, the theologian from Samarqand had already debated the Muʿtazilites on this controversial topic; besides, al-Māturīdī was earlier (*aqdam*) than al-Ashʿarī, and what is more, had taken the entire concept from earlier Ḥanafite theology, without creating anything new on his part.[4]

These last sentences clearly lay close to al-Pazdawī's heart. This is why it would have been helpful had he explained and documented the importance of the Ḥanafites' long record of teachings on the divine attributes as well al-Māturīdī's seniority over al-Ashʿarī. This he does not do. The context of his comments is only understood if Abū l-Muʿīn al-Nasafī is brought into the picture, since he goes into an unusually broad explanation of the entire problem and sketches out the central points of the debate with the Ashʿarites with more precision.[5]

According to al-Nasafī, three different Ashʿarite theologians were responsible for advancing vehement attacks against the Transoxanian Ḥanafites. Two of them only spread brief polemics against the Ḥanafites, while the third was

4 *Uṣūl*, 70.5ff.
5 *Tabṣira*, vol. 1, 310–372.

striking in his persistence and impertinence: He put together arguments from the Qur'ān, jurisprudence, grammar, and rational theology in order to denigrate the Ḥanafite position. But to top it all of he crowned his tirade with yet another insidious insinuation. According to him, the Ḥanafite theologians he attacked were merely blaspheming innovators at work in Transoxania, since what they said on the attribute of "creating" was not professed by any early authority and not a single one of the pious forebears (*al-salaf*). This was nothing but a recently invented heresy, which only arose after the year 400/1010 in northeastern Iran.

The accusation was rather grave, and compelled Abū l-Muʿīn al-Nasafī to react. He did so with the required detail, by presenting an extensive excursus into history.[6] In essence, he says that the doctrine in question is not new, but had always been professed by Abū Ḥanīfa's followers. In order to prove this claim, almost all Ḥanafite authorities are invoked by name. It is critical for al-Nasafī, however, that the Ḥanafites not only thought this way in Iraq or in other Islamic territories, but also followed this teaching in Transoxania, where he viewed the city of Samarqand as playing a key role. To this effect, he lists quite a number of Samarqandian scholars of the second and third centuries AH, and explains that they had all professed the eternality of the divine attributes of action. He then concludes with the pivotal sentences mentioned earlier: "(However), if there had been among them only the Imām Abū Manṣūr al-Māturīdī, who dove into the sea of knowledge to bring forth its pearls … this would have sufficed." Anyone who surveyed al-Māturīdī's achievements could only come to the conclusion that God had singled him out with miracles (*karāmāt*), gifts of grace (*mawāhib*), divine assistance (*tawfīq*), and guidance (*irshād, tasdīd*). This is so because in the normal course of things (*fī l-ʿādāt al-jāriya*), many scholars together do not possess the knowledge that was assembled in him alone.[7]

As mentioned at the beginning of this study, these remarks served to emphasize the continuity of the Samarqand school. This is why al-Nasafī was concerned with al-Māturīdī's name being mentioned in a long list of other prominent scholars. But at the same time, he cannot help singling him out among this list with every word he says. This is because Abū l-Muʿīn, as we have come to know, considered al-Māturīdī superior to all the other theologians on the list, and wrote works such as the *Tamhīd*, the *Baḥr al-kalām*, and the *Tabṣirat al-adilla*, which all stand completely in the tradition of al-Māturīdī's *K. al-Tawḥīd*. With these he laid the foundations for further development,

---

6 Ibid., vol. 1, 355.12ff.

7 Ibid., 358.15–359.11.

which quickly took its course. Only a few years after his death Najm al-Dīn al-Nasafī wrote his famous creed, which reproduced al-Māturīdī's doctrine in Abū l-Muʿīn's formulation. And thus a new tradition was established, which henceforth set the tone for posterity. It still bore the name of *aṣḥāb Abī Ḥanīfa*, but really referred back to the man from Samarqand, such that it could truthfully be called Māturīdīya.

Our last considerations then, end up back at the Ashʿarites, since they were the ones who provoked al-Nasafī to place al-Māturīdī's legacy in the foreground. However, this was not undertaken in the spirit of harmony with al-Ashʿarī, but actually on the basis of a standing rivalry in the context of unmistakable disputation. Thus, one can maintain as the final facet of our study that Ḥanafite theology in Transoxania was shaken up twice, changing qualitatively both times as a result: first, at the beginning of the fourth/tenth century through the rise of the Muʿtazila, against whom al-Māturīdī formulated his own *kalām*; and second, in the fifth/eleventh century through the Ashʿarite challenge, which contributed to the formation of the Māturīdites as a distinct theological school.

Appendix
Inauthentic and Doubtful Texts

After al-Māturīdī found general recognition, there was a great attempt to adorn oneself with his name. This is certainly the reason why he is named as the author of a series of smaller texts that have been transmitted to us in manuscript form; what all of these works have in common is that they are not mentioned by any of our bio-bibliographical sources as having been written by al-Māturīdī. This alone is grounds for suspicion and suggests the hypothesis that we are dealing strictly with pseudepigrapha. Nevertheless, one must distinguish between different cases. Most of these texts can clearly be shown to come from a later time; however, in regard to one of them we can only assert that al-Māturīdī's authorship is very improbable, but not completely ruled out.

1 Inauthentic Texts

1.1 Sharḥ al-Fiqh al-akbar

The work which has long found the greatest attention from among these texts is without a doubt the so-called *Sharḥ al-Fiqh al-akbar*. It is ascribed to al-Māturīdī in a Yemeni manuscript, and was thus printed under his name in the *Rasāʾil al-sabʿa*. Several voices immediately objected to this attribution,[1] but for a long time, the text could not be more precisely examined because there was no edition in which its complex history of transmission could be assessed. This situation has changed in the meantime, since we now possess a edition by H. Daiber. He edited the *Sharḥ* on the basis of seven manuscripts and added a detailed commentary to it.[2] Thus the text has become accessible for the first time in a way that allows us to reflect on its historical dating.

As Daiber confirms in the introduction to the edition, al-Māturīdī's authorship of the *Sharḥ* is out of the question. There are a number of important indications that rule out such a thesis,[3] among which is the observation that the *Sharḥ* contradicts a point

1 Cf., for example, Madelung, "The Spread," 122n3; van Ess, Review of *Kitāb al-Tawḥīd*, 557n2; Sezgin also does not mention it among al-Māturīdī's works (*GAS*, vol. 1, 604–606).

2 Hans Daiber, *The Islamic Concept of Belief in the 4th/10th Century: Abū l-Layth al-Samarqandī's Commentary on Abū Ḥanīfah (died 150/767) al-Fiqh al-absaṭ* (Tokyo, 1995). In the introduction (ibid., 1ff.) Daiber discusses the manuscripts, the question of authorship, and the foundational theological orientation of the work; this is followed by the Arabic text (ibid., 27ff.), then a theological commentary (ibid., 211ff.), and detailed indexes (ibid., 253). Unfortunately I was not able to refer to this edition, when I myself examined and cited the *Sharḥ* (e.g., 59f.).

3 Daiber, *Islamic Concept*, 5ff.

 | DOI 10.1163/9789004261846_012

in al-Māturīdī's doctrine.[4] One could suffice with this reason alone to dismiss the text as a pseudepigraphical work. Nevertheless, it was an important text for Transoxania's subsequent theological development, and thus the question of its date and authorship merits a closer look.

Daiber argued for the presumption of Abū l-Layth al-Samarqandī as the author of the *Sharḥ*; this was a thesis that had already been proposed several times before. He mentions three arguments in particular to justify this. First, two of the manuscripts explicitly name Abū l-Layth as the author; second, the text itself names him as an authority two times (lines 188 and 412 of the Daiber edition); and third, the content of the *Sharḥ* confirms this attribution because in various places it supposedly shows literary parallels with the teachings of Abū l-Layth in his Qur'ān commentary.[5]

Nevertheless, Daiber does add that these indications are not weighty enough to dispel any possible doubt.[6] This is why he adds that the text was perhaps "lightly reworked" by later Māturīdite transmitters.[7] He thereby brings into play the influence of a later period, which is plausible given everything we have ascertained on the development of the Māturīdites, since on the basis of our previous observations it can hardly be assumed that Abū l-Layth wrote the *Sharḥ al-fiqh al-akbar*. It is much more probable that the text was only written after the middle of the fifth/eleventh century. The arguments for this are as follows:

1) The fact that two of the seven manuscripts claim Abū l-Layth as the author means little. Both of these copies actually carry a later dating than the others,[8] while in the two oldest manuscripts, another as of yet unidentifiable author (Abū Ibrāhīm Ismāʿīl b. Isḥāq al-Khāṭirī?) is named.
2) That the text mentions teachings from Abū l-Layth several times is also not a watertight argument. These parallels are always short and also few in number. This does not argue for Abū l-Layth having written the work, but merely indicates that his teachings were known to the author of the *Sharḥ*.
3) It is significant in this context that one can also find a contradiction between the statements of the *Sharḥ* and Abū l-Layth's views. This is the case in regard to the question of whether prophets ever sin. The *Sharḥ* holds this to be possible (for small offenses);[9] Abū l-Layth, however, believed that a prophet is always completely free of sin.[10]

4 Ibid., 7ff.
5 Ibid., 7.
6 Ibid., 9.
7 Ibid., 10.
8 Cf. ibid., 17ff.
9 Cf. ibid., lines 679–680 of text.
10 Abū l-Layth, *ʿAqīda* I 222.4–223.4 = *ʿAqīda* II 271.11–16.

4) In two places the author of the *Sharḥ* admits that the scholars in Samarqand preferred another formulation from the one that he chooses.[11] This suggests that he himself was not located in Samarqand, but in another city.
5) The theological opponents with which the *Sharḥ* contends most seriously are the Ashʿarites.[12] This alone ought to rule out a fourth/tenth-century origin for this text. As al-Nasafī reported, the dispute with them began only after 400/1010,[13] and came to dominate the discussion only within his lifetime.
6) This later time period is also indicated by an additional piece of evidence, namely the fact that al-Māturīdī is mentioned by name in the *Sharḥ*. This argues for the text being composed only after the middle of the fifth/eleventh century. Only then did the idea emerge of recognizing al-Māturīdī as a prominent authority, which as we have come to know, hinged directly on antagonism with the Ashʿarites in the region.

Given the resemblance of the text's argumentation to that of al-Pazdawī and Abū l-Muʿīn al-Nasafī in its emphasis of al-Māturīdī's importance and its antagonism toward the Ashʿarites, it would seem that the *Sharḥ* belongs to the phase in which the Māturīdīya were establishing themselves,. If this presumption is accepted, then even more features of the text may be explained; positions that cannot be associated with al-Māturīdī or Abū l-Layth, but instead are noticeably closer to the views of al-Pazdawī.

7) These begin with a position that was just mentioned: the view of the *Sharḥ* that prophets are not free of smaller sins.[14] This is found as well with al-Pazdawī,[15] while we know that Abū l-Layth had a divergent opinion.
8) Another parallel is found in a section on the divine attributes.[16] There, the *Sharḥ* reports a dispute that is supposed to have broken out among the Transoxanian Ḥanafites. Some were of the view that God was "knowing through His knowledge." Others disapproved of this and preferred the formulation "God is knowing and possesses knowledge." The *Sharḥ* places itself in the first camp[17] and thus shows its proximity to al-Pazdawī again. Al-Pazdawī was of the same view and furthermore reports to us the same intra-Ḥanafite dispute in very similar wording.[18]

11 Daiber, *Islamic Concept*, line 579ff. and 600f. of text.
12 Cf. ibid., line 286ff., 537ff., 603ff. and elsewhere.
13 *Tabṣira*, vol. 1, 310.11f.
14 Daiber, *Islamic Concept*, lines 679–688.
15 *Uṣūl*, 243.6f.
16 Daiber, *Islamic Concept*, lines 579ff.
17 Ibid., line 574.
18 *Uṣūl*, 34.6–9.

9) Three further commonalities may be added to conclude. The first is that both authors similarly separate the uncreated Qur'ān from the created means of its presentation (i.e., the written letters or voice of the reciter).[19] The second is even more idiosyncratic, dealing with speculation on the rank of Muḥammad over Adam.[20] But the third commonality is most interesting of all, since it relates to human actions. Here a theme is discussed which was struggled with considerably. The *Sharḥ* is quite clear on this; human beings actually act, and not metaphorically so;[21] but they only have access to one capacity of action (*istiṭāʿa*), which is only given to them directly at the time of the action (*maʿa al-fiʿl*).[22] The same view was held by al-Pazdawī,[23] as we have already seen; and in abiding by this position he basically stood alone among the late Transoxanian Ḥanafites. All the other authors whom we know held different views: Abū l-Layth did not address the question of the capacity to act at all; al-Māturīdī, Abū Salama, and Abū l-Muʿīn al-Nasafī spoke of two capacities to action; and Abū Shakūr al-Sālimī even spoke of three.

These clues lead us to a relatively straightforward conclusion. We may presume that the *Sharḥ* was probably written in the late fifth/eleventh century. At that time, theological discussions (especially with the Ashʿarites) were in the state which the text assumes as a backdrop. There had also developed a rivalry between the scholars of Samarqand and those of other cities, which is also indicated in the *Sharḥ*. Furthermore, at this time both al-Pazdawī and al-Nasafī developed their theology on similar lines, though it may be observed that the traditional creed such as the one al-Pazdawī propagated was clearly preferred by the author of the *Sharḥ*.[24]

19 Cf. Daiber, *Islamic Concept*, lines 594ff. with *Uṣūl*, 53.9ff. and 62.13ff.

20 Cf. Daiber, *Islamic Concept*, lines 720ff. with *Uṣūl*, 202f.

21 Daiber, *Islamic Concept*, line 270.

22 Ibid., line 249.

23 *Uṣūl*, 244.2f.

24 This also fits with the fact that the *Sharḥ* seeks to distance itself from al-Māturīdī on one issue (cf. Daiber, *Islamic Concept*, lines 548ff. and 572ff.); this does not accord with al-Nasafī's attitude, whereas al-Pazdawī occasionally does criticize al-Māturīdī (cf. *Uṣūl*, 207.12ff. and 211.17ff.). Furthermore, it can be added that Abū l-Layth is highly esteemed in the *Sharḥ*; he also happens to have been known as a more traditional Ḥanafite. For the time being we cannot conclude from the indications described here that the *Sharḥ* came from Bukhārā. Al-Pazdawī continually brings up Bukhārā and provokes the impression that a more traditionally oriented theology was adhered to there for which he had a certain amount of sympathy.

1.2 Risāla fī l-ʿaqāʾid

Another shorter manuscript which names al-Māturīdī as its author is a short creedal work.[25] It summarizes in 43 articles the main teachings adhered to by the *ahl al-sunna wa-l-jamāʿa*, i.e., the Transoxanian Ḥanafites. This work, too, was certainly not written by al-Māturīdī; instead, it is a compilation of teachings heavily indebted to the *Sharḥ al-fiqh al-akbar*.[26] In this light, it is enough to state that the *Risāla fī l-ʿaqāʾid* was written even later. But this conclusion is in principle also quite interesting: it demonstrates that people tried since the time of al-Nasafī and al-Pazdawī to spread theological teachings under al-Māturīdī's name. It also demonstrates what an important role the text of the *Sharḥ* played in this.

1.3 Kitāb al-Tawḥīd

What we have ascertained for the *Risāla* is likewise true for a third text. It bears the highbrow title of *K. al-Tawḥīd*, but is really an *ʿaqīda* that is even shorter than the *Risāla*.[27] The only theme treated in the text is the description of God. There the style of presentation shows that the state of the discourse is also relatively developed. Thus we are probably dealing with another rather late date of authorship, which is confirmed again by the fact that various elements evocative of the *Sharḥ al-fiqh al-akbar* may be detected.[28]

1.4 Risāla fī-mā lā yajūz al-waqf ʿalayhi

The case is somewhat different with the fourth work that is falsely attributed to al-Māturīdī. It does not deal with issues of dogma, but instead with the *qirāʾa*, or proper recitation of the Qurʾān.[29] The text is quite short and concentrates on a single theme. Its author's main intention is to assert which Qurʾānic verses it is forbidden to stop in the middle of (*al-waqf*) while reading. The type of draconian penalties he threatens in the case of someone's neglect of these rules are striking. He does not just hold the erring person's prayer to be invalid as a result (fol. 44a3 and elsewhere); he even believes that whoever breaks up the recitation at the wrong place becomes a disbeliever (fol. 44a3, 44a6 and elsewhere).

---

25 On the manuscripts, cf. *GAS*, vol. 1, 605. The work was available to me in the Gotha manuscript and in the edition by Yörükan.

26 Daiber has already collected the extensive evidence of this. Cf. his commentary on the *Sharḥ al-fiqh al-akbar* (*Islamic Concept*, 211ff.), where at the end of each section the parallels between the two texts are given (e.g., ibid., 214, 215, 218, 222 and elsewhere).

27 Ed. Yörükan from MS Feyzullah 2155.

28 Cf. *Tawḥīd*, 3.6 ult. with *Sharḥ* 539; *Tawḥīd* 4.17ff. with *Sharḥ* 528ff.; *Tawḥīd* 5.21ff. with *Sharḥ* 574ff.

29 On the manuscripts, cf. *GAS*, vol. 1, 606. My exposition is based on the MS Köprülü III 705, fols. 44a–44b.

It seems absolutely ruled out that al-Māturīdī would have said such things. It not only contradicts his general maxims, but particularly those on belief and sin. Most critical for him was that one turn to God with one's heart;[30] this led him to the opinion that not even a grave sinner loses their belief. Thus, it could hardly be assumed that he viewed someone as a disbeliever because of a mistaken pause in the recitation of the Qurʾān. This means, consequently, that the *Risāla fī-mā lā yajūz al-waqf ʿalayhi* cannot be an authentic work of our theologian either.

2 Doubtful Texts

Fawāʾid

The fifth text with which we must close our discussion poses a different case. It is not written in Arabic, but Persian.[31] This makes it immediately more interesting, because in al-Māturīdī's context the New Persian language had just developed.[32] In regard to the content, however, the text is anything but sensational, since no original themes are taken up there. It represents a conventional piece of popular ethical and edificational literature (*andarz*) as can often be found in Iran. Some of the advice which the author gives us has a thoroughly religious character. The author tells us, for example, that it is worth having fear of God in one's life, because *tawḥīd* is our "capital."[33] Other exhortations, however, are more profane and worldly, such as when it is pointed out that one should not undertake anything which will be detrimental to one's own status and wealth.[34]

Such simplistic pieces of advice can hardly be reconciled with our image of al-Māturīdī. They correspond neither to the thematization nor the formalistic standard that is otherwise characteristic for him. Nevertheless, it cannot be completely ruled out

---

30 *Tawḥīd*, 373.9f.

31 Sezgin names two manuscripts for the text (*GAS*, vol. 1, 606). The MS Fatih 5426, fols. 235–240a was available to me, where the work is provided with the title *Fawāʾid*. The same title is clearly used in the second manuscript from Bursa, as Afshār states in his edition ([Ps.-] Māturīdī, *Pandnāme*, ed. Īrāj Afshār, *Farhang-i Īrān Zamīn* 9 (1961): 47.2). He certainly has other reasons for providing the edition with the supertitle *Pandnāme*; he clearly intends to state which genre of literature the text belongs to.

32 The text must actually be quite old, as is shown by certain reminiscences of Middle-Persian; cf. for example, fol. 235b13 *farēshtah*, which is imprecisely reproduced by Afshār in [Ps.-]Māturīdī, *Pandnāme*, 48.3.

33 Such pious exhortations are found especially in the first chapter of the work (fol. 235b3–236a3 = [Ps.-]Māturīdī, *Pandnāme*, 47–49), but also in the appendix, provided with the title *Munājāt* (239 b ult.ff.; cf. [Ps.-]Māturīdī, *Pandnāme*, 66, comments by Afshār).

34 Cf. the beginning of the third chapter (236a19f. = [Ps.-]Māturīdī, *Pandnāme*, 51.6ff.).

that our theologian did at one point author a popular work or basic sermon. We do not possess any indication that proves the inauthenticity of the text with certainty. For this reason, we do not present it here among the pseudepigrapha, but instead as a doubtful text. At the same time, we may add that the work, even if authored by al-Māturīdī, gives absolutely no indication of his theological views.

Bibliography

ʿAbd al-Jabbār b. Aḥmad al-Qāḍī. *K. Faḍl al-iʿtizāl wa-ṭabaqāt al-Muʿtazila wa-mubāyanatihim li-sāʾir al-mukhālifīn*. In Sayyid, *Faḍl al-iʿtizāl*, 135–350.

———. *Al-Mughnī fī abwāb al-tawḥīd wa-l-ʿadl*. Edited by ʿAbd al-Ḥalīm Maḥmūd and Sulaymān Dunyā. 16 vols. Cairo, 1960–1965.

ʿAbd al-Jalīl b. Abī l-Ḥusayn al-Qazwīnī al-Rāzī. *K. al-Naqḍ, maʿrūf bi baʿḍ mathālib al-nawāṣib fī naqḍ baʿḍ faḍāʾiḥ al-rawāfiḍ*. Edited by Jalāl al-Dīn Ḥusaynī ʿUrmawī. Tehran, 1952.

Abdel Haleem, M.A.S. *Chance or Creation? God's Design in the Universe*. Reading, UK, 1995.

Abū Bakr Muḥammad b. al-Yamān al-Samarqandī. *Maʿālim al-dīn*. MS Mashhad 2605, 365 foll. Without pagination.

Abū Ḥanīfa. *Risāla ilā ʿUthmān al-Battī* [= *Risāla I*]. In al-Kawtharī, *al-ʿĀlim wa-l-mutaʿallim*, 34–38.

Abū l-Layth al-Samarqandī. *ʿAqīdat al-uṣūl*. In Juynboll, "Een Moslimsche Catechismus," 215–231 [= *ʿAqīda* I]. Second edition, *ʿAqīdat al-uṣūl*. In Juynboll, "Samarḳandī's Catechismus," 267–284 [= *ʿAqīda* II].

———. *Asrār al-Waḥy*. In Hell, *Von Mohammed bis Ghazâlî*, 61–74.

———. *Bustān al-ʿārifīn*. See idem, *Tanbīh al-ghāfilīn*.

———. *Al-Tafsīr*. Edited by ʿAbd al-Raḥīm Aḥmad al-Ziqqa. 3 vols. Baghdad, 1985.

———. *Tanbīh al-ghāfilīn, wa bi-hāmishihi Bustān al-ʿārifīn*. Cairo, 1302.

[Ps.-] Abū l-Layth al-Samarqandī. *Hal al-īmān makhlūq aw ghayr makhlūq*. MS British Museum Add. 9509, fols. 162a–162b. Edited in al-ʿOmar: "The Doctrines," 238–242 [= excerpt from: Muṣṭafā b. Zakarīyāʾ b. Aidoġmuš al-Qaramānī, *al-Tawḍīḥ*].

Abū Muqātil al-Samarqandī. *K. al-ʿĀlim wa-l-mutaʿallim*. See Qalʿajī, *Al-ʿĀlim*.

Abū Muṭīʿ al-Balkhī. *Al-Fiqh al-absaṭ*. In Kawtharī, *al-ʿĀlim wa-l-mutaʿallim*, 39–60.

Abū Naṣr Ṭāhir b. Muḥammad al-Khānaqāhī. *Guzīda dar akhlāq u taṣawwuf*. Edited by Īrāgh Afshār. Tehran, 1347/1968.

Abū Rashīd al-Nīsābūrī. *Al-Masāʾil fī l-khilāf bayna al-Baṣrīyīn wa-l-Baghdādīyīn*. Edited by Maʿn Ziyāda and Riḍwān al-Sayyid. Beirut, 1979. See partial edition in Biram, *Die atomistische Substanzenlehre*.

Abū Shakūr al-Sālimī, Muḥammad b. ʿAbd al-Sayyid b. Shuʿayb. *Al-Tamhīd fī bayān al-tawḥīd*. MS Berlin 2456, fols. 1–170b.

Abū Salama Muḥammad b. Muḥammad al-Samarqandī. *Jumal uṣūl al-dīn*. Edited by Ahmet Saim Kılavuz as *Ebû Seleme es-Semerkandî ve Akâid Risâlesi*. Istanbul, 1989.

Abū Ṭāhir Khāja Samarqandī. *Samarīya dar bayān-i awṣāf-i ṭabīʿī u mazārāt-i Samarqand*. Edited by Īrāj Afshār. Tehran, 1343/1965.

Abū ʿUdhba, al-Ḥasan b. ʿAbd al-Muḥsin. *Al-Rawḍa al-bahīya fī-mā bayna al-Ashāʿira wa-l-Māturīdīya*. Hyderabad, 1322.

Allard, Michel. *Le problème des attributs divins dans la doctrine d'al-Ašʿarī et de ses premiers grands disciples*. Beirut, 1965.

al-Anṣārī Harawī, ʿAbdallāh. *Ṭabaqāt al-ṣūfīya*. Edited by ʿAbd al-Ḥayy Ḥabībī. Kabul, 1341/1962.

Āqḥiṣārī, Kāfī Ḥasan Efendī. *Rawḍat al-jannāt fī uṣūl al-iʿtiqādāt*. MS Berlin 1841, fols. 91b–107b.

ʿAqīda I = First edition of the *ʿAqīdat al-uṣūl* by Abū l-Layth al-Samarqandī; see Juynboll.

ʿAqīda II = Second edition of the *ʿAqīdat al-uṣūl* by Abū l-Layth al-Samarqandī; see Juynboll.

Aristotle. *Opera*. Edited by Immanuel Bekker. 2 vols. Berlin, 1831.

al-Ashʿarī, Abū l-Ḥasan ʿAlī b. Ismāʿīl. *Al-Ibāna ʿan uṣūl al-diyāna*. Edited by F.H. Maḥmūd. Cairo, 1977. Translated by W.C. Klein as *Abū l-Ḥasan ʿAlī ibn Ismāʿīl al-Ashʿarī's al-Ibānah ʿan uṣūl al-diyānah* (*The Elucidation of Islam's Foundation*). New Haven, 1940.

———. *al-Lumaʿ*. Edited by Robert J. McCarthy as *The Theology of al-Ashʿarī*. Beirut, 1953.

———. *Maqālāt al-Islāmīyīn wa-ikhtilāf al-muṣallīn*. Edited by Hellmut Ritter. Wiesbaden, 1963.

———. *Risāla ilā ahl al-thaghr*. Edited by Muḥammad al-Sayyid al-Julaynid as *Uṣūl ahl al-sunna wa-l-jamāʿa al-musammā bi-risālat ahl al-thaghr*. Cairo, 1987.

Badawī, ʿAbd al-Raḥmān, ed. *Aflūṭīn ʿinda al-ʿArab*. Cairo, 1966.

Badeen, Edward. *Sunnitische Theologie in osmanischer Zeit*. Würzburg, 2008.

al-Baghdādī, Abū Manṣūr ʿAbd al-Qāhir b. Ṭāhir. *K. al-Farq bayna al-firaq*. Edited by Muḥammad Badr. Cairo, 1328/1910.

al-Baghdādī, Ismāʿīl Bāshā. *Hadīyat al-ʿārifīn, asmāʾ al-muʾallifīn wa-āthār al-muṣannifīn*. Edited by Kilisli Rifat Bilge and Ibnülemin Mahmut Kemal Inal. 2 vols. Istanbul, 1951–55.

al-Balkhī, Abū Zayd. *K. Maṣāliḥ al-abdān wa-l-anfus*. Edited by Fuat Sezgin. Frankfurt a.M. 1984.

Barthold, Wilhelm. *Turkestan down to the Mongol Invasion*. London, 1977.

Baumstark, Anton. *Geschichte der syrischen Literatur mit Ausschluß der christlichpalästinenischen Texte*. Bonn, 1922.

al-Bayāḍī, Kamāl al-Dīn Aḥmad b. al-Ḥasan. *Ishārāt al-marām min ʿibārāt al-imām*. Edited by Yūsūf ʿAbd al-Razzāq. Cairo, 1368/1949.

Beck, Edmund. *Ephräms Polemik gegen Mani und die Manichäer im Rahmen der zeitgenössichen griechischen Polemik and der des Augustinus*. Louvain, 1978.

Bernand, Marie. "La critique de la notion de nature (Ṭabʿ) par le Kalām." *SI* 51 (1980): 59–105.

———. "Le Kitāb al-Radd ʿalā l-bidaʿ d'Abū Muṭīʿ Makḥūl al-Nasafī." *Annales Islamologiques* 16 (1980): 39–126.

Biesterfeldt, Hans-Hinrich. "Ibn Farīghūn's Chapter on Arabic Grammar in his Compendium of the Sciences." In *Studies in the History of Arabic Grammar II*, edited by Kees Versteegh and Michael G. Carter, 49–56. Amsterdam/Philadelphia, 1990.

———. "Die Zweige des Wissens: Theorie und Klassifikation der Wissenschaften im mittelalterlichen Islam in der Darstellung des Ibn Farīghūn." Unpublished Habilitationsschrift, Bochum, 1985.

Biram, Arthur. *Die atomistische Substanzenlehre aus dem Buch der Streitfragen zwischen Basrensern und Bagdadensern*. Berlin, 1902.

al-Bīrūnī, Abū l-Rayḥān Muḥammad. *Al-Āthār al-bāqiya ʿan al-qurūn al-khāliya*. Edited by Eduard Sachau as *Chronologie orientalischer Völker*. Leipzig, 1878. Translated into English by Eduard Sachau as *The Chronology of Ancient Nations*. London, 1879.

Bivar, A.D.H. "The History of Eastern Iran." In *The Cambridge History of Iran* III (1). Edited by E. Yarshater, 181–231. Cambridge, 1983.

Bosworth, Clifford Edmund. "Al-Ḫwārazmī on Theology and Sects: The Chapter on Kalām in the Mafātīḥ al-ʿulūm." *BEO* 29 (1977): 85–95.

———. *The Islamic Dynasties*. Edinburgh, 1967.

Boyce, Mary. *Zoroastrians: Their Religious Beliefs and Practices*. London, 1979.

Browne, Edward Glanville. *A Supplementary Hand-List of the Muhammadan Manuscripts including all those written in the Arabic Character, Preserved in the Libraries of the University and Colleges of Cambridge*. Cambridge, 1922.

Brunschvig, Robert. "Devoir et Pouvoir: Histoire d'un Problème de Théologie musulmane." *SI* 20 (1964): 5–46.

———. "Muʿtazilisme et optimum." *SI* 39 (1974): 5–23.

al-Bukhārī, Abū Isḥāq al-Ṣaffār. *Talkhīṣ al-adilla li-qawāʿid al-tawḥīd*. Edited by Angelika Brodersen. Beirut, 2011.

Bulliet, Richard W. *Conversion to Islam in the Medieval Period: An Essay in Quantitative History*. Cambridge, MA/London, 1979.

Calmard, Jean: "Le chiisme imamite en Iran à l'époque seldjoukide, d'après le *Kitāb al-Naqḍ*." In *Le monde iranien et l'Islam. Sociétés et cultures* 1 (1971): 43–67.

Cerić, Mustafa. *Roots of Synthetic Theology in Islam: A Study of the Theology of Abū Manṣūr al-Māturīdī (d. 333/944)*. Kuala Lumpur, 1995.

Cheikho, Louis. "Mimar li Tadurus Abi Qurrah fi Wugud al-Haliq wa d-Din al-Qawim." *al-Machriq* 15 (1912): 757–74, 825–842.

Colpe, Carsten. "Iranische Traditionen." In *Orientalisches Mittelalter*, edited by Wolfhart Heinrichs, 68–85. Wiesbaden, 1990.

———. "Literatur im Jüdischen and Christlichen Orient." In *Orientalisches Mittelalter*, edited by Wolfhart Heinrichs, 86–122. Wiesbaden, 1990.

Cook, Michael. *Early Muslim Dogma: A Source-critical Study*. Cambridge, 1981.

Daccache, Salim. *Le problème de la création du monde et son contexte rationnel et historique dans la doctrine d'Abū Manṣūr al-Māturīdī (333/944)*. Beirut, 2008.

Daiber, Hans. *The Islamic Concept of Belief in the 4th/10th Century: Abū l-Layth al-Samarqandī's Commentary on Abū Ḥanīfah (died 150/767) al-Fiqh al-absaṭ*. Tokyo, 1995.

———. Review of *Kitāb al-Tawḥīd* by Abū Manṣūr Muḥammad al-Māturīdī, edited by Fathallah Kholeif. *Der Islam* 52 (1975): 299–313.

———. *Das theologisch-philosophische System des Muʿammar ibn ʿAbbād al-Sulamī (gest. 830 n. Chr.)*. Beirut, 1975.

Davidson, Herbert A. "John Philopenus as a Source of Medieval Islamic and Jewish Proofs of Creation." *JAOS* 89 (1969): 357–391.

———. *Proofs for Eternity, Creation and the Existence of God in Medieval Islamic and Jewish Philosophy*. New York/Oxford, 1987.

al-Dhahabī, Abū ʿAbd Allāh Muḥammad b. Aḥmad. *Al-ʿIbar fī khabar man ghabar*. Edited by Ṣalāḥ al-Dīn al-Munajjid. 5 vols. Kuwait, 1960–66.

———. *Mīzān al-iʿtidāl fī naqd al-rijāl*. Edited by ʿAlī Muḥammad al-Bajāwī. 4 vols. Cairo, 1381/1963.

———. *Al-Mushtabih fī l-rijāl: asmāʾihim wa-ansābihim*. Edited by ʿAlī Muḥammad al-Bajāwī. 2 vols. [with continuous pagination]. Cairo, 1962.

Dhanani, Alnoor. *The Physical Theory of Kalām: Atoms, Space, and Void in Basrian Muʿtazilī Cosmology*. Leiden, 1994.

Drijvers, H.J.W. *Bardaisan of Edessa*. Assen, 1966.

Emmerick, Ronald E. "Buddhism among Iranian Peoples." In *The Cambridge History of Iran* III (2), edited by E. Yarshater, 949–964. Cambridge, 1983.

Endreß, Gerhard. *Proclus Arabus: Zwanzig Abschnitte aus der Institutio theologica*. Beirut, 1973.

———. "Die wissenschaftliche Literatur." *Grundriss der arabischen Philologie* II, edited by Helmut Gätje, 400–506. Wiesbaden, 1987.

Ephraem Syrus. *Contra haereses*. Edited and translated by Edmund Beck as *Des heiligen Ephraem des Syrers Hymnen Contra Haereses*. 2 vols. Louvain, 1957. Translated by Adolf Rücker as *Des heiligen Ephräm des Syrers Hymnen gegen die Irrlehren*. Munich, 1928.

van Ess, Josef. "Ḍirār b. ʿAmr und die "Cahmīya. Biographie einer vergessenen Schule." *Der Islam* 43 (1967): 241–279 and *Der Islam* 44 (1968): 1–70.

———. *Die Erkenntnislehre des ʿAḍudaddīn al-Īcī. Übersetzung und Kommentar des ersten Buches seiner Mawāqif*. Wiesbaden, 1966.

———. "Al-Fārābī und Ibn ar-Rēwandī." *Hamdard Islamicus* 3 (1980): 3–15.

———. *Die Gedankenwelt des Ḥārit al-Muḥāsibī*. Bonn, 1961.

———. "Ibn ar-Rēwandī, or the Making of an Image." *Al-Abḥāth* 28 (1978): 5–26.

———. "Kritisches zum Fiqh akbar." *REI* 54 (1986): 327–338.

———. Review of *Kitāb al-Tawḥīd* by Abū Manṣūr Muḥammad al-Māturīdī, edited by F. Kholeif. *Oriens* 27–28 (1981): 556–565.
———. "Kullu muǧtahid muṣīb." In *Dirāsāt islāmīya*, edited by F. Jadʿan, 123–141. Irbid, 1983.
———. *Une lecture à rebours de l'histoire du muʿtazilisme*. Paris, 1984. Originally published in *REI* 46 (1978): 163–240 and *REI* 47 (1979): 19–69.
———. "The Logical Structure of Islamic Theology." In *Logic in Classical Islamic Culture*, edited by G.E. von Grunebaum, 21–50. Wiesbaden, 1970.
———. *Theologie und Gesellschaft im 2. und 3. Jahrhundert Hidschra. Eine Geschichte des religiösen Denkens im frühen Islam*. 6 vols. Berlin/New York, 1991–96.
———. *Ungenützte Texte zur Karrāmīya. Eine Materialsammlung*. Heidelberg, 1980.
———. *Zwischen Ḥadīt und Theologie. Studien zum Entstehen prädestinatianischer Überlieferung*. Berlin/New York, 1975.
Fiqh absaṭ = *Al-Fiqh al-absaṭ*; see Abū Muṭīʿ al-Balkhī.
Flashar, Hellmut. "Aristotles." In *Grundriss der Geschichte der Philosophie. III: Ältere Akademie—Aristotles—Peripatos*, edited by H. Flashar, 175–457. Basel/Stuttgart, 1983.
Flügel, Gustav. "Die Classen der hanefitischen Rechtsgelehrten." *Abhandl. d. Königl. Sächs. Ges. d. Wiss. VIII*, 269–358. Leipzig, 1860.
Frank, Richard M. "Al-Ashʿarī's Conception of the Nature and Role of Speculative Reasoning in Theology." In *Proceedings of the VIth Congress of Arabic and Islamic Studies (Visby-Stockholm 1972)*, edited by Frithiof Rundgren, 136–164. Stockholm, 1975.
———. *Beings and Their Attributes: The Teaching of the Basrian School of the Muʿtazila in the Classical Period*. Albany, NY, 1978.
———. "The Divine Attributes According to the Teaching of Abu 'l-Hudhayl al-ʿAllaf." *Le Muséon* 82 (1969): 451–506.
———. "The Neoplatonism of Ǧahm Ibn Ṣafwān." *Le Muséon* 78 (1965): 395–424.
———. Review of *Kitāb al-Tawḥīd* by Abū Manṣūr Muḥammad al-Māturīdī, edited by F. Kholeif. *OLZ* 71 (1976): 54–56.
———. "Notes and Remarks on the *ṭabāʾiʿ* in the Teaching of al-Māturīdī." In *Mélanges d'Islamologie: Volume dédié à la mémoire de Armand Abel par ses collègues, ses élèves et ses amis*, edited by P. Salmon, 137–149. Leiden, 1974.
———. "Reason and Revealed Law: A Sample of Parallels and Divergences in kalâm and falsafa." In *Recherches d'Islamologie. Recuil d'articles offert à Georges C. Anawati et Louis Gardet par leurs collègues et amis*, 123–138. Louvain, 1977.
Frye, Richard N. *Bukhara: The Medieval Achievement*. Norman, OK, 1965.
———, ed. "The Sāmānids." In *The Cambridge History of Iran* IV, 136–161. Cambridge, 1975.
———. See Narshakhī, *Tārīkh-i Bukhārā*.

Fück, Johann. "Some hitherto Unpublished Texts on the Muʿtazilite Movement from Ibn al-Nadīm's Kitāb al-Fihrist." In *Professor Muhammad Shafiʿ Presentation Volume*, edited by S.M. Abdallah, 51–74. Lahore, 1955.
Gätje, Helmut. *Koran und Koranexegese*. Zürich/Stuttgart, 1971.
al-Ghālī, Belqāsim. *Abū Manṣūr al-Māturīdī: Ḥayātuhu wa-ārāʾuhu al-ʿaqdīya*. Tunis, 1989.
Galli, Ahmad Mohamed Ahmad. "The Place of Reason in the Theology of al-Māturīdī and al-Ashʿarī." PhD dissertation, Edinburgh, 1976
———. "Some Aspects of al-Māturīdī's Commentary on the Qurʾān." *IS* 21 (1982): 3–21.
Gardet, Louis and M.M. Anawati. *Introduction à la théologie musulmane: Essai de théologie comparée*. Paris, 1981.
Gibb, H.A.R. *The Arab Conquests in Central Asia*. New York, 1923.
Gilliot, Claude. "L'embarras d'un exégète musulman face à un palimpseste. Māturīdī et la sourate de l'Abondance (*al-Kawthar*, sourate 108), avec une note savante sur le commentaire coranique d'Ibn al-Naqīb (m. 698/1298)." In *Words, Texts and Concepts Cruising the Mediterranean Sea: Studies on the Sources, Contents and Influences of Islamic Civilization and Arabic Philosophy and Science Dedicated to Gerhard Endress on his Sixty-fifth Birthday*, edited by R. Arnzen and J. Thielmann (Leuven: Peeters, 2004), 33–69.
———. "Muqātil, grand exegete, traditionniste et théologien maudit." *JA* 279 (1991): 39–92.
Gimaret, Daniel. "Bibliographie d'Ashʿarī: un réexamen." *JA* 273 (1985): 223–292.
———. "Bouddha et les bouddhistes dans la tradition musulmane." *JA* 257 (1969): 273–316.
———. *La doctrine d'al-Ashʿarī*. Paris, 1990.
———. "Un document majeur pour l'histoire du kalām: le Muğarrad maqālāt al-Aŝʿarī d'Ibn Fūrak." *Arabica* 32 (1985): 185–218.
———. *Les noms divins en Islam. Exégèse lexicographique et théologique*. Paris, 1988.
———. "Pour un rééquilibrage des etudes de théologie musulmane." *Arabica* 38 (1991): 11–18.
———. *Théories de l'acte humain en théologie musulmane*. Paris, 1980.
Gimaret, Daniel and Guy Monnot. *Shahrastani. Livre des religions et des sects. I Traduction avec introduction et notes*. Peeters/Unesco, 1986.
Givony, Joseph. "The Murjiʾa and the Theological School of Abū Ḥanīfa: A Historical and Ideological Study." PhD dissertation, Edinburgh, 1977. British Thesis, No. D 50955–84.
Goldziher, Ignaz. "Le dénombrement des sects mahométanes." *RHR* 26 (1892): 129–137.
———. *Die Richtungen der islamischen Koranauslegung*. Leiden, 1920.
———. *Vorlesungen über den Islam*. Edited by Frank Babinger. Heidelberg, 1925.
Götz, Manfred. "Māturīdī und sein Kitāb Taʾwīlāt al-Qurʾān." *Der Islam* 41 (1965): 27–70.

Graeser, Andreas. *Die Philosophie der Antike 2. Sophistik und Sokratik, Plato und Aristoteles*. Munich, 1993.

Graf, George. Die Arabischen Schriften des Theodor Abû Qurra. Paderborn, 1910.

Gutas, Dimitri. "Plato's Symposion in the Arabic Tradition." *Oriens* 31 (1988): 36–60.

Guttmann, Jacob. *Die Religionsphilosophie des Saadia*. Göttingen, 1882.

Guttmann, Julius. *Die Philosophie des Judentums*. Munich, 1933.

Hadot, Ilsetraut. "La vie et l'œuvre de Simplicius d'après des sources grecques et arabes." In *Simplicius—sa vie, son œuvre, sa survie*, edited by I. Hadot, 2–39. Berlin, 1987.

Hadot, Pierre and Claude Rapin. "Les texts littéraires grecs de la Trésorerie d'Aï Khanoum." *BCH* 111 (1987): 225–266.

Hage, Wolfgang. "Das Nebeneinander christlicher Konfessionen im mitteralterlichen Zentralasien." In *ZDMG* Suppl. 1, 2 (1969): 517–525.

Ḥājjī Khalīfa, Muṣṭafā b. ʿAbd Allāh. *Kashf al-ẓunūn ʿan asāmī l-kutub wa-l-funūn*. Edited by Mehmet Şerefettin Yaltkaya and Kilisli Rifat Bilge as *Keşf el-zunun. Kâtib Çelebi*. 2 vols. Istanbul, 1941–43.

al-Ḥakīm al-Samarqandī, Abū l-Qāsim Isḥāq b. Muḥammad. *K. al-Sawād al-aʿẓam*. Būlāq, 1253/1837–38 [= main version cited in book as *K. al-Sawād*].

———. Istanbul, 1304/1886–7.

———. Istanbul undated (after 1304/1886–7).

———. [Persian translation]. Edited by ʿAbd al-Ḥayy Ḥabībī. Tehran, 1348/1969.

———. [Tatar translation] Kazan, 1881.

———. [English translation] see al-ʿOmar, "The Doctrines" of the Māturīdite School.

al-Ḥalīmī, Abū ʿAbd Allāh al-Ḥusayn b. al-Ḥasan. *K. al-Minhāj fī shuʿab al-īmān*. Edited by Ḥalīmī Muḥammad Fūda. 3 vols. Beirut, 1399/1979.

Halm, Heinz. *Die Ausbreitung der šāfiʿitischen Rechtsschule von den Anfängen bis zum 8./14./Jahrhundert*. Wiesbaden, 1974.

———. *Kosmologie und Heilslehre der frühen Ismāʿīlīya. Eine Studie zur islamischen Gnosis*. Wiesbaden, 1978.

———. *Die Schia*. Darmstadt, 1988.

Haussig, Hans Wilhelm. *Die Geschichte Zentralasiens und der Seidenstraße in vorislamischer Zeit*. Darmstadt, 1983.

Heinzmann, Richard. *Philosophie des Mittelalters*. Stuttgart, 1992.

Hell, Joseph. *Von Mohammed bis Ghazâlî*. Jena, 1915.

Horten, Max. *Die philosophischen Systeme der spekulativen Theologen im Islam nach Originalquellen dargestellt*. Bonn, 1912.

Ibn Abī Ḥātim al-Rāzī, ʿAbd al-Raḥmān. *K. al-Jarḥ wa-l-taʿdīl*. 9 vols. Hyderabad, 1371–73/1952–53.

Ibn Abī l-Wafāʾ al-Qurashī, ʿAbd al-Qādir b. Muḥammad. *Al-Jawāhir al-muḍīʾa fī ṭabaqāt al-Ḥanafīya*. 2 vols. Hyderabad, 1332/1913.

Ibn al-Athīr. *Al-Lubāb fī tahdhīb al-ansāb*. 3 vols. Cairo, 1357–60

Ibn al-Dāʿī al-Rāzī, al-Sayyid al-Murtaḍā. *K. Tabṣirat al-ʿawāmm fī maʿrifat maqālat al-anām*. Edited by ʿAbbās Iqbāl. Tehran, 1313/1934.

Ibn Fūrak, Abū Bakr. *Mujarrad maqālāt al-Ashʿarī*. Edited by D. Gimaret. Beirut, 1987.

Ibn Ḥajar al-ʿAsqalānī, Aḥmad b. ʿAlī. *Lisān al-mīzān*. 7 vols. Hyderabad, 1329–31 (repr. Beirut 1390/1971).

———. *Tahdhīb al-tahdhīb*. 12 vols. Hyderabad, 1325–27 (repr. Beirut, 1968).

Ibn Ḥibbān al-Bustī, Muḥammad. *K. al-Majrūḥīn*. Edited by al-Ḥāfiẓ Begh. Hyderabad, 1390/1970.

Ibn Khaldūn. *Al-Muqaddima*. Beirut, 1967 (As vol. 1 of *Taʾrīkh al-ʿAllāma Ibn Khaldūn*. Edited by Y.A. Daghir. Beirut, 1965–67). Translated by Franz Rosenthal as *The Muqaddimah: An Introduction to History*. 3 vols. (New York, 1958).

Ibn Mattawayh, Abū Muḥammad. *K. al-Majʿmūʿ fī l-muḥīṭ bi-l-taklīf*. Edited by J.J. Houben and Daniel Gimaret. 2 vols. Beirut, 1965–81.

Ibn al-Murtaḍā, Aḥmad b. Yaḥyā. *Ṭabaqāt al-Muʿtazila: Die Klassen der Muʿtaziliten*. Edited by Susanna Diwald-Wilzer. Beirut/Wiesbaden, 1961.

Ibn al-Nadīm, Muḥammad b. Isḥāq. *Al-Fihrist*. Edited by G. Flügel, completed after his death by J. Rödiger and A. Müller. 2 vols. Leipzig, 1871–72. Translated by Bayard Dodge as *The Fihrist of al-Nadīm: A Tenth-century Survey of Muslim Culture*. 2 vols. (New York, 1970).

Ibn Qutayba, Abū Muḥammad ʿAbd Allāh b. Muslim al-Dīnawarī. *K. al-Maʿārif*. Edited by Tharwat ʿUkāsha. Cairo, 1960.

Ibn Quṭlūbughā, Abū l-ʿAdl Zayn al-Dīn Qāsim. *Tāj al-tarājim*. Baghdad, 1962.

Ibn Shayba b. al-Ḥusayn al-Sindī, Masʿūd. *Muqaddimat Kitāb al-taʿlīm*. Edited by Muḥammad ʿAbd al-Rashīd al-Nuʿmānī. Hyderabad, 1384/1965.

Ibrahim, Lutpi. "Al-Māturīdī's Arguments for the Existence of God." *Hamdard Islamicus* 3 (1980): 17–22.

al-Isbarī Qāḍīzāde, Muḥammad. *Mumayyizat madhhab al-Māturīdīya ʿan al-madhāhib al-ghayrīya*. MS Berlin 2492, fols. 68b–76a.

Īshoʿdād of Merw. *Commentaire d'Išoʿdad de Merv sur l-Ancien Testament. I: Genèse*. Edited by J.M. Vosté and C. van den Eynde. Louvain, 1950. Translated by C. van den Eynde as *Commentaire d'Išoʿdad de Merv sur l'Ancien Testament. I: Genèse* (Louvain, 1955).

Işik, Kemal. *Mâtürîdînin Kelâm Sisteminde İman, Allah ve Peygamberlik*. Ankara, 1980.

Ivry, Alfred L. *Al-Kindi's Metaphysics: A Translation of Yaʿqūb ibn Isḥāq al-Kindī's Treatise "On First Philosophy (fī l-Falsafah al-Ūlā)."* Albany, NY, 1974.

Izutsu, Toshihiko. *The Concept of Belief in Islamic Theology: A Semantic Analysis of îmân and islâm*. Tokyo, 1965.

Jacob of Edessa. *Hexaemeron*. Edited by I.-B. Chabot. Louvain, 1953. Translated into Latin by A. Vaschalde as *Iacobi Edesseni Hexaemeron seu In opus creationis libri* (Louvain, 1953).

Jettmar, Karl. *Die Religionen des Hindukusch*. Stuttgart, 1975.

John of Damascus [Johannes Damascenus]. *Die Schriften des Johannes von Damaskos II: Expositio fidei*. Edited by B. Kotter. Berlin/New York, 1973.

Juynboll, A.W.T. "Een Moslimsche Catechismus in het Arabish met eene Javaansche interlineaire vertaling in pegonschrift uitgegeven en in het Nederlandsch vertaald." In *Bijdragen tot de Taal-Land-en Volkenkunde van Nederlandsch-Indië*, ser. IV, vol. 5 (1881): 215–231 [= *ʿAqīda* I].

———. "Samarḳandī's Catechismus opnieuw besproken." In *Bijdragen tot de Taal-Land-en Volkenkunde van Nederlandsch-Indië*, ser. IV, vol. 5 (1881): 267–284 [= *ʿAqīda* II].

al-Juwaynī, ʿAbd al-Mālik b. ʿAbd Allāh. *Al-Kāfiya fī l-jadal*. Edited by Fawqiya Ḥusayn Maḥmūd. Cairo, 1399/1979.

al-Kaʿbī, Abū l-Qāsim al-Balkhī. *Maqālāt al-Islāmīyīn*. In Sayyid, *Faḍl al-iʿtizāl*, 63–118.

al-Kaḥḥāla, ʿUmar Riḍā. *Muʿjam al-muʾallifīn*. 15 vols. Damascus, 1957–61.

al-Kalābādhī, Abū Bakr Muḥammad. *Al-Taʿarruf li-madhhab ahl al-taṣawwuf*. Edited by ʿAbd al-Ḥalīm Maḥmūd and Ṭāhā ʿAbd al-Bāqī Surūr. Cairo, 1380/1960.

al-Karābīsī al-Samarqandī, Abū l-Faḍl Muḥammad b. Ṣāliḥ. *K. al-Furūq*. MS Feyzullah 921/1, fols. 1–25b.

al-Kawtharī, Muḥammad Zāhid, ed. *Al-ʿĀlim wa-l-mutaʿallim*. Cairo, 1368/1949.

Kern, Fr. "Murǵitische und antimurǵitische Tendenztraditionen in Sujūṭī's al laʾāli al-maṣnūʿa fī l aḥādīt al mauḍūʿa." *ZA* 26 (1912): 169–174.

al-Khalīfa al-Naysābūrī, Aḥmad b. Muḥammad. *Talkhīṣ-i Tārīkh-i Nīshābūr*. Edited by Bahman Karīmī. Tehran, 1340.

Kharpūtī, ʿAbd al-Ḥamīd. *K. al-Simṭ al-ʿabqarī fī sharḥ al-ʿiqd al-jawharī fī l-farq bayna kasbay al-Māturīdī wa-l-Ashʿarī*. Istanbul, 1305 AH.

al-Khaṭīb al-Baghdādī, Abū Bakr Aḥmad b. ʿAlī. *Taʾrīkh Baghdād*. 14 vols. Cairo, 1349/1931.

al-Khayyāṭ, Abū l-Ḥusayn b. ʿUthmān. *K. al-Intiṣār wa-l-radd ʿalā Ibn ar-Rāwandī al-mulḥid*. Edited and translated by Albert Nader. Beirut, 1957.

al-Khwārizmī, Abū ʿAbd Allāh Muḥammad b. ʿAlī. *Mafātīḥ al-ʿulūm*. Edited by G. van Vloten. Leiden, 1895.

al-Kindī, Abū Yūsuf Yaʿqūb b. Isḥāq. *Rasāʾil al-Kindī al-falsafīya*. Edited by Muḥammad ʿAbd al-Hādī Abū Riḍā. 2 vols. Cairo, 1369–72/1950–53.

———. *Cinq Epîtres*. Edited by Daniel Gimaret. Paris, 1976 [Five texts in commentated French translation].

———. *Fī l-Falsafa al-ūlā*; see Ivry, *Al-Kindī's Metaphysics*.

Kitāb al-ʿĀlim = *Kitāb al-ʿālim wa-l-mutaʿallim*; see Abū Muqātil al-Samarqandī.

Klimkeit, Hans-Joachim. "Buddhistische Übernahmen im iranischen und türkischen Manichäismus." In *Synkretismus in den Religionen Zentralasiens*, edited by W. Heissig and H.J. Klimkeit, 58–75. Wiesbaden, 1987.

———. *Hymnen und Gebete der Religion des Lichts. Iranische und türkische liturgische Texte der Manichäer Zentralasiens*. Opladen, 1989.

———. "Der Manichäismus in Iran und Zentralasien." In *Japanische Studien zum östlichen Manichäismus*, edited by H.J. Klimkeit and H. Schmidt-Glintzer, 3–15. Wiesbaden, 1991.

Kraus, Paul. "Beiträge zur islamischen Ketzergeschichte. Das "Kitāb az-Zumurrud" des Ibn ar-Rāwandī." *RSO* 14 (1933–34): 93–129 and 335–379 (reprint in P. Kraus, *Alchemie, Ketzerei, Apokryphen im frühen Islam. Gesammelte Aufsätze*, edited by R. Brague, 109–190, Hildesheim, 1994).

al-Laknawī, Muḥammad ʿAbd al-Ḥayy. *Al-Fawāʾid al-bahīya fī tarājim al-Ḥanafīya*. Cairo, 1324/1906 (together with *al-Taʿlīqāt al-sanīya*).

Laoust, Henri. "La classification des sectes dans le farq d'Al-Baghdâdî." *REI* 29 (1961): 19–59.

Lieu, Samuel N.C. *Manichaeism in the Later Roman Empire and Medieval China: A Historical Survey*. Manchester, 1985.

Luna, Concetta. Review of *Simplikios und das Ende der neuplatonischen Schule in Athen*, by R. Thiel. *Mnemosyne* 54 (Aug. 2001): 482–504.

Madelung, Wilferd. "Abū ʿĪsā al-Warrāq über die Bardesaniten, Marcioniten und Kantäer." In *Studien zur Geschichte und Kultur des Vorderen Orients. Festschrift für Bertold Spuler zum siebzigsten Geburtstag*, edited by Hans R. Roemer and Albrecht Noth, 210–224. Leiden, 1981 (reprint in Madelung, *Religious Schools*, XX).

———. "Bemerkungen zur imamitischen Firaq-Literatur." *Der Islam* 43 (1967): 37–52 (reprint in Madelung, *Religious Schools*, XV).

———. "The Early Murji'a in Khurāsān and Transoxania and the Spread of Ḥanafism." *Der Islam* 59 (1982): 32–39 (reprint in Madelung, *Religious Schools*, III).

———. "Early Sunnī Doctrine Concerning Faith as Reflected in the Kitāb al-īmān of Abū ʿUbayd al-Qāsim b. Sallām (d. 224/839)." *SI* 32 (1970): 233–254 (reprint in Madelung, *Religious Schools*, I).

———. *Der Imam al-Qāsim ibn Ibrāhīm und die Glaubenslehre der Zaiditen*. Berlin, 1965.

———. "Imāmism and Muʿtazilite Theology." In *Le Shîʿisme imâmite*, edited by T. Fahd, 13–29. Paris, 1979 (reprint in Madelung, *Religious Schools*, VII).

———. "Der Kalām." In *Grundriss der arabischen Philologie II*, edited by Helmut Gätje, 326–337. Wiesbaden, 1987.

———. Review of *Kitāb al-Tawḥīd* by Abū Manṣūr Muḥammad al-Māturīdī, edited by F. Kholeif. *ZDMG* 124 (1974): 149–151.

———. "The Origins of the Controversy Concerning the Creation of the Koran." In *Orientalia Hispanica sive studia F.M. Pareja octogenario dedicata*, edited by J.M. Barral, 504–525. Leiden, 1974 (reprint in Madelung, *Religious Schools*, V).

———. "Ar-Rāġib al-Iṣfahānī und die Ethik al-Ġazālīs." In *Islamwissenschaftliche Abhandlunden Fritz Meier zum sechzigsten Geburtstag*, edited by Richard Gramlich, 152–163. Wiesbaden, 1974 (reprint in Madelung, *Religious Schools*, IV).

———. *Religious Schools and Sects in Medieval Islam*. London, 1985.

———. *Religious Trends in Early Islamic Iran*. Albany, NY, 1988.

———. "The Shiite and Khārijite Contribution to Pre-Ashʿarite Kalām." In *Islamic Philosophical Theology*, edited by Parviz Morewedge, 120–139. Albany, NY, 1979 (reprint in Madelung, *Religious Schools*, VIII).

———. "The Spread of Māturīdism and the Turks." In *Actas do IV Congresso de Estudos Árabes e Islâmicos, Coimbra-Lisboa 1968*. Leiden, 1971. 109–168 (reprint in Madelung, *Religious Schools*, II).

———. "Sonstige religiöse Literatur." In *Grundriss der arabischen Philologie II*, edited by Helmut Gätje, 379–383. Wiesbaden, 1987.

Maḥmūd b. ʿUthmān. *Firdaws al-murshidīya fī asrār al-ṣamardīya*. Edited by Fritz Meier as *Die Vita des Scheich Abū Isḥāq al-Kāzarūnī*. Leipzig, 1948.

Makḥūl al-Nasafī, Abū Mutīʿ. *K. al-Radd ʿalā ahl al-bidaʿ wa-l-ahwāʾ*; see Bernand, "Le Kitāb al-Radd."

Malaṭī, Muḥammad b. Aḥmad. *Al-Tanbīh wa-l-radd ʿalā ahl al-ahwāʾ wa-l-bidaʿ*. Edited by Muḥammad Zāhid al-Kawtharī. Baghdad, 1388/1968.

Mardānfarrūkh-i Ohrmazdād. *Škand-gumānīg wizār*. Edited and translated by P.J. de Menasce. Fribourg en Suisse, 1945.

Massignon, Louis. *Essai sur les origins du lexique technique de la mystique musulmane*. Paris, 1954.

al-Masʿūdī, Abū l-Ḥasan ʿAlī b. al-Ḥusayn. *K. al-Tanbīh wa-l-ishrāf*. Edited by M.J. de Goeje. Leiden, 1894.

al-Māturīdī, Abū Manṣūr Muḥammad b. Muḥammad. *K. al-Tawḥīd*. Edited by Fatholla Kholeif. Beirut, 1970.

———. *Kitâbü't-Tevhîd*. Edited by Bekir Topaloğlu and Muhammed Aruçi. Ankara, 2003.

———. *Taʾwīlāt ahl al-sunna*. Edited by I. and S. ʿAwaḍayn. Cairo, 1971.

———. *Taʾwīlāt ahl al-sunna*. Edited by M.M. Rahman. Dhaka, 1982.

———. *Taʾwīlāt al-Qurʾān*. Edited by Fāṭima Yūsuf al-Khaymī. 5 vols. Beirut, 2004.

———. *Taʾwīlāt al-Qurʾān* [= *Taʾwīlāt*]. Edited by Bekir Topaloğlu et al. 18 vols. Istanbul, 2005–11.

———. *Taʾwīlāt al-Qurʾān*. Edited by Ahmet Vanlıolu.

Ps.-Māturīdī. *Fawāʾid*. MS Fatih 5426, fols. 235b–240a. Edited by Īrāgh Afshār as *Pandnāme* in *Farhang-i Īrān Zamīn* 9 (1961): 46–67.

———. *Risāla fī l-ʿaqāʾid*. Edited by Y.Z. Yörükan. *Ankara Üniversitesi Ilahiyat Fakültesi Yayınlarından* 5 (1953): 7–22 = *Kitāb al-Uṣūl*. MS Gotha 100, fols. 1a–15b.

———. *Risāla fī mā lā yajūz al-waqf ʿalayhi*. MS Köprülü III 705, fols. 44a–44b.

———. *Sharḥ al-Fiqh al-akbar* [= *Sharḥ*]. In *al-Rasāʾil al-sabʿa*, 1–28. See Daiber, *The Islamic Concept*, 31–209.

———. *K. al-Tawḥīd*. Edited by Y.Z. Yörükan. *Ankara Üniversitesi Ilahiyat Fakültesi Yayınlarından* 5 (1953): 2–6.

McDermott, Martin J. "Abū ʿĪsā al-Warrāq on the Dahriyya." *MUSJ* 50 (1984): 385–402.

Minorsky, Vladimir, ed. and trans. *Ḥudūd al-ʿālam: The Regions of the World*. Oxford, 1937.

Monnot, Guy. "Māturīdī et le manichéisme." *MIDEO* 13 (1977): 39–66 (reprint in Monnot, *Islam et Religions*, 129–156).

———. *Penseurs musulmans et religions iraniennes. ʿAbd al-Jabbār et ses devanciers*. Paris, 1974.

———. *Islam et Religions*. Paris, 1986.

———. See Gimaret-Monnot.

Moses bar Kepha. *Hexaemeronkommentar*; see Schlimme, Lorenz.

Mudīr-Shānačī, Kāẓim, ʿAbdallāh Nūrānī, and Taqī Bīnīsh. *Fihrist-i nuskhahā-yi khaṭṭī-i du kitābkhāna-i Mashhad*. Tehran, 1351 AH.

Mullā ʿAbd al-Ḥakīm Tājir. *Qandīya dar bayān-i mazārāt-i Samarqand*. Edited by Īrāgh Afshār. Tehran, 1334/1955.

Muqaddasī, Muḥammad b. Aḥmad. *K. Aḥsan al-taqāsīm fī maʿrfat al-aqālīm*. Edited by M.J. de Goeje. Leiden, 1906.

al-Muqammiṣ, Dāwūd b. Marwān. *ʿIshrūn maqāla*. Edited and translated by Sarah Stroumsa. Leiden, 1989.

Muṭahhar b. Ṭāhir al-Maqdisī. *Al-Badʾ wa-l-tārīkh*. Edited by Clément Huart. 6 vols. Leroux, 1899–1919.

al-Murādī, Muḥammad Khalīl. *Silk al-durar fī aʿyān al-qarn al-thānī ʿashar*. 4 vols. Cairo, 1291–1301/1874–84.

al-Murtaḍā l-Zabīdī, al-Sayyid Muḥammad b. Muḥammad al-Ḥusaynī. *K. Itḥāf al-sāda al-muttaqīn bi-sharḥ asrār Iḥyāʾ ʿulūm al-dīn*. 10 vols. Cairo, 1311/1893–94.

Nader, Albert. *Le système philosophique des Muʿtazila*. Beirut, 1956.

Nagel, Tilman. *Die Festung des Glaubens. Triumph und Scheitern des islamischen Rationalismus im 11. Jahrhundert*. Munich, 1988.

———. *Geschichte der islamischen Theologie*. Munich, 1994.

———. *Der Koran. Einführung. Texte. Erläuterungen*. Munich, 1983.

Narshakhī, Abū Bakr Muḥammad b. Jaʿfar. *Tārīkh-i Bukhārā*. Edited by C. Shefer as *Description topographique et historique de Boukhara par Mohammed Nerchakhy suivie de textes relatifs à la Transoxanie*. Paris, 1892. Translated by Richard N. Frye as *The History of Bukhara: Translated from a Persian Abridgement of the Arabic Original by Narshakhi* (Cambridge, 1954).

al-Nasafī, Abū l-Muʿīn Maymūn b. Muḥammad. *K. Baḥr al-kalām*. Cairo, 1329/1911. Translated by Arthur Jeffery in *A Reader on Islam: Passages from Standard Arabic Writings Illustrative of the Beliefs and Practices of Muslims*, 375–456 (S-Gravenhage, 1962).

———. *Tabṣirat al-adilla*. Edited by Claude Salamé. 2 vols. Damascus, 1990–93.

———. *K. al-Tamhīd li-qawāʿid al-tawḥīd*. Edited by Jīb Allāh Ḥasan Aḥmad. Cairo, 1986.

al-Nasafī, Abū Mutīʿ Makḥūl. *K. al-Radd ʿalā ahl al-bidaʿ wa-l-ahwāʾ*; see Bernand, "Le radd."

al-Nasafī, Najm al-Dīn Abū Ḥafṣ ʿUmar b. Muḥammad. *Al-ʿAqāʾid*. Edited by William Cureton, as *Pillar of the Creed of the Sunnites*. London, 1843. Translated into German by Joseph Schacht in *Der Islām mit Auschluss des Qorʾāns* (see Schacht, Joseph), 81–87.

Neuwirth, Angelika. "Koran." In *Grundriss der arabischen Philologie* II, edited by Helmut Gätje, 96–135. Wiesbaden, 1987.

al-ʿOmar, Farouq ʿUmar ʿAbdallāh. "The Doctrines of the Māturīdite School with Special Reference to As-Sawād al-Aʿẓam of al-Ḥakīm as-Samarqandī." PhD dissertation, Edinburgh, 1974.

El Omari, Racha Moujir. "The Theology of Abū l-Qāsim al-Balḫī/al-Kaʿbī (d. 319–931): A Study of its Sources and Reception." PhD dissertation, Yale University, 2006.

Ortiz de Urbina, Ignatius. *Patrologia Syriaca*. Rome, 1965.

al-Pazdawī, Abū l-Yusr Muḥammad. *K. Uṣūl al-dīn*. Edited by Hans Peter Linss. Cairo, 1383/1963.

Pessagno, J. Meric. "Intellect and Religious Assent: The View of Abū Manṣūr al-Māturīdī." *MW* 69 (1979): 18–27.

———. "Irāda, Ikhtiyār, Qudra, Kasb: The View of Abū Manṣūr al-Māturīdī." *JAOS* 104 (1984): 177–191.

———. "The Murjiʾa, Īmān and Abū ʿUbayd." *JAOS* 95 (1975): 382–394.

———. "The Reconstruction of the Thought of Muḥammad ibn Shabīb." *JAOS* 104 (1984): 445–453.

———. "The Uses of Evil in Maturidian Thought." *SI* 60 (1984): 59–82.

Pines, Shlomo. *Beiträge zur islamischen Atomenlehre*. Berlin, 1936.

Plotinus. *Opera*. Edited by P. Henry and H.R. Schwyzer. 3 vols. Paris/Brussels, 1951–73. [In vol. 2:] Plotiniana Arabica ad codd. fidem anglice vertit G. Lewis.

Poonawala, Ismail K. *Biobibliography of Ismāʿīlī Literature*. Malibu, CA 1977.

Pretzl, Otto. "Die frühislamische Atomenlehre. Ein Beitrag zur Frage über die Beziehungen der frühislamischen Theologie zur griechischen Philosophie." *Der Islam* 19 (1931): 116–130.

Qalʿajī, Muḥammad Rawās and ʿAbd al-Wahhāb al-Hindī l-Nadwī, eds. *Al-ʿĀlim wa-l-mutaʿallim* [ascribed to Abū Ḥanīfa]. Aleppo, 1972.

Al-Qurʾān. Cairo, 1380/1961.

Radd = *K. al-Radd ʿalā ahl al-bidaʿ wa-l-ahwāʾ* by Abū Mutīʿ Makḥūl al-Nasafī; see Bernand, "Le Kitāb al-Radd."

Radtke, Bernd. "Theologen und Mystiker in Ḫurāsān und Transoxanien." In ZDMG 136 (1986): 536–569.

Raḥman, Muḥammad Mustafizur. *An Introduction to al-Maturidi's Taʾwilat Ahl al-Sunna*. Dhaka, 1981.

Al-Rasāʾil al-sabʿa fī l-ʿaqāʾid. Hyderabad, 1980.

al-Rāzī, Abū Bakr Muḥammad b. Zakarīyāʾ. *Rasāʾil falsafīya*. Edited by P. Kraus. Cairo, 1939.

Risāla I = *Risāla ilā ʿUthmān al-Battī*; see Abū Ḥanīfa.

Ritter, Helmut. "Philologika. III. Muhammedanische Häresiographien." *Der Islam* 18 (1929): 34–55.

Rosenthal, J. *Ḥīwī al-Balkhī: A Comparative Study*. Philadelphia, 1949.

Rudolph, Ulrich. "Christliche Bibelexegese und muʿtazilitische Theologie. Der Fall des Moses bar Kepha (gest. 903 n. Chr.)." *Oriens* 34 (1994): 299–313.

———. *Die Doxographie des Pseudo-Ammonios. Ein Beitrag zur neuplatonischen Überlieferung im Islam*. Stuttgart, 1989.

———. "Das Entstehen der Māturīdīya." ZDMG 147 (1997): 393–404.

———. "Ratio und Überlieferung in der Erkenntnislehre al-Ašʿarī's und al-Māturīdī's." ZDMG 142 (1992): 72–79.

Saʿadyā Gaon. *K. al-Amānāt wa-l-iʿtiqādāt*. Edited by S. Landauer. Leiden, 1881. Translated into English by Samuel Rosenblatt as *The Book of Beliefs and Opinions* (New Haven, 1948).

Ṣābūnī, Nūr al-Dīn Aḥmad b. Maḥmūd. *K. al-Kifāya fī l-hidāya*. MS Yale Univ. Library 849, fols. 55b–259.

Sadighi, Gholam Hossein. *Les mouvements religieux iraniens au IIe et au IIIe siècle de l'hégire*. Paris, 1938.

Ṣafadī, Ṣalaḥ al-Dīn Khalīl b. Aibak. *K. al-Wāfī bi-l-wafayāt*. Edited by Hellmut Ritter and Sven Dedering. Istanbul/Damascus/Wiesbaden, 1949.

al-Samʿānī, ʿAbd al-Karīm b. Muḥammad. *K. al-Ansāb*. Edited by Abd al-Rahman ibn Yahyā Muʿallimī. 13 vols. Hyderabad, 1962–82.

Sayyid, Fuʾād, ed. *Faḍl al-iʿtizāl wa-ṭabaqāt al-Muʿtazila*. Tunis, 1974.

K. al-Sawād = *K. al-Sawād al-aʿẓam*, Būlāq edition; see al-Ḥakīm al-Samarqandī, Abū l-Qāsim Isḥāq b. Muḥammad.

Sbath, Paul. *Vingt traités philosophiques et apologétiques d'auteurs arabes chrétiens du IXème au XIVème siècle*. Cairo, 1925.

Schacht, Joseph. "An Early Murciʾite Treatise: The Kitāb al-ʿĀlim wa-l-mutaʿallim." *Oriens* 17 (1964): 96–117.

———. *Der Islām mit Ausschluss des Qorʾāns*. Tübingen, 1931.

———. "New Sources for the History of Muhammadan Theology." *SI* 1 (1953): 23–42.

———. *The Origins of Muhammadan Jurisprudence*. Oxford, 1950.

———. "Aus zwei arabischen Furūq-Büchern." *Islamica* 2 (1926): 505–537.

Schimmel, Annemarie. *Mystical Dimensions of Islam*. Chapel Hill, NC, 1975.

Schlimme, Lorenz. *Der Hexaemeronkommentar des Moses bar Kepha. Einleitung, Übersetzung und Untersuchungen*. 2 vols. Wiesbaden, 1977.

Sezgin, Fuat. *Geschichte des arabischen Schrifttums*. Leiden, 1967ff.

Shaban, Moshe A. "Khurāsān at the time of the Arab conquest." In *Iran and Islam* (*Festschrift Minorsky*), edited by C.E. Bosworth, 479–490. Edinburgh, 1971.

al-Shahrastānī, Abū l-Fatḥ Muḥammad. *Al-Milal wa-l-niḥal*. Edited by William Cureton. 2 vols. London, 1942–46.

Sharḥ = *Sharḥ al-Fiqh al-akbar*; see [Ps.-] Māturīdī.

Shaykhzāde, ʿAbd al-Raḥīm b. ʿAlī. *Naẓm al-farāʾid wa-jamʿ al-fawāʾid fī bayān al-masāʾil allatī waqaʿa fīhā l-ikhtilāf bayna al-Māturīdīya wa-l-Ashʿarīya fī l-ʿaqāʾid*. Cairo, 1317/1899.

Simon, Heinrich and Marie Simon. *Geschichte der jüdischen Philosophie*. Munich, 1984.

Spiro, Jean. "La Théologie d'Aboû Manṣoûr al-Mâtourîdy." In *Verhandlungen des XIII. Internationalen Orientalisten-Kongresses* (*Hamburg 1902*), 292–295. Leiden, 1904.

Spitta, Wilhelm. *Zur Geschichte Abū 'l-Ḥasan al-Aśʿarī*'s. Leipzig, 1876.

Spuler, Bertold. "Die nestorianische Kirche." In *Religionsgeschichte des Orients in der Zeit der Weltreligionen*, 120–169. Leiden/Köln, 1961.

Stern, Samuel Miklos. *Studies in Early Ismāʿīlism*. Jerusalem, 1983.

Stroumsa, Sarah. "From Muslim Heresy to Jewish-Muslim Polemics: Ibn al-Rāwandī's Kitāb al-Dāmigh." *JAOS* 107 (1987): 767–772.

al-Subkī, Tāj al-Dīn Abū Naṣr ʿAbd al-Wahhāb. *Ṭabaqāt al-Shāfiʿīya al-kubrā*. Edited by ʿAbd al-Fattāḥ Muḥammad al-Ḥulw and Maḥmūd Muḥammad al-Ṭanāḥī. 2 vols. Cairo, 1964–76.

al-Sulamī, Abū ʿAbd al-Raḥmān Muḥammad b. al-Ḥusayn. *K. Ṭabaqāt al-ṣūfīya*. Edited by J. Pedersen. Leiden, 1960.

al-Suyūṭī, Jalāl al-Dīn. *Al-Laʾālīʾ al-maṣnūʿa fī l-aḥādīth al-mawḍūʿa*, 2 vols. Cairo, undated.

al-Ṭabarī, Abū Jaʿfar Muḥammad b. Jarīr. *Taʾrīkh al-rusul wa-l-mulūk*. Edited by M.J. de Goeje, as *Annales*. 2 vols. Leiden, 1879–1901.

Tabṣira = *Tabṣirat al-adilla*; see al-Nasafī, Abū l-Muʿīn Maymūn b. Muḥammad.

al-Ṭaftāzānī, Saʿd al-Dīn Masʿūd b. ʿUmar. *Sharḥ al-ʿaqāʾid al-nasafīya*. Edited by Claude Salamé. Damascus, 1974. Translated into English by Edgar Elder as *A Commentary on the Creed of Islam: Saʿd al-Dīn al-Taftāzānī on the Creed of Najm al-Dīn al-Nasafī* (New York, 1950).

al-Tancî, Muḥammad b. Tavît. "Abû Mansûr al-Mâturîdî." *Ankara Ilahiyat Fakültesi Dergisi* 4 (1955): 1–12.

Tardieu, Michel. "Les calendriers en usage à Ḥarrān d'après les sources arabes et le commentaire de Simplicius à la Physique d'Aristote." In *Simplicius—sa vie, son oeuvre, sa survie*, edited by I. Hadot, 40–57. Berlin, 1987.

———. "Ṣābiens coraniques et "Ṣābiens" de Ḥarrān." *JA* 274 (1986): 1–44.

Ta'rīkh Baghdād; see al-Khaṭīb al-Baghdādī.

Tarn, W.W. *The Greeks in Bactria and India*. Cambridge, 1951.

Ta'wīl = *Ta'wīlāt al-Qur'ān*, Topaloğlu edition; see Māturīdī, Abū Manṣūr Muḥammad b. Muḥammad.

Tawḥīd = *K. al-Tawḥīd*, Kholeif edition; see Māturīdī, Abū Manṣūr Muḥammad b. Muḥammad.

Ṭāshköprüzāde, Aḥmad b. Muṣṭafā. *Miftāḥ al-saʿāda wa-miṣbāḥ al-siyāda*. 3 vols. Hyderabad, 1356.

Theodor Abū Qurra. *Mīmar fī wujūd al-khāliq wa-l-dīn al-qawūm*. Edited by I. Dick. Jūniya, 1982.

Theodor bar Koni. *Liber scholiorum* [Seert recension]. Edited by Addaï Scher. 2 vols. Louvain, 1954. Translated into French by Robert Hespel and René Draguet as *Théodore bar Koni, Livre des scolies* (*recension de Séert*). 2 vols. Louvain, 1981–82.

———. *Théodore bar Koni, Livre des scolies* (*recension d'Urmiah*). Edited and translated into French by Robert Hespel. 2 vols. Louvain, 1983.

———. *Théodore bar Koni, Livre des scolies* (*recension d'Urmiah*): *Les collections annexes par Sylvain de Qardu*. Edited and translated into French by Robert Hespel. 2 vols. Louvain, 1984.

al-Tirmidhī, al-Ḥakīm. *Drei Schriften des Theosophen von Tirmid.* Edited by B. Radtke. Beirut, 1992.

Tritton, A.S. "An Early Work from the School of al-Māturīdī." *JRAS* 3/4 (1966): 96–99.

———. *Muslim Theology*. London, 1947.

al-Ūshī, ʿAlī b. ʿUthmān. *Al-Qaṣīda al-lāmīya fī l-tawḥīd*. Istanbul, 1302/1884–85.

Uṣūl = *K. Uṣūl al-dīn*; see al-Pazdawī, Abū l-Yusr Muḥammad.

Vadet, Jean-Claude. "Le karramisme de la Haute-Asie au carrefour de trois sectes rivales." *REI* 48 (1980): 25–50.

Vajda, Georges. "Autour de la théorie de la connaissance chez Saadia." *REJ* 126 (1967): 135–189 and 275–397.

———. "Le problème de l'unité de Dieu d'après Dāwāud ibn Marwān al-Muqammiṣ." In *Jewish Medieval and Renaissance Studies*, edited by A. Altmann, 49–73. Cambridge, MA, 1967.

———. "Le témoignage d'al-Māturīdī sur la doctrine des Manichéens, des Dayṣānites et des Marcionites." *Arabica* 13 (1966): 1–38 and 113–128.

Versteegh, Kees. “Grammar and Exegesis: The Origins of Kufan Grammar and the Tafsīr Muqātil.” *Der Islam* 67 (1990): 206–242.

Wāʿiẓ-i Balkhī = Ṣafī al-Milla wa-l-Dīn Abū Bakr ʿAbd Allāh b. ʿUmar b. Muḥammad b. Dāwūd Wāʿiẓ-i Balkhī. *Faḍāʾil-i Balkh*. [Translated into Persian by ʿAbd Allāh Muḥammad Ḥusaynī Balkhī.] Edited by ʿAbd al-Ḥayy Ḥabībī. Tehran, 1350/1972.

Wakīʿ, Muḥammad b. Khalaf. *Akhbār al-quḍāh*. Edited by ʿAbd al-ʿAzīz Muṣṭafā l-Marāghī. 3 vols. Cairo, 1366–69/1947–50.

Wakin, Jeanette. *The Function of Documents in Islamic Law: The Chapters on Sales from Ṭāhāwī's Kitāb al-Shurūṭ al-Kabīr*. Albany, NY, 1972.

Walker, Paul E. *Early Philosophical Shiism: The Ismaili Neoplatonism of Abū Yaʿqūb al-Sijistānī*. Cambridge, 1993.

Wansbrough, John. *Quranic Studies: Sources and Methods of Scriptural Interpretation*. Oxford, 1977.

Watt, W. Montgomery. *The Formative Period of Islamic Thought*. Edinburgh, 1973.

———. *Der Islam II*. Stuttgart, 1985.

———. “The Problem of al-Māturīdī.” In *Mélanges d'Islamologie: Volume dédié à la mémoire de Armand Abel par ses collègues, ses élèves et ses amis*, edited by P. Salmon, 264–269. Leiden, 1974.

Watt, W. Montgomery and Alford T. Welch, *Der Islam I*. Stuttgart, 1980.

Weinberger, J. “The Authorship of Two Twelfth-century Transoxanian Biographical Dictionaries.” *Arabica* 33 (1986): 369–382.

Wensinck, Arent Jan. *Concordance et indices de la tradition musulmane*. 8 vols. Leiden, 1936–88.

———. *The Muslim Creed: Its Genesis and Historical Development*. Cambridge, 1932.

Widengren, Geo. *Mani und der Manichäismus*. Stuttgart, 1961.

Yāqūt, Yaʿqūb b. ʿAbd Allāh. *K. Muʿjam al-buldān*. Edited by F. Wüstenfeld as *Jacut's geographisches Wörterbuch*. 6 vols. Leipzig, 1866–60 (reprint, Leipzig, 1924).

Yazıcıoğlu, Mustafa Said. “Mâtürîdî Kelâm Ekolünün İki Bükük Simasi: Ebû Mansûr Mâtürîdî ve Ebu 'l-Muîn Nesefî.” *Ankara Ilahiyat Fakültesi Dergisi* 127 (1985): 281–298.

———. *Mâtürîdî ve Nesefi'ye Göre Insan Hürriyeti Kavrami*. Ankara, 1988.

Zimmermann, Friedrich W. “The Origins of the So-called Theology of Aristotle.” In *Pseudo-Aristotle in the Middle Ages: The Theology and Other Texts*, edited by J. Kraye, W.F. Ryan, and C.B. Schmitt, 110–240. London, 1986.

al-Ziriklī, Khayr al-Dīn. *Al-Aʿlām*. Beirut, 1984.

Zysow, Aron. “Two Unrecognized Karrāmī Texts.” *JAOS* 108 (1988): 577–587.

Index of People

ʿAbbād b. Sulaymān 151, 278
ʿAbd al-Jabbār b. Aḥmad al-Qāḍī 163, 176, 182, 219
ʿAbd al-Jalīl b. Abī l-Ḥusayn al-Qazwīnī al-Rāzī 77, 85
ʿAbduh, Muḥammad 305
Abraham 121
Abū Bakr (Caliph) 115, 121
Abū Bakr Muḥammad b. al-Yamān al-Samarqandī 72–75, 77, 106, 133, 146, 153
Abū Ḥafṣ al-Bukhārī 138
Abū Ḥafṣ al-Kabīr 138
Abū Ḥanīfa 4–7, 13, 19f., 23f., 27–44, 46–48, 53–57, 62–64, 72, 77, 79, 84f., 98, 105f., 127, 141, 147f., 155, 165, 187, 195f., 211f., 224, 261, 265f., 279, 288f., 302f., 305, 308–310, 313f., 317, 322
Abū Hāshim al-Jubbāʾī 1, 183, 280
Abū l-Hudhayl 62, 160, 241, 244, 273, 282, 311
Abū ʿĪsā al-Warrāq cf. Warrāq
Abū l-Layth al-Samarqandī 31, 61, 134, 137, 139, 156, 160, 188f., 195, 248, 258, 307, 310, 320, 326–328
Abū Muqātil al-Samarqandī 42–53, 105, 107, 133, 147, 153f., 225, 266, 310
Abū Muṭīʿ al-Balkhī 39, 45, 53–71, 84, 105, 107, 147, 153, 225, 279, 288f., 294, 302f., 310
Abū Naṣr Ṭāhir b. Muḥammad al-Khānaqāhī 100
Abū l-Qāsim Isḥāq b. Muḥammad al-Ḥakīm al-Samarqandī cf. Ḥakīm al-Samarqandī
Abū Salama Muḥammad b. Muḥammad al-Samarqandī 15, 38, 139f., 147, 160, 191, 194, 247f., 307, 312, 320, 328
Abū Shakūr al-Sālimī, Muḥammad b. ʿAbd al-Sayyid b. Shuʿayb 61, 248, 258f., 307, 320f., 328
Abū Ṭāhir Khāja Samarqandī 101, 130
Abū l-Ṭayyib al-Balkhī 157
Abū ʿUdhba, al-Ḥasan b. ʿAbd al-Muḥsin 9, 12
Abū Yūsuf 30, 53, 76, 147
Abū Zayd al-Balkhī cf. Balkhī
Adam 79, 114, 328
Aḥmad b. Sahl 158, 190
ʿAlāʾ al-Dīn al-Kāsānī 184
ʿAlāʾ al-Dīn Muḥammad b. Aḥmad al-Samarqandī 184f., 188, 191
ʿAlī (Caliph) 33, 35f., 65, 67, 89, 115, 120, 136
ʿAmmār al-Baṣrī 242
Āqḥiṣārī, Kāfī Ḥasan Efendi 191, 195
Aristotle 149, 169f., 176f., 207, 221, 240, 246, 254
Aṣamm, Abū Bakr ʿAbdarraḥmān b. Kaysān 149, 243
Ashʿarī, Abū l-Ḥasan ʿAlī b. Ismāʿīl 1–3, 6–9, 11–13, 18, 20, 73, 78, 82f., 125–127, 159, 162–164, 166, 182f., 189, 201, 219, 232, 236, 239f., 241, 244, 248f., 252, 254, 260, 265, 273, 277f, 297f., 301, 317–319, 321, 323
Athanasius 242
Awzāʿī 196
Ayyāshī, Muḥammad b. Masʿūd 156, 181, 188
Azdī, Abū ʿAbdallāh Muḥammad b. Aslama 129

Baghdādī, ʿAbd al-Qāhir b. Ṭāhir 3, 80, 162f., 182
Bāhilī, Abū ʿUmar Saʿīd b. Muḥammad 159f., 180, 245
Balkhī, Abū Muṭīʿ cf. Abū Muṭīʿ
Balkhī, Abū l-Qāsim al-Kaʿbī cf. Kaʿbī
Balkhī, Abū l-Ṭayyib cf. Abū l-Ṭayyib
Balkhī, Abū Zakarīyāʾ Yaḥyā b. Muṭarraf 31
Balkhī, Abū Zayd 144, 159, 174, 260, 277
Balkhī, Burhān al-Dīn ʿAlī b. al-Ḥusayn 45f.
Balkhī, Ḥīwī cf. Ḥīwī
Balkhī, Ibrāhīm cf. Ibrāhīm
Balkhī, ʿIṣām b. Yūsuf cf. ʿIṣām
Balkhī, Nuṣayr b. Yaḥyā al-Faqīh cf. Nuṣayr
Bardesanes 151, 172, 174–176, 222
Bayāḍī, Kamāl al-Dīn Aḥmad b. al-Ḥasan 7, 11, 47, 126–128, 130, 142f., 318
Bilbaysī, Majd al-Dīn Ismāʿīl b. Ibrāhīm b. Muḥammad al-Kinānī 126
Birkawī, Muḥammad b. Pīr ʿAlī 10
Bīrūnī, Abū l-Rayḥān Muḥammad 151, 172
Bishr al-Marīsī 165, 196, 281

Bishr b. al-Muʿtamir 244, 311
Bukhārī, Abū ʿIṣma 138, 147
Burghūth, Muḥammad b. ʿĪsā al-Baṣrī 149, 164f., 206, 243, 262, 274
Bustī, Abū Saʿīd Muḥammad b. Abī Bakr 31

Dāwūd b. Marwān al-Muqammiṣ 151, 163, 177, 219f.
Dhahabī, Abū ʿAbdallāh Muḥammad b. Aḥmad 43, 55
Ḍirār b. ʿAmr 165f., 170, 218, 243, 251, 253, 257, 261, 311

Ephraem Syrus 175

Fārisī, Abū l-Ḥasan ʿAlī b. Aḥmad 31, 55, 147
Fūrakī, Abū Bakr 320

Ghazālī, Abū Ḥāmid 293

Ḥājjī Khalīfa, Muṣṭafā b. ʿAbdallāh 101, 126f., 129, 133, 136, 143, 184
Ḥakīm al-Samarqandī, Abū l-Qāsim Isḥāq b. Muḥammad 19, 39, 61, 77, 88, 97–121, 126, 130f., 135, 137–139, 142, 147, 153, 261, 281, 290f., 293–295, 302f., 311
Ḥakīm al-Tirmidhī cf. Tirmidhī
Ḥalīmī, Abū ʿAbdallāh al-Ḥusayn b. al-Ḥasan 155f.
Ḥārith b. Surayj 26
Hārūn al-Rashīd 53
Ḥasan al-Baṣrī 120, 187
Hiob of Edessa 242
Hishām b. al-Ḥakam 243
Ḥīwī al-Balkhī 153
Ḥusayn al-Najjār, Abū ʿAbdallāh vgl. Najjār

Ibn ʿAbbās 120, 187
Ibn Abī l-Wafāʾ al-Qurashī, ʿAbd al-Qādir b. Muḥammad 46, 54, 81, 107, 126f., 141, 184
Ibn al-Dāʿī al-Rāzī, al-Sayyid al-Murtaḍā 7, 77, 85, 164
Ibn Farīghūn 142, 300
Ibn Fūrak, Abū Bakr 55, 183, 219, 273, 320
Ibn al-Hayṣam, Muḥammad 77, 80
Ibn Ḥazm 3
Ibn Karrām, Muḥammad 75–80, 83–87, 106, 131, 154, 157, 266, 278, 288–290, 294, 314
Ibn Khaldūn 3
Ibn al-Malāḥimī 172
Ibn Mattawayh, Abū Muḥammad 163, 219
Ibn al-Murtaḍā, Aḥmad b. Yaḥyā 163
Ibn al-Nadīm, Muḥammad b. Isḥāq 58, 152, 171–173, 226
Ibn Qāḍī al-ʿAskar, Abū l- Ḥasan ʿAlī b. Khalīl 45f.
Ibn Qutayba 32
Ibn Quṭlūbughā, Abū l-ʿAdl Zayn al-Dīn Qāsim 54, 126f.
Ibn al-Rāwandī 149f., 153, 160–162, 196, 209, 225–228, 230, 235, 315
Ibn Shabīb, Muḥammad 16, 149, 151f., 154, 162–164, 173f., 179, 207, 209, 218, 226–230, 241, 247, 257, 262, 297, 315
Ibn Sallām, Abū ʿUbayd al-Qāsim 33
Ibn Samāʿa, Abū ʿAbdallāh Muḥammad 30, 147
Ibn Shayba b. al-Ḥusayn al-Sindī, Masʿūd 77
Ibrāhīm al-Balkhī 157
Ibrāhīm b. Yūsuf al-Balkhī 76
ʿIṣām b. Yūsuf al-Balkhī 45, 147
Isbarī Qāḍizāde, Muḥammad 11
Isfarāyīnī, Abū Isḥāq 320
Īshoʿdād from Marw 174, 176
Iskāfī, Abū Jaʿfar 241, 244
Ismāʿīl b. Aḥmad (Sāmānid) 98f., 107, 191
ʿIyāḍī, Abū Aḥmad Naṣr 127, 135, 137–140, 147
ʿIyāḍī, Abū Bakr Muḥammad 135, 138, 147
ʿIyāḍī, Abū Naṣr 72, 99, 107, 128–130, 132, 134–138, 147, 157, 164, 283

Jacob 35
Jaʿfar b. Ḥarb 149, 157, 163, 208
Jaʿfar al-Ṣādiq 120
Jāḥiẓ, Abū ʿUthmān ʿAmr b. Baḥr 272
Jahm b. Ṣafwān 26, 54, 90, 149, 152–154, 175, 196, 204, 206, 277–279, 310
Jesus 68, 209f.
John Philoponus 240
Jubbāʾī, Abū ʿAlī 1, 160, 183, 229, 232, 244f.
Juwaynī, ʿAbd al-Mālik b. ʿAbdallāh 55, 58
Jūzjānī, Abū Bakr Aḥmad b. Isḥāq 45, 72, 127–129, 132–134, 147
Jūzjānī, Abū Sulaymān Mūsā 45, 72, 127, 129, 133, 147
Jūzjānī, ʿAṭāʾ b. ʿAlī 62

Kaʿbī, Abū l-Qāsim al-Balkhī 1, 150f., 157–160, 163, 180–183, 188, 190, 202, 204f., 211–213, 227–230, 245, 262, 283–285, 292–295, 297, 301, 304, 306, 308, 315
Kalābādhī, Abū Bakr Muḥammad 131f., 276
Kamālpashazāde 10, 126–128
Karābīsī al-Samarqandī, Abū l-Faḍl Muḥammad b. Sāliḥ 99
Kashshī, Muḥammad 156
Khālid Ḍiyāʾ al-Dīn 10
Kharpūtī (actually Khartabirtī), ʿAbd al-Ḥamīd 10
Khaṭīb al-Baghdādī 53f., 129, 133
Khāṭirī (?), Abū Ibrāhīm Ismāʿīl b. Isḥāq 326
Khayyāṭ, Abū l- Ḥusayn b. ʿUthmān 157f., 177, 241
Khwārizmī, Abū ʿAbdallāh Muḥammad b. ʿAlī 144, 151, 160, 162, 245
Kindī, Abū Yusūf Yaʿqūb b. Isḥāq 159, 174, 240, 260, 277, 301

Laknawī, Muḥammad ʿAbd al-Ḥayy 107, 126, 128

Makḥūl al-Nasafī cf. Nasafī, Abū Muṭīʿ Makḥūl b. Faḍl
Malaṭī, Ibrāhīm b. Ismāʿīl 62
Malaṭī, Muḥammad b. Aḥmad 152
Mālik b. Anas 196
Mani 151, 167, 174–176, 222
Marcion 151, 167, 172–176
Mardānfarrukh-ī Ohrmazddād 177
Marwazī, al-Ḥusayn b. ʿAlī 190
Marwazī, Muḥammad b. Naṣr 98
Moses 35, 68, 223
Moses bar Kepha 176, 220–223
Muʿammar b. ʿAbbād al-Sulamī 160, 218, 244
Muḥammad (Prophet) 35, 50–52, 111, 114–117, 121, 201f., 209, 213, 245, 309, 328
Muḥāsibī, al-Ḥārith 131, 272f.
Mullā ʿAbd al-Ḥakīm Tājir 101, 130
Muqaddasī, Muḥammad b. Aḥmad 77, 164
Muqammiṣ, Dāwūd b. Marwān cf. Dāwūd
Muqātil b. Ḥayyān 188
Muqātil b. Sulaymān 86, 142, 149f., 154, 187f.
Muqtadir (Caliph) 171
Murtaḍā al-Zabīdī, al-Sayyid Muḥammad b. Muḥammad al-Ḥusaynī 126–128, 130, 184

Nābulūsī, ʿAbd al-Ghanī 10
Najjār, Abū ʿAbdallāh al-Ḥusayn 23, 136, 149, 154, 163–167, 187, 205f., 211f., 222, 227f., 230, 243, 251, 253, 261, 274, 282f., 294, 300, 304f., 315
Nasafī, Abū Maymūn Muḥammad 45, 145
Nasafī, Abū l-Muʿīn Maymūn b. Muḥammad 4–7, 13, 15, 31, 45–47, 72, 77, 81, 107, 125–127, 132f., 142f., 145, 182–185, 191f., 195f., 249–253, 257, 261, 289, 307, 312, 321–323, 327–329
Nasafī, Abū Muṭīʿ Makḥūl b. Faḍl 39, 80–97, 106, 136, 145, 153–157, 164, 266, 280f., 289, 302f., 311, 314
Nasafī, Muḥammad b. Aḥmad (Ismāʿīlī) 98, 151, 170, 181, 190, 227, 229
Nasafī, Muḥammad b. Makḥūl b. Faḍl 81
Nasafī, Najm al-Dīn Abū Ḥafṣ ʿUmar b. Muḥammad 10, 28, 141, 195, 252, 258, 308, 312, 323
Nasafī al-Makḥūlī, Abū l-Maʿālī Muʿtamad 81
Nasafī al-Makḥūlī, Aḥmad 81
Naṣr I b. Aḥmad (Sāmānid) 98, 129, 134
Nawʿī, Yaḥyā b. ʿAlī b. Naṣūḥ 11
Naẓẓām, Abū Isḥāq 149, 152, 157f., 160, 162f., 207, 218, 229, 240f., 243, 253, 257, 262, 281
Nūḥ b. Manṣūr (Sāmānid) 100
Nūḥ b. Naṣr (Sāmānid) 98, 100
Nūr al-Dīn (Zangid) 2
Nuṣayr b. Yaḥyā al-Faqīh al-Balkhī 30f., 55, 128, 147

Paul 271
Pazdawī, ʿAbd al-Karīm b. Mūsā 45f., 144–148
Pazdawī, Abū l-Ḥasan, Fakhr al-Islām 145, 184f.
Pazdawī, Abū l-Yusr Muḥammad 4–7, 38, 45–47, 55, 58, 61, 77, 79, 125, 127, 130–132, 142, 145, 184, 191f., 194, 248, 257, 265, 307, 310f., 321, 327–329
Plotinus 175, 276
Proclus 221, 276

Qāḍī l-ʿAskar, Abū l-ʿAbbās 8
Qāḍīzāde cf. Isbarī
Qallās, Muḥammad b. Khuzayma 99

Rammāḥ, ʿUmar b. Maymūn 27
Rāzī, ʿAbdallāh b. Sahl 100

Rāzī, Muḥammad b. Muqātil 45, 128f., 133, 147
Rāzī, Muḥammad b. Zakarīyā' 159
Rustughfanī, Abū l-Ḥasan ʿAlī b. Saʿīd 140–144, 147

Saʿadyā Gaon 151, 177, 219f.
Ṣābūnī, Nūr al-Dīn 145, 195, 252, 258
Ṣaffār, Yaʿqūb b. Layth (Ṣaffārid) 98
Sāmān-Khudā 98
Samʿānī, ʿAbd al-Karīm b. Muḥammad 99, 107, 130
Samarqandī, Abū Bakr Muḥammad b. al-Yamān cf. Abū Bakr
Samarqandī, Abū l-Faḍl Muḥammad b. Sāliḥ al-Karābīsī cf. Karābīsī
Samarqandī, Abū l-Layth cf. Abū l-Layth
Samarqandī, Abū Muqātil cf. Abū Muqātil
Samarqandī, Abū l-Qāsim Isḥāq b. Muḥammad al-Ḥakīm cf. Ḥakīm
Samarqandī, Abū Salama cf. Abū Salama
Samarqandī, Abū Ṣāliḥ Muḥammad b. al-Ḥusayn 31
Samarqandī, Abū Ṭāhir Khāja cf. Abū Ṭāhir
Samarqandī, ʿAlā' al-Dīn cf. ʿAlā' al-Dīn
Sanūsī, Muḥammad b. Yūsuf 195
Shāfiʿī, Muḥammad 135, 155, 196
Shahrastānī, Abū l-Fatḥ Muḥammad 3, 80, 162f., 166, 182, 289
Shaʿrāwī, Muḥammad 305
Shaybānī, Muḥammad b. al-Ḥasan 5, 31, 147
Shaykhzāde, ʿAbd al-Raḥīm b. ʿAlī 10
Shirāzī, Nūr al-Dīn Muḥammad b. Abī l-Ṭayyib 9
Sighnāqī, Ḥuṣām al-Dīn 31
Siyālkūtī, ʿAbd al-Ḥakīm 10
Subkī, Tāj al-Dīn Abū Naṣr ʿAbd al-Wahhāb 7–9, 12, 318
Suyūṭī, Jalāl al-Dīn 44, 195

Ṭabarī, Abū Gaʿfar Muḥammad b. Jarīr 25f., 187f., 273
Taftāzānī, Saʿd al-Dīn Masʿūd b. ʿUmar 252, 308
Ṭahāwī, Aḥmad b. Muḥammad 8, 195
Tāshköprüzāde 126f.
Tawḥīdī, Abū Ḥaiyān 163
Theodor Abū Qurra 177
Theodor bar Kōnī 176
Tirmidhī, al-Ḥakīm 175, 276

ʿUmar (Caliph) 115, 121
ʿUmar b. ʿAbd al-ʿAzīz (Caliph) 67
Ūshī, ʿAlī b. ʿUthmān 258
ʿUthmān (Caliph) 33, 35f., 65, 115, 136
ʿUthmān al-Battī 28–34, 36f., 40, 47, 55, 63, 73, 157, 217, 265, 279, 302f., 308, 311, 317

Wāʿiẓ-i Balkhī, Ṣafī al-Milla wa-l-Dīn Abū Bakr ʿAbdallāh 27
Warrāq, Abū Bakr 100
Warrāq, Abū ʿĪsā 149, 161, 172f., 209, 225

Zabīdī, al-Sayyid al-Murtaḍā cf. Murtaḍā
Zamakhsharī, Abū l-Qāsim 187
Zoroaster 167

Index of Religious and Political Movements

ahl al-ʿadl (wa-l-sunna) 24, 33f., 36, 50, 61, 118
ahl al-ijbār 38–40, 303
ahl al-sunna wa-l-jamāʿa 61, 70, 79, 329
ahl al-tafwīḍ 38–40, 303
Anthropomorphists cf. "Mujassima" and "Mushabbiha"
Aristotelians 171
aṣḥāb Abī Ḥanīfa 5–7, 323
aṣḥāb al-hayūlā 149, 169, 177, 222
aṣḥāb al-nujūm 169
aṣḥāb al-ṭabāʾiʿ 149, 169, 176, 206, 254f., 274
Ashʿarites 6, 8f., 55, 83, 126f., 245, 257, 265, 268, 278, 285, 297, 319–321, 323, 327f.
Ayyūbids 3

Bardesanites (or Daiṣānīya) 149, 163, 167, 173, 176f., 208, 226
"Bāṭinīya" 170; cf. also Ismāʿīlīs
Buddhists 152

Christians 50f., 120, 149, 153f., 170, 175f., 181, 206, 209, 220, 240, 274

"Dahrīya" 108, 149, 151, 163, 166–171, 174–180, 204–207, 216, 220f., 226, 233, 236, 255, 267, 274, 285
Dayṣānīya cf. Bardesanites
Dualists 149, 166f., 169–171, 175–180, 206–208, 210, 216, 220, 226, 255, 260, 269f., 272, 274, 297f., 304

Ḥanafites passim; cf. also aṣḥāb Abī Ḥanīfa
Ḥanbalites 265, 318
Ḥarrānians 175
"Ḥarūrīya" 87, 89, 91
"Ḥashwīya" 136, 150, 154f., 214, 309f.
al-ḥukamāʾ (the philosophers) 149, 223, 301

Ibāḍites 166
Imāmites 87, 156, 181; cf. also "Rawāfiḍ(a)"
Ismāʿīlīs 98, 149, 170, 174f., 178, 181, 190, 204–206, 227, 260, 277, 285

"Jabrīya" 38–40, 83, 85, 87, 89f., 94f., 106, 108, 112, 118, 121, 150, 154, 164f., 210, 212, 214, 302, 304, 306; cf. also ahl al-ijbār
Jacobites 220
Jahmites 54, 69, 86f., 89f., 95f., 108, 114f., 119, 153f., 156, 166, 279f.
al-jamāʿa 83, 87–89
Jews 50f., 120, 149, 153f., 177, 206, 209, 219, 240, 274

Karrāmites 74f., 77f., 80, 83–88, 97, 108, 116, 119, 133, 149, 153, 214, 261, 274, 278, 280, 290, 302f., 305f., 309–311
Khārijites 32f., 35, 47, 49, 51f., 67, 87, 108, 118, 121, 149, 153, 212–214, 224, 308–310; cf. also "Ḥarūrīya" and Ibāḍites

"Māhānīya" 173
Mālikites 8
Mamlūks 3, 7, 9, 12
Mandaeans 151
Manichaeans 149, 151, 161, 167, 171f., 176–178, 208, 226, 245, 260, 273
Marcionites 149, 167, 172f., 176f., 208, 226
Materialists cf. aṣḥāb al-hayūlā and "Dahrīya"
Māturīdites 5, 7f., 10, 12f., 17, 20, 31, 44, 46, 55, 61, 72, 78, 81, 84, 86, 102, 137, 141, 145, 185, 194, 252, 257, 285, 299, 308, 319–323, 326f.
"Mujassima" 77
Murjiʾites 23–27, 32–34, 36, 49, 54, 78, 87, 89, 91, 96f., 104, 106, 108, 119, 121, 135f., 142f., 150, 154f., 162, 165, 210, 213f., 308
"Mushabbiha" 84, 86f., 150, 154, 206, 274, 289, 293
"Mutaqashshifa" 77
Muʿtazilites 5, 32f., 35, 62, 78, 83, 108, 113f., 121, 136, 138, 149f., 154, 156–166, 172, 177, 179–181, 186–190, 204–206, 208, 210–214, 218–221, 227–229, 240f., 245, 247f., 250, 257f., 260, 262, 265, 267f., 274, 277f., 282–285, 291–293, 296–299, 304f., 308–311, 315, 317f., 320f., 323

Najjārites 164, 274
Naturalists (or Natural philosophers) cf. asḥāb at-ṭabāʾiʿ und "Ṭabāʾiʿīya"
Nestorians 153, 175

"Qadarīya" 39, 66, 69, 83, 85, 87, 89f., 93, 106, 108, 112–114, 118, 150, 154, 210–212, 224f., 302–304, 306; cf. also ahl al-tafwīḍ
Qarmatians 170; cf. also Ismāʿīlīs

"Rawāfiḍ(a)" 87, 89, 93, 108, 156

Sabians 149–151, 176, 208
Ṣaffārids 98
Sāmānids 98f., 125, 129, 134, 144, 170, 191f., 311
Seljuks 2
Shāfiʿites 2, 7f., 98f., 135, 155f.
Shīʿites 38, 49, 141, 156, 170, 188; cf. also Imāmites und Ismāʿīlīs
Skeptics 177, 207, 226
Sophists 149–151, 156, 163, 176–178, 207, 222
Stoics 271
"Sumanīya" 149–152, 156, 163, 207
Sunnites passim

"Ṭabāʾiʿīya" 258
Ṭāhirids 98
Traditionists 106, 119, 135, 156, 269, 297, 316, 318; cf. also "Ḥashwīya"

Zangids 2
Zoroastrians 108, 120, 149, 167, 171, 176–178, 208, 211f., 226

Index of Arabic Terms

[ʾ j l] *ajal* lifespan 116, 143
[ʾ kh dh] *akhadha biʾl-nawāṣī* to take by the forelocks 41
[ʾ z l] *azal* preeternity 286; *azalī* preeternal (divine attributes) 280f.
[ʾ ṣ l] *aṣl* pl. *uṣūl* foundation, principle 5, 133, 181f., 259, 263, 267f.; material basis 168; principle (of Muʿtazilism) 218–220; *uṣūl al-dīn* principles of religion 251
[ʾ l h] *ilāh* God 282; *ulūhīya* divinity 192
[ʾ l f] *al-muʾallaf / al-muʾtalif* unified (the body, from two parts) 244; *taʾlīf* unification 248
[ʾ m m] *imām al-aʾimma* the guide of guides (Abū Ḥanīfa) 7; *imām ahl al-arḍ* the imam of the world's inhabitants (Kaʿbī according to the Muʿtazilites) 158
[ʾ m r] *amr* command (of God) 69, 93, 112; *amīr* commander (of the faithful) 92, 97, 113; *al-amr biʾl-maʿrūf waʾl-nahy ʿan al-munkar* commanding the correct and forbidding the reprehensible 53f., 65, 67, 92, 97
[ʾ m n] īmān faith/belief 33, 35, 49, 65f., 89, 196, 214, 291; *muʾmin ḥaqqan* truly a believer (without qualifications) 67; *muʾmin ḍāll* a believer who has gone astray 32, 34
[ʾ w l] *āla* (the intellect as) instrument (God-given for the sake of knowledge) 299; *ālāt* organs (of the body) 258; *awwalīya* beginninglessness 192
[ʾ y] *āyāt* signs (of God in the creation) 92, 266; signs (of prophethood) 209
[ʾ y n] "Where?" (as a question of God's location) 68, 71, 206, 288–291, 294–296
[b d ʾ] *ibtidāʾ* (the One as) principle (of numbers) 269
[b d ʿ] *bidʿa* innovation, heresy 33f., 111; *tabdīʿ* to hereticize 9, 11; *mubtadiʿ* innovator, heretic 291; *dalāla badīʿa* amazing sign (in the creation) 263
[b r ʾ] *barāʾa* disassociation (from disbelievers) 52
[b r d] *burūda* cold (as an elemental quality) 255
[b s ṭ] *al-arkān al-basīṭa* the simple elements 246, 253
[b ṣ r] *baṣar* seeing (as an attribute of God) 285
[b ṭ n] *bāṭin* hidden, inner meaning; opposite of ẓāhir 121
[b ʿ d] *abʿād thalātha* three dimensions 246; *tabāʿud* dispersal 234, 254
[b ʿ ḍ] *abʿāḍ* parts (from which a body is composed) 243, 253
[b q y] *baqāʾ* persistence (in belief) 120; perpetuity (without end) 235, 262
[b h m] *ibhām fiʾl-maʿnā* vagueness of meaning 185
[b y n] *bayān* clarification/ exposition 276
[t b ʿ] *tabaʿ* (action as a) consequence (of knowledge) 48
[th b t] *thabata li-* to apply to 249; *thawābit* the fixed stars 275; *ithbāt* proof of existence 94
[th n y] *istithnāʾ* qualification (of faith, by adding the expression "if God wills") 70, 96, 105, 111f., 155, 214, 310
[j b r] *jabr* compulsion 38, 259; *jabbār* omnipotent (God) 259; *majbūr* compelled 258
[j ḥ d] *juḥūd* denial (of the existence of God) 50
[j r ḥ] *jāriḥa* pl. *jawāriḥ* body parts 71, 258
[j z ʾ] *juzʾ* part 275; *al-juzʾ alladhī lā yatajazzaʾ* atom 244f., 248; *ajzāʾ wa-abʿāḍ* parts (of which bodies are composed) 234, 253
[j z y] *jizya* headtax 24–26
[j s m] *jism* pl. *ajsām* bodies 203, 206, 234, 244, 246, 248f., 252, 270, 278; *jismīya* corporeality 192
[j l l] *jalāl* might (of God) 275
[j m ʿ] *jamāʿa* community 67f., 83, 87–89, 111; *ijtamaʿa* unification (of opposites in bodily substances) 259; *mujtamiʿ* unified 242, 244
[j h d] *ijtihād* independent reasoning (in law) 141
[j h l] *jahl* ignorance (denied of God) 270; *jāhil* ignorant (and sinful person, who is nevertheless a believer) 35

[j w d] *jūd* generosity (of God) 285
[j w z] *bi'l-majāz* metaphorically 114, 117, 282
[j w h r] *jawhar* pl. *jawāhir* entity, substance (corresponding to the Greek *ousia*) 242, 245, 253f., 315; atom 244, 248f., 252; body, corporeal entity (corresponding to *ʿayn*) 245f., 258f., 299
[ḥ b b] *ḥubb* love (of God) 93
[ḥ j j] *ḥujja* argument, justification (for humans with God) 40, 118; *ḥujaj* proofs (for the existence of God) 92, 266; *maḥajja* (correct) path, conduct 40
[ḥ d d] *ḥadd* pl. *ḥudūd* limit 290, 293; *ḥudūd* commands (of God) 65; *maḥdūd* limited (body) 246
[ḥ d th] *ḥadatha* originate temporally 234, 256, 280; *ḥadath* temporal origination 235, 263; *ḥadathīya* temporality 192; *muḥdith* Creator 263; *muḥdath* created in time 249, 252, 258
[ḥ r r] *ḥarāra* heat (as an elemental quality) 255
[ḥ r ṣ] *ḥaraṣa ʿalā* to be keen on (sin) 41
[ḥ r k] *ḥaraka* movement (opposite of stillness) 234, 237
[ḥ s s] *ʿilm al-ḥiss* knowledge by the senses 236f.; *maḥsūs* perceivable by the senses 237, 254
[ḥ s b] *ḥisāb* reckoning (after death) 114f.; *al-ḥussāb* mathematicians 250
[ḥ s n] *iḥsān* proper (human) behavior 65
[ḥ q q] *ḥaqq* rights (of God towards man and vice versa) 71; property/characteristic 234, 254; true/correct 291f.; *ḥaqīqa* pl. *ḥaqāʾiq* essence (of a thing) 250f.; *bi'l-ḥaqīqa* in an actual sense 114, 117, 282; *ḥaqīqīya* essentiality 192
[ḥ k m] *ḥukm* decree (of God) 41; *aḥkām* legal rulings 63, 65; *ḥikma* wisdom (of God) 263, 270, 296–300; *ḥikam* wisdom sayings 100; *ḥakīm* wise (God) 296; *al-ḥukamāʾ* the philosophers 149, 223, 301; *ḥākim* judge (referring to the intellect in regard to good and evil) 299; *muḥkam* unambiguous (material from transmission) 210
[ḥ l l] *ḥalla* to inhere in 258; *maḥall* substrate 244, 247, 259
[ḥ w j] *ḥāja* necessity 250; *ḥāja* pl. *ḥawāʾij* need/dependency (of the creation) 234f. (cf. *muḥtāj* 290)
[ḥ w l] *ḥāl* state (unchanging in regard to God) 266, 281; *aḥwāl al-rubūbīya* states (referring to God's unique characteristics) 271
[ḥ y z] *mutaḥayyiz* that which occupies space 244; *taḥayyuz* spatiality 261
[ḥ y y] *ḥayāt* life 116; *al-ḥayy al-nāṭiq al-mayyit* the rational mortal lifeform (definition of a human being) 254, 300; *al-ḥayyāt* living (beings) 299; *al-ḥayawānāt* lifeforms 259
[kh b r] *akhbara* inform (from God to humanity) 239; *akhbār* transmission (religious and profane) 232
[kh dh l] *khadhala* (and *khidhlān*) forsaking (by God of humans, when they will evil) 38, 41, 112, 118, 303
[kh r ʿ] *ikhtaraʿa* to create 242
[kh ṣ ṣ] *takhṣīṣ* particularization (by God) 93
[kh l f] *khilāf* difference (opposite of *mithl*) 267; *khilāfāt* differences (between theological schools) 8; *ṭabāʾiʿ mukhtalifa wa-mutaḍādda* differing and opposing natures 234 (cf. 254)
[kh l q] *khalq* the act of creation 211, 280, 283, 302, 305; *khāliqīya* and *khāliqūqīya* capacity to create 280; *khāliq* Creator 234, 280f., 312; *khāliq azalī* Eternal Creator 91, 280; *makhlūq* created 283; *khuluq* (unique) character trait (of the Prophet Muḥammad) 116; *makārim al-akhlāq* noble characteristics of the prophets and angels 49; *khilqa* natural disposition, created nature 246; *takhlīq* creating 90, 93
[kh l w] *takhlīya* to allow to happen (by God) 41
[kh y r] *ikhtiyār* free choice (by God) 93, 202, 204, 284f.; free choice (by humans) 111, 211, 305f.
[d b r] *tadbīr* direction and providence (by God of the creation) 270, 272f., 298
[d kh l] *mudākhala* and *tadākhul* mutual penetration (of bodies, according to the theory of al-Naẓẓām) 243

[d r k] *idrāk* comprehend (in contrast to seeing) 205, 293
[d ʿ w] *daʿwa* the (Ismāʿīlī) mission 190
[d l l] *dalāla* and *dalāʾil* sign (of God in the creation) 263f.; *dalālat al-shāhid ʿalā al-ghāʾib* the inferrability of the unseen from the seen 266; *dalālat al-ʿaql* the indication of the intellect 269; *dalālat al-istidlāl biʾl-khalq* indication of what may be known by inference through creation (via impressions of the senses) 269; *ʿilm al-istidlāl* knowledge through rational inference 237
[d h r] *dahr* beginningless time 167
[d y n] *dīn* religion (in the sense of faith, in contrast to religious duties and laws) 35, 49, 63; religion (in the sense of personal relationship to God, in contrast to meticulous theological speculation) 250, 253, 316
[dh w] *dhāt* essence (of an existing thing) 94; essence (of God) 275; *bi-dhātihi* essentially, on account of one's self (referring to God's being powerful and knowledgeable) 117, 282, 286
[r ʾ y] *biʾl-raʾy* by personal opinion 121; *ruʾya(t Allāh)* the vision (of God in the hereafter), the visio beatifica 116, 205, 287, 290–293; *murāʾāt* ostentation 51
[r b b] *rubūbīya* lordship 270f.
[r j ʾ] *irjāʾ* pushing back (of judgment) 51; (equation with *wuqūf*) 155, 165, 214, 224
[r kh ṣ] *rukhṣa* concession (from God) 119
[r z q] *rizq* provision 116, 119, 143
[r sh d] *irshād* guidance 131, 322
[r ḍ y] *raḍiya* pleased (describing God) 69; *riḍā* approbation (by God) 69–71, 93, 112, 115, 279, 281
[r f ʿ] *rifʿa* high rank (of God, symbolized by oneness) 269
[r k b] *tarkīb* composition (of bodies) 248; *murakkab* composed 253
[r k ʿ] *rakʿa* and *rukūʿ* bending at the torso (in prayer) 82, 120
[r k n] *rakina* to base one's self (on a teaching) 251; *al-arkān al-basīṭa* the simple elements (i.e., accidents or qualities as opposed to bodies) 246, 253
[r w d] *irāda* will (of God) 41, 204, 212, 285
[r w y] *riwāya* chain of transmission 30f., 44–46, 55, 145
[z h d] *zāhid* ascetic 131
[s b b] *sabab* pl. *asbāb* corporeal means; *istiṭāʿat al-asbāb waʾl-aḥwāl* capacity over (corporeal) means and conditions (as first capacity to act/ *istiṭāʿa* according to al-Māturīdī) 306
[s kh ṭ] *sukhṭ* wrath (of God) 71
[s d d] *tasdīd* guidance 131, 322
[s r r] *sarīr* bed, throne (of God, according to Karrāmite interpretation of the word *ʿarsh*) 294
[s f l] *asfal* low (in contrast to *aʿlā*) 288
[s k n] *sukūn* stillness (in contrast to movement) 234, 256
[s l f] *al-salaf* the pious forebears 6, 322
[s l m] *salāmat al-asbāb* soundness of (corporeal) means (as first capacity to act/ *istiṭāʿa* according to al-Māturīdī) 306; *taslīma* greeting of peace (in prayer) 120; *muslim* Muslim (made equivalent with a believer/*muʾmin*) 35
[s l ṭ n] *sulṭān* dominion (of God, symbolized by His oneness) 269, 275
[s m ʿ] *samʿ* transmission (religious and profane) 203, 232, 269; hearing (as an attribute of God) 285
[s n d] *isnād* chain of transmitters 43–46, 55, 72, 88, 129, 146
[s n n] *sunna* pl. *sunan* traditions (of the Prophet) 33f., 36, 48, 65, 88, 97, 111
[s m w] *ahl al-samāʾ* angels 35; *fīʾl-samāʾ* in heaven (referring to God above us; according to the earlier Ḥanafites and the Karrāmites) 68, 288–290
[s m y] *asmāʾ* names (of God) 204
[sh b h] *ashbāh* likenesses (not applicable to God) 275; *tashbīh* likening (God to humans) 119, 205; *mutashābih* pl. *mutashābihāt* equivocal expressions, verses (in the Qurʾān) 94, 106, 119, 210, 291, 293
[sh r ʿ] *sharīʿa* pl. *sharāʾiʿ* religious law (not an integral part of belief) 49, 89; law (learning it as the greatest insight) 65; laws (consisting of prayer, alms, fasting, pilgrimage, and purification) 65

[sh r f] *ʿaql min jihat al-sharaf* a noble intellect (unique to the Prophet Muḥammad; according to al-Ḥakīm al-Samarqandī) 116
[sh r k] disbelief (cause for punishment with no exception) 50; *fī arḍ al-shirk* outside the domain of Islam 65
[sh h d] *shahida* witness (by God) 35; *shahāda* testimony (of God, made by angels and believers) 65, 91, 96, 120; testimony (uncreated, in the Qurʾān, spoken by humans, according al-Ḥakīm al-Samarqandī) 113, 311
[sh h w] *shahawāt* desires 254
[sh y ʾ] *shāʾa* will (by God) 279; *mashīʾa* the will (of God) 41, 69, 93, 111f., 302; *shayʾ* pl. *ashyāʾ* thing, existent 71, 90, 94, 202f., 206, 275, 278, 286, 293; (created) thing 234, 244, 246, 312; *shayʾīya* existence (according to al-Māturīdī), thingness, being-a-thing (in the terminology of the Muʿtazilites) 192 (with references to *K. al-Tawḥīd*)
[ṣ ḥ ḥ] *ṣiḥḥa(t al-ālāt)* soundness (of bodily organs; as first capacity to act/*istiṭāʿa* acording to al-Māturīdī) 306
[ṣ ḥ b] *ṣāḥib* (*al-kitāb*) author (of the book) 43, 55
[ṣ d q] *taṣdīq* affirmation (of revealed truth; an integral part of faith, carried out with the heart/*qalb*) 35, 49, 89, 111, 120, 214, 309; *ahl al-taṣdīq* believers 35
[ṣ r ṭ] *ṣirāṭ* bridge (over Hell) 115
[ṣ l ḥ] *al-aṣlaḥ* the best, optimum (which God always does, according to the Muʿtazilites) 205, 267, 297–299; *iṣṭilāḥ* compromise (with another; ruled out in regard to an omnipotent God) 270
[ṣ n f] *aṣnāf al-ʿulūm* categories of knowledge 144
[ṣ w b] *al-iṣāba* hitting the mark (part of the discussion of God's wisdom) 299
[ḍ d d] *ḍidd* pl. *aḍdād* opposition (between natures and thus in corporeal entities as well) 259; (God has no) opposite 275; *al-istiṭāʿa li'l-ḍiddayn* the capacity to two contrary actions 66, 305; *taḍādda* to be mutually opposed 242; *ṭabāʾiʿ mukhtalifa wa mutaḍādda* (the world is composed of) varying and opposing natures 234; *ṭabāʾiʿ mukhtalifa wa-wujūh mutaḍādda* various natures and opposing aspects 254; *al-qābil li'l-mutaḍāddāt* that which can take on contrary qualities (part of the definition of an atom according to Abū'l-Muʿīn al-Nasafī) 249
[ḍ r r] *ḍarūra* (corporeal substances are subject to) compulsion 234; *ḍarūrī* necessary (knowledge, as opposed to acquired/*muktasab* knowledge; according to al-Jubbāʾī) 229, 232, 237; *al-ḥayyāt wa'l-jawāhir al-ḍārra* (God's wisdom in) harmful life-forms and substances 298f.
[ḍ r b] *iḍṭirāb* striking together (of bodies to create heat) 256
[ḍ ʿ f] *ḍuʿf* weakness (of creatures) 266
[ḍ l l] *muʾmin ḍāll* a believer who has gone astray 32, 34; *ḍāll* astray 35
[ḍ m r] *ḍamīr* pl. *ḍamāʾir* hearts (probing them is left to God; a position of the Karrāmīya) 91
[ḍ y f] *iḍāfa* attribution, association 305
[ṭ b ʿ] *ṭabīʿa* pl. *ṭabāʾiʿ* natures (i.e. the elementary qualities such as heat, cold, moisture, and dryness, from which the material world is composed) 16, 94, 210, 234, 238, 242, 253–260, 262, 270, 273, 300; *kāna al-ʿālam bi-aṣlihi mabnīyan ʿalā ṭabāʾiʿa mukhtalifatin wa-wujūhin mutaḍāddatin* the world is (materially) made up of various natures and opposing aspects 254; *ṭabāʾiʿ mukhtalifa wa-mutaḍādda* varying and opposing natures 234; *bi'l-ṭabʿ* according to its nature, obligatorily 254f., 257, 285; *ṭibāʿ* natural disposition 210
[ṭ r q] *ṭarīqānī* two ways (by which divine wisdom is expressed) 299
[ṭ l b] *ṭalaba* (God has no) request (of the people) 71
[ṭ n b] *iṭnāb* long-winded talk 247
[ṭ w ʿ] *istiṭāʿa* capacity (for human action) 63, 66, 84, 90, 93f., 118 (in assocation with *quwwat al-ʿamal*) 227, 303, 328; distinction between two capacities according to al-Māturīdī: 1) the capacity of means and states

(*istiṭāʿat al-asbāb wa'l-aḥwāl*), identified with soundness (*salāma*) and health (*ṣiḥḥa*) of the body and mind, and which the human must possess before the action (*qabla al-fiʿl*) 2) the actual capacity to act (*istiṭāʿat al-fiʿl*) which he only receives from God at the time of the act (*maʿa al-fiʿl*) 211, 306–308
[ṭ w q] *ṭawwaqa* (*taṭwīq*) (God's) giving (humans) the power to act (by planting in them a capacity; according to the Karrāmite conception) 93f., 303
[ṭ w l] *ṭawīl* long (a dimension of bodies) 244
[ṭ y n] *ṭīna* (preexisting) material 169, 204
[ẓ h r] *ẓāhir* apparent, outward, perceivable (meaning; opposite of *bāṭin*) 121
[ʿ b d] *ʿibāda* worship (of God) 47, 52
[ʿ b r] *ʿibra* pl. *ʿibar* (admonitory and instructive) sign/example (in the creation) 92, 266
[ʿ j z] *ʿajz* weakness, inability (of the creation) 266; (ruled out in regard to God) 270
[ʿ d l] *ʿadl* justice (of God) 113, 116, 299; (as a theological leitmotif of Abū Ḥanīfa) 33f., 36; (as the second principle of the Muʿtazila) 218
[ʿ d m] *al-maʿdūm* the non-existent (in Muʿtazilite thought) 205, 274
[ʿ r j] *miʿrāj* heavenly journey (of the Prophet) 114
[ʿ r sh] *ʿarsh* throne (of God) 204, 287f., 294
[ʿ r ḍ] *ʿaraḍ* pl. *aʿrāḍ* accident 236–238, 242–246, 248, 250, 253, 280; *ʿaraḍ muḥdath majbūr* an accident created in time which is compelled (as a definition of natures/ *ṭabāʾiʿ*) 258; (two types of) accidents (according to al-Māturīdī) 259f.; *ʿaraḍīya* the quality of being an accident 192; *ʿarīḍ* wide (a dimension of bodies) 244
[ʿ r f] *maʿrifa* knowledge (in the heart as a component of belief) 49, 89, 113, 214; *taʿrīf* bestowing knowledge (by God) 113
[ʿ ṣ y] *ʿaṣā* to disobey 35; *maʿṣīya* pl. *maʿāṣin* sins 112
[ʿ ṭ l] *taʿṭīl* negation (of God's characteristics) 119, 291
[ʿ ṭ w] *ʿaṭāʾ* (belief as a) gift (from God) 113; *ʿaṭāʾī* (type of intellect) gifted (by God to the believers alone; according to the conception of al-Ḥakīm al-Samarqandī) 116
[ʿ ẓ m] *ʿaẓama* majesty (of God; symbolized through His oneness) 269, 275
[ʿ q l] *ʿaql* intellect 203, 232, 254; (five types of) intellect (according to al-Ḥakīm al-Samarqandī) 116; *dalālat al-ʿaql* indications of the intellect 269
[ʿ l l] *al-ʿilla al-ūlā* (God as) the first cause 241
[ʿ l q] *ʿalaqa* embryo 239
[ʿ l m] *ʿalima* know, recognize 292; *ʿilm* knowledge (of God) 204, 279, 282, 285; knowledge (of humans) 48, 229; (transmitted human) knowledge 63, 135; *ʿilm al-ḥiss* knowledge by the senses 236f.; *ʿilm al-istidlāl* knowledge by inference (of the intellect) 237; *ʿālim* knowing (God) 279, 282; *ʿālam* the (material) world 254; *ʿālam ṣaghīr* microcosm (the human being) 254, 301
[ʿ l w] *ʿulūw* elevation (of God) 275; *ʿalā* (God is) on (the throne, but not above/ *fawqa* it) 119, 290; *aʿlā* (God may only be described with) highness 288
[ʿ m q] *ʿamīq* deep (a dimension of bodies) 244
[ʿ m l] *ʿamila* act, carry out an action 41, 94; *ʿamal* deed(s do not belong to faith) 35, 89; (can only be a consequence/*tabaʿ* of knowledge) 48
[ʿ n y] *maʿnawī* matter of content 9, 11
[ʿ y n] *ʿayn* pl. *aʿyān* bodily substance; concrete, created, entity 234f., 237f., 242, 245f., 249f., 252–254, 270; *al-aʿyān al-murakkaba* composed bodily substances (i.e. bodies) 246; *ʿayn al-qalb* the eye of the heart 291; *ʿiyān* seeing (as pars pro toto for sense perception) 231
[gh r z] *gharaza* (God has) planted (the capacity to act in human beings; according to Karrāmite doctrine) 94, 304; *gharīzī* from natural disposition (referring to a type of intellect; according to al-Ḥakīm al-Samarqandī) 116

[gh ḍ b] *ghaḍab* anger (of God) 70, 115, 279, 281
[gh l q] *ighlāq fi'l-lafẓ* obscurity in expression 185
[gh n y] *ghinan* and *ghanāʾ* autarchy, self sufficiency (possessed only by the pre-eternal) 234
[gh y r] *ghayrīya* otherness, differentness 192
[f ʾ] *al-fiʾa al-bāghiya* the aggressive group (referring to conflict between religious parties) 67f.; *al-fiʾa al-ʿādila* the righteous group 68
[f r ḍ] *farḍ* religious obligation 251, 291; *farāʾiḍ* religious duties (do not belong directly to belief) 35, 49; (in contrast with superogatory works/*nawāfil* and sins/ *maʿāṣin*) 112
[f r ʿ] *farʿ* pl. *furūʿ* branch, derivative (in contrast with principles/*uṣūl*) 5, 133, 181, 267
[f s r] *tafsīr* commentary of the Qurʾān 186–189, 292; explanation, exegesis (of ambiguous verses is forbidden; according to al-Ḥakīm al-Samarqandī) 119, 291; (must be in accordance with the transmitted interpretations of the Prophet's Companions and scholars; also according to al-Ḥakīm al-Samarqandī) 121
[f ṭ r] *fiṭra* (all humans possess belief as) natural disposition (in a Karrāmite context) 92
[f ḍ l] *faḍl* grace, beneficence (of God), excellence 41, 113, 116f., 269, 299; a "supplement" (given to the prophets in their reward of the next life, in comparison with other believers; from the teachings of al-Ḥakīm al-Samarqandī) 49; *faḍāʾil* merits (which humans can achieve in addition to their fulfillment of religious obligations) 93; *afḍal* the maximum good (not applicable to God's actions) 299
[f ʿ l] *fiʿl* pl. *afʿāl* action (of God) 206, 270, 280; deed, action (by humans) 112, 142, 211, 303, 305, 312; *qabla al-fiʿl* (the human capacity to act) before the act 211, 303, 306; *maʿa al-fiʿl* with the act 211, 303, 306, 328
[f q h] *fiqh* insight 63–65; jurisprudence 23, 28, 31f., 43, 53, 73, 75, 77, 85, 99f., 102, 111, 141, 182; *faqīh* pl. *fuqahāʾ* jurisprudent 128, 133, 196
[f h m] *fahm* pl. *afhām* understanding, intellect 276
[f w ḍ] *fawwaḍa* and *tafwīḍ* (God's) delegating (power to humans over their actions; a doctrine of the Qadarites/ Muʿtazilites) 38–40, 66, 90
[f w q] *fawqa* (God is on/*ʿalā* the throne, but not) above (it) 68, 119, 290; (God is) above (us in heaven; teaching of the Karrāmites) 289; (God has a hand, other than the hands of creation) above (them) 71
[q b l] *qabila* accept (accidents) 247; *al-qābil li'l-mutaḍāddāt* cf. *mutaḍāddāt*; *qabla al-fiʿl* cf. *fiʿl*; *ahl al-qibla* Muslims (and thus believers) 91
[q d r] *qadar* determination, decree (of action by God) 39f., 65f., 71, 90, 93, 112, 212, 302; *qudra* power (of God) 90, 204, 275, 279, 282, 285, 290; capacity (to act by humans; synonymous with *istiṭāʿa*) 211, 306; *qādir* powerful (God) 279; *taqdīr* determination (used like *qadar*) 112
[q d m] *qidam* pre-eternity 234; *qadīm* pre-eternal 114; *qadīm dāʾim* without beginning or end 91; *aqdam* (according to al-Pazdawī, al-Māturīdī was) earlier (than al-Ashʿarī) 321
[q r ʾ] *qirāʾa* Qurʾān recitation 329
[q r r] *qarār* stability (and stillness produce coldness) 256; *iqrār* affirmation (of revealed truth is an integral part of belief undertaken with the tongue/*lisān*) 35, 49, 111, 113, 309; (in the Karrāmite view is sufficient for the constitution of belief) 85f., 89, 214
[q ḍ y] *qaḍāʾ* decision (of God) 90, 93, 112, 212, 302; *qāḍin* judge 7–9, 27, 30, 44, 53f., 73, 100, 129
[q l b] *qalb* heart 89, 291, 309
[q l d] *taqlīd* (religion may not be based on) belief in authority 203, 231; (leads to the emergence of false doctrines) 206
[q h r] *qahara* (God has) subjugated (opposing natures such that they unite) 242

[q w t] *qūt* provision 94
[q w l] *qawl* (belief is) speech (according to Karrāmite teachings) 89
[q w m] *qāma bi-* exist in/through (something) 244, 249, 251, 258, 275, 290
[q w y] *quwwa* capacity (by humans to act; according to Abū Ḥanīfa) 38, 41, 303, 307 (cf. *istiṭāʿa* and *qudra*)
[q y s] *qiyās* analogy 49f., 52; inference of analogy (between the visible and unseen) 266
[k b r] *kibriyāʾ* glory (of God; symbolized by His oneness) 275
[k dh b] *biʾl-kadhib* an untrue manner, deceptively 117, 282; *takdhīb* denial (of God's truth is disbelief) 50
[k r m] *karam* magnanimity (of God) 285; *karāma* pl. *karāmāt* miracle (of holy men) 116, 131, 322; *makārim al-akhlāq* virtuous characteristics (of prophets and angels) 49
[k s b] *kasb* earning (a livelihood) 119; aquiring (of actions) 211; *muktasab* acquired (knowledge; in contrast with necessary/*ḍarūrī* knowledge according to al-Jubbāʾī) 229, 232, 237
[k f r] *kufr* disbelief 50, 302; *kufr al-niʿam* (disbelief through) rejection of God's blessing 53, 67, 302; *takfīr* to declare a disbeliever 9
[k l l] *kull* totality 275
[k l f] *kallafa* (God) places duty (on humans to perform correct actions, and gives them the capacity to do so) 42; *kullifa* (humans are) given reponsibility (for their actions) 118; *takallufī* (an intellect) sharpened by effort (according to al-Ḥakīm al-Samarqandī) 116
[k m n] *kāmin* (a body) hidden (in another; according to al-Naẓẓām) 243
[k n h] *kunh* true nature (of the creation) 263, 298
[k w n] *al-kawn baʿda an lam yakun* existing after not existing 235; *kawwana li-tukawwana al-ashyāʾu ʿalā mā takūnu* (God has eternally) created so that things come to exist as they are 286; *takwīn* creating (as an eternal attribute of God) 142, 204, 285–287, 321f.
[k y f] *bi-lā kayfa* without (being able to say) "how," in an unknowable way 70f., 205, 293; *bi-lā mithāl wa-lā kayfa* without being able to say how and without clear comparison 116, 291; *kayfīya* "howness" 206
[l z m] *lāzim* necessary 292
[l s n] *lisān* language (fails when communicating about God) 276, 309
[l ṭ f] *luṭf* (God's) good will 270
[l f ẓ] *lafẓī* merely lexical, dealing with expression (i.e. not in regard to content/ *maʿnawī*) 9, 11
[l q b] *biʾl-laqab* as a title (i.e., not truly) 282
[mā] *mā* what (as a question about God's essence) 206; *māʾīya* essence 263, 315
[m th l] *mithl* likeness, equal 266f., 275; *mithāl* cf. kayfa
[m ḥ n] *miḥna* (humans are created for) testing 210
[m ḍ gh] *muḍgha* fetus 239
[m ḍ y] *amḍā* (God) allows (good human actions) to occur 39, 41
[m ʿ] *maʿa al-fiʿl* cf. *fiʿl*
[m l k] *mulk* dominion (of God) 279; *mālik* ruling, a ruler (God) 279; *amlaka* (God) made (humans) possess their actions (in the view of the Qadarites/ Muʿtazilites) 93
[m n ʿ] *tamānuʿ* mutual incapacitation (of two assumed deities) 269, 271–273
[n b w] *min jihat al-nubuwwa* (an intellect) bound with prophethood (according to al-Ḥakīm al-Samarqandī) 116
[n s b] *nasaba* ascribing (actions to human agents; according to Karrāmite doctrine) 90; *nisba* a toponym 31, 44, 81, 130, 140
[n ṣ ṣ] *naṣṣ* (authoritative, revealed) text 51
[n ṭ f] *nuṭfa* sperm 239
[n ṭ q] *manṭiq* logic 169
[n ẓ r] *naẓar* rational inquiry 207, 231; *naẓīr* similar 266
[n f r] *tanāfur* mutual repulsion (of natures/ *ṭabāʾiʿ*) 234, 242, 254
[n f s] *nafs* self 71; *bi-nafsihi* (God acts) on His own (without assistance) 286
[n f ʿ] *manfaʿa* pl. *manāfiʿ* benefits 235, 247
[n f q] *nifāq* hypocrisy 51

[n q ḍ] *naqaḍa* (the heretics have) negated (this God-given insight) 274
[n k r] *inkār* rejection (of God is disbelief) 50
[n h y] *nihāya* pl. *nihāyāt* (God's goodness has no) end 299; limit (of a body) 246; *ajzāʾ mutanāhiya* limited parts 234; *ghayr mutanāhin* infinite 234
[n w ʿ] *nawʿāni* two types (of created things) 246; *anwāʿ al-ʿulūm* the categories of knowledge 144
[n w y] *nawā* (human) intending (an action) 41; *nīya* intention 38
[hast] *hastīya* existence 192
[h w] *huwīya* being, existing 192, 206
[h w y] *hawan* pl. *ahwāʾ* passions 254
[h y l] *hayūlā* primordial material 149, 169
[w t r] *ṣalāt al-witr* the odd-numbered prayer 120
[w th q] *mīthāq* (primordial) covenant (between God and humans) 79, 86, 92
[w j d] *wujūd* being, existence 192, 244; coming into existence 256
[w j h] *wajh* face (of God) 86f.; *wujūh mutaḍādda* opposing aspects (of bodies) 254; *ʿalā wujūh* in various ways 293; *jihāt* sides (of bodies) 246; aspects (of actions) 305
[w ḥ d] *al-wāḥid* one, the one 269, 273–275, 278; the One (God) 268–277; *tawḥīd* monotheism passim; (whoever denies the prophethood of Muḥammad is no adherent to true monotheism) 50; *tawaḥḥud* singularity (of God) 275
[w r ʿ] *waraʿ* scrupulous observation (of religious duties) 135
[w ṣ f] *ṣifa* pl. *ṣifāt* attribute (of God) 275, 278–282; quality (in contrast with a body; identified with an accident/*ʿaraḍ*) 246, 248f.
[w ḍ ḥ] *wāḍiḥ* (and *awḍaḥ*) (more) evident 267
[w ḍ ʿ] *waḍaʿa* (God) sets (things in place) 299; *waḍʿu kulli shayʾin mawḍiʿahu* putting everything in its (proper) place (as definition of God's wisdom) 299
[w f q] *tawfīq* assistance (from God) 38, 41, 112f., 118, 131, 303, 322
[w q f] *waqafa* (and *wuqūf*) to refrain from judgement 51, 114; *waqf* to pause (during recitation of the Qurʾān) 329; *al-wuqūf ʿalā ḥudūd al-shayʾ* grasping the limits of a thing (as definition of comprehending/*idrāk*) 293
[w q y] *taqīya* religious dissimulation 49
[w l d] *wallada* (movement) brings forth (heat) 256
[w l y] *walāya* assocation (with the believers) 52; *walī* pl. *awliyāʾ* friend of God, saint 116, 131
[w h b] *mawhiba* pl. *mawāhib* gifts of grace (from God) 131, 322
[w h m] *wahm* pl. *awhām* imagination (fails before God) 276; delusion 11, 286
[y s r] *yasīr* (a) slight (reckoning for those who commit minor sins) 114
[y q n] *yaqīn* certainty 49, 120
[y w m] *yawm al-mīthāq* the day of the (primordial) covenant (between God and humanity) 92